THE ROUGH GUIDE TO

New York City

written and researched by

Martin Dunford, Stephen Keeling and Andrew Rosenberg

ROUGH
GUIDES

roughguides.com

Contents

Introduction to
New York City

No superlative, no cliché does New York City justice. It may not serve as the official capital of the US or even New York State, but it's the undisputed capital of the world. High finance, media, art, architecture, food, fashion, popular culture… it's all here, in plenitude and peak form. Best of all for visitors, you don't have to look too hard for any of it – often, it's just staring you right in the face. The money fortresses of Wall Street. The raised torch of the Statue of Liberty. The iconic Empire State Building. The hype and hustle of Times Square. Fifth Avenue's foot traffic. The proud lions of the Public Library. For energy and dynamism, cultural impact and sheer diversity, New York cannot be beat. Resilient, too, as responses to 2012's Hurricane Sandy and, a little over a decade before that, 9/11 have proved.

The city demands more than just a scratch at a familiar surface. Dig deeper – stay a week or two; move past Central Park and the famous museums, past the historical highlights of downtown and Midtown, and on to less-well-known neighbourhoods, buildings, green spaces and art collections; let yourself be diverted by a tree-lined street or stray path, a glimpse of an Art Deco detail, a hole-in-the-wall serving soul food or fried dumplings – and you'll start to feel a new rhythm.

New York bristles with brash bursts of energy, for certain, but it also emits a slow-burning charm. Hidden gardens next to postmodern skyscrapers; priceless art tucked away in medieval cloisters; a waterfront – seemingly in continuous redevelopment – where you can bike, kayak or just stroll along to take in the view. Wandering through the patchwork of neighbourhoods is as great a thrill as any single sight. Frantic Chinatown edges stylish Soho, which is but a stone's throw from the quiet, angled lanes of the once-bohemian West Village. A perfect espresso in a shabby-chic Williamsburg café, a rooftop view from Chelsea's High Line or a ride on the "A" to Far Rockaway is worth much more than an "I Love New York" handbag.

ABOVE CENTRAL PARK

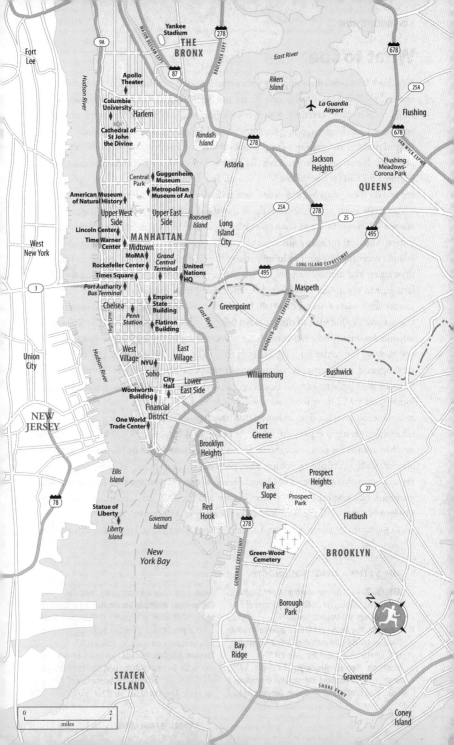

What to see

New York City officially comprises the central island of Manhattan and four outer boroughs – Brooklyn, Queens, the Bronx and Staten Island. For many, **Manhattan** simply is New York; certainly, whatever your interests, you'll probably spend most of your time here. Understanding the intricacies of Manhattan's layout, especially beyond its grid pattern, and getting a grasp on its subway and bus systems should be top priorities. New York is very much a city of neighbourhoods, most compact enough to be explored on foot (at least below 59th Street). For an overview of each district, plus what to see and do there, turn to "Itineraries" (see p.18) and to the introduction of each chapter.

This guide starts at the southern tip of the island and moves north. The **Harbour Islands** – Liberty, Ellis and Governors islands – were the first glimpses of New York (and indeed America) for many nineteenth-century immigrants, a legacy celebrated in Ellis Island's excellent Museum of Immigration. The **Financial District** encompasses the skyscrapers and historic buildings of Manhattan's southern reaches, including the tallest structure in town, One World Trade Center, rising from the ashes of Ground Zero. Immediately east of here is **City Hall**, New York's well-appointed municipal centre, and the massive Gothic span of the **Brooklyn Bridge**, while to the west is swanky **Tribeca**, a loft-filled residential district with plenty of happening restaurants. **Soho**, just to the north, was a big centre for art galleries in the 1970s and 80s; it's better known today for its shops and street scene, as well as some historic cast-iron buildings. East of here is **Chinatown**, Manhattan's most densely populated ethnic neighbourhood and a vibrant locale great for Chinese food and mooching around. Now more a haven for pasta-and-red-sauce tourist traps than Italians, **Little Italy** next door is slowly being swallowed by Chinatown's hungry expansion, while the **Lower East Side**, traditionally the city's gateway neighbourhood for new immigrants – whether German, Jewish or Hispanic – has been almost totally gentrified by young urban professionals, but preserves its history in the thought-provoking Tenement Museum. The **East and West villages** are known for their gorgeous, tree-lined streets, bohemian history and their hip bars, restaurants and shops. **Chelsea** has displaced the West Village as the heart of Manhattan's gay scene, scooped Soho for exciting gallery spaces and added outdoor gems in the High Line and Hudson

---

TOP 5 ETHNIC NEIGHBOURHOODS

Astoria, Queens All sorts of groups have settled here, but it's most famous for its Greek population and the Hellenic shops and tavernas. See p.241.

Belmont, the Bronx Home to far more Italians than touristy Little Italy; the main drag, Arthur Avenue, hops with salumerias and bakeries. See p.254.

Brighton Beach, Brooklyn Since the 1970s, Brighton Beach has been a strong Russian enclave; a walk down Brighton Beach Avenue takes you by food emporia and cheap electronic stores. See p.234.

Chinatown, multiple boroughs Busy restaurants pepper Mott Street in Manhattan's Chinatown; Main Street in predominantly Cantonese Flushing has street food stalls and mini-malls. See p.70 & p.247.

Jackson Heights, Queens Best known for its Indian population, focused on 74th Street between Roosevelt and 37th Street, but Roosevelt Avenue east of there is like a Latin American bazaar. See p.244.

OPPOSITE FROM ABOVE CENTRAL PARK; TIMES SQUARE

River Park developments. The areas around **Union Square** and **Gramercy Park** feature some lovely skyscrapers, including the Flatiron Building, that nicely complement the green spaces, as well as an exciting eating scene. This is where the avenues begin their march north through the busy, regimented blocks of **Midtown**. In its eastern portion, it's dotted with some of the city's most impressive sights, including the Empire State Building, Grand Central Terminal and the Museum of Modern Art. Modern and postmodern skyscrapers punctuate this business district. To the west, **Times Square** and the **Theater District** provide a commercialized look at the popular image of New York City, while **Hell's Kitchen**, along Ninth and Tenth avenues, at least harkens back to a slightly grittier day.

Beyond the high-rise blocks of Midtown, the character of the city changes quite rapidly. The neck-cricking architecture and flagship stores along Fifth Avenue run into 59th Street, where the classic Manhattan vistas are broken by the broad expanse of **Central Park**, a supreme piece of nineteenth-century landscaping. Flanking the park, the **Upper East Side** is wealthy and grandiose, with many of its nineteenth-century millionaires' mansions now transformed into a string of magnificent museums known as **"Museum Mile"**; the most prominent of these is the vast Metropolitan Museum of Art. The residential neighbourhood boasts some of the swankiest addresses in Manhattan, as well as a nest of designer shops along Madison Avenue in the seventies.

On the other side of the park, the largely residential, less patrician enclave of the **Upper West Side** is worth a visit, mostly for Lincoln Center, the American Museum of Natural History and Riverside Park along the Hudson River; studenty Morningside Heights, home to Columbia University, tops off the neighbourhood. Immediately north of Central Park, **Harlem**, the historic black city-within-a-city, numbers elegant brownstones, Baptist churches, jazz landmarks and a strong community spirit among its high points. Still farther north, past residential Hamilton Heights and Washington Heights, a largely Hispanic enclave that few visitors ever venture to visit, stands Inwood at the tip of the island. It's here you'll find the Cloisters, a nineteenth-century mock-up of a medieval monastery, packed with great European Romanesque and Gothic art and (transplanted) architecture – in short, one of Manhattan's must-sees.

It's a good thing that, more and more, visitors (even those on a limited trip) venture off Manhattan Island to one or more of the outer boroughs: **Brooklyn**, **Queens**, **The Bronx**

TOP 5 ARCHITECTURAL NEIGHBOURHOODS

Harlem Some of the most beautiful residential architecture in the city, exemplified by blocks of brownstones and other styles south of 125th Street, and developments farther north like Strivers' Row and Hamilton Heights. See p.196.

Midtown Manhattan A smorgasbord of twentieth-century architectural styles, including some of the city's greatest skyscrapers (the Empire State and GE buildings) and Modernist masterpieces (the Seagram Building and Lever House). See p.121.

Park Slope This tranquil, wealthy Brooklyn district is crammed with fabulous neo-Romanesque and neo-Gothic brownstones and mansions built in the 1880s and 1890s. See p.228.

Soho The largest collection of cast-iron buildings in the world, with incredibly ornate, Neoclassical facades. See p.65.

West Village Still home to the city's best and oldest domestic architecture, with quiet mews and handsome Federal row houses from the 1830s. See p.94.

and **Staten Island**. In addition to the points of historical and contemporary interest in each, some of the city's most vibrant ethnic neighborhoods (and consequently best food) can be found out here: the Greek restaurants of the Astoria district in Queens, for example, or the Italian bakeries and trattorias of the Bronx's Belmont section. Individual sights like the New York Botanical Garden in the Bronx and Museum of Moving Image in Queens have plenty of pull, too, and a ride on the Staten Island Ferry is a free thrill that's hard to beat. It's Brooklyn, however, that tends to steal the show and is more or less Manhattan's equal – or at least rival. You can sample locally made food and buy snappy duds in hip Williamsburg, wander the brownstone-lined streets of Cobble Hill and Brooklyn Heights, view cutting-edge exhibits at the Brooklyn Museum, ride a rickety roller coaster and soak up the old-world charm of Coney Island or hit Central Park's counterpart, activity-filled Prospect Park.

When to go

New York City's climate ranges from sticky, hot and humid in midsummer to very cold in January and February: be prepared to freeze or boil accordingly if you decide to visit during these periods. **Spring** is gentle, if unpredictable and often wet, while **autumn** is perhaps the most beguiling season, with crisp, clear days and warmish nights – either period is a great time to schedule a visit. Whenever you're visiting, plan to dress in layers, as it's the only way to combat overheated buildings in winter and overactive, icy air-conditioning come summertime.

18

things not to miss

It's not possible to see everything that New York City has to offer in one trip – and we don't suggest you try. What follows, in no particular order, is a selective taste of highlights: mind-blowing feats of engineering and design, waterfront amusements, hallowed art collections and, of course, plenty of eating, shopping and nightlife. All entries have a page reference to take you straight into the Guide, where you can find out more.

1

5

4 GRAND CENTRAL TERMINAL
Page 133
Take a free lunchtime tour (Wed or Fri) of this magnificent building to learn the history of the station's majestic concourse.

5 BASEBALL
Page 389
A summertime treat: enjoy a hot dog, a cold beer and America's pastime in the Yankees' or Mets' homes – or for a more intimate experience, see a Cyclones game in Coney Island.

6 MUSEUM OF MODERN ART
Page 128
Simply put, MoMA holds the most comprehensive collection of modern art in the world.

7 FINE DINING VS. FOOD TRUCKS
Page 286
After splashing out at a celebrity chef spot like *Le Bernardin* (see p.313), save some cash – and still eat like a king – at one of the city's many mobile food trucks.

7

 ROCKEFELLER CENTER

If anywhere can truly claim to be the centre of New York, this stylish piece of twentieth-century urban planning is it.

 LIVE JAZZ

New York's jazz scene is vibrant, but Harlem is first choice for characterful venues and late-night jam sessions.

10 **STATUE OF LIBERTY**

There's no greater symbol of the American dream than the magnificent statue that graces New York Harbor.

11 **BAR HOPPING IN WILLIAMSBURG**

Haute food, house-made bitters, vintage arcade games, a beer or three at a beloved local brewery – it all adds up to a night of good fun.

 THE FRICK COLLECTION

He may have been a ruthless coal baron, but Henry Frick's eye for art and the elegance of his collection's setting make this one of the city's best galleries.

 BROOKLYN FLEA
Page 221
An array of funky crafts, clothes and antique vendors coupled with local food purveyors have made this weekend event a new institution.

 THE HIGH LINE
Page 106
This Chelsea walkway offers a unique perspective on the city below and on the power of progressive urban renewal.

 CENTRAL PARK
Page 149
The world's most iconic swathe of green: take a boat ride, watch Shakespeare in the Park or enjoy a Conservatory Garden picnic after a morning spent in a museum.

 STATEN ISLAND FERRY
Page 52
Savour Manhattan's skyline and the Statue of Liberty from a boat's-eye view – absolutely free.

 LONG ISLAND CITY ART
Page 239
MoMA PS1 is the focal point, but there are cool smaller galleries and, on the periphery, a funky sculpture park.

 CONEY ISLAND
Page 233
A ride on the Wonder Wheel or Cyclone, high above the boardwalk, is an old-timey thrill.

16

17

18

Itineraries

These themed itineraries are not meant to be followed slavishly or sequentially; instead, let them lead you to unusual city sights, flavours and corners. Choose a few that interest you and you'll see a side of New York well away from the typical big-ticket attractions.

A NEIGHBOURHOOD TOUR

These neighbourhoods absorb (or create) the new while retaining a character all their own – making them great places to understand the city today.

Greenpoint Cool cafés and progressive parks peppered around an old Polish community. **See p.236**

Red Hook Feels like a world apart – or at least an independent waterfront town – with artisanal food and drink producers and galleries in its industrial spaces. **See p.224**

Harlem America's foremost African-American community is a neighbourhood on the rise, its gospel churches and soul food complimented by new bars, restaurants and galleries. **See p.197**

NoMad Boasting the latest in chic Manhattan hotels and dining, NoMad also has the new Museum of Mathematics. **See p.118**

Lower East Side Former immigrant enclave now home to vintage boutiques such as Edith Machinist and the restaurants of Wylie Dufresne and Keith McNally. **See p.80**

A DAY IN THE VILLAGE

Take a day to explore historic Greenwich Village (aka the West Village), the artistic, bohemian heart of New York since the 1920s and now one of its richest, most sought after neighbourhoods.

Wander along historic Bedford Street One of the most beautiful streets in Manhattan drips with history, from the thinnest house to the oldest house (and that one from *Friends*). **See p.103**

Coffee in Caffe Reggio Take in the Italian antiques, paintings and sculptures at this 1927 coffee shop, where Tennessee Williams once sipped espresso. **See p.281**

Bleecker Street snacking Sample the prosciutto balls at *Faicco's*, cannoli at *Rocco's*, finest *fromage* at *Murray's Cheese*, cheap slices at *Joe's Pizza* and cupcakes from *Magnolia Bakery*. **See p.102**

The 4th Street Courts Witness some high-quality street basketball at "The Cage", magnet for NBA wannabes from all over the city. **See p.102**

Kayaking and sunset on the Hudson Enjoy the free kayaking at Pier 40, before strolling along the Hudson River Park as the sun sets behind New Jersey. **See p.104**

Pints at the White Horse Grab a pint in this classic 1880 watering hole, the haunt of Kerouac, Mailer and Hunter S. Thompson, and the pub where Dylan Thomas supped his last drink. **See p.334**

Live jazz Check out the dynamic West Village jazz scene at underground venue *Bar Next Door* or cosy dive *Smalls Jazz Club*. **See p.346**

Late-night visit to Village Chess Can't sleep? Pay a visit to 24-hour Village Chess Shop, where serious aficionados gather to view the antique sets and discuss strategy – at 2.30am. **See p.372**

ABOVE ICE CREAM AT EATALY; MUSEUM OF MATHS **OPPOSITE** KEITH HARING MURAL AT BROOKLYN MUSEUM

EAT NEW YORK CITY

Something New York does better than pretty much anywhere else? Food, in all tastes and varieties. Eat your way around the city by visiting some of its top marketplaces and street-food centres.

Eataly (Flatiron District) Celebrity-chef-run spot for immaculate produce, fresh breads and Italian groceries, plus numerous spots for meals and quick bites, with a rooftop beer garden to boot. **See p.385**

Smorgasburg (Williamsburg) This offshoot of the Brooklyn Flea, full of inventive food vendors, also spends time in Dumbo and South Street Seaport. **See p.235**

Chelsea Market (Chelsea) Lots of deliciousness under one roof: gooey brownies and just-from-the-ocean lobster are among the highlights. **See p.384**

Essex Street Market (Lower East Side) Dominican fruit and veg stalls rub shoulders with New York classics (Shopsin's) and hip newcomers (Saxelby Cheesemongers and Beurre & Sel). **See p.385**

Hester Street Fair (Lower East Side) Spring and summer Saturday market showcasing speciality foods from lobster rolls to ice cream sandwiches. **See p.384**

OFF THE BEATEN TRACK

Getting out to these stops (in one case, by ferry) is part of the adventure. Once there, you're likely to be surrounded by locals enjoying some of the city's less-advertised highlights.

Hispanic Society, Washington Heights New York's under-visited art gem is like a Castilian palace, crammed with paintings by Goya, Velázquez, El Greco and the spectacular mural series *Vision of Spain*. **See p.208**

Keith Haring murals, Harlem & West Village Check out the iconic Keith Haring mural *Crack is Wack* in Harlem, and his Carmine Street mural overlooking the public swimming pool in the Village. **See p.103 and p.201**

Governors Island This bucolic retreat sits in the harbour a short ferry ride from Wall Street, though its leafy parks and stately buildings are more New England than New York. **See p.39**

Flushing Meadows–Corona Park, Queens Science and art museums, a skating rink and other sports facilities, and proximity to Flushing's Chinatown… what's not to like? **See p.246**

Green-Wood Cemetery, Brooklyn The final resting place of many local notables, Greenwood adds a rural flair to the urban landscape, and its hills afford great views of Manhattan. **See p.229**

NEW YORK GRAFFITI

Basics

Getting there

Getting to New York is easy. There are three international airports (⑩panynj .gov) that serve the city: John F. Kennedy (JFK), LaGuardia (LGA) and Newark (EWR). The city is on every major airline's itinerary, and is also a regional hub for train and bus travel. Expressways surround Manhattan, making driving another viable option.

Flights from the US and Canada

From most places in North America, flying is the most convenient way to reach New York. Airfares to New York depend on the season and can fluctuate wildly. The highest prices are generally between May and September; you'll get the best prices by booking months in advance or flying during the low season, November to February (excluding late Nov until early Jan, the holiday season). The lowest round-trip fares from the West Coast tend to average around $400–450; from Chicago or Miami it's about $300–350. Nonstop flights from Canada are always more expensive; reckon on paying Can$350–400 from Toronto or Montréal and at least Can$500–600 from Vancouver.

Flights from the UK and Ireland

Flying to New York from the UK takes about seven hours; flights tend to leave Britain in the morning or afternoon and arrive in New York in the afternoon or evening, though the odd flight does leave as late as 8pm. Coming back, most flights depart in the evening and arrive in Britain early next morning; flying time, due to the prevailing winds, is usually a little shorter.

As far as **scheduled flights** go, Virgin Atlantic and British Airways offer the most direct services each day from London's Heathrow to JFK and Newark. American Airlines, Delta and United also fly direct on a daily basis; there is not much difference in the prices on the different airlines. Round-trip fares (nonstop) also fluctuate wildly, averaging £400–500 for off-peak tickets bought in advance, to £700 and up in the summer. United flies nonstop to Newark from Birmingham, Manchester and Glasgow. Aer Lingus, Delta and United all fly nonstop services to New York from Dublin – expect to pay at least €800 in the summer. United also flies nonstop from Shannon Airport for around €775, and nonstop from Belfast for about the same rates.

Flights from Australia, New Zealand and South Africa

It's not yet possible to take a nonstop flight between New York and Australia or New Zealand, though Qantas offers a direct service from Sydney, with a two-and-a half hour layover in Los Angeles (meaning you won't have to change planes). Most Aussies and Kiwis reach the eastern United States by way of LA and San Francisco (flying time is approximately ten hours to the West Coast, with another six-hour flight to New York). The best connections tend to be with United, Delta, Air New Zealand and Qantas; from Auckland, Air New Zealand connects with United flights in LA.

Fares from eastern Australian state capitals are generally the same: return flights for most of the year start at around Aus$1600 but can go up to more than Aus$2500 in December, when most Australians tend to visit; fares from Perth and Darwin can be up to Aus$500 more all year, and it's usually about the same from New Zealand (NZ$2500). If you intend to take in New York as part of a world trip, a **round-the-world** ticket offers the best value for money, working out just a little more than an all-in ticket.

South African Airways flies nonstop from Johannesburg to JFK (15hr 35min) from around R13,500; you can get cheaper rates (from R9500) by shopping around for indirect flights via Qatar (Qatar Airways), Dubai (Emirates), or Amsterdam and London.

By train

New York is connected to the rest of the continent by several **Amtrak train lines** (☎1-800/USA-RAIL, ⑩amtrak.com). The most frequent services are along the Boston–Washington, DC corridor; there is also one daily train between Montréal and New York. Fares from Boston and DC start at around $100 round-trip, or $200 for the Acela Express, which saves 30–35 minutes on either route. Fares from Canada usually start around Can$130. Like planes, train fares are often based on availability; with the exception of peak travel times (ie Christmas), seats are much cheaper months in advance. Although it's possible to haul yourself long-distance from the West Coast, the Midwest or the South, it's an exhausting trip (three days-plus from California) and fares are expensive.

By bus

Going by bus is usually the cheapest, but also the most time-consuming and least comfortable mode of travel. The best reason to take the bus for more than a few hours is if you're going to make a number of stops en route; if this is the case, you might check out **Greyhound's Discovery Pass**, which is good for unlimited travel within a set period of time.

Unlike most parts of the country, where Greyhound is the only game in town, in the busy northeast corridor there is fierce competition between bus operators. One-way from either DC or Boston to New York can go for as little as $30 on one of the major lines. **Peter Pan Bus Lines** often has $25 one-way fares from New York to Boston and DC. Buses arrive in New York at the Port Authority Bus Terminal, Eighth Avenue and 42nd Street.

For the best bargains along the East Coast check **Bolt Bus** and **Mega Bus**, which sometimes offer tickets for $1 (Mega Bus also runs buses to Toronto from around $40); the newest entrant is **Yo! Bus**, running between New York Chinatown, Boston and Philadelphia from just $12. Other cheap options (with the oldest buses) include **Lucky Star**, which runs nonstop between the Chinatowns of Boston and New York for $15–20 each way.

AIRLINES

Aer Lingus Ⓦ aerlingus.com
Air Canada Ⓦ aircanada.com
Air France Ⓦ airfrance.com
Air Jamaica Ⓦ airjamaica.com
Air New Zealand Ⓦ airnz.co.nz
Alaska Airlines Ⓦ alaskaair.com
Alitalia Ⓦ alitalia.com
Allegiant Air Ⓦ allegiantair.com
American Airlines Ⓦ aa.com
British Airways Ⓦ ba.com
Caribbean Airlines Ⓦ caribbean-airlines.com
Cathay Pacific Ⓦ cathaypacific.com
Delta Air Lines Ⓦ delta.com
El Al Ⓦ elal.co.il
Emirates Ⓦ emirates.com
Frontier Airlines Ⓦ flyfrontier.com
Hawaiian Airlines Ⓦ hawaiianairlines.com
Icelandair Ⓦ icelandair.co.uk
JAL (Japan Air Lines) Ⓦ jal.com
JetBlue Ⓦ jetblue.com
KLM (Royal Dutch Airlines) Ⓦ klm.com

Korean Air Ⓦ koreanair.com
LanChile Ⓦ lan.com
Lufthansa Ⓦ lufthansa.com
Porter Airlines Ⓦ flyporter.com
Qantas Airways Ⓦ qantas.com
Singapore Airlines Ⓦ singaporeair.com
South African Airways Ⓦ flysaa.com
Southwest Airlines Ⓦ southwest.com
Spirit Airlines Ⓦ spiritair.com
United Airlines Ⓦ united.com
Virgin America Ⓦ virginamerica.com
Virgin Atlantic Ⓦ virgin-atlantic.com
WestJet Ⓦ westjet.com

AGENTS AND OPERATORS

Amtrak Vacations US ☎ 1 800 654 5748, Ⓦ amtrakvacations .com. Rail, accommodation and sightseeing packages.

Contiki US ☎ 1 888 266 8454, Ⓦ contiki.com. 18- to 35-year-olds-only tour operator. Runs highly social sightseeing trips to New York that focus on major tourist attractions.

Delta Vacations US ☎ 1 800 654 6559, Ⓦ deltavacations.com. Offers packages to New York that include mid-range to upscale accommodation, plus optional sightseeing and airport transfers.

International Gay and Lesbian Travel Association US ☎ 1 800 448 8550, Ⓦ iglta.org. Trade group with lists of gay-owned or gay-friendly travel agents, accommodation and other travel businesses.

Maupintour US ☎ 1 800 255 4266, Ⓦ maupintour.com. Luxury tours. Runs trips to New York, with city tours, show tickets and upscale meals.

New York City Vacation Packages US ☎ 1 888 692 8701, Ⓦ nycvp.com. All sorts of short, reasonably priced New York vacations, from spa weekends to Broadway shows.

North South Travel UK ☎ 01245 608 291, Ⓦ northsouthtravel .co.uk. Friendly, competitive travel agency, offering discounted fares worldwide. Profits are used to support projects in the developing world, especially the promotion of sustainable tourism.

STA Travel US ☎ 1 800 781 4040, UK ☎ 0871 2300 040; Ⓦ statravel.com. Worldwide specialists in independent travel; also student IDs, travel insurance, car rental, rail passes and more. Good discounts for students and under-26s.

Trailfinders UK ☎ 0845 058 5858, Republic of Ireland ☎ 01 677 7888; Ⓦ trailfinders.com. One of the best-informed and most efficient agents for independent travellers.

Viator US ☎ 1 866 648 5873 Ⓦ viator.com. Books local tours and sightseeing trips within New York.

A BETTER KIND OF TRAVEL

At Rough Guides we are passionately committed to travel. We believe it helps us understand the world we live in and the people we share it with – and of course tourism is vital to many developing economies. But the scale of modern tourism has also damaged some places irreparably, and climate change is accelerated by most forms of transport, especially flying. All Rough Guides' flights are carbon-offset, and every year we donate money to a variety of environmental charities.

BUS AND RAIL CONTACTS

Amtrak ☎ 1 800 872 7245, 🖥 amtrak.com
Bolt Bus ☎ 1 877 265 8287, 🖥 boltbus.com
Greyhound ☎ 1 800 231 2222, Canada ☎ 1 800 661 8747, 🖥 greyhound.com
Lucky Star ☎ 617 426 8802, 🖥 luckystarbus.com
Mega Bus ☎ 1 877 462 6342, 🖥 megabus.com
Peter Pan ☎ 1 800 343 9999, 🖥 peterpanbus.com
Yo! Bus ☎ 1 855 669 6287, 🖥 yobus.com

Arrival

Most visitors to New York arrive at one of the three major international airports that serve the city: John F. Kennedy (Queens), LaGuardia (Queens) and Newark (in New Jersey). All three share a website at 🖥 panynj.gov. You can find general information about getting to and from the airports on the website or by calling ☎ 1 800 247 7433. Amtrak trains arrive at Penn Station, and most buses at the Port Authority Bus Terminal, both of which are in Midtown, Manhattan.

By plane

Whichever airport you arrive at, one of the simplest ways into Manhattan is by **bus**. All airport bus services operate from one of two terminals in Manhattan: **Grand Central Terminal** (at Park Ave and 42nd St) and the **Port Authority Bus Terminal** (Eighth Ave at 34th St, ☎ 212 564 8484). Grand Central is more convenient for the east side of the island. The Port Authority Bus Terminal isn't as good a bet for Manhattan (as it entails carrying luggage from bus to street level), though you'll find it handy if you're heading for the west side of the city or out to New Jersey (by bus). Some airport buses also stop at **Penn Station** at 32nd Street between Seventh and Eighth avenues, where you can catch the Long Island Railroad (LIRR), as well as Amtrak long-distance trains to other parts of America. More convenient than the bus but cheaper than a taxi, the **GO Airport Shuttle** is a minibus that offers a drop-off service anywhere in the city (shared with other riders).

Taxis are the most convenient option if you are travelling in a group or are arriving at an antisocial hour. Ignore the individual touts vying for attention as you exit the baggage claim; these "gypsy cab" operators are notorious for ripping off tourists. Any airport official can direct you to the taxi stand, where you can get an official New York City yellow taxi. A few car services have direct phones near the exits; they're competitive in price with taxis (they charge set rates). Remember to add a fifteen- to twenty-percent tip for the driver of any taxi.

If you're not so pressed for time and want to save some money, it is also possible to take the **train**, commuter or subway, from Newark or JFK, and a **city bus** from LaGuardia.

JFK

The **NYC Airporter** (☎ 718 777 5111, 🖥 nycairporter .com) runs airport buses between JFK and Grand Central Terminal, Port Authority Bus Terminal, Penn Station and Midtown hotels every 20 to 30 minutes between 5am and 11.30pm. Journeys take 45 to 60 minutes, depending on time of day and traffic conditions. The fare is $16 one-way, $29 round-trip; discounts are available. **Go Airport Shuttle** (🖥 goairportshuttle.com) offers shared minibus services to your hotel door ($18.94 to Manhattan), but you need to reserve this in advance and be a little flexible on times.

The **AirTrain** (🖥 panynj.gov/airtrain) runs every few minutes, 24 hours daily, between all JFK terminals and the Jamaica and Howard Beach stations in Queens. You pay $5 when you exit, which can be debited from your MetroCard (see p.25). The fastest onward connection into Manhattan is to take the **LIRR** (Long Island Rail Road) from Jamaica to Penn Station ($7 off-peak, $9.50 peak; 20min); buy tickets at the station, as fares are almost double if purchased on board. You can also take the **subway** (E, J, Z from Jamaica, and A from Howard Beach) for just $2.50 on MetroCard ($2.75 single-ride ticket), anywhere in the city. In the daytime or early evening this is a cheap, viable option, although late at night it isn't the best choice – trains run infrequently and can be deserted. Travel time to Manhattan is usually a little under an hour. **Taxis** charge a flat rate of $52 to anywhere in Manhattan from JFK (plus the state tax surcharge of 50¢). There is no $1 peak time or 50-cent night surcharge for these trips. Tolls are payable however, and some drivers will try to increase the $52 rate by claiming you must take a toll route. Insist on $52; there are no toll roads between JFK and Manhattan, and all the bridges are **free**. The only toll is payable on the **Midtown Tunnel** ($7.50 or just $5.33 if your taxi has an electronic E-ZPass), but unless you are in a real hurry (if you are heading to Midtown the tunnel is slightly faster), you can insist on taking one of the bridges instead. All non-Manhattan trips should be on the meter; expect to pay $59–64 for downtown Brooklyn.

LaGuardia

The **NYC Airporter** (☎718 777 5111, ⓦnycair porter.com) runs express buses between LaGuardia and Grand Central Station, Port Authority Bus Terminal and Penn Station every 20 to 30 minutes between 5am and 11.30pm. Journey time is 45 to 60 minutes, depending on traffic. The fare is $13 one-way, $23 round-trip. **Go Airport Shuttle** (ⓦgoairportshuttle.com) offers shared minibus services to your hotel door (around $15.59 to Manhattan), but you need to reserve this in advance and be a little flexible on times.

You can also travel from the airport by **city bus**. The best bargain in New York airport transit is the #M60 bus, which for $2.50 by MetroCard ($2.75 for single ticket, exact change) takes you into Manhattan, across 125th Street and down Broadway to 106th Street. Ask for a transfer (see opposite) when you get on the bus and you can get almost anywhere. Journey time from LaGuardia ranges from 20 minutes late at night to an hour in rush-hour traffic. Alternatively, you can take the #M60 bus to Astoria Boulevard. There you can transfer to the N subway, which runs through Manhattan and south to Brooklyn.

Taxis from LaGuardia use the meter; reckon on $25–37 into mid-Manhattan plus tip and surcharges (Mon–Fri 4–8pm $1; daily 8pm–6am $0.50). Tolls are also extra, but you can insist on avoiding the Midtown Tunnel (see p.26).

Newark

Newark Airport Express (☎877 863 9275, ⓦcoachusa.com) runs buses to Grand Central Station, Port Authority Bus Terminal and Penn Station every 30 minutes daily between 4am and 1am (every 15min 6.45am–11.15pm). In the other direction, buses run from the same locations just as frequently between 4.45am and 1.45am. In either direction, the journey takes 30 to 45 minutes depending on the traffic. The fare is $16 one-way, $28 round-trip. **Go Airport Shuttle** (ⓦgoairportshuttle.com) offers shared minibus services to your hotel door (around $17.43 to Manhattan), but you need to reserve this in advance and be a little flexible on times.

From any of the terminals you can also take the short **AirTrain** ride to Newark Liberty International Airport Train Station and connect with frequent NJ Transit or Amtrak trains heading into Manhattan. The AirTrain runs 24 hours (every 3–15min) and nominally costs $5.50, but this is included when you buy an NJ Transit or Amtrak ticket from machines in the AirTrain terminals or at the main station – there's no need to pay separately for the AirTrain.

Heading into Manhattan (Penn Station; 30min) the fare for NJ Transit is $12.50 (Amtrak trains are more expensive). If you really want to save a few dollars (and have plenty of time), take an NJ Transit train ($8.25) to Newark Penn Station (not to be confused with Penn Station in Manhattan) and transfer to the PATH system (☎1 800 234 7284, ⓦpanynj.gov/path), with connections to Downtown and Midtown Manhattan (30–40min) for just $2.25. The PATH train runs 24 hours, but service is limited between midnight and 7am.

Taxis from Newark into Manhattan charge according to an expensive fixed schedule of rates, clearly listed at terminal taxi ranks – the dispatcher will confirm the rate before you get in. For points south of Central Park the rate is $50–55 ($60–70 further north), plus $5 for locations on the east side of the island and a $5 peak-time surcharge (Mon–Fri 6–9am & 4–7pm, Sat & Sun noon–8pm). On top of that you need to add $1 per suitcase, a tip and any tolls incurred; you can ask the driver to avoid toll roads in New Jersey but to get to Manhattan you'll need to take the Lincoln or Holland toll tunnels ($13 or $8.25–10.25 if your driver has an electronic E-ZPass). Note, though, that this toll is only paid going into Manhattan, so even though you are obliged to pay "round-trip" tolls, the charge should only be a maximum $13.

By train, bus and car

Amtrak trains arrive at Penn Station, at West 32nd Street between Seventh and Eighth avenues, which is connected to the subway system and has plenty of taxis outside. If you come to New York by Greyhound or any other long-distance **bus** line (with the exception of the Chinatown buses, which arrive in Chinatown, and Mega Bus and Bolt Bus, which drop you off on Midtown streets), you arrive at the **Port Authority Bus Terminal** at West 42nd Street and Eighth Avenue – this is also connected to the subway system and it's fairly easy to catch a taxi outside.

If you're coming from the East Coast (or if you don't mind long journeys), **driving** is an option, but note that you probably won't need (or want) a car once you're in the city. Major highways come in from most directions (I-87 and -95 from the north; I-95 from the south; and I-80 from the west). In terms of tolls, crossing the Hudson River costs $13, while bridges over the East River are free; the Midtown Tunnel is $7.50.

City transport

Public transit in New York is excellent, extremely cheap and covers most conceivable corners of the city, whether by subway or bus. Don't be afraid to ask someone for help if you're confused. You'll no doubt find the need for a taxi from time to time, especially if you feel uncomfortable in an area at night; you will rarely have trouble tracking one down in Manhattan or on major Brooklyn avenues – the ubiquitous yellow cabs are always on the prowl for passengers. And don't forget your feet – New Yorkers walk everywhere.

By subway

The New York subway (☎718 330 1234, ⓦmta .info) is initially incomprehensible, but it's also the fastest and most efficient way to get from place to place in Manhattan and to the outer boroughs. Put aside your qualms: it's much safer and user-friendly than it once was, and it's definitely not as difficult to navigate as it seems. Nonetheless, it pays to familiarize yourself with the subway system before you set out. Study the map in this book, or get a free map at any information kiosk. Though the subway runs daily 24 hours, some routes operate at certain times of day only; read any service advisories carefully.

SUBWAY ESSENTIALS

Tickets The subway costs $2.50 per ride anywhere on the system if you purchase a MetroCard ($1) from a vending machine (in the subway station) or a subway teller, available in denominations between $5 and $80; a $20 purchase gives you $21 on your card. Vending machines accept all credit and debit cards, but keep some fresh bills on hand in case you have a problem. Single-ride tickets are also sold at vending machines, but cost $2.75 and are not really worth it if you intend to use the subway more than once. Unlimited-ride cards – almost always the best deal if you intend to be on the go – allow unlimited travel for a certain period of time: a seven-day pass for $30 and 30-day pass for $112 (there is no one-day pass).

Trains and routes Trains run uptown or downtown in Manhattan, following the great avenues. Crosstown routes are few. Trains and their routes are identified by a number or letter (not by their colour). There are two types of train: the express, which stops only at major stations, and the local, stopping at every station. Be aware that service changes due to track repairs and other maintenance work are frequent (especially after midnight and on weekends) and confusing.

Safety By day the whole train is safe, but don't go into empty cars if you can help it. Some trains have doors that connect between cars, but do not use them other than in an emergency, because this is dangerous and illegal. Keep an eye on bags (and especially iPods, which can get snatched) at all times, especially when sitting or standing near the doors. With all the jostling in the crowds near the doors, this is a favourite spot for pickpockets. At night, always try to use the centre cars, because they tend to be more crowded. Yellow signs on the platform saying "During off hours train stops here" indicate where the conductor's car will stop. If you are lost, go to the subway teller or phone ☎718 330 1234. State your location and destination; the teller or operator will tell you the most direct route.

By bus

The **bus system** (☎718 330 1234, ⓦmta.info) is simpler than the subway, as you can see where you're going and hop off at anything interesting. There are many crosstown routes and most services run 24 hours. The major disadvantage is that buses can be extremely slow due to traffic – in peak hours almost down to walking pace.

Anywhere in the city the fare is $2.50, payable on entry with a MetroCard (the most convenient way) or with the correct change – coins only (no pennies). Bus maps can be obtained at the main concourse of Grand Central Terminal or at visitor information centres. There are routes on almost all the avenues and major streets. Most buses with an M designation before the route number travel exclusively in Manhattan; others may show a B for Brooklyn, Q for Queens, Bx for the Bronx or S for Staten Island. The crosstown routes are the most useful, especially the ones through Central Park. Also good are the buses that take you to east Manhattan where subway coverage is sparse. Most crosstown buses take their route number from the street they traverse, so the #M14 will travel along 14th Street. Buses display their number, origin and destination up front.

There are three types of bus: **local**, which stop every two or three blocks at five- to ten-minute intervals; **limited stop**, which travel the same routes but stop at only about a quarter of the local stops; and **express**, which cost extra ($6) and stop hardly anywhere, shuttling commuters in and out of the outer boroughs and suburbs.

Bus stops are marked by a tall, round sign with a bus emblem and route number. Once you're on board, to signal that you want to get off a bus, press the yellow strip between the windows or one of the "stop" buttons on the grab bars; the driver will stop at the next official bus stop. Between 10pm and

5am you can ask to get off on any block along the route, whether or not it's a regular stop (not available on limited routes).

Transfers

If you're going to use buses a lot, it pays to understand the **transfer system**. A transfer allows a single fare to take you, one-way, anywhere in Manhattan, within two hours of your first ride. Pay by Metrocard and the transfer will apply automatically on the next bus/subway (no need to ask for it). If you pay with coins, ask your driver for a transfer (free) – you'll get a single-use MetroCard to use on your connecting bus/subway. Because few buses go up and down and across, you can transfer from any bus to almost any other that continues your trip. (You can't use transfers for return trips.) If you're unsure where to get off to transfer, consult the map on the panel behind the driver, or ask the driver for help.

By taxi

Taxis are always worth considering, especially if you're in a hurry or it's late at night. There are two types of taxi; in Manhattan, you'll generally be using **medallion cabs**, recognizable by their yellow paintwork and medallion up top. Before you hail a cab, work out exactly where you're going and if possible the quickest route there – a surprising number of cabbies are new to the job and speak little English. If you feel the driver doesn't seem to know your destination, point it out on a map. An illuminated sign atop the taxi indicates its availability. If the words Off Duty are lit, the driver won't pick you up (see also box below).

TAXI TIPS: BEATING THE CHANGE-OVER

One problem that often catches out foreign visitors to New York is the notorious taxi "change-over" time, usually around 3.30–5pm, when most drivers end their shift (and hand the car over to another driver). Unless you are going in their direction they will refuse to pick you up – getting to the airport is often impossible at this time, so always book a private car instead. Chinese-run taxi firms usually offer the cheapest rates; try New Golden Horse (☎718 762 8888). Otherwise Carmel (☎1 866 666 6666) and Dial 7 (☎212 777 7777) offer dependable services.

The alternative is to take a **"gypsy cab"** (which looks like a regular car), roughly divided into two types: licensed livery cabs (identified by a "T" on the number plate), only permitted to pick up passengers on call by telephone, but which often illegally seek passengers on the street; and completely unlicensed, uninsured operators who tout for business wherever tourists arrive. Avoid these drivers like the plague – they will rip you off (and can be unsafe). Their main hunting grounds are outside tourist arrival points like Grand Central. If you're looking for a cab in Harlem or the outer boroughs at night however, you'll have little choice but to opt for a livery cab (preferably a licensed one); if you call ahead or pick one up on the street, always fix the fare in advance (ask someone before you head out, for a rough idea).

Fares

Up to four people can travel in an ordinary medallion cab. Fares are $2.50 for the first fifth of a mile plus New York State Tax surcharge of 50¢ per ride, and 50¢ for each fifth of a mile thereafter or for each minute in stopped or slow traffic. An additional **surcharge** of 50¢ is payable daily between 8pm and 6am, and $1 Monday to Friday 4 to 8pm. When you take a cab outside the city limits you must agree on a flat fare with the driver before the trip begins (metered fare rules only apply to New York City; drivers can set prices to other destinations as they see fit). Note that this does not apply to trips to Westchester and Nassau counties, for which there are previously determined fare rules. Trips to Newark Airport are on the meter plus $17.50 and tolls. Note also that all trips from Manhattan to JFK should be a flat $52 (plus the state tax surcharge of 50¢), though drivers sometimes try and use the meter.

Trips outside Manhattan can incur **toll fees** (which the driver will usually pay through E-ZPass and which will be added to your fare); the only river crossings into Manhattan that cost money both ways are the Hugh L. Carey Tunnel and Queens Midtown Tunnel ($7.50 each; $5.33 with E-ZPass). Tolls for the Holland Tunnel, Lincoln Tunnel and George Washington Bridge (all $13; $8.25–10.25 with E-ZPass) are paid coming into Manhattan only. All the other bridges are free.

The **tip** should be fifteen to twenty percent of the fare; you'll get a dirty look if you offer less. Drivers don't like splitting anything bigger than a $20 bill, and are in their rights to refuse a bill over $20. Drivers are required to accept American Express, MasterCard, VISA and Discover for all fares.

If they refuse, you may call ☎311 and report the medallion number.

Rules

Certain regulations govern taxi operators. A driver can ask your destination only when you're seated (this is often breached) – and must transport you (within the five boroughs), however undesirable your destination may be. You may face some problems, though, if it's late and you want to go to an outer borough. Also, if you request it, a driver must pick up or drop off other passengers, turn on the air conditioning, and turn the radio down or off. Many drivers use a cell phone while driving; this is common but prohibited, and while you can ask him or her to stop, don't expect compliance. If you lose something in a taxi, or you have a problem with a driver, get the license number from the right-hand side of the dashboard, or the medallion number from the rooftop sign or from the print-out receipt for the fare, and file a complaint at ☎311 or ⓦci .nyc.ny.us/apps/311.

By ferry

Manhattan is connected to New Jersey, Staten Island, Queens and Brooklyn by a web of **ferry services**. These generally serve commuters, but some routes are worth checking out for a relatively cheap opportunity to get onto the water. New York Water Taxi (ⓦnywatertaxi.com) runs a daily hop-on hop-off ferry service (April–Oct 9am–6.15pm; Nov– March 9am–5.30pm) around south Manhattan, linking West 44th Street with Battery Park and Dumbo in Brooklyn (day-pass $28, kids $16; tickets also valid on the NYWT Express tour bus through Midtown). Water Taxi also runs a daily shuttle from Wall Street's Pier 11 in Manhattan to Brooklyn's Ikea superstore in Red Hook (Mon–Fri 2–8pm, Sat & Sun 11.20am–9.20pm), an efficient way to reach this neighbourhood. The service is free on weekends, and $5 weekdays (if you spend over $10 in Ikea the ferry is free). In the summer (May–Sept) ferries from Pier 11 also zip across to Rockaway Beach (see p.393) and Sandy Hook on the Jersey Shore.

NY Waterway (ⓦnywaterway.com) runs the excellent-value East River Ferry, which connects Midtown at 34th Street with various destinations in Brooklyn, Queens and Governors Island. One-way trips are $4, an all-day pass is $12.

None of these options beats the bargain of the free Staten Island Ferry (☎718 727 2508, ⓦsiferry .com), which leaves from its own terminal in Lower Manhattan's Battery Park and provides stunning views of New York Harbour around the clock. It's also a commuter boat, so avoid crowded rush hours if you can. Departures are every 15 to 20 minutes during rush hours (7–9am and 5–7pm), every 30 minutes during the day, and every 60 minutes late at night (the ferry runs 24hr) – weekends less frequently. Few visitors spend much time on Staten Island; it's easy to just turn around and get back on the ferry, although there's plenty to see if you stay.

By bike

Cycling is becoming a viable form of transportation around New York, most enjoyable if you stick to the city's two hundred miles of **bike lanes**, as well as the cycle paths along the waterfront and in parks. Wear all possible safety equipment including pads and a helmet (required by law). When you park, double-chain and lock your bike (including wheels) to an immovable object if you'd like it to be there when you return.

In May 2013 New York started a **bike share scheme** dubbed **Citi Bike** (ⓦcitibikenyc.com), with 10,000 bikes at 600 stations all over the city. There are three payment options: 24-Hour Pass ($9.95), 7-Day Pass ($25) or annual membership ($95). You may make as many trips as you want during your pass period. Pay at any Citi Bike station kiosk with a credit card; you'll be given a code that will unlock a bike so you can begin your trip – end at another station and relock the bike. Trips of less than 30 minutes are free with your pass, but over 30 minutes overtime fees are incurred (starting at $4).

Traditional **bike rentals** start at about $15 per hour or $40 per day – which means opening to closing (9.30am to 6.30pm for instance) – though the bike share scheme may shake things up. See Chapter 31, "Sports and outdoor activities", for more information on bicycle rental.

The media

Generally acknowledged as the media capital of the world, New York is the headquarters of just about all the country's major television news organizations and book and magazine publishers. This means that there is a newsstand on nearly every corner selling a wonderful variety of newspapers and magazines, as well as frequent opportunities to take part in television-show tapings (see box, p.356).

Newspapers and magazines

Although it's still the most vibrant news market in the US, only four newspapers remain. *The New York Times* ($2.50; ⓦnytimes.com), an American institution, prides itself on being the "paper of record" – America's quality national paper (it has the third-largest circulation in the US). It has solid international coverage, and places much emphasis on its news analysis. The Sunday edition ($5) is a thumping bundle of newsprint divided into a number of supplements that take a full day to read.

It takes serious coordination to read the sizeable *Times* on the subway, one reason many turn to the *Daily News* and the *Post*. Tabloids in format and style, these rivals concentrate on local news. The *Daily News* (75¢; ⓦnydailynews.com) is a "picture newspaper" with many racy headlines. The *New York Post* ($1; ⓦnypost.com), the city's oldest newspaper, started in 1801 by Alexander Hamilton, has been in decline for many years. Known for its solid city news and consistent conservative-slanted sermonizing, it also takes a fairly sensationalist approach to headlines.

The other New York-based daily newspaper is *The Wall Street Journal* ($2; ⓦwsj.com), in fact a national paper (with the largest circulation in the US) that also has strong, conservative national and international news coverage – despite an old-fashioned design that eschews the use of photographs.

Weeklies and monthlies

Of the **weekly** papers, the *Village Voice* (Tues; free; ⓦvillagevoice.com) is the most widely read, mainly for its comprehensive arts coverage and investigative features. It offers opinionated stories that often focus on the media, gay issues and civil rights. It's also one of the best pointers to what's on around town (including the most interesting, inexpensive cuisine and shopping). Its main competitor until 2011 was the *New York Press* (ⓦnypress.com), now only published online.

Other leading weeklies include *New York* magazine ($5.99; ⓦnymag.com), which has reasonably good listings and is more of a society and entertainment journal, and *Time Out New York* ($4.99; ⓦtimeouty.com) – a clone of its London original, combining the city's most comprehensive "what's on" listings with New York-slanted stories and features. The venerable *New Yorker* ($5.99; ⓦnewyorker.com) has good highbrow listings, and features poetry and short fiction alongside its much-loved cartoons. The wackiest, and perhaps best, alternative to the *Voice* is *Paper* (ⓦpapermag.com), a monthly that carries witty and well-written rundowns on city nightlife and restaurants as well as current news and gossip. If you want a weekly with more of a political edge, there's the ironic *New York Observer* (Wed; $2; ⓦobserver.com) and the *Forward* ($1; ⓦforward.com), a century-plus-old Jewish publication that's also published in Russian and Yiddish editions.

Many neighbourhoods and ethnic communities have their own weeklies, led by the politically oriented African-American *Amsterdam News* ($1; ⓦamsterdamnews.org), and the *Brooklyn Paper* (free every Fri; ⓦbrooklynpaper.com).

International publications

British, European, Latin American and Asian newspapers are widely available, usually a day after publication – except for the *Financial Times*, which is printed (via satellite) in the US and sold on most newsstands. If you want a specific paper or magazine, try any Universal News or Hudson News, sprinkled throughout the city. Barnes & Noble superstores stock magazines and international newspapers, which you can peruse for **free** over coffee (not free).

Television

Any American will find on TV in New York mostly what they find at home, plus several multilingual stations and some wacky public access channels. Channels 13 and 21 are given over to **PBS** (Public Broadcasting Service), which has earned the nickname "Purely British Station" for its fondness of British drama series, although it excels at documentaries and educational children's shows. The 70-plus stations available on cable in most hotel rooms may be a bit more fascinating for foreign travellers; most cable channels are no better than the major networks (**ABC**, **CBS**, **NBC** and **Fox**), although a few of the specialized channels can be fairly interesting. NY1 is the city's 24-hour local news channel, available exclusively on cable.

Radio

The FM dial is crammed with local stations of varying quality and content. *The New York Times* lists highlights daily; explore on your own and you're sure to come across something interesting.

Incidentally, it's possible to get BBC World Service programmes on WNYC (ⓦwnyc.org) at 93.9FM or 820AM. BBC (ⓦbbc.co.uk/worldservice), Radio Canada (ⓦrcinet.ca) and Voice of America (ⓦvoa.gov) list all their frequencies around the globe.

Tourist information

There is a veritable torrent of information available for visitors to New York City. In the unlikely event it's not in this book, chances are that the answers to any questions you may have are readily accessible on a website or in a brochure.

General information

The central **NYC Information Center** is in Midtown at 810 Seventh Ave at West 53rd Street (Mon–Fri 8.30am–6pm, Sat & Sun 9am–5pm; ☎ 212 484 1222, Ⓦ nycgo.com). It has bus and subway maps, information on hotels and accommodation (including discounts), and up-to-date leaflets on what's going on in the arts and elsewhere. You'll find other small tourist information centres and kiosks all over the city, starting with the airports, Grand Central and Penn stations, and Port Authority Bus Terminal.

INFORMATION CENTRES AND KIOSKS

Brooklyn Tourism and Visitors Center Brooklyn Borough Hall, 209 Joralemon St ☎ 718 802 3846, Ⓦ visitbrooklyn.org. Mon–Fri 10am–6pm.
Dairy Visitor Center & Gift Shop Central Park (mid-park at 65th St) ☎ 212 794 6564, Ⓦ centralparknyc.org. Daily 10am–5pm. Check also Ⓦ nycparks.org, the official word on all of the obscure, famous and thrilling events in the city's parks.
Federal Hall Information Center Federal Hall National Memorial, 26 Wall St. Mon–Fri 9am–5pm; closed federal holidays.
Lower East Side Visitor Center 54 Orchard St, between Hester and Grand sts ☎ 866 226 9010, Ⓦ lowereastsideny.com. Mon–Fri 9am–5pm, Sat & Sun 10am–4pm.
Official NYC Information Center–Harlem Studio Museum, 144 W 125th St, between Powell and Malcolm X blvds ☎ 212 222 1014. Mon–Fri noon–6pm, Sat & Sun 10am–6pm (closed holidays).
Official NYC Information Kiosk–Chinatown Junction of Canal, Walker and Baxter sts ☎ 212 484 1222. Daily 10am–6pm, holidays 10am–3pm.
Official NYC Information Kiosk–City Hall Southern end of City Hall Park, Broadway at Park Row ☎ 212 484 1222. Mon–Fri 9am–6pm, Sat & Sun 10am–5pm, holidays 9am–3pm.
Times Square Museum & Visitors Center 1560 Broadway, entrance on Seventh Ave between W 46th and W 47th sts ☎ 212 452 5283, Ⓦ timessquarenyc.org. Daily 8am–8pm.

Maps

Other than our maps, the best maps of New York City are the free bus maps (ask any subway teller or librarian for one), as well as the huge, minutely detailed neighbourhood maps found fixed to the wall near the teller booth of subway stations. A great selection of New York City maps is available at Ⓦ randmcnally.com. Street atlases of all five boroughs cost around $10–15; if you're after a map of one of the individual outer boroughs, try those produced by Geographia or Hagstrom, on sale online and in bookshops for $5–15.

Tours

There are many different ways to take in the city. First-time visitors may be interested in taking a tour – they come in all kinds of lengths, themes and modes of transportation.

Bus tours

Bus tours can provide a good way to orient yourself with the city. Gray Line New York, Port Authority Terminal at 42nd Street and Eighth Avenue (☎ 800 669 0051 or ☎ 212 445 0848, Ⓦ newyorksightseeing .com), runs a large number of popular **hop-on/ hop-off bus tours** that range from $44 for just the Downtown Loop to two-day passes that cover all loops ($54). Discounts are available for children under 12. Call or look at the website for complete information and to book a tour.

Helicopter tours

A more exciting option is to look at the city by helicopter. This is very expensive, but you won't easily forget the experience. **Liberty Helicopter Tours** (☎ 212 967 6464, Ⓦ libertyhelicopter.com), at the Wall Street Heliport at Pier 6 (near the Staten Island Ferry), offers tours from around $150 per person for 12 to 15 minutes, to $215 per person for 20 minutes. Helicopters take off regularly between 9am and 6pm every day unless winds and visibility are bad. Reservations are required; times vary on Sundays and holidays. New York Helicopter offers slightly cheaper rates from the same location (around $139 for a 12–15min tour; Ⓦ newyorkhelicopter.com).

Boat tours

A great way to see the island of Manhattan is to take one of many **harbour cruises** on offer. The **Circle Line** (☎ 212 563 3200, Ⓦ circleline42.com) sails from Pier 83 at West 42nd Street and Twelfth Avenue, circumnavigating Manhattan and taking in everything from the Statue of Liberty to Harlem, complete with a live commentary; the three-hour tour runs year-round ($38, seniors $33, under-12s $25). The evening two-hour **Harbor Lights Cruise**

BIG APPLE GREETER

If you're nervous about exploring New York, or would just like to meet a local, contact **Big Apple Greeter**, 1 Centre St, Suite 2035 (☎212 669 8159, ⓦbigapplegreeter.org), one of the best – and certainly cheapest – ways to see the city. This not-for-profit organization matches visitors with their active corps of trained volunteer "greeters". Specify the part of the city you'd like to see, indicate an aspect of New York life you'd like to explore, or plead for general orientation – whatever your interests, chances are they will find someone to take you around. Visits have a friendly, informal feel, and generally last a few hours. The service is free. You can call once you're in New York, but it's better to contact the organization as far in advance as possible.

(March–Sept; $34, seniors $30, under-12s $23) offers dramatic views of the skyline. Thrill-seekers should try *The Beast* (May–Sept; adults & seniors $27, under-12s $21), a speedboat painted to look like a shark that will throw you around for thirty minutes at a wave-pounding 45 miles per hour.

Circle Line Downtown (☎1 866 925 4631, ⓦcirclelinedowntown.com) runs harbour cruises from Downtown Manhattan's South Street Seaport; on *Zephyr* (1hr; adults $28, seniors $24, children $17), and speedboat rides on the *Shark* May to September (30min; adults $24, seniors $22, children $17). Alternatively, check the **NY Waterway** website (☎800 533 3779, ⓦnywaterway.com) for a range of speciality cruises. You can also cruise the harbour in style aboard one of the historic yachts based at the South Street Seaport (p.55) or Chelsea Piers (see p.394). **Bateaux New York** (ⓦbateauxnewyork.com) offers posh dining cruises from $90–125/person.

SPECIALIST TOUR COMPANIES

★ **Big Apple Jazz Tours** ☎718 606 8442, ⓦ bigapplejazz.com. Insider Gordon Polatnick offers a fabulous introduction to the Harlem jazz scene, with walking and bus tours that typically take in some of the lesser-known clubs and plenty of jazz history. Wed, Thurs, Fri & Sun ($99; 4hr, 2 sets) and Sun ($149; 5hr & 3 clubs).

★ **Big Onion Walking Tours** ☎212 439 1090, ⓦ bigonion.com. Guided by local history grad students, venerable Big Onion specializes in tours with an ethnic and historical focus: pick one, or take the "Immigrant New York" tour and learn about everyone. Cost is $20; the food-included "Multi-Ethnic Eating Tour" costs $25. Tours last about two hours.

Greenwich Village Literary Pub Crawl ☎212 613 5796, ⓦ literarypubcrawl.com. Local actors lead you to several of the most prominent bars in literary history and read from associated works. Tours meet every Sat at 2pm at the *White Horse Tavern* in Manhattan (see p.334). Reservations are required: $20, students and seniors $15.

★ **Harlem Heritage Tours** ☎212 280 7888, ⓦ harlemheritage .com. Local Neal Shoemaker runs cultural tours of this historic neighbourhood, ranging from Harlem Gospel ($39) to Harlem Renaissance-themed walking tours ($25). The tours sometimes include food, a cultural performance, film clips and/or bus service.

★ **Hush Hip Hop Tours** ☎ 212 391 0900, ⓦ hushtours.com. Illuminating bus tours of the home of hip-hop, given by legends such as

GrandMaster Caz, DJ Red Alert, Kurtis Blow and DJ Kool Herc, from the South Bronx to Harlem and Brooklyn ($32–78).

Municipal Arts Society ☎212 935 3960, ⓦ mas.org/tours. Incredibly detailed historical and architectural tours in Manhattan, Brooklyn, Queens and the Bronx ($20). They also offer free tours of Grand Central Terminal (Wed at 12.30pm; from the information booth).

NoshWalks ☎ 212 222 2243, ⓦ noshwalks.com. Weekend ethnic culinary tours of neighbourhoods in Manhattan, Queens, Brooklyn and the Bronx, incorporating local history and culture, by the author of two NYC food guidebooks. $50 plus food. Reservations recommended.

Scott's Pizza Tours ☎ 212 209 3370, ⓦ scottspizzatours.com. Yes, New York really does boast specialized pizza tours, and this is one of the best; Scott Wiener knows his slices and leads gut-busting bus tours ($60) or walks ($38) of the best pizza joints all over the city – slices included.

Wall Street Experience ☎ 212 608 0130, ⓦ thewallstreet experience.com. Edifying tours (90min–2hr) of the Financial District from Wall Street insiders (founder Andrew Luan was a trader at Deutsche Bank). Local history is enhanced with easy-to-understand segments on the 2008 financial crisis, 9/11 Memorial and the Wall Street Crash. Most tours range $35–50.

Travel essentials

Costs

On a moderate budget, expect to spend at least $200–250 per night on accommodation in a mid-range, centrally located hotel in high season, plus $30–40 per person for a moderate sit-down dinner each night and about $20 more per person per day for takeaway and grocery meals. Getting around will cost $30 per person per week for unlimited public transportation, plus $7–10 for the occasional cab ride. Sightseeing, drinking, clubbing, eating haute cuisine and going to the theatre have the potential to add exponentially to these costs. The combined New York City and State sales **tax** is 8.875 percent, payable on just about everything. Hotel rooms are subject to an additional 5.875 percent tax (for a total of 14.75 percent) and a $2 per night "occupancy tax" for rooms over $40 per night.

You're expected to **tip** in restaurants, bars, taxicabs, hotels (both the bellboy and the cleaning staff) and even some posh restrooms. In restaurants in particular, it's unthinkable not to leave the minimum (15 percent of the bill) – even if you hated the service.

Crime and personal safety

In two words: don't worry. New York has come a long way since the early 1990s. While the city can sometimes feel dangerous, the reality is somewhat different. As far as per capita crime rates go, New York is America's safest city with a population over one million; in 2012, there were 414 homicides, the lowest number since at least 1963 (statistics before that are unreliable). Areas such as Brownsville or East New York in Brooklyn remain sketchy (as is Bedford-Stuyvesant at night), but you are highly unlikely to end up in either place. Take the normal **precautions** and you should be fine; carry bags closed and across your body, don't let cameras dangle, keep wallets in front – not back – pockets, and don't flash money around. You should also keep a firm grip on your phone/iPod/tablet on the subway (these are occasionally snatched just as the doors close). Mugging can and does happen, but rarely during the day. Avoid wandering empty streets or the subway late at night (especially alone). If you are unlucky enough to be mugged, try to stay calm and hand over the money. File the theft at the nearest police station and take the incident report to claim on your insurance back home.

Note that possession of any "controlled substance" is absolutely **illegal**. Should you be found in possession of a very small amount of marijuana, you probably won't go to jail – but you can expect a hefty fine and, for foreigners, deportation.

Each area of New York has its own police precinct; to find the nearest station, call ☎646 610 5000 (during business hours only) or ☎311, or check the phone book. In emergencies, phone ☎911 or use one of the outdoor posts that give you a direct line to the emergency services. This information, plus crime stats, is available at ⓦnyc.gov/nypd.

Electricity

US electricity is **110V AC** and most plugs are two-pronged. Unless they're dual voltage (most mobile phones, cameras, MP3 players and laptops are), all Australian, British, European, Irish, New Zealand and South African appliances will need a voltage transformer as well as a plug adapter (older hair-dryers are a common problem for travellers).

USEFUL NUMBERS
Police, fire or ambulance ☎911
Non-emergency queries ☎311

Entry requirements

Under the Visa Waiver Program, citizens of Australia, Ireland, New Zealand and the UK do **not** require visas for visits to the US of ninety days or less. You will, however, need to obtain **Electronic System for Travel Authorization (ESTA)** online before you fly (at ⓦesta.cbp.dhs.gov/esta/), which involves completing a basic immigration form in advance, on the computer. There is a processing fee of $4, and a further $10 authorization fee once the ESTA has been approved (all paid via credit card online). Once given, authorizations are valid for multiple entries into the US for around two years – it's recommended that you submit an ESTA application as soon as you begin making travel plans (in most cases the ESTA will be granted immediately, but it can sometimes take up to 72hr to get a response). You'll need to present a machine-readable passport to Immigration upon arrival. Note that ESTA currently only applies to visitors arriving by air: crossing the **land border from Canada or Mexico** those qualifying for the Visa Waiver Program do not need to apply for ESTA – instead you must fill in an I-94W form and pay $6, though this may change in future. Canadians now require a passport to cross the border, but can travel in the US for up to a year without a visa or visa waiver.

CONSULATES IN NEW YORK CITY

Australia 34/F, 150 E 42nd St ☎212 351 6500, ⓦnewyork.usa.embassy.gov.au

Canada 1251 Sixth Ave, at W 50th St ☎212 596 1628, ⓦcanadainternational.gc.ca/new_york/index.aspx

Ireland 17/F, 345 Park Ave, between E 51st and E 52nd sts ☎212 319 2555, ⓦconsulateofirelandnewyork.org

New Zealand 222 E 41st St, Suite 2510, between Second and Third aves ☎212 832 4038, ⓦnzembassy.com/usa

South Africa 333 E 38th St, between First and Second aves ☎212 213 4880, ⓦsouthafrica-newyork.net/consulate

UK 845 Third Ave, between E 51st and E 52nd sts ☎212 745 0200, ⓦukinusa.fco.gov.uk

Health

There are few health issues specific to New York City, short of the common cold. Pharmacies can be found every few blocks – CVS and Duane Reade are the city's major chains, many open 24hr (such as the Duane Reade at 1470 Broadway, near Times Square).

If you do get sick or have an accident, things can get incredibly **expensive**; organize **insurance** before your trip, just in case. It will cost upwards of $100 to simply see a doctor or dentist, and prescription drugs can be very pricey – if you don't have US medical insurance (as opposed to normal overseas travel insurance), you'll have to cough up the money and make a claim when you get home.

Should you find yourself requiring a doctor or dentist, ask if your hotel has links to a local practice, or look in the *Yellow Pages* under "Clinics" or "Physicians and Surgeons". Doctors in Manhattan often have long waiting lists however, and will be reluctant to see a new patient at short notice – if you have an accident or need immediate attention head to the **24-hour emergency rooms** at these and other Manhattan hospitals: New York Presbyterian (Cornell), East 70th Street at York Avenue (❶212 746 5050, ❿nyp.org); and Mount Sinai, Madison Avenue at East 100th Street (❶212 241 7171, ❿mountsinai.org).

Should you be in a serious accident, a medical service will pick you up and charge later. Note that basic emergency care will cost at least $200, ranging to several thousand dollars for serious trauma – that's in addition to fees for drugs, appliances, supplies and the attendant physician, who will charge separately.

Insurance

You will want to invest in **travel insurance**. A typical travel-insurance policy usually provides cover for the loss of baggage, tickets, and – up to a certain limit – cash or cheques, as well as cancellation or curtailment of your journey. Many policies can be chopped and changed to exclude coverage you don't need – for example, sickness and accident benefits can often be excluded or included at will. Before you take out a new policy, however, it's worth checking whether you are already covered: some all-risks home-insurance policies may cover your possessions when overseas, and many private medical schemes include cover when abroad.

Internet

Wireless is king in New York, with free wi-fi hotspots in places like Times Square and Bryant Park, complimentary connections at cafés like *Starbucks* and most hotels offering it for no charge. If you're travelling without your own computer, accessing your email is still possible at internet cafés, though their numbers are dwindling. Try the Cyber Café, at 250 West 49th St between Broadway and Eighth Avenue (Mon–Fri 8am–11pm, Sat & Sun 11am–11pm; ❶212 333 4109, ❿cyber-cafe.com), which charges $6.40 per 30 minutes, or 90 Bowery Internet Café in Chinatown (at 90 Bowery and Grand St).

A handy alternative is to stop by a branch of the New York City Public Library, where free wi-fi (network "NYPL") and free computer internet access are available. To use the computers you first need to get a guest pass at the Stephen A. Schwarzman Building (the main library building; Mon & Thurs–Sat 10am–6pm, Tues & Wed 10am–8pm, Sun 1–5pm), at 42nd Street and Fifth Avenue; or Mid-Manhattan Library, 455 Fifth Ave (at 40th St; Mon–Thurs 8am–11am, Fri 8am–8pm, Sat & Sun 10am–6pm). Bring proof of identity and your current home address. With the pass, you can reserve time slots at computers at any branch in person or via ❿nypl.org.

Laundry

Hotels do it but charge a lot. You're much better off going to an ordinary **laundromat** or dry cleaner, of which you'll find plenty listed in the *Yellow Pages* under "Laundries". Most laundromats also offer a very affordable drop service, where, for about $1 per 1lb (0.45kg) or less, you can have your laundry washed, dried and tidily folded – often the same day (there's usually an $18–20 minimum though). Some budget hotels, YMCAs and hostels also have coin-operated washers and dryers.

ROUGH GUIDES TRAVEL INSURANCE

Rough Guides has teamed up with WorldNomads.com to offer great **travel insurance** deals. Policies are available to residents of over 150 countries, with cover for a wide range of **adventure sports**, 24hr emergency assistance, high levels of medical and evacuation cover and a stream of **travel safety information**. Roughguides.com users can take advantage of their policies online 24/7, from anywhere in the world – even if you're already travelling. And since plans often change when you're on the road, you can extend your policy and even claim online. Roughguides.com users who buy travel insurance with WorldNomads.com can also leave a positive footprint and donate to a community development project. For more information go to ❿**roughguides.com/travel-insurance**.

Living and working in New York

It's not easy to live and work in New York, even for US residents. For anyone looking for **short-term** work, the typical urban employment options are available – temporary office work, waiting tables, babysitting, etc – as well as some quirkier opportunities, like artists' modelling in Chelsea. For ideas and positions, check the employment ads in *The New York Times*, *New York Press*, *Village Voice*, Craigslist NYC (Ⓦnewyork .craigslist.org) and the free neighbourhood tabloids available throughout the city.

If you're a foreigner, you start at a disadvantage. Unless you already have family in the US (in which case special rules may apply), you need a **work visa**, and these can be extremely difficult to get. The US visa system is one of the world's most complex, with a bewildering range of visa types to suit every circumstance (a "green card" refers to permanent resident status, meaning you can work without a visa, but this is hard to obtain without working or living here first) – most people hire a lawyer to do the paperwork ($2000 and up). Essentially, you'll need a firm offer of work from a US company; however, unless you have a special skill, few companies will want to go through the hassle of sponsoring you. Since tourists are not supposed to seek work, legally you'll have to apply for jobs from overseas. Plenty of foreigners do manage to work for short periods illegally in New York (typically cash-in-hand jobs, bar work or freelancing); be warned however that the penalties for doing so can be harsh (deportation and being barred from the US for up to ten years), and that if you repeatedly enter the country on a visa waiver, you are likely to be severely questioned at Immigration. For further visa information, go to Ⓦtravel.state.gov/visa.

Finding a place to **stay** is tricky for everyone. A studio apartment – a single room with bathroom and kitchen – in a popular neighbourhood in Manhattan can go for upwards of $1800 per month. Many newcomers share studios and one-bedrooms among far too many people; it makes more sense to look in the outer boroughs or the nearby New Jersey towns of Jersey City and Hoboken. However, even some of these neighbourhoods are becoming expensive, and to find a real deal you must hunt hard and check out even the most unlikely possibilities. It frequently takes up to a month or two to find a place.

Most people employ the services of an agent, though they usually work for a fee based on a percentage of the first month's rent. Citi Habitats is one of the biggest agencies (Ⓦciti-habitats.com). Watch also the ads in the *Village Voice*, *The New York Times* and on Ⓦnewyork.craigslist.org (actually a great resource for all kinds of classified listings in New York). Try commercial and campus bulletin boards too, where you might secure a temporary apartment or sublet while the regular tenant is away.

Left luggage

The best place to leave luggage is with your **hotel concierge**, but you can also use Schwartz Travel Services ($7–10/day per item; ☎212 290 2626, Ⓦschwartztravel.com) at 355 West 36th St, near Penn Station, and 34 West 46th St, between Fifth and Sixth avenues near Grand Central (both daily 8am–11pm).

Lost property

For things lost on **buses** or on the **subway**: NYC Transit Authority, at the West 34th Street/Eighth Avenue Station on the lower level-subway mezzanine (Mon, Tues & Fri 8am–3.30pm, Wed & Thurs 11am–6.30pm; ☎212 712 4500). For things lost in a cab call ☎311; try to get the cab's medallion number (printed on your receipt).

Mail

Post offices in New York City are generally open Monday to Friday 9am to 5pm (though some open earlier) and Saturday from 9am to noon or later. The main post office in Midtown is at 421 Eighth Ave, at West 33rd Street (☎212 967 8585) and is open 24 hours, seven days a week. **Ordinary mail** within the US costs 46¢ for letters weighing up to an ounce, and 33¢ for postcards; addresses must include a **zip code** (postal code) and a return address in the upper left corner of the envelope. International letters and postcards will usually take about a week to reach their destination; rates are currently $1.10 for letters and postcards to all other countries. To find a post office or check up-to-date rates, see Ⓦusps.com or call ☎1 800 275 8777.

Money

US currency comes in bills of $1, $5, $10, $20, $50 and $100, plus various larger (and rarer) denominations. The dollar is made up of 100 cents (¢) in coins of 1 cent (usually called a penny), 5 cents (a nickel), 10 cents (a dime), 25 cents (a quarter) and rarely, 50 cents (a half-dollar) and one dollar. Change – especially quarters – is needed for buses, vending machines and telephones, so always carry plenty.

Most people on holiday in New York withdraw cash as needed from **ATMs**, which are at any bank branch and at many convenience stores and delis in the city, though the latter can charge fees of up to $3 for the service (in addition to bank charges). If you're visiting from abroad, make sure you have a personal identification number (PIN) that's designed to work overseas. A credit card is a must; American Express, MasterCard and Visa are widely accepted, and are almost always required for deposits at hotels. Most banks are open Monday to Friday 8.30am to 5pm, and a few have limited Saturday hours (major Citibank branches tend to open Sat 9am–3pm).

The value of the US dollar tends to vary considerably against other currencies. At press time, one dollar was worth 0.70 British pounds (£), 0.77 euros (€), 1.03 Canadian dollars (Can$), 0.96 Australian dollars (Aus$), 1.22 New Zealand dollars (NZ$) and 9.24 South African Rand (R). For current exchange rates, check Ⓦxe.com.

Opening hours

The opening hours of specific attractions are given throughout the Guide. As a general rule, most **museums** are open Tuesday to Sunday, 10am to 5/6pm, though most have one night per week where they stay open at least a few hours later. **Government offices** are open during regular business hours, usually 9am to 5pm. **Shop** hours vary widely, depending on the kind of shop and what part of town you're in, though you can generally count on their being open Monday to Saturday from around 10am to 6pm, with limited Sunday hours. Many of the larger chain or department stores will stay open to 9pm or later, and you generally don't have to walk more than a few blocks anywhere in Manhattan to find a 24-hour deli. On national public holidays (see box below), banks and offices are likely to be closed all day, and most shops will be closed or have reduced hours.

Phones

International visitors who want to use their mobile phones in New York will need to check with their phone provider to make sure it will work, and what the call charges will be. Unless you have a tri-band phone, it is unlikely that a mobile bought for use outside the US or Canada will work inside the States (all iPhones should be OK). Even if your phone does work you'll need to be extra careful about **roaming charges**, especially for data, which can be extortionate; even checking voicemail can result in hefty charges. Many travellers turn off voicemail and data roaming before they travel. If you have a compatible (and **unlocked**) GSM phone and intend to use it a lot, it can be much cheaper to **buy a US SIM card** ($10 or less) to use during your stay (you can also buy a micro-SIM for iPhone 4, 4S, or any compatible smartphone, or a nano-SIM for iPhone 5). AT&T (Ⓦatt .com) is your best bet (unlimited calls from $2/day; unlimited calls and data for 1 month $85). Some networks also sell basic phones (with minutes) for as little as $15 (no paperwork or ID required).

Public telephones are becoming harder to find due to the popularity of mobile phones. The cost of a local call (within New York) is 25¢ for three or four minutes, depending on the carrier (each phone company runs its own booths). Calls elsewhere within the US are usually 25¢ for one minute; overseas long-distance rates are pricier, and you're better off using a prepaid calling card ($5, $10 and $20), which you can buy at most grocery stores and newsstands.

There are five area codes in use in New York: ☎212 and ☎646 for Manhattan, ☎718 and ☎347 for the outer boroughs and ☎917 for (mostly) mobile phones. You must dial the area code, even if you're calling a number from a phone within the same area. For directory assistance, call ☎411.

Smoking

Since 2003 smoking has been banned in virtually all indoor public areas (including malls, bars, restaurants and most work places) in New York – fines start at around $100 for breaking this law, though it

---

PUBLIC HOLIDAYS

New Year's Day Jan 1
Martin Luther King, Jr's Birthday Third Mon in Jan
Presidents' Day Third Mon in Feb
Memorial Day Last Mon in May
Independence Day July 4

Labor Day First Mon in Sept
Columbus Day Second Mon in Oct
Veterans' Day Nov 11
Thanksgiving Day Fourth Thurs in Nov
Christmas Day Dec 25

CALLING HOME FROM THE US

Note that the initial zero is omitted from the area code when dialling the UK, Ireland, Australia, and New Zealand from abroad. The US country code (which it shares with Canada) is 1.

Australia 011 + 61 + city code + local number.
Canada city code + local number.
New Zealand 011 + 64 + city code + local number.
UK 011 + 44 + city code + local number.
Republic of Ireland 011 + 353 + city code + local number.

is rarely enforced in late-night bars and clubs (the onus is on the owner to stop you smoking). In 2011, smoking was also prohibited at all parks, beaches and pedestrian plazas.

Time

New York City is on Eastern Standard Time (EST), which is five hours behind Greenwich Mean Time (GMT), three hours ahead of Pacific Standard Time, fourteen to sixteen hours behind East Coast Australia (variations for Daylight Savings) and sixteen to eighteen hours behind New Zealand (variations for Daylight Savings).

Travellers with disabilities

New York City has had disabled access regulations imposed on an aggressively disabled-unfriendly system. There are wide variations in accessibility, making navigation a tricky business. At the same time, you'll find New Yorkers surprisingly willing to go out of their way to help you. If you're having trouble and you feel that passers-by are ignoring you, it's most likely out of respect for your privacy – never hesitate to ask for assistance.

For wheelchair users, getting around on the **subway** is next to impossible without someone to help you, and even then is extremely difficult at most stations. Several, but not all, lines are equipped with elevators, but this doesn't make much of a difference. The Transit Authority is working to make stations accessible, but at the rate they're going it won't happen soon. **Buses** are another story, and are the first choice of many disabled New Yorkers. All MTA buses are equipped with wheelchair lifts and locks. To get on a bus, wait at the bus stop to signal the driver you need to board; when he or she has seen you, move to the back door, where he or she will assist you. For travellers with other mobility difficulties, the driver will lower a special ramp to allow you easier access.

For wheelchair users, **taxis** are less of a possibility unless you have a collapsible chair, in which

case drivers are required to store it and assist you; the unfortunate reality is that most drivers won't stop if they see you waiting. If you're refused, try to get the cab's medallion number and report the driver at ☎311. Most major hotels in New York have wheelchair-accessible rooms, including roll-in showers.

SERVICES

Big Apple Greeter (see p.30).
The Lighthouse 111 E 59th St ☎ 212 821 9200,
Ⓦ lighthouse.org. General services for the visually impaired.
The Mayor's Office for People with Disabilities 100 Gold St, 2nd floor ☎ 212 788 2830, Ⓦ nyc.gov/html/mopd/home.html. General information and resources.
Traveler's Aid ☎ 202 546 1127, Ⓦ travelersaid.org. Nonprofit organization with professional and volunteer staff who provide emergency assistance to disabled or elderly travellers at JFK airport: you can find volunteers at the Ground Transportation Counters in each terminal or via their main office in the arrivals area of Terminal 6 (daily 10am–6pm). They also operate at Newark airport.

Women travellers

Women travelling alone or with other women in New York City should attract no more attention than in any other urban destination in the US. As always, the usual precautions should suffice; a big part of visiting New York is to look as if you know what you're doing and where you're going. If someone's bugging you, either turn away, leave, or let them know your feelings loudly and firmly. Avoid getting noticeably intoxicated unless you are with a trusted friend. If you are being followed, turn around and look at the person following you, and step off the pavement and into the street; attackers hate the open. If you're unsure about the area where you're staying, ask other women's advice. However, don't avoid parts of the city just through hearsay – you might miss out on what's of most interest – and learn to expect New Yorkers (Manhattanites in particular, many of whom feel incorrectly that anywhere outside of the borough shouldn't be risked) to sound alarmist; it's part of the culture.

The Harbor Islands

The southern tip of Manhattan, together with the shores of New Jersey, Staten Island and Brooklyn, enclose the broad expanse of New York Harbor. When the Dutch arrived in 1624, it was teeming with fish, seals, whales and half of the world's oysters. With the water heavily polluted, the last oyster bed was closed in 1927, and though things are much improved (the harbour is officially clean enough to swim and fish), it will take many generations to recover its former glory. For now, the main attractions lie above water, where ferries provide dazzling views of New York's celebrated skyline. Take a boat to Liberty, Ellis or Governors islands (the only way to get to any of the Harbour Islands is by ferry) or, if you're feeling less purposeful, catch the Staten Island Ferry, which traverses the harbour for free.

ARRIVAL AND DEPARTURE

Ferries to Liberty and Ellis islands Take the #1 train to South Ferry, R to Whitehall or the #4 or #5 trains to Bowling Green, then walk to Castle Clinton in Battery Park where you can buy tickets (round-trip $17, seniors $14, children 4–12 $9). The best way to avoid the long wait (you must line up to buy tickets, and then again to clear security before boarding the ferry), is to buy tickets in advance online, preferably reserving the 9am slot, and have them emailed to you; you can then go straight to the security queue. From the nearby pier, Statue Cruises goes to Liberty, then on to Ellis Island (daily, every 30–45min 9.30am–4.45pm; ☎ 201 604 2800, ⓦ statuecruises.com). You must be at security thirty minutes before departure.

Ferries to Governors Island Ferries run from the Battery Maritime Building at Slip 7 just northeast of the Staten Island Ferry Terminal (late May–late Sept: Wed–Fri guided tours only; Sat & Sun hourly 10am–5pm; last ferry back 7pm; free). Access is on a first-come, first-served basis, and limited to 400 people per trip. Call ahead or check the websites (☎ 212 825 3045, ⓦ nps.gov/gois & ⓦ govisland.com) for the up-to-date schedule. The East River Ferry service (see p.27) also connects Governors Island with Wall St/Pier 11 and other locations along the East River in season.

Ferries to Staten Island The Staten Island Ferry (free; ⓦ siferry.com) departs every half an hour and shuttles between Manhattan and its namesake island (see p.52). While it provides a beautiful panorama of the harbour and downtown skyline, it doesn't actually stop at any of the Harbour Islands.

INFORMATION

Tickets The basic ferry ticket to Liberty and Ellis islands allows entry to Ellis Island and Liberty Island grounds only. If you want to visit the museum at the base of the Statue of Liberty and the pedestal observation deck (168 steps up), you need a "pedestal/museum ticket" (no extra charge). To enjoy the cramped but spectacular views from the crown of the statue, buy a special "crown ticket" ($20, seniors $17, children 4–12 $12; includes round-trip ferry) in advance and climb a total of 354 steps – note that you must go through another security screening before entry to the statue.

Timing your visit Give yourself at least half a day to see both Liberty and Ellis islands. Liberty Island needs at least one hour (that's only if you're walking around the island, and not going inside the statue), and Ellis requires at least two hours to do its museum justice. Start out as early as possible: keep in mind that if you take the last ferry of the day to Liberty Island, you won't be able to get over to Ellis. Allow at least two hours for a leisurely amble around Governors Island.

The Statue of Liberty

Daily 9.30am–5pm • Free with ferry ticket (extra $3 for "crown ticket"); ranger-guided tours of Liberty Island are offered throughout the day (free) • ☎ 212 363 3200, ⓦ nps.gov/stli

Of all America's symbols, none has proved more enduring than the **Statue of Liberty**, looming over the harbour from its pedestal on tiny **Liberty Island**. Indeed, there is probably no more immediately recognizable profile in existence than that of Lady Liberty, who stands with torch in hand, clutching a stone tablet. Measuring some 305ft from her pedestal base, she has acted as the figurehead of the American Dream for more than a century. When the first waves of European refugees arrived in the mid-nineteenth century, it was she who greeted them – the symbolic beginning of a new life.

The **statue** itself, which depicts Liberty throwing off her shackles and holding a beacon to light the world, is the creation of French sculptor **Frédéric Auguste Bartholdi**,

---

A BEACON TO THE WORLD

These days, an immigrant's first view of the US is more likely to be the customs check at JFK Airport, but the Statue of Liberty nevertheless remains a stirring sight. **The New Colossus** by American Jewish poet Emma Lazarus, inspired by the new immigrant experience and inscribed on a tablet on the pedestal, is no less quotable now than when it was written in 1883: "Give me your tired, your poor, Your huddled masses yearning to breathe free, The wretched refuse of your teeming shore. Send these, the homeless, tempest-tost to me, I lift my lamp beside the golden door!"

1

who crafted it a hundred years after the American Revolution, supposedly to commemorate the solidarity between France and America. (Actually, he originally intended the statue for Alexandria, Egypt.) Bartholdi built Liberty in Paris between 1874 and 1884, starting with a terracotta model and enlarging it through four successive versions to its present size of 151ft. The final product is a construction of thin copper sheets bolted together and supported by an iron framework designed by **Gustave Eiffel**. The statue had to be taken apart into hundreds of pieces in order to ship it to New York, where it was finally reassembled, although it was another two years before it could be properly unveiled. Only through the efforts of newspaper magnate Joseph Pulitzer, a keen supporter of the statue, were the necessary funds raised and Liberty was formally dedicated by President Cleveland on October 28, 1886, amid a patriotic outpouring that has never really stopped. Indeed, fifteen million people descended on Manhattan for the statue's centennial celebrations, and some three million people make the pilgrimage here each year.

The **museum** is definitely worth a look, the downstairs lobby containing the original torch and flame (completed first and used to raise funds for the rest of the statue), and the small exhibition upstairs telling the story of Lady Liberty with prints, photographs, posters and replicas. At the top of the pedestal, you can look up into the centre of the

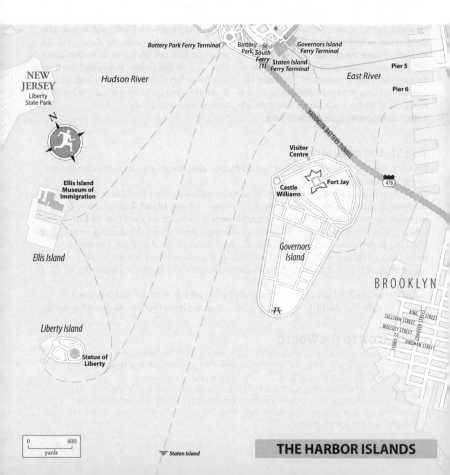

THE HARBOR ISLANDS

statue's skirts – make sure you get a glance of her riveted and bolted interior, and her fire-hazard staircase. After you've perused the statue's interior offerings, take a turn around the balcony outside – the views are predictably superb.

Ellis Island Museum of Immigration

Daily 9.30am–5.15pm • Free • Hourly 45min ranger-guided tours (free); audio tours (free); documentary film *Island of Hope, Island of Tears* (30min) shown throughout the day (free) • ☎ 212 363 3200, ⓦ ellisisland.org & ⓦ nps.gov/elis

Just across the water from Liberty Island, and fifteen minutes farther from Manhattan by ferry, sits **Ellis Island**, the former arrival point for over twelve million immigrants to the US. After $162 million was donated for its restoration, the main complex reopened in 1990 as the impressive **Ellis Island Museum of Immigration**, which eloquently recaptures the spirit of the place with artefacts, photographs, maps and personal accounts that tell the story of the immigrants who passed through here on their way to a new life in America – some 100 million Americans can trace their roots to those who arrived on the island.

On the first floor, the excellent permanent exhibit "Peopling of America" chronicles four centuries of immigration, offering a statistical portrait of those who disembarked here – who they were, where they came from and why they came. The huge, vaulted Registry Room on the second floor, scene of so much immigrant trepidation, elation and despair, has been left imposingly bare, with just a couple of inspectors' desks and American flags. In the side halls, a series of interview rooms re-creates the process that immigrants went through on their way to naturalization; the white-tiled chambers are soberingly bureaucratic. Each room is augmented by recorded voices of those who passed through Ellis Island, recalling their experiences, along with photographs, explanatory text and small mementoes – train timetables, toiletries and toys from home.

The museum's **American Family Immigration History Center** (same times as museum) holds a database of over 22 million immigrants who passed through New York between 1892 and 1924. Outside, the names of over 700,000 of these immigrants are engraved in copper; while the "Wall of Honor" (ⓦ wallofhonor.org) is always accepting new submissions, it controversially requires families to pay $150 to be included on the list.

Governors Island

Late May to late Sept Sat & Sun 10am–7pm • Free • 2hr guided tours Wed–Fri (free; see website for details) • ☎ 212 825 3045, ⓦ nps.gov/gois & ⓦ govisland.com

"Nowhere in New York is more pastoral," wrote travel writer Jan Morris of **Governors Island**, a 172-acre tract of land across from Brooklyn with unobstructed views of the Financial District and New York Harbor. With its village greens and colonial architecture reminiscent of a New England college campus, a visit here makes for an intriguingly offbeat and bucolic day-trip, offering a dramatic contrast to the skyscrapers across the water. Ferries arrive at Soissons Landing, where you'll find the small **visitors' centre** (with maps and information about the island) and a gift shop. From here you can explore on foot or by bike (Bike and Roll; $20/half-day, $25/day; ☎ 212 260 0400, ⓦ bikenewyorkcity.com), or simply head to the tiny artificial beach at **Governors Beach Club** (to the right), which comes with food-and-drink tent, various events, live bands, volleyball and stupendous views (ⓦ governorsbeachclub.com).

When the Dutch arrived in 1624, they actually made camp here first before cautiously occupying Manhattan, and "purchased" what they called Noten Island from the Native Americans in 1637 (only to lose it to the British in the 1660s). Set aside for the "benefit and accommodation of His Majesty's Governors", Governors Island formally received its current name in 1784. Between 1794 and 1966, the US Army occupied the island, and for the following thirty years it was the US Coast Guard's

1

THE IMMIGRANT EXPERIENCE

Up until the 1850s, there was no official **immigration process** in New York, but a surge of Irish, German and Scandinavian immigrants forced authorities to open an immigration centre at Castle Clinton in Battery Park. By the 1880s, millions of desperate immigrants (mostly southern and eastern Europeans) were leaving their homelands in search of a new life in America. The Battery Park facilities proved totally inadequate, and in 1892 Ellis Island became the new immigration station.

The immigrants who arrived on Ellis Island were all **steerage-class passengers**; richer immigrants were processed at their leisure on-board ship. Though the processing centre had been designed to accommodate 500,000 immigrants per year, double that number arrived during the early part of the twentieth century; as many as 11,747 immigrants passed through the centre on a single day in 1907. Once inside, each family was split up – men sent to one area, women and children to another – while a series of checks weeded out the undesirables and the infirm. The latter were taken to the second floor, where doctors would check for "loathsome and contagious diseases" as well as signs of insanity. Those who failed medical tests were marked with a white cross on their backs and either sent to the hospital or put back on the boat; only two percent of all immigrants were ever rejected, and of those, many jumped into the sea and tried to swim to Manhattan, or committed suicide. Eighty percent of immigrants were processed in less than eight hours, after which they headed either to New Jersey and trains to the West, or into New York City. After 1924, Ellis Island became primarily a **detention facility** (during World War II, some seven thousand German, Italian and Japanese people were detained here), before finally closing in 1954.

largest and most extensive installation. In 2003, 22 acres of the island were sold to the National Park Service as the Governors Island National Monument. In 2010, the New York Harbor School (a public high school) opened here.

It's a short stroll from the dock up to **Fort Jay**, completed in 1794. Reinforced in 1806, its dense stone walls helped to deter the British from attacking the city in 1812. Nearby, you can wander the shady lanes of **Nolan Park**, home to some beautifully preserved, bright yellow Neoclassical and Federal-style mansions dating from 1857 to 1902 (occupied by officers during the army period), notably the Governor's House and Admiral's Mansion, site of the Reagan–Gorbachev Summit in 1988. Many of these are gradually being opened, or converted into art studios.

At the southern end of Nolan Park and facing the grassy **Parade Ground**, the grey stone Episcopalian **Chapel of St Cornelius & the Centurion** was completed in 1907. To the south, the humble white-clapboard **Our Lady of the Sea Chapel** served as the Roman Catholic house of worship from 1942. The southern side of the Parade Ground is taken up by **Colonels' Row**, another collection of historic redbrick housing built between 1893 and 1917 (used for officers' housing) backed by the impressive bulk of **Liggett Hall**, a barracks completed in 1929. Heading back to the waterfront you'll see **Castle Williams**, a circular fort completed in 1811 to complement the near-identical Castle Clinton in Battery Park. Used as a prison until 1966, the tiny cells inside held as many as a thousand Confederate soldiers during the Civil War.

The island also has plenty of green spaces in which to lounge in the sun, as well as a breezy promenade with stellar views of Manhattan – you can stroll right down to the southern tip, dubbed **Picnic Point**, or enjoy the open spaces of **Liggett Terrace**, **Hammock Grove** and the **Play Lawn**, which all opened in 2013. On summer evenings the island is increasingly being used as a concert, DJ and event venue: see Ⓦ governorsislandalliance.org for the latest schedule.

NEW YORK STOCK EXCHANGE

The Financial District

With its dizzying assemblage of skyscrapers, the Financial District has long been synonymous with the New York of popular imagination. This is where New Amsterdam was founded in the 1620s, and today the heart of the world's financial markets is still home to some of the city's most historic streets and sights. Over time, the area has seen more than its fair share of destruction and renewal; indeed, thanks to landfill, today's Financial District is double the size of that first Dutch colony, and many of the early colonial buildings burned down in either the Revolutionary War or the Great Fire of 1835. In September 2001, the character of the Financial District was altered radically once again after the attack on the Twin Towers, while Hurricane Sandy wreaked further devastation in 2012.

Yet the regeneration of the area is startling: the new One World Trade Center now towers above the city, and a spate of ambitious projects from parks and office towers to transport hubs and new hotels pepper the area. Though some banks still maintain headquarters here, the most dramatic change is in the increase of residential development, as new condos and luxury conversions (many from former bank buildings) prove that the Financial District is once again in the process of integrating its present and future into its past.

2

Wall Street and around
Subway #2, #3, #4, #5 to Wall St

Associated with money since the eighteenth century, **Wall Street** takes its name from the wooden stockade built by the Dutch in 1653 to protect themselves from the British colonies further north (the wall was dismantled in 1699). Though it remains the apex of the global financial system thanks to the Stock Exchange, most of the street was closed to traffic after 9/11, and fitness studios and condos have replaced almost all the banks that were once based here.

Trinity Church
79 Broadway, at Wall St • Mon–Fri 7am–6pm, Sat 8am–4pm, Sun 7am–4pm; museum Mon–Fri 9am–5.30pm (closed during the 12.05pm service), Sat & Sun 9am–3.45pm • Free • ☎ 212 602 0800, ⓦ trinitywallstreet.org • Subway #4, #5 to Wall St

Perched at Wall Street's western end on Broadway is **Trinity Church**, a stoic onlooker of the street's dealings. The church held its first service in 1698, but this stern Gothic Revival structure – the third model – went up in 1846. It was the city's tallest building for fifty years, a reminder of how relatively recently high-rise Manhattan has sprung up. Trinity has the air of an English country church (hardly surprising, given its architect, Richard Upjohn, was English), especially in the

---

GREED IS GOOD: THE RISE AND FALL OF WALL STREET

Admired, feared and generally despised by most Americans at the time, **J.P. Morgan** is considered the godfather of US merchant banking (that is, banking for governments and big companies rather than individuals), presiding over New York's gradual replacement of London (largely bailed out by Morgan-led banks during World War I) as the world's biggest financial market from his base on **Wall Street** between 1858 and 1913. Wall Street and its merchant banks (also "investment banks") boomed in the 1920s, survived the Great Depression and regulation of the 1930s and led the world with innovative products such as "junk bonds" and derivatives into the 1990s. Yet today, all the big investment banks have gone and most of Wall Street has been converted into condos – so where did it all go wrong?

A series of crashes, starting with the dot-com bust and 9/11 attacks in 2001, battered the markets and began the physical move away from the Financial District and Wall Street (as much for security as high rental costs). The **2008–2009 financial crisis** proved the hardest blow. Investment banks had arranged hundreds of CDOs (Collateralized Debt Obligations), essentially bonds secured by subprime mortgages, since 1987; when overextended borrowers began to default on their mortgages all over the US, the money dried up. Insurer AIG was bailed out by the US government to the tune of $186 billion, and one by one the investment banks failed, unable to cope with mind-boggling losses. Lehman Brothers, founded in 1850, collapsed with debts of over $700 billion (the largest bankruptcy in US history), and Bear Stearns and Merrill Lynch were sold to JPMorgan Chase and Bank of America respectively. Finally, Goldman Sachs and Morgan Stanley (the last heir to JP's empire) converted to traditional bank holding companies (thus allowing them access to federal funds), ending the era of merchant banks on Wall Street.

The financial sector remains a huge part of the New York economy, but these days hedge funds, not banks, tend to manage the biggest portfolios, and trading rooms are as likely to be based in Connecticut and New Jersey as Manhattan.

sheltered **graveyard**, the resting place of many early Manhattanites: Alexander Hamilton (see box, p.207), famed diarist and lawyer George Templeton Strong and steamboat king Robert Fulton among them. As you enter the church itself, note the ornate bronze doors designed by Richard Morris Hunt in the 1890s, a memorial to John Jacob Astor III. Towards the back you'll find a small but enlightening **museum** that shows temporary exhibits, from thought-provoking art installations to the history of the church.

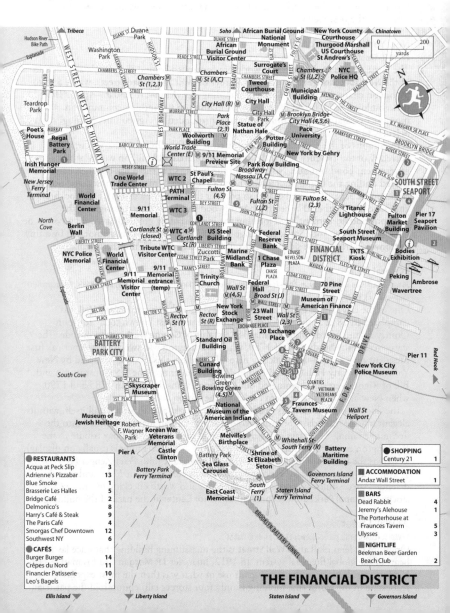

● RESTAURANTS	
Acqua at Peck Slip	3
Adrienne's Pizzabar	13
Blue Smoke	1
Brasserie Les Halles	5
Bridge Café	2
Delmonico's	8
Harry's Café & Steak	9
The Paris Café	4
Smorgas Chef Downtown	12
Southwest NY	6

● CAFÉS	
Burger Burger	14
Crêpes du Nord	11
Financier Patisserie	10
Leo's Bagels	7

● SHOPPING	
Century 21	1

■ ACCOMMODATION	
Andaz Wall Street	1

■ BARS	
Dead Rabbit	4
Jeremy's Alehouse	1
The Porterhouse at Fraunces Tavern	5
Ulysses	3

■ NIGHTLIFE	
Beekman Beer Garden Beach Club	2

THE FINANCIAL DISTRICT

1 and 14 Wall Street

1 & 14 Wall St • Closed to the public • Subway #2, #3, #4, #5 to Wall St

Opposite Trinity Church, the soaring Bank of New York building at **1 Wall Street** is an Art Deco wonder, topping out at 654ft in 1931. From the outside, you can just about make out the shimmering mosaic lobby interior (sadly closed to the public). On the other side of the street, the old Bankers Trust Building at **14 Wall Street** (539ft) was completed in 1912 and is best known for its ostentatious step-pyramid top, modelled on the Greek Mausoleum at Halicarnassus – wander down Broad Street for the best views.

New York Stock Exchange

11 Wall St • Closed to the public • Ⓦ nyse.com • Subway #2, #3, #4, #5 to Wall St

The purse strings of the capitalist world are controlled behind the Neoclassical facade of the **New York Stock Exchange** at the corner of Wall and Broad streets, where $35 to 50 billion changes hands on an average trading day (Mon–Fri 9.30am–4pm). The main building at 18 Broad St, with its six mammoth Corinthian columns and monumental statues representing Integrity surrounded by Agriculture, Mining, Science, Industry and Invention, dates from 1903.

The origins of the exchange lie in the aftermath of the Revolutionary War, when Secretary of the Treasury Alexander Hamilton offered $80 million worth of government bonds for sale. Not only did the public snap them up, but merchants also started trading the bonds, along with bills of exchange, promissory notes, and other commercial paper. Trading became so popular that in 1792 a group of 22 stockbrokers and merchants gathered beneath a buttonwood tree on Wall Street, signing the "**Buttonwood Agreement**" and forming the initial trading group that would go on to be renamed the New York Stock Exchange in 1817. The event is commemorated by a tiny **buttonwood tree** on the sidewalk in front of 18 Broad St (it's not the original).

Federal Hall

26 Wall St, at Nassau St • Mon–Fri 9am–5pm • Free; free 30min tours 10am, 11am, 1pm, 2pm & 3pm • ☎ 212 825 6990, Ⓦ nps.gov/feha • Subway #2, #3, #4, #5 to Wall St

One of the city's finest examples of Greek Revival architecture, **Federal Hall** was completed in 1842 as the US Customs House, but is best known today for John Quincy Adams Ward's monumental 1883 **statue of George Washington** outside. The statue recalls the heady days of 1789, when Washington was sworn in as America's first president on a second-floor balcony here – back then, this site was occupied by New York's second City Hall (demolished in 1812). Elements of the US Constitution and Bill of Rights were also hammered out by Congress inside between 1785 and 1790, when New York was the de facto capital of the nation.

The documents and exhibits inside are worth a look, as is the main hall itself, with its elegant marble rotunda, Corinthian columns and Cretan maidens worked into the decorative railings. Displays cover the history of the building and pay tribute to the Washington connection (the Bible he used in the 1789 ceremony is usually on display), as well as the landmark libel case of German immigrant John Peter Zenger (1697–1746), who was arrested for exposing government corruption in 1734, and was defended successfully by Andrew Hamilton. It's also worth checking out the well-stocked **National Parks of New York Harbor Visitor Center** at the back of the building.

23 Wall Street

23 Wall St • Closed to the public • Subway #2, #3, #4, #5 to Wall St

Opposite Federal Hall at **23 Wall Street** is the unassuming building that once lay at the heart of the global financial system. In 1912, financier **J.P. Morgan** had his marble-clad headquarters built here; the extravagant use of what was then the most expensive real-estate in the world (the building is only four storeys tall) epitomized the patrician aloofness of the period – the bank didn't even bother adding its name to the facade. J.P. Morgan had been based on this spot since 1873, taking his father's words to heart – "always be a bull on America". In 1920, a horse-drawn cart blew up out front, killing 38 and wounding over a hundred. The bombing has never been explained, though the most popular theory holds that the blast was planned by Italian anarchists taking revenge for the arrest of Sacco and Vanzetti. The shrapnel marks on the building's wall have never been repaired, out of respect for the victims. In 2003, JPMorgan sold the building for $100 million, with part of the structure absorbed by the conversion of 15 Broad Street into luxury condos by Philippe Starck.

2

Trump Building
40 Wall St · Closed to the public · Subway #2, #3, #4, #5 to Wall St

Further along Wall Street, the former Bank of Manhattan Trust building was briefly the world's tallest skyscraper in 1930 (at 927ft), before being topped by the Chrysler Building (whose designers secretly increased the height of their tower after no. 40 was completed). Today, it's known as the **Trump Building** after the flamboyant tycoon who bought it for just $1 million in 1995 (he has claimed it is worth at least $600 million since then).

The Museum of American Finance
48 Wall St · Tues–Sat 10am–4pm · $8 · ☎ 212 908 4110, ⓦ moaf.org · Subway #2, #3, #4, #5 to Wall St

Across William Street from the Trump Building, the former Bank of New York & Trust building is now home to the **Museum of American Finance**. Housed in the fittingly opulent former main banking hall completed in 1929, this illuminating museum is the best place to gain an understanding of what's really going on outside: stocks, bonds and futures trading are demystified through multimedia presentations and a stack of rare artefacts that include a 1792 bond signed by Washington, an 1850s gold ingot and a stretch of ticker tape from the opening moments of 1929's Great Crash. Financial pioneer Alexander Hamilton (see box, p.207) is commemorated with his own room, while documentaries on Wall Street are shown throughout the day.

20 Exchange Place
20 Exchange Place · Closed to the public · Subway #2, #3 to Wall St

One block south of Wall Street on William Street, **20 Exchange Place** is a truly stupendous Art Deco tower (741ft), built for City Bank-Farmers Trust in 1931 and now a series of luxury apartments. The main entrance is adorned by eleven stone impressions of coins from the countries where the bank had offices, while the nineteenth floor is circled by fourteen "Giants of Finance", helmeted figures that look like classical Greek warriors.

Delmonico's
56 Beaver St, at William St · Mon–Fri 11.30am–10pm, Sat 5–10pm · ☎ 212 509 1144, ⓦ delmonicosrestaurantgroup.com · Subway #2, #3 to Wall St

Venerable **Delmonico's** is technically the oldest restaurant in the country, although it's been closed for prolonged periods and has exchanged owners several times over the

---

FROM FIRE TO FINE DINING ON STONE STREET

The best-preserved block of nineteenth-century architecture in the Financial District is narrow, cobblestone **Stone Street**, between Hanover Square and Coenties Alley – also the Financial District's best place to eat and drink. It's a vast open-air beer garden packed with a party-hardy Wall Street crowd on summer nights, when places like *Ulysses* (see p.330) and *Adrienne's Pizzabar* (see p.296) cover the street with picnic tables. Many of the Greek Revival-style counting houses here were built in the wake of the Great Fire of 1835, which destroyed much of the area.

2

years. The Swiss-born Delmonico brothers opened their first café on William Street in 1827, and moved here ten years later when eating options in New York were generally restricted to British-style taverns; in addition to the usual array of Astors and Morgans, Charles Dickens, French exile Louis-Napoléon and generals Grant and Sherman all dined here. The current building (completed in 1891), is a bastion of opulence, with its grand portico supported by columns brought from the ruins of Pompeii and a menu that features many of the restaurant's culinary inventions (see p.295).

Queen Elizabeth II September 11th Garden

Hanover Square, Pearl St and Stone St • 24hr • Free • ☎ 212 682 7945, ⓦ queenelizabethgarden.org • Subway #2, #3 to Wall St

Just to the south of *Delmonico's*, the **Queen Elizabeth II September 11th Garden** is dedicated to the 67 British and other Commonwealth citizens killed on 9/11 (Australia lost 11, Canada lost 24). Queen Elizabeth II paid her respects here in 2010 – the rounded "Braemar" stone and cairn at the south end of the garden comes from her Balmoral estate, inscribed with the distance from here to Aberdeen (3281 miles). Overlooking the garden is the majestic **India House**, completed in 1853 for Hanover Bank and subsequently used by the New York Cotton Exchange (1870–1885). It's now an exclusive club for august financial types, and houses the more accessible *Harrys Café* (see p.296).

70 Pine Street

70 Pine St • Closed to the public • Subway #2, #3 to Wall St

One block north of Wall Street on Pearl Street, **70 Pine Street** (952ft) was completed in 1932 for Cities Service Company (the precursor of Venezuelan oil and gas conglomerate CITGO). It is one of New York's most graceful and iconic Art Deco towers, though it can be frustratingly hard to get a decent view – head down Cedar Street for the best glimpse. Insurance giant **AIG** bought the building in 1976, but as a consequence of the 2008 financial crisis sold it for around $150 million – it was sold again in 2011 for $205 million and is expected to be converted to luxury condos by 2014.

Federal Reserve Bank

33 Liberty St (enter at 44 Maiden Lane) • Mon–Fri 10am–4.30pm self-guided visits; on the hour until 3pm (on line reservation required) • Free • ☎ 212 720 6130, ⓦ newyorkfed.org • Subway A, C, #2, #3 to Fulton St

Three blocks north of Wall Street lies the **Federal Reserve Bank of New York**. Completed in 1924 and the largest of America's twelve reserve banks, there's good reason for the building's fortress-like exterior (based on Florentine palazzos): stashed 80ft below street level is ten percent of the world's gold reserves – seven thousand tonnes of it (worth over $360 billion in 2013). Yet as impressive as all this sounds, gold has played a minor part in global finance since 1971 (when President Nixon ended trading gold at the fixed price of $35/ounce), and today the reserve is used primarily by foreign governments for bookkeeping and reporting purposes.

Even if you decide not to take the guided tour (see box, below), you can make an online reservation to visit the multimedia **exhibitions** inside, housed in the vaulted former banking hall: "**FedWorks**", naturally enough, explains how the Fed system

---

FEDERAL RESERVE BANK TOURS

Gold Vault Tours (45min; free) are given Monday to Friday (11.15am, noon, 12.45pm, 1.30pm, 2.15pm & 3pm), but you must reserve these online at least one week in advance. You'll see a couple of introductory videos then the vault itself, but only through the bars at the entrance; you'll only get close to one gleaming heap of gold bricks. You'll need to arrive twenty minutes early with your e-ticket and photo ID, such as a driving licence or passport; taking pictures or videos is not allowed.

SEPTEMBER 11 AND ITS AFTERMATH

At 8.46am on September 11, 2001, a hijacked plane slammed into the north tower of the **World Trade Center**; seventeen minutes later another hijacked plane struck the south tower. As thousands looked on in horror – in addition to hundreds of millions more viewing on TV – the south tower collapsed at 9.50am, its twin at 10.30am. All seven buildings of the World Trade Center complex eventually collapsed, and the centre was reduced to a mountain of steel, concrete and glass rubble. As black clouds billowed above, the whole area was covered in a blanket of concrete dust many inches thick; debris reached several hundred feet into the air. The devastation was staggering. While most of the fifty thousand civilians working in the towers had been evacuated before the towers fell, many never made it out of the building; hundreds of firemen, policemen and rescue workers who arrived on the scene when the planes struck were crushed when the buildings collapsed. In all, **2977 people perished** at the WTC and the simultaneous attack on the Pentagon in Washington DC, in what was, in terms of casualties, the largest foreign attack on American soil in history. Radical Muslim Osama bin Laden's terrorist network, al-Qaeda, claimed responsibility for the attacks.

Dominating Lower Manhattan's landscape from nearly any angle, the 110-storey **Twin Towers** always loomed over their surroundings. The first tower went up in 1972 and the second a year later, and while becoming integral parts of the New York skyline, they also evolved into emblems of American power in the eyes of Islamic extremists.

In the days after the attack, downtown was basically shut down, and the seven-square-block area immediately around the WTC was the focus of an intense rescue effort. New Yorkers lined up to give blood and volunteered to help the rescue workers; vigils were held throughout the city, most notably in Union Square, which was peppered with candles and makeshift shrines. Then-Mayor **Rudy Giuliani** cut a highly composed and reassuring figure as New Yorkers struggled to come to terms with the assault on their city. In 2011, hundreds gathered again at Ground Zero to celebrate the killing of Osama bin Laden, though most New Yorkers greeted the news more soberly, remembering those who were lost ten years earlier.

MOVING FORWARD

In 2003, Polish-born architect **Daniel Libeskind** was named the winner of a competition held to determine the overall design for the new World Trade Center, though his plans were initially plagued with controversy and he's had little subsequent involvement with the project. In 2006, a modified design, still incorporating Libeskind's original 1776ft-high Tower of Freedom (now **One World Trade Center**), was finally accepted, supervised by architect David Childs. The whole multibillion-dollar scheme, which also involves a Santiago Calatrava-designed transport hub, a Performing Arts Center designed by Frank Gehry and four subsidiary towers conceived by Norman Foster, Richard Rogers, Fumihike Maki and the firm Kohn Pedersen Fox, should be complete by 2014–16 (the target has been continually put back). In addition, the project includes the **National September 11 Memorial and Museum**, designed by Michael Arad and Peter Walker (see p.48).

To get an idea what all this will look like, visit the **9/11 Memorial Preview Site** (daily 9am–7.30pm; free; ⊛911memorial.org) at 20 Vesey St, at Church St.

works, allowing visitors to participate in monetary policy simulations and to identify counterfeit notes. You'll need a photo ID and your e-ticket to pass through security.

Ground Zero and around

⊛wtc.com • Subway A, C, #2, #3, #4, #5 to Fulton St, E to World Trade Center, R to Cortland St, #1 to Rector St

The former location of the Twin Towers, **Ground Zero** remains a vast construction site, with hundreds of workers labouring away at the new **World Trade Center** complex. Seven buildings in total were destroyed as a result of the 2001 terrorist attacks, but today the area is booming, invigorated by the huge surge in investment as part of the regeneration of Lower Manhattan.

The whole complex (including four other towers) is unlikely to be completed before 2016, though glass-plated **7 World Trade Center** (741ft) on the north side at 250 Greenwich St opened in 2006. You can admire Jenny Holzer's intriguing lobby installation from the street outside: digital poetry text moving across wide plastic panels (the 65ft-long wall changes colour according to the time of day).

One World Trade Center

72 Vesey St • ⦿ onewtc.com • Subway A, C, #2, #3, #4, #5 to Fulton St, E to World Trade Center, R to Cortland St, #1 to Rector St

The tallest skyscraper in the US (and third highest in the world, if the spire is included), **One World Trade Center** (1776ft) finally topped out in 2012, a gleaming pinnacle of glass and steel. The tower is expected to be complete in 2014, when a restaurant and an enclosed **observation deck** should be open to the public.

National September 11 Memorial & Museum

Entrance at Albany St and Greenwich St • Daily: mid-March to mid-Sept 10am–8pm (last entry 7pm); mid-Sept to mid-March 10am–6pm (last entry 5pm) • Free, with a reserved visitor pass (see website) • ☎ 212 266 5211, ⦿ 911memorial.org • Subway A, C, #2, #3, #4, #5 to Fulton St, E to World Trade Center, R to Cortland St, #1 to Rector St

The incredibly moving **National September 11 Memorial & Museum** was dedicated on 11 September 2011 to commemorate the ten-year anniversary of the 9/11 attacks. The two memorial pools, representing the footprints of the original towers, are each around one acre in size, with 30ft waterfalls tumbling down their sides. The names of the 9/11 victims – some women listed with their "unborn children" – are inscribed on bronze parapets surrounding the pools, while the contemplative eight-acre Memorial Plaza is filled with nearly four hundred oak trees. The underground **9/11 Memorial Museum**, in between the two pools, should be open sometime in 2014; it will use artefacts (including two FDNY fire trucks and the heavily inscribed "Last Column", the last piece of structural steel to be removed from the site in 2002), and poignant exhibits to tell the story of September 11.

Tribute WTC Visitor Center

120 Liberty St, between Greenwich and Church sts • Mon–Sat 10am–6pm, Sun 10am–5pm (last ticket sold 30min before closing) • $15; tours Mon–Fri & Sun 11am, noon, 1pm, 2pm & 3pm, Sat 11am, noon, 1pm, 2pm, 3pm & 4pm ($10; $20 with Tribute Center admission) • ☎ 1 866 737 1184, ⦿ tributewtc.org • Subway A, C, #2, #3, #4, #5 to Fulton St, E to World Trade Center, R to Cortland St, #1 to Rector St

The poignant **Tribute WTC Visitor Center** houses five small galleries that commemorate the attacks of September 11, beginning with a model of the Twin Towers and a moving section about that chilling day, embellished with video and taped accounts of real-life survivors. A handful of items found on the site – a pair of singed high-heel shoes, pieces of twisted metal – make heart-rending symbols of the tragedy. The centre also offers daily walking **tours** (1hr 15min) of the National September 11 Memorial (includes Memorial pass).

St Paul's Chapel

209 Broadway, at Fulton St • Mon–Sat 10am–6pm, Sun 7am–6pm • Free • ☎ 212 233 4164 • Subway A, C, #4, #5 to Fulton St, E to World Trade Center

Both the oldest church and the oldest building in continuous use in Manhattan, **St Paul's Chapel** dates from 1766, making it almost prehistoric by New York standards. The main attraction inside is **Unwavering Spirit**, a moving exhibition on September 11. For eight months after the 9/11 attacks, St Paul's Chapel served as a sanctuary for the rescue workers at Ground Zero, providing food, a place to nap and spiritual support. The exhibit chronicles the church's role in these recovery efforts, with a touching ensemble of photos, artefacts and testimonies from those involved. The church itself was based on London's St Martin-in-the-Fields, with a handsome interior of narrow Corinthian columns and ornate chandeliers, though even **George Washington's pew**, preserved shrine-like from 1789–1790 (when New York was the US capital), forms part of the September 11 exhibition (it served as a foot treatment chair for firefighters). Outside, the historic cemetery is worth a wander, sprinkled with colonial headstones and the **Bell of Hope**, a gift from London in 2002; the bell is rung every September 11.

Battery Park City

Between West Side Hwy and the Hudson River, from Battery Park to Chambers St • 📞 212 417 2000, 🌐 batteryparkcity.org • Subway R, #1 to Rector St

The hole dug for the foundations of the former World Trade Center threw up a million cubic yards of earth and rock, which was then dumped into the Hudson River to the west to form the 23-acre base of **Battery Park City**. This self-sufficient development of office blocks, apartments, chain boutiques and landscaped esplanade feels a far cry from the rest of Manhattan. Battery Park City's southern end is anchored by **Robert F. Wagner Jr Park**, a refuge from the ferry crowds – you can follow the **Esplanade** up the Hudson from here as far as Chelsea.

2

Brookfield Place (World Financial Center)

250 Vesey St • 📞 212 945 2600, 🌐 brookfieldplaceny.com

The centrepiece of the Battery Park development is the **World Financial Center**, a rather grand and imposing fourteen-acre business, shopping and dining complex that looks down onto Ground Zero from just across West Street. Originally designed by César Pelli in the 1980s, an ambitious $250 million renovation of the whole complex, which will officially be known as **Brookfield Place**, should be complete by 2014. Inside, the **Winter Garden**, a ten-storey, glass-ceilinged public plaza, brings light and life into a mall full of shops and restaurants. Decorated by sixteen 45ft-high Washingtonia palms from Florida, the plaza is a veritable oasis, and connects with the **North Cove** yacht harbour on the Hudson River side. Don't miss the small chunk of the **Berlin Wall** tucked away on the south side of the cove, donated by the German Consulate in 2004.

The Irish Hunger Memorial

290 Vesey St • Daily 8am–6.30pm • Free • Subway A, C, #1, #2, #3 to Chambers St, E to World Trade Center

Just north of the World Financial Center, facing the Hudson at the end of Vesey Street, the **Irish Hunger Memorial** is a sobering monument to the more than one million Irish people who starved to death during the Great Famine of 1845–52. The tragedy sparked a flood of Irish immigration to the US, mostly through New York. An authentic famine-era stone cottage, one of many abandoned in the west of Ireland, was transported from County Mayo by artist Brian Tolle and set on a raised embankment overlooking the water. The passageway underneath echoes with haunting Irish folk songs, and you can follow the meandering path through the grassy garden and stones 25ft to the top.

Poets House

10 River Terrace • Tues–Fri 11am–7pm, Sat 11am–6pm • Free • 📞 212 431 7920, 🌐 poetshouse.org • Subway A, C, #1, #2, #3 to Chambers St, E to World Trade Center

To the north of the Irish Hunger monument, the **Poets House** contains a fabulous 50,000-volume reference library, reading room and audio collection dedicated to poets of every nationality. Historic recordings include readings from W.H. Auden, e.e. cummings, T.S. Eliot, Allen Ginsberg and Ezra Pound (and it has free wi-fi) – it's a relaxing place to end an afternoon.

Battery Park and around

Battery Place and State and Whitehall sts • **Park** Daily sunrise–1am • Free • 📞 212 344 3491, 🌐 thebattery.org **Castle Clinton** Daily 8.30am–5pm • Free • 📞 212 344 7220, 🌐 nps.gov/cacl • Subway R to Whitehall St, #1 to South Ferry, #4, #5 to Bowling Green

Lower Manhattan lets out its breath in **Battery Park**, a breezy, 25-acre swathe of grass and gardens littered with monuments and fine views of the Statue of Liberty across the harbour. Dating back to 1693, the park is named after the gun batteries that once protected the city from here. Before landfill closed the gap in the 1850s, **Castle Clinton**, the redbrick fort on the west side of the park, was on an island. Built in 1811, it was ceded to the city in 1823, finding new life as a prestigious concert venue known as Castle Garden before doing service (pre-Ellis Island) as the drop-off point for arriving immigrants; from 1855 to 1890, eight million people passed through its doors. After serving as an aquarium, the squat fortress is now the place to buy **tickets for the Statue of Liberty and Ellis Island** (see p.37); it also contains a small exhibit on the history of the site, though the whole thing was badly damaged by **Hurricane Sandy** in 2012. South of Castle Clinton stands the **East Coast Memorial**, a series of granite slabs inscribed with the names of all the American seamen who were killed in World War II. On the other side of Castle Clinton, poking into the harbour, **Pier A** is a lavish nineteenth-century relic dating from 1886 – a mammoth renovation should be complete by 2014, with a mix of shops, beer garden and restaurants occupying the old wooden structure. One of the newest park attractions is the **SeaGlass Carousel**, a futuristic aquatic-themed ride that should be open by 2014.

Bowling Green

Broadway • 24hr • Free • Subway R to Whitehall St, #1 to South Ferry, #4, #5 to Bowling Green

The southern end of Broadway meets tiny but momentous **Bowling Green** just before Battery Park. The city's oldest public garden, this is supposedly the location of the most famous real-estate deal in history, when Peter Minuit, the newly arrived director-general of the Dutch colony of New Amsterdam, bought the whole island from the Native Americans for a bucket of trade goods worth sixty guilders in 1626 (the figure of $24 was calculated in the 1840s). Though we don't know for sure who "sold" the island to Minuit (it was probably a northern branch of the Lenni Lenape), the other side of the story (and the part you never hear) was that the concept of owning land was utterly alien to Native Americans – they had merely agreed to support Dutch claims to use the land, as they did. The green was formally established in 1733, when it was used for lawn bowling by colonial Brits, on a lease of "one peppercorn per year". The encircling iron fence is an original from 1771, though the crowns that once topped the stakes were removed during the Revolutionary War, as was a statue of George III. The statue was melted into musket balls – little bits of the monarch that were then fired at his troops.

Just north of the green on the Broadway partition is a sculpture of a **Charging Bull** – not originally envisioned as a symbol of a "bull market" for Wall Street stocks, though that's how it is perceived by New Yorkers today. As the story goes, on December 15, 1989, Arturo Di Modica installed his sculpture in the middle of Broad Street. The city removed the sculpture the next day, but was forced to put it here when public support of the statue was surprisingly vocal. The bull stands opposite the former headquarters of John D. Rockefeller's **Standard Oil Company** at 26 Broadway. Originally constructed in 1885, when Rockefeller moved here from Cleveland, most of the elaborate, pyramid-topped building you see today was added in the 1920s, the pinnacle serving as a lighthouse for ships entering New York Harbor. You'll get the best views from Battery Park.

National Museum of the American Indian

1 Bowling Green • Daily 10am–5pm, Thurs until 8pm • Tours daily 1pm (free) • **National Archives** Mon–Fri 10am–5pm, first Sat of the month 10am–4pm • Free • ☎ 212 514 3700, ⓦ nmai.si.edu • Subway R to Whitehall St, #1 to South Ferry, #4, #5 to Bowling Green

Bowling Green sees plenty of office folk picnicking in the shadow of Cass Gilbert's stately US Customs House, the former site of Fort Amsterdam and now (not without some irony) the only part of Manhattan dedicated to Native Americans,

CLOCKWISE FROM TOP LEFT TRINITY CHURCH (P.42); GEORGE WASHINGTON STATUE (P.44); WALL STREET (P.42); TRIBUTE WTC (P.48) >

CROSSING THE HARBOUR

The **Staten Island ferry** (☎ 718 727 2508, ⚙ siferry.com) sails from the modern Whitehall Ferry Terminal on the east side of Battery Park, built directly above the equally smart South Ferry subway station (at the end of the #1 line and accessible via R trains to Whitehall Street). The #4 and #5 trains to Bowling Green also let you off within easy walking distance. Weekday departures are scheduled every fifteen to twenty minutes during rush hours (7–9am & 5–7pm), every half-hour through the rest of the day and evenings, and every hour late at night (the ferry runs 24hr). On weekends, boats run every half-hour from Manhattan, but slightly less frequently on the return trip.

The 25-minute ride is truly New York's best bargain: it's absolutely free, with wide-angle views of the city and the Statue of Liberty becoming more spectacular as you retreat. You also pass very close to Governors Island (near Manhattan, left of the boat) and the 1883 Robbins Reef Lighthouse (closer to Staten Island, off to the right). By the time you arrive on **Staten Island** (see p.259), the Manhattan skyline stands mirage-like: the city of a thousand and one posters, its skyscrapers almost bristling straight out of the water.

---

the Smithsonian **National Museum of the American Indian**. The main galleries lie on the second floor, where temporary exhibits focus on various aspects of Native American culture as well as shows by contemporary artists. Most exhibits last at least six months, though **Infinity of Nations: Art and History in the Collections of the National Museum of the American Indian** is expected to be permanent, highlighting artefacts from the Smithsonian's vast collection representing almost every Native American tribe from Patagonia to the Arctic; it was largely assembled by one man, George Gustav Heye (1874–1957), who travelled through the Americas picking up such works for over fifty years. On the first floor, the **Diker Pavilion** serves as an additional performance and exhibition space, while **The National Archives at New York City** on the third floor contains a small exhibition featuring a changing selection of original documents from the National Archives.

Completed in 1907 and in use until 1973, the Beaux Arts **Customs House** is itself part of the attraction; the facade is adorned with elaborate statuary representing the major continents (carved by Daniel Chester French) and the world's great commercial centres, while the spectacular marble-clad Great Hall and Rotunda inside are beautifully decorated; the sixteen murals covering the 135ft dome were painted by Reginald Marsh in 1937.

The Skyscraper Museum

39 Battery Place • Wed–Sun noon–6pm • $5 • ☎ 212 968 1961, ⚙ skyscraper.org • Subway R to Whitehall St, #4, #5 to Bowling Green

Given the Financial District's love affair with soaring towers of steel and limestone, it's fitting that the **Skyscraper Museum** should be located down here, just behind the *Ritz-Carlton Hotel* on the northern edge of Battery Park. The core display area is usually taken up with temporary exhibits, but always with skyscraper focus – recent displays have featured the Woolworth Building and New York's Garment District. Permanent exhibits are dedicated to "Supertall" (over 380m) towers, One World Trade Center and the Twin Towers, and hand-carved miniature wooden models of Downtown and Midtown Manhattan created by Michael Chesko.

The Museum of Jewish Heritage

36 Battery Place • Mon, Tues, Thurs & Sun 10am–5.45pm, Wed 10am–8pm, Fri 10am–5pm; Oct–March museum closes at 3pm on Fri; closed Jewish holidays • $12 or $17 with audio guide; free Wed 4–8pm • ☎ 646 437 4202, ⚙ mjhnyc.org • Subway R to Whitehall St, #4, #5 to Bowling Green

Jewish culture remains a key component of New York's identity, and on the north side of Battery Park **The Museum of Jewish Heritage** stands as a memorial to the Holocaust; its six sides represent both the six million dead and the Star of David. The moving and informative collection, which covers three floors of permanent exhibits and multimedia installations, begins with the rituals and practical accoutrements of everyday Eastern European Jewish life pre-1930, before moving on to the horrors of the Holocaust and ending with the establishment of Israel and subsequent Jewish achievements. Some of the more memorable installations include a fine hand-painted Sukkah cover from 1930s Hungary, and a heart-rending display commemorating the children murdered by the Nazis. Temporary exhibits also fill the upper floors, while the Zen-like "Garden of Stones" stands on the second-floor terrace. Be sure to also visit the innovative **Keeping History Center** on the third floor, where the "Voices of Liberty" exhibit features testimony from Holocaust survivors and immigrants via iPod-like audio guides.

2

Shrine of St Elizabeth Ann Seton

7 State St • Daily 7am–5pm • ☎ 212 269 6865, ⓦ setonshrine.com • Subway R to Whitehall St, #1 to South Ferry #4, #5 to Bowling Green

A rounded, redbrick facade on the east side of Battery Park identifies the **Shrine of St Elizabeth Ann Seton**, honouring the first native-born American to be canonized. The shrine comprises a working Catholic chapel, the Church of Our Lady of the Rosary, built in 1965 in Georgian style with a small room at the front containing a statue of the saint and rather pious illustrations of her life. Before moving to Maryland to found a religious community, St Elizabeth lived briefly (1801–03) in a small house on this site. You enter through the adjacent porticoed building, completed in 1793 and known as **Watson House**, one of only a few old buildings in the area have has survived the modern onslaught. Seton (1774–1821) was canonized in 1975, principally in recognition of her work establishing the Sisters of Charity and schools for poor women and children.

Cut through the buildings to Pearl Street from here and you'll see the small memorial marking the site of **Herman Melville's birthplace**; the author of *Moby Dick* was born in a small townhouse on this spot in 1819, now long gone.

Fraunces Tavern Museum

54 Pearl St, at Broad St • Daily noon–5pm • $7 • ☎ 212 425 1778, ⓦ frauncestavernmuseum.org • Subway R to Whitehall St, #1 to South Ferry, #4, #5 to Bowling Green

For a window into eighteenth-century Manhattan, check out the **Fraunces Tavern Museum**. The ochre-and-red-brick building was constructed in 1719 and became the Queen's Head Inn after Samuel Fraunces purchased the property in 1762; having survived extensive modifications, several fires and a brief stint as a hotel in the nineteenth century, the three-storey Georgian house was almost totally reconstructed by the Sons of the Revolution in the early part of the twentieth century to mimic how it appeared on December 4, 1783. It was then that a weeping George Washington took leave of his assembled officers, intent on returning to rural life in Virginia: "I am not only retiring from all public employments," he wrote, "but am retiring within myself." With hindsight, it was a hasty statement – six years later he was to return as the new nation's president. The **Long Room** where the speech was made has been faithfully decked out in the style of the time, while the adjacent Federal-style **Clinton Room** is smothered in rare and florid French wallpaper from 1838. The tavern's upper floors contain a permanent exhibit tracing the site's history, a room with over two hundred flags and an expansive collection of Revolutionary War artefacts; look out for a lock of Washington's hair, preserved like a holy relic. Fascinating temporary exhibits are also held here, usually on related themes (such as the influence of the Magna Carta on the Revolution). The *Porterhouse* restaurant and pub occupies the lower floors (see p.329), but have a peek at the historic murals in the **Bissell Room** (at the back), and the plaque commemorating the bomb that killed four people here in 1975 (the Puerto Rican nationalist group FALN claimed responsibility).

The old Stadt Huys

85 Broad St • 24hr • Free • Subway R to Whitehall St, #1 to South Ferry, #4, #5 to Bowling Green

In the shadow of 85 Broad St (Goldman Sachs' old headquarters), are the oldest remnants of colonial New York. This was the site of the city's first tavern,

2

transformed into the **Stadt Huys** or City Hall in 1653 when New Amsterdam was officially incorporated – the city government still dates its foundation from this year. Nothing remains from that period, but archeologists have uncovered the foundations of **Governor Lovelace's Tavern**, a British pub dating from the 1670s, preserved under glass panels just off the street; the outlines of where both buildings once stood are marked by coloured bricks. At nearby Coenties Slip you can turn left to reach historic **Stone Street** (see box, p.45), or turn right to the **Vietnam Veterans Memorial**, a modern assembly of glass blocks etched with troops' letters home. The mementoes are sad and often haunting, but the place is a peaceful spot for contemplation.

New York City Police Museum

100 Old Slip • Mon–Sat 10am–5pm, Sun noon–5pm • $8 • ☎ 212 480 3100, ⓦ nycpolicemuseum.org • Subway R to Whitehall St, #2, #3 to Wall St, #4, #5 to Bowling Green

Walk up South Street to Old Slip and you'll find the small but ornate Italianate building (completed by the sons of Richard Morris Hunt in 1911) that once housed the **First Precinct Police Station**, now home to the **New York City Police Museum**. Three floors of exhibits showcase the history of New York's Finest, a force established in 1845; as well as historic uniforms, guns and vehicles such as a 1972 Plymouth patrol car, special displays cover weapons used by the likes of Al Capone and his mentor Frankie Yale, and Lieutenant Petrosino, one of the first and most successful Italian-American officers to tackle the "Black Hand" gangs of the early 1900s (see p.78). A special multimedia exhibit commemorates the NYPD's role in **September 11**, when 23 officers were killed, and the Hall of Heroes honours all officers who have died in the line of duty. Finally, a display documents how the NYPD has reduced crime levels in the city by over fifty percent since the 1990s. Note that the museum was badly damaged by **Hurricane Sandy** and remained closed through 2013 – check the website for the latest.

South Street Seaport

Fulton St and South St • Subway A, C, J, #2, #3, #4, #5 to Fulton St

New York's original dockyards were located on Manhattan's southern tip between Battery Park and Fulton Street, and today a tiny part of this heritage is preserved as the touristy **South Street Seaport**. This area was particularly hammered by **Hurricane Sandy** in 2012 – almost all the shops and restaurants remained closed well into 2013.

Created by the Dutch in the 1620s, the port boomed in the nineteenth century, favoured by sea captains for providing shelter from the westerly winds and the ice that floated down the Hudson River during winter. **Robert Fulton** started a ferry service from here to Brooklyn in 1814, leaving his name for the street and then its market, New York's largest (the fish market moved to the Bronx in 2006). After World War II, containers came to dominate shipping, and Manhattan effectively ceased being a port in the 1970s; ships were handled in New Jersey and Staten Island, and the docks were left as rotting eyesores. Beginning in 1966, a private initiative rescued some of the remaining warehouses, creating the historical seaport you see today; a mix of attractively restored buildings and ships, with fairly standard main-street stores and cafés. Weather permitting, you can also enjoy the **Beekman Beer Garden Beach Club** (89 South St; daily noon–3am; ⓦ beekmanbeergarden.com), a small strip of imported sand with tables, food, drinks and weekend dance parties. Finally, one of the best-kept tourist secrets is here: a **TKTS box office** (corner of John and Front sts; Mon–Sat 11am–6pm, Sun 11am–4pm). Like its counterpart in Times Square (see p.145), it sells same-day half-price tickets to **Broadway shows**, but the queues here are usually a fraction of those in Midtown.

CRUISING, OLD SCHOOL

The South Street Seaport Museum runs a programme of leisurely **cruises** around New York Harbor on its handsome 1885 schooner, the *Pioneer*. Two-hour cruises usually run May–Oct Tues–Fri 3–5pm, 7–9pm & 9.30–11pm and Sat & Sun 1–3pm, 4–6pm, 7–9pm & 9.30–11.30pm (Sat only). Tickets are $45 (seniors and children 3–12 $35). Call in advance for the latest information: ☎ 212 748 8786, ⓦ nywatertaxi.com/tours/pioneer-tour.

2

The South Street Seaport Museum

12 Fulton St • Jan–March Thurs–Sun 10am–5pm; April–Dec Tues–Sun 10am–6pm • $10 • ☎ 212 748 8600, ⓦ southstreetseaportmuseum.org • Subway A, C, J, #2, #3, #4, #5 to Fulton St

Housed in a series of painstakingly restored warehouses, the **South Street Seaport Museum** offers illuminating maritime art and trades exhibits and a spread of refitted ships and chubby tugboats (the largest collection of sailing vessels – by tonnage – in the US). The main ticket office and galleries lie on Fulton Street, housed in **Schermerhorn Row**, a unique ensemble of Federal-style warehouses dating to about 1811. The interiors have been hollowed out to accommodate the galleries, with exposed brick and ceiling timbers sensitively restored – recent temporary exhibitions have focused on the SS *Normandie* and maritime-related folk art.

In the spring and summer, your ticket also includes a look around the **Ambrose** (a 1908 lightship) at the end of Fulton Street on Pier 17, which remained in service until 1964 having spent much of its working life in New York Harbor. Exhibits tackle the history of the vessel, navigation and the role of lightships in general – you can also view the engine room and sailors' quarters. On the other side of the dock the **Peking** is massive in comparison – built as a German merchant ship, it became a British training boat in the 1930s and ended up here in 1975. Ongoing repairs mean this ship is likely to be off limits for several years. The **Wavertree**, a graceful tall-ship built in 1885, is still being restored and is expected to open in 2014.

Pier 17

Fulton St and South St • ⓦ southstreetseaport.com • Subway A, C, J, #2, #3, #4, #5 to Fulton St

The Seaport is planning a major expansion in the next few years (slated for completion in 2015), but until then the **Pier 17 Pavilion** will remain the focal point of the district, created from the old fish-market wharf that was demolished and then restored in 1982. The three-storey glass-and-steel pavilion houses all kinds of restaurants and shops; more interesting is the outdoor promenade, where you'll find the museum ships and booths selling cruise and water-taxi tickets. Circle Line Downtown (☎ 1 866 925 4631, ⓦ circlelinedowntown.com) runs **harbour cruises** from April to December on *Zephyr* (1hr; $28, seniors $24, children $17), and speedboat rides on *Shark* from May to September (30min; $24, seniors $22, children $17). The views of the Brooklyn and Manhattan bridges from the promenade are fantastic (and free) at any time of year.

Bodies

11 Fulton St • Mon–Thurs & Sun 10am–7pm, Fri & Sat 10am–9pm • $28.85, seniors $24.60, children (4–12) $22.32 • ☎ 646 747 5663, ⓦ bodiestheexhibition.com/newyork • Subway A, C, J, #2, #3, #4, #5 to Fulton St

Just across from the South Street Seaport Museum, the old Fulton Market Building contains the ever-popular **Bodies** exhibition, with its presentation of twenty real human bodies and 260 organs, polymer-preserved in fascinating but slightly disturbing detail. Opened in 2005, the exhibition has been extended indefinitely, though a 2007 *New York Times* article claimed that such displays have created "a ghastly new underground mini-industry" in China, the origin of the preserved cadavers. Note that Bodies was closed at the time of research due to Hurricane Sandy damage.

BROOKLYN BRIDGE

City Hall Park and Brooklyn Bridge

City Hall Park has been the seat of New York's municipal government since 1812, but in the seventeenth century it was just communal pasture. An almshouse for the poor stood on this site from 1736 to 1797, and during the Revolutionary War (1776–83) the British used the nearby debtors' prison to hold prisoners, hanging 250 of them. Today the park contains stately City Hall, with Tweed Courthouse just to the north, while the towers of Park Row and the Woolworth Building loom nearby. The Municipal Building watches over Police Plaza and the city's courthouses; from here the Brooklyn Bridge, a magnificent feat of engineering, soars over the East River. In stark contrast, the African Burial Ground National Monument is a poignant and powerful reminder of the city's early African population.

City Hall

City Hall Park • Free tours Thurs 10am (must reserve in advance at ☎ 212 788 2656, ⓦ nyc.gov/html/artcom) & Wed noon (sign up at the NYC information kiosk, opposite the Woolworth Building; Mon–Fri 9am–6pm, Sat & Sun 10am–5pm) • Subway J, Z to Chambers St, R to City Hall, #2 or #3 to Park Place, #4, #5 or #6 to Brooklyn Bridge-City Hall

Towards the northern end of City Hall Park sits **City Hall** itself, a gleaming white marble palace with Neoclassical columns, arches and furnishings virtually unchanged since it was completed in 1812. It's the oldest city hall in the US to retain its original government function; the **mayor's office** and the chambers of the New York City Council are inside. Increased security means the building is fenced off from the rest of the park, and the only way you can admire the magnificent interior is to take a **free guided tour** offered by Art Commission experts, well worth your time (tours take just over one hour).

Tours begin in the elegant triple-arcaded lobby, which opens up to the **rotunda**, one of the most sensational pieces of architecture in the city; the all-white coffered dome (topped with a skylight and invisible from the outside), is ringed by ten Corinthian columns and a floating marble staircase that spirals up to the second floor. Up here you'll see the **Council Chamber**, where the city council meets once a month; the ceiling is covered in a giant allegorical mural representing New York. Most of the decor dates back to 1898, when the chamber was redesigned to take in the newly expanded city boroughs. An 1825 portrait of the Marquis de Lafayette by Samuel Morse (later of Morse Code fame) hangs on the wall.

More nineteenth-century portraits by John Trumbull adorn the **Governor's Room**, an immaculate French Regency-style reception room containing George Washington's writing desk and a rare mahogany table from 1814. The room hosted President-elect Abraham Lincoln in 1861 (who shook hands for eight hours straight), and served as the backdrop in 1865 when Lincoln's body lay in state for 120,000 sorrowful New Yorkers to file past.

Tweed Courthouse

52 Chambers St • Free guided tours Fri noon; 1hr; must reserve in advance at ☎ 212 788 2656, ⓦ nyc.gov/html/artcom • Subway J, Z to Chambers St, R to City Hall, #2 or #3 to Park Place, #4, #5 or #6 to Brooklyn Bridge-City Hall

If City Hall is the acceptable face of New York's municipal bureaucracy, the spectacular **Tweed Courthouse**, just to the north, is a reminder of the city government's infamous corruption in the nineteenth century. The man behind this former county courthouse, **William Marcy "Boss" Tweed**, worked his way up from nowhere to become chairman of the Democratic Central Committee in 1856. Tweed embezzled the city's revenues (even the courthouse's budget, which rolled up from $3 million to $12 million during its construction between 1861 and 1881), until political cartoonist Thomas Nast and the editor of *The New York Times* (who'd refused a $500,000 bribe to keep quiet) turned public opinion against him in the early 1870s. Fittingly, Tweed was finally tried in an unfinished courtroom in his own building in 1873, and died in 1878 in Ludlow Street Jail – a prison he'd had built while he was Commissioner of Public Works.

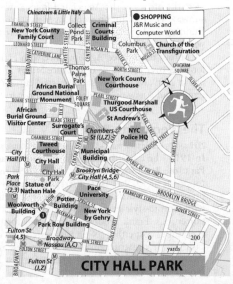

CITY HALL PARK

Tweed's monument to greed, which now houses the Department of Education and a kindergarten, looks more like a mansion than a municipal building, especially after the lavish $85 million restoration completed in 2001. To get a look at its fabulous interior, you need to take a **free guided tour**, arranged by the Art Commission, which begins in the 75ft monumental **rotunda**, soaring upward to the stained-glass skylight. Here it's easy to spot the contrasting styles of the two architects who worked on the building; the cast-iron floors, doors and stairways have been skilfully blended with a series of exposed red-and-white brick Romanesque arches – indeed, this is the most developed cast-iron interior in the city. The jarring Roy Lichtenstein moulded fibreglass installation **Element E** dominates the space, emphasizing that this is also a modern place of work – offices now occupy all the old courtrooms. The tour takes in one of these high-ceilinged halls with ornate plasterwork and giant chandeliers, as well as the remarkable southern **annexe**, a confection of polished granite columns, white marble and English ceramic tile floors; the upper floors feature elaborate exposed-brick vaulting.

Park Row

Park Row, between Broadway and Frankfort St • Subway J, Z to Chambers St, R to City Hall, #2 or #3 to Park Place, #4, #5 or #6 to Brooklyn Bridge-City Hall

City Hall Park is flanked on either side by impressive early twentieth-century skyscrapers. **Park Row**, the eastern edge of the park, was once known as "Newspaper Row". From the 1830s to the 1920s, the city's most influential publishers, news services and trade publications had their offices on this street or surrounding blocks. *The New York Times* operated from no. 41, a handsome Romanesque-Revival structure that grew from twelve storeys in 1889 to sixteen in 1904 (Pace University moved here in 1952). The wildly ornamented **Potter Building** at no. 38 dates from 1886, when it was a pioneer in fireproofing, thanks to its ironclad lower floors and durable terracotta trim. Today, as with much of downtown, it's been converted into high-end apartments (with a *Starbucks* on the first floor).

The **Park Row Building**, at no. 15, was completed in 1899; at 391ft, it was the tallest office building in the world. Behind the elaborate limestone-and-brick facade were the offices of the Associated Press as well as the headquarters of the IRT subway. The building towered over its surroundings until 1908, when the Singer Building, at 165 Broadway (now demolished), surpassed it – it's now primarily filled with expensive apartments.

Contrast this Gilded Age opulence with Frank Gehry's contemporary masterpiece, looming over Park Row at 8 Spruce St; his 77-storey **New York by Gehry** (870ft) topped out in 2009, its rippling stainless-steel curtain wall containing nine hundred luxury rentals and a new public elementary (primary) school at its base.

The Woolworth Building

233 Broadway • Closed to the public • J, Z to Chambers St, R to City Hall, #2 or #3 to Park Place, #4, #5 or #6 to Brooklyn Bridge-City Hall

In 1913, the tallest building in the world was on the opposite side of City Hall Park: the **Woolworth Building** (792ft) held the title until the Chrysler Building topped it in 1929. Cass Gilbert's "Cathedral of Commerce" oozes money and prestige. The soaring, graceful lines are covered in white terracotta tiles and fringed with Gothic-style gargoyles and decorations that are more whimsical than portentous. Frank Woolworth made his fortune from his "five and dime" stores – everything cost either 5¢ or 10¢, strictly no credit. True to his philosophy, he paid cash for the construction of his skyscraper, and reliefs at each corner of the ornate lobby (sadly, now closed to sightseers) show him doing just that: counting out the money in nickels and dimes.

HIDDEN GEMS: CITY HALL PARK AND BROOKLYN BRIDGE

African Burial Ground See below
Hot dog stand, NY County Courthouse See below

Park Row Building See opposite
The Rotunda, City Hall See opposite
Tweed Courthouse tours See p.57

The Municipal Building

1 Centre St • Mon–Fri 9am–4.30pm (City Store) • Free • ⓦ nyc.gov • Subway J, Z to Chambers St, R to City Hall, #2 or #3 to Park Place, #4, #5 or #6 to Brooklyn Bridge-City Hall

At the east end of Chambers Street, across Centre Street, stands the imposing 580ft bulk of the **Municipal Building**, looking a bit like an oversized chest of drawers. Built between 1909 and 1914, it was the first skyscraper constructed by the well-known architectural firm McKim, Mead, and White, although it was actually designed by one of the firm's younger partners, William Mitchell Kendall. At its top, an extravagant "wedding cake" tower of columns and pinnacles, including Adolph Weinman's frivolous 25ft gilt sculpture *Civic Fame*, attempts to dress up the no-nonsense home of public records and much of the city government's offices. The shields decorating the moulding above the colonnade represent the various phases of New York as colony, city and state: the triple-X insignia is the Amsterdam city seal, and the combination of windmill, beavers and flour barrels represents New Amsterdam and its first trading products, images used on the city seal today. There's little to see inside, but the City Store at the base sells New York City maps, books and souvenirs.

New York Court District

Subway J, Z to Chambers St

To the north of City Hall Park lies New York's court district, familiar to fans of *Law & Order* and countless other crime shows and dominated by the grandiose 590ft tower of the **Thurgood Marshall US Courthouse**. Designed by Cass Gilbert and completed in 1936 at 40 Centre St, the building still serves as a federal courthouse. The adjacent building, at 60 Centre St, is the **New York County Courthouse** (daily 9am–5pm), now one of the state's supreme courts. A massive hexagonal Neoclassical structure completed in 1927, it merits a quick peek into the lobby to see its elaborate rotunda, decorated by Attilio Pusterla in the 1930s with storybook murals illustrating the history of justice (you'll have to pass through security to get a good look, but as it's a public building you are allowed to go in). The columned facades of the courthouses look onto **Foley Square**, named for the sheriff and saloonkeeper Thomas "Big Tom" Foley, one of the few admirable figures in the Tammany Hall era. The focal point of the wide concrete plaza is Lorenzo Pace's three-hundred-tonne black granite sculpture, *The Triumph of the Human Spirit*, a tribute to the many thousands of enslaved Africans who died on American soil – particularly those whose bodies were discovered in the African Burial Ground just off the west side of the square.

African Burial Ground National Monument

Duane St, at Elk St • Daily 9am–5pm • Free • ☏ 212 637 2019, ⓦ nps.gov/afbg • Subway A, C, J, Z to Chambers St, R to City Hall

In 1991, construction of a federal office building at 290 Broadway uncovered one of the most important US archeological finds of the twentieth century – the remains of 419 skeletons in what was once a vast African burial ground. Today, the **African Burial Ground National Monument** occupies a tiny portion of a cemetery that covered five blocks between the 1690s and 1794. Then outside the city boundary, this was the only place Africans could be buried. After being examined at Howard University, the skeletons, along with artefacts (such as beads) buried with them, were reinterred at this

THE NOTORIOUS FIVE POINTS

East of Foley Square is the area once known as **Five Points**, named for the intersection of Mulberry, Worth, Park, Baxter and Little Water streets, the last of which no longer exists. A former pond here known as the Collect was filled in as part of a public-works project around 1812, but the fetid, damp location soon became a massive slum as a relentless influx of immigrants, sailors and criminals sought refuge here, and toxic industries were shunted to this unlovely side of town. In 1829, the local press started using the Five Points moniker, and by 1855, when immigrants formed 72 percent of the population, its muddy streets – called Bone Alley, Ragpickers' Row and other similarly inviting names – were lined with flimsy tenements. Diseases such as cholera skipped easily from room to overcrowded room.

The neighbourhood was further marred by vicious pitched battles among the district's numerous **Irish gangs**, including the Roach Guards, the Plug Uglies and the Dead Rabbits (depicted with flair in Martin Scorsese's *The Gangs of New York*). After the Civil War, when the area's Irish majority gave way to the new waves of Italian and Chinese immigrants, the gangs consolidated to form the Five Pointers.

Upper-class sightseers like Charles Dickens (who came here in 1842), both fascinated and repelled by Five Points, invented the concept of "slumming" in their tours of the neighbourhood. They made lurid note of the crime, filth and other markers of obvious moral depravity, but most New Yorkers were not gravely concerned until 1890, when police reporter and photographer Jacob A. Riis published *How the Other Half Lives*, a report on the city's slums. In particular, his gripping images, which retained his subjects' dignity while graphically showing the squalor all around them, helped convince readers that these people were not poor simply due to moral laxity. The book was remarkably successful in its mission to evoke sympathy for the plight of this troubled community, and it's in large part thanks to Riis that Five Points was razed by 1895, eventually replaced by a park and a towering courthouse.

site in 2003, marked by seven grassy mounds and a highly polished, black granite monument. The soaring **Ancestral Chamber** in the centre is a symbolic counterpoint to the infamous "Gate of No Return" on Gorée Island in Senegal, through which slaves would leave Africa for the New World. Instead of captivity and departure, this gateway represents spiritual freedom and return, facing east towards Africa.

The spiral path into the **Ancestral Libation Court**, 4ft below street level, is engraved with signs and symbols of the African Diaspora, inspired by the discovery of what might be one symbol, the *sankofa*, on the coffin of a former slave – heart-rending evidence that despite their situation, slaves maintained spiritual links with their homeland (the *sankofa* symbolized "returning to your roots"). Despite its relatively small size, the curving walls and mystical symbols create a meditative, temple-like atmosphere, in utter contrast to its skyscraper-bound surroundings.

African Burial Ground Visitor Center

290 Broadway • Tues–Sat 10am–4pm, closed federal holidays • Free • ☎ 212 637 2019, ⓦ nps.gov/afbg • Subway A, C, J, Z to Chambers St, R to City Hall

To learn more about the African Burial Ground on Duane Street, walk around the corner to the **African Burial Ground Visitor Center**; look for the dedicated doorway just along from the main 290 Broadway entrance. A twenty-minute video (played throughout the day) introduces the site, while an interactive exhibition with touch-screen computers and replicas of the artefacts found here trace not just the history of the cemetery but of slavery in New York. Experts believe as many as fifteen thousand free and enslaved blacks were buried here, and examination of the bones revealed a cycle of back-breaking toil that began in childhood. One of the reasons the site is considered so significant is that slavery (and the cruelty that went with it) is something many people associate with the Deep South. In reality, New York had the second-largest enslaved population outside of South Carolina in 1776, and slave labour built much of the colonial city. Maya Angelou alluded to this misconception at the emotional reinterment ceremony: "You may bury me in the bottom of Manhattan. I will rise. My people will get me. I will rise out of the huts of history's shame." Slavery was abolished in New York State in 1827.

From here, if you retrace your steps to Foley Square and down Centre Street, you'll see the footpath that runs over the Brooklyn Bridge.

The Brooklyn Bridge

Subway J, Z to Chambers St, R to City Hall, #2 or #3 to Park Place, #4, #5 or #6 to Brooklyn Bridge-City Hall

One of several spans across the East River, the **Brooklyn Bridge** is today dwarfed by lower Manhattan's skyscrapers, but in its day, the bridge was a technological quantum leap, its elegant gateways towering over the brick structures around it. For twenty years after its opening in 1883, it was the world's largest and longest suspension bridge, and – for many more years – the longest single-span structure. To New Yorkers, it was an object of awe, the concrete symbol of the Great American Dream. Italian immigrant painter Joseph Stella called it "a shrine containing all the efforts of the new civilization of America". Indeed, the bridge's meeting of art and function, of romantic Gothic and daring practicality, became a sort of spiritual model for the next generation's skyscrapers. On a practical level, it expanded the scope of New York City, paving the way for the incorporation of the outer boroughs and the creation of a true metropolis.

The bridge didn't go up without difficulties. Early in the project, in 1869, architect and engineer John Augustus Roebling crushed his foot taking measurements for the piers and died of tetanus less than three weeks later. His son Washington took over, only to be crippled by the bends after working in an insecure underwater caisson; he subsequently directed the work from his sickbed overlooking the site. Some twenty workers died during the construction, and a week after the opening day, twelve people were crushed to death in a panicked rush on the bridge's footpath. Despite this tragic toll (as well as innumerable suicides over the years), New Yorkers still look to the bridge with affection, celebrating its milestone anniversaries with parades and respecting it as a civic symbol on a par with the Empire State Building.

The **view** from below (especially on the Brooklyn side) as well as from the top is undeniably spectacular. You can **walk across** its wooden planks from Centre Street, but resist the urge to look back until you're at the midpoint, when the Financial District's giants stand shoulder to shoulder behind the spidery latticework of cables. You can follow the pedestrian path straight to its end, at the corner of Adams and Tillary streets in **Downtown Brooklyn** (see p.214), behind the main post office. More convenient for sightseeing, however, is to exit the bridge at the first set of stairs: walk down and bear right to follow the path through the park at Cadman Plaza. If you cross onto Middagh Street, you'll be in the core of **Brooklyn Heights** (see p.218); or follow Cadman Plaza West down the hill to Old Fulton Street and the **Fulton Ferry District** (see p.216).

VARIAZIONI
NYC

PRINCE STREET BOUTIQUE, SOHO

Tribeca and Soho

The adjoining neighbourhoods of Tribeca and Soho, north of the Financial District, are home to wealthy New Yorkers with a taste for retro-industrial cool and the stores that cater to them. Nineteenth-century warehouses have been converted into vast lofts, and the area's cast-iron buildings (and their enormous ground-floor windows) make it a perfect spot for purveyors of fine art, fashion and luxury goods. The art scenes that flourished here in the 1970s and 1980s have generally moved on to Chelsea and the outer boroughs, and today Tribeca feels more residential, its streets populated by stylish mums and their hip kids. Soho is also the haunt of fashionable Hollywood types, though the focus here is on dining and, especially, shopping.

Tribeca

#1 train to Canal St (for the north edge), Franklin St (centre) and Chambers St for the south side; the #2 and #3 also stop here

Tribeca (try-BECK-a), the Triangle below Canal Street, is a former wholesale-food district that has become an enclave of urban style; its old industrial buildings house the spacious loft apartments of the area's gentry. Less a triangle than a crumpled rectangle, the neighbourhood is bounded by Canal and Murray streets to the north and south, and Broadway and the Hudson River to the east and west. The name is a mid-1970s invention of real-estate brokers who thought it better suited to the neighbourhood's increasing trendiness; rapper Jay-Z, Mariah Carey and Gwyneth Paltrow are among a long list of celebrities who own apartments here. Another big name in the neighbourhood is Robert De Niro, who helped found both the **Tribeca Film Center**, a state-of-the-art building catering to producers, directors and editors, and the **Tribeca Film Festival** in 2002. It can be an intriguing area to explore, but most visitors who trek to Tribeca do so for its **restaurants** (see p.297).

Chambers Street to the Hudson River

Subway A, C, #1, #2, #3 to Chambers St

Heading west from City Hall Park, you'll get a taster of Tribeca's historic roots at the triangular intersection between Chambers Street and West Broadway, known as the Bogardus Triangle. Here, the **James Bogardus Viewing Garden** is dedicated to James Bogardus (1800–74), an architect and inventor who put up the city's first cast-iron building in 1849. You can see one of his few remaining creations at 85 Leonard St between Church Street and Broadway, a graceful structure completed in 1868.

4

Head up Hudson Street from the Bogardus Triangle to equally compact **Duane Park**, a sliver of green between Duane, Hudson and Greenwich streets. Established in 1797 as the second-oldest park in New York City (after Bowling Green), it was also once the site of the city's egg, butter and cheese markets – the original depots (mostly posh restaurants and shops today), alternating with new residential buildings, form a picturesque perimeter around the little triangle.

Walk across to Greenwich Street and you'll reach the top end of **Washington Market Park**, a pleasant green space that pays tribute, in name at least, to the neighbourhood's old function; today it's mainly a playground for Tribeca's stroller set. Next door, the **Tribeca Performing Arts Center** (see p.353) is the largest arts complex in Lower Manhattan.

From here you can continue up Greenwich Street to the thoroughly incongruous **Harrison Street Row**, such a contrast to the surrounding concrete that its nine Federal-style houses seem like reproductions. Though three of these late eighteenth-century homes were moved here in the 1970s, all are original, rare reminders of the area's pre-industrial past. Immediately to the west lies the traffic-choked West Side Highway (aka West St) and the eminently more appealing **Hudson River Park** beyond, a landscaped promenade that stretches north towards Chelsea and Midtown; you can also wander south to the tip of the island along the shady **Battery Park City Esplanade**.

Hook and Ladder Company #8

Subway #1 to Franklin St

Just north of Leonard Street, Varick Street splits off from West Broadway, one of Tribeca's main thoroughfares, and angles northwest, becoming Seventh Avenue once it crosses Houston Street. The New York City Fire Department's **Hook and Ladder Company #8**, 14 North Moore St, at Varick, operates from an 1865 brick-and-stone fire station dotted with white stars. Movie buffs may recognize the building from the *Ghostbusters* films of the 1980s (note the mural on the pavement outside); more recently, it played a role in the rescue efforts of September 11. As it is a working fire station, you can't do more than admire it from the outside.

SHOPPING
Agent Provocateur	19
Alexander Wang	40
Amarcord	20
Anna Sui	17
Apple Store	12
Bliss	8
Burberry	25
Calypso St Barth's	35
Camper	11/14
DKNY	22
Dean & Deluca	16
Eastern Mountain Sports	28
Housing Works Thrift Shop	4
John Varvatos	30
Kate's Paperie	36
Kate Spade	34
Kiosk	26
Kirna Zabête	24
Leica Store Soho	5
MAC	7
Marc Jacobs	1
Marni	7
MiN New York Apothecary & Atelier	9
Miu Miu	15
MoMA Design Store	29
The Mysterious Bookshop	42
Prada	13
Rag & Bone	21
Ricky's	3
Sabon	27
Selima Optique	33
Sephora	23
Shibui Spa	41
Soho Sanctuary	21
Stella McCartney	18
Supreme	10
Swarovski Crystallized	32
Topshop	37
Vera Wang	6
Victoria's Secret	2
Vivienne Tam	39
What Comes Around Goes Around	38

CAFÉS
Balthazar Bakery	14
Chobani SoHo	8
Dominique Ansel Bakery	12
Hampton Chutney	9
Once Upon a Tart	2

ACCOMMODATION
Cosmopolitan Hotel	7
Crosby Street Hotel	4
The James	3
The Mercer	5
Room in Soho Loft	1
Smyth Tribeca	8
Soho Grand	2
Tribeca Grand	6

BARS
Bubble Lounge	10
Café Noir	6
Ear Inn	4
Fanelli Café	2
Kenn's Broome Street Bar	5
M1-5 Lounge	8
Puffy's Tavern	11
The Room	1
Toad Hall	7

NIGHTLIFE
City Winery	3
Santos Party House	9

RESTAURANTS
Aquagrill	13
Balthazar	14
Blaue Gans	25
Blue Ribbon Sushi	10
Bouley	24
Bubby's	19
City Hall	26
Corton	18
Cupping Room Café	16
Dos Caminos	1
The Dutch	4
Harrison	23
Kelley and Ping	3
L´Ecole	17
Locanda Verde	20
Lure Fishbar	6
Mercer Kitchen	5
Nobu	21
Omen	11
Pakistan Tea House	27
Raoul's	7
Spring Street Natural Restaurant	15
Tribeca Grill	22

TRIBECA AND SOHO

JACKIE ROBINSON MUSEUM

Note that the long-anticipated **Jackie Robinson Museum**, commemorating the famous African-American baseball player, will open at One Hudson Square, 75 Varick St at Canal St, pending funds being raised; see ⓦjackierobinson.org for the latest progress.

New York City Fire Museum

278 Spring St • Daily 10am–5pm • $8; seniors, students and children $5 • ☎ 212 691 1303, ⓦ nycfiremuseum.org • Subway C, E to Spring St, #1 to Houston St

Housed in a 1904 Beaux Arts fire station just off Varick Street, the **New York City Fire Museum** displays old fire trucks dating back to the 1840s and plenty of art and NYFD memorabilia, but also acts as a touching memorial to the 343 firefighters who died on September 11. The NYFD lost 778 men in the line of duty between 1865 and September 10, 2001, but the devastating losses of the following day drew worldwide sympathy. Photos, videos and artefacts found at the site record the disaster, and tiles commemorate those lost.

Dahesh Museum of Art

145 Sixth Ave • Tues–Sat 11am–7pm • Free • ☎ 212 759 0606, ⓦ daheshmuseum.org • Subway C, E to Spring St, #1 to Houston St

A rare and little-known collection of European academic paintings of the nineteenth and twentieth centuries, the **Dahesh Museum of Art** is largely the creation of Lebanese writer Saleem Moussa Ashi (1909–84). Sadly, the museum has been without a permanent home since 2008, and this location is little more than an arty gift-shop with a few examples from the collection on display (a new permanent location is being sought). The merchandise is good quality, though, and the museum also runs an enlightening programme of free talks and events in the evenings (check the website).

Soho

The R and N trains to Prince St drop you at Prada's front door; the B, D or F to Broadway-Lafayette St deposits you a block north at Houston. For access to the west side of the neighbourhood, take the C or E to Spring St

Like Tribeca, **Soho** (short for *So*uth of *Ho*uston) has also undergone a series of transformations in the past few decades. In the 1980s, Soho was the centre of New York's art scene, but today a mostly non-resident crowd uses the area between Houston and Canal streets and Sixth Avenue and Lafayette Street as an enormous outdoor shopping mall. By day a place to buy trendy labels, at night the neighbourhood becomes a playground for gangs of well-groomed bistro- and bar-goers.

Despite the commercialism, Soho's artistic legacy hasn't been completely eradicated. If anything, it has been incorporated into the neighbourhood's new character. Check out **The Wall** (1973) by Forrest Myers, a giant installation of 42 aluminium bars, painted turquoise and bolted to a periwinkle blue wall at Houston and Broadway, or just cruise the visionary **Prada boutique** (Mon–Sat noon–8pm, Sun 11am–7pm), designed by Dutch architect Rem Koolhaas. The store, at Prince Street and Broadway, acts as a sort of gatekeeper to the area's myriad shopfronts, which showcase everything from avant-garde home decor to conceptual fashion.

Broadway

Subway B, D, F, M to Broadway-Lafayette St; N, R to Prince St

Any exploration of Soho's streets entails crisscrossing and doubling back, but an easy enough starting point is the intersection of Houston Street and Broadway. **Broadway** reigns supreme as downtown's busiest drag, and numerous storefronts, most of them jazzed-up chain shops trying to compete with Soho's pricey designer boutiques, make it easy to get swept up in the commercial frenzy. Broadway is also the place to start a tour

---

HIDDEN GEMS: SOHO AND TRIBECA

Broome Street Building See below
The New York Earth Room See p.67
Broken Kilometer See p.68
Ear Inn See p.330
Housing Works Used Books See p.374

City Walls trompe l'oeil mural
See p.67
Kiosk Gallery See p.372
All-you-can-eat mussels at
Petite Abeille See p.297

---

of Soho's distinctive **cast-iron architecture**, best appreciated from the outside – many are now shops, and the interiors have usually been substantially remodelled.

New Museum Building

583 Broadway • Subway B, D, F, M to Broadway-Lafayette St, N, R to Prince St

Making a handsome introduction to Soho's architectural charms, the ornate Beaux-Arts **New Museum Building** was built in 1896 on the site of the house where John Jacob Astor, America's original tycoon, died in 1848. Originally filled by apparel and hat manufacturers, it's now occupied by condos.

Little Singer Building

561 Broadway • Mango store Mon–Sat 10am–8.30pm, Sun 11am–7.30pm • Subway B, D, F, M to Broadway-Lafayette St, N, R to Prince St

One of the later examples of Soho's cast-iron architecture is the **Little Singer Building**, which is actually an L-shaped structure with a second front at 88 Prince St. The twelve-storey terracotta-tiled office and warehouse of the sewing-machine company was erected in 1904 by architect Ernest Flagg, who went on to build the record-breaking Singer Tower in the Financial District in 1908, thus rendering this earlier creation "little" in comparison. Here, Flagg used wide plate-glass windows set in delicate iron frames, a technique that pointed the way to the glass curtain wall of the 1950s. Today, the first floor is a Mango fashion store while the rest is a residential co-op – units were selling for $5–6 million in 2013.

Haughwout Building

488–492 Broadway, at Broome St • Bebe store Mon–Sat 10am–9pm, Sun 11am–8pm • Subway N, R to Prince St, #6 to Spring St

The magnificent 1857 **Haughwout Building** is the oldest cast-iron structure in the city, as well as the first building of any kind to boast a passenger elevator – the lift, designed by Elisha Otis, was steam-powered. Despite its dreary grey colour, the facade of the former housewares emporium (it's now a Bebe fashion store) is still mesmerizing; 92 colonnaded arches are framed behind taller columns and the whole building looks more like an elaborate sculpture.

Broome Street Building

451 Broome St, at Broadway • Subway N, R to Prince St, #6 to Spring St

Diagonally opposite the Haughwout Building and equally impossible to ignore, the ostentatious wedding-cake exterior of the **Broome Street Building** was completed in 1896. By the turn of the century, this was known as the Silk Exchange, but the building is mostly residential today – Britney Spears owned the penthouse before selling it in 2006.

Greene Street

Subway A, C, E, N, Q, R to Canal St

If you continue down Broadway to Grand Street and turn right (west), you'll be in a prime position to appreciate a couple of architectural beauties on **Greene Street**. First dip south to **no. 28–30**, the building known as the "**Queen of Greene Street**" (store open Mon–Fri 10am–6pm, Sat noon–6pm). Architect Isaac Duckworth's five-storey

---

SOHO'S CAST-IRON ARCHITECTURE

In vogue from around 1860 to the turn of the twentieth century, the **cast-iron architecture** that is visible all over Soho initiated the age of prefabricated buildings. With mix-and-match components moulded from iron, which was cheaper than brick or stone, a building of four storeys could go up in as many months. The heavy iron crossbeams could carry the weight of the floors, allowing greater space for windows.

The label can be confusing at first, as you won't see any obvious sign of metal (other than fire escapes); another major appeal for architects was that it was easy to disguise the iron with remarkably **decorative facades**. Almost any style or whim could be cast in iron, painted or plastered and pinned to the front of an otherwise dreary building to resemble marble: instant face-lifts for Soho's existing structures, and the birth of a whole new generation of beauties. Glorifying Soho's sweatshops, architects indulged themselves in Baroque balustrades and forests of Renaissance columns. But as quickly as the trend took off, it fell out of favour. Stricter building codes were passed in 1899, when it was discovered that iron beams, initially thought to be fireproof, could easily buckle at high temperatures. At the same time, steel proved an even cheaper building material.

With nearly 150 structures still standing, Soho contains one of the largest collections of cast-iron buildings in the world, and the **Soho Cast-Iron Historic District**, from Houston Street south to Canal Street and from West Broadway to Crosby Street on the east, helps preserve the finest examples.

French Second Empire extravagance dates from 1873 and was tastefully renovated in 2010 by trendy Swiss-based USM Modular Furniture. Retrace your steps and head north across Broome to see more of Duckworth's artistry at **no. 72–76** Greene St. Thanks to its mass of columns and peaked cornice, this palatial creation, completed just prior to no. 28–30, has naturally been given the title "**King of Greene Street**". The building was sold for a cool $41.5 million in 2012 (Dedon Furniture and Alicia & Olivia fashion boutique occupy the retail spaces).

One block west, at 35 Wooster St, between Grand and Broome streets, the **Drawing Center** (Wed & Fri–Sun noon–6pm; Thurs noon–8pm; ⓦdrawingcenter.org) hosts contemporary and historical drawing exhibits. Masters including Marcel Duchamp and Richard Tuttle, as well as emerging and unknown artists, are shown together.

The Cast-Iron Historic District
Subway N, R to Prince St, #6 to Spring St

Farther north, beyond Spring Street, you enter the heart of the **Cast-Iron Historic District**, where you'll see vivacious facades, as well as curlicue bishop's-crook cast-iron lampposts. None is quite as splendid as Duckworth's, but all are beautifully preserved and make excellent display cases for the high-end retail offerings inside. The busiest shop in this area is one of the few not devoted to fashion, cosmetics or high-end art (and is not cast iron): the landmark **Apple Store** (Mon–Sat 9am–9pm, Sun 9am–7pm), occupying the former post office on the corner of Greene and Prince streets. Look out also for the **City Walls** (1975) trompe l'oeil mural at 112 Prince St (at Greene St) by Richard Haas, a solid wall craftily made to look like windows.

The New York Earth Room
141 Wooster St • Wed–Sun noon–3pm & 3.30–6pm; closed mid-June to mid-Sept • Free • ⓦ diaart.org/sites/main/earthroom • Subway B, D, F, M to Broadway-Lafayette St, N, R to Prince St

Wander north of Prince Street to see **The New York Earth Room**, a permanent installation by land artist Walter De Maria. Since 1977, this second-floor loft has been some of the most squandered real estate in NYC, as it is covered in almost two feet of moist brown earth, all of which weighs some 127 tonnes. Commissioned and maintained by the Dia Art Foundation, the dirt is periodically aerated and cleaned,

THE SOHO ART SCENE

These days the pristine cobbled streets of Soho attract hordes of happy shoppers at the weekends, but its transformation into high-end fashion mall is relatively recent. The deceptively plain former **Soho Gallery** building at 420 West Broadway was the home of the most influential **art galleries** in the city between the 1970s and 1990s. In 1971, art dealers Leo Castelli, André Emmerich and John Weber, along with Castelli's ex-wife Ileana Sonnabend, moved here from their offices uptown, jump-starting an art boom in what was then a largely derelict area of warehouses. Perhaps the most over-the-top exhibition occurred in 1991 in Sonnabend's gallery, when **Jeff Koons** debuted his *Made in Heaven* collection, a series of sexually explicit photos and sculptures featuring his then-wife, Italian porn-star/politician, La Cicciolina. The art-market bubble burst a year later, and the galleries started to leave Soho; though all the original dealers at 420 West Broadway have since died, their galleries remain in the Upper East Side and Chelsea (Koons still lives and works on the Upper East Side). Today, the old Soho Gallery building is occupied by a DKNY store and luxury apartments.

to keep mushrooms and bugs from flourishing. The grey-door entrance is easy to miss; press the buzzer for 2B and walk up to the second floor. You're not allowed to take photographs.

West Broadway and the South Village

Subway C, E to Spring St; N, R to Prince St

4

The north–south avenue of **West Broadway**, lined on either side with stately buildings, is the edge of the cast-iron district and was once the traditional boundary of Soho, though these days the blocks to the west are usually considered part of the area. Smaller and more residential, this section was once known as the **South Village**, its primarily Italian residents an extension of the Greenwich Village community until Robert Moses' brutal widening of Houston Street in 1940 effectively split them in two. The change in architecture is obvious, as the high-rise cast-iron warehouses give way to older Federal and Greek Revival row houses and cafés. At the top of Sullivan Street, **St Anthony of Padua Church** was built in 1888 by the oldest Italian congregation in the US. The church hosted the 2005 funeral of local resident and mafioso Vincent Gigante, better known as "The Oddfather" because he feigned mental illness for years to avoid prison. Walk back down to **116 Sullivan Street** to find one of the oldest homes in the neighbourhood, an elegant Federal-style townhouse completed in 1832 and particularly noted for its carved wooden doorway. Further south, below Spring Street, **83 & 85 Sullivan Street** are the oldest homes in the neighbourhood, completed in 1819.

Broken Kilometer

393 West Broadway • Wed–Sun noon–3pm & 3.30–6pm, closed mid-June–mid-Sept • Free • ⓦ diaart.org/sites/main/brokenkilometer; subway C, E to Spring St; N, R to Prince St

Just south of Spring Street on West Broadway you can find **Broken Kilometer**, another mind-bending installation by Walter De Maria dating from 1979. This collection of five hundred carefully arranged brass rods, each 2m long, is a slightly disorienting study in scale and perspective, as well as a testament to the sturdiness of cast-iron buildings – the collected rods weigh more than seventeen tonnes.

SHOPPING IN CHINATOWN

Chinatown, Little Italy and Nolita

Life has always been tough for Chinese immigrants in New York, but they've been coming to the city – and prospering – since at least the 1850s, making this Chinatown one of the oldest and biggest in the Western hemisphere. Indeed, with around five hundred restaurants and over 100,000 residents, Chinatown is Manhattan's most densely populated ethnic neighbourhood. Since the 1980s it has pushed into the smaller enclave of Little Italy, and has begun to sprawl east across Division Street and East Broadway. Little Italy itself, now squeezed into a narrow strip along Mulberry Street, is far more touristy than Chinatown, but both neighbourhoods are fun places to eat. Just to the north, the quarter known as Nolita is home to a number of chic restaurants, bars and boutiques.

5

INFORMATION

You can pick up maps, brochures and coupon booklets at the information kiosk (daily 10am–6pm) at Canal and Baxter streets. Staff here also speak Mandarin and Cantonese.

Chinatown

J, N, Q, R, Z or #6 train to Canal St

Walk through the crowded streets of **Chinatown** at any time of day and you'll find packed restaurants; storefronts displaying heaps of shiny squid, clawing crabs and fresh lobsters; and street markets overflowing with piles of exotic fruits, vegetables and ginger root. Beneath the neighbourhood's prosperous facade, however, is a darker legacy. Since 9/11, some of the most regrettable institutions associated with the area – namely non-union sweatshops – have closed, or at least moved (rising rents in Manhattan have forced these factories out to satellite Chinatowns in Queens and Brooklyn) but other sharp practices continue to flourish. Organized crime is prevalent, illegal immigrants are commonly exploited, and living conditions can be abysmal for poorer Chinese.

Outsiders, however, won't see anything sinister. The neighbourhood is a melange of vintage storefronts, modern Chinese graffiti and tourist-oriented kitsch. Lined with tacky shops and frequently a pedestrian traffic jam, the unappealing east–west thoroughfare of **Canal Street** is unfortunately often all visitors ever see of Chinatown – perhaps along with the inside of a dim sum palace on **Mott Street**. Explore the narrow side-streets, though, and you will be rewarded with a taste of a Chinatown that functions more for its residents than for tourists and retains many of its older traditions. Mott Street is the main north–south avenue, although the streets around it – Pell, Bayard, Doyers and the Bowery – also host a glut of restaurants, tea-and-rice shops and grocery stores that are fun to browse. Nowhere in this city can you eat so well, and so much, for so little.

Brief history

The first known **Cantonese** immigrant to New York arrived in 1858, and settled on Mott Street. He was not joined by significant numbers of his countrymen – and they were virtually all men – until the 1870s. By 1890, the census recorded about twelve thousand Chinese. Most of these men had previously worked out West on the transcontinental railroad or in gold mines, and few intended to stay in the US. Their idea was simply to make a nest egg, then return to their families and (hopefully) a far easier life in China; as a result, the neighbourhood around the intersection of Mott and Pell streets became known as the "bachelor society". Inevitably, money took rather longer to accumulate than expected, and though some did go back, Chinatown soon became a permanent settlement. Residents made their livings as cooks, cigar vendors, sailors and operators of fan-tan parlours and opium dens.

By the end of the nineteenth century, the quarter was notoriously violent, in large part due to its Triad-like "tongs". These Chinese organized-crime operations doubled as municipal-aid societies and thrived on prostitution, gambling and the opium trade. Beginning in the waning years of the nineteenth century, the **Tong Wars** raged well into the 1930s in the form of intermittent assassinations.

Growing resentment led to the Chinese Exclusion Act of 1882, which completely forbade entry to Chinese workers for ten years, and in the early twentieth century additional **immigration quotas**, particularly the 1924 National Origins Provision (NOP), further restricted the flow of Asians to America. In 1965, the Immigration Act did away with the NOP, and some twenty thousand new Chinese immigrants, many of them women, began to arrive in Chinatown. Local businessmen took advantage of the declining midtown garment business and made use of the new, unskilled female workforce to open garment factories of their own.

The early 1990s saw another major shift, as large numbers of illegal immigrants from the Fujian province of China arrived. Unlike the established Cantonese, the **Fujianese**

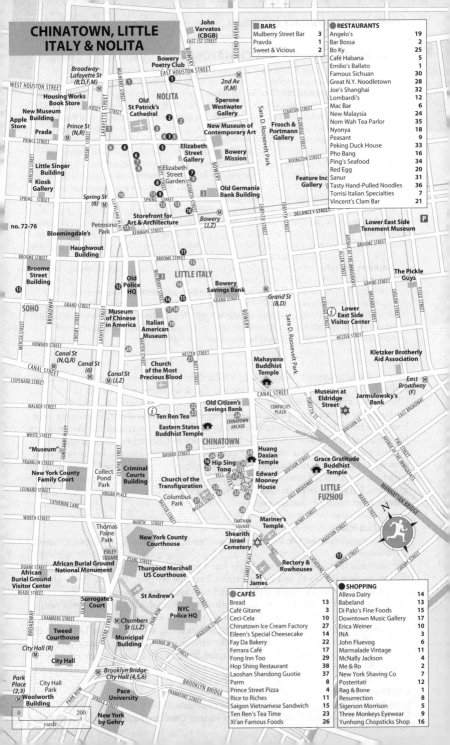

5

BEFORE CHINATOWN WAS CHINATOWN

As is true for many of the neighbourhoods in New York City, the area that is now known as Chinatown has undergone several transformations. The first trace of another culture is the **cemetery of Congregation Shearith Israel**, just south of Chatham Square on St James Place. The oldest Jewish congregation in North America, Shearith Israel was established in New York in 1654 by a small group of Sephardim from Brazil, descendants of Jews who had fled the Spanish Inquisition. This small graveyard was in use from 1683 to 1833, but all that remains today is a collection of seventeenth- and eighteenth-century headstones. The cemetery is opened every year around Memorial Day, when a special ceremony pays tribute to those Jews interred here who died in the Revolutionary War; at other times you can just peer through the iron railings.

Just around the corner on St James Street, the **St James Church** marks the arrival of the Irish in the mid-nineteenth century. A big Greek Revival brownstone, the church was the gathering place of the first American division of the Ancient Order of Hibernians, an Irish-Catholic brotherhood, in 1836. True to the cultural mixing that is characteristic of Manhattan's slums, St James Church was founded with the help of a Cuban priest, Félix Varela, who was also instrumental in the early Catholic period of the Church of the Transfiguration on Mott Street. If you walk around the corner from St James Church to Oliver Street, you'll see the former church rectory in a row of tenement-style homes, as well as the much-worse-for-wear **Mariners' Temple**, completed in 1845 and the oldest Baptist church in Manhattan (both churches tend to open only for services).

Perhaps the most overlooked anachronism is the **Edward Mooney House**, a tiny Georgian-style brick building at 3 Pell St, on the corner of the Bowery, that looks very out of step with its plastic-facade neighbours. Built around 1785, it's the oldest surviving row house in New York City, erected by a merchant who saw this neighbourhood's future as a centre for commerce – today, it's occupied by Summit Mortgage Bankers.

---

were largely uneducated labourers who spoke their own dialects along with Mandarin. Cultural and linguistic differences made it difficult for them to find work in Chinatown, and a large number turned to more desperate means. By 1994, Fujianese-on-Fujianese violence comprised the majority of Chinatown's crime, prompting local leaders to break the neighbourhood's traditional bond of silence and call in city officials for help. Today, Cantonese is still the lingua franca of Chinatown; though many well-off Cantonese have moved to the outer boroughs, they remain the district's most important customers, and businesses remain largely Cantonese-owned. This combined with high rents has led many Mandarin-speaking "mainlanders" (immigrants from mainland China) to settle in Brooklyn's Sunset Park, though the southern half of **East Broadway** remains a Fujianese enclave.

Columbus Park

Baxter St, Mulberry St, Bayard St and Worth St • Daily 24hr • Free • ☎ 212 639 9675, ⓦ nycgovparks.org • Subway J, N, Q, R, Z, #6 to Canal St, J, Z to Chambers St

The southern limits of Chinatown begin just a few blocks north of City Hall Park at the intersection of Worth and Baxter streets, once the centre of the Five Points slum (see p.60). From here, **Columbus Park** stretches north, a green sward away from Chinatown's hectic consumerism. It's favoured by the neighbourhood's elderly, who congregate for morning *t'ai chi* and marathon games of *xiangqi* (Chinese chess). The park was laid out by Calvert Vaux, of Central Park fame, and opened in 1897, but little of his original plan remains – ball fields take up one end, while craggy rock-gardens are the backdrop on the north side. Facing Bayard Street, an open-air concert pavilion is a relic of the late nineteenth century.

Chatham Square

Bowery, Park Row and Worth St • Subway J, N, Q, R, Z, #6 to Canal St, J, Z to Chambers St

Southeast of Columbus Park, Worth Street ends at **Chatham Square**, really a concrete triangle hemmed in by traffic, where Fujianese civic organizations have erected a statue of **Lin Zexu**, a Qing-dynasty official who is revered in China for cracking down on the opium trade. Lin arrested thousands of Chinese opium dealers, destroyed 1180 tonnes of the drug and kicked out the British opium merchants in 1839, thereby precipitating the Opium Wars. The Fujianese have cast their hero as a "pioneer in the war against drugs", according to the inscription. Also in Chatham Square, the **Kimlau Memorial Arch** pays tribute to Chinese-Americans killed in World War II. Just to the north looms **Confucius Plaza**, a 1970s housing complex that's still considered some of the best living quarters in Chinatown; a statue of the Chinese philosopher was erected outside in 1976.

Little Fuzhou

East Broadway • Subway F to East Broadway, J, N, Q, R, Z, #6 to Canal St

East from Chatham Square is the "new" Chinatown – the district expanded by the Fujianese and other mainland immigrants in the past few decades. East Broadway, often dubbed **Little Fuzhou**, is the main commercial avenue, an earthy, authentic blend of bakeries, restaurants and markets.

Grace Gratitude Buddhist Temple

48 East Broadway • Daily 10am–5pm • Free • ☎ 212 925 1335 • Subway F to East Broadway, J, N, Q, R, Z, #6 to Canal St

Founded in 1974 by revered Chinese monk Master Fayun, the **Grace Gratitude Buddhist Temple** is one of the oldest Chan (Zen) Buddhist temples in the city, a serious place of worship maintained by resident monks. The architecture is typically modern, but there's a shrine to Buddhist bodhisattva Guanyin (known as the "Goddess of Mercy") in the lobby, and the main hall is dominated by gold statues representing three incarnations of Buddha.

Pell and Doyers streets

Subway J, N, Q, R, Z, #6 to Canal St

Just to the north of Chatham Square, on the corner of **Pell Street** and the Bowery, you'll find the **Huang Daxian Temple** (daily 9am–6pm; free; ☎212 349 6221), one of Chinatown's few Taoist temples and, like most of them, a converted shop front. This one is dedicated to Huang Daxian, a quasi-historical figure who is said to have lived in China in the fourth century, worshipped today for his supposed powers of healing. Better known as Wong Tai Sin in Cantonese, he remains one of the most popular Taoist deities in Hong Kong. On the other side of Pell Street stands the venerable **Edward Mooney House** (see box, opposite).

Further along Pell Street itself, no. 16 is the headquarters of the United in Victory Association, also called the **Hip Sing Tong**, where some seventy people were killed when the rival On Leong group raided the building in 1924 (the doorway is next to the Foot Rub place). Halfway along Pell is crooked **Doyers Street**. Once known as the "Bloody Angle" for its role as a battleground during the Tong Wars, there's little more malicious than barber shops operating here now.

Mott Street

Subway J, N, Q, R, Z, #6 to Canal St

At first glance, **Mott Street**, the "dragon's spine" of Chinatown, is a strip of tacky gift shops and countless modern teashops. Look past the kitsch, though, and you'll also find herbal-medicine vendors, traditional furniture dealers and barely renovated tenements – this is the oldest section of Chinatown.

Church of the Transfiguration

29 Mott St, at Mosco St • Sat 2–5pm, otherwise services only • Free • ☎ 212 962 5157, ⊕ transfigurationnyc.org • Subway J, N, Q, R, Z, #6 to Canal St

This green-domed church is an elegant Georgian building known as the "church of immigrants" for good reason. Established here in 1801 as a Lutheran parish, it was

5

sold to Irish Catholics fifty years later; the plaque honouring those killed in World War I lists primarily Italian names, while today, Mass is said daily in Cantonese, English and Mandarin.

Eastern States Buddhist Temple

64 Mott St • Daily 8am–6pm • Free • ☎ 212 966 6229 • Subway J, N, Q, R, Z, #6 to Canal St

This is the oldest Chinese temple on the East Coast. Established in 1962 by the Ying family (originally from Ningbo, China), the room's linoleum floors and dropped ceiling make it more functional than fancy. The main deity here is Sakyamuni Buddha, but note also the glass-encased gold statue of the "four-faced Buddha", a replica of the revered image in Bangkok's Erawan Shrine.

Ten Ren's Tea

75 Mott St • Daily 10am–8pm • Free • ☎ 212 349 228, ⓦ tenrenusa.com • Subway J, N, Q, R, Z, #6 to Canal St

Tea lovers should cross the street from the Eastern States Buddhist Temple to this lauded Taiwanese tea merchant, established in the 1950s, which sells everything from cheap green tea to expensive oolongs (semi-fermented tea); try the delicious "Oriental Beauty".

Canal and Grand streets

Subway J, N, Q, R, Z, #6 to Canal St

Say "Canal Street" to most New Yorkers, and they'll think not of a real canal (which this busy thoroughfare was until 1820), but of counterfeit handbags, watches and designer sunglasses, which you'll see on sale in nearly every shop you pass. A casual stroll here is impossible; the streets are lined with food vendors, souvenir stalls and hawkers talking up their knock-off bargains – foot traffic often grinds to a halt. Canal Street channels its eastbound traffic onto the **Manhattan Bridge**, completed in 1909, which crosses the East River to Brooklyn via the grand Beaux Arts arch over the centre lanes (modelled on the Porte St-Denis in Paris).

Citizens Savings Bank

58 Bowery, at Canal St • Mon–Fri 8.30am–5pm, Sat 10am–2pm • ☎ 800 975 4722 • Subway J, N, Q, R, Z, #6 to Canal St

The former **Citizens Savings Bank** is something of a local landmark, its neo-Byzantine bronze dome looming majestically above the chaotic streets of Chinatown. Completed in 1924, it now functions as a branch of HSBC. Enter on Canal Street to take a peek at the interior of the dome and its four surviving murals: Thrift, Success, Safety and Wisdom (no photography allowed).

Mahayana Buddhist Temple

133 Canal St • Daily 8am–6pm • Free • ☎ 212 925 8787 • Subway J, N, Q, R, Z, #6 to Canal St

Chinese influence is obvious at this gilded temple, which is much more opulent than its counterpart on Mott Street (it was established in 1997 by the same family). Candlelight and blue neon glow around the giant gold Buddha on the main altar, while along the walls are 32 plaques that tell the story of Buddha's life. Despite the assault of red and gold, it's a surprisingly peaceful place. The entrance hall contains a smaller shrine to Guanyin (see p.73) and the small shop upstairs sells books and statues.

Bowery Savings Bank

130 Bowery • Closed to the public • ☎ 212 334 5500, ⓦ capitaleny.com • Subway N, Q, R, #6 to Canal St, J, Z to Bowery

This lavish Roman Classical-style structure lies two blocks north of Canal Street, at the corner of Grand Street (the city's main east–west avenue in the 1800s). Designed by celebrated architect Stanford White in 1894, today the building is a posh location for private dinners and functions known as **Capitale**, and sadly off-limits to visitors.

5

HIDDEN GEMS: CHINATOWN, LITTLE ITALY AND NOLITA

Prince Street Pizza See p.279
Linguini at Vincent's See p.300
Three Monkeys Eyewear See p.378
Yunhong Chopsticks Shop See p.372

Huang Daxian Temple See p.73
"Museum" See below
Croissants at Ceci-Cela See p.278
Eileen's Special Cheesecake See p.278

Museum of Chinese in America

215 Centre St at Grand St • Tues, Wed & Fri–Sun 11am–6pm, Thurs 11am–9pm • $10, free Thurs • ☎ 212 619 4785, ⓦ mocanyc.org • Subway J, N, Q, R, Z, #6 to Canal St

Designed by Maya Lin (best known for her Vietnam Memorial in Washington, DC), the slickly presented **Museum of Chinese in America** provides a historical overview of the Chinese-American experience from 1784 to the present, through an evocative blend of multimedia displays, artefacts and filmed interviews of real people. Some of the issues tackled are the Chinese Exclusion Act of 1882, the emergence of "Chop-Suey" restaurants and bigoted "Yellowface" movies in the 1930s, and the identity of second-generation Chinese-Americans since the 1960s. Galleries are arranged around a sunlit courtyard reminiscent of a traditional Chinese house, and also include temporary exhibitions of Chinese and Chinese-American art.

Museum

Cortlandt Alley, between Franklin and White sts • Sat & Sun 11am–7pm • Free • No phone, ⓦ museumm.com • Subway J, N, Q, R, Z, #6 to Canal St

Technically in Tribeca but just a short walk south of Canal Street, the creatively named **Museum** is a quirky New York sight not to be missed. Tucked away down a scruffy alley, it occupies just a single old warehouse elevator. Exhibits rotate (think New York City tip jars, international toothpaste tubes and fake vomit from around the world), but the permanent collection includes what claims to be one of the shoes thrown at George Bush in Iraq in 2008 (the US military said it destroyed both shoes). Check the website for current opening times; even if it's closed you can see most of the goofy treasures inside through the windows.

Little Italy

Subway J, N, Q, R, Z, #6 to Canal St

Bounded roughly by Canal Street to the south, Houston Street to the north, Mulberry Street to the east and Broadway to the west, **Little Italy** is light years away from the solid ethnic enclave of old, but it's still fun for a stroll and a decent cappuccino on the hoof.

If you walk north on Mulberry from Chinatown to get here, the transition from the throngs south of Canal to the kitsch of today's Little Italy can be a little difficult to stomach. The red, green and white tinsel decorations along Mulberry Street and the suited hosts who aggressively lure out-of-town visitors to their restaurants are undeniable signs that the neighbourhood is little more than a tourist trap. Few Italians still live here, though a number still visit for a dose of nostalgia, some Frank Sinatra and a plate of fully *Americano* spaghetti with red sauce. For a more vibrant, if workaday, Italian-American experience, you'll want to head to Belmont in the Bronx (see p.254).

This is not to advise missing out on Little Italy altogether. Some original bakeries and *salumerias* (Italian speciality food stores) do survive, and here, amid the imported cheeses, sausages and salamis hanging from the ceiling, you can buy sandwiches made with slabs of mozzarella or eat slices of fresh focaccia. In addition, you'll still find plenty of places to indulge with an espresso and a pastry, not least of which is *Ferrara's*, at 195

5

Grand St, the oldest and most popular café. Another establishment of note is the belt-defying *Lombardi's*, at 32 Spring St, which is not only the city's oldest pizzeria but also one of its finest.

Brief history

The area was settled in the latter half of the nineteenth century by a huge influx of Italian immigrants, who supplanted the district's earlier Irish inhabitants and, like their Chinese and Jewish counterparts, clannishly cut themselves off to re-create the Old Country; even streets were claimed by different regions, with settlers from Campania and Naples on Mulberry, Sicilians on Elizabeth, and Mott Street divided between Calabrians (south end) and immigrants from Puglia (north end). After World War II, the Italians started moving out of the city (though Martin Scorsese and Robert De Niro roamed the area in the 1950s), and the neighbourhood is much smaller and more commercial than it once was, with Chinatown encroaching on three sides – Mulberry Street is the only Italian territory south of Broome Street.

Mulberry Street

Subway J, N, Q, R, Z, #6 to Canal St

Little Italy's main strip, **Mulberry Street** is an almost solid row of restaurants and cafés – and is therefore filled with tourists. The street is particularly lively, if a bit like a theme park at night, when the lights come on and the streets fill with restaurant hosts who shout menu specials at passers-by. If you're here in mid-September, the eleven-day **Festa di San Gennaro** (see p.402) is a wild and tacky celebration of the patron saint of Naples, held here since 1926. Italians from all over the city converge on Mulberry Street, and the area is filled with street stalls and numerous Italian fast-food and snack vendors. The festivities centre on the 1892 **Church of the Most Precious Blood**, at 109 Mulberry St (main entrance on Baxter St), providing visitors with a chance to see the inside of this small church, which is normally closed.

None of the eating places around here really stands out, but 129 Mulberry St at Hester Street, the former site of *Umberto's Clam House* (now relocated on the other side of the street), was quite notorious in its time: in 1972, it was the scene of a vicious gangland murder when "Crazy Joey" Gallo was shot dead while celebrating his birthday with his wife and stepdaughter. Gallo, a big talker and ruthless businessman, was keen to protect his interests in Brooklyn; he was alleged to have offended a rival family and so paid the price. Today, the space is occupied by run-of-the-mill *Da Gennaro* restaurant. For a more tangible Mafia vibe, you can't beat the 1908 *Mulberry Street Bar*, at no. 176 1/2, where the back room, all fogged mirrors and tile floors, has been the setting for numerous Mob movies and episodes of *The Sopranos*.

Incidentally, the very real Gambino crime family ran operations from the **Ravenite Social Club**, at 247 Mulberry St, between Prince and Spring (now a posh shoe shop); boss John Gotti went to jail in 1992 (his son John Gotti Jr claims to have renounced crime).

At the corner of Mulberry and Grand streets, **Alleva** (Mon–Sat 8.30am–6pm, Sun 8.30am–3pm; free; ☎ 212 226 7990, ⓦ allevadairy.com) was established in 1892 and claims to be the oldest cheese-maker in the US – perhaps true if the definition of cheese is limited to mozzarella and ricotta.

Italian-American Museum

155 Mulberry St, at Grand St • Sat & Sun noon–6pm • Donation $5 • ☎ 212 965 9000, ⓦ italianamericanmuseum.org • Subway J, N, Q, R, Z, #6 to Canal St, B, D to Grand St

To learn more about the historic roots of the area, stop by the **Italian-American Museum** housed in the former Banca Stabile. The bank opened in 1885 and offered services to immigrants, including translation, letter writing, wire transfers and travel booking. The

FROM TOP NEW MUSEUM OF CONTEMPORARY ART (P.79); MUSEUM OF CHINESE IN AMERICA (P.75) >

5

building still contains the old vault and banking machines, enhanced by small but enlightening exhibits on the old neighbourhood and Stabile family business – though the bank closed in 1932, the family maintained their other businesses here until the 1960s. Look out for a brutal extortion note from 1914, written by a member of the "Black Hand" to a local business owner, and the display about Giuseppe Petrosino, one of the first Italian-American NYPD officers, who was murdered working a case in Sicily in 1909. The museum hopes to expand into the adjacent buildings over the next few years.

Old Police HQ

240 Centre St, at Grand St • Closed to the public • Subway J, N, Q, R, Z, #6 to Canal St, B, D to Grand St

The **Old Police Headquarters** is a palatial 1909 Neoclassical construction a short walk from Mulberry Street. Meant to cow would-be criminals into obedience with its high-rise copper dome and lavish ornamentation, it was more or less a complete failure: the blocks immediately surrounding the edifice were some of the most corrupt in the city in the early twentieth century. Police headquarters moved to a bland modern building near City Hall in 1973, and the overbearing palace was converted in 1987 into luxury condominiums; one-bedroom apartments were selling for $2–3 million in 2013.

Nolita

Subway N, R to Prince St, #6 to Spring St

The blocks surrounding St Patrick's Old Cathedral, particularly north to Houston Street and east to the Bowery, were rechristened **Nolita** ("North of Little Italy") by savvy real-estate developers in the late 1990s. Stylish shop-owners are the newest variety of immigrant here, as numerous tiny boutiques have taken over former Italian haunts. Most are above Spring Street, but the trendiness has spread south too. Although this district is not cheap by any means, it is a bit more personal and less status-mad than much of neighbouring Soho. The shops showcase handmade shoes, custom swimwear and items with vintage flair, often sold by the designers themselves, or at least by obsessive buyers who have strong affection for the goodies they've collected from elsewhere.

If you're not interested in shopping, you should definitely check out the **New Museum of Contemporary Art** on the Bowery, a stylish showcase for the latest trends in multimedia art. Nolita is also an appealing place to put your feet up after a long walking tour. Choose from any of the numerous restaurants (p.300), or head to the café inside the **McNally Jackson** bookstore, at 52 Prince St (Mon–Sat 10am–10pm, Sun 10am–9pm), or the **Housing Works Bookstore Café**, at 126 Crosby St (Mon–Fri 10am–9pm, Sat & Sun 10am–5pm).

Basilica of St Patrick's Old Cathedral

263 Mulberry St, at Prince St • Daily except Wed 8am–6pm • Free • ☎ 212 226 8075, ⓦ oldcathedral.org • Subway N, R to Prince St, #6 to Spring St

The **Basilica of St Patrick's Old Cathedral** was once the spiritual heart of Little Italy and the oldest Catholic cathedral in the city. When it was consecrated in 1815, it actually served the Irish community and hosted the Roman Catholic archdiocese in New York. Catholic leadership has moved uptown to a newer St Patrick's Cathedral on Fifth Avenue at 50th Street, relegating "old St Pat's" to the status of a parish church. It now serves English-, Spanish- and Chinese-speaking worshippers. Designed by Joseph-François Mangin, the architect behind City Hall, the building is grand Gothic Revival, with an 85ft vault, a gleaming gilt altar and a massive pipe organ that was installed in 1868, when the church was restored following a terrible fire. The Vatican awarded Basilica status to the Old Cathedral in 2010, a title that confers increased ceremonial privileges.

Equally notable is the **cemetery** behind the church, which is ringed with a brick wall that the Ancient Order of Hibernians used as a defence in 1835, when anti-Irish rioters threatened to burn down the church. The cemetery is almost always locked, but try to peek through one of the gates – you may recognize the view from a scene in Martin Scorsese's *Mean Streets* (one of the few parts of the movie actually shot here, even though the film was set in Little Italy).

The Bowery
Subway B, D to Grand St, J to Bowery

Forming the boundary between Nolita and the Lower East Side, **the Bowery** was until relatively recently a byword for poverty and destitution, America's original **skid row**. At its peak in 1949, around fourteen thousand homeless people could be found here, most dossing down in hostels known as flophouses. Today, only a few flophouses remain, and these mostly cater to Chinese labourers at the southern end of the Bowery. The street runs north from Chatham Square in Chinatown to Cooper Square in the East Village, where it is increasingly lined with smart, contemporary buildings (see p.89).

The current gentrification of this wide thoroughfare is just the latest of many changes over the years: the street takes its name from *bouwerie*, the Dutch word for farm, when it was the city's main agricultural supplier. In the nineteenth century, it was flanked by music halls, opera houses, vaudeville theatres, hotels and middle-market restaurants, drawing people from all parts of Manhattan – including opera lover **Walt Whitman** (see box, p.218). The good times did not last, and by the early twentieth century the street was becoming associated with crime and poverty, attracting religious and social welfare institutions like the **Bowery Mission**, which opened in 1880.

The Bowery's notoriety immortalized it in literature, with many writers making use of its less than stellar reputation. Theodore Dreiser closed his 1900 tragedy *Sister Carrie* with a suicide in a Bowery flophouse, while fifty years later William S. Burroughs alluded to the area in a story that complained of undesirables waiting to "waylay one in the Bowery". The Great Depression signalled a low-point in the Bowery's fortunes, and between the 1940s and 1980s the whole strip was synonymous with alcoholics and the homeless. Those days are largely gone, and though pockets of the old Bowery remain (check out the graffiti-smothered walls of the 1899 **old Germania Bank Building**, at no. 190, at the corner of Spring Street, actually the home of photographer Jay Maisel), wine stores, galleries and high-end apartments are becoming far more prevalent.

New Museum of Contemporary Art
235 Bowery, opposite Prince St • Wed, Fri–Sun 11am–6pm, Thurs 11am–9pm • $14, free for age 18 and under & Thurs 7–9pm • Free guided tours Wed–Fri 12.30pm, Sat & Sun 12.30pm & 3pm; free audio tours available for download on the website • ☏ 212 219 1222, ⓦ newmuseum.org • Subway N, R to Prince St, #6 to Spring St, F to Second Ave-Lower East Side

Two blocks east of St Patrick's Old Cathedral, the **New Museum of Contemporary Art** is a powerful symbol of the Bowery's rebirth. The building itself is as much the attraction as the avant-garde work inside, a stack of seven shimmering aluminium boxes designed by Tokyo-based architects Kazuyo Sejima and Ryue Nishizawa.

An industrial elevator glides between the four main floors, each holding one exhibition space. The warehouse-like galleries, all brilliant white with shiny concrete floors, are spacious but still small enough to digest without overdosing on the often thought-provoking and diverse range of temporary exhibits inside. The **shop** in the lobby has a fabulous book section and café, while the **Sky Room** on the seventh floor opens at weekends for rare views across the Lower East Side and Nolita.

The Lower East Side

Historically the epitome of the American ethnic melting pot, the Lower East Side – bordered to the north by Houston Street, the south by East Broadway, the east by the East River and the west by the Bowery – is one of Manhattan's most enthralling downtown neighbourhoods. A fair proportion of its inhabitants are Dominicans and Chinese, but among them you're also likely to find small Jewish communities, students, moneyed artsy types and hipster refugees from the more gentrified areas of Soho and the East Village. Many visitors come for the shopping; some of the city's best vintage-clothing and furniture stores are here, which has in turn attracted a number of emerging designers as well. The plethora of drinking, dancing and food options also draws large crowds every night of the week.

INFORMATION

Tourist information For details about local events and tours, visit the Lower East Side Visitor Center at 54 Orchard St, between Hester and Grand streets (Mon–Fri 9.30am–5.30pm, Sat & Sun 9.30am–4pm; ☎212 226 9010, ⓦlowereastsideny.com).

Local tours For tours of the neighbourhood's Jewish heritage (and to gain entrance into some of the otherwise private synagogues), contact the Lower East Side Conservancy (☎212 374 4100, ⓦnycjewishtours .org).

Brief history

Most of this area was owned by the pro-British DeLancey family until 1787, when it was confiscated and sold off by the new American government. The first tenement buildings in the city were constructed here in 1833, and the development of **Kleindeutschland** (Little Germany) followed closely behind. By 1860, Irish immigrants had started to dominate the neighbourhood, and by the end of the nineteenth century it was attracting international humanitarian attention as an insular slum for over half a million **Jews**. Mainly from Eastern Europe, these refugees came to America in search of a better life, but instead found themselves scratching out a living. By the 1880s, the area had become America's **garment capital** – today, there are still over one hundred small garment factories in the Lower East Side. For many Jews, the entertainment industry was the only way out; comedian George Burns, composer George Gershwin, and William Fox, founder of the Fox Film Corporation, all grew up here.

Low standards of hygiene and abysmal housing made disease rife and life expectancy low: in 1875, the infant mortality rate was forty percent, mainly due to cholera. It was conditions like these that spurred reformers like Jacob Riis and Stephen Crane to record the plight of the city's immigrants in writing and photographs, thereby spawning not only a whole school of journalism but also some notable changes in urban planning.

The **Chinese** and **Dominicans** moved into the area in the 1980s, but it wasn't until the 1990s that retro clubs, chic bars, gourmet restaurants and unique boutiques sprouted up all over. Despite the changes, about forty percent of the people living here were born in another country, with a quarter of residents Spanish-speaking, and around twenty percent from China and other parts of East Asia.

Houston Street to Grand Street

South of Houston Street, **Jewish** immigrants indelibly stamped their character on the Lower East Side with their shops, delis, restaurants and synagogues. Even now, with Chinatown overflowing into the neighbourhood, the area exhibits remnants of its Jewish past: on Houston itself, you'll find *Katz's Deli* (see p.301) at no. 205, at the corner of Ludlow Street; *Russ & Daughters* (see p.279) at no. 179, at the corner with Orchard Street; and venerable knish-maker *Yonah Schimmel* (see p.279), farther west at no. 137. South of Houston, **Orchard Street** is centre of the so-called **Bargain District**. This area is at its best on Sundays, when the street is closed to traffic between Houston

THE BEAUTIFUL LOSERS

When a few artsy types discovered the then run-down, shabby **Ludlow Street** in the early 1990s, it sparked a hipster migration south from the East Village. Between 1992 and 1997, Aaron Rose ran the **Alleged Gallery** at 172 Ludlow St between Houston and Stanton streets, a dynamic focal point for urban artists involved with skateboarding, graffiti and independent film dubbed "The Beautiful Losers": Thomas Campbell, Cheryl Dunn, Shepard Fairey, Harmony Korine, Geoff McFetridge, Barry McGee, Margaret Kilgallen, Mike Mills, Steven "Espo" Powers and Ed Templeton among them. The artists are long gone, and today the street is home to fashion boutiques, speciality stores (no. 172 is now Ludlow Guitars), cafés and bars.

and Delancey, and it's filled with stalls and storefronts hawking discounted designer clothes and accessories.

Lower East Side Tenement Museum

97 Orchard St • Tenement is accessible only by various themed guided tours (every 15–30min, 10.30am–5pm; 1hr; $22); for tickets, go to the museum's visitor centre at 103 Orchard St (daily 10am–6pm) • ☎ 212 431 0233, Ⓦ tenement.org • Subway B, D to Grand St, F, J, M, Z to Delancey St/Essex St

Even if you don't have the time to tour the Lower East Side extensively, make sure you visit the **Lower East Side Tenement Museum**, an 1863 tenement building restored by the museum founders in the 1990s (it had been abandoned since 1935). If you've visited Ellis Island (see p.38), this museum continues the immigrant story: guides do a brilliant job bringing to life the building's (and the neighbourhood's) past and present, aided by documents, photographs and artefacts found on site, concentrating on the area's multiple ethnic heritages. This will probably be your only chance to see the claustrophobic, crumbling interior of a tenement, with its deceptively elegant, though ghostly, entry hall and two communal toilets for every four families. Various apartments inside have been renovated with period furnishings to reflect the lives of its tenants, from the mid-nineteenth century when there was no plumbing (or indoor toilets), electricity or heat, to the mid-twentieth century when many families ran cottage industries out of their apartments.

At the **visitor centre** you can buy tickets, watch a couple of introductory videos (20min, on permanent loop), peruse the excellent bookshop, visit the demonstration kitchen for culinary programmes and view art exhibitions. **Tours** include "Hard Times", which focuses on a German-Jewish family and an Italian family in the depression years of 1863 and 1935; "Irish Outsiders", which examines the grim life of an Irish family 1868–69; and "Sweatshop Workers", which highlights the Levine family's garment workshop. The newest tour is "Shop Life", which explores a restored nineteenth-century German saloon at street level, and discusses other businesses located in that space. The museum also offers a 1hr 30min **walking tour** of the neighbourhood (daily 12.30pm & 2pm; $22); this is designed to complement the tenement tours, so it's best to do it second. For all tours, come early or book in advance.

Kehila Kedosha Janina Synagogue

289 Broome St, at Allen St • Sun 11am–4pm • Free • ☎ 212 431 1619, Ⓦ kkjsm.org • Subway B, D to Grand St, F, J, M, Z to Delancey St/Essex St

Two blocks east of the tenement museum along Broome Street, the beautifully preserved **Kehila Kedosha Janina Synagogue and Museum** has been the home of the region's Romaniote Jews since 1927, an obscure branch of Judaism with roots in Roman-era Greece. Enthusiastic volunteers are on hand to provide background and introduce Jewish art and various exhibits, including costumes from Janina (the Romaniote capital of Greece), alephs (hand-painted birth certificates), and the first Holocaust Memorial to Greek Jews.

Delancey and Essex streets

Subway F to Delancey St, J, M, Z to Essex St

Orchard Street bisects **Delancey Street**, once the horizontal axis of the old Jewish Lower East Side, now a tacky boulevard leading to the **Williamsburg Bridge** and Brooklyn. Two blocks east, at Delancey and Essex, sprawls the **Essex Street Market** (Mon–Sat 8am–7pm, Sun 10am–6pm; Ⓦ essexstreetmarket.com), erected under the aegis of Mayor LaGuardia in 1939, when pushcarts were made illegal. Here you'll find all sorts of fresh fruit, fish and vegetables, along with artisan chocolates, cheese and *Shopsin's* restaurant (see p.301). Two blocks south of Delancey, 49 Essex St is home to **The Pickle Guys** (Mon–Thurs & Sun 9am–6pm, Fri 9am–4pm; ☎ 212 656 9739, Ⓦ pickleguys .com), where people line up outside the store to buy fresh home-made pickles, olives and other yummy picnic staples from huge barrels of garlicky brine.

Rivington Street

Subway F to Delancey St, J, M, Z to Essex St

Just one block north of Delancey Street, **Rivington Street** epitomizes the fashionable face of the Lower East Side, with a string of hip bars and restaurants – it's supposedly Lady Gaga's favourite place for a drink (the fashion-forward singer got her start in the Lower East Side).

■ BARS

Back Room	14
Barramundi	8
Barrio Chino	17
The Delancey	15
Experimental Cocktail Club	13
Libation	11
Magician	12

■ NIGHTLIFE

Arlene's Grocery	6
bOb Bar	4
Bowery Ballroom	16
Cake Shop	10
The Living Room	9
Mercury Lounge	1
Pianos	5
Rockwood Music Hall	3
Sapphire Lounge	2
Slipper Room	7

● RESTAURANTS

Cibao Restaurant	11
Congee Village	18
Georgia's Eastside Barbeque	5
Katz's Deli	2
Meatball Shop	6
Mission Chinese Food	10
Pok Pok Phat Thai	14
Sammy's Roumanian Steakhouse	17
Schiller's Liquor Bar	15
Shopsin's	16
Stanton Social	7
WD-50	9

● CAFÉS

Bluestockings	8
Cheeky Sandwiches	23
Doughnut Plant	22
Il Laboratorio del Gelato	1
Kossar's	21
Mikey's Burger	13
Pop Karma	19
Russ & Daughters	3
Sugar Sweet Sunshine	12
Vanessa's Dumpling House	20
Yonah Schimmel Knish Bakery	4

■ ACCOMMODATION

Blue Moon	1
Hotel 91	2

● SHOPPING

Babeland	4
Economy Candy	3
Edith Machinist	2
Essex Street Market	5
Hester Street Fair	7
Mooshoes	6
Yumi Kim	1

THE LOWER EAST SIDE

Walking east along Rivington beyond Suffolk Street takes you to **Streit's** (Mon–Thurs 9am–4.30pm; ⓦstreitsmatzos.com), at 148 Rivington St, maker of fine *matzo* (a cracker-like flatbread) and kosher foods for Passover on this spot since 1925 – another survivor of the old Jewish neighbourhood.

ABC No Rio

156 Rivington St • ☎ 212 254 3697, ⓦ abcnorio.org • Subway F, J, M, Z to Delancey St/Essex St

The welded gate composed of old gears and scrap metal marks the entrance to ABC No Rio, a long-downtrodden but still vibrant community arts centre that has hosted gallery shows, raucous concerts, a 'zine library, art installations and the like since 1980. Despite an extensive and ongoing ecofriendly renovation, the centre still runs Hardcore/Punk Matinees every Saturday at 3.30pm, and the Sunday Open Series of poetry readings at 3pm each week, featuring new works by local neighbourhood poets and writers.

Angel Orensanz Center

172 Norfolk St • Mon–Fri 10am–5pm by appointment • Free • ☎ 212 529 7194, ⓦ orensanz.org • Subway F, J, M, Z to Delancey St/Essex St

One block north of Rivington, the **Angel Orensanz Center** was originally the Gothic Revival-style **Anshe Chesed Synagogue**, built in 1849 for the German Jewish community and the oldest surviving synagogue building in New York. Abandoned in the 1970s, Spanish sculptor and painter Angel Orensanz purchased the property in 1986 and converted it into an art gallery and performance space. Today the third and fourth floors serve as a museum displaying the work of Orensanz (who still maintains a studio here) while the Shul of New York, a liberal Reform synagogue, uses the main space for services. Sarah Jessica Parker and Matthew Broderick, both half Jewish, were married here in super-secret in 1997 (though in a Christian service). To see the gorgeous interior you must make an appointment or check the website for upcoming events.

Canal Street and around

Though the southern part of the Lower East Side has largely been absorbed by Chinatown, the area used to be an important hub for the Jewish community. To get a feel for the old quarter, start on **Canal Street** at Eldridge Street, two blocks west of Orchard Street.

Museum at Eldridge Street

12 Eldridge St, just south of Canal St • Mon–Thurs & Sun 10am–5pm, Fri 10am–3pm • $10, free Mon; by half-hourly guided tours only (last tour 4pm; 1hr) • ☎ 212 219 0888, ⓦ eldridgestreet.org • Subway B, D to Grand St, F to East Broadway

Completed in 1887 as the first **synagogue** constructed by Eastern European Orthodox Jews in the US, this painstakingly restored site opened as a museum in 2007. It's still one of the neighbourhood jewels: the facade is a grand brick and terracotta hybrid of Romanesque, Moorish and Gothic influences, but the real highlight is the **main sanctuary** upstairs, a gasp-inducing space with rich woodwork, painted ceiling, giant chandelier and original stained-glass windows, including the west-wing rose window – a spectacular Star of David roundel. The **women's balcony** offers a closer view of the artwork, while displays show just how dilapidated the synagogue had become by the early 1970s. The synagogue is a functioning house of worship, but you can visit the interior on **guided tours**, which provide plenty of entertaining stories about the neighbourhood. Tours begin at the lower level, where the **Bes Medrash** or "House of Study" also serves as a synagogue, and there's a shop and the Limud Center; the interactive computer displays here offer further insights into the history of the building.

HIDDEN GEMS: THE LOWER EAST SIDE

Breakfast at Shopsin's See p.301
Knish at Yonah Schimmel See p.279
Kehila Kedosha Janina Synagogue
    See p.82

Bialystoker Synagogue See below
Live music at Arlene's Grocery
    See p.344
Pok Pok Phat Thai See p.302

Sender Jarmulowsky's Bank

6

54 Canal St • Closed to the public • Subway B, D to Grand St, F to East Broadway

Above a row of food and electrical stores is the ornate facade of **Sender Jarmulowsky's Bank**, dwarfing the buildings around it. Founded in 1873 by a Russian-Jewish peddler who made his fortune reselling ship tickets, the bank catered to the financial needs of the area's non-English-speaking immigrants. Jarmulowsky, who was dubbed the "East Side J.P. Morgan", and became the first president and key benefactor of the Eldridge Street Synagogue (see opposite), died less than a month after the current building was completed in 1912. As the threat of war in Europe grew, the bank was plagued by runs and riots, and in 1917 it finally collapsed; on its closure, thousands lost what little savings they had accumulated. The building is currently being converted into a boutique hotel.

East Broadway and Shtiebel Row

Subway F to East Broadway

Canal Street ends at **East Broadway**, now almost exclusively a Fujianese enclave but once a thriving Jewish neighbourhood. At the junction between the two streets, the handsome **Forward Building** at 175 East Broadway became the headquarters of the influential Jewish daily *The Forward* in 1912, with adjacent Straus Square a hangout for radicals and activists (the building features carved bas-relief portraits of Karl Marx and Friedrich Engels).

The section of East Broadway between Clinton and Montgomery streets is known as **Shtiebel Row**, once home to dozens of storefront *shtieblach* (small congregations) but now lined by ugly housing projects on the north side. Several remain in the historic row houses on the south side of the street, however, often marked by small signs in Hebrew; the **Congregation Beth Hachasidim De Polen**, a branch of Agudath Israel of America, a leading Orthodox organization, is at 233 East Broadway. The best way to see inside any of the *shtieblach* is to contact the Lower East Side Conservancy (see p.81). Look out also for the huge **Jewish Ethnic Mural** (1973) by Susan Caruso-Green, peeling but still visible on the east side of 232 East Broadway.

Bialystoker Synagogue

7 Willett St, near the junction of Grand St and East Broadway • Mon–Thurs 7–10am (to visit you must call in advance) • Free • ☎ 212 475 0165, ⓦ bialystoker.org • Subway F, J, M, Z to Delancey St/Essex St

This synagogue was built in 1826 as a Methodist church and purchased by the Beth Haknesseth Anshe Bialystok Congregation in 1905. Sombre grey stone on the outside, hemmed in by grim housing projects, the synagogue's sanctuary is a trove of stained glass, gold leaf and exuberant murals of zodiac signs, all beautifully restored. There's also a balcony door that was used to hide slaves as part of the Underground Railway, and a memorial plaque to the gangster Bugsy Siegel (aka Benjamin Siegel), who worshipped here as a child.

ST MARK'S CHURCH-IN-THE-BOWERY

The East Village

The East Village, which extends east from Broadway to the East River and north from Houston Street to 14th Street, is one of New York's most fashionable neighbourhoods, home to some of the best bars, restaurants and independent theatres in the city. Once a working-class refuge for immigrants, New York's nonconformist intelligentsia were sent scurrying here when rents began to rise in Greenwich Village, and by the 1960s the East Village was at the height of its creative and often lawless period. Since the 1990s, the area's flourishing culinary and bar scene (and its proximity to NYU), has ensured that rents here are almost as insane as in neighbouring West Village. Thoughtful resistance to the status quo can still be found, however, through a smattering of independent boutiques, thrift stores, record shops and alternative performance spaces.

ARRIVAL AND INFORMATION

Arrival The East Village can be reached by taking the #6 train to Astor Place, the L train to Third or First Ave, or the R and N trains to 8th Street.

Information The East Village Visitor Center, 75 E 4th St, between Bowery and Second Ave (☎212 228 4670, ⓦfacebook.com/EastVillageVisitorsCenter), was being renovated at the time of research.

Noho

Squashed between Astor Place, the Bowery, Broadway and Houston Street, **Noho** (North of Houston) was considered part of the East Village until the name was invented by a group of local activists in the 1970s. Tucked in-between the old warehouses now being transformed into trendy offices and galleries, just south of Astor Place on Lafayette Street, is the beautifully restored brownstone-and-brick building that was once the **Astor Library**. Built with a bequest from John Jacob Astor between 1853 and 1881 (in a belated gesture of *noblesse oblige*), it was the first public library in New York. It became the **Public Theater** in 1967; pop into the lobby to see Ben Rubin's *Shakespeare Machine*, a chandelier installation with 37 fan-like LED screens displaying text from the Bard's work.

7

Merchant's House Museum

29 E 4th St • Mon & Thurs–Sun noon–5pm • $10 • ☎ 212 777 1089, ⓦ merchantshouse.com • Subway N, R to 8th St, #6 to Astor Place

Constructed in 1832, this elegant Federal-style row house offers a rare and intimate glimpse of domestic life in New York during the 1850s. The house was purchased by Seabury Tredwell in 1835, a successful metal merchant. Remarkably, much of the

---

EAST VILLAGE REBELS: FROM REDS TO RENT

Over the years, the East Village has been home to its share of **radical artists**, **politicos** and **literati**. In 1916, the short-lived Communist journal *Novy Mir* operated from the basement at 77 St Mark's Place, numbering among its contributors **Leon Trotsky**, who lived in New York for three months (1916–17) – **W.H. Auden** lived in the same building between 1953 and 1972. At 208 E 13th St historical markers commemorate **Emma Goldman**, who lived here 1903 to 1913 while publishing her anarchist paper *Mother Earth* (she was deported to the Soviet Union in 1919). Blues pioneer **Leadbelly** died in 1949 while living in a tenement that still stands at 414 East 10th St (just off Ave C). In the 1950s, the East Village became one of the main New York haunts of the **Beat poets** – Kerouac, Burroughs, Ginsberg – who, when not riding trains across the country, would get together at Ginsberg's house on East 7th Street for declamatory readings; **Ginsberg** wrote *Kaddish* at 170 E 2nd St in 1961, as tribute to his mother, Naomi. **Andy Warhol** debuted the Velvet Underground at the Fillmore East (105 Second Ave at East 6th St), which played host to just about every band you've ever heard of between 1968 and 1971, before becoming *The Saint* (also now defunct), a gay disco famous for its three-day parties (1980–90). In 1973, Puerto Rican artists established the **Nuyorican Poets Café** on East 3rd St (see p.360), a haven for up-and-coming New York poets and writers. By the 1980s, the East Village was best known for its **radical visual artists**, including Keith Haring, Jeff Koons and Jean-Michel Basquiat, while gay icon **Quentin Crisp** lived at 46 E 3rd St from 1981 until his death in 1999. In the early 1980s **Madonna** lived at 230 E 4th St, while Chinese artist and activist **Ai Weiwei** lived on East 7th and East 3rd streets between 1983 and 1993, his apartments becoming a hub for other Chinese artists and intellectuals (Chen Kaige and Tan Dun among them).

Towards the end of the 1980s, the neighbourhood was the centre of a different kind of attention: the city evicted the homeless from Tompkins Square Park, and the neighbourhood's many dead-broke squatter artists were forced out, a story memorialized in the hit Broadway musical **Rent**. With suitable irony, the show has made millions of dollars since its debut in 1996, and was successfully adapted for the big screen in 2005 – its Broadway run finally ended in 2008.

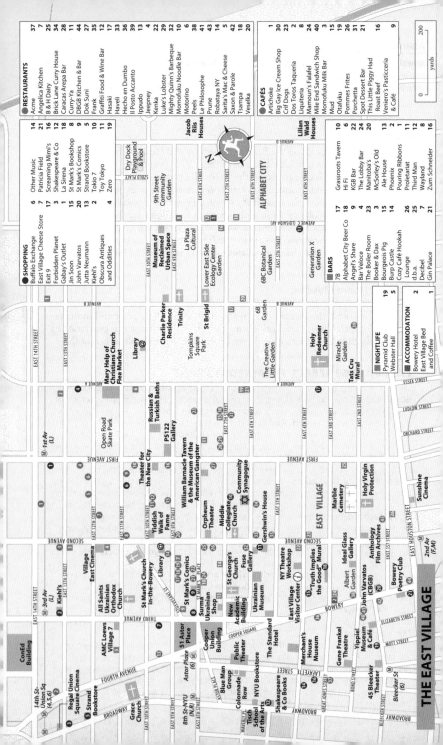

THE EAST VILLAGE

● RESTAURANTS

Acme	37
Angelica Kitchen	25
B & H Dairy	34
Brick Lane Curry House	28
Caracas Arepa Bar	11
Curry-Ya	44
DBGB Kitchen & Bar	27
Dok Suni	35
Frank	12
Graffiti Food & Wine Bar	17
Hasaki	33
Haveli	36
Hecho en Dumbo	39
Il Posto Accanto	13
Ippudo	4
Jeepney	22
Kenka	29
Luke's Lobster	32
Mighty Quinn's Barbeque	10
Momofuku Noodle Bar	6
Motorino	38
Peels	41
Le Philosophe	43
Prune	14
Robataya NY	5
Santa's Mac & Cheese	42
Saxon & Parole	18
Tsampa	20
Veselka	

● SHOPPING

Buffalo Exchange	14
East Village Cheese Store	16
Exit 9	12
Forbidden Planet	18
Gabay's Outlet	15
Jin Soon	20
John Varvatos	13
Jutta Neumann	10
Kiehl's	19
Obscura Antiques and Oddities	
Other Music	6
Patricia Field	7
Screaming Mimi's	1
Shakespeare & Co	
La Sirena	
St Mark's Bookshop	9
St Mark's Comics	
Strand Bookstore	
Tokio 7	
Toy Tokyo	
Zero	

● CAFES

Artichoke	1
Big Gay Ice Cream Shop	30
Crif Dogs	23
Dos Toros Taqueria	2
Liquiteria	8
Mamoun's Falafel	24
Mile End Sandwich Shop	40
Momofuku Milk Bar	3
Mud	15
Otafuku	19
Pommes Frites	26
Porchetta	31
This Little Piggy Had Roast Beef	16
Veniero's Pasticceria & Café	9

BARS

7B	10
Alphabet City Beer Co	6
Angel's Share	22
Bar Veloce	24
The Boiler Room	20
Booker & Dax	
Bourgeois Pig	
Burp Castle	
Cozy Café Hookah Lounge	
d.b.a.	
Decibel	
Gin Palace	
Grassroots Tavern	17
Hi Fi	18
KGB Bar	9
The Lobby Bar	23
Manitoba's	3
McSorley's Old Ale House	15
Phoenix	14
Pouring Ribbons	26
Proletariat	25
Third Man	7
Wayland	8
Zum Schneider	16

NIGHTLIFE

Pyramid Club	19
Webster Hall	5

ACCOMMODATION

Bowery Hotel	2
East Village Bed and Coffee	1

0 ——— 200 yards

mid-nineteenth-century interior remains in pristine condition, largely thanks to Seabury's daughter Gertrude, who lived here until 1933 – it was preserved as a museum three years later. Folders loaded with information provide ample material for a self-guided tour of the house, providing fascinating background, anecdotes and quotes from the family, their servants and neighbours. Highlights include furniture fashioned by New York's best cabinet-makers, the mahogany four-poster beds upstairs (where both Gertrude and Seabury passed away) and the tiny brass bells in the basement, used to summon the servants.

CBGB

315 Bowery • John Varvatos store open Mon–Sat noon–9pm, Sun noon–7pm • ☎ 212 358 0315 • Subway N, R to 8th St, #6 to Bleecker St

The site of the legendary underground music club **CBGB** is just a few blocks south of the Merchant's House Museum, along the Bowery. The New York **punk-rock** scene began here in the 1970s, famously hosting bands such as **the Ramones**, **Blondie**, **Patti Smith** and **Talking Heads**. In 2003, the city renamed the corner of East 2nd Street and the Bowery "Joey Ramone Place", in honour of the late punk legend. The club finally closed in 2006, and in a sign of the times has become a John Varvatos fashion boutique; designer clothes and vinyl records are displayed in the original, dimly lit interior, with walls plastered with punk memorabilia.

Yippie! Museum and Café

9 Bleecker St • Café daily 10am–7.30pm (closing times vary for events) • ☎ 212 677 5918, ⓦ 9bleecker.com, ⓦ harmonykitchennyc.com • Subway N, R to 8th St, #6 to Bleecker St

Another vestige of the East Village's radical past lies on Bleecker Street close to the Bowery, where the **Yippie! Museum and Café** hosts informal concerts, comedy shows and readings in the evenings (typically from 8pm). The museum moniker is slightly misleading, but it's still an interesting place to visit, with the Harmony Kitchen café offering vegan food, free wi-fi and a cosy lounge loaded with radical magazines and flyers. The counterculture/anti-war group, led by Abbie Hoffman (who died in 1989), has been based here since 1973, despite being regularly faced with eviction.

Astor Place

Subway N, R to 8th St, #6 to Astor Place

Between Broadway and Third Avenue lies **Astor Place**, a street that forms a busy crossroads as it intersects with the Bowery, Third and Fourth avenues and St Mark's Place/East 8th Street, where students, tourists and teenagers mill around, wolfing pizza, drinking cheap beer or skateboarding. It's named for real-estate tycoon John Jacob Astor, the wealthiest person in the US at the time of his death in 1848 (worth $115 billion in modern terms). Beneath the replicated old-fashioned kiosk of the Astor Place subway station, the platform walls sport reliefs of beavers, recalling Astor's first big killings – in the fur trade. The balancing black steel cube in the centre of the intersection is the *Alamo* (1967) by Tony Rosenthal.

Cooper Square

Just south of Astor Place, between the Bowery and Third Avenue, is **Cooper Square**, dominated by the brownstone mass of the Foundation Building of the **Cooper Union for the Advancement of Science and Art** (☎ 212 353 4100, ⓦ cooper.edu), a college for the poor established in 1859 by the wealthy entrepreneur Peter Cooper (1791–1883). Today, Cooper Union is a prestigious art, engineering and architecture school, whose nineteenth-century glory is evoked with a statue of the benevolent Cooper by Augustus Saint-Gaudens just in front. From the entrance

LANDMARKS OF ST MARK'S

St Mark's Place isn't just a cool place to eat and drink. Check out these notable landmarks, walking east from Third Avenue. As you stroll along the street, note the mosaic-encrusted lampposts, part of the **Mosaic Trail** created by Jim Power, aka "Mosaic Man" (ⓦ mosaicmannyc.com).

St Mark's Comics 11 St Marks Place between Third and Second aves. One of the few iconic stores to have survived since the street's punk heyday in the early 1980s (see p.375).

German-American Shooting Society Clubhouse (Deutsch-Amerikanische Schuetzen Gesselschaft) 12 St Mark's Place. A rare German Renaissance-style beauty, built in 1889 when St Mark's was the heart of Kleindeutschland, or Little Germany (it's now a yoga studio and apartments).

Gem Spa 36 St Mark's Place at Second Ave. This tiny newspaper/magazine shop dates back to 1900 (the current incarnation opened in 1957, but is best known as the birthplace of the authentic New York City-style egg cream (chocolate or vanilla syrup, milk and seltzer water; no eggs; $2.50). It also featured on the back of the New York Dolls' eponymous debut album. **Open 24hr.**

Physical Graffitea 96 St Mark's Place, east of First Ave. A teashop housed in the tenement that featured on the cover of the 1975 Led Zeppelin album *Physical Graffiti*. **Mon–Fri noon–11pm, Sat & Sun 11am–11pm.**

hall, the guards will normally allow you to walk downstairs to the **Great Hall**, where historical exhibits are displayed in the gallery outside. The hall itself is not particularly exciting, though it's where, in 1860, Abraham Lincoln wowed an audience of New Yorkers with his "right makes might" speech, criticizing the pro-slavery policies of the Southern states – before going to *McSorley's* on East 7th Street (see p.333) to quench his thirst.

You should also check out the gleaming **New Academic Building** at 41 Cooper Square across the street, completed in 2009 with a contemporary, environmentally friendly design by LA-based Thom Mayne; however, it's usually closed to the public.

St Mark's Place

East from Cooper Square, between Third Avenue and Avenue A, East 8th Street is known as **St Mark's Place**, lined with souvenir stalls, punk and hippie-chic clothiers and newly installed chain restaurants, signalling the end of the gritty atmosphere that had dominated this thoroughfare for years. Indeed, the sections closest to Third Avenue have a discernable Asian/Japanese vibe these days, with noodle bars and fashions more akin to parts of Tokyo than 1970s New York. To the south of St Mark's Place, East 6th Street between First and Second avenues is known as **"Curry Row"** after the preponderance of restaurants here from the Indian Subcontinent (not to be confused with Curry Hill on Lexington Avenue; see p.120).

Museum of the American Gangster

80 St Mark's Place (go through the gate and up the stairs of no. 78) • Daily 1–6pm • $15 • ☎ 212 228 5736, ⓦ museumoftheamericangangster.org • **William Barnacle Tavern** Mon–Thurs & Sun 6pm–midnight, Fri & Sat 6pm–2am • ☎ 212 388 0388 • Subway #6 to Astor Place

One of the newest attractions on St Mark's, the **Museum of the American Gangster** is also one of the oddest, housed above what used to be an illegal speakeasy run by gangster Walter Scheib in the 1920s (now the **William Barnacle Tavern**, owned by the same folks). Though the two exhibition rooms contain a handful of rare gangster-related curios (a John Dillinger death mask, and the bullet that killed Pretty Boy Floyd for example), there's not much to see, and it's the **guided tours** by enthusiastic owner Lorcan Otway that make this worth considering. He'll lead you into the basement (where the illicit boozers once hid) and regale you with tales of prohibition, Cosa Nostra and Frank Sinatra, though again, you won't see anything especially exciting.

Little Ukraine

Just behind Cooper Square is an area long inhabited by New York's Ukrainian community, most evidenced by the lavishly adorned exterior of **St George Ukrainian Catholic Church** at 30 East 7th St (rebuilt in the 1970s), and the **Ukrainian Museum**. You can also grab a bite nearby at *Streecha Ukrainian Kitchen*, at 33 East 7th St (Fri–Sun noon–4pm; ☎ 212 674 1615), or *Veselka* (see p.304), and buy Ukrainian music, newspapers, cards and icons at **Surma Ukrainian Shop**, at 11 East 7th St (Mon–Fri 11am–6pm, Sat 11am–4pm).

Ukrainian Museum

222 East 6th St · Wed–Sun 11.30am–5pm · $8 · ☎ 212 228 0110, ⓦ ukrainianmuseum.org · Subway #6 to Astor Place

This small but beautifully maintained museum is primarily a collection of Ukrainian folk costumes and textiles, as well as modern art from respected Ukrainian artists such as Nikifor (1896–1960) and Vasyl Krychevsky (1873–1952). You'll also see examples of the country's famous painted Easter eggs, known as *pysanky*. You can buy them at *Surma* (see above).

Yiddish Theater District

On Second Avenue, between East 5th and 6th streets, the apartment on the second floor of no. 91 was the childhood home of the **Gershwin** brothers, one of the greatest musical partnerships in history. George and Ira grew up in the heart of the **Yiddish Theater District**, centred on Second Avenue, which by World War I rivalled Broadway in scale and quality. The Immigration Act of 1924 signalled the end, however, and today all that remains of this once exuberant art form is the **Yiddish Walk of Fame**, like the stars on Hollywood Boulevard, at the corner of East 10th Street.

St Mark's Church-in-the-Bowery

131 East 10th St, at Second Ave · Office hours Mon–Fri 10am–4pm · Free · ☎ 212 674 6377, ⓦ stmarksbowery.org · Subway L to Third Ave, #6 to Astor Place

Opposite the Yiddish Walk of Fame is **St Mark's Church-in-the-Bowery**, the second-oldest church in the city. **Peter Stuyvesant**, the last Dutch Director-General of the New Netherlands, who arrived in what was then New Amsterdam in 1647 and surrendered the city to the English in 1664, built a small chapel here in 1660. The chapel was close to his farm, and he was laid to rest inside twelve years later. The box-like Episcopalian house of worship that currently occupies this space was completed in 1799 over his tomb, and sports a Neoclassical portico by James Bogardus (see p.63) that was added fifty years later – Stuyvesant's tombstone is now set into the outer walls. Nearby is a bust of the Director-General donated by the Dutch in 1915, looking far nobler than the crude, early English caricatures of "Peg-leg Pete" suggest.

The church is normally locked – walk up to the office on the second floor (via a side door on the right side) and someone will let you in to see the vivid stained-glass windows inside. In 1966, the **St Mark's Poetry Project** (☎ 212 674 0910, ⓦ poetryproject.org) was founded here by Allen Ginsberg and friends to ignite artistic and social change. Today, the church remains an important cultural rendezvous, with poetry readings Monday and Wednesday evenings at 8pm and most Fridays at 10pm (all $8), dance performances by the **Danspace Project** (ⓦ danspaceproject.org), and theatre from the **Incubator Arts Project** (ⓦ incubatorarts.org).

Tompkins Square Park

Aves A to B, and East 7th to East 10th sts · Daily 6am–midnight · Free · ☎ 212 674 6377, ⓦ nycgovparks.org; · Subway L to First Ave, #6 to Astor Place

A great green square in the heart of the East Village, **Tompkins Square Park** has long been a focus for the local community as well as one of New York's great centres for

THE TOMPKINS SQUARE RIOTS

Until 1991, Tompkins Square Park was more or less a shantytown (known locally as "Tent City" or "Needle Park"). Hundreds of homeless people slept on benches or under makeshift shelters between the paths. In the winter, only the really hardy or truly desperate lived here, but when the weather got warmer the numbers swelled, as activists, anarchists and all manner of statement-makers descended on the park. Things came to a head in the 1988 **Tompkins Square Riots**, when massive demonstrations against a 1am curfew for the previously 24-hour park led the police, badges covered and batons drawn, to attempt to clear the square of people. In the ensuing battle, 44 demonstrators and bystanders were hurt; the investigation that followed heavily criticized the police for the violence. It wasn't the first disturbance here – a far larger riot occurred in **1874**, when police crushed a demonstration involving thousands of unemployed. In 1991 the park was temporarily closed and dozens of homeless people who had been living here were relocated. The park was subsequently overhauled, its winding pathways and playground restored; the changes are enforced by a midnight lock-up and police surveillance.

7

political protest (see box, above). In recent years the park has evolved like the rest of the Village, and is now a desirable outdoor space that appeals to everyone, from local families to drag queens. The cleaned-up park features handball courts, a dog run and free concerts, a regular summer pastime for locals. Near the centre of the park is the **Prabhupada elm tree**, the site of the **Hare Krishna** movement's first ceremony outside of India, held in 1966, and named after the founder Swami Prabhupada (Allen Ginsberg was in attendance that day). Jazz legend **Charlie Parker** lived at 151 Ave B (closed to the public) on the east side of the park from 1950 until his death in 1954; the free **Charlie Parker Jazz Festival** features concerts in the park on the last weekend in August (see ⓦcityparksfoundation.org).

Slocum Memorial Fountain

Tompkins Square Park, near East 10th St • Daily 6am–midnight • Free • ⓦ nycgovparks.org • Subway L to First Ave, #6 to Astor Place

Just inside the brick enclosure on the north side of the park, the **Slocum Memorial Fountain** (1906) is a 9ft pink-Tennessee-marble column showing two children gazing forlornly out to sea. In 1904, the local community, then mostly made up of German immigrants, was devastated by the burning and sinking of a cruise ship, the **General Slocum**, in Long Island Sound. In the aftermath, most of the traumatized German-Americans in the neighbourhood moved away, many to Yorkville (see p.179). The monument commemorates the 1021 lives lost, mostly women and children, with a moving quote from Shelley's poem *Revolt of Islam*.

Tenth Street Russian and Turkish Bath

268 E 10th St, between First Ave and Ave A • Mon, Tues, Thurs, Fri noon–10pm, Wed 10am–10pm, Sat 9am–10pm, Sun 8am–10pm; men only Thurs noon–5pm, Sun 8am–2pm; women only Wed 10am–2pm; co-ed otherwise (shorts are mandatory) • $30 • ☎ 212 473 8806, ⓦ russianturkishbaths.com • Subway L to First Ave, #6 to Astor Place

The old steam rooms at the redbrick **Tenth Street Russian and Turkish Bath** have been active since 1892; you can enjoy the steam baths, sauna and an ice-cold pool all day for $35 (includes soap, towel, robe, razor and slippers), though it's extra to get beaten with an oak-leaf broom ($40) or chow down on some borscht or herring (both $4) in on-site *Anna's Restaurant*.

Alphabet City

East of Tompkins Square Park and north of Houston Street is **Alphabet City**, one of the most dramatically revitalized areas of Manhattan. Deriving its name from the grid of avenues lettered A–D, Alphabet City is also known to its remaining Puerto Rican

THE EAST VILLAGE GARDENS

In the 1970s, huge parts of the East Village burned to the ground after cuts in the city's firefighting budget closed many of the local fire stations. Since then, **Green Thumb** (🌐 greenthumbnyc.org), founded in 1978 on the back of work by local (mostly female) activists, has helped the community transform these neglected and empty lots from rubble-filled messes into some of the prettiest and most verdant spaces in lower Manhattan. In 1995, NYC Parks & Recreation began managing the programme, but a dramatic reversal in city policy in 1998 – to convert garden land into real estate – almost scuppered the whole project. Despite a last-minute agreement that ensured the safety of 114 of the neighbourhood's 600-plus gardens in 1999, the battle reached fever pitch in February 2000, when **El Jardin de la Esperanza** (Hope Garden) on East 7th Street between avenues B and C was bulldozed to make way for market-priced housing. Around thirty local residents were arrested while protesting the action; the city began to bulldoze the garden while the last resister was being removed – a mere forty minutes before an injunction was issued to prevent the city from destroying any further community gardens. The final 2002 agreement guaranteed the preservation of an additional two hundred community gardens.

The fight seems to have been well worth it. There is no nicer way to spend a summer afternoon than by picnicking among the lush trees and carefully planted foliage of these spaces, though sadly, many gardens were badly damaged by **Hurricane Sandy** in 2012. Of particular note is the **6th & B Garden** (May–Oct Sat & Sun 1–6pm; 🌐 6bgarden.org), which lost its willow tree but remains overgrown with wildflowers, vegetables and roses. The garden also provides a space for yoga classes in the morning and performance art in the evening during the summer, as well as a forum for bake sales, sing-alongs and other community events. Other gardens include the very serene and lush **6 B/C Botanical Garden** (May–Oct Wed 6–8pm, Sat & Sun noon–11pm; 🌐 6bc.org) on East 6th Street between B and C; **Generation X Garden** (May–Oct Sat & Sun 8am–8pm) on East 4th Street between B and C; the **Parque de Tranquilidad** (April–Oct Tues–Fri 11am–1.30pm, Sat & Sun 10am–6pm) on East 4th Street between C and D; and **La Plaza Cultural** (April–Oct Sat & Sun noon–5pm) on East 7th Street between B and C. Note that alcohol is not permitted inside the gardens.

7

residents as **Loisaida** (a Spanglish rendering of "Lower East Side"). Like Tompkins Square Park, this used to be a notoriously unsafe corner of town run by drug pushers and gangsters; today, the crime rate is way down, many of the old buildings have been renovated, and the streets are increasingly the haunt of 20-somethings and edgier tourist youth. Comestibles aside, it's worth wandering around this part of town just to see some of the **murals** by the likes of Antonio "Chico" Garcia, as well as the numerous **community gardens** (see box, above). One definite cultural highlight is the **Nuyorican Poets Café**, at 236 East 3rd St (📞 212 505 8183, 🌐 nuyorican.org), where you can catch some of the biggest stars of the spoken-word scene.

Museum of Reclaimed Urban Space

155 Ave C, at E 10th St • Tues & Thurs–Sun 11am–7pm • Free, suggested donation $5; tours $20 • 📞 973 818 8495, 🌐 morusnyc.org • Subway L to Third Ave

Alphabet City's tradition of resistance is commemorated at the tiny **Museum of Reclaimed Urban Space**, housed in a nineteenth-century tenement that has been a punk squat since 1986. Inside you'll find photographs, posters, exhibits, a bicycle activism timeline and articles chronicling the history of social activism, community gardens and squatting in the East Village. Check the website for details of guided tours.

WASHINGTON SQUARE PARK

The West Village

Greenwich Village (now commonly called the West Village or just "the Village") has been the artistic, bohemian heart of New York since the 1920s, and though still one of the more progressive neighbourhoods in the city, it has attained a moneyed status over the last four decades and is definitely the place for those who have "arrived". Celebrities seem to snap up properties left, right and centre – the likes of Nicole Kidman, Philip Seymour Hoffman, Hugh Jackman and Sarah Jessica Parker, for example – attracted for the same reasons as the intelligentsia a century ago: quaint side-streets, charming brownstones and brick townhouses unrivalled elsewhere in Manhattan. It's quiet and residential, but with a busy streetlife that keeps humming later into the night than in many other parts of the city.

Brief history

Greenwich Village was a rural retreat until the yellow fever epidemic of 1822, when it became highly sought-after as a wealthy refuge from infected downtown streets. At the close of the nineteenth century, German, Irish and Italian immigrants moved in, rents plummeted and the neighbourhood took on a much more working-class atmosphere. The area's large but cheap houses proved a fertile hunting ground for struggling artists and intellectuals, and by the end of World War I, the Village had become **New York's Left Bank**; writer e.e. cummings, playwright Eugene O'Neill and dancer Isadora Duncan made their homes here.

In the 1950s, the Village became a hub for the **Beat Movement**, a loose collection of writers, poets, artists and students, and by the 1960s the area harboured rebellious, countercultural groups and activities – **Bob Dylan** was resident here for much of his early career. The mystique and allure of the Village was further enhanced by radicals such as the **Weather Underground** (see box, p.102) and history-changing events like the **Stonewall Riots** (see box, p.104). In recent decades, the Village has grown up, leaving its impassioned youth behind to become the fashionable, historic and increasingly expensive corner of Manhattan that it is today.

Washington Square Park

Fifth Ave, Waverly Place, West 4th St and MacDougal St • Daily 6am–midnight • Free • ☎ 212 998 6780, ⓦ nycgovparks.org • Subway A, C, E, F or M to West 4th St

The best way to see the Village is to walk, and by far the best place to start is its natural centre, **Washington Square Park**. Memorialized in Henry James's 1880 novel *Washington Square*, the city completed an extensive renovation of the park in 2011.

8

The park was established in 1827 on the site of a former cemetery and execution ground (up to ten thousand bodies are reputed to be buried here and the **Hangman's Elm** continues to grow in the park today). For years, the square was something of an open-air drug bazaar, but in the 1990s a heavy undercover police presence put an end to most of that activity. During the spring and summer months, the square becomes a combination of running track, performance venue, giant chess tournament and social club, boiling over with life as skateboards flip, dogs run and guitar notes crash through the urgent cries of performers calling for the crowd's attention.

The most imposing monument in the park itself is Stanford White's **Washington Memorial Arch**, built in 1892 to commemorate the centenary of George Washington's presidential inauguration. On the northern side of the park, only the row of elegant Greek Revival mansions – the "solid, honourable dwellings" that James described – remind visitors of the area's more illustrious past. The author based much of the novel on his grandmother's house at **no. 19**, while James himself was born around the corner on Washington Place (the house had already been torn down when he returned to the city in 1906, much to his disgust). Further along Washington Square

---

THE TRIANGLE SHIRTWAIST FIRE

One of New York's most infamous tragedies occurred on March 25, 1911, at the corner of Washington Place and Greene Street, when a fire started on the eighth floor of the **Triangle Shirtwaist garment factory**, one of the city's notorious sweatshops. A terrible combination of flammable fabrics, locked doors, collapsing fire escapes and the inability of fire-truck ladders to reach higher than the sixth floor, resulted in the deaths of 146 workers – almost all women, primarily immigrants, and some only 13 years old – in less than fifteen minutes. The fire led to legislation requiring improved safety standards, and helped spur the growth of the International Ladies' Garment Workers' Union. The site is now known as the Brown Building and forms part of NYU, with flowers left in front of the plaque commemorating the disaster on March 25 each year.

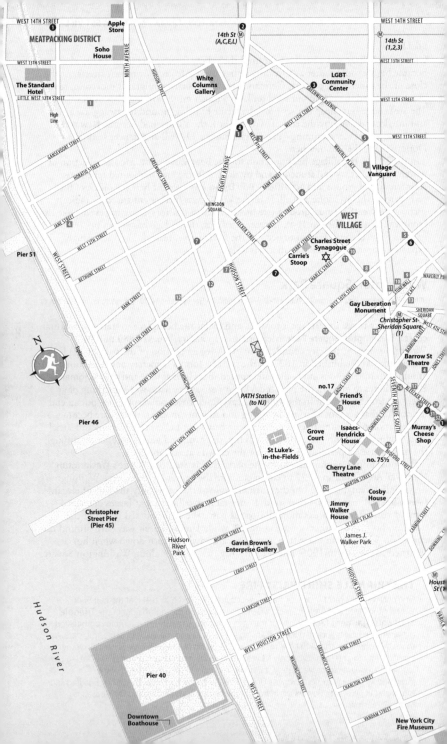

THE WEST VILLAGE

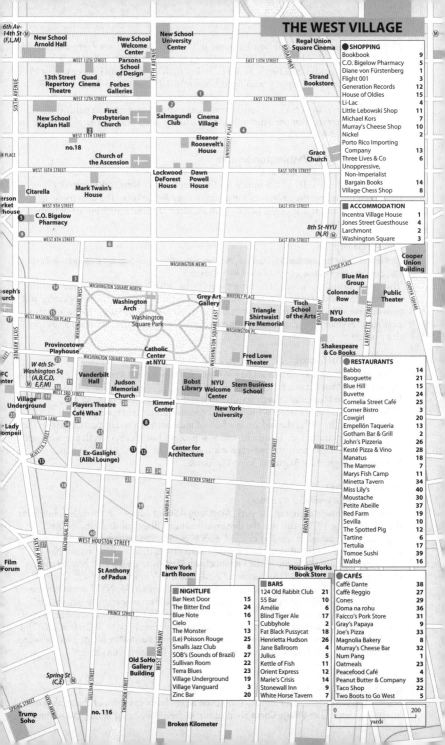

6th Av-14th St (F,L,M)

New School Arnold Hall

New School Welcome Center

New School University Center

Regal Union Square Cinema

WEST 13TH STREET

EAST 13TH STREET

Parsons School of Design

13th Street Repertory Theatre

Quad Cinema

Forbes Galleries

Strand Bookstore

WEST 12TH STREET

EAST 12TH STREET

First Presbyterian Church

New School Kaplan Hall

Salmagundi Club

Cinema Village

WEST 11TH STREET

Eleanor Roosevelt's House

no.18

Church of the Ascension

Grace Church

WEST 10TH STREET

EAST 10TH STREET

Lockwood DeForest House

Dawn Powell House

Citarella

Mark Twain's House

WEST 9TH STREET

EAST 9TH STREET

C.O. Bigelow Pharmacy

WEST 8TH STREET

EAST 8TH STREET

8th St-NYU (N,R)

Cooper Union Building

WASHINGTON MEWS

WASHINGTON SQUARE NORTH

Astor Place

Blue Man Group

Colonnade Row

Public Theater

Grey Art Gallery

WAVERLY PLACE

Washington Arch

Washington Square Park

Triangle Shirtwaist Fire Memorial

Tisch School of the Arts

NYU Bookstore

Cooper Square

WASHINGTON PL.

Provincetown Playhouse

Catholic Center at NYU

Fred Lowe Theater

Shakespeare & Co Books

WASHINGTON SQUARE SOUTH

W 4th St-Washington Sq (A,B,C,D, E,F,M)

Vanderbilt Hall

Judson Memorial Church

Bobst Library

NYU Welcome Center

Stern Business School

Village Underground

WEST 3RD STREET

Players Theatre

Café Wha?

Kimmel Center

New York University

MINETTA LANE

Ex-Gaslight (Alibi Lounge)

Center for Architecture

BLEECKER STREET

BOND STREET

MERCER STREET

BROADWAY

LA GUARDIA PLACE

MACDOUGAL STREET

WEST HOUSTON STREET

Film Forum

St Anthony of Padua

New York Earth Room

Housing Works Book Store

PRINCE STREET

SPRING STREET

Spring St (C,E)

Old SoHo Gallery Building

Trump Soho

no.116

Broken Kilometer

● SHOPPING

Bookbook	9
C.O. Bigelow Pharmacy	5
Diane von Fürstenberg	1
Flight 001	3
Generation Records	12
House of Oldies	15
Li-Lac	4
Little Lebowski Shop	11
Michael Kors	7
Murray's Cheese Shop	10
Nickel	2
Porto Rico Importing Company	13
Three Lives & Co	6
Unoppressive, Non-Imperialist Bargain Books	14
Village Chess Shop	8

■ ACCOMMODATION

Incentra Village House	1
Jones Street Guesthouse	4
Larchmont	2
Washington Square	3

● RESTAURANTS

Babbo	14
Baoguette	21
Blue Hill	15
Buvette	24
Cornelia Street Café	25
Corner Bistro	3
Cowgirl	20
Empellón Taqueria	13
Gotham Bar & Grill	2
John's Pizzeria	26
Kesté Pizza & Vino	28
Manatus	18
The Marrow	7
Marys Fish Camp	11
Minetta Tavern	34
Miss Lily's	40
Moustache	30
Petite Abeille	37
Red Farm	19
Sevilla	10
The Spotted Pig	12
Tartine	6
Tertulia	17
Tomoe Sushi	39
Wallsé	16

■ NIGHTLIFE

Bar Next Door	15
The Bitter End	24
Blue Note	16
Cielo	1
The Monster	13
(Le) Poisson Rouge	25
Smalls Jazz Club	8
SOB's (Sounds of Brazil)	27
Sullivan Room	22
Terra Blues	23
Village Underground	19
Village Vanguard	3
Zinc Bar	20

■ BARS

124 Old Rabbit Club	21
55 Bar	10
Amélie	6
Blind Tiger Ale	17
Cubbyhole	2
Fat Black Pussycat	18
Henrietta Hudson	26
Jane Ballroom	4
Julius	5
Kettle of Fish	11
Marie's Crisis	14
Orient Express	12
Stonewall Inn	9
White Horse Tavern	7

● CAFÉS

Caffè Dante	38
Caffè Reggio	27
Cones	29
Doma na rohu	36
Faicco's Pork Store	31
Gray's Papaya	9
Joe's Pizza	33
Magnolia Bakery	8
Murray's Cheese Bar	32
Num Pang	1
Oatmeals	23
Peacefood Café	4
Peanut Butter & Company	35
Taco Shop	22
Two Boots to Go West	5

0 — 200 yards

North, **no. 11** served as Will Smith's home in the 2007 movie *I am Legend* (much of it shot in the area), while Edith Wharton lived at **no. 7** in 1882. Later, **no. 3** became known as the "studio building", home to artists such as William Glackens, Guy Pène du Bois and Edward Hopper, who lived here from 1913 until his death in 1967. Today, all these buildings, like most of the property around the square, belong to New York University (NYU) – unless you charm your way past the guard, the reverently preserved **Hopper Studio** (no. 3) is usually open only in October on Open House weekend (see ⓦohny.org).

NYU and south of Washington Square

Subway A, C, E, F or M to West 4th St; N, R to 8th St

The south and east sides of the square are lined with bulky **New York University** buildings, including the university's innovative **Grey Art Gallery**. The university dates back to 1831, and is one of the largest (and wealthiest) private institutions of higher education in the US.

Grey Art Gallery

100 Washington Square East • Tues, Thurs & Fri 11am–6pm, Wed 11am–8pm, Sat 11am–5pm • Suggested admission $3 • ☎ 212 998 6780, ⓦ nyu.edu/greyart • Subway A, C, E, F or M to West 4th St, N, R to 8th St

This space hosts top-notch travelling exhibitions, which rotate every three months and feature a wide range of media, including sculpture, painting, photography and provocative video art. Temporary exhibits are also assembled from the university's permanent collection, especially strong in American painting from the 1940s to the present.

Judson Memorial Church

55 Washington Square South • Only open before and after services Wed 6–8pm & Sun 10.30am–1.30pm • ☎ 212 477 0351, ⓦ judson.org • Subway A, B, C, D, E, F, M to West 4th St, N, R to 8th St

Elegant **Judson Memorial Church** stands out amid a messy blend of modern architecture, one of Stanford White's most beautiful Italianate creations. Built as a Baptist church in 1892, the Judson is a hub of local activism today, particularly in the areas of immigration, Fair Trade and anti-war protest, but it's also worth a look inside for its seventeen gorgeous stained-glass windows by John La Farge and a small baptistery designed by Augustus Saint-Gaudens.

MacDougal Street

Subway A, B, C, D, E, F, M to West 4th St; N, R to 8th St

From the southwest corner of the park, **MacDougal Street** cuts south towards Soho; from the 1920s to the 1970s, this was the dynamic heart of Village cultural life (see box, opposite), and though it remains clogged with bars and cafés, its patrons these days are more likely to be NYU students looking for cheap drinks than aspiring artists. No. 133–139 was once the home of the **Provincetown Playhouse** established here by the Provincetown Players in 1918; Eugene O'Neill, Edna St Vincent Millay and Djuna Barnes were all key members. Despite vociferous local opposition, NYU demolished most of the building in 2009, retaining a portion of the facade for a new university theatre.

Continuing south brings you to venerable *Caffè Reggio* at 119 MacDougal St, one of the first and most atmospheric Village coffeehouses, dating back to 1927 (see p.281). The brick row house opposite at no. 130–132 is where **Louisa May Alcott** lived between 1867 and 1870; it's thought she wrote most of *Little Women* (1868) here.

Thompson Street

Subway A, B, C, D, E, F, M to West 4th St; N, R to 8th St

South of Judson Memorial Church, **Thompson Street** harbours some of the area's most intriguing shops. The **Village Chess Shop** (24hr; ⓦchess-shop.com) at no. 230 is more like

FROM BEBOP TO GAGA: MUSIC IN THE WEST VILLAGE

The West Village has been a breeding ground for innovative musicians since the 1930s, when jazz club **Village Vanguard** opened at 178 Seventh Ave – **Sonny Rollins** made a legendary recording here in 1957 and **John Coltrane** followed in 1961 (see p.347). In the early 1940s the **Almanac Singers** (which included Pete Seeger and Woody Guthrie) held "hootenannies" at 130 West 10th St ("Almanac House"), and in 1961, **Bob Dylan** played his first professional gig at legendary **Gerde's Folk City**, at 11 West 4th St (long ago absorbed by NYU buildings), while supporting John Lee Hooker. In 1970 Gerde's moved to 130 West 3rd St before finally closing in 1987 – the space is currently occupied by live venue *Village Underground*.

The infamous **Gaslight Café** opened in 1958 in the basement of 116 MacDougal St, closing in 1971. Next door at no. 114, the *Kettle of Fish* pub opened in 1950 and was where many performers hung out between sets – it later moved to Christopher Street (see p.104), where you can still see the original neon "Bar" sign inside, with which a drunken Jack Kerouac was famously photographed in 1957. At the corner of Bleecker Street, 93 MacDougal St was the site of the raucous **San Remo Café**, which Jack Kerouac turned into *The Masque* in his novel *The Subterraneans* (these days, it's a branch of *Coffee Bean*). The original **Fat Black Pussycat** around the corner on Minetta Street – where Dylan allegedly wrote *Blowin' in the Wind* in 1962 – is *Panchito's* today.

Jimi Hendrix and **Bill Cosby** began their careers at **Café Wha?**, at 115 MacDougal St, one of the few MacDougal venues still open. Hendrix lived for a time at 59 West 12th St, while Dylan had digs at 161 West 4th St and later at 92–94 MacDougal St.

By the 1970s, new musical genres such as disco, punk, salsa and hip-hop were emerging elsewhere in New York, though there are still several **jazz clubs** in the Village (see p.347), and venues such as the **Bitter End** at 147 Bleecker St (see p.344) occasionally nurture future stars: **Lady Gaga** was a struggling regular here in 2007.

8

a museum of chess, with hundreds of chess sets on display. At no. 215, the **Little Lebowksi Shop** (Mon, Wed & Thurs noon–9pm, Fri & Sat noon–11pm, Sun noon–7pm; Ⓦlittlelebowskishop.com) has garnered a cult following with its cool retro T-shirts and tributes to the movie The *Big Lebowksi* (the owner wanders around in his dressing gown).

Center for Architecture

536 LaGuardia Place • Mon–Fri 9am–8pm, Sat 11am–5pm • Free • ☎ 212 683 0023, Ⓦ aiany.org • Subway A, B, C, D, E, F, M to West 4th St

Two blocks south of Washington Square Park, the innovative **Center for Architecture** hosts temporary exhibitions highlighting every aspect of architectural design, from Modernism to specific shows on New York themes (like the 1964 World's Fair). The centre itself, operated by the American Institute of Architects, is a bright and stylish hub for evening programmes, conferences, lectures, film screenings and off-site tours (check the website for details).

North of Washington Square Park

Subway A, B, C, D, E, F, M to West 4th St, N, R to 8th St

Running between University Place and Fifth Avenue just north of the park, the small cobblestone street and old pastel buildings of **Washington Mews** seem out of place amid the grand brownstones that abut the square. This alley was used to stable horses until it was redesigned in 1916 to stable humans, and most recently NYU professors.

Stroll along the streets off Fifth Avenue and you'll find some of the best-preserved, early nineteenth-century townhouses in the Village, with the exception of the rebuilt facade of **18 West 11th St** (see box, p.102). Perhaps the most picturesque is the exotic-looking facade of the **Lockwood de Forest house**, at 7 East 10th St (now the NYU Jewish student centre) – the ornate oriel window of intricate filigree is made from teak carved in India in the 1880s. Writer **Dawn Powell** lived next door at 9 East 10th St from 1931 to 1942, where a plaque declares "all but forgotten after her death, her work enjoyed an extraordinary revival in the 1990s". In stark contrast, **Mark Twain** lived the life of a national celebrity at 14 West 10th St between 1900 and 1902, while poet **Emma Lazarus** lived at no. 18 from 1883 to her untimely death here just four years later. **Eleanor Roosevelt** kept an apartment at 20 East 11th St between 1933 and 1942, but since this period coincided with her husband's presidency, it's probable that she spent more time talking domestic and foreign policies than playing bridge with her West Village neighbours.

Church of the Ascension

36–38 Fifth Ave, at 10th St • Mon–Sat noon–1pm; Sun services only at 9am, 11am, 6pm • Free • ☎ 212 254 8620, ⓦ ascensionnyc.org • Subway N, Q, R, L, #4, #5, #6 to Union Square/14th St

If you head north up Fifth Avenue from Washington Square Park, you'll pass a couple of imposing churches. On the corner of West 10th Street stands the Episcopal **Church of the Ascension**, built in 1841 by Richard Upjohn (the Trinity Church architect), where a vast but gracefully toned La Farge altar painting and some fine stained glass dominate an interior designed by Stanford White in the 1880s.

First Presbyterian Church

12 West 12th St • Mon–Fri noon–12.30pm • Free • ☎ 212 675 6150, ⓦ fpcnyc.org • Subway N, Q, R, L, #4, #5, #6 to Union Square/14th St

Continuing the Gothic theme, Joseph Wells's bulky, chocolate-brown **First Presbyterian Church**, just across 11th Street from the Church of the Ascension, was completed in 1845 with a crenellated tower modelled on the one at Magdalen College in Oxford, England. Inside, you'll find carved black-walnut pews, a soaring altarpiece and a fabulous Tiffany rose window.

Salmagundi Club

47 Fifth Ave, between E 11th and E 12th sts • Mon–Fri 1–6pm, Sat & Sun 1–5pm, Thurs till 8pm • Free • ☎ 212 255 7740, ⓦ salmagundi. org • Subway N, Q, R, L, #4, #5, #6 to Union Square/14th St

Housed in a graceful 1852 Italianate brownstone opposite First Presbyterian, the members-only **Salmagundi Club** was founded in 1871 as one of the nation's foremost art associations – members have included William Merritt Chase, Childe Hassam, John LaFarge, Augustus Saint-Gaudens, Louis Comfort Tiffany and Stanford White. Take a peek inside the public galleries to view rotating exhibitions from contemporary members and items from the permanent collection.

Forbes Galleries

62 Fifth Ave, at West 12th St • Tues, Wed, Fri & Sat 10am–4pm • Free • ☎ 212 206 5548, ⓦ forbesgalleries.com • Subway N, Q, R, L, #4, #5, #6 to Union Square/14th St

One of the city's quirkiest small museums is the **Forbes Galleries**, which contains a rather whimsical collection of treasures assembled by the Forbes family, owners of the publishing empire. The 10,000-strong host of tin soldiers, over five hundred model boats and early Monopoly boards will appeal primarily to aficionados and kids, though the galleries also hold temporary exhibitions of a diverse range of art work, from cartoons to rare Art Deco gems.

Parsons The New School for Design

Sheila C. Johnson Design Center 68 Fifth Ave, between W 12th and W 13th sts • Daily noon–6pm, Thurs till 8pm • Free • ☎ 212 229 8919, ⓦ newschool.edu/parsons • Subway N, Q, R, L, #4, #5, #6 to Union Square/14th St

One of the most prestigious art and design colleges in the world, **Parsons The New School for Design** was founded by American Impressionist William Merritt Chase in 1896, and now forms part of the New School, a private university. Like NYU, its campus is spread around the West Village, but you can visit the two public art galleries in the **Sheila C. Johnson Design Center** on Fifth Avenue – expect an eclectic programme of high-quality contemporary exhibitions.

CLOCKWISE FROM TOP LEFT GREENWICH VILLAGE; MACDOUGAL STREET (P.98); BLEECKER STREET (P.102); WASHINGTON ARCH (P.95) >

THE WEATHERMEN

In 1969, disillusioned by the failure of peaceful protest to stop the Vietnam War, a militant faction of pressure group Students for a Democratic Society set up a bomb factory in the basement of the Henry Brevoort-designed house at 18 West 11th St. Known as the **Weathermen** (after the Bob Dylan lyrics, "you don't need a weatherman to know which way the wind blows"), the group aimed to bomb a military ball to be held at Fort Dix, New Jersey, but the plan backfired disastrously. On March 6, 1970, the house's arsenal exploded, killing three of the group (two escaped). The organization went into hiding soon after, becoming the **Weather Underground** and evading capture by the FBI, despite being on their Most Wanted List. While the group was responsible for several bombings in the 1970s, the loss of life was studiously avoided – though buildings in New York and Washington, DC, were damaged, the group's most notorious exploit was busting counterculture guru Timothy Leary out of prison in 1970. By 1980, most of the group had surrendered to the authorities, though few were ever charged; the FBI had broken so many laws trying to catch them, most evidence was inadmissible.

Incidentally, the Weathermen's neighbour at the time of the 11th Street bomb was actor Dustin Hoffman, whose home at no. 16 suffered extensive damage from the blast.

Sixth Avenue and around

Subway A, B, C, D, E, F, M to West 4th St, #1 to Christopher St

Although **Sixth Avenue** is for the most part lined with mediocre stores, restaurants and modern buildings, there are some exceptions, like the unmistakeable clock tower of the nineteenth-century **Jefferson Market Courthouse**.

Across the street from the courthouse and opening onto West 10th Street, **Patchin Place** is a tiny mews constructed in 1848 (you can only peer through the gate). The rowhouses were home to the reclusive author Djuna Barnes for more than forty years; supposedly, Barnes's long-time neighbour e.e. cummings used to call her "just to see if she was still alive". Patchin Place has also been home to Marlon Brando, Ezra Pound and Eugene O'Neill. Heading south, look out for **C.O. Bigelow Pharmacy**, at 414 Sixth Ave, just north of West 8th Street, founded in 1838 and probably the city's oldest drugstore, and a few blocks further on (at Sixth Avenue and 3rd Street), the **West 4th Street Courts**. Known as "The Cage" for the physical style of basketball typically on display here, the courts attract amateur players from all over the city and regularly host high-quality street tournaments.

Jefferson Market Courthouse

425 Sixth Ave, at West 10th St • Mon & Wed 9am–8pm, Tues & Thurs 9am–7pm, Fri & Sat 10am–5pm • Free • Subway N, Q, R, L, #4, #5, #6 to Union Square/14th St

Completed in 1877 by Central Park co-designer Calvert Vaux and English-born Frederick Clarke Withers on the site of a former market, this imposing Victorian Gothic edifice served as a district courthouse until 1945; the murderer of architect Stanford White (see p.119) was tried here in 1906, as was Mae West, arrested for appearing in an "immoral" play (*Sex*) in 1927. It's been a public library since 1967, and is worth a quick peek inside; stroll up to the second floor via the spiral stone staircase to see the original ceiling and stained-glass windows, still reminiscent of a Gothic church despite the rows of books.

Bleecker Street

Subway A, B, C, D, E, F, M to West 4th St, #1 to Christopher St

Off Sixth Avenue's west side are some of the Village's prettiest residential streets, where you can easily spend a couple of hours strolling and soaking up the neighbourhood's charms. To start exploring, cross Father Demo Square on Sixth Avenue and walk up **Bleecker Street**, past the Italian Renaissance-style **Our Lady of Pompeii Church** (Mon, Tues, Thurs & Fri 7am–5.30pm, Wed & Sun 7am–7pm, Sat 7am–6pm; free), built in 1929 – check out the florid interior, replete with marble columns, stained glass and murals that evoke the spirit, if not quite the artistry, of classical Italy. Until the 1970s there was an Italian open-air marketplace on this stretch, and it's still lined by a few Italian stores and cafés, notably **Faicco's** (see p.282) and **Rocco's** (best known for its nut-sprinkled cannoli), as well as celebrated deli **Murray's Cheese Shop** (see p.385). If folk music is your thing, **Bob Dylan** lived for a time at 161 West 4th St, and the cover of his 1963 *Freewheelin'* album was shot a few paces away on Jones Street, just off Bleecker, a scene faithfully re-created in the Cameron Crowe movie *Vanilla Sky*.

St Luke's Place

Subway A, B, C, D, E, F, M to West 4th St, #1 to Houston St

If you turn down Leroy Street at Bleecker Street, and continue west across Seventh Avenue, you'll come to St Luke's Place; no. 10 was used as the exterior of the **Cosby house**, while no. 6 (recognizable by the two gas lamps at the bottom of the steps) is the ex-residence of **Jimmy Walker**, mayor of New York in the 1920s. Walker was for a time the most popular of mayors, a big-spending wisecracker who gave up working as a songwriter for politics and lived an extravagant lifestyle that rarely kept him out of the gossip columns – he resigned in 1932, accused of corruption.

Bedford Street

Subway A, B, C, D, E, F, M to West 4th St, #1 to Christopher St

Just north of St Luke's Place, **Bedford Street** runs west off Seventh Avenue to become one of the quietest and most desirable Village addresses. Edna St Vincent Millay, the young poet and playwright, lived at no. 75 1/2 in the 1920s; at only 9ft wide, it is one of the narrowest houses in the city – but was still sold for $3.25 million in 2013. The brick and clapboard structure next door at no. 77 is the **Isaacs-Hendricks House**, built in 1799 and the oldest house in the Village.

Grove Street

Subway A, B, C, D, E, F, M to West 4th St, #1 to Christopher St

The building at 90 Bedford St, right on the corner of **Grove Street** (above the *Little Owl*), served as the exterior for Monica's apartment in *Friends*, though the TV series was shot entirely in L.A. studios. Opposite is **17 Grove St**, built in 1822 and one of the most complete wood-frame houses in the city. Turn left here down Grove Street and you'll find **Grove Court** just off the road, one of the neighbourhood's most attractive and exclusive little mews (you have to peer through the gate).

Heading back to Seventh Avenue on Grove Street, *Marie's Crisis Café* at no. 59 was the site of the rented rooms where English revolutionary writer and philosopher **Thomas Paine** died in 1809. Paine, who was reviled in England for his support of both the American and French revolutions, was the author of the eighteenth century's three bestselling pamphlets, his *Common Sense* of 1776 generally credited for turning public opinion in favour of US independence. Cantankerous and conceited to the end, Paine made plenty of enemies, and after the publication of the *Age of Reason*, many Americans assumed he was an atheist (he was actually a deist). By the time he died here, he was poverty stricken and abandoned by his former friends. The current building dates from 1839, the café named in part after Paine's masterful essay *The American Crisis*.

KEITH HARING'S CARMINE STREET MURAL

New York-based Pop artist Keith Haring painted several wall murals in the city, with one of the most magnificent examples overlooking the public swimming pool at the back of the Tony Dapolito Recreation Center (at Clarkson and Seventh Ave). You can get a decent view of the iconic work, painted in 1987, from the street. Check out, too, the *Crack is Wack* mural (see p.201).

STONEWALL RIOTS

On June 27, 1969, police raided the **Stonewall gay bar** (see p.364) and started arresting its occupants – for the local gay community, simply the latest occurrence in a long history of harassment. Spontaneously, word got around to other bars in the area, and before long the Stonewall was surrounded by hundreds of angry protestors, resulting in a siege that lasted the better part of the night and ended with several arrests and a number of injured policemen. Though hardly a victory for their rights, it was the first time that gay men had stood up en masse to police persecution and, as such, formally inaugurated the gay-rights movement. The event is honoured by the Annual Lesbian, Gay, Bisexual and Transgender March (usually just referred to as the **Gay Pride March**). Typically the last Sunday in June, this parade is one of the city's most exciting and colourful (see p.400).

Christopher Street
Subway A, B, C, D, E, F, M to West 4th St, #1 to Christopher St

Christopher Street runs west from Jefferson Market Courthouse past **Christopher Park**, the traditional centre of the city's gay community. Confusingly, the park contains a pompous-looking statue of Civil War cavalry commander General Sheridan, though Sheridan Square is actually the next space down, where West 4th Street meets Washington Place. Historically, the area is better known as the scene of one of the worst and bloodiest of New York's **Draft Riots** (see p.413), when a marauding mob assembled here in 1863 and attacked members of the black community, several of whom were lynched. Violence also erupted in 1969, when the **gay community** wasn't as readily accepted as it is now (see box, above). The riots are commemorated by George Segal's **Gay Liberation Monument** in the park, four life-size white-painted figures (two males, two females), unveiled in 1992. Nowadays, however, the gay community is fairly synonymous with Village life.

The Far West Village
Subway L to Eighth Ave, #1 to Christopher St, #1, #2, #3 to 14th St

The area northwest of Sixth Avenue, dubbed the **Far West Village** by those ever-creative estate agents, contains some of the most appealing and expensive residential streets in the city. Most of the gorgeous townhouses here are owned, not rented, and a bevy of unique stores, coffee bars and restaurants cater to its upwardly mobile and moneyed residential community – including plenty of Hollywood stars. Much to the chagrin of locals, you'll probably see small groups of excited fans taking photos at **66 Perry St**, between Bleecker and West 4th Street, used as the exterior of Carrie's apartment in *Sex and the City* ("Carrie's Stoop"), while almost constant lines form outside lauded **Magnolia Bakery** at Bleecker and West 11th Street (see p.282). The historic **White Horse Tavern** (see p.334), over at West 11th Street and Hudson, was frequented by Norman Mailer and Hunter S. Thompson among others, and is where legend claims Dylan Thomas had his last drink – you'll see a portrait of the poet and various memorabilia in the wood-panelled room named after him. The area has its rock connections, too; between 1971 and 1973, John Lennon and Yoko Ono lived in relative obscurity at **105 Bank St**, a block from the *White Horse* at Greenwich Street, before moving uptown (see p.188). And in 1979, a 21-year-old Sid Vicious took a lethal dose of heroin at **63 Bank St**, between Bleecker and West 4th streets.

These days, a stroll along leafy **Hudson River Park** is more likely to reveal joggers and pushchairs than punks, though **Pier 45** (aka the Christopher Street Pier) remains a lively hangout for gay youth, especially at night. For a closer look at the water, head over to the **Downtown Boathouse** at Pier 40, at the end of Houston Street (see p.394), which offers free **kayaking** at the weekends; you can only paddle around the piers in the immediate vicinity, but the sensational views, fresh air and chance to work off all those cupcakes make this a fabulous deal.

THE HIGH LINE

Chelsea

A grid full of renovated tenements, row houses and warehouses, Chelsea lies west of Broadway between 14th and 30th streets. For years, its stock of dreary, overlooked buildings, coupled with bare streets, gave off an atmosphere of neglect. Over the past few decades, however, quite the opposite has been the case: the arrival of a large gay community in the late 1980s and early 1990s, the decamping of the art scene from Soho to Chelsea's western reaches and, finally, the transformation of the High Line park – which starts in the now-fashionable Meatpacking District – have ushered in a new era of desirability and development. The result: affluent townhouses, daring condo conversions, cutting-edge galleries, public parks and shops of every variety pepper the scene.

9

Brief history

The neighbourhood, developed on former farmland, began to take shape in 1830 thanks to Clement Clarke Moore, famous as the author of the surprise poetic hit *A Visit from St Nick* (popularly known as *'Twas the Night Before Christmas*), whose estate comprised most of what is now Chelsea. That year, Moore, anticipating Manhattan's movement uptown, laid out his land for sale in broad lots. However, stuck as it was between the ritziness of Fifth Avenue, the hipness of Greenwich Village and the poverty of Hell's Kitchen, the area never quite made it onto the shortlist of desirable places to live. Manhattan's chic residential focus leapfrogged over Chelsea to the East 40s and 50s, and the arrival of the slaughterhouses, an elevated railroad and working-class poor sealed Chelsea's reputation as a rough-and-tumble no-go area for decades.

The last few decades have seen a totally new Chelsea emerge. New York's drifting art scene has been extremely significant in the neighbourhood's transformation. In the early 1990s, a number of respected **galleries** began making use of the large spaces available in the low-rise warehouses in far west Chelsea, securing the area's cultural bent. This influx has been counterbalanced by the steadily expanding presence of retail superstores, especially along **Sixth Avenue**; the building of the **Chelsea Piers** mega-sized sports complex; and high-rise apartments and hotels springing up north of 23rd Street. Now crowded with shoppers, restaurant-goers and the like, the lively neighbourhood shows no signs of quietening down.

Meatpacking District

Creating a buffer between the West Village and Chelsea proper, the **Meatpacking District** between Gansevoort Street and West 15th Street, west of Ninth Avenue, has seen the majority of its working slaughterhouses converted to French bistros, late-night (and hard-to-breach) clubs, wine bars and fancy galleries. Though a few wholesale meat companies remain, the area is now very much designer territory, with Diane Von Furstenberg, Tory Burch and Helmut Lang among the fashion boutiques lining the cobblestone streets. The opening of the High Line has added much to the area's appeal, providing a tranquil greenway right into the heart of Chelsea.

The High Line

Gansevoort St to 34th St, between Tenth and Eleventh aves; entrances at Gansevoort, 14th, 16th, 18th, 20th, 23rd, 26th, 28th and 30th sts • Daily spring & summer 7am–11pm, autumn 7am–10pm, winter 7am–7pm; Tues at dusk April–early Sept stargazing nights, weather permitting • Free, though some organized tours $15 • ☎ 212 500 6035, ⊕ thehighline.org • Subway A, C, E, to 14th St, L to Eighth Ave or C, E to 23rd St

An ambitious renewal project that spans – and unites – the Meatpacking District, West Chelsea and a no-man's-land near the West Side rail yards, the **High Line** asserts itself as a new form of urban park. It's a stunning transformation of a disused railway that was built between 1929 and 1934, once moving goods and produce around lower Manhattan, then going on to spend a number of years rusted, overgrown and threatened with demolition. Concerned activists fought to stave off what seemed inevitable, but it wasn't until two locals formed the **Friends of the High Line** in 1999 that the tide improbably began to turn. A deal with the city ensued, construction began in 2006, and the first phase opened in summer of 2009 to big crowds and rave reviews; a second section debuted in June 2011; a third is on the way for 2014.

Much more than an elevated promenade-cum-public-park some thirty feet in the air, the High Line forges a balance between the West Side's industrial tradition and its design-focused present. It pays proper homage to its history – steel rails peek out from the ground; smooth pavement and wood echo the lines of train tracks and sometimes slope right up onto the benches; like the old line did, it cleverly cuts through the middle of buildings and blocks – for example, the *Standard Hotel* (see p.267), and the structure that holds the Chelsea Market (see p.108) – and many wild growth patches

CHELSEA

BARS

Barracuda	9
Boxer's NYC	10
The Eagle NYC	2
El Quinto Pino	5
Frying Pan	4
G Lounge	13
GYM	14
Half King	7
Peter McManus Café	11
Smithfield	1
Tia Pol	8
XES	6

NIGHTLIFE

Big Apple Ranch	12
Cielo	16
High Line Ballroom	15
Samba New York	3

CAFÉS

Amy's Bread	19
Billy's Bakery	11
Doughnut Plant	10
Eleni's Cookie's	20
Empire Cake	17
Kofoo	1
Lobster Place	16
Rocket Pig	6
Sullivan Street Bakery	4

RESTAURANTS

Bottino	3
Cafeteria	15
Co.	18
Colicchio & Sons	6
Cookshop	12
East of Eighth	8
El Quijote	9
La Lunchonette	14
La Nacional	23
La Taza de Oro	21
The Old Homestead	22
Paradou	24
Red Cat	7
Rocking Horse	13
Txikito	5

SHOPPING

Alexander McQueen	13
Center for Book Arts	1
Chelsea Market	11
Comme des Garçons	5
Housing Works Thrift Shop	8
Jazz Record Center	9
Jeffrey	12
Loehmann's	10
Nasty Pig	7
Nickel	14
Rainbows and Triangles	4
Revolution Books	2
Universal Gear	6
Utrecht Art Supplies	3

ACCOMMODATION

Chelsea International Hostel	5
Chelsea Lodge	6
Chelsea Pines Inn	7
Colonial House Inn	4
Comfort Inn Chelsea	14
Gansevoort	9
Hotel Americano	6
Inn on 23rd St	1
The Standard	8

FLATIRON DISTRICT

West 25th Street Market
Eataly
Edith Wharton Birthplace
Flatiron Building
Forbes Galleries
Quad Cinema
First Presbyterian Church
no.18

FLOWER MARKET
Antiques Garage Flea Market
Rubin Museum of Art

FIT Museum
Chelsea Hotel

CHELSEA GALLERY DISTRICT
Chelsea Park
London Terrace Apartments
General Theological Seminary
Oldest House in Chelsea
Cushman Row
Joyce Theater

CHELSEA
Chelsea Market
Apple Store

MEATPACKING DISTRICT
Soho House
The Standard Hotel
High Line
Future site of Whitney Museum
White Columns Gallery

High Line
HL 23
180 Tenth Avenue
100 Eleventh Avenue
IAC Building
200 Eleventh Avenue

Pier 66
Pier 62
Pier 61
Pier 60
Pier 59
Chelsea Piers
Hudson River Bike Path

Hudson River

0   200
yards

9

HIDDEN GEMS: CHELSEA HIGH LINE

Viewing spur See below
Tuesday stargazing nights See p.106
Water feature, near 15th St See below

Cutout See below
Lunch from Lobster Place or Rocket Pig See p.283

---

have been left as is. At various intervals on the line are art installations and some select food vendors (most of the latter congregate at West 15th Street).

The park

The initial completed stretch runs from Gansevoort to 20th Street. It's at its most untamed at the southernmost end, becoming a bit more elegant and organized above 14th Street. A subtle water feature between 14th and 15th streets is followed a block north by a spur that overlooks a horticultural preserve and an amphitheatre that offers a cinematic view up Tenth Avenue. The views shift just as the path does: move your gaze from the Hudson to the eclectic architecture of a neighbourhood in transition, some of its old factories and warehouses giving way to quite daring modernist residences (see p.110).

The second phase, between 20th and 30th streets, moves off Tenth Avenue to cut a swathe through the middle of the block, about a hundred feet west of the road. It's more intimate in feel; a walk here at times seems like you're tracing a narrow path along Chelsea's rooftop gardens. At 22nd Street, a grassy lawn beneath a faded brick facade is one of the few places you can divert from the path. Further on, the walkway rises and falls, at one point elevating about eight feet up on a metal catwalk to put you right up in the trees. A neat feature at 26th Street, the "viewing spur", places you as the subject in an advertising sign, for street onlookers – and also frames the neighbourhood for your benefit. As you approach 30th Street you'll pass the "cutout", which lets you see the inner workings of the old line below, before winding up face to face with the railyards – a part of the city few previously ventured to (or wished to venture to, for that matter).

Thus begins the last segment, the so-called High Line at the West Rail Yards, a stretch that curves around the rail terminus and is set to open in 2014. The yards themselves are in line to be massively redeveloped and become almost a "city within a city", with an extension of the #7 train connecting them to the rest of Manhattan.

In addition, the **Whitney Museum of American Art** has broken ground on a new indoor-outdoor exhibition space designed by Renzo Piano (of Morgan Library and the new New York Times Building fame), back down at the Gansevoort Street entrance; it's slated to open in 2015 and replace Whitney's Upper East Side location (see p.173).

West Chelsea

The far west of Chelsea, from **Ninth Avenue** over to the waterfront, holds many of the more scenic blocks, best galleries and most intriguing merchants the district has to offer. It's a part of the city in rapid development, thanks in large part to the popularity and revitalizing effect of the High Line: cutting-edge residential architecture, a varied restaurant-and-bar scene, and even a sprinkling of hotels have sprung up to complement the sturdy old warehouses.

Chelsea Market

75 Ninth Ave, between 15th and 16th sts • Mon–Sat 7am–9pm, Sun 8am–8pm • ⓦ chelseamarket.com • Subway A, C, E, to 14th St or L to Eighth Ave

A high-class food temple, the redbrick **Chelsea Market** is housed in the old National Biscuit Company (aka "Nabisco") factory, where legend has it the Oreo cookie was created. Many of the factory's features remain, including pieces of rail track used to transport provisions. The hand-picked retailers inside – some thirty or so of them – sell fresh fruit, fish, bread, wine, brownies and flowers (see p.384); the building also serves as home to the Food Network, though unfortunately there's no access to the taping of shows.

Chelsea Historic District

West 20th, 21st and 22nd sts between Ninth and Tenth aves • Subway C, E to 23rd St

A few blocks north of Chelsea Market, the **Chelsea Historic District** boasts a picturesque variety of predominantly Italianate and Greek Revival row houses. Dating from the 1830s to the 1890s, they demonstrate the faith some early developers had in Chelsea as an up-and-coming New York neighbourhood. The **oldest house** in the area, at 404 West 20th St (just off Ninth Ave), stands out with its 1829 wood siding, predating as it does the all-brick constructions of James Wells, Chelsea's first real-estate developer. The ornate iron fencing heading west along this block, known as **Cushman Row**, is original and quite impressive. Closer to Tenth Avenue, Jack Kerouac lived at 454 20th St in 1951 with his wife Joan Haverty, while he wrote *On the Road*.

General Theological Seminary

175 Ninth Ave, on the block bounded by 20th and 21st sts, entrance on 21st Street, about midway between Ninth and Tenth • Mon–Fri 10am–3pm • Free • ☎ 212 243 5150, ⓦ gts.edu • Subway C, E to 23rd St

The 1817 **General Theological Seminary** is one of Chelsea's secrets. Clement Clarke Moore, author of *'Twas the Night Before Christmas*, donated this island of land to the institute, and today the harmonious assembly of ivy-clad Gothic structures surrounding a green feels like part of a college campus. Though some of the buildings still house a working Episcopal seminary – the oldest in the United States – others have been sold off to help solidify the seminary's flagging finances: the grey stone pile at 455 W 20th St has been turned into condos, and 180 Tenth Ave is the new *High Line Hotel*. Nevertheless you can get in to explore the site as long as you sign in and keep quiet.

London Terrace

The block bounded by 23rd and 24th sts, and Ninth and Tenth aves • Subway C, E to 23rd St

Just north of the historic district is one of New York's premier residences for those who believe in understated opulence. **London Terrace**, two rows of apartment buildings a full city block long, surrounds a private interior garden (the corner Towers and interior Gardens units are managed separately). The buildings had the misfortune of being completed in 1930 at the height of the Great Depression, and despite a swimming pool and other posh amenities, many of the 1665 apartments stood empty for several years. The first management, wanting to evoke thoughts of Britain, made the doormen wear London-style police uniforms, thereby giving the building its name. The apartments were later nicknamed "The Fashion Projects" because of their designer, photographer and model residents (past and present names include Isaac Mizrahi, Debbie Harry, Tim Gunn and Annie Leibovitz).

Chelsea's gallery district

Tenth Avenue serves as a dividing line between Chelsea's more historic and quainter side to the east and its industrial past to the west. For years there was not much to see or do along this stretch – that is, until the galleries started swarming in. Along 22nd Street between Tenth and Eleventh avenues, as well as farther north up to West 29th, lie the few hundred **galleries and warehouse spaces** that house one of New York's most vibrant art scenes (see p.368). Even the ovular entryway to **Comme des Garçons** – the store is just west of Tenth Avenue at 520 West 22nd St – masquerades as art in this part of town. The buildings used by Chelsea's galleries are especially imposing above West 23rd Street, and in some cases even stretch for a whole block.

9

Chelsea Piers

West 18th to West 23rd sts, on the West Side Highway • ☎ 212 336 6666, ⓦ chelseapiers.com • Subway C, E to 23rd St

Chelsea Piers, a glitzy, family-friendly, and somewhat incongruous entertainment development, stretches along the West Side Highway from piers 59 to 62. Its first incarnation opened in 1910, as the place where passengers would disembark from the great transatlantic liners (it was en route to the Chelsea Piers that the *Titanic* sank in 1912). By the 1960s, however, the piers had fallen into decay through disuse, and as late as the mid-1980s an official report condemned them as "shabby, pathetic reminders of a glorious past". Since then, money and effort have been poured into the revival of the area. Reopened in 1995, the new Chelsea Piers, whose commercial aura begs comparison with South Street Seaport (see p.54), is primarily a huge sports complex, with ice rinks and open-air roller rinks, as well as a skate park, bowling alley and a landscaped golf driving range (see p.395).

Around the piers

Just north of Chelsea Piers are the latest instalments in the continuation of **Hudson River Park** (see p.104), which have added large green spaces, a carousel, art displays and a skate park to piers 62, 63 and 64.

Across from the piers, at the end of 19th Street, warehouses and car parks have given way to the billowing, fluid walls of Frank Gehry's **IAC Building**, one of New York's most fanciful examples of contemporary architecture. It's right next to Jean Nouvel's similarly striking **100 Eleventh Avenue**, a glittering patchwork of glass that holds luxury condos. More new buildings with a strong design focus have followed: **515 West 23rd Street**, or **HL23**, an extremely close neighbour of the High Line (it hangs right over it, close enough to touch), is a slick steel-and-glass work by cutting-edge architect Neil Denari; and **200 Eleventh Avenue**, at the corner of 24th Street, is designed in keeping with the area's industrial past. Each condo in this stainless steel mini-skyscraper has its own en-suite parking garage (reached by internal car elevator).

Eighth Avenue

Double back east along 23rd Street to Chelsea's main drag, **Eighth Avenue**, which is full of vibrant retail energy, if nothing of particular note. Along here, dozens of trendy bars, restaurants, health-food stores, gyms, bookstores and clothes shops cater to Chelsea's large, out and proud gay population.

Hotel Chelsea

222 East 23rd St, between Seventh and Eighth aves • ☎ 646 918 8770, ⓦ hotelchelsea.com • Subway C, E to 23rd St

One of the neighbourhood's major claims to fame is the **Hotel Chelsea**. Originally built as a luxury co-operative apartment building in 1884 and partially converted to a hotel in 1903, the building has served as the undisputed residence of the city's harder-up literati and its musical vagabonds. Mark Twain, Tennessee Williams, Dylan Thomas and Thomas Wolfe all spent time here, and in 1951 Jack Kerouac, armed with a specially adapted typewriter (and a lot of Benzedrine) supposedly typed the first draft of *On the Road* nonstop onto a 120ft roll of paper… though it more likely happened at his house nearby (see p.109). William Burroughs (in a presumably more relaxed state) completed *Naked Lunch* at the Chelsea, and Arthur C. Clarke wrote *2001: A Space Odyssey* while in residence.

In the 1960s, the Chelsea entered a wilder phase. Andy Warhol and his doomed protégées Edie Sedgwick and Candy Darling holed up here and made the film *Chelsea Girls*. In probably the hotel's most infamous moment, Sid Vicious stabbed Nancy Spungen to death in 1978 in their suite, a few months before he fatally overdosed on heroin. The photographer Robert Mapplethorpe and Patti Smith also lived here in the late 1960s and early 1970s, and the hotel inspired Joni Mitchell's song *Chelsea Morning* and Leonard Cohen's *Chelsea Hotel No.2*.

With a pedigree like this it's easy to forget the hotel itself, which has a down-at-heel Edwardian grandeur all its own – not that you'll likely be able to see any of it past the exterior. After declaring bankruptcy in late 2010, the hotel was sold in the summer of 2011 to a developer, who closed it up and began renovations, which keep going and going. Speculation as to whether it would continue on as a hotel or be converted to condos, and what would become of long-term residents, remained just that. A call to the hotel received the following answer about when it will reopen: "Not soon".

East Chelsea

Sandwiched between infinitely more interesting blocks, the eastern edge of Chelsea has become a buzzing strip of commerce, concentrated mostly along **Sixth Avenue** between West 17th and 23rd streets. A crush of discount emporiums like Best Buy and TJ Maxx, along with mediocre chain restaurants, have done their best to drive out the independent mom-and-pop businesses, and, on weekends especially, Sixth Avenue teems with bargain hunters lugging oversized bags from places like Bed, Bath and Beyond, the Container Store and the Sports Authority. Fortunately a few indoor flea markets remain.

Rubin Museum of Art

150 West 17th St, between Sixth and Seventh aves • Mon & Thurs 11am–5pm, Wed 11am–7pm, Fri 11am–10pm, Sat & Sun 11am–6pm • $10, free on Fri 6–10pm • ⓦ rmanyc.org • Subway F, M, #1, #2, #3 to 14th St or #1 to 18th St

For a brief escape from Chelsea's commercialism, visit the **Rubin Museum of Art**. The serene museum is one of the city's lesser-visited gems, a collection of two thousand paintings, sculptures and textiles from the Himalayas and surrounding regions. The permanent exhibits on the second and third floors are organized and labelled with great care and thought, essential for a subject that will be familiar to few. While a few pieces manage to stand out – don't miss the small room on the third floor devoted to the fascinating, colourful Lukhang murals, taken from the Dalai Lama's temple – the thrust is less about individual artists and objects and more about understanding how and why art is created. The stylish ground-floor *Serai Café* serves Himalayan food and, on Friday nights, becomes the *K2 Lounge*, which hosts regular performances; there's a film series as well.

Flower Market

The area around West 28th Street is Manhattan's **Flower Market** – not really a market as such, more the warehouses and storefronts where potted plants and cut flowers are stored before brightening offices and atriums across the city. The district, which has atrophied against a tide of gentrifications, still manages to surprise, its greenery bursting out of the drab blocks in a welcome touch of life.

West 28th Street's historical background couldn't be more at odds with its present incarnation: from the mid-1880s until the 1950s, the short block between Sixth Avenue and Broadway was the original **Tin Pan Alley**, where music publishers would peddle songs by the likes of Irving Berlin and George Gershwin to artists and producers from vaudeville and Broadway. The name came from the piano-playing racket coming out of the publishing houses here at any time of the day, a sound that one journalist compared to banging on tin pans.

Museum at the Fashion Institute of Technology (FIT)

Seventh Ave at 27th St • Tues–Fri noon–8pm, Sat 10am–5pm • Free • ⓦ fitnyc.edu • Subway #1 to 28th St

A block west of the Flower Market, the **Museum at the Fashion Institute of Technology (FIT)** covers two levels; you'll find rotating exhibits on contemporary design and fashion history, often pulled from their extensive permanent collection. The buildings that make up the campus have some architectural interest too: take a quick walk along 27th Street to admire – or sniff at – the cold Modernist facades.

UNION SQUARE

Union Square, Gramercy Park and the Flatiron District

This knot of close-knit neighbourhoods east of Fifth Avenue has some of the city's best restaurants and shops and several of New York's most historically significant buildings and landmarks. Chief among the latter is Union Square, between 14th and 17th streets, a bustling space that breaks up Broadway's pell-mell dash north. To the northeast is the posh neighbourhood of Gramercy, with its private clubs and a members-only park. Straddling Broadway northwest of Union Square and running up to 23rd Street, the Flatiron District was once Manhattan's shopping hub and still has a certain elegance and energy; from there, the up-and-coming neighbourhood of "NoMad" (north of Madison Square Park) takes over, with its hip hotels and exclusive eateries.

Union Square and around

Located at the confluence of Broadway, Fourth and Park avenues between 14th and 17th streets, **Union Square** is an inviting public space. Among the statues here are George Washington as equestrian; Gandhi; a Lafayette by Bartholdi (more famous for the Statue of Liberty); and, at the centre of the green, a massive flagstaff base whose bas-reliefs symbolize the forces of Good and Evil in the American Revolution. Opened as a park in 1839, the square is surrounded by a crush of commerce and serves as a welcome respite from crazed taxi-drivers and rushed pedestrians on 14th Street. Mostly, however, Union Square is beloved for its **farmers' market** (one in a citywide network known as Greenmarket, to which each is also commonly referred as) – the largest in Manhattan – that sells all sorts of seasonal produce, wine, meats and nonedible products, like hand-spun wools and flowers (see p.386).

The square is flanked by a range of excellent restaurants, as well as by buildings in a mismatched hotchpotch of architectural styles, not least of which is the old **American Savings Bank** at 20 Union Square East – now the **Daryl Roth Theatre** – of which only the grandiose columned exterior survives, completed in 1923 and designed by Henry Bacon. The pedimented **Union Square Theater** just north of here at 17th Street became the second Tammany Hall in 1929, once headquarters of the Democratic Party and a fine example of Colonial-Revival architecture.

Decker Building

33 Union Square West • Subway L, N, Q, R, #4, #5, #6 to 14th St-Union Square

The narrow **Decker Building**, on the west side of the park, was where Andy Warhol moved his **Factory** in 1968, occupying the sixth floor until 1973; the artist was shot by Valerie Solanas here shortly after the move. The building itself, completed in 1893, is a lavish, Moorish-inspired skyscraper.

Irving Place

East of Union Square, the six graceful blocks of **Irving Place** head north towards Gramercy Park. Irving Place was named for Washington Irving, the early nineteenth-century writer best known for his creepy tale of the Headless Horseman, *The Legend of Sleepy Hollow*, and also for supposedly being the first American to earn a living from his writing. The claims that he lived for a short time at no. 49 (trumpeted in a plaque outside the quaint house) are spurious; he did, at the least, frequently visit his nephew's house on East 21st Street, and a bust of Irving stands in front of the early nineteenth-century Washington Irving High School at East 17th Street.

Another celebrated author, Pulitzer Prize-winning short-story writer O. Henry, did live at no. 55 between 1902 and 1910. Again in the mythmaking vein, O. Henry reputedly dreamed up and wrote *The Gift of the Magi* at **Pete's Tavern** (see p.335), at 18th Street and Irving Place, one of New York's oldest bars. The legend serves the place and its atmosphere well.

SQUARE ROOTS ACTIVISM

Like the generally more rambunctious Washington Square in the West Village, Union Square Park is also often the site of **civil demonstrations**. After 9/11, hundreds of vigils were held here, and the entire square became a makeshift memorial to the victims until it was finally ordered dismantled by then-Mayor Rudy Giuliani. The park's southern boundary serves as the informal centre of Manhattan protest against miscellaneous causes, everything from the wars in the Middle East and repression in Iran to legalized marijuana, with raggedly dressed protesters brandishing megaphones at passers-by day and night.

ConEd building

4 Irving Place • Subway L, N, Q, R, #4, #5, #6 to 14th St-Union Square

The **Consolidated Edison** (or **ConEd**) building, which anchors the southern end of Irving Place, is home to the company responsible for providing the city with both energy and steaming manholes. The majestic Warren & Wetmore-designed tower, completed in 1929, is topped by a 38ft-high bronze lantern (itself atop a colonnaded mini-temple and pyramid roof), a memorial to employees killed in World War I.

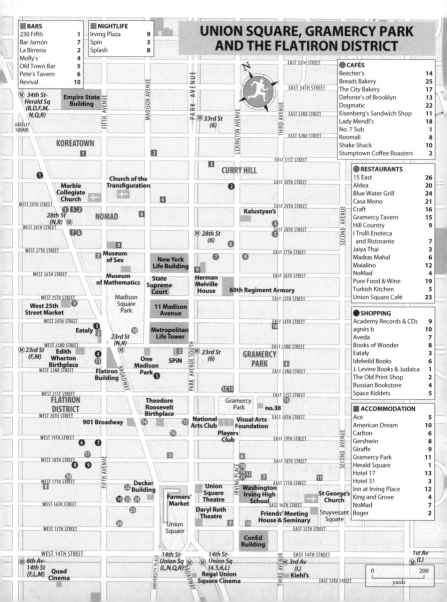

UNION SQUARE, GRAMERCY PARK AND THE FLATIRON DISTRICT

▮ BARS	
230 Fifth	1
Bar Jamón	7
La Birreria	2
Molly's	4
Old Town Bar	5
Pete's Tavern	6
Revival	10

▮ NIGHTLIFE	
Irving Plaza	9
Spin	3
Splash	8

● CAFÉS	
Beecher's	14
Breads Bakery	25
The City Bakery	17
Defonte's of Brooklyn	13
Dogmatic	22
Eisenberg's Sandwich Shop	11
Lady Mendl's	18
No. 7 Sub	1
Roomali	8
Shake Shack	10
Stumptown Coffee Roasters	2

● RESTAURANTS	
15 East	26
Aldea	20
Blue Water Grill	24
Casa Mono	21
Craft	16
Gramercy Tavern	15
Hill Country	9
I Trulli Enoteca and Ristorante	7
Jaiya Thai	3
Madras Mahal	6
Maialino	12
NoMad	4
Pure Food & Wine	19
Turkish Kitchen	5
Union Square Café	23

● SHOPPING	
Academy Records & CDs	9
agnès b	10
Aveda	7
Books of Wonder	8
Eataly	3
Idelwild Books	6
J. Levine Books & Judaica	1
The Old Print Shop	2
Russian Bookstore	4
Space Kiddets	5

▮ ACCOMMODATION	
Ace	5
American Dream	10
Carlton	6
Gershwin	8
Giraffe	9
Gramercy Park	11
Herald Square	1
Hotel 17	13
Hotel 31	3
Inn at Irving Place	12
King and Grove	4
NoMad	7
Roger	2

Map labels: EAST 35TH STREET, EAST 34TH STREET, EAST 33RD STREET, EAST 32ND STREET, EAST 31ST STREET, EAST 30TH STREET, EAST 29TH STREET, EAST 28TH STREET, EAST 27TH STREET, EAST 26TH STREET, EAST 25TH STREET, EAST 24TH STREET, EAST 23RD STREET, EAST 22ND STREET, EAST 21ST STREET, EAST 20TH STREET, EAST 19TH STREET, EAST 18TH STREET, EAST 17TH STREET, EAST 16TH STREET, EAST 15TH STREET, EAST 14TH STREET, EAST 13TH STREET

WEST 29TH STREET, WEST 28TH STREET, WEST 27TH STREET, WEST 26TH STREET, WEST 25TH STREET, WEST 24TH STREET, WEST 23RD STREET, WEST 22ND STREET, WEST 21ST STREET, WEST 20TH STREET, WEST 19TH STREET, WEST 18TH STREET, WEST 17TH STREET, WEST 16TH STREET, WEST 15TH STREET, WEST 14TH STREET

34th St-Herald Sq (B,D,F,M,N,Q,R), Empire State Building, GREELEY SQUARE, KOREATOWN, Marble Collegiate Church, Church of the Transfiguration, CURRY HILL, 28th St (N,R), NOMAD, Kalustyan's, 28th St (6), Museum of Sex, New York Life Building, Museum of Mathematics, State Supreme Court, Herman Melville House, 69th Regiment Armory, West 25th Street Market, Madison Square Park, 11 Madison Avenue, Eataly, Metropolitan Life Tower, 23rd St (N,R), 23rd St (F,M), Edith Wharton Birthplace, One Madison Park, SPiN, 23rd St (6), GRAMERCY PARK, Flatiron Building, FLATIRON DISTRICT, Theodore Roosevelt Birthplace, Gramercy Park, no.38, 901 Broadway, National Arts Club, Visual Arts Foundation, Players Club, Decker Building, Union Square Theatre, Washington Irving High School, St George's Church, Farmers' Market, Daryl Roth Theatre, Friends' Meeting House & Seminary, Stuyvesant Square, Union Square, ConEd Building, 6th Av-14th St (F,L,M), Quad Cinema, 14th St-Union Sq (L,N,Q,R), Regal Union Square Cinema, 14th St-Union Sq (4,5,6,L), 3rd Av (L), Kiehl's, 1st Av (L)

FIFTH AVENUE, MADISON AVENUE, PARK AVENUE, LEXINGTON AVENUE, THIRD AVENUE, SECOND AVENUE, BROADWAY, PARK AVENUE SOUTH, IRVING PLACE, UNIVERSITY PLACE

0   200
yards

HIDDEN GEMS: UNION SQUARE

Supreme Appellate Court hearings
See p.119
Garden, Church of the Transfiguration
See p.120

National Arts Club See p.116
Molly's See p.335
The Old Print Shop See p.376

10

Stuyvesant Square

The area between Irving Place and the East River is something of a no-man's-land, with a clutch of nondescript apartment buildings and businesses. It is, however, a good place for a stroll, even if only to hop off the beaten path and to check out the neighbourhood's few historical points of interest. The land that makes up **Stuyvesant Square**, between East 15th and 17th streets, was gifted to the city in 1836 by **Peter Gerard Stuyvesant**, a descendant of the last Director-General of New Amsterdam (see p.412). The park contains Gertrude Vanderbilt Whitney's bronze statue of the Director-General (replete with peg-leg), unveiled in 1941, and a sculpture of Czech composer **Antonín Dvořák**, who lived nearby on East 17th Street in the 1890s.

Though framed by the buildings of Beth Israel Medical Centre and bisected by bustling Second Avenue, the park still retains something of its secluded quality, especially on the western side. Here you'll find the **Friends' Meeting Houses and Seminary** (1860), whose austere Greek Revival facade contrasts with the grand Romanesque brownstone of St George's Episcopal Church next door, completed in 1856.

St George's Episcopal Church

4 Rutherford Place, between Second and Third aves • Normally open for services only (Sun 9.30 & 11.15am), but you can schedule a weekday tour with the parish office • ☎ 646 723 4178 • Subway L to First or Third aves

The most famous member of the **St George Episcopal Church** congregation was J.P. Morgan, who lived just up the road (see p.131). Remembered as the most powerful and ruthless banker of the Gilded Age, Pierpont, as he was commonly known, was also a devout Episcopalian; in St George's, says Morgan biographer Ron Chernow, "he seemed mesmerized by ritual and lapsed into reveries of mystic depth". His funeral, held here in 1913, was more akin to that of a head of state, and was conducted by an unprecedented three bishops (the tycoon is buried in Hartford, Connecticut). The interior is worth a quick peek for its soaring wood-beam roof, monument to Henry Bacon – designer of the Lincoln Memorial in Washington, DC, and of the American Savings Bank (see p.113) – and the carved pulpit, dedicated to J.P.

Gramercy Park and around

Irving Place comes to an end at the ordered open space of **Gramercy Park**. This former "little crooked swamp" (which is what the Dutch called it before the name was Anglicized) between East 20th and 21st streets is one of the city's prettiest squares. It is beautifully manicured and, most noticeably, completely empty for much of the day – principally because it is the city's last private park, and the only people who can gain access are those rich or fortunate enough to live here. Famous past key-holders have included Mark Twain, Uma Thurman and Julia Roberts, as well as a host of Kennedys and Roosevelts. Despite the park's exclusivity, it's well worth a walk around the edge for a glimpse of the trim, historic area that was once the city's main theatre district.

Inside the park gates stands a statue of the actor **Edwin Booth** (brother of Lincoln's assassin, John Wilkes Booth) in the guise of Hamlet, one of his most famous roles. (Ironically, Edwin rescued Lincoln's son, Robert, from a train accident years before John's fatal action.)

10

The Players Club

16 Gramercy Park South • ☎ 212 475 6116, ⓦ theplayersnyc.org • Subway #6 to 23rd St

In 1888, aided by architect (and Gramercy Park resident) Stanford White, Edwin Booth turned his home into the private club **The Players**. The porch railings on this rather forbidding building are decorated with distinctive figures representing Comedy and Tragedy. In the nineteenth century, actors and theatre types were not accepted in general society, so Booth created the club for play and socializing – neglecting, however, to admit women, who were not allowed in until 1989. Later members included the Barrymores, Frank Sinatra and (oddly) Sir Winston Churchill, while more recent inductees are Morgan Freeman, Edie Falco and (current board member) Martha Plimpton. These days it seems to be the club that is trying to keep regular society out rather than vice versa, though you can show up for Food for Thought productions – one-act plays, with lunch (2pm; days vary; $65), featuring the odd big name in theatre.

National Arts Club

15 Gramercy Park South • ☎ 212 475 3424, ⓦ nationalartsclub.org • Subway #6 to 23rd St

The patrician **National Arts Club** is fittingly located in the rather grand Tilden Mansion. Built in 1840, the mansion was Victorianized in the 1870s by Central Park co-designer Calvert Vaux at the request of owner Governor Samuel Tilden, and is studded with terracotta busts of Shakespeare, Milton and Franklin, among others. Charles de Kay, a *New York Times* art critic, founded the club in 1898 to create a meeting place for artists, patrons and audiences of all the arts; it moved here in 1906. Nonmembers are permitted to visit the temporary art exhibitions inside, usually open Monday to Friday 11am to 5pm, but call or check the website to confirm.

The rest of the park perimeter

On the other side of The Players is the **Visual Arts Foundation** at no. 17, occupying the former home of Joseph Pulitzer, while at no. 38 on the northeast corner of the square is the mock-Tudor building in which John Steinbeck, then a struggling reporter for the now-defunct *New York World*, lived from 1925 to 1926 (it took getting fired from that job to plunge him into fiction). The brick-red structure at no. 34 was one of the city's very **first building co-operatives**.

At 2 Lexington Ave and Gramercy Park North is the imposing 1920s bulk of the **Gramercy Park Hotel** (see p.267), whose elite early residents included Mary McCarthy, a very young John F. Kennedy and Humphrey Bogart. Lastly, lining Gramercy Park West is a splendid row of brick **Greek Revival townhouses** from the 1840s with ornate wrought-iron work; James Harper, of the publishing house Harper & Row, lived at no. 4 until his death in 1869.

The Flatiron District

The small district north and northwest of Union Square, between Fifth and Park avenues up to 23rd Street, is generally known as the **Flatiron District**, taking its name from the distinctive early skyscraper on the southwest corner of Madison Square Park (see p.118). The area is a nice enough place to stroll around in, though there's little to see. This stretch of Broadway was once the heart of the so-called "**Ladies' Mile**", which during the mid-nineteenth century was lined with fancy stores and boutiques. It started losing its lustre around the turn of the twentieth century, and by World War I, Ladies' Mile had all but disintegrated due to the department stores' uptown migration. However, a few sculpted facades and curvy lintels remain as mementoes of that gilded age, including Lord & Taylor's Victorian wedding-cake of a building at 901 Broadway at 20th Street, now converted into pricey apartments (the current store, itself a hundred-year-old landmark, is at 424 Fifth Ave, at 38th St).

FLATIRON BUILDING (P.118) >

Theodore Roosevelt's Birthplace

28 East 20th St • Tues–Sat 9am–5pm, tours on the hour (except at noon) 10am–4pm • Free • ☎ 212 260 1616, ⓦ nps.gov/thrb • Subway N, R to 23rd St

Standing apart from its rather commercial surroundings is **Theodore Roosevelt's Birthplace**, or at least a reconstruction of it, viewable on an obligatory guided tour. In 1923, the house was rebuilt as it would have been when Roosevelt was born there in 1858, the rooms restored to reflect their appearance between 1865 and 1872. The rather sombre (if just recently renovated, in 2013) mansion contains mostly original furnishings: a brilliant chandelier in the parlour, obelisks from a family trip to Egypt, young "Teedie's" crib and more. A room at the top of the house holds some of TR's hunting trophies; a gallery on the ground floor displays photos and documents from the life of the 26th President – still the only one born in New York City.

The Flatiron Building

Broadway, Fifth Avenue and 23rd Street • Subway N, R to 23rd St

The lofty, elegant and decidedly anorexic **Flatiron Building** (originally the Fuller Construction Company, later renamed in honour of its distinctive shape) is set on a narrow, triangular plot of land at a manic intersection. It is one of the city's most famous buildings, evoking images of Edwardian New York. Though it's hard to believe today, the Flatiron was the city's first true skyscraper (a fact hotly debated by architectural-history buffs), hung on a steel frame in 1902 with its full twenty storeys dwarfing all the other buildings around. Its uncommonly thin, tapered structure creates unusual wind currents at ground level; according to lore, the cry "23 Skidoo!" came from policemen warning off voyeurs gathering to watch the wind raise the skirts of women passing by. Such behaviour would presumably have horrified novelist **Edith Wharton**, who was born in 1862 at 14 West 23rd St, just around the corner. Her parents' townhouse has been altered many times since then, and is currently occupied (on its ground floor, that is) by a *Starbucks*.

Madison Square Park and NoMad

Just northeast of the Flatiron Building, between Park and Fifth avenues, lies **Madison Square Park**. Though enveloped by a maelstrom of cars, cabs, buses and dodging pedestrians, because of the stateliness of the surrounding buildings and its peaceful green spaces it possesses a grandiosity and neat seclusion that Union Square has long since lost – be sure to grab a burger at *Shake Shack*, near the southeast entrance (see p.284), or something from Eataly, across the street (see p.385), while you're taking it in. Surrounding the park are a few monumental buildings; north of it, the trendy neighbourhood of **NoMad** takes over, with a few unusual museums and lots of fashionable places to eat, drink and stay.

Around Madison Square Park

On Madison Square Park's east side, at 5 Madison Ave, stands the tiered, stately **Metropolitan Life Tower**, which at 700ft was the world's tallest building between 1909 and 1913, when it was surpassed by the Woolworth Building (see p.58). It was sold to a developer in 2007 for $200 million, and, following an area trend, is being converted into high-end residential apartments – and has been rechristened Madison Avenue Clocktower. Of course, **One Madison Park**, the new mirrored glass condo across the way, at 23 East 22nd St, nearly foreclosed before it was finished, so nothing in the way of real estate development is guaranteed.

MetLife also once owned **11 Madison Avenue**, across East 24th Street (it now houses Credit Suisse), connected to the tower building by a sky-bridge. Completed in 1929, the onset of the Great Depression quashed MetLife's plans to make this section a mind-blowing hundred storeys high – viewed from the park, you can see how it was designed to be the base for something much bigger.

STANFORD WHITE AND THE OLD MADISON SQUARE GARDEN

Stanford White, a partner in the illustrious architectural team of McKim, Mead, and White, which designed many of the city's great Beaux Arts buildings, including the General Post Office and the old Penn Station, as well as the second incarnation of Madison Square Garden (at 26th St and Madison; now demolished), was by all accounts something of a rake. His dalliance with millionaire Harry Thaw's future wife, Evelyn Nesbit, a Broadway showgirl (who was unattached at the time), had been well publicized – even to the extent that the naked statue of the goddess Diana on the top of the Madison Square Garden building was said to have been modelled on her. Violent and possessive, Thaw could never accept his wife's past, and one night in 1906 he burst into the roof garden of White's Madison Square Garden tower apartment, found the architect surrounded, as usual, by doting women and admirers, and shot him in the head. Thaw was carted away after trial to a mental institution, which he was subsequently in and out of for around a third of his remaining years, while his wife's show-business career took a tumble: she resorted to drugs and prostitution, dying in 1967 in Los Angeles.

10

On the other side of 25th Street, at 27 Madison Ave, the Appellate Division of the **New York State Supreme Court** boasts a marble facade, resolutely righteous with its statues of Justice, Wisdom and Peace. The chamber inside where arguments are heard (open to the public Tues–Thurs 2pm; free) is almost rococo in its detail.

The grand structure opposite is the **New York Life Building**, the work of Cass Gilbert, creator of the Woolworth Building downtown. It went up in 1928 on the site of the original **Madison Square Garden** (see box, above), renowned scene of drunken and debauched revels of high and Broadway society. Some believe that the junction nearby, at Madison and West 27th Street, is the birthplace of baseball, as the members of the country's first ball club, the New York Knickerbockers, started playing in a vacant sandlot here in 1842.

Museum of Mathematics

11 E 26th St, between Fifth and Madison aves • Daily 10am–5pm • $15, 12 and under $9 • ☎ 212 542 0566, ⓦ momath.org • Subway N, R, #6 to 23rd St or 28th St

Somewhere between a high-minded institution and an interactive romper room, the **Museum of Mathematics** debuted in late 2012 with the goal of making maths fun and accessible to kids – and adults. Featuring roughly thirty exhibits on two floors (one, the multiplication-oriented String Product, extends over both via a spiral staircase), the gallery puts a focus on experience and engagement over understanding, with the idea that the latter will naturally follow. Whimsical details abound – the pi-shaped door handles, the numbering of the floors ("0" and "−1"), the geometric sinks in the bathrooms – evidence that the museum's directors are not "museum people". There's the occasional lack of context or explanatory aid, but the overall effect is refreshing. Posing in front of the Human Tree, the most popular exhibit (though tucked away in a far corner of the lower level), throws up dazzling special effects projected on screen; taking a smooth ride on the Square-Wheeled Trike or Coaster Rollers will get you wondering about catenaries (even if you didn't know that was the name for the curves in the roadway). After you've seen how fractals relate to the real world, take a breather in the *Enigma Café* – for sustenance, there are puzzles rather than coffee and baked goods.

Museum of Sex

233 Fifth Ave, at 27th St • Mon–Thurs & Sun 10am–8pm, Fri & Sat 10am–9pm • $17.50, ages 18 and over only • ☎ 212 689 6337, ⓦ museumofsex.com • Subway N, R, #6 to 28th St

One of the city's more provocative institutions, the **Museum of Sex** attempts to bring serious study to its subject but is more of interest for its singularity than any new light it might shed. The first floor has temporary exhibitions on subjects like pornography and the sex lives of animals, while upstairs features a mishmash of items from the permanent collection (much of which has been donated), such as early vibrators, sex dolls and so forth, which look anything but titillating in this setting – presumably part of the point.

Church of the Transfiguration

1 East 29th St, just off Fifth Ave • Chapel open daily 8.30am–6pm, Tues lunchtime music performances • ⓦ littlechurch.org • Subway N, R, #6 to 28th St

10

The lone reminder of the time when this area was New York's theatreland is the **Church of the Transfiguration**. Built in 1849, this dinky, rusticated church, made of brown brick, topped with copper roofs, and set back from the street, has long been a traditional place of worship for showbiz people and various social misfits. It was not until 1870, though, that members of the theatre profession started coming here to pray. That year, the place was tagged with the name "The Little Church Around the Corner" after a devout priest from a larger, stuffier church had refused to officiate at the funeral of an actor named George Holland, sending the bereaved here instead. Since then, the church has been a haven for actors, and there is even an Episcopal Actors' Guild. The chapel itself is an intimate little building in a gloriously leafy garden, providing comfort and solace away from the skyscrapers on Fifth Avenue. Its interior is furnished in warm wood and lit with soft candlelight. The figures of famous actors (most notably Edwin Booth as Hamlet) are memorialized in the stained glass.

Marble Collegiate Church

1 West 29th St • Mon–Fri 10am–noon & 2–4pm • ⓦ marblechurch.org • Subway N, R, #6 to 28th St

Across Fifth Avenue from the Church of the Transfiguration is another house of worship, the 150-year-old **Marble Collegiate Church**, which in addition to having two Tiffany stained-glass windows in its sanctuary (plus a number of later knock-offs), was where preacher-cum-pop-psychologist Norman Vincent Peale held the pulpit for years.

Lexington Avenue

Two blocks east of Madison, **Lexington Avenue**, which begins its long journey north at Gramercy Park, passes the lumbering **69th Regiment Armory** at 26th Street (ⓦ sixtyninth.net). The site of the famous "Armory Show" of 1913, which brought modern art to New York, and a very early home to the Knicks' basketball team, it retains its original function as the headquarters of the National Guard's "Fighting Sixty-Ninth", though its drill hall is still used for events and exhibitions.

Just west of the Armory, on the corner of Park Avenue, 104 East 26th St was once the brownstone home of **Herman Melville**, long since replaced with a modern office building but remembered with a small plaque. The author moved here in 1863, and lived in the spot for nearly thirty years, toiling at the New York Custom House and, later, working on the unfinished *Billy Budd* before his death in 1891. The nearby intersection is named **Herman Melville Square** in his honour.

North of the Armory lies what is sometimes dubbed **Curry Hill**, a collection of Indian restaurants, snack shops and stores along Lexington Avenue between East 27th and 30th streets – blink and you might miss it altogether. Most of New York's Indian population lives in Queens, but the cluster of businesses here (many of them Tamil) just about warrants the moniker.

CHRYSLER BUILDING

Midtown East

The largely corporate and commercial area known as Midtown East rolls north from the 30s to the 50s, and east to the river from Sixth Avenue. Some of the city's most determinedly modish boutiques, richest Art Deco facades and most sophisticated Modernist skyscrapers are in this district, primarily scattered along Fifth, Madison and Park avenues. You'll find the Empire State Building, the soaring symbol of New York City; the grand Neoclassicism of the New York Public Library's main branch; the Art Deco, automobile-inspired Chrysler Building; the rambling, geometric bulk of the United Nations complex; and the peerless Museum of Modern Art. Affordable places to eat and good nightlife spots may be relatively thin on the ground, but you can spend plenty of worthwhile daylight hours here.

ARRIVAL AND DEPARTURE

By train and subway Grand Central is probably the best spot to emerge in this neighbourhood: it's not just a subway (the #4, #5, #6, #7 and S all stop here) and commuter rail hub, but an elegant introduction to Midtown architecture. Fifth Avenue is just a stone's throw away.

Fifth Avenue

For the last two centuries, an address on **Fifth Avenue** has signified prosperity, respectability and high social standing. Whether around Washington Square or far uptown around the Harlem River, the boulevard has traditionally been the home to Manhattan's finest mansions, hotels, churches and stores. Thanks to its show of wealth and opulence, Fifth Avenue has always drawn crowds, nowhere more than on the stretch between 34th and 59th streets, home to grand institutions like **Rockefeller Center** and the **New York Public Library**. The streets nearly reach a standstill at Christmas, with shoppers stalled at elaborate window displays; at other times, it plays host to some of the city's biggest processions (see pp.398–403).

The Empire State Building

350 Fifth Ave, between 33rd and 34th sts • **Observatory** Daily 8am–2am, last trip 1.15am • $25, ages 6–12 $19, 5 and under and military personnel free; audio tour $8; you can buy tickets online or, for an extra $20, express to skip lines • ☎ 212 736 3100, ⓦ esbnyc.com • **New York Skyride** Daily 8am–10pm • Tickets bought online $29, youths and seniors $19; more at box office; combined tickets for New York Skyride and the Observatory $47 • ☎ 212 279 9777 or ☎ 1 888 759 7433, ⓦ skyride.com • Subway B, D, F, M, N, Q, R to 34th St-Herald Square

For two different eras the city's tallest skyscraper, the **Empire State Building** has easily been the most potent and evocative symbol of New York since its completion in 1931. The building occupies what has always been a prime piece of real estate, originally the site of the first Waldorf-Astoria Hotel, built by William Waldorf Astor and opened in 1893; its current Art Deco home lies on Park Avenue (see p.269).

Wall Street visionary John Jacob Raskob and his partner Alfred E. Smith, a former governor, began accumulating funds in October 1929, just three weeks before the stock market crash. Despite the ensuing Depression, the Empire State Building proceeded full steam ahead and came in well under budget after just fourteen months. Since the opening, the building has seen its share of celebrity and tragedy: King Kong clung to it while grabbing at passing aircraft; in 1945, a B-25 bomber negotiating its way through heavy fog crashed into the building's 79th storey, killing fourteen people; and in 1979, two Englishmen parachuted from its summit to the ground, only to be carted off by the NYPD for disturbing the peace. The darkest moment in the building's history came in February 1997, when a man opened fire on the observation deck, killing one tourist and injuring seven others; that's but one reason there is tight security upon entrance, with metal detectors, package scanners and the like (though this only solves part of the problem: in 2010, a Yale student scaled the barrier on the main observation deck and jumped to his death).

The building

From toe to TV mast including antennas, the building is 102 storeys and 1454ft tall, but its height is deceptive, rising in stately tiers with steady panache. Indeed, standing on Fifth Avenue below, it's quite easy to walk right by without even noticing it's there. From elsewhere in the city, it can seem ubiquitous, especially at night, when lit in various colours until the wee hours of morning (view the lighting schedule online at ⓦ esbnyc.com/current_events_tower_lights.asp).

Retrofitted since 2009 to make it more energy efficient (for example, all 6514 windows were taken out and reused after being turned into super-insulating windows on-site), the Empire State uses 38 percent less energy than it did a few years ago. The building is filled with Art Deco touches: the restored grand ceiling in the lobby with its cosmic gold murals; the elevator doors; the chandeliers in the new cocktail lounge, the *Empire Room*,

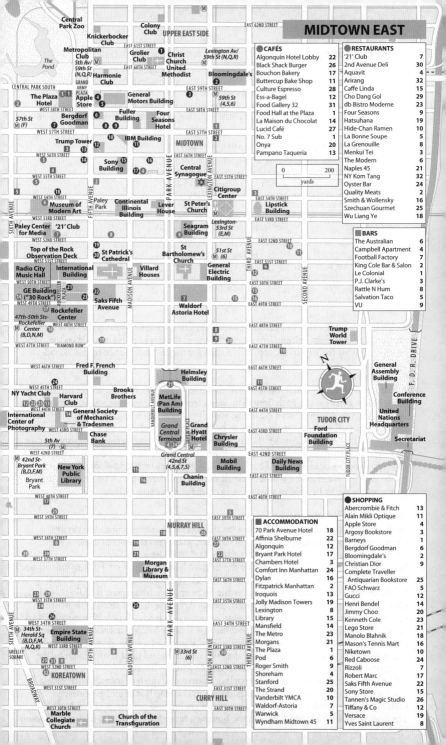

MIDTOWN EAST

● CAFÉS

Algonquin Hotel Lobby	22
Black Shack Burger	26
Bouchon Bakery	17
Buttercup Bake Shop	11
Culture Espresso	28
Ess-a-Bagel	12
Food Gallery 32	31
Food Hall at the Plaza	1
La Maison du Chocolat	14
Lucid Café	27
No. 7 Sub	1
Onya	20
Pampano Taqueria	13

● RESTAURANTS

'21' Club	7
2nd Avenue Deli	30
Aquavit	4
Arirang	32
Caffe Linda	15
Cho Dang Gol	29
db Bistro Moderne	23
Four Seasons	9
Hatsuhana	19
Hide-Chan Ramen	10
La Bonne Soupe	5
La Grenouille	8
Menkui Tei	3
The Modern	6
Naples 45	21
NY Kom Tang	32
Oyster Bar	24
Quality Meats	2
Smith & Wollensky	16
Szechuan Gourmet	25
Wu Liang Ye	18

Scale: 0 — 200 yards

■ BARS

The Australian	6
Campbell Apartment	4
Football Factory	7
King Cole Bar & Salon	2
Le Colonial	1
P.J. Clarke's	3
Rattle N Hum	8
Salvation Taco	5
VU	9

● SHOPPING

Abercrombie & Fitch	13
Alain Mikli Optique	11
Apple Store	4
Argosy Bookstore	3
Barneys	1
Bergdorf Goodman	6
Bloomingdale's	2
Christian Dior	9
Complete Traveller Antiquarian Bookstore	25
FAO Schwarz	5
Gucci	12
Henri Bendel	14
Jimmy Choo	20
Kenneth Cole	23
Lego Store	21
Manolo Blahnik	18
Mason's Tennis Mart	16
Niketown	10
Red Caboose	24
Rizzoli	7
Robert Marc	17
Saks Fifth Avenue	22
Sony Store	15
Tannen's Magic Studio	26
Tiffany & Co	12
Versace	19
Yves Saint Laurent	8

■ ACCOMMODATION

70 Park Avenue Hotel	18
Affinia Shelburne	22
Algonquin	12
Bryant Park Hotel	17
Chambers Hotel	3
Comfort Inn Manhattan	24
Dylan	16
Fitzpatrick Manhattan	2
Iroquois	13
Jolly Madison Towers	19
Lexington	8
Library	15
Mansfield	14
The Metro	23
Morgans	21
The Plaza	1
Pod	6
Roger Smith	9
Shoreham	4
Stanford	25
The Strand	20
Vanderbilt YMCA	10
Waldorf-Astoria	7
Warwick	5
Wyndham Midtown 45	11

11

SKYSCRAPERS

New York is one of the best places in the world to see **skyscrapers**. There are only two main clusters – Midtown and the Financial District – but the concentration is high: the iconic, almost medieval skyline traces over forty buildings higher than 200m (roughly 650ft), a number of them more than eighty years old. In a small grid, Art Deco masterpieces such as the Chrysler Building and Rockefeller Center rub shoulders with Modernist masterpieces like the Seagram Building and Lever House.

NEW YORK'S TALLEST BUILDINGS 1846–PRESENT

1846–1890 Trinity Church – Financial District (284ft/87m)
1890–1899 World Building – demolished 1955 (348ft/106m)
1899–1908 Park Row Building – City Hall Park (391ft/119m)
1908–1909 Singer Building – demolished 1968 (612ft/187m)
1909–1913 MetLife Tower – Madison Square Park (700ft/213m)
1913–1930 Woolworth Building – Financial District (792ft/241m)
1930 Bank of Manhattan Trust – Financial District (927ft/283m)
1930–1931 Chrysler Building – Midtown (1046ft/319m)
1931–1972 Empire State Building – Midtown (1250ft/381m)
1972–2001 World Trade Center – destroyed 2001 (1368ft/417m)
2001–2012 Empire State Building – Midtown (1250ft/381m)
2012– Present One World Trade Center – Financial District (1776ft/541m)

---

which is in the space that once held a post office. On the second floor is the **New York Skyride**, a pricey, eight-minute simulated flight over the city's landmarks. Of course, most people come for the trip to the top, rather than for the cocktail lounge or the Skyride.

Getting to the top

A first set of elevators takes you to the 80th floor, where you transfer to get up to the main observatory on the **86th floor**. The views from the outdoor walkways here are as stunning as you'd expect; on a clear day, visibility can be up to eighty miles, but given the city's air pollution, it's more likely to be between ten and twenty. You get a great vantage point over the Chrysler Building, completed not long before the Empire State, and over the surprisingly elegant Queensboro Bridge beyond that. For an additional $15, a second set of elevators will take you to the glassed-in **102nd-floor observatory**, the base of the radio and TV antennas; all things considered, it's an unnecessary trip, unless you want to be able to say you've been as far up as you can go.

New York Public Library

Fifth Ave and 42nd St • Mon & Thurs–Sat 10am–6pm, Tues & Wed 10am–8pm, Sun 1–5pm (except summer) • Tours start at the information desk in Astor Hall, the main lobby (1hr; Mon–Sat 11am & 2pm, Sun 2pm; free) • ☎ 212 930 0800 or ☎ 917 275 6975, ⓦ nypl .org • Subway B, D, F, M to 42nd St-Bryant Park, #7 to Fifth Ave, #4, #5, #6, #7, S to Grand Central

Several unexceptional blocks north of the Empire State Building on Fifth Avenue is one of Midtown Manhattan's most striking buildings: the hundred-year-old **New York Public Library** (more formally known as the Stephen A. Schwarzman Building), which stretches between 40th and 42nd streets. Beaux Arts in style and faced with white marble – recently restored for the centennial; approach from Library Way, or East 41st Street, for the most eye-catching introduction – it is the headquarters of the largest public-library system in the world. It's also in the midst of a controversial overhaul, one that will replace the celebrated stacks that run underground (and move much of the collection to New Jersey) with a more accessible lending library.

To explore, either walk around yourself or take one of the **free tours**, which give a good all-round picture of the building, taking in the **Map Room** and evocative **Periodicals Room**, with its stunning faux-wood ceiling and paintings of old New York. The undisputed highlight of the library, however, is the large, coffered 636-seat **Reading**

Room on the third floor. Authors Norman Mailer and E.L. Doctorow worked here, as did Leon Trotsky during his brief sojourn in New York just prior to the 1917 Russian Revolution. It was also here that Chester Carlson came up with the idea for the Xerox copier and Norbert Pearlroth searched for strange facts for his "Ripley's Believe It or Not!" cartoon strip in the famed research library.

Bryant Park

Between 40th and 42nd streets, bordered by the New York Public Library and Sixth Ave • **Park** Hours vary but roughly 7am–10pm, closes earlier in Feb, March & Oct, later May–Sept **Ice skating** Nov–Feb daily 8am–10pm, midnight on weekends • $14 for skate rental • ☎ 212 768 4242, ⓦ bryantpark.org • Subway B, D, F, M to 42nd St-Bryant Park, #7 to Fifth Ave

Bryant Park, just behind the library, is Midtown's busiest outdoor space. Transformed a few decades ago from seedy eyesore to beautiful, grassy block filled with trees, flowerbeds and inviting chairs, it's a welcoming place to relax with a coffee or book on a warm day – or engage in any number of more organized activities. A sandwich and coffee kiosk in the northwest corner and alfresco bar in the southwest provide on-site refreshments.

In summertime, free activities abound: dance and yoga classes, Monday evening movies and table tennis to name a few (there are also areas to play chess and petanque). Lectures and rallies take place in the park; there's a carousel ($2) for children, and in winter the park's Citi Pond turns into an ice-skating rink. Donning your blades in the shadow of the library and giant Christmas tree rivals the more popular scenes at Rockefeller Center and Central Park for atmosphere.

North to Rockefeller Center

The **Chase Bank**, on the southwest corner of West 43rd Street and Fifth Avenue, is an eye-catcher. An early glass'n'gloss box, it teasingly displays its vault (no longer in use) to passers-by. Around the next corner, West 44th Street contains several old-guard New York institutions. The Georgian-style **Harvard Club**, at no. 35 (☎ 212 840 6600, ⓦ hcny .com), has an interior so lavish that lesser mortals aren't even allowed to enter (you must be a Harvard alumnus/a). Built in 1894, it was the first of several elite associations in the neighbourhood.

The **New York Yacht Club**, at 37 West 44th Street (☎ 212 382 1000, ⓦ nyyc.org), chartered in 1844, is just next door. In its current location since 1901, this playfully eccentric exterior of bay windows is moulded as ships' sterns; waves and dolphins complete the effect of tipsy Beaux Arts fun. For years, this has been the home of the America's Cup, a yachting trophy first won by the schooner *America* in 1851. Across the street at no. 20, the 230-year-old **General Society of Mechanics and Tradesmen** occupies a late nineteenth-century building; step inside to peruse the library (Mon–Thurs 11am–7pm, Fri 10am–5pm; free; ⓦ generalsociety.org) and to examine their amazing collection of locks (by appointment ☎ 212 840 1840; $10 admission).

THE ROUND TABLE

All across the globe, the period between World War I and World War II saw an incredible outpouring of creative energy. In America, one of the groups involved in this burst of productivity was the so-called **Round Table**, which originated at the *Algonquin Hotel*. Several writers, many of whom had worked together for the Army newspaper *Stars and Stripes*, met in June 1919 at the hotel to roast *New York Times* drama critic Alexander Woollcott. They had so much fun that they decided to return the following afternoon; it wasn't long before their meeting became a ritual. At the heart of the group were Dorothy Parker, Robert Benchley, Robert Sherwood, Irving Berlin, Harold Ross (founder of *The New Yorker* magazine), George Bernard Shaw and George S. Kaufman, among others. Outspoken and unafraid to comment on the state of the postwar world, they wielded an increasing influence on social issues through the 1920s; when the Round Table spoke, the country listened. Then the Great Depression arrived, and a decade after its inception, it finally faded from the scene.

"Dammit, it was the twenties and we had to be smarty," said Dorothy Parker of the sharp-tongued wits known as the Round Table (see box, p.125), whose members lunched and drank regularly at the **Algonquin Hotel**, at 59 West 44th Street (see p.268). Recent refurbishments have shut the hotel's legendary *Oak Room*, but you can still find an excuse to pop in for a tea or just a look round.

It's worth ducking into the **Fred F. French Building** at 551 Fifth Avenue. The colourful mosaics near the top of the building's exterior are a mere prelude to the combination of Art Deco and Middle Eastern imagery on the vaulted ceiling and bronze doors of the lobby.

Diamond District

West 47th Street, or the **Diamond District** (marked by the diamond-shaped lamps mounted on pylons at the Fifth- and Sixth-avenue ends of the street), is a diverting side-trip from Fifth Avenue, a strip of wholesale and retail shops chock-full of gems and jewellery first established in the 1920s. These shops are largely managed by Hasidic Jews, who impart much of the street's workaday vibe, making the row feel less like something just off ritzy Fifth Avenue and more like the Garment District, by way of the Middle East. Come here to get jewellery fixed at reasonable prices.

Rockefeller Center

Taking up the blocks between Fifth and Sixth aves and 48th and 51st sts • Leaflets for self-guided tours available from GE Building lobby desk or online • ☎ 212 332 6868 or ☎ 212 632 3975, ⓦ rockefellercenter.com • Subway B, D, F, M to 47-50th sts-Rockefeller Center

Rockefeller Center is one of the finest examples of urban planning in New York. Built between 1930 and 1939 by John D. Rockefeller Jr, son of the oil magnate, its offices, cafés, theatre, underground concourse and rooftop gardens work together with an intelligence and grace rarely seen. The main part of the Center is along the block between 49th and 50th streets, though just across 50th Street on the corner of Sixth Avenue stands the Art Deco-style **Radio City Music Hall**, arguably the most famous theatre in the United States.

GE Building ("30 Rock")

30 Rockefeller Plaza • **Ice rink** Mon–Thurs 8.30am–10.30pm, Fri 8.30am–midnight, Sat 8am–midnight, Sun 8am–10.30pm • $25, 10 and under $12, $10 skate rental ☎ 212 332 7654, ⓦ therinkatrockcenter.com • Subway B, D, F, M to 47-50th sts-Rockefeller Center

From Fifth Avenue, the gentle slope of the **Channel Gardens** leads to the focus of the Center – the **GE Building** (formerly the RCA Building), nicknamed "30 Rock". Rising 850ft, its monumental lines echo the scale of Manhattan, though they are softened by symmetrical setbacks to prevent an overpowering expanse of wall. At the foot of the building, the Lower Plaza holds a sunken restaurant in the summer months – a great place for afternoon cocktails – linked visually to the downward flow of the building by **Paul Manship**'s sparkling sculpture *Prometheus*. In winter this recessed area becomes an **ice rink**, and following a New York tradition that dates to 1931, a huge tree is displayed at Christmas time, drawing hordes of gawkers, especially the night it's initially lit (first week of Dec).

Inside, the GE Building is no less impressive. **José Maria Sert**'s lobby murals, *American Progress* and *Time*, are faded but still in tune with the 1930s ambience – presumably more so than the original paintings by Diego Rivera, which were

---

FIVE UNIQUE CITY VIEWS

Top of the Rock and the Empire State Building are obvious places to go for panoramic **views** of New York, but you can find interesting angles on the city at any of the following:

Brooklyn Bridge See p.61
Cantor Rooftop Garden See p.165
Brooklyn Bridge Park's Main Street Lot See p.217

The High Line See p.106
The Panorama of the City of New York See p.247

removed by John D.'s son Nelson Rockefeller when the artist refused to scrap a panel glorifying Lenin.

NBC Studios

30 Rockefeller Plaza • 1hr 10min behind-the-scenes tours every 15min Mon–Thurs 8.30am–5.30pm, Fri & Sat 8.30am–6pm, Sun 9.15am–4.30pm; reservations at the NBC Experience Tour Desk • $24, ages 6–12 $21; call ☏ 212 664 3700 to reserve or buy a combination ticket with Rockefeller Center tour, ⓦ nbcstudiotour.com • For information on show tapings, visit ⓦ nbc.com/tickets or call the ticket line on ☏ 212 664 3056 (see p.356) • Subway B, D, F, M to 47-50th sts-Rockefeller Center

Among the GE Building's many offices is **NBC Studios** on 49th Street between Fifth and Sixth avenues, which produces, among other things, the long-running sketch-comedy hit *Saturday Night Live* and the popular morning programme the *Today Show*. To become part of the throng that appears (and waves frantically) when the anchors step outside, all one has to do is show up – the earlier the better. This is especially true on summer Fridays when the *Today Show* hosts concerts, which begin at 7am.

Top of the Rock

30 Rockefeller Plaza • Daily 8am–midnight, last elevator at 11pm • $25, ages 6–12 $16; "Sun & Stars" $38, children $20 • ☏ 212 698 2000, ⓦ topoftherocknyc.com • Subway B, D, F, M to 47-50th sts-Rockefeller Center

The observation deck on the top of Rockefeller Center, first opened in 1933, fell into disuse and was closed in the 1980s. The owners returned to John D.'s original vision by restoring the platform on the structure's 70th storey in November 2005. In contrast to the Empire State Building, **Top of the Rock** offers completely unobstructed views, and the timed-entry scheme, multiple observation decks and decent square-footage of the viewing platforms make a visit seem less like a cattle call. The panorama allows you to examine the layout of Central Park, how built-up downtown Manhattan is compared to the north and offers a vertiginous look at St Patrick's Cathedral below – not to mention of the Empire State Building nearby. A "Sun & Stars" ticket option allows particularly dedicated visitors to scale the building twice in one day and experience the city in two different veils of light.

Radio City Music Hall

1260 Sixth Ave • "Stage Door" walking tours (1hr), daily 11am–3pm every 30min • $23.70 • For tickets, call ☏ 212 307 7171, tour info ☏ 212 247 4777, ⓦ radiocity.com • Subway B, D, F, M to 47-50th sts-Rockefeller Center

On the northeast corner of Sixth Avenue and 50th Street is **Radio City Music Hall** =(see p.343), a sweeping and dramatic Art Deco jewel box that represents the last word in 1930s luxury. The staircase is positively regal, the chandeliers are the world's largest, and the auditorium looks like an extravagant scalloped shell: "Art Deco's true shrine", as critic Paul Goldberger rightly called it. You're unlikely to be taking in a show here – with a couple of exceptions, the venue rarely books the type of cool acts that once made it such a hot ticket – so to explore, take a tour. In addition to the behind-the-scenes look at the building, the tour includes a brief meeting and photo-op with a Rockette (the "house" dancers that are part of the Christmas Spectacular, the big annual event at RCMH).

North to Central Park

Fifth Avenue has another sumptuous Art Deco component in the Rockefeller Center, the **International Building**. The lobby looks out on **Lee Lawrie**'s bronze *Atlas*, which rules the space – a thorough cleaning in the summer of 2008 returned its lustre – and the muscleman gazes toward **St Patrick's Cathedral** across the avenue. Designed by James Renwick and completed in 1888, St Patrick's sits on the corner of 50th Street amid the glitz like a misplaced bit of moral imperative, painstakingly detailed yet – notwithstanding the mysticism of **Lady Chapel** to the rear – spiritually lifeless. Despite its shortcomings, St Patrick's is still an essential part of the Midtown landscape, a foil for Rockefeller Center and one of the most important Catholic churches in America.

Across the street from St Patrick's are the striped awnings of **Saks Fifth Avenue** at no. 611, one of the last of New York's premier department stores to relocate to Midtown from Herald Square. With its columns on the ground floor and graceful pathways through high-end fashion collections, Saks is every bit as glamorous today as it was when it opened in 1924.

Paley Center for Media

25 West 52nd St, between Fifth and Sixth aves • Wed & Fri–Sun noon–6pm, Thurs noon–8pm • $10, 13 and under $5 • ☎ 212 621 6800, ⓦ paleycenter.org • Subway B, D, F, M to 47th-50th sts-Rockefeller Center

If your body needs the kind of rejuvenation only an hour in front of a television can offer, visit the **Paley Center for Media**. Formerly known as the Museum of Television & Radio, the space was renamed in 2007 with a nod to the eventual inclusion of digital media. In a building designed by Philip Johnson, the organization preserves an archive of 150,000, mostly American, TV shows, radio broadcasts and commercials, accessible via an excellent computerized reference system. Regular screenings and panel discussions take place in the downstairs theatre.

The '21' Club

21 West 52nd St • ☎ 212 582 7200, ⓦ 21club.com • Subway B, D, F, M to 47th-50th sts-Rockefeller Center

Right next door to the Paley Center is the **'21' Club**, which has been providing food (and drink) since the days of Prohibition, and remains an Old Boys' institution. Founded by Jack Kriendler and Charlie Berns, the club quickly became one of the most exclusive establishments in town, a place where young socialites and local celebrities could spend wild nights dancing the Charleston and enjoying wines and spirits of the finest quality. Although '21' was raided more than once, federal agents were never able to pin anything on Jack and Charlie. At the first sign of a raid, they would activate an ingenious system of pulleys and levers, which would sweep bottles from the bar shelves and hurl the smashed remains down a chute into the New York sewer system.

Museum of Modern Art

11 West 53rd St, just off Fifth Ave • Daily 10.30am–5.30pm, Fri till 8pm • $25, 16 and under free and free for all Fri 4–8pm • ☎ 212 708 9400, ⓦ moma.org • Subway E, M to 5th Ave-53rd St, B, D, F, M to 47-50th Sts-Rockefeller Center

New York City's **Museum of Modern Art – MoMA** to its friends – offers the finest and most complete collection of late nineteenth- and twentieth-century art anywhere, with a permanent collection of more than 150,000 paintings, sculptures, drawings, prints and photographs, as well as a world-class film archive. Despite its high admission price, it's an essential stop for anyone even remotely interested in the world of modern art.

Founded in 1929 by three wealthy women, including Abby Aldrich Rockefeller (wife of John D., Jr), as the very first museum dedicated entirely to modern art, MoMA moved to its present home ten years later. Philip Johnson designed expansions in the 1950s and 1960s, and in 1984 a steel-pipe and glass renovation by Cesar Pelli doubled gallery space. The latest renovation was completed in 2004 by Japanese architect Yoshio Taniguchi, doubling the exhibition space yet again and creating new and vibrant public areas; another expansion is already in the works – gallery space in a soaring new skyscraper next door that will be one of the city's tallest structures. Also included in the expansion plans is the space that once held the American Folk Art Museum (see p.185), a striking work of architecture that MoMA purchased – and demolished – barely a decade after its construction.

The layout

MoMA's building is quite clever: it's easy to navigate, but it also constantly and deliberately gives glimpses of other levels, like the sculpture garden, the lobby and the spacious second-floor landing where large canvases or installations are often displayed.

The core collection – at least in the Painting and Sculpture galleries – is arranged more or less in chronological order and is somewhat stable, though pieces do go in and out (to and from the archive, set up for special exhibitions, out on loan, etc), and there's been a bit more rearrangement activity in recent years. At least it is more consistent than the substantial collections of photography, drawings, architectural design and contemporary art on the second and third floors, which rotate with frequency within their own galleries; temporary exhibitions are also afforded their own dedicated areas.

Despite all this space, the main galleries in MoMA can still feel very crowded, especially during weekends and holidays (not to mention the free admission time on Friday evenings) and queues can be long at the entrance, cloakroom, cafés and for audio guides. You can avoid waiting in line by booking tickets in advance on the website or by getting here either first thing or late in the afternoon, to avoid the worst of it. Note also that you must check-in large shopping bags and backpacks of any size – don't bring them if you want to avoid another wait for the cloakroom.

Painting and Sculpture I

11

The core of the collection is the Painting and Sculpture galleries, numbered from 1 to 25. Most visitors head directly for the fifth floor – to **Painting and Sculpture I**, which covers 1880 to 1940. Gallery 1 opens with the **Post-Impressionists** of the late nineteenth century, with works by **Cézanne**, **Seurat**, **Van Gogh** (visitors always mill around his *Starry Night*) and **Gauguin** mixed in with vivid early paintings by **James Ensor** and **Henri Rousseau** that already hint at a more Modernist perspective. This is developed in the next gallery by **Picasso**, most notably with his seminal *Les Demoiselles d'Avignon*, as well as by some of his later, more Cubist pieces; you can also contrast his *Bather* with Cézanne's take on the same subject from the previous gallery. The big swirling colours of **Boccioni**, **Severini** and the Italian Futurists follow in Gallery 3, with Gallery 4 holding an "artist's choice" selection which is nominally ongoing, though it does go on hiatus and can move galleries from installation to installation. Gallery 5 is given over to **Munch**; *The Scream* takes centre stage, but other works of his hold interest, most notably *The Storm*, almost a practice run for his most famous image. Gallery 6 is entirely devoted to **Matisse**. Featured are the flat, almost primitive *Dance I*; his *Red Studio*; and *The Moroccans*, at once still and rhythmic.

After Matisse is a so-called **"Crossroads" gallery** (Gallery 7), which houses some of the most recognizable works of the modern age – Picasso's *Three Women at the Spring*, the same artist's *Three Musicians* and Léger's *Three Women*, all painted the same year (1921), as well as some haunting exercises in perspective by **de Chirico**. After Monet's *Water Lilies* (Gallery 8), the adjoining room is devoted to the paintings of the Dutch De Stijl movement, with **Malevich** heavily featured in Gallery 9; you can trace the development of the movement's leading light, **Mondrian**, right up to the pure colour abstract of his late-era *Broadway Boogie Woogie*, painted in New York in 1943. Gallery 10 picks up with the Bauhaus, namely the symbols and scribbles of **Klee**. Gallery 11 is another artist's choice room, a breather before the Surrealists make their presence felt in Gallery 12. Many of the works here will be familiar from popular reproductions: the vivid creations of **Miró**, **Magritte**'s *The Menaced Assassin* and the famously drooping clocks of **Dalí**'s *Persistence of Memory*, astonishingly detailed for its compact size; the last of those is often on loan to other galleries. Tiny Gallery 13 features **Jacob Lawrence**'s *Migration Series*, a shorthand history of

THE MOMA SHUFFLE

While a number of the pieces and painters that we cover will (almost) always be on display, don't bank on the order or selections; recent trends have included, more mixing of eras and artists in Painting and Sculpture I, a stronger emphasis on recent Conceptual Art in Painting and Sculpture II, and an ongoing dedication to rethinking the canon and its sacred cows.

FIVE MIDTOWN RETREATS

With the crush of skyscrapers and street traffic in Midtown, it's nice to find private (well, public really, but they can feel otherwise) nooks to have a coffee and snack, read or just take a contemplative break from the hustle.

Ford Foundation Building atrium
See p.137
IBM Building atrium See p.132

Paley Park See p.132
Sony Building atrium See p.132
Sutton Place Park See p.138

---

the African-American shift from the rural south to the urban north. Gallery 14 surrounds the staircase and typically holds a couple of representative works.

Painting and Sculpture II

11

Painting and Sculpture II, the next floor down, displays work from the 1940s to 1970s and inevitably has a more American feel. Gallery 15 features a few artists influenced by New York in the 1940s, namely **Louise Bourgeois** and **Yves Tanguy**; the latter's surrealist canvases capture the confusion of the times. In Gallery 16, the large canvases of Abstract Expressionist giants hold sway: the "zips" of **Barnett Newman**; the "multiforms" of **Rothko**; and, of course, the splatterings of **Pollock**. **De Kooning**'s fierce *Woman I* is also on hand. **Jasper Johns**' *Flag* and **Robert Rauschenberg**'s mixed-media paintings, including the barely-constrained bald eagle of *Canyon*, fill Gallery 17. The remaining galleries survey Pop Art (**Warhol**'s soup cans and *Marilyn Monroe* in 19), Minimalism (look for **Donald Judd**'s *Untitled* wall-mounted box sculpture in 20) and various subsequent movements.

Photography, Architecture and Design, Drawings

The other sections of the museum's collection are just as impressive and shouldn't be missed. On the third floor, the **Photography** galleries are devoted to a rotating selection of exceptional work from visiting artists and the museum's permanent collection – everything from the candid street photos of Paris by **Cartier-Bresson** and **Richard Avedon**'s penetrating portraits of well-known figures to **Helen Levitt**'s colourful shots of unwitting New York characters.

Architecture and Design, on the same floor, hosts revolving exhibits showcasing every aspect of design from the mid-nineteenth century to the present. You'll find illustrations of buildings, works of interior design, lots of glass and ceramics, high-backed chairs and early electronics, and a series of neat large-scale objects like vintage cars, bikes, surfboards, even helicopters.

The **Drawing** galleries, also on the third floor, show revolving exhibitions by a glittering array of twentieth-century artists, including **Pollock**, **Rauschenberg**, **de Kooning**, **Warhol**, **Jasper Johns** and **Roy Lichtenstein**. Finally, the second-floor galleries give MoMA the chance to show its **Contemporary art** in all media, and usually displays works from the 1980s onward, including provocative pieces by **Jeff Koons** and **Gilbert & George**.

53rd Street to Grand Army Plaza

Northward from MoMA, Fifth Avenue's ground floors shift from mundane offices to an elegant stretch of exclusive shops and art galleries. Taking ostentatious wealth to the extreme is **Trump Tower** (not to be confused with Trump World Tower over by the UN, or any other number of "Trump" city properties), at no. 725 at 56th Street. Perfumed air, polished marble panelling and a five-storey waterfall are calculated to knock you senseless with expensive "good taste". The building itself is clever: a neat little outdoor garden is squeezed high in a corner, and each of the 230 apartments above the atrium provides views in three directions. Another atrium, complete with piped-in sounds, connects the tower to the IBM Building (see p.132).

The stores on these blocks are as much sights as shops, with **Gucci**, **Tiffany & Co** and **Bergdorf** among the gilt-edged names (see pp.377–382). At 59th Street, Fifth Avenue reaches **Grand Army Plaza** and the fringes of Central Park, where a golden statue of William Tecumseh Sherman stands guard amid all the highbrow shopping, and the copper-edged 1907 **Plaza Hotel** (see p.269) lords it over the square's western border.

Madison Avenue

Madison Avenue parallels Fifth with some of the grandeur but less of the excitement. In the East 30s, the avenue runs through the heart of the mundane and residential **Murray Hill** neighbourhood, an area distinguished mostly by the presence of the **Morgan Library & Museum**. Heading north to the East 40s and the Upper East Side, you encounter the Madison Avenue of legend, the centre of the international advertising industry in the 1960s and 1970s. Today, this section of town is a major high-end shopping boulevard.

Murray Hill

Madison Avenue is the main artery of **Murray Hill**, a tenuously tagged residential area (no commercial building was allowed until the 1920s) of statuesque, canopy-fronted buildings bounded by East 34th and 40th streets, and lacking any real centre or sense of community. Indeed, you're likely to pass through without even realizing it.

When Madison Avenue was on a par with Fifth as the place to live, Murray Hill was dominated by the Morgan family, including the crusty old financier J.P. and his offspring, who at one time owned a clutch of properties here. Morgan Junior lived in the brownstone house on the corner of 37th Street and Madison (after his death, it became headquarters of the American Lutheran Church, but the Morgan Library eventually bought it back), his father in a house that was later pulled down to make way for an extension to his library next door.

Morgan Library & Museum

225 Madison Ave at E 36th St • Tues–Thurs 10.30am–5pm, Fri 10.30am–9pm, Sat 10am–6pm, Sun 11am–6pm • $15, free Fri 7–9pm, 16 and under $10 • ☎ 212 685 0008, ⓦ themorgan.org • Subway #6 to 33rd St

The uplifting **Morgan Library & Museum**, housed across multiple buildings on properties of industrial magnate J.P. Morgan, is dedicated largely to artefacts of the written and printed word. Morgan would often come to his library, a mock-Roman villa, to luxuriate among the art treasures he had acquired on his trips to Europe: manuscripts, paintings, prints and furniture. A stunning piazza-style gathering space, created by Pritzker Prize-winner Renzo Piano, brings together the building in which Morgan stored his collection, designed by noted architects McKim, Mead, and White, an annexe designed in somewhat similar fashion (that replaced Morgan's old townhouse) and Morgan Junior's brownstone. Piano's renovation, completed in 2006, also doubled the exhibition space and added several new features to the building, including a main entrance on Madison Avenue (you should still head around the corner on E 36th Street to get the best exterior perspective), a subterranean performance hall and a naturally lit reading-room.

The collection of some ten thousand drawings and prints by such greats as Da Vinci, Degas and Dürer is augmented by rare literary manuscripts by Dickens, Austen and Thoreau as well as handwritten correspondence between Ernest Hemingway and George Plimpton, letters from Virginia Woolf and J.R.R. Tolkien, and musical scribblings by everyone from Haydn to Dylan. The museum also typically displays a copy of the Gutenberg Bible (it owns three out of the eleven that survive). Morgan's personal library and study, the crucial pieces of the McKim building, were recently restored; poke around them to see Morgan's extensive personal book archive, various paintings and exquisite office furniture, and take note of the newly opened North Room, which showcases the museum's ancient and medieval holdings. Peek into the vault within his private study – the prizes of his manuscript collection were once held behind the combination-locked door.

11

North of Murray Hill

Leaving behind the relative quiet of Murray Hill, Madison Avenue becomes progressively more commercial the further north one goes. Several good stores – some specializing in men's haberdashery, shoes and cigars – still cater to the needs of the more aristocratic consumer. **Brooks Brothers**, traditional clothiers of the Ivy League and inventors of the button-down collar, occupies a corner of East 44th Street. Between 50th and 51st streets the **Villard Houses**, a replica collection of Italian palazzos (ones that didn't quite make it to Fifth Ave) by McKim, Mead, and White, merit more than a passing glance. The houses have been surgically incorporated into the *New York Palace Hotel*, and the interiors polished up to their original splendour.

Madison's most interesting sight comes in a four-block strip above 53rd Street. The tiny, vest-pocket-sized **Paley Park** is on the north side of East 53rd between Madison and Fifth avenues. Its soothing mini-waterfall and transparent water tunnel are juxtaposed with a haunting five-panel section of the former Berlin Wall. Around the corner, the **Continental Illinois Center** looks like a cross between a space rocket and a grain silo.

A few streets up at East 57th Street, at no. 41–45, is the eye-catching **Fuller Building**. Black-and-white Art Deco, it has a fine entrance and tiled floor. Cut east on 57th Street to no. 57 to find the **Four Seasons Hotel**, notable for sweeping marble and limestone design by I.M. Pei.

Sony Building

550 Madison Ave, between 55th and 56th sts • Subway E, M to Fifth Ave-53rd St

The **Sony Building** (formerly the AT&T Building) has grabbed headlines since its construction thirty years ago – and just managed to make its latest, with the completion of its sale for an astounding $1.1 billion. A Johnson–Burgee collaboration, it follows the postmodernist theory of borrowing from historical styles: a Modernist skyscraper is sandwiched between a Chippendale top and a Renaissance base. The grand, oversized entrance makes you feel quite small indeed, though around the corner, an atrium provides a pleasant enough place to park yourself. The **Sony Wonder Technology Lab**, on the first few floors (see p.407), is a great place for the children, though they can also get some kicks trying out the latest games down in the lower level of the **Sony Store** (see p.408). Of course, these will go, with whatever plans and renovations the new owners put in place.

IBM Building

590 Madison Ave, between 56th and 57th sts • Subway E, M to Fifth Ave-53rd St

The green-tinted faceted **IBM Building** has a far more user-friendly plaza than the Sony Building; note the unusual shape of the structure, too – a pentagonal wedge, with a street-level cutaway. In its calm, glass-enclosed atrium, tinkling music, tropical foliage, a coffee bar and comfortable seating make for an uplifting experience – it also links to the Trump Tower (see p.130).

Park Avenue

In 1929, author Collinson Owen wrote that **Park Avenue** is "where wealth is so swollen that it almost bursts". Things have changed little since. The focal point of the avenue is the hulking **Grand Central Terminal**, at 42nd Street. South of Grand Central, Park Avenue narrows in both width and interest, but to the north of the building it becomes an impressively broad boulevard. Built to accommodate elevated rail tracks, the area quickly became a battleground, as corporate headquarters and refined residences jostled for prominence. Whatever your feelings about conspicuous wealth, from the 40s north, Park Avenue is one of the city's most awesome sights. Its sweeping expanse, genteel facades and sculpture-studded medians capture both the gracious and grand sides of New York in one fell swoop.

TOURS OF GRAND CENTRAL TERMINAL

You'll no doubt find plenty to please the eye just wandering around Grand Central by yourself, but for some context and the odd inside secret, opt for one of the excellent tours run by the **Municipal Arts Society** (every Wed 12.30pm; 1hr 15min; $10 suggested donation; ⓦ mas .org), meeting at the info booth on the main concourse, or the **Grand Central Partnership** (Fri 12.30pm; 1hr 30min–2hr; free; ⓦ grandcentralpartnership.org), which meets across 42nd Street in the atrium at 120 Park Ave. Both will clue you in on the building's architecture and history; the latter walk takes you to a few nearby spots outside Grand Central as well. A third option is a **self-guided audio tour**; pick it up at GCT Tour windows on the main concourse (daily 9am–6pm; $7).

Grand Central Terminal

87 East 42nd St, between Lexington and Vanderbilt aves • ⓦ grandcentralterminal.com • Subway S, #4, #5, #6, #7 to Grand Central-42nd St

Park Avenue hits 42nd Street at Pershing Square, where it lifts off the ground to make room for the massive **Grand Central Terminal**. More than just a train station, the terminal is a full-blown destination in itself. When it was constructed in 1913 (on the site of the original station built by Cornelius Vanderbilt), the terminal was a masterly piece of urban planning. After the electrification of the railways made it possible to reroute trains underground, the rail lines behind the existing station were sold off to developers and the profits went towards the building of a new terminal – built around a basic iron frame but clothed with a Beaux Arts skin. While Grand Central soon took on an almost mythical significance, today its traffic consists mainly of commuters speeding out to Connecticut, Westchester County and upstate New York, and any claim to being a gateway to an undiscovered continent is purely symbolic.

The building

The most spectacular aspect of the building is its **size**, though the MetLife Building (see p.134) dwarfs it in height. The station's main concourse is one of the world's finest and most imposing open spaces, 470ft long and 150ft high. The **barrel-vaulted ceiling** is speckled like a Baroque church with a painted representation of the winter night sky, its 2500 stars shown back to front – "as God would have seen them", the French painter Paul Helleu reputedly remarked. Stand in the middle and you realize that Grand Central represents a time when stations were seen as miniature cities. Walking around the marble corridors and feeling the subtle shifts in dynamics, mood and pace is an elegant and instructive experience you're unlikely to forget.

In addition to its architectural and historical offerings, there are fifty shops here, including those in the tantalizing **Grand Central Market**, which sells every gourmet food imaginable, and more than thirty restaurants, many of which are on the terminal's lower concourse. Chief among the eateries is the *Grand Central Oyster Bar* (see p.310), which is located in the vaulted bowels of the station and is one of the city's most celebrated seafood spots. Just outside of the restaurant is something that explains why the *Oyster Bar's* babble is not solely the result of the people eating there: two people can stand on opposite sides of any of the vaulted spaces and hold a conversation just by whispering, an acoustic fluke that makes this the loudest eatery in town.

For a civilized cocktail, stop into the *Campbell Apartment* (see p.336). The grand one-time home of the terminal's architect, it is found near the terminal's west-side taxi stand.

Around Grand Central

Across East 42nd Street to the south, the former **Bowery Savings Bank**, now one of Harry Cipriani's upscale restaurants, echoes Grand Central's grandeur. **The Grand Hyatt Hotel**, meanwhile, next to Grand Central Terminal on the south side of 42nd Street, is another notable instance of excess, and perhaps the best (or worst) example in the city of all that is truly vulgar about contemporary American interior design. The thundering waterfalls, lurking palms and gliding escalators represent plush-carpeted bad taste at its most meretricious. Meanwhile, the Chrysler Building (see p.136) towers over the station a block east on Lexington Avenue.

MetLife Building

200 Park Ave • Subway S, #4, #5, #6, #7 to Grand Central-42nd St

Just north of Grand Central stands the Bauhaus bulk of the **MetLife Building**, built in 1963 as the Pan Am Building and impressive more for its size than its grandeur. Bauhaus guru Walter Gropius had a hand in designing the structure; the critical consensus is that he could have done better. As the headquarters of the now-defunct international airline, the building, in profile, was meant to suggest an airplane wing. The blue-grey mass certainly adds drama to the cityscape, although it robs Park Avenue of its southern views, sealing off 44th Street and sapping much of the vigour of the surrounding buildings.

11 Helmsley Building

230 Park Ave, at 46th St • Subway S, #4, #5, #6, #7 to Grand Central-42nd St

The high altar of the New York Central Building (built in 1928 and years later rechristened the **Helmsley Building**), a delicate construction with a lewdly excessive Rococo lobby, rises up directly in the middle of Park Avenue; twin tunnels allow traffic to pass beneath it. In its mid-twentieth-century heyday it formed a punctuation mark to the avenue, but its thunder was stolen in 1963 by the completion of the MetLife Building, which looms above and behind it.

St Bartholomew's Church

325 Park Ave, at 51st St • Ⓦ stbarts.org • Subway #6 to 51st St

Crouching just across 50th Street from the Waldorf, **St Bartholomew's Church** is a low-slung Byzantine hybrid with portals designed by McKim, Mead, and White; it adds an immeasurable amount of character to the area, lending the lumbering skyscrapers a much-needed sense of scale. The church fought against developers for years, and ultimately became a test case for New York City's landmark preservation law. Today, its congregation thrives – services are held throughout the week and four times on Sundays – and its members sponsor many community-outreach programmes; the church also serves as a prime place to hear sacred music, with a summer festival dedicated to the genre (June & July), not to mention the largest pipe organ in the city.

Seagram Building

375 Park Ave between 52nd and 53rd sts • Subway E, M to Lexington Ave-53rd St

It may be difficult at first to see the originality of the **Seagram Building**, among the architectural ostentation of its neighbours. Designed by Mies van der Rohe and Philip Johnson, and built in 1958, this was the seminal curtain-wall skyscraper: deceptively simple and cleverly detailed, with floors supported internally rather than by the building's walls, allowing a skin of smoky glass and whisky-bronze metal. Although the facade has now weathered to a dull black, it remains the supreme example of Modernist reason. The **plaza**, an open forecourt designed to set the building apart from its neighbours and display it to advantage, was such a success as a public space that the city revised the zoning laws to encourage other high-rise builders to supply similar plazas.

Lever House

390 Park Ave, between 53rd and 54th sts • Subway E, M to Lexington Ave-53rd St

Across Park Avenue between 53rd and 54th streets is **Lever House**, the building that set the Modernist ball rolling on Park Avenue when it was constructed in 1952. Back then, the two right-angled slabs that form a steel-and-glass bookend seemed

FROM TOP ST PATRICK'S CATHEDRAL (P.127); GRAND CENTRAL TERMINAL (P.133) >

revolutionary when compared with the surrounding buildings. Its vintage appeal helps to make *Casa Lever*, the Italian restaurant on the ground floor (and one with some funky design touches itself), a welcome spot for a drink or meal.

Lexington Avenue

One block east of Park Avenue, **Lexington Avenue** marks a sort of border between East Side elegance and the everyday avenues closer to the East River. It roars into life around 42nd Street and the Chrysler Building, and especially through the mid-40s, where commuters swarm around Grand Central Terminal. From there, Lexington lurches northward past 53rd Street and the towering aluminium-and-glass **Citigroup Center**, to the bulk of **Bloomingdale's** department store at 59th Street, which marks the end of the avenue's Midtown stretch of highlights.

Chrysler Building

11

405 Lexington Ave, at 42nd St • Lobby Mon–Fri 8am–6pm • Subway S, #4, #5, #6, #7 to Grand Central-42nd St

The **Chrysler Building** dates from 1930, a time when architects married prestige with grace and style. For a fleeting moment, this was the world's tallest building; it was surpassed by the Empire State Building in 1931, and is currently tied with the new Times building for third-tallest in the city. However, since the rediscovery of Art Deco, it has become one of Manhattan's best-loved structures. The building's car-motif friezes, hood-ornament gargoyles, radiator-grille spire, and the fact that the entire building is almost completely fashioned from stainless steel, evokes the golden age of motoring. Its designer, William Van Alen, indulged in a feud with an erstwhile partner, H. Craig Severance, who was designing a building at 40 Wall St at the same time. Each was determined to have the higher skyscraper. Van Alen secretly built the stainless-steel spire inside the Chrysler's crown, and when 40 Wall St finally topped out a few feet higher than the Chrysler, Van Alen popped the 185-foot spire out through the top of the building and won the day.

The Chrysler Corporation moved out decades ago, and for a while the building was allowed to decline by a company that didn't wholly appreciate its spirit; fortunately, buyers in the late 1990s took more care and began restoration, while also renovating the **Chrysler Building East** (666 Third Ave), to a plan by Philip Johnson. The lobby (of the main Chrysler Building, that is), once a car showroom, is all you can see, but that's enough in itself. The opulent walls are covered in African marble; the ceiling shows a realistic, if rather faded, study of airplanes, machines and brawny builders who worked on the tower; and the lift doors have magnificent inlaid-wood designs.

Chanin and Mobil buildings

On the south side of 42nd Street flanking Lexington Avenue are two more noteworthy buildings. The **Chanin Building**, at 122 East 42nd St, on the right, is another Art Deco monument, cut with terracotta carvings of leaves, tendrils and sea creatures. Also interesting is the design of the weighty **Mobil Building** at no. 150. Built in 1956, it was the first metal-clad office building in the world at the time. Made with seven thousand panels of chromium-nickel stainless steel, it was designed to enable the wind to keep it clean.

General Electric Building

570 Lexington Ave, at 51st St • Subway #6 to 51st St

Directly behind St Bartholomew's Church (see p.134), the spiky-topped **General Electric Building** seems like a wild extension of the church, its slender shaft rising to a meshed crown of abstract sparks and lightning strokes that symbolize the radio waves used by its original owner, RCA. Not to be confused with the GE Building, better known as 30 Rock (see p.126), this is another Art Deco delight, with nickel-silver ornamentation, carved red marble and a lobby with a vaulted ceiling.

Citigroup Center

153 East 53rd St, between Lexington and Third aves • Subway E, M to Lexington Ave-53rd St

Just as the Chrysler Building dominates the lower stretches of Lexington Avenue, the chisel-topped **Citigroup Center** (better known by its former name of Citicorp Center) towers above northern Midtown. Opened in 1978, the building, now one of New York's most conspicuous landmarks, looks as if it is sheathed in shiny graph paper. Its slanted roof was designed to house solar panels and provide power, but the idea was ahead of the technology and Citicorp, as the company was previously called, had to satisfy itself by adopting the distinctive top as a corporate logo.

St Peter's Lutheran Church

619 Lexington Ave, at 54th St • ⊕ saintpeters.org • Subway E, M to Lexington Ave-53rd St

Hiding under one corner of Citigroup Center is **St Peter's Lutheran Church**, known as "the Jazz Church" for being the venue of many a jazz musician's funeral. It's also host to a long-running jazz-tinged vespers service at 5pm, and there are jazz performances lunchtime on Wednesdays, as well as on Thursdays through summer, plus the occasional evening concert. The tiny church was built to replace the one demolished to make way for Citicorp, and part of the deal was that the church had to stand out from the Center – which explains the granite material. The minimalist, thoroughly modern interior includes sculptor Louise Nevelson's white-walled **Erol Beker Chapel of the Good Shepherd**. Another Nevelson sculpture (*Night Presence IV*) can be seen at East 92nd Street, on the median running down Park Avenue.

Central Synagogue

652 Lexington Ave, at East 55th St • Tours Tues & Wed noon–2pm • Free • ☎ 212 838 5122, ⊕ centralsynagogue.org • Subway E, M to Lexington Ave-53rd St

Striking in its Moorish appearance, the landmark structure that's home to the Reformed **Central Synagogue** was built in 1870–72 by German immigrant Henry Fernbach. The oldest continually used Jewish house of worship in the city, it was nearly razed to the ground in a 1998 blaze; only the ark, a few pews and some of the floor tiles remained, give or take. After three years of extensive rebuilding it reopened, with remade stained-glass windows, a new organ and a markedly different interior design.

Third, Second and First avenues

The construction of the Citigroup Center spurred the development of **Third Avenue** in the late 1970s. One 1980s postmodern entry on that stretch, the so-called **Lipstick Building** at no. 885, is a tiered, oval-shaped steel tower created by Philip Johnson and John Burgee; it also holds the former offices of disgraced (and incarcerated) Ponzi-scheme broker Bernard Madoff. Nightlife, however, congregates on **Second Avenue**, which also has some architectural attractions lying on or around 42nd Street.

Daily News Building

220 East 42nd St • Closed Sat & Sun • Subway S, #4, #5, #6, #7 to Grand Central-42nd St

The stone facade of the sombre yet elegant former **Daily News Building** fronts a surprising Art Deco interior. The most impressive remnant of the original 1929 decor is a large globe encased in a lighted circular frame (with updated geography), made famous by Superman movies when the Daily News Building appropriately housed the Daily Planet. The tabloid after which the building is named has since moved to 450 West 33rd Street.

Ford Foundation Building

320 East 43rd St, between First and Second aves • Subway S, #4, #5, #6, #7 to Grand Central-42nd St

Just north and around the corner from the Daily News Building is one of the city's most peaceful (if surreal) spaces – the **Ford Foundation Building**. Built in 1967, the building featured the first of the atria that are now commonplace across Manhattan. Structurally, the atrium is a giant greenhouse, gracefully supported by soaring granite columns and edged with two walls of offices visible through the windows. This subtropical garden, which changes with the seasons, was one of the first attempts to create a "natural" environment inside a building, and it's astonishingly quiet. Forty-second Street is no more than a murmur outside, and all you can hear is the burble of water, the echo of voices, and the clipped clack of feet on the brick walkways. The indoor/outdoor experience here is one of New York City's great architectural coups.

Tudor City

At the east end of 42nd Street, steps lead up to the 1925 **Tudor City**, which rises behind a tiny tree-filled park. With coats of arms, leaded glass and neat neighbourhood shops, this area is the very picture of self-contained residential respectability. It's an official historic district to boot.

11

United Nations Headquarters

First Ave, between 45th and 46th sts • Guided tours Mon–Fri 9.45am–4.45pm; tours last 45min • $16, ages 5–12 $9; bring ID and call ahead to see if anything is off-limits that day • ☎ 212 963 8687, ⓦ visit.un.org • Subway S, #4, #5, #6, #7 to Grand Central-42nd St

Some see the **United Nations Headquarters** – built after World War II, when John D. Rockefeller, Jr donated $8.5 million to buy the eighteen-acre East River site – as one of the major sights of New York. Others, usually those who've been there, are not so complimentary: despite the symbolism of the UN, few buildings are quite so dull to walk around.

The complex consists of three main sites – the thin, glass-curtained slab of the **Secretariat**; the sweeping curve of the **General Assembly Building**, whose chambers can accommodate more than 191 national delegations; and the low-rise **Conference Wing**, which connects the other two structures. Construction on the complex began in 1949 and finished in 1963, the product of a suitably international team of architects that included Le Corbusier – though he pulled out before work was completed.

Council chambers visited on the tour include the **Security Council**, the **Economic and Social Council** and the **Trusteeship Council** – all of which are similarly retro (note the clunky machinery of the journalists' areas) and sport some intriguing Marxist murals. More revealing are some thoughtful exhibition spaces and artful country gifts on view, including an intricate ivory carving from China and a huge (12ft by 15ft) stained-glass window by artist Marc Chagall, commissioned in 1964 as a memorial to Dag Hammarskjold, the second Secretary-General of the United Nations. Once you've been whisked around all these sites and have seen examples of the many artefacts that have been donated to the UN by its various member states, the tour is more or less over and will leave you in the basement of the General Assembly Building. Where the UN HQ has real class is in its beautiful **gardens**, with their modern sculpture and views of the East River.

Beekman Place and Sutton Place

Outside of the environs of the UN, **First Avenue** has a certain looseness that's a relief after the concrete claustrophobia of Midtown. **Beekman Place** (49th to 51st sts between First Ave and the East River) is quieter still, a beguiling enclave of garbled styles. Similar, though not quite as intimate, is **Sutton Place**, which stretches from 53rd to 59th streets between First Avenue and the East River. Originally built for the lordly Morgans and Vanderbilts in 1875, Sutton Place increases in elegance as you move north. The UN Secretary-General has an official residence at 3 Sutton Place – some 14,000 square feet of living space – and current and past residents include the likes of Sigourney Weaver and I.M.Pei. For the real *crème de la crème*, **Riverview Terrace**, off 58th Street at the river, is a (very) private block-long street filled with a handful of pricey townhouses, though you can sit in (the public) Sutton Place Park for a view of the houses and the river.

TIMES SQUARE

Midtown West

Between West 30th and 59th streets and west of Sixth Avenue, much of Midtown Manhattan is enthralling, noisy and garish, packed with attractions meant to entertain legions of tourists. The heart of Midtown West is Times Square, where jostling crowds and huge neon signs assault the senses, and New York City reaches its commercial zenith. South of Times Square is the business-oriented Garment District, while just north of the once "naughty, bawdy 42nd Street", the Theater District offers the most impressive concentration of live theatre in the world. West beyond Eighth Avenue, the buzzing forces of gentrification are hard at work in Hell's Kitchen and back over in the centre of the island, Sixth Avenue's blend of cultural and corporate New York is good for a stroll.

By public transport Nearly every subway, save the East Side's #4/#5/#6, goes to Midtown West. Central stops include: the B, D, F, M, N, Q, R to 34th St-Herald Square; the N, Q, R, S, #1, #2, #3, #7 to 42nd St-Times Square; and, at the northern end, the A, B, C, D, #1 to Columbus Circle-59th St. And, of course, this is the spot for arrivals and departures to and from Penn Station (trains) and Port Authority (buses).

The Garment District

Squeezing in-between Sixth and Eighth avenues from West 30th to 42nd streets, the **Garment District** (sometimes referred to as the Fashion District), home to the twin modern monsters of Penn Station and Madison Square Garden, offers little of interest to the casual visitor.

With the rise in foreign production, fewer and fewer garments are put together in this tiny (and ever-diminishing) quarter, though it's still responsible for a high percentage of American-made clothing. Walking around, you might just think nothing at all is going on: outlets are almost entirely wholesale and don't bother to woo customers, and the only visible evidence of the industry is the racks of clothes shunted around on the street and occasional bins of off-cuts that give the area the look of an open-air rummage sale.

One of the benefits of walking through this part of town, though, is taking advantage of the designers' sample sales, where floor samples and models' castoffs are sold to the public at cheap prices (see box, p.383).

Greeley Square

Sixth Avenue collides with Broadway just below West 34th Street, making an unremarkable triangle with the somewhat overblown title of **Greeley Square**, in honour of Horace Greeley, founder of the *New York Tribune* newspaper. One could make the case that Greeley deserves better: known for his rallying call to the youth of the nineteenth century ("Go West, young man!"), he also supported the rights of women and trade unions, denounced slavery and capital punishment, and commissioned a weekly column from Karl Marx.

Herald Square

Herald Square opposes Greeley Square across 34th Street, in a continuation of the once fierce rivalry between the *New York Herald* newspaper and Horace Greeley's *Tribune*. (The two papers merged in 1924 to form the *New York Herald Tribune*, which was published until 1967.) During the 1890s, this was the Tenderloin area, with dance halls, brothels and rough bars like Satan's Circus and the Burnt Rag thriving beside the elevated railway that ran up Sixth Avenue. These days its streets are congested with consumers, many heading for the massive Macy's department store adjacent to the square.

Macy's

151 West 34th St • Mon–Fri 9am–9.30pm, Sat 10am–9.30pm, Sun 11am–8.30pm • ☎ 212 695 4400, ⓦ macys.com • Subway B, D, F, M, N, Q, R to 34th St-Herald Square

Macy's bills itself as "the world's largest store", which is only somewhat hyperbolic, considering the building takes up an entire city block and offers well over one million square feet of selling space (the South Korean flagship of Shinsegae actually holds the title). Founded in 1858, the store moved to its current location in 1902, although it wasn't until the 1980s that Macy's went fashionably upmarket, with designers – such as Tommy Hilfiger – building their own shops in-store. Macy's fortunes declined dramatically, however, when the economy went into a tailspin in 1990, but scrambled out of its 1992 bankruptcy in the nick of time, complete with a debt-restructuring plan that allowed it to continue financing its famed annual Thanksgiving Day Parade (see p.403). That nadir seems a far cry from the $400 million renovation the store is

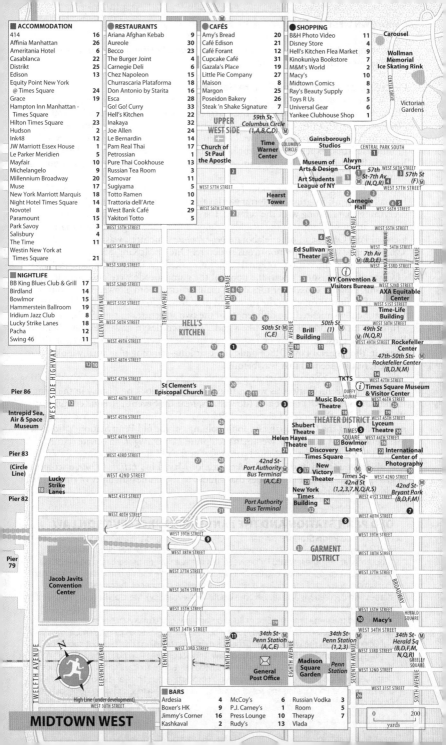

■ ACCOMMODATION

414	16
Affinia Manhattan	26
Ameritania Hotel	6
Casablanca	22
Distrikt	25
Edison	13
Equity Point New York @ Times Square	24
Grace	19
Hampton Inn Manhattan - Times Square	7
Hilton Times Square	23
Hudson	2
Ink48	12
JW Marriott Essex House	1
Le Parker Meridien	5
Mayfair	10
Michelangelo	9
Millennium Broadway	20
Muse	17
New York Marriott Marquis	18
Night Hotel Times Square	14
Novotel	8
Paramount	15
Park Savoy	3
Salisbury	4
The Time	11
Westin New York at Times Square	21

■ NIGHTLIFE

BB King Blues Club & Grill	17
Birdland	14
Bowlmor	15
Hammerstein Ballroom	19
Iridium Jazz Club	8
Lucky Strike Lanes	12
Pacha	12
Swing 46	11

● RESTAURANTS

Ariana Afghan Kebab	9
Aureole	30
Becco	23
The Burger Joint	4
Carnegie Deli	6
Chez Napoleon	15
Churrascaria Plataforma	18
Don Antonio by Starita	16
Esca	28
Go! Go! Curry	33
Hell's Kitchen	22
Inakaya	32
Joe Allen	24
Le Bernardin	14
Pam Real Thai	17
Petrossian	1
Pure Thai Cookhouse	13
Russian Tea Room	3
Samovar	11
Sugiyama	5
Totto Ramen	10
Trattoria dell'Arte	2
West Bank Café	29
Yakitori Totto	5

● CAFÉS

Amy's Bread	20
Café Edison	21
Café Forant	12
Cupcake Café	31
Gazala's Place	19
Little Pie Company	27
Maison	8
Margon	25
Poseidon Bakery	26
Steak 'n Shake Signature	7

● SHOPPING

B&H Photo Video	11
Disney Store	4
Hell's Kitchen Flea Market	9
Kinokuniya Bookstore	7
M&M's World	2
Macy's	10
Midtown Comics	8
Ray's Beauty Supply	3
Toys R Us	5
Universal Gear	6
Yankee Clubhouse Shop	1

■ BARS

Ardesia	4	McCoy's	6
Boxer's HK	9	P.J. Carney's	1
Jimmy's Corner	16	Press Lounge	10
Kashkaval	2	Rudy's	13
		Russian Vodka Room	3
		Therapy	7
		Vlada	5

MIDTOWN WEST

undergoing today, which has already added the "world's largest shoe floor" – boasting a staff of more than four hundred.

Penn Station and Madison Square Garden

The blocks between Seventh and Eighth aves, and W 31st and W 33rd sts • Subway A, C, E, #1, #2, #3 to 34th St-Penn Station

The most prominent landmark in the Garment District, the **Penn Station and Madison Square Garden** complex is a combined box-and-drum structure. At the same time its train-station belly swallows up millions of commuters, its above-ground facilities, expensively refurbished in the past three years, house Knicks' basketball and Rangers' hockey games, as well as professional wrestling and boxing matches (see p.389).

There's nothing memorable about Penn Station (or Pennsylvania Station, as it is formally known); its grimy **subterranean levels** are an example of just about everything that's wrong with the subway. The original 1910 train station, which brought an air of dignity to the neighbourhood and set the stage for the ornate General Post Office and other elaborate *belle époque* structures, was demolished in 1963 to make way for this monstrous structure. One of McKim, Mead, and White's greatest designs, the station's original edifice reworked the ideas of the Roman Baths of Caracalla to awesome effect: the floors of the grand arcade were pink marble, the walls pink granite. Glass floor tiles in the main waiting room allowed light from the glass roof to flow through to the trains and platforms below. Architectural historian Vincent Scully lamented the differences in the two structures in the 1960s, saying, "Through it one entered the city like a god... One scuttles in now like a rat." Some of Penn Station's lost lustre may be restored when – or rather, if – an expanded station opens in the General Post Office building; that long-standing plan finally looks set to happen, but it's seemed that way before.

Glimpses of the **original structure** are visible in photos hanging in the Amtrak waiting area of today's Penn Station, as well as in the four-faced clock on display in the Long Island Railroad (LIRR) ticket area (downstairs, near the Seventh Avenue entrance at West 32nd Street). Andrew Leicester's 1994 *Ghost Series* lines the walls: five terracotta murals saluting the Corinthian and Ionic columns of the old Penn Station. Also look for a rendering of Adolph A. Weinman's sculpture *Day & Night*, an ornate statue surrounding a clock that welcomed passengers at the old station's entrance. Be sure to look above your head in the LIRR ticket area for Maya Lin's *Eclipsed Time*, a sculpture of glass, aluminium and fibre optics that alludes to the immeasurability of time with random number patterns.

12

OLD PENN STATION AND THE LANDMARKS PRESERVATION LAW

When the old **Penn Station** was demolished in 1963 to expand the Madison Square Garden sports complex, the notion of conservation was only a gleam in the eye of its middle-class supporters, at the time few and far between, but ten years later a broad-based power group. Despite the vocal opposition of a few, "modernization" was the theme of the day – so much so that almost nothing of the original building was saved. A number of the carefully crafted statues and decorations actually became landfill for New Jersey's Meadowlands complex just across the Hudson River.

At around the same time, the Singer Building, an early, graceful skyscraper in the Financial District, was demolished to make way for the hulking US Steel Building. In the end, it was public disgust with the wanton destruction of these two buildings that brought about the passing of the **Landmarks Preservation Law**. This act ensures that buildings granted landmark status – a designation based on aesthetic value or historical importance – cannot be destroyed or even altered. The law goes beyond protecting buildings, and also applies to districts, such as Fort Greene and Soho, as well as "scenic" landmarks, including Verdi Square at Broadway and West 73rd Street.

General Post Office

421 Eighth Ave, between 31st and 33rd sts • Mon–Fri 7am–10pm, Sat 9am–9pm, Sun 11am–7pm • Subway A, C, E, #1, #2, #3 to 34th St-Penn Station

Immediately behind Penn Station, the **General Post Office** (aka the James A. Farley Post Office) is a 1913 McKim, Mead, and White structure that survived the push for modernization, and stands as a relic from an era when municipal pride was all about making statements – the block-and-a-half-long building is fronted by twenty Corinthian columns and steps spanning the length of the colonnade. There's still a working post-office branch here – one where you'll find plenty of taxpayers filing up until midnight on April 15 – although the main sorting stations have moved into more modern spaces farther west; a few scattered displays on postal history flesh things out. That said, the building is no architectural dinosaur: there are plans for a new Penn Station for Amtrak to be built inside, keeping the original exterior preserved, though these and other redevelopment plans have been all over the place. Construction finally began in late 2010 to improve the connections between this site (which will be called **Moynihan Station**, after the late New York State Senator Daniel Patrick Moynihan) and Penn Station; this part of the redevelopment is due to be complete in 2016.

Port Authority Bus Terminal

625 Eighth Ave, from W 40th to W 42nd sts • Subway A, C, E to 42nd St-Port Authority Bus Terminal

One of Midtown's more reviled landmarks, the **Port Authority Bus Terminal Building** crouches on Eighth Avenue for a few city blocks. Not long ago, it served as a magnet for down-and-outs, but it is spruced up and remarkably safe now, even if not a place to hang around – unless you're in the mood for some bowling (see p.395). Greyhound buses leave from here, as do several other regional services.

12

Times Square

Forty-second Street meets Broadway at the southern outskirts of **Times Square**, the fulcrum for the Theater District, where the constantly pulsating neon conjures up the notion of a beating heart for Manhattan. The area is certainly always alive with activity. Traditionally a melting pot of debauchery, depravity and fun, for decades the quarter was a place where out-of-towners provided easy pickings for petty criminals, drug dealers and prostitutes. Most of Times Square's legendary pornography and crime are long gone, replaced by sanitized superstores, high-rise office buildings and boutique hotels that have killed off the square's historically greasy appeal. This doesn't mean, though, that the area is without charm, and hundreds of thousands of people still mass here every New Year's Eve, when a giant sparkling ball drops from the top of Times Tower on the stroke of midnight. If you have never seen Times Square, plan your first visit for after dark. Without passing through the square, take a taxi to 57th and Broadway (or the subway to, say, Columbus Circle) and start walking south. The spectacle will open out before your eyes, slowly at first, and then with a rush of energy and animation.

Orientation

Not actually a square at all, Times Square is formed by the intersection between arrow-straight Seventh Avenue and left-leaning Broadway; the latter more or less follows true north through much of the island, which tilts to the northeast. So narrow is the angle between these two thoroughfares that Broadway, which meets Seventh Avenue at 43rd Street, does not begin to strike off on its own again until 48th Street, just above the traffic island of Duffy Square. That stretch has been made into a pedestrianized plaza in an effort to improve traffic flow; there's seating along the way as well. On and off the street are the theatres that host big plays and musicals.

Brief history

Like nearby Greeley and Herald squares, Times Square took its name from a newspaper – the *New York Times* built its offices here in 1904. While the *Herald* and *Tribune* fought each other in ever more vicious circulation battles, the *Times* stood on more restrained ground under the banner "All the news that's fit to print", a policy that has enabled both its survival and its current status as the most powerful newspaper in the country. The newspaper's old headquarters, Times Tower, is at the southernmost end of the square on a small block between 42nd and 43rd streets. Originally an elegant building modelled on Giotto's campanile in Florence, the famous zipper sign displaying the news of the world was added in 1928. In 1965, the building was "skinned" and covered with the lifeless marble slabs visible today. The paper's offices have long since moved, most recently to a 52-storey Renzo Piano tower across from the Port Authority, and most of the printing is done in New Jersey.

Discovery Times Square Exposition

224 West 44th St • Mon–Thurs & Sun 10am–8pm, Fri & Sat 10am–9pm • $27.50, ages 4–12 $19.50 • Tickets ☎ 866 987 9692, exhibition info ☎ 646 368 6759, ⓦ discoverytsx.com • Subway N, Q, R, S, #1, #2, #3, #7 to Times Square-42nd St or A, C, E to 42nd St-Times Square

Not quite a museum, the **Discovery Times Square Exposition** puts on large-scale, specialized exhibits (just a couple a year) in a space once occupied by *The New York Times*. Prices are quite high, but if you don't want to miss that travelling King Tut or Harry Potter spectacular you've been hearing so much about, this site is likely to be your best – that is to say, only – bet to see it.

Times Square Museum and Visitor Center

1560 Broadway, enter on Seventh Ave between 46th and 47th sts • Daily 8am–8pm • Free • ☎ 212 869 1890, ⓦ timessquarenyc.org • Subway N, Q, R, S, #1, #2, #3, #7 to Times Square-42nd St

Home to the usual information dispensers and gift shop, the **Times Square Museum and Visitor Center** goes the extra mile with a small exhibit on the area's history, including some peep-show technology, hats from Broadway shows like *Chicago* and *Cabaret*, a short film on Times Square and, of most interest, the 2008 edition of the ball that drops on New Year's Eve. A sound-and-light show re-creating the celebrated drop takes place every twenty minutes.

The Theater District

Though many of the theatres hosting big-budget musicals and dramas considered to be "Broadway shows" are not technically on that avenue, they are, for the most part,

---

FIVE DISTINCTIVE BROADWAY THEATRES

When choosing a **Broadway show**, you won't necessarily be doing it by virtue of the venue; nevertheless, these theatres all stand out in various ways – regardless of what's on. The Lyceum, Music Box and Shubert are among the 25 Broadway theatres that are designated landmarks.

Helen Hayes Theatre 240 W 44th St, between Seventh and Eighth aves. This modest 1912 theatre is the smallest of the Broadway houses and is done in simple Federal-style architecture.

Lyceum Theatre 149 W 45th St, between Broadway and Seventh Ave. Original facade intact, the Lyceum is one of the few area theatres whose lobby you can poke around without having bought a ticket.

New Victory Theater 209 W 42nd St, between Seventh and Eighth aves. First of the historic theatres to be refurbished – and sanitized – (by Disney) for the new-look Times Square almost twenty years ago; its programming is family oriented (see p.408).

Music Box Theatre 239 W 45th St between Seventh and Eighth aves. The exterior looks like it forms a stage, and the box office marquee is a cool, Deco touch.

Shubert Theater 225 W 44th St, between Seventh and Eighth aves. This playhouse, which hosted *A Chorus Line* during its fifteen-year run (the longest-running show when it closed, though that record has since been surpassed multiple times), has a magnificent interior that belies its simple outward appearance.

WHERE THE STREETS HAVE TWO NAMES

Throughout Midtown (and all the city, really), you'll find **secondary street names** of all stripes: some descriptive, like **Little Brazil** (W 45th between Fifth and Sixth aves) and **Diamond and Jewelry Way** (47th St between Fifth and Sixth aves); some honorary, say, **Jerry Orbach Way** (W 53rd St, at Eighth Ave) or **W.C. Handy Place** (52nd St between Sixth and Seventh aves), and some a bit nonsensical. Take **Sixth-and-a-Half Avenue**, a pedestrianized passageway that cuts through buildings from 51st Street up to 57th Street, in between Sixth and Seventh avenues. It was officially created in 2012 for the benefit of walkers, but the space had of course existed for years – this just put the secret to light. No traffic lights, middle-of-the-street crosswalks… and, of course, easier access to the commercial establishments tucked along the way.

located within a couple of blocks of it in the West 40s (concentrated on 44th and 45th sts), the heart of New York's **Theater District**. The majority of the great venues have been destroyed to make way for office buildings; however, some of the old grandeur still survives in the forty or so that remain (see box, opposite).

The famous neon, so much a signature of Times Square, was initially confined to the theatres and spawned the term "the Great White Way". Today, the illumination is not limited to theatres. Myriad ads, forming one of the world's most garish nocturnal displays, promote hundreds of products and services. Businesses that rent offices here are actually required to allow signage on their walls – the city's attempt to retain the square's traditional feel, paradoxically enough, with the most advanced technology possible.

12

Duffy Square

Bordered by Broadway and Seventh Ave, 45th and 47th sts • Subway N, Q, R, S, #1, #2, #3, #7 to Times Square–42nd St

Not much to look at itself, **Duffy Square** offers an excellent view of Times Square's lights, mega-hotels, theme stores and restaurants. A glass "stairway to nowhere", modest in comparison, is balanced on the renovated **TKTS booth**, which sells half-price, same-day tickets for Broadway shows, whose exorbitant prices these days make a visit to TKTS a necessity (see p.351). A lifelike statue of Broadway's doyen George M. Cohan looks on, while at eye level you can find enough gifts in the souvenir shops for your five hundred closest friends.

Brill Building

1619 Broadway at 49th St • Subway #1 to 50th St or N, R to 49th St

For years a crucial hub in New York's entertainment business, the **Brill Building** is synonymous with the pop music sound of the 1960s. Here (and at a few nearby offices), songwriters such as Burt Bacharach and Hal David, Carole King, Barry Mann and Phil Spector cranked out hit after hit that your parents loved, like "You've Lost That Lovin' Feelin'" and "Walk on By". Unfortunately, running those songs through your head is about all you can do here, save for admire the fine entrance.

Ed Sullivan Theater

1697 Broadway between 53rd and 54th sts • Subway B, D, E to Seventh Ave

Past 50th Street, it's the **Ed Sullivan Theater** that attracts the most people on this stretch of Broadway. Queues wrap around 53rd Street for standby tickets to see the *Late Show with David Letterman* (see p.356), just as they might have fifty years ago for the Ed Sullivan variety show shot on the same stage.

Hell's Kitchen

Sprawling across the blocks west of Times Square to the Hudson River, between 30th and 59th streets, lies Clinton (named for nineteenth-century Governor Dewitt

Clinton), more famously known as **Hell's Kitchen**, an area centred on the restaurants, bars and ethnic delis of Ninth Avenue – the staging set for the excellent Ninth Avenue International Food Festival (@ninthavenuefoodfestival.com) each May.

From Eighth Avenue, walk west on 46th Street, so-called Restaurant Row – the area's preferred haunt for pre- and post-theatre dining, even though most of the strip's eateries are mediocre at best – to arrive in the neighbourhood. The Gothic, red **St Clement's Episcopal Church**, at 423 West 46th Street (@stclementsnyc.org), doubles as a community theatre, very much in keeping with the local vibe.

Brief history

Among New York's most violent and lurid neighbourhoods at one time, Hell's Kitchen was purportedly named for a tenement at 54th Street and Tenth Avenue. More commonly, the term has been attributed to a veteran policeman who went by the sobriquet "**Dutch Fred the Cop**". In response to his young partner's comment – while watching a riot – that the place was hell, Fred reportedly replied, "Hell's a mild climate. This is Hell's kitchen." The area originally contained slaughterhouses and factories that made soap and glue, with sections named "Misery Lane" and "Poverty Row". Irish immigrants were the first inhabitants; Greeks, Puerto Ricans and African-Americans soon joined them. Amid the overcrowding, tensions rapidly developed between (and within) ethnic groups – the rough-and-tumble neighbourhood was popularized in the musical *West Side Story* (1957). A violent Irish gang, the Westies, claimed the streets in the 1970s and early 1980s, but the area has since been cleaned up and is far less dangerous than it ever has been – though as ever you should still keep your wits about you. Trim residential streets counter the odd tatty block, and construction and renovation of luxury apartments and hotels occurs at sometimes breakneck speed. Along with other gentrifiers, there's now a substantial gay community, with nearly as many gay bars and nightspots as in Chelsea or the East Village.

Intrepid Sea, Air & Space Museum

W 46th St and Twelfth Ave at Pier 86 • April–Sept Mon–Fri 10am–5pm, Sat & Sun 10am–6pm; Oct–March Tues–Sun 10am–5pm • $24, ages 7–17 $19, ages 3–6 $12 • ☎ 212 245 0072, @intrepidmuseum.org • Subway A, C, E to 42nd St-Port Authority or C, E to 50th St

If you continue west to the river from Times Square, you'll reach the **Intrepid Sea, Air & Space Museum**. This huge (900ft-long) old aircraft carrier has a distinguished history: it picked up capsules from the Mercury and Gemini space missions and made several tours to Vietnam. It holds an array of modern and vintage air- and sea-craft, including the A-12 *Blackbird*, the world's fastest spy plane, and the USS *Growler*, the only guided-missile submarine open to the public. Interactive exhibits and simulators dominate the interior, but make sure to explore further into the bowels of the carrier, where you can see the crew's dining and sleeping quarters, the anchor room and a lot of navigational gadgets. A retired *Concorde*, formerly operated by British Airways, is also at the pier, though the stats about the aircraft are more remarkable than an inspection of the craft itself. It shares pride of place with the latest big-time addition, the space shuttle *Enterprise*; built in 1976 as a test orbiter, it was never space-ready and has spent the last 25-plus years as property of the Smithsonian Institution. If you're visiting at the end of May, **Fleet Week** (the week leading up to Memorial Day) is a big deal here, and deservedly so, with ships visiting from all corners of the globe, as well as military demonstrations and competitions. In early September (Labor Day weekend), an annual **tugboat festival** (@tugboatroundup.com) is held at the pier next door.

Sixth Avenue

East of Times Square, **Sixth Avenue** is officially named Avenue of the Americas but no New Yorker ever calls it that. While there's little of the ground-floor glitter of Fifth or the razzmatazz of Broadway, the street does more or less separate the business side of

Midtown East from the theatre side of Midtown West (even though Fifth Avenue is where the east–west addresses switch).

International Center of Photography

1133 Sixth Ave at 43rd St • Tues–Thurs, Sat & Sun 10am–6pm, Fri 10am–8pm • $14, 11 and under free; pay what you wish Fri after 5pm • 📞 212 857 0000, 🌐 icp.org • Subway B, D, F, M to 42nd St-Bryant Park or N, Q, R, S, #1, #2, #3, #7 to Times Square-42nd St

Just north of Bryant Park, the **International Center of Photography** was founded in 1974 by Cornell Capa (brother of war photographer Robert Capa). This exceptional museum and school sponsors around twenty exhibits a year dedicated to "concerned photography", avant-garde works and retrospectives of modern masters. Many of the shows focus on holdings from their own extensive permanent collection, which contains basically all of Robert Capa's photography, as well as that of New York sensationalist Weegee.

Rockefeller Center Extension

1211–1271 Sixth Ave, between 47th and 51st sts

The **Rockefeller Center Extension** defines the Sixth Avenue stretch from 47th to 51st streets and gives it whatever visual excitement exists. Following the **Time & Life Building** at 50th Street, three near-identical buildings went up in the 1970s: **Exxon Building**, at no. 1251, **McGraw-Hill Building II**, at no. 1221, and **News Corp Building**, at no. 1211. Though they have none of the romance or style of their predecessor, they at least possess the monumentality. Backing onto Rockefeller Center proper (see p.126), the repeated statement of each building comes over with some power.

AXA Equitable Center

Occupying the block bordered by Sixth and Seventh aves and 51st and 52nd sts • Subway B, D, F, M to 47-50th sts-Rockefeller Center or B, D, E to Seventh Ave

The **AXA Equitable Center** has plenty for the eye in the form of its public art. The entrance to the UBS Building (one part of the Center), at 1285 Sixth Avenue, has a small gallery that occasionally rotates exhibits; the mid-block galleria, connecting pedestrians to the Equitable Tower, is highlighted by a series of Sol Lewitt murals, while Roy Lichtenstein's *Mural with Blue Brushtroke* provides a rush of colour for the atrium at 787 Seventh Avenue.

12

AXA financial office

1290 Sixth Ave, between 50th and 51st sts • Subway B, D, F, M to 47-50th sts-Rockefeller Center

The **AXA financial office** displays Thomas Hart Benton's *America Today* murals. This creation (1931) was celebrated for its representation of ordinary pre-Depression-era Americans from a variety of classes, shown both at work and at leisure. It spurred an interest in murals as public art, and lent momentum to the Federal Arts Project (which provided both employment for artists suffering through the decade, and a morale boost for the rest of the public) in the 1930s. North of here, Sixth Avenue proceeds grandly and placidly for several blocks before reaching the green expanse of Central Park.

57th Street

The area just around **57th Street** from Broadway over to Fifth Avenue competes with Soho and Chelsea as a centre for upmarket art sales. **Galleries** here (see p.369) are noticeably snootier than their downtown relations, and some require appointments for viewings.

Hearst Tower

300 W 57th St, at Eighth Ave • Subway A, B, C, D, #1 to 59th St-Columbus Circle

If you head west from Carnegie Hall on 57th Street, at the intersection with Eighth Avenue you'll hit the **Hearst World Headquarters**, which had its 597ft, Norman

---

HIDDEN GEMS: MIDTOWN WEST

Cheap pints and free hot dogs at
Rudy's See p.337
Japanese snacks at Yakitori Totto
See p.313
Atrium at AXA Equitable Center
See p.147
Wu Liang Ye See p.311

Unfettered art viewing at Art
Students League See below
Cheap Cuban cuisine at Margon
See p.286
Ball drop, Times Square Visitor Center
See p.144

Foster-designed **tower** completed in June 2006. The faceted steel-and-glass skyscraper, with its distinctive triangular pattern, is incongruously attached atop a multi-style six-storey base of precast limestone (built eighty years earlier). It is certified as one of the most environmentally friendly high-rise buildings ever constructed, employing technologies to reduce pollution and energy consumption, while fully utilizing renewable energy sources.

Art Students League of New York

215 W 57th St, between Broadway and Seventh Ave • Mon–Fri 9am–8.30pm, Sat & Sun 9am–4pm (Sun Sept–Dec only) •
ⓦ theartstudentsleague.org • Subway N, Q, R to 57th St

One gallery that provides something other than a quick, uncomfortable browse is the **Art Students League**, built in 1892 by Henry J. Hardenbergh (who later built the *Plaza Hotel*) to mimic Francis the First's hunting lodge at Fontainebleau. Its pedigree is impressive; Ben Shahn and Donald Judd are among the artists who trained here. Besides offering inexpensive art classes to the public, the League allows visitors the chance to observe the instructors and students in action.

Carnegie Hall

57th St at Seventh Ave (there are separate entrances for the box office, museum and Zankel Hall) • Tours Oct–May only, typically Mon–Fri
11.30am, 12.30pm, 2pm & 3pm, Sat 11.30am & 12.30pm, Sun 12.30pm, though call or check web for current schedule, as it can change
with frequency; 1hr; $10 • Tours ☎ 212 903 9765, concert tickets ☎ 212 247 7800, ⓦ carnegiehall.org • Subway N, Q, R to 57th St

Stately **Carnegie Hall** is one of the world's greatest concert venues, revered by musicians and audiences alike. The Renaissance-inspired structure was built in the 1890s by steel magnate and self-styled "improver of mankind" Andrew Carnegie, and the still-superb acoustics ensure full houses most of the year. Tchaikovsky conducted the programme on opening night and Mahler, Rachmaninov, Toscanini, Frank Sinatra and Judy Garland have all performed here (not to mention Duke Ellington, Billie Holiday, the Beatles, Spinal Tap and Lady Gaga). If you're not here for a show, you can take a tour, which concludes in the small, second-floor gallery of memorabilia – a part that's actually open to the public for free.

North to Central Park

A few Carnegie Hall-vicinity apartment buildings are worth a gander on the way to Central Park. An absolute riot of terracotta embellishments cover the facade of **Alwyn Court**, at 180 West 58th Street, though unfortunately you can't enter the building to see the mural and skylight in the courtyard. Around the corner is the **Gainsborough Studios** building, at 222 Central Park South, between Broadway and Seventh Avenue. Built in 1905, it became an official city landmark in 1988 and is notable for the Moravian tiles that dominate the top two floors, as well as the double-storey windows that peer onto Central Park. Note the bust of the building's namesake, English artist **Thomas Gainsborough**, which hovers above the entrance on the facade.

Central Park

"All radiant in the magic atmosphere of art and taste", raved *Harper's* magazine on the occasion of the opening of Central Park in 1876. A slight overstatement, perhaps, although today few people could imagine New York City without this beloved green parcel. Devotedly used by locals and visited by nearly everyone who spends a few days here, it serves purposes as varied as the individuals who take advantage of it: it's an environmental haven; a beach; a playground; a running track; a venue for pop music, opera, theatre and street entertainers; and much more. The Reservoir divides Central Park in two. The larger southern park holds most of the attractions (and people), but the northern park (above 86th Street) is well worth a visit for its wilder natural setting and dramatically quieter ambience.

Brief history

Poet and newspaper editor **William Cullen Bryant** is credited with first publicizing the idea for an open public space in Manhattan in 1844; seven years later, City Hall finally agreed to carry out his plan, paying $5 million for 840 acres north of the (then) city limits at 38th Street, a desolate swampy area occupied at the time by scattered shantytowns whose residents were evicted as planning began to pick up speed.

After a fierce design contest, **Frederick Law Olmsted and Calvert Vaux** were chosen to create the rural paradise they called "Greensward", an illusion of the countryside smack in the heart of Manhattan. They designed 36 elegant bridges, each unique, and planned an ingenious system of four sunken transverse roads to segregate different kinds of traffic.

It took sixteen years and $14 million ($270 million in today's money) to construct the entire park, though the sapling trees planted here didn't reach their full height for five decades. Central Park opened to the public in 1876. At its opening, the powers that be emphasized that Central Park was a "**people's park**", available to all. Though most of the impoverished masses for whom it was allegedly built had neither the time nor the money to travel up to 59th Street from their downtown slums and enjoy it, people eventually started flooding in as the city grew in size and wealth.

The park hit rock bottom in 1973, by which point it had degenerated into a vandalized, crime-infested eyesore on which the bankrupt city had no money to spare. It was only the suggestion that the park would be turned over to the National Park Service that mobilized both politicians and local citizens to find funds to refit it. The ongoing effort is now overseen by a feisty nonprofit group called the **Central Park Conservancy** (see box, opposite), which works in conjunction with the city government to maintain the park.

ARRIVAL AND DEPARTURE

By subway The park can be accessed from the east or west sides roughly every six or seven blocks; to see the greatest concentration of sights, your most logical starting places include the A, B, C, D and #1 stop at 59th St–Columbus Circle; the N, Q, R at Fifth Ave–59th St; and the B, C stop at 72nd St.

INFORMATION

Visitor centres The nonprofit Central Park Conservancy (☎ 212 310 6600, ⓦ centralparknyc.org), founded in 1980, is dedicated to preserving and managing the park. It runs five visitor centres, which have free maps and other helpful literature. The centres are: the Chess & Checkers House (64th St at mid-park; 10am–5pm: Nov–March Wed–Sun; April–Oct Tues–Sun; ☎ 212 794 4064); the Dairy (65th St at mid-park; daily 10am–5pm; ☎ 212 794 6564); Belvedere Castle (79th St at mid-park; daily 10am–5pm; ☎ 212 772 0210); the North Meadow Recreation Center (mid-park at 97th St; 10am–5pm: April–Oct Tues–Sun; Nov–March Wed–Sun; ☎ 212 348 4867); and the Charles A. Dana Discovery Center (110th St off Fifth Ave; 10am–5pm: April–Oct Tues–Sun; Nov–March Wed–Sun; ☎ 212 860 1370).

Restrooms Heckscher Playground (61st St at mid-park), Arsenal (64th St at Fifth Ave), *Tavern on the Green* (67th St near Central Park West), the Boat Pond (Conservatory Water), Mineral Springs House (northwest end of Sheep's Meadow), Bethesda Terrace, Loeb Boathouse, the Delacorte Theater, the East 85th Street Playground (aka the Ancient Playground, near Fifth Ave), the Tennis House (94th St at mid-park), the North Meadow Recreation Center, the Conservatory Garden, the Robert Bendheim Playground (East 100th St at Fifth Ave), the Great Hill and the Charles A. Dana Discovery Center.

Urban Park Rangers ☎ 212 628 2345, ⓦ nycpgovparks .org. Rangers lead walking tours, give directions, provide necessary first-aid and even organize camping trips.

Safety You should be fine during the day, though always be alert to your surroundings and try to avoid being alone in an isolated part of the park. After dark, stick to busy areas. If you're there for a public event in the evening, make sure to leave when the crowds do. Emergency phone boxes can be found throughout the park and along the four transverses; they connect to the Central Park Precinct.

NAVIGATING THE PARK

Central Park is so enormous that it's nearly impossible to miss entirely and as impossible to cover in one visit. The intricate **footpaths** that meander through the park are some of its greatest successes. If you've lost your way among them, though, there are several tricks to finding it again. Every feature has a name in order that a rendezvous can be precise. Even the bodies of water are differentiated (a loch, a pool, a lake and even a meer) so that there can never be confusion. But if you do need **to figure out where you are**, find the nearest lamppost. The first two digits on the post indicate the number of the nearest cross street, while the last two show whether you're nearer the east side (odd numbers) or west side (even). You can pick up free maps at any of the visitor centres (see above) or two dozen freestanding unmanned kiosks throughout the park. Organized walking tours (see above) are available from a number of sources, including the Urban Park Rangers and the visitor centres, but almost any stroll, formal or informal, will invariably lead to something interesting.

CYCLING

To make their way around from place to place, people typically either walk (there are no bus routes within the park) or don rollerblades and glide there. Other options include **renting a bike** – West Drive, East Drive and the 72nd Street Cross Drive all have specified car-free hours, allowing you to create various loops around the park in relative freedom. All bicycle rental shops require a credit card or refundable cash deposit.

Bike and Roll 59th St and Columbus Circle ☎ 212 260 0400, ⓦ bikeandroll.com. Offers bike hire from the southwest corner of the park ($12–20 /hr, $39–69/day).

Loeb Boathouse E 72nd St and Park Drive North ☎ 212 517 2233, ⓦ thecentralparkboathouse .com. Bicycles are available for hire from this lakeside shop for $9–15/hr, $45–50/day (see p.154).

Master Bike Shop NYC 265 W 72nd, between Broadway and West End Ave ☎ 212 580 2355, ⓦ masterbikeshop.com. Reputable spot (also well placed for Riverside Park) with very good rates – adult bikes start at $20/4hr and $40/day.

Metro Bicycles 1311 Lexington Ave at 88th St ☎ 212 427 4450, ⓦ metrobicycles.com. Just east of the park, Metro Bicycles offer cheap hourly rates, at $9/hr ($45–55/day). Look online for their other shops, since another may be closer to you.

HORSE AND CARRIAGE

Since 1994 a law protects the horses pulling the carriages ($34 for 30min; ☎ 212 736 0680, ⓦ centralparkcarriages.com). They must get fifteen-minute rest breaks every two hours, and they cannot work more than nine hours a day or in temperatures above 90ºF (32ºC).

13 The southern park: 59th to 86th streets

Many visitors enter the park at Grand Army Plaza (Fifth Ave and 59th St); the sights below are roughly organized as a tour from there up to 86th Street, though you can obviously dip in and out from neighbouring points along the Upper East and West sides. Highlights in this busier part of the park include Central Park Zoo and Strawberry Fields, a tribute to John Lennon.

Wollman Memorial Rink and Victorian Gardens

63rd at mid-park • **Ice-skating** Nov–March Mon & Tues 10am–2.30pm, Wed & Thurs 10am–10pm, Fri & Sat 10am–11pm, Sun 10am–9pm • Mon–Thurs $11, Fri–Sun $17; skate rentals $7 • ☎ 212 439 6900, ⓦ wollmanskatingrink.com • **Amusement park** Late May–early Sept; check website for opening hours as can vary, although generally Mon–Thurs 11am–7pm, Fri 11am–8pm, Sat 10am–9pm, Sun 10am–8pm • $7 weekdays, $8 weekends; rides extra • ⓦ victoriangardensnyc.com • Subway N, Q, R to Fifth Ave-59th St

Just north of **The Pond**, with its tiny nature sanctuary in the far southeast corner of Central Park, is the Trump-run **Wollman Memorial Rink**. Don blades for some of the city's most atmospheric ice-skating; you're surrounded by onlookers, trees and, beyond that, a brilliant view of Central Park South's skyline. In summers, the rink becomes **Victorian Gardens**, a small amusement park with rides and carnival-style entertainment.

Central Park Zoo

64th St and Fifth Ave • April–Oct Mon–Fri 10am–5pm, Sat, Sun & holidays 10am–5.30pm; Nov–March daily 10am–4.30pm • $12, ages 3–12 $7, 2 and under free • ☎ 212 439 6500, ⓦ centralparkzoo.com • Subway N, Q, R to Fifth Ave-59th St

The small, welcoming **Central Park Zoo** has over a hundred species on view in mostly natural-looking homes. The animals are as close to the viewer as possible: the penguins, for example, swim around at eye level in Plexiglas pools. Other highlights include giant polar bears, a humid tropical zone filled with exotic birds, and the sea lions, which cavort in a pool right by the zoo entrance. This complex also boasts the **Tisch Children's Zoo**: there's a petting area, interactive displays and a musical clock just outside the entrance that draws rapt children at the start of each hour. The zoo is a charming stop-off for an hour or two, but if you're a dedicated animal-lover or have older children, you're better off heading to the Bronx Zoo (see p.254).

Dairy

65th St at mid-park • Daily 10am–5pm • Check ⓦ centralparknyc.org for weekend walking tours times and routes

Close to Central Park Zoo stands the **Dairy**, a cutesy yellow neo-Gothic chalet built in 1870 as a café. Despite local lore, there were never any cows here, though it did sell milk for children. It's now one of the park's visitor centres (see p.151): weekend walking tours often leave from it and you can also pick up pieces for the **Chess and Checkers Pavilion** (itself another visitor centre), near the zoo as well.

Carousel

64th St at mid-park • Daily 10am–6pm weather permitting (call in winter months) • $2.50 • ☎ 212 439 6900 • Subway A, B, C, D, #1 to 59th St-Columbus Circle

Just west of the Dairy, an octagonal brick building houses the **Carousel**. Built in 1903 and moved to the park from Coney Island in 1951, this is one of the park's little gems. There are fewer than 150 such vintage handmade carousels left in the country (others in New York City are in Prospect Park, Dumbo, Flushing-Meadows Park and Forest Park). A ride on it is a magical experience: its wood-carved, colourfully painted jumping horses are accompanied by the music of a military-band organ.

The Mall

Heading north from the Dairy, you'll pass through the avenue of trees known as **The Mall**. The trees, whose branches tangle together to form a "roof" (hence its nickname, "The Cathedral"), are elms, a rarity in America. The statues that line the avenue are all literary and artistic greats: Shakespeare arrived first, and others from across the world

13

soon followed, often privately funded by the appropriate immigrant groups – hence Italy's Mazzini and Germany's Beethoven. At the base of The Mall is one of only two acknowledgements to either park architect: a small memorial garden in Frederick Law Olmsted's name. Poor Calvert Vaux wasn't commemorated anywhere until April 2008, when the 72nd Street transverse was rechristened "Olmsted & Vaux Way".

Sheep Meadow

Between 66th and 69th sts • **Bowling and croquet** $30 • Permits are available from the Arsenal at Fifth Ave and 64th St • ☎ 212 360 8133 (permit info only) • **Volleyball courts** Free (although you'll need to bring your own ball) • Subway B, C to 72nd St

West of The Mall lies the **Sheep Meadow**, fifteen acres of commons where sheep grazed until 1934, when they were banished to Brooklyn's Prospect Park. In the summer, the meadow is crowded with picnickers, sunbathers and Frisbee players. Two grass bowling and croquet lawns are maintained on a hill near the Sheep Meadow's northwest corner; to the southeast are a number of very popular volleyball courts. On warm weekends, an area between the Sheep Meadow and the north end of The Mall is usually filled with rollerbladers dancing to funk, disco and hip-hop – one of the best free shows in town.

Bethesda Terrace and Fountain

72nd St at mid-park • Subway B, C to 72nd St

At the northernmost point of The Mall lie the **Bandshell** and **Rumsey Playfield**, the sites of the free SummerStage performance series (see box, p.156). There's also the **Bethesda Terrace and Fountain**, one of the few formal elements planned by Olmsted and Vaux. The crowning centrepiece of the fountain is the nineteenth-century *Angel of the Waters* sculpture, the only statue included in the original park design. Its earnest puritanical angels were recently made famous again by Tony Kushner's Pulitzer Prize-winning play *Angels in America*, of which the last scene is set here. The subterranean arcade boasts a series of intricate, multihued Minton tiles on its ceiling, a star turn of the park's original design.

Cherry Hill Fountain

West of Bethesda Terrace, along 72nd St at mid-park • Subway B, C to 72nd St

Originally a turnaround point for carriages, the **Cherry Hill Fountain** was designed to have excellent views of the Lake, The Mall and the Ramble. One of the pretty areas paved by city planner Robert Moses in the 1930s for use as a car park, it was restored to its natural state in the early 1980s.

Strawberry Fields

72nd St and Central Park West • Subway B, C to 72nd St

Strawberry Fields is a peaceful area dedicated to John Lennon, who was murdered in 1980 in front of his home at the Dakota Building, across the street on Central Park West (see p.188). Strawberry Fields is typically crowded with those here to remember Lennon, at no time more so than on December 8, the anniversary of his murder. Near the West 72nd Street entrance to the park is a round Italianate mosaic with the word "Imagine" at its centre, donated by Lennon's widow, Yoko Ono, and frequently covered with flowers. This is also a favourite spot for picnickers.

TAVERN ON THE GREEN

In headier days, *Tavern on the Green* was not just one of the city's best-known restaurants; it was one of the country's highest-grossing. Festooned with Christmas lights, familiar from appearances in *The Out of Towners* and *Ghostbusters*, among many more films, it was a celebrity hangout and party spot *du jour* – though after a few scandals and an economic downturn, the party was snuffed out in 2009. The rambling building, at West 66th Street and Central Park West, was briefly reborn as a park visitor centre but is now revived as a (slightly less formal and pricey) restaurant, albeit one opening too late for review in this book.

13

> ### PICNICKING IN THE PARK
> Central Park has ample **picnicking opportunities**, the most obvious of which is the hectic, perpetually crowded expanse of the Sheep Meadow. For (a very little) more peace and quiet, you might try one of these other fine locations: the western shore of the Lake, near Hernshead; the lawn in front of Turtle Pond, which has a nice view of Belvedere Castle; the Conservatory Garden; the lawn immediately north of the Ramble; Strawberry Fields; the Arthur Ross Pinetum; Cherry Hill; and the areas around the Delacorte Theater.

Lake

72nd to 77th sts at mid-park • **Boat rental** April–Nov daily 10am–dusk, weather permitting • Rowboats $12 for the first hr, $2.50 each 15min thereafter, $20 refundable cash deposit • **Gondola rides** Daily 5–9pm • $30 per 30min (up to six people per boat), reservation required • ☎ 212 517 2233, ⓦ thecentralparkboathouse.com • Subway B, C to 72nd St

Bethesda Fountain overlooks the **Lake**, where you can go for a Venetian-style gondola ride or rent a rowboat from the **Loeb Boathouse** on the eastern bank. You can also rent bikes here. The narrowest point on the lake is crossed by the elegant cast-iron-and-wood **Bow Bridge**.

Boat Pond

72nd to 75th sts and Fifth Ave • Subway #6 to 77th St • **Model-boat races** Sat mornings in the summer; participate by showing up at the green boat-rental kiosk near the Kerbs Memorial Boat House (generally Mon–Fri & Sun 11am–7pm, Sat 1–7pm, though sometimes later on weekends) • $11 for 30min • ☎ 917 522 0054, ⓦ sailthepark.com • **Storytelling** June–Sept Sat 11am–noon • Free

To the east of Bethesda Terrace is the **Boat Pond** – or Conservatory Water – where **model-boat races** are held every Saturday morning in the summer; you can show up to watch that or participate yourself any other time. The fanciful *Alice in Wonderland* statue at the northern end of the pond was donated by publisher George Delacorte and is a favourite climbing spot for kids. In the summer, the Hans Christian Andersen Storytelling Center sponsors Saturday-morning **storytelling** sessions for children at the *Hans Christian Andersen* statue on the west side of the pond.

The Ramble

Take the Bow Bridge if you want to amble to **The Ramble** on the Lake's northern banks, a 37-acre area of unruly woodland, filled with narrow winding paths, rocky outcrops, streams and an array of native plant life. Once a favourite spot for drug dealers and anonymous sex, it is now a great place to watch for one of the park's two-hundred-plus species of bird or take a quiet daytime stroll. Clean-up notwithstanding, steer clear of this area at night.

Great Lawn

81st St at mid-park • Subway B, C to 81st St-Museum of Natural History

Behind the **Metropolitan Museum of Art** (see p.157) stands the **Obelisk**, the oldest structure in the park, which dates from 1450 BC. It was a gift to the city from Egypt in 1881 and, like its twin on the Thames River in London, is nicknamed "Cleopatra's Needle". Immediately west of the needle is the **Great Lawn**. It was the site of the park's original reservoir from 1842 until 1931, when the water was drained to create a playing field. Years later, the lawn became a popular site for free concerts and rallies (Simon & Garfunkel, Elton John, Garth Brooks, Sting, and the Pope, who celebrated Mass here in 1995, have all attracted crowds numbering over half a million), but it was badly overused and had serious drainage problems. Reopened in late 1997 after a massive two-year, $18-million reconstruction, the lawn's engineering and sandy soil now mean that even if there's a heavy downpour at lunchtime, the grass will be dry by evening. Rebuilt, reseeded and renewed, it will hopefully stay that way by only hosting the more sedate, free New York Philharmonic and Metropolitan Opera concerts (see box, p.156). The lawn features eight softball fields and, at its northern end, basketball and volleyball courts and an eight-mile running track; a four-acre pine-tree stand is at the northwest corner.

13

Turtle Pond

The refurbished **Turtle Pond** is at the southern end of the Great Lawn, with a new wooden dock and nature blind designed for better views of the aquatic wildlife (yes, there actually is wildlife here, including ducks, fish and frogs). Note the massive statue of fourteenth-century Polish king **Wladyslaw Jagiello** on the southeast corner of the pond, donated by the Polish government as a Holocaust memorial.

Delacorte Theater and Shakespeare Garden

Southwest of the Great Lawn is the **Delacorte Theater**, the venue of the annual free Shakespeare in the Park festival (see box, p.156). In another of the park's Shakespearean touches, the theatre features Milton Hebald's sculptures of Romeo and Juliet and *The Tempest's* Prospero, while the tranquil **Shakespeare Garden** next door claims to hold every species of plant or flower mentioned in the Bard's plays.

Belvedere Castle and Vista Rock

Daily 10am–5pm

The grey stone pile of **Belvedere Castle**, a mock medieval citadel erected on top of **Vista Rock** in 1869 as a lookout on the highest point in the park, edges just south of Turtle Pond. It's still a splendid viewpoint – its terraces prime perches for birdwatchers – and houses the New York Meteorological Observatory's weather centre; there's also a handy visitor centre here (see p.151).

Swedish Cottage Marionette Theatre

79th St at mid-park • Most of the year Mon–Fri 10.30am & noon plus an extra show on Wed afternoon, Sat & Sun 1 & 3pm • $10, 12 and under $7 • ☎ 212 988 9093 • Subway B, C to 81st-Museum of Natural History

For plays of the puppet kind, check out the wooden **Swedish Cottage Marionette Theatre** at the base of Vista Rock, which holds fun shows aimed at young kids. The structure was imported from Sweden in 1876 for a world's fair and placed in the park in 1877; it's been redone a few times since.

The northern park

There are fewer attractions – but more open spaces – above the Great Lawn. Much of the northern park is taken up by the **Reservoir** (86th–97th sts at mid-park, main entrance at 90th St and Fifth Ave), a 107-acre, billion-gallon reservoir originally designed in 1862 and no longer active. It's a favourite for sporty uptown residents: the raised 1.58-mile track is a great place to get 360-degree views of the skyline. North of the reservoir are a tennis-court complex (☎212 280 0205 for reservations; see p.393) and the soccer and baseball fields of the **North Meadow Recreation Center** (97th St at mid-park; ☎212 348 4867). The landscape north of here, in the aptly named North Woods, feels more like upstate New York than Manhattan: the ninety-acre area contains man-made but natural-looking stone arches plus the **Loch**, which is now more of a stream, and the **Ravine**, which conceals five small waterfalls.

Conservatory Garden

East 104th–106th sts along Fifth Ave with entrance at 105th • Daily 8am–dusk • Subway #6 to 103rd St

If you see nothing else in the park above 86th Street, don't miss the **Conservatory Garden**. Filled with flowering trees and shrubs, planted flowerbeds, fanciful fountains and shaded benches, the space actually houses three gardens, each landscaped in a distinct style. You'll first walk through the Italian garden, a reserved oasis with neat lawns and trimmed hedges. To the south is the English area, enhanced by the Burnett Fountain, which depicts the two children from F.H. Burnett's classic book *The Secret Garden*. The French garden, the northernmost of the three, hosts sculptor Walter Schott's *Three Dancing Maidens* – as well as some twenty thousand tulips in spring.

13

TOP FIVE SUMMER PARK EVENTS

Central Park holds **events** throughout the year, but summer is undoubtedly the busiest and most popular time for such celebrations. Best of all, most of the events are free and open to anyone willing to brave a queue, the crowds, the heat or whatever else might get thrown your way.

Harlem Meer Performance Festival 110th St between Fifth and Lenox aves ☎ 212 860 1370. Offers fairly intimate and enjoyable free performances of jazz and salsa music outside the Charles A. Dana Discovery Center on Sun (mid-June to early Sept 2–4pm).

Metropolitan Opera in the Park ☎ 212 362 6000, ⓦ metoperafamily.org. This could be the least stuffy way to enjoy a night at the opera. Performances occur in city parks in July & Aug; here, it might be at SummerStage or on the Great Lawn.

New York Philharmonic in the Park ☎ 212 875 5709, ⓦ nyphil.org. The Philharmonic holds a few evenings of classical music in the summer, usually in July on the Great Lawn (some in other parks around the boroughs) and often with a booming fireworks display to usher the crowds home.

Shakespeare in the Park ☎ 212 539 8750, ⓦ shakespeareinthepark.org. Probably the most anticipated annual happening, Shakespeare in the Park takes place at the open-air Delacorte Theater (performances Tues–Sun at 8pm, approx early June–early Aug; see p.155). Pairs of free tickets are distributed daily at 1pm for that evening's performance, but you'll have to get in line early, as a crowd often gathers by 7am. Alternatively, pick them up at the Public Theater, at 425 Lafayette St (see p.352), from 1pm on the day of the performance or try for a ticket via their online draw—register on the website.

SummerStage Rumsey Playfield near 72nd St and Fifth Ave ☎ 212 360 2777, ⓦ cityparksfoundation .org/summerstage. SummerStage presented its inaugural Central Park concert in 1986, with Sun Ra performing to an audience of fifty people. When he returned with Sonic Youth six years later, the audience numbered ten thousand. Musical acts cover pretty much every genre during the festival's mid-June to mid-Aug run. Dance performances, DJ sets and (paid admission) benefit shows also share the stage.

Harlem Meer

East 106th–110th sts, near Fifth Ave • Subway #2, 3 to Central Park North-110th St

At the top of the park is the **Charles A. Dana Discovery Center**, an environmental education centre and visitor centre (see p.151). Crowds of locals fish in the adjacent **Harlem Meer**, an eleven-acre pond stocked with more than fifty thousand fish. The Discovery Center provides free bamboo fishing poles and bait.

Lasker Pool and Rink

North end of the park, near 110th St and Lenox Ave entrance • **Ice rink** Nov–March Mon, Wed & Thurs 10am–3.45pm, Tues 10am–3.30pm & 8–10pm, Fri 10am–5.15pm & 7–11pm, Sat 1–11pm, Sun 12.30–4.30pm • $7, 11 and under $4, skate rentals $6 • **Pool** July & Aug daily 11am–3pm & 4–7pm • Free

Just south of Harlem Meer, the **Lasker Rink** provides another place to ice-skate in the park – usually less crowded than Wollman Rink save for the occasional school group. The pool opens during a few months in summer; bring a lock with you to store your stuff.

Duke Ellington monument

110th St and Fifth Ave

In the extreme northeast of the park is a 1997 monument to **Duke Ellington**, the esteemed musician and composer of such classics as *Mood Indigo*. On top of the three columns that summon the nine Muses, the Duke stands before his grand piano, symbolically looking toward Harlem for the next generation of musical vanguards.

Blockhouse

In the park's northwestern corner stands the **Blockhouse**, one of the few landmarks still awaiting renovation: one of several such houses built as a lookout over pancake-flat Harlem during the War of 1812, it's the only one which remains. Now a ruin perched atop a small hill, it's a picturesque but iffy place to visit even during the daytime – stick to seeing it on one of the park's scheduled tours.

The Metropolitan Museum of Art

One of the greatest collections of art treasures in the world, the Metropolitan Museum of Art, or the Met, as it's usually called, owns over two million works of art spanning five thousand years of world culture – almost every civilization on earth is represented. The range is staggering: enough gold, bronze and marble to sink an aircraft carrier, Persian daggers, Baroque arquebuses, Art Deco sofas, Old Masters by the tonne, whole interiors of homes, palaces and chapels, an entire Egyptian temple and Impressionists by the hundreds. Take your time: recent renovations have made the Met a real joy to explore, with plenty of sun-lit courtyards and cafés strategically placed for rest and contemplation.

The main entrance to the museum leads to the **Great Hall**, a deftly lit Neoclassical cavern where you can consult floor plans (including room-by-room gallery maps for the European Paintings and Nineteenth-Century Paintings collections), check tour times and pick up info on the Met's excellent lecture listings. Straight across from the entrance is the **Grand Staircase**, which leads to, for many visitors, the museum's single greatest attraction – the European Paintings galleries.

Brief history

14

The Met was created in 1870 by the New York State Legislature as a kind of civic education project, opening in a brownstone downtown two years later. It decamped to its present site in Central Park, a Gothic Revival building designed by Jacob Wrey Mould and Calvert Vaux, in 1880. Over time, various additions to the site have completely surrounded the original structure; the museum's familiar multi-columned, wide-stepped facade on Fifth Avenue was conceived by Richard Morris Hunt and completed in 1902, while the north and south wings were added by McKim, Mead, and White between 1911 and 1913.

ARRIVAL AND DEPARTURE

By subway Take subway #4, #5 or #6 to 86th St-Lexington Ave, and walk one block west to Fifth Ave.

The museum is at 1000 Fifth Ave, at E 82nd St, set into Central Park.

INFORMATION

Opening hours Mon–Thurs & Sun 10am–5.30pm, Fri & Sat 10am–9pm; ☏ 212 535 7710, ⦿ metmuseum.org. Note that the Met is so big that some sections may be closed for renovation when you visit.

Tickets There is no set admission price, but the suggested donation is $25, $17 for senior citizens and $12 for students. Includes admission to the Cloisters (see p.210). These suggested amounts are exactly that: whether you pay $1 or $10, the cashier won't flinch, so if you can, spread out your exploration over several days. Audio guides are $7.

Tours The museum runs free guided tours daily. Call or check the website for schedules.

European Paintings

The Met's **European Paintings galleries** (600–632), located on the second floor at the top of the Grand Staircase, are organized roughly by nationality and period. They begin with huge works by **Tiepolo** (Gallery 600) and a room full of eighteenth-century French portraits by the likes of Elizabeth Vigée-Lebrun, Marie-Denise Villers and Jacques-Louis David (Gallery 601).

Spanish paintings

Turning right at Gallery 601 brings you to the **Spanish** section; highlights include **Goya**'s widely reproduced portrait of a toddler in a red jumpsuit, *Manuel Osorio Manrique de Zuniga*, in Gallery 623; **Velázquez**'s piercing and sombre *Portrait of Juan de Pareja* in Gallery 618; and a room of freaky, dazzling canvases by **El Greco** (Gallery 619), each of which underscores the jarring modernism of his approach. In solitary contrast is his wraith-like *View of Toledo*, one of the best of his works displayed anywhere in the world.

Italian paintings

The central galleries contain **Italian paintings**, with **Duccio**'s sublime *Madonna and Child* currently holding court in Gallery 602. Described by the Met as "one of the great single acquisitions of the last half century", the delicately crafted painting is an extremely rare example of early Renaissance art, acquired by the Met in 2004 for around $45 million. The collection continues with the Sienese School before moving into the High Renaissance, with **Botticelli**'s tiny *Last Communion of St Jerome* one of the few high points (Gallery 605); other standouts include works by **Mantegna** and

METROPOLITAN MUSEUM OF ART

14

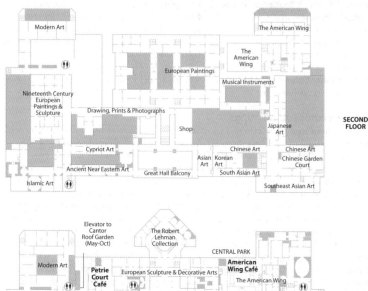

SECOND FLOOR

Modern Art

The American Wing

The American Wing

European Paintings

Musical Instruments

Nineteenth Century European Paintings & Sculpture

Drawing, Prints & Photographs

Japanese Art

Shop

Cypriot Art

Chinese Art

Chinese Art

Chinese Garden Court

Ancient Near Eastern Art

Asian Art

Korean Art

Great Hall Balcony

South Asian Art

Islamic Art

Southeast Asian Art

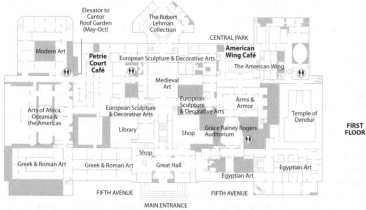

FIRST FLOOR

Elevator to Cantor Roof Garden (May–Oct)

The Robert Lehman Collection

CENTRAL PARK

Modern Art

Petrie Court Café

European Sculpture & Decorative Arts

American Wing Café

The American Wing

Medieval Art

Arts of Africa, Oceania & the Americas

European Sculpture & Decorative Arts

European Sculpture & Decorative Arts

Arms & Armor

Temple of Dendur

Library

Shop

Grace Rainey Rogers Auditorium

Greek & Roman Art

Greek & Roman Art

Shop

Great Hall

Egyptian Art

Egyptian Art

FIFTH AVENUE

FIFTH AVENUE

MAIN ENTRANCE

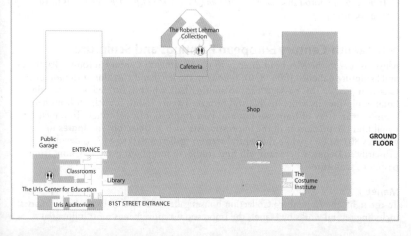

GROUND FLOOR

The Robert Lehman Collection

Cafeteria

Shop

Public Garage

ENTRANCE

Classrooms

Library

The Uris Center for Education

The Costume Institute

Uris Auditorium

81ST STREET ENTRANCE

Carlo Crivelli (Gallery 606), as well as an outstandingly preserved chunk of **Ghirlandaio fresco**, *St Christopher and the Infant Christ*, in Gallery 607. As for later pictures, there's Mannerist master **Bronzino**'s dapper but haughty *Portrait of a Young Man* and a showy **Raphael**, *Madonna and Child Enthroned with Saints*, which features his signature, pin-up-pretty *Virgin Mary* (both in Gallery 608). There are also rooms filled with massive works by **Titian** and **Tintoretto** (Gallery 609), though it's **Veronese**'s raunchy and artfully composed *Mars and Venus United by Love* that's especially appealing among the Venetians (also Gallery 609). Also in Gallery 609 is the much-reproduced painting of **Christopher Columbus** attributed to Sebastiano del Piombo, though many scholars now doubt its authenticity.

Northern European paintings

Galleries dedicated to Northern European schools surround the Italian rooms, with **Vermeer** particularly well represented. Most haunting of all is his *Study of a Young Woman* in Gallery 616; she's an odd-looking creature with huge, doleful eyes and twinkly earrings, her enigmatic expression making her Vermeer's own *Mona Lisa*. While Vermeer's paintings focused on stillness and light, the portraits of **Hals** and **Rembrandt** burst with life. At first, galleries 614 and 615 simply seem full of men in jaunty hats and ruffles, but the personalities of the sitters emerge on closer inspection, from the heavy-lidded world-weariness of Rembrandt's *Portrait of a Man* to his deeply reflective *Aristotle with a Bust of Homer* (next to each other in Gallery 614).

Other highlights include Flemish Painting from the fifteenth and sixteenth centuries. Particularly prominent are the paintings of **Jan Van Eyck**, who is usually credited with beginning the tradition of North European realism. The freestanding panels of *The Crucifixion* and *The Last Judgement* in Gallery 625 were painted early in his career and are full of scurrying, startled figures, tightly composed with expressive and even horrific detail. Another great Northern Gothic painter, **Gerard David**, used local settings for his religious scenes; the background of his exquisite *Virgin and Child with Four Angels* is medieval Bruges and *The Rest on the Flight to Egypt* features a forest glade, again with the turrets of Bruges visible down below (both in Gallery 626). Head to adjacent Gallery 627 and **Pieter Bruegel the Elder**'s *Harvesters* to see how these innovations were assimilated. Made charming by its snapshot ordinariness (check the sprawling figure napping under a tree), this is one of the Met's most reproduced pictures.

The Met's elegant collection of **English paintings**, in Gallery 617, is also worth seeking out. Here you see modest works from **Hogarth**, **Reynolds** and **Thomas Lawrence**, as well as **Thomas Gainsborough**'s *Cottage Children* (*The Wood Gatherers*), one of his most famous paintings.

Nineteenth-Century European Paintings and Sculpture

Most visitors to the Met head directly to the **Nineteenth-Century European Paintings and Sculpture galleries** (800–830), following the left-hand corridor at the top of the Grand Staircase. This passage leads to another hall, which is littered with stunning **Rodin** sculptures in white marble and bronze. Twenty rooms branch off from here, leading to an array of Impressionist and Post-Impressionist paintings. To the far left, you'll find the precursors of the **Impressionists** such as **Delacroix** and **Ingres** in galleries 801 to 803, while the central section (galleries 810 to 817) is devoted primarily to **Degas**, where fans will find studies in just about every medium, from pastels to sculpture.

Manet

To the right, the Annenberg Collection houses galleries dedicated to all the big names, including several works by **Manet**, the Impressionist movement's most influential predecessor, whose early style of contrasting light and shadow with modulated shades of black can be firmly linked to the traditions of Hals, Velázquez and Goya. *Boating* evokes a vividly fresh, spring morning, while the influential *Spanish Singer* is a vigorous and realistic portrayal of a guitar player (both in Gallery 810).

Monet
Monet was one of the Impressionist movement's most prolific painters, returning again and again to a single subject in order to produce a series of images capturing different nuances of light and atmosphere. The Met's hoard runs like Monet's greatest hits: the museum has a canvas from almost every major sequence by the artist, including *Water Lilies*, *Rouen Cathedral (The Portal)*, *The Houses of Parliament (Effect of Fog)* and *Haystacks (Effect of Snow and Sun)*, all in Gallery 819.

Renoir
Though there's also work here by every Impressionist from **Berthe Morisot** to **Pissarro**, it's **Renoir** who is perhaps the best represented. Sadly, most of his works are from after 1878, when he began to move away from the techniques he'd learned while working with Monet and toward the chocolate-boxy soft focus that plagued his later work. Of these, *The Daughters of Catulle Mendès* (Gallery 824) is a likeable enough piece, one whose affectionate tone manages to sidestep the sentimentality of this period.

Cézanne
Cézanne is regarded as bridging the gap between Impressionism and early twentieth-century art movements, and his technique was very different from Monet's – he laboured long to achieve a painstaking analysis of form and colour. Of his few portraits, the jarring, almost Cubist angles and spaces of the rather plain *Mme Cézanne in a Red Dress* (Gallery 825) seem years ahead of their time: she looks clearly pained, as if she'd rather be anywhere than under her husband's gaze. Look out also for one of Cézanne's five famed portraits of the *Card Players* in the same gallery.

Post-Impressionists
Paintings of the **Post-Impressionists**, logically enough, lie beyond these first galleries. One of the highlights of the collection is **Gauguin**'s masterly *La Orana Maria* in Gallery 826. This Annunciation-derived scene, a Renaissance staple, has been transferred to a different culture in an attempt to unfold the symbolism, and perhaps voice the artist's feeling for the native South Sea islanders.

Also in Gallery 826 there are more than half a dozen canvases by **Van Gogh**, including his *Self-Portrait with Straw Hat* and famed *Irises*, and Pointillist work by the master of the technique, **Georges-Pierre Seurat** – the sparkling night-time scene *Circus Sideshow* was the first attempt to replicate artificial light using multicoloured dots. Gallery 830 contains work from **Picasso** and **Matisse** – the former's portrait of *Gertrude Stein* was the Met's first Picasso (donated by Stein in 1947).

Asian Art
Also on the second floor are the **Asian Art** galleries, an impressive, schizophrenic collection that includes works in various media from most major Asian civilizations.

Ancient Near Eastern Art
From the **Great Hall Balcony**, turning right leads to the **Ancient Near Eastern Art** galleries (400–406), with art from Central Asia, Cyprus and the Near East, including some exceptional silver and gold pieces from Iran (Gallery 405) and an impressive hall (Gallery 401) of huge ninth-century BC carvings from the Palace of Assyrian king Ashurnasirpal II, in Nimrud.

Arts of Arab Lands (Islamic Art)

Beyond Near Eastern Art lies the **Arts of Arab Lands** and associated **Islamic Art** section (galleries 450–464) in an elegant series of galleries laced with rare Islamic texts, richly patterned carpets, Ottoman armour, ceramics and jewellery. Highlights include the vast Simonette Carpet (Gallery 459) from sixteenth-century Egypt, and the gorgeous reception room from Damascus (Gallery 461), dating from 1707 and saved after the French bombing of Syria in 1925.

14

Southeast Asian and Chinese Art

Turning left at the balcony takes you to the main **Southeast Asian and Chinese Art** galleries, beginning with the serene, 12ft-high *Stele with Buddha Dipankara* from the Northern Wei dynasty (386–495) and a 14ft-high Bodhisattva from China's Northern Qi Dynasty (550–577) in Gallery 206. The focal point, however, is the enormous (and exquisite) fourteenth-century mural, *The Pure Land of Bhaisajyaguru* (also known as the "Medicine Buddha"). This piece was carefully reconstructed after being severely damaged in an earthquake and is a study in calm reflection – it was created in China during the Yuan Dynasty (c.1319).

Take the left fork here for more Chinese art and the real highlight of the Asian collection, the **Chinese Garden Court** (aka Astor Court, Gallery 217) a serene, minimalist retreat, and the adjacent **Ming Reception Room** (Gallery 218), a typical salon decorated in period style with wooden lattice doors. Assembled by experts from China, the naturally lit garden is representative of one found in wealthy Chinese homes of the Ming Dynasty: a pagoda, small waterfall and stocked goldfish pond landscaped with limestone rocks, trees and shrubs conjure up a sense of peace.

Korean and South Asian Art

Take the right fork from Gallery 206 for **Korean Art** (Gallery 233) and **South Asian Art** (galleries 234–243). There's a vast, if rather monotonous, range of **statues** of Hindu and Buddhist deities here, alongside numerous pieces of friezes, many of which still possess exceptional detail despite years of exposure. *The Great Departure and the Temptation of the Buddha*, carved in the third century AD (Gallery 235), is particularly lively: Siddhartha sets out on his spiritual journey, chased by a harem of dancing girls and grasping cherubs.

Japanese Art

The **Japanese Art** galleries (223–232) contain objects from the prehistoric to the present, ordered not chronologically but thematically, with rotating exhibits divided by medium: ceramics, textiles, paintings and prints. The undeniable showstoppers here are the seventeenth- and eighteenth-century hand-painted **Kano screens**, often elaborate scenes of historical allusion and divine fervour. Since all the exhibited paintings, calligraphy and scrolls of Asian art are rotated every six months or so, the objects change, but their beauty remains constant.

The American Wing

Close to being a museum in its own right, the **American Wing** (galleries 703–772) is a thorough introduction to the development of fine art in America, with a vast collection of paintings, period furniture, glass, silverware and ceramics. The spectacular **courtyard** reopened in 2009, studded with sculpture from the likes of Daniel Chester French and Augustus Saint-Gaudens – you can also grab a snack at the **café** here.

To view the Wing's **period rooms** in chronological order, begin on the third floor (Gallery 709) with the interior of a dark, low-beamed Jacobean beauty from Ipswich, Massachusetts, dating from 1680, and end with the Frank Lloyd Wright Room (Gallery 745), built in Minnesota (1912–14). Don't miss the collection of florid Tiffany glass in Gallery 743.

American Painting

The core **American Painting** galleries lie on the second floor, containing some real gems of New World artistry. Galleries 747 and 748 contain fine examples of colonial portraiture, featuring the work of **John Singleton Copley**, while Gallery 753 is primarily a homage to George Washington, with much-reproduced portraits by **John Trumbull**, **Charles Willson Peale** and **Gilbert Stuart** (Stuart's famed Lansdowne portrait of America's first president resides in Gallery 755). Galleries 759 and 761 are dedicated to the **Hudson Valley School** (1825–1875), who glorified the landscape in their vast lyrical canvases; English-born **Thomas Cole**, the school's doyen, is represented by *The Oxbow*, while his pupil **Frederic Church** also has work here and in Gallery 760, where the immense *Heart of the Andes* combines the grand sweep of the mountains with minutely depicted flora. Gallery 760 also contains **Albert Bierstadt**'s monumental *The Rocky Mountains, Lander's Peak* but the real star here is *Washington Crossing the Delaware* by **Emanuel Leutze**, the celebrated image of Washington escaping across the river in the winter of 1776.

14

Post-Civil War painting

Winslow Homer is also well represented in the collection, from his early illustrations of the Civil War (Gallery 762) to his late, quasi-Impressionistic seascapes, of which *Northeaster* is one of the finest (Gallery 767). Look out, too, for the painters of the American West – **Frederic Remington**'s *On the Southern Plains* (Gallery 765) helped create the popular image of the swashbuckling Seventh Cavalry. Other highlights of the late nineteenth and early twentieth centuries include **Thomas Eakins'** subdued, almost ghostly *Max Schmitt in a Single Scull* (Gallery 767) and **William Merritt Chase**'s *For the Little One* (Gallery 770), an Impressionist study of his wife sewing. American Impressionism (1880–1920) is explored more fully in Gallery 769 with the work of **Childe Hassam** and **William Merritt Chase**, and in Gallery 770 with **John Singer Sargent**, **John H. Twachtman** and **J. Alden Weir**.

Medieval Art

Although you could move straight to **Medieval Art** (galleries 300–307) from the American Wing, you'd miss out on the museum's carefully planned approach. Instead, enter these galleries via the corridor from the western end (or rear) of the Great Hall behind the main staircase. There you'll see displays of the sumptuous Byzantine metalwork and jewellery that financier **J.P. Morgan** donated to the museum in its early days. At the end of the corridor is the **main sculpture hall** (Gallery 305), piled high with religious statuary and carvings; it's divided by a 52ft-high *reja* – a decorative open-work, iron altar screen – from Valladolid Cathedral in Spain. If you're here in December, you'll see a highlight of New York's Christmas season: a beautifully decorated, 20ft-high Christmas tree lit up in the centre of the sculpture hall. The **medieval treasury** (Gallery 306) to the right of the hall has an all-encompassing display of objects religious, liturgical and secular.

Egyptian Art

The Met hogs a collection of more than 35,000 objects from **ancient Egypt** (galleries 100–138), most of which are displayed to their full potential. Brightly efficient corridors steer you through the treasures of the museum's own digs during the 1920s and 1930s, as well as other art and artefacts from 3000 BC to the Byzantine period of Egyptian culture.

Prepare to be awed as you enter from the Great Hall on the first floor: the large **statuary**, **tombs** and **sarcophagi** in the first few galleries are immediately striking. As you move into the interior galleries, arranged chronologically, the smaller, quieter

14

THE TEMPLE OF DENDUR

At the end of the Egyptian section sits the **Temple of Dendur**, housed in the vast and airy Gallery 131, lined with photographs and placards about the temple's history and its original site on the banks of the Nile. Built by the Emperor Augustus in 15 BC for the goddess Isis of Philae, the temple was moved here as a gift from the Egyptian government during the construction of the Aswan High Dam in 1965 – otherwise, it would have drowned. Though you can't walk all the way inside, you can go in just far enough to get a glimpse of the interior rooms, their walls chock-full of hieroglyphs and the scrawls of nineteenth-century **graffiti** artists (though "J Livingston" is no relation to the famous explorer). The entire gallery is glassed-in on one side, and looks out onto Central Park; the most magical time to view the temple is when it's illuminated at night and the gallery seems to glow, lending it an air of mystery that's missing during the day.

---

sculptural pieces are also quite eye-catching. Don't miss the finely crafted models of ships, a brewery and a cattle stable in Gallery 105, offerings found in the **Tomb of Meketre**. Incredibly well preserved, they look as if they were made yesterday, not four thousand years ago, and offer a rare insight into everyday Egyptian life. Look, too, for the dazzling collection of **Princess Sithathoryunet jewellery** in Gallery 111, a pinnacle in Egyptian decorative art from around 1830 BC.

Greek and Roman Art

Thanks to a magnificent renovation completed in 2007, one of the largest collections of Greek and Roman art in the world occupies some of the most attractive wings of the museum (galleries 150–172). Enter from the southern end of the Great Hall, and you'll find yourself in the wonderfully bright **Greek Sculpture Court** (Gallery 153), a fittingly elegant setting for sixth- to fourth-century BC marble sculptures. The adjacent galleries display Greek art from the prehistoric era through to the fourth century BC. Look out for the tiny but fanciful **Minoan vase** in the shape of a bull's head from around 1450 BC (Gallery 151) and the **Marble Statue of a Kouros** (Gallery 154) – one of the earliest examples of a funerary statue (*kouros* means "youth") to have survived intact. Dating from 580 BC and originally from Attica, it marked the grave of the son of a wealthy family, created to ensure he would be remembered.

Beyond here, the hefty **Sardis Column** from the Temple of Artemis marks the entrance into the stunning **Leon Levy and Shelby White Court** (Gallery 162), a soaring two-storey atrium of **Roman sculpture** from the first century BC to the second century AD, with mosaic floors, Doric columns and a glass ceiling – take a moment to soak up your surroundings at the fountain in the centre. Highlights include the incredibly detailed Badminton Sarcophagus towards the back, and beyond this a small but enigmatic bust of the Emperor Caracalla from the third century.

Arts of Africa, Oceania and the Americas

Michael C. Rockefeller, son of Governor Nelson Rockefeller, disappeared during a trip to West New Guinea in 1961. In 1969, Nelson donated the entire contents of his missing son's **Museum of Primitive Art** – over 3300 works, plus library and photographic material – to the Met. This wing, on the first floor past the Greek and Roman galleries, stands as a memorial to Michael. It includes many Asmat tribal objects, such as carved *mbis* (memorial poles), figures and a canoe from Irian Jaya, alongside the Met's comprehensive collection of art from **Africa**, **Oceania and the Americas**.

It's a superb set of galleries – the muted, understated decor throwing the exhibits into sharp and often dramatic focus. The **African galleries** (350–352) offer an overview of the major geographic regions and their cultures, though West Africa is better represented than the rest of the continent. Particularly awe-inspiring is the display of art from the Kingdom of Benin (in present-day Nigeria) – tiny carved ivory figures, created with astonishing detail (Gallery 352).

The **Pacific collection** (galleries 353–355) covers the islands of Melanesia, Micronesia, Polynesia and Australia, and contains a wide array of objects, including wild, somewhat frightening wooden masks with all-too-realistic eyes. Sadly, **Mexico**, **Central America and South America** (galleries 357–358) get somewhat short shrift, though there is a respectable collection of pre-Columbian jade, Mayan and Aztec pottery and Mexican ceramic sculpture; the best part by far, however, is the **Jan Mitchell Treasury** (Gallery 357), an entire room filled with South American gold jewellery and ornaments – particularly the exquisite hammered-gold nose ornaments and earrings from Peru and the richly carved, jewelled ornaments from Colombia.

14

Modern and Contemporary Art

The Met's **Modern and Contemporary Art** collection (galleries 900–926) – housed over two floors in the Lila Acheson Wallace Wing (named in honour of the founder of *Reader's Digest*) – is another fine hoard that includes several stunning individual works, from mid-century experimental and abstract canvases to contemporary sculpture.

1905 to 1945
Work on the first floor is arranged roughly by school and period, covering **American and European art from 1905 to 1945**. The first galleries on the right side are dedicated to American art, beginning with **Edward Hopper** and the mural-like images of Broadway and Wall Street by **Florine Stettheimer** (Gallery 908), and including the paintings of **Charles Sheeler** (Gallery 911), and **Georgia O'Keeffe**, whose moody *From the Faraway, Nearby* (Gallery 910) resembles a progressive-rock album cover.

Beyond here, the European galleries begin with the Surrealists, with work from **Miró** and **Dalí** giving way to **Picasso**, **Bonnard**, **Braque** and **Modigliani**. Picasso is particularly well represented, his work sprinkled throughout the first floor, from his Blue Period, through his Cubist Period, to more familiar skewed-perspective portraits. Following a small room dedicated to **Paul Klee** (Gallery 903), the galleries end with the Fauvism of **Derain** and **Soutine** and more Cubism from Picasso, Braque and **Gris**. Note that some of the most famous pieces in the collection – **Modigliani**'s firm-breasted *Reclining Nude* for example – are often moved around or on loan elsewhere.

1945 to the present
The mezzanine and second floors contain **European and American art from 1945 to the present**, from installations to vast abstracts. The mezzanine level (Gallery 915) displays

---

THE CANTOR ROOF GARDEN

From May to October, you can ascend to the **Cantor Roof Garden**, located on top of the Modern Art section. The leafy garden is an outdoor gallery, and each summer it's used to showcase contemporary sculpture; it's also a café (Tues–Thurs & Sun 10am–4.30pm, Fri & Sat 10am–8pm) and martini bar (Fri & Sat 5.30–8pm), though the pricey snacks and drinks aren't the main reason to come here. The views are what draw most visitors – from this height, you can grasp how vast Central Park truly is; you're also within close view of Cleopatra's Needle. By far the best time to come for a cocktail is October, when the weather's cooler and the foliage has begun to turn.

To reach the garden, head for the southwest elevators on the first floor, just outside the Modern Art gallery – to get to the elevators, walk behind the main marble stairs in the Great Hall, into the the main Medieval sculpture hall (Gallery 305), and turn left towards the Modern Art section.

the work of **Chuck Close**, whose *Lucas* has the characteristic intense stare of his giant portraits, as well as **Andy Warhol**'s monumental *Mao* and **David Hockney**'s *Mount Fuji & Flowers*. The second floor is filled with giant, abstract canvases from artists such as **Mark Rothko** (galleries 921 and 922), with an entire room (Gallery 919) devoted to grumpy Abstract Expressionist **Clyfford Still**, who once "repossessed" a picture by knifing it from its frame when he fell out with the owner. The iconic *White Flag* by **Jasper Johns** holds court in Gallery 922, while you'll find **Jackson Pollock**'s swirling *Autumn Rhythm (No. 30)* in Gallery 921; if you stand up close, the painting seems to suck you in, and you'll spot far more colours than at first glance.

14

European Sculpture and Decorative Arts

Most people pass right through the **European Sculpture and Decorative Arts** section (galleries 500–556) on their way between the Modern and Medieval art galleries, but there are a couple of reasons to pause. The **European Sculpture Court** (Gallery 548) is a gorgeous sunlit courtyard studded with grand marble statues, notably *Andromeda and the Sea Monster* by **Domenico Guidi** and the agonizing *Ugolino and his Sons* by **Carpeaux**, depicting the Pisan traitor from Dante's *Inferno*. There's also a cast of **Rodin**'s *Burghers of Calais*, an impressive bronze ensemble recalling the Hundred Years War. The **Decorative Arts section** – furniture, ceramics, glassware and the like – is less appealing, but displayed in some opulent Baroque- and Rococo-style rooms reminiscent of a French palace.

The Robert Lehman Collection

Another of the Met's many treasures, the **Robert Lehman Collection** (galleries 950–965) was tacked on to the rear of the museum in 1975 to house the holdings of Robert Lehman, a relentless collector and scion of the Lehman Brothers banking family. Lehman bequeathed his entire collection with the stipulation that the galleries retain the appearance of a private home, and parts of this extension – an octagonal building centred on a brilliantly lit atrium – do resemble rooms in his former mansion. The walls around the atrium (galleries 961 and 962) are lined with mostly uninteresting **nineteenth-century** works from **Braque**, **Derain**, **Matisse**, **Renoir** and **Sisley**, though **Balthus**'s creamy and disturbing *Nude with a Mirror* (Gallery 961) is worth a longer look.

Italian Renaissance art

Lehman's artistic interests fill important gaps in the Met's collection, notably the **Italian Renaissance**. This period was his passion, with Gallery 950 containing one of the most celebrated collections of Italian **maiolica** (glazed ceramics) in the world. Fourteenth- and fifteenth-century Florentine and Sienese work features in Gallery 952, by masters such as **Simone Martini** and **Ugolino da Siena**. The red-velvet-walled Gallery 956 is home to more Sienese paintings while Lehman's personal hoard also includes some standout Italian works in Gallery 959, such as the tiny, easily missed *Annunciation* by **Botticelli**. More impressive are the Venetian works, including a glassy *Madonna and Child* by **Bellini** in which Mary looks like a 1920s screen goddess (also Gallery 959).

Northern European and Spanish art

Gallery 953 houses **Northern Renaissance art**, from the likes of **Petrus Christus** and **Gerard David**, while eighteenth- and nineteenth-century paintings from France and England hold court in Gallery 957; Lehman evidently liked **Ingres**, whose languid, sculptural portrait of the Princesse de Broglie in her bright-blue dress sparkles on the wall. Similarly impressive is **El Greco**'s *Christ Carrying the Cross* (Gallery 958), though one picture stands out from them all in this gallery: **Rembrandt**'s creepy *Portrait of Gerard de Lairesse*, his bug eyes and snout-like nose evidence of the ravages of congenital syphilis.

GUGGENHEIM MUSEUM

The Upper East Side

The defining characteristic of Manhattan's Upper East Side – a two-square-mile grid that runs from 59th to 96th streets between Fifth Avenue and the East River – is wealth. Despite the lowering of rents in recent years and an influx of young professionals, this area has been an enclave of New York's upper class since the 1890s, when dynasties such as the Rockefellers, Whitneys and Astors built mansions here. Today, Martin Scorsese, Spike Lee, long-time resident Woody Allen and Madonna call the Upper East Side home, a world aptly portrayed in movies such as *Breakfast at Tiffany's*, and more recently in TV shows *Sex and the City and Gossip Girl*. Farther east, in the middle of the East River, sits Roosevelt Island, an area distinctly different from the rest of the city.

ARRIVAL AND DEPARTURE

By subway For the Upper East Side Historic District take Subway F to Lexington Ave/63rd St or #6 to 68th St or 77th St. For Museum Mile, Carnegie Hill and Yorkville take the #4, #5 or #6 to 86th St or the #6 to 96th St.

Upper East Side Historic District

Subway F to Lexington Ave/63rd St, #6 to 68th St or 77th St

Encompassing 59th to 78th streets, between Fifth and Lexington avenues, the **Upper East Side Historic District** has been the haughty patrician face of Manhattan since the late nineteenth century. Wealthy families built their fashionable residences on **Fifth Avenue** overlooking Central Park, lavish Neoclassical mansions cluttered with columns and classical statues.

Today, the area is jam-packed with museums: Henry Clay Frick's mansion at East 70th Street, marginally less ostentatious than its neighbours, is now the intimate and tranquil home of the **Frick Collection**, one of the city's must-see spots, while the modern exhibits at the **Whitney** are across at 74th Street and Madison.

15

The Grolier Club

47 East 60th St, just off Park Ave • Mon–Sat 10am–5pm; closed Aug • Free • ☎ 212 838 6690, ⓦ grolierclub.org • Subway N, Q, R to Fifth Ave/59th St, #4, #5, #6 to 59th St

North of **Grand Army Plaza**, Fifth Avenue and its opulent side-streets are dotted with **private clubs** that served and still cater to the city's wealthy (see box, p.170). One of the few open to the public (at least partly) is the relatively modest **Grolier Club**. There are four public art shows a year in the main ground-floor gallery, usually with a literary or artistic theme utilizing paintings, books and sculpture; recent displays have focused on American "little magazines" of the 1890s, and the life of Count Guglielmo Libri. Established in 1884 as a literary club, the Grolier's current premises date from 1917.

Christ Church United Methodist

520 Park Ave, at East 60th St • Mon–Fri 7am–6pm; Sun services only • Free • ☎ 212 838 3036, ⓦ christchurchnyc.org • Subway N, Q, R to Fifth Ave/59th St, #4, #5, #6 to 59th St

Christ Church United Methodist looks relatively plain from the outside, but the interior is one of the most memorable in New York. Ralph Adams Cram started work on this Romanesque masterpiece in 1931, but the lavish Byzantine interior wasn't completed until 1949. The apse and vaulted ceiling are smothered in dazzling gold-leaf mosaics – parts of the choir screen date from 1660 and were once owned by Tsar Nicholas II of Russia. The altar itself is carved from Spanish marble, with the nave columns hewn from veined, purple Levanto marble.

Museum of American Illustration

128 East 63rd St, between Park and Lexington aves • Tues 10am–8pm, Wed–Fri 10am–5pm, Sat noon–4pm • Free • ☎ 212 838 2560, ⓦ societyillustrators.org • Subway F to Lexington Ave/63rd St

Fans of cartoon art should walk one block east from Park Avenue to the **Museum of American Illustration**, New York's shrine to the genre. Rotating selections from the museum's permanent collection of more than two thousand illustrations include everything from wartime propaganda to contemporary ads. Exhibitions are based on a theme or illustrator; designed primarily for aficionados, they are nonetheless accessible, well presented and topical. **Sketch Night** (Tues & Thurs 6.30–9.30pm; $15) is lots of fun for budding artists, with live music and models to draw (supplies available for sale).

Park Avenue Armory

643 Park Ave • Guided tours (1hr 15min) Tues & Thurs 10am (reservations required) • $10 • ☎ 212 616 3930, ⓦ armoryonpark.org • Subway #6 to 68th St

The vast hulk of the **Park Avenue Armory** dominates the block of Park Avenue between East 66th and 67th streets. Completed in 1881 for the National Guard's Seventh

THE UPPER EAST SIDE

Museum of the City of New York

EL BARRIO

Mount Sinai Hospital

East Meadow

Icahn Medical Institute

St Nicholas Russian Orthodox Cathedral

Islamic Cultural Center

The Reservoir

Main Entrance for Reservoir Track & NY Road Runners Club Booth

Jewish Museum

Otto and Addie Kahn Mansion

Cooper-Hewitt National Design Museum

CARNEGIE HILL

Ruppert Park

Church of Heavenly Rest National Academy of Design

Guggenheim Museum

Church of the Holy Trinity

Gracie Mansion

AMC Lower Cinemas

Henderson Place

Carl Schurz Park

Neue Galerie

E 86th St Cinemas

Schaller and Weber

YORKVILLE

Park Avenue Christian Church

St Ignatius Loyola

Metropolitan Museum of Art

Institute for the Study of the Ancient World

New York Society Library

Comic Strip Live

Ukrainian Institute

Alexander Calder Sidewalk

Orwasher's Handmade Bread

UPPER EAST SIDE

Cherokee Apartments

John Jay Park

Leo Castelli Gallery

Temple Israel

St Jean Baptiste

Loeb Boathouse

Whitney Museum of American Art

Church of the Resurrection

Czech Center

Conservatory Pond

Frick Collection

St James's Church

Asia Society

Sotheby's

Rumsey Playfield (Summerstage)

Union Club

Hunter College

68th St-Hunter College (6)

Park East Synagogue

Tisch Children's Zoo

Cosmopolitan Club

Park Avenue Armory

St Vincent's Church

Temple Emanu-El

Roosevelt House

China Institute

Central Park Zoo

Central Presbyterian Church

Museum of American Illustration

Lexington Av/ 63rd St (F)

Roosevelt Island

Knickerbocker Club

Colony Club

Christ Church United Methodist

Mount Vernon Hotel Museum & Garden

The Pond

5th Av/ 59th St (N,Q,R)

Metropolitan Club

Lexington Av/ 59th St (N,Q,R)

Bloomingdale's

Roosevelt Island Tramway

Roosevelt Island (F)

Harmonie Club

Grolier Club

59TH STREET BRIDGE

QUEENSBORO BRIDGE

East River

0   200
yards

● SHOPPING
Barneys New York	14
Bloomingdale's	18
Calvin Klein	16
Carolina Herrera	5
Chloé	17
Dolce & Gabbana	9
Donna Karan	11
DKNY	15
Giorgio Armani	12
Intermix	3
Kitchen Arts & Letters	1
Polo Ralph Lauren	8
Pookie & Sebastian	4/13
Scoop	7
Shakespeare & Co	10
Super Runners Shop	2
Zitomer	6

● RESTAURANTS
Beyoglu	13
Café Boulud	16
Candle Café	17
Cascabel Taqueria	14
Daniel	25
Donguri	8
E.A.T.	12
Flex Mussels	11
Heidelberg	6
Hospoda	22
JG Melon Restaurant	20
Jojo	29
King's Carriage House	10
Maya	27
Naruto Ramen	2
Ottomanelli's 86th St Café	7
Paola's	1
Pastrami Queen	15
Penrose	9
Persepolis	21
Pig Heaven	14

■ ACCOMMODATION
Franklin	1
Mark	2
Pierre	4
Sherry-Netherland	5
Surrey	3

● CAFÉS
Alice's Tea Cup	28
Café Sabarsky	4
FP Pâtisserie	18
Maison Kayser	19
Maison Ladurée	23
Mitchel London Foods	26
Neil's Coffee Shop	24
Shake Shack	5
Serendipity 3	30
Tal Bagels	3

■ BARS
ABV	2
Balcony Bar	4
Bar Pléiades	6
Bemelmans Bar	5
Brandy's Piano Bar	3
Earl's Beer & Cheese	4
Roof Garden Café	4
Stir	7
Subway Inn	8

■ NIGHTLIFE
Café Carlyle	5

15

MEMBERS ONLY

The traditional **gentlemen's club** originated in London in the eighteenth century but was quickly transported to North America, becoming especially popular among the burgeoning wealthy classes of nineteenth-century New York. Founded in 1836, the **Union Club**, at 101 East 69th St at Park Ave, is the second-oldest in the nation (the current building opened in 1933), its 135 founders very much the city's social elite; J.P. Morgan, Cornelius Vanderbilt, William Randolph Hearst and John Jacob Astor IV would all become members. Equally exclusive is the still-male-only **Knickerbocker Club**, a handsome Federal-style structure on the corner of Fifth Ave and East 62nd St, founded in 1871 by Union Club members who thought the club's standards of admission had dropped (the building dates from 1915), and attracting a bevy of Astors, Roosevelts and Rockefellers.

Indeed, in the 1890s established society still looked askance at bankers and industrialists – the city's new money. When Union Club member J.P. Morgan proposed his friend Frank King, the latter was blackballed because he had done manual labour in his youth. Not one to be slighted, Morgan resigned and commissioned Stanford White to design a club for him – one that would be bigger, better and grander than all the rest. Such was the birth of the **Metropolitan Club**, at 1 East 60th St at Fifth Ave, an exuberant Italian Renaissance confection by Stanford White, completed in 1894 with a marvellously outrageous gateway: just the thing to greet its affluent members (both then and now).

Another group of New Yorkers unwelcome in the elite clubs, prosperous German Jews, founded the elegant **Harmonie Club** in 1852, hiring Stanford White to build a new home at 4 East 60th St (across the road from the Metropolitan Club) in 1905.

All the clubs, both restrictive and lax, refused to open their doors to women. In 1903, with the opening of the **Colony Club**, at 564 Park Ave at East 62nd St, the ladies fought back, founding the first social club for members of their sex (this building dates from 1916). The ornate **Cosmopolitan Club**, with its New Orleans-style balconies at 122 East 66th St between Lexington and Park avenues, also opened as a women's institution in 1909 (the building dates from 1932, and is unmarked from the street).

Regiment, the exterior features pseudo-medieval crenellations, and the interior a grand double staircase and spidery wrought-iron chandeliers. The most reliable way to get a peek at the lavish rooms inside is take a **guided tour** or to attend one of the frequent art and antique shows staged here (it's normally closed otherwise); you'll usually have to pay to attend the shows (which showcase the enormous **drill hall**), but the period rooms on the first floor will be open for **free self-guided tours**. Highlights include the incredibly opulent **Veterans Room** and **Library**, designed by Stanford White and decked out with Tiffany interiors and stained glass – the fireplace in the former is particularly fine, framed with blue glass tiles and murals. Check out also the portraits in the **Colonel's Reception Room**, where George Washington and compatriot Marquis de Lafayette would no doubt be mortified to find themselves on display with a very regal King George VI. The website is the best place to find out about upcoming exhibitions.

China Institute

125 East 65th St • Daily 10am–5pm (open to 8pm Tues & Thurs) • $7, free Tues & Thurs 6–8pm • ☎ 212 744 8181, Ⓦ chinainstitute.org • Subway F to Lexington Ave/63rd St, #6 to 68th St

This educational and cultural institution was founded in New York in 1926, and is worth a visit for its high-quality temporary exhibitions, on everything from the latest contemporary Chinese art to bronze vessels dating back three thousand years.

Temple Emanu-El

1 East 65th St, at Fifth Ave • Sun–Thurs 10am–4.30pm • Free • ☎ 212 744 1400, Ⓦ emanuelnyc.org • Subway F to Lexington Ave/63rd St, #6 to 68th St

Overlooking Central Park sits the awe-inspiring **Temple Emanu-El**, completed in 1929. Still America's largest Reform Jewish synagogue, this Romanesque-Byzantine cavern – a

THE ROOSEVELTS

President FDR and Eleanor Roosevelt loved the Upper East Side. Eleanor was born at 56 West 37th St in 1884, but moved into 49 East 65th St with her husband in 1908 (a wedding gift from FDR's overbearing mother). The couple owned the property until 1941; after a spell in the West Village, Eleanor (now a widow) moved to 211 East 62nd St in 1953 and then to 55 E 74th St in 1959 – she died there three years later.

vast, moody and contemplative place – manages to feel even bigger inside than it looks from the outside (you can only take a quick look, usually escorted by a member of staff). The entrance is on 65th Street, where there's also the **Herbert & Eileen Bernard Museum of Judaica** on the second floor (same hours; free); its three rooms hold both temporary exhibits on religious themes like the Kabbalah as well as an artefact-heavy history of the temple itself. Despite the official opening hours, both the temple and museum are often closed – **call ahead** to confirm times.

15

The Frick Collection

1 East 70th St, at Fifth Ave • Tues–Sat 10am–6pm, Sun 11am–5pm • $18, pay what you wish Sun 11am–1pm • ☎ 212 288 0700, ⓦ frick.org • Subway #6 to 68th St

A spectacular feat of acquisitive good taste, the **Frick Collection** is one of New York's finest sights. The collection comprises the art treasures amassed by **Henry Clay Frick** (1849–1919), one of New York's most ruthless robber-barons, and is housed in the sumptuous mansion he had built in 1914. The legacy of his ill-gotten gains – he spent millions on the best of Europe's art – is a superb assembly of work.

Opened in 1935, for the most part the museum has been kept as it looked when the Fricks lived here. What sets it apart from most galleries is that it strives hard to be as unlike a museum as possible. There is no wall text describing the pictures, though you can dial up info on most pieces using the hand-held guides available in the lobby (included with the price of admission). There are few ropes, fresh flowers on every table, and chairs provided for weary visitors, even in the most lavishly decorated rooms. Make sure you pay a visit to the enclosed central **Garden Court**, where marble floors, fountains and greenery, all simply arranged, exude serenity.

Start your visit with the **introductory film** (22min) shown every hour in the Music Room, which provides background on Frick's coke and steel empire and his ravenous appetite for acquiring art, which really got going in the 1890s.

The South Hall to Fragonard Room

With its magnificent array of Old Masters, the collection rivals to a certain extent the much larger holdings of the Met, especially in the quality of Italian Renaissance pieces, an area in which the Met is comparatively weak. Don't rush; even the initial corridors beyond the entrance hold some exceptional pieces. The **South Hall** contains Renoir's beguiling *Mother and Children* and two fabulous Vermeers: *Girl at Her Muse* and *Officer and Laughing Girl*, the latter in particular a masterful play on light. Look out, too, for the elegant French Rococo furniture here – though paintings take the limelight, Frick also collected antique tables, chests and chairs, spread liberally throughout the mansion.

Keep an open mind as you enter the eighteenth-century **Boucher Room**. With its flowery walls, overdone furniture and Boucher's Rococo representations of the Arts and Sciences in gilded frames, it is not to modern tastes. More reserved English paintings pack the **Dining Room**: giant portraits by Romney and Gainsborough, whose *St James's Park* is a study in social mores – there isn't a woman walking under the trees who isn't assessing the competition. The nearby **Fragonard Room** contains the French painter's typically florid *Progress of Love* series, painted for Louis XV's mistress Madame du Barry but discarded by her soon afterwards.

15

The Living Hall

The **Living Hall** houses one of the most impressive Renaissance pictures anywhere in America: Bellini's sublime *St Francis in the Desert*. Stunningly well preserved, the picture suggests Francis's vision of Christ. This canvas unfairly overshadows the rest of the pieces in the room, although also notable are a couple of knockout portraits by Hans Holbein the Younger: his masterpieces *Thomas Cromwell* and *Sir Thomas More*, Tudor adversaries that now seem to stare at each other. More's world-weariness is graphically evidenced by the bags under his eyes and his five-o'clock shadow, while the two are separated by El Greco's restrained *St Jerome*.

Library and North Hall

Move into the **Library** to see more English paintings, such as Turner's *Fishing Boats entering Calais Harbour*, Reynolds' *Lady Taylor*, who's dwarfed by her huge blue ribbon and feather hat, and one of Constable's *Salisbury Cathedral* series; there's also a portrait of Frick himself here, as a white-bearded old man, and one of Frick's rare American paintings, a portrait of *George Washington* by Gilbert Stuart. Across in the **North Hall**, look for the gorgeous but chill-inducing *Vétheuil in Winter* by Monet, and a classic Degas, *The Rehearsal*.

The West and East galleries

The **West Gallery** is another important space: the long, elegant room is decorated with dark-green walls, a concave glass ceiling and ornately carved wood trim. There's a clutch of snazzy Dutch pictures here, including Rembrandt's enigmatic *Polish Rider* and his most magnificent self-portrait, regal robes contrasting with his sorrowful, weary expression. Look out for a couple of uncharacteristically informal portraits of Frans Snyders and his wife by Van Dyck, Frick's favourite artist, and Turner's vast canvases of Dieppe and Cologne. This gallery is also the location of the last picture Frick himself bought before his death in 1919: Vermeer's seemingly unfinished *Mistress and Maid*, a tantalising snapshot of an intimate moment.

At the far end of the West Gallery is the tiny **Enamel Room**, named for the exquisite set of mostly sixteenth-century Limoges enamels on display. There's also a collection of small altarpieces by Piero della Francesca; it's another sign of Frick's good taste that he snapped up work by this artist, who is now one of the acknowledged Italian masters but was little regarded in the nineteenth century. The **Oval Room** at the other end of the West Gallery is filled with a quartet of pretty portraits by James McNeill Whistler, the only US painter admired by Frick, as well as the incredibly detailed "*Fraga Philip*", a portrait of Spain's King Philip IV by Velázquez.

Finally, the **East Gallery** displays a mishmash of styles and periods; highlights are Reynolds' bug-eyed but dashing *General Burgoyne*, the vigorous *Forge* by Goya, and Manet's unusually cropped *Bullfight*. The modern **basement gallery** displays temporary exhibits from other museums; accessible only by a steep spiral staircase just to the left beyond the entry hall, it's easy to miss unless you're looking for it.

St James' Church

865 Madison Ave, at East 71st St • Tues–Sun 8am–8pm • Free • ☎ 212 288 4100, ⓦ stjames.org • Subway #6 to 68th St

One block east of the Frick Collection is the stately and elaborate neo-Gothic facade of **St James' Church**. This Episcopal church was first constructed in 1885, but what you see today dates mostly from the 1920s, including the graceful, gilded reredos above the marble altar, designed by Ralph Adams Cram.

Asia Society

725 Park Ave, at East 70th St • Tues–Sun 11am–6pm, Fri until 9pm mid-Sept to June • $10, free Fri 6–9pm • ☎ 212 517 2742, ⓦ asiasociety.org • Subway #6 to 68th St

A prominent educational resource founded by John D. Rockefeller III, the **Asia Society** offers two floors of small but nevertheless enthralling exhibition spaces dedicated to both traditional and contemporary art from all over Asia. In addition to the usually worthwhile temporary exhibits, ranging from Japanese lacquerware to ancient Buddhist sculpture, a variety of intriguing performances, political roundtables, lectures, films and free events are frequently held here.

Czech Center

321 East 73rd St • Mon–Fri 10am–6pm (Tues till 7pm) • Free • ☎ 212 988 1733, Ⓦ bohemiannationalhall.com • Subway #6 to 77th St

The grand old Bohemian National Hall, completed in 1897, now functions as the **Czech Center**, home to the Czech Consulate, enticing Czech restaurant *Hospoda* (see p.315) and a series of public art galleries well worth checking out. Exhibits change every few months, featuring notable names in Czech contemporary art.

Whitney Museum of American Art

945 Madison Ave, at East 75th St • Wed, Thurs, Sat & Sun 11am–6pm, Fri 1–9pm • $18, pay what you wish Fri 6–9pm • ☎ 1 800 944 8639, Ⓦ whitney.org • Subway #6 to 77th St

In a grey, arsenal-like building designed in 1966 by Marcel Breuer, the **Whitney Museum of American Art** offers intelligent, challenging art exhibitions, garnered from its outstanding collection of twentieth-century American art – note that the museum is relocating downtown at the end of 2014 (see box, below).

The Whitney is best known for its superb **temporary exhibitions.** Many of these are retrospectives of established artists or debuts of their lesser-known counterparts: Jasper Johns, Cy Twombly and Cindy Sherman were all given their first retrospectives here, and hipster photographer Ryan McGinley also had a solo show. The most thought-provoking exhibitions, however, push the boundaries of art as a concept – strong showings of late have been in the realms of video installation (incorporating names such as Bill Viola and Nam June Paik) and computer and digital technology.

Without a doubt, though, the Whitney is most famous for its **Biennial**, which was first held in 1932 and continues to take place between March and June in even-numbered years. Designed to give a provocative overview of what's happening in contemporary American art, it's often panned by critics, sometimes for good reason. Nonetheless, the Biennial is always packed with visitors, so catch it if you can.

15

Brief history

Gertrude Vanderbilt Whitney (1875–1942), a sculptor and champion of American art, founded the Whitney Studio in 1914 to exhibit the work of living American artists who could not find support in established art circles – she was the first to exhibit Edward Hopper, in 1920. By 1929, she had collected more than five hundred works by various artists, all of which she offered, with a generous endowment, to the Met. When her offer was refused, she set up her own museum in Greenwich Village in 1930, with her collection as its core exhibit, relocating to its current spot in 1966. The Brutalist building was initially a controversial addition to the neat townhouses of the Upper East Side, but it's a sign of how beloved the structure has become that plans to wreck its integrity with a Neoclassical addition were shouted down in the late 1990s.

The collection

The museum owns more than 18,000 paintings, sculptures, photographs and films by

THE WHITNEY GOES DOWNTOWN

Note that the Whitney Museum of American Art will only be open in the Upper East Side until late 2014 – the museum is planning to relocate to new premises near the High Line in 2015 (see p.106). Once the Whitney moves out of 945 Madison Ave, the **Metropolitan Museum of Art** plans to hold exhibitions and educational programmes here for eight years, with the possibility of extending.

almost two thousand artists such as Calder, Nevelson, O'Keeffe, de Kooning, Rauschenberg and LeWitt. For an overview of its holdings, see **American Legends: From Calder to O'Keeffe**, a permanent installation of the Whitney's best on display on the fifth floor. The works are rotated, but the collection is particularly strong on **Edward Hopper** (two thousand of his works were bequeathed to the museum in 1970) and several of his best paintings are usually on show. The eerie *Early Sunday Morning* is a typical example: it focuses on light and shadow, a bleak urban landscape, uneasily tense in its lighting and rejection of topical detail. The street could be anywhere (in fact it's Seventh Ave); for Hopper, it becomes universal. Look out also for **Joseph Stella**'s Futurist *Brooklyn Bridge*; **Jackson Pollock**'s explosion of colour, *Number 27*; and **Jasper Johns**' celebrated *Three Flags*, which erases the emblem of patriotism and replaces it with ambiguity.

As if to balance the figurative works that formed the nucleus of the original collection, more recent purchases have included an emphasis on abstract art. **Marsden Hartley**'s *Painting, Number 5* is a jarring work painted in memory of a German officer friend killed in the early days of World War I. **Georgia O'Keeffe**'s *Abstraction* is gentler, though with its own darkness: it was suggested by the noises of cattle being driven to slaughter. The **Abstract Expressionists** are also a strong presence, with great works by masters **Pollock** and **de Kooning**, **Mark Rothko** and the **Color Field** painters – though you need a sharp eye to discern any colour in **Ad Reinhardt**'s *Black Painting*. In a different direction, **Warhol**, **Johns** and **Oldenburg** each subvert the meaning of their images. Warhol's silk-screened *Coke Bottles* fade into motif; and Oldenburg's lighthearted *Soft Sculptures*, with its toilets and motors, falls into line with his declaration, "I'm into art that doesn't sit on its ass in a museum."

St Jean Baptiste Church

184 East 76th St, at Lexington Ave • Daily 7am–7pm • Free • ☎ 212 288 5082, ⓦ stjeanbaptisteny.org • Subway #6 to 68th St

Built in 1913 to serve the local French-Canadian community, **St Jean Baptiste Church** is an opulent Italian Baroque and Neoclassical confection with a magnificent 175ft dome. Though the main towers are being restored you still can admire the interior and the rare Chartres stained-glass windows. The church is also the **national shrine for St Anne** (Mary's mother), with a special chapel on the right side, and an important pilgrimage site for American Catholics.

Museum Mile and Carnegie Hill

Subway #4, #5 or #6 to 86th St, #6 to 96th St

Upper Fifth Avenue is nicknamed **Museum Mile**, home to New York's greatest concentration of museums, several of which are housed in the area's few remaining mansions. North of the Met (covered in Chapter 14), the neighbourhood is known as **Carnegie Hill** after steel magnate Andrew Carnegie, who constructed his mansion on Fifth Avenue and 91st Street; it's now the Cooper-Hewitt National Design Museum (see p.178). Note that the Museo del Barrio and the new Museum for African Art are covered in the Harlem chapter (see p.206).

Ukrainian Institute

2 East 79th St • Tues–Sun noon–6pm • $5 donation suggested • ☎ 212 288 8660, ⓦ ukrainianinstitute.org • Subway #4, #5, #6 to 86th St

Inevitably overshadowed by the Met just up the road, the **Ukrainian Institute** boasts a small but intriguing art collection – temporary exhibits from modern Ukrainian artists take up the second floor, but the upper levels contain some real gems. Still life from Sergei Belik, abstract work from Alexander Archipenko and paintings from David Burliuk, the one-eyed "father of Russian Futurism". The real highlights are the huge Soviet Socialist Realist canvases, saved from destruction in the 1990s by collector Jurii Maniichuk and on loan here till 2018; think Khrushchev meeting Yuri Gagarin in *Motherland Greets a Hero*. The building itself is a gorgeous example of Fifth Avenue opulence, built for wealthy banker Isaac Fletcher by C.P.H. Gilbert in 1899 but more famous for being the home of scandal-prone oilman Harry Sinclair in the 1920s.

Institute for the Study of the Ancient World

15 East 84th St, near Madison Ave • Tues–Thurs, Sat & Sun 11am–6pm, Fri 11am–8pm • Free • ☎ 212 992 7843, ⓦ nyu.edu/isaw • Subway #4, #5, #6 to 86th St

Primarily a cutting-edge research facility, NYU's **Institute for the Study of the Ancient World** also hosts thought-provoking exhibitions on prehistory – anything from mysterious Central European objects dating back five thousand years to ancient grave goods from the Republic of Georgia. Exhibitions usually last five months, but sometimes there are gaps between shows, so check in advance.

Park Avenue Christian Church

1010 Park Ave, at East 85th St • Daily 8am–5pm • Free • ☎ 212 288 3246, ⓦ parkavenuechristian.com • Subway #4, #5, #6 to 86th St

The Upper East Side's surfeit of spectacular churches continues with Gothic **Park Avenue Christian Church**, completed in 1911 by the ubiquitous firm of Ralph Adams Cram to mimic La Sainte-Chapelle in Paris – an audacious comparison that, incredibly, it almost pulls off. The magnificent Tiffany windows are the showstoppers here, a blend of figurative and symbolic coloured panels.

One block south at 980 Park Ave lies the incredibly opulent **Church of St Ignatius Loyola** (same hours), a grand Italian Baroque masterpiece of marble and vibrant murals that successfully re-creates Italy's High Renaissance (despite being completed in 1898).

15

Neue Galerie

1048 Fifth Ave, at East 86th St • Thurs–Mon 11am–6pm • $20, free first Fri of the month 6–8pm • ☎ 212 628 6200, ⓦ neuegalerie.org • Subway #4, #5, #6 to 86th St

Dedicated to early twentieth-century art from Austria and Germany, the small but enchanting **Neue Galerie** occupies an ornate Georgian-style mansion on the corner of East 86th Street. The house was completed in 1914 for industrialist William Starr Miller, but became the residence of formidable New York socialite Grace Vanderbilt between 1944 and 1953, after the death of her millionaire husband, Cornelius Vanderbilt III. In 2001, it was transformed into the museum, thanks largely to the work of New York art collectors Serge Sabarsky and Ronald S. Lauder.

The exhibits tend to rotate, but the collection contains some real gems. The galleries begin on the wood-panelled second floor, where the undoubted star is **Gustav Klimt**'s *Portrait of Adele Bloch-Bauer I* (1907), a resplendent portrait from Klimt's "Golden Period". The Bloch-Bauers were one of Vienna's richest Jewish families; the painting was looted by the Nazis in 1938 but descendants sued the Austrian government and had the painting returned in 2006 – the gallery is said to have paid $135 million for it soon after. On this floor, dedicated to art from Vienna circa 1900, you'll also find exceptional work by **Egon Schiele** and **Max Oppenheimer**, while the third floor is usually reserved for rotating German work from various movements of the early twentieth century: look out for Paul Klee (of the Blaue Reiter and Bauhaus movements), Ernst Ludwig Kirchner (of Die Brücke) and Otto Dix (of the Neue Sachlichkeit). At the Neue's *Café Sabarsky* (see p.286), you can pause for exquisite Viennese pastries before heading back to Museum Mile.

Guggenheim Museum

1071 Fifth Ave, at East 89th St • Sun–Wed & Fri 10am–5.45pm, Sat 10am–7.45pm • $22, pay what you wish Sat 5.45–7.45pm; multimedia tours free; free apps for iPhone and iPod Touch; guided tours daily 11am & 1pm (free) • ☎ 212 423 3500, ⓦ guggenheim.org • Subway #4, #5, #6 to 86th St

Multistorey car park or upturned beehive? Whatever you may think of the collection, it's the **Guggenheim Museum** building that steals the show. The structure, designed by **Frank Lloyd Wright** specifically for the museum, caused a storm of controversy when it was unveiled in 1959, bearing, as it did, little relation to the statuesque apartment buildings of this most genteel part of Fifth Avenue. Reactions ranged from disgusted disbelief to critical acclaim – "one of the greatest rooms erected in the twentieth century", wrote Philip Johnson, himself no slouch in the architectural genius stakes. Time has been kinder than his contemporaries were – nearly half a century later, the museum is now a beloved New York landmark.

The institution's namesake, **Solomon R. Guggenheim** (1861–1949), was one of America's richest men, thanks to his silver and copper mines. Although abstract art was considered little more than a fad at the time, Guggenheim, always a man with an eye for a sound investment, began collecting modern paintings with fervour. He bought wholesale the canvases of **Kandinsky**, then added works by **Chagall**, **Klee** and **Léger**, among others, and exhibited them to a bemused American public in his suite of rooms in the *Plaza Hotel*. The Guggenheim Foundation was created in 1937; after exhibiting the collection in various rented spaces, it commissioned Wright to design a permanent home. The museum's holdings have been bolstered since Guggenheim's day via acquisitions and donations. A significant gift came in 1976 when collector **Justin K. Thannhauser** handed over more works by Cézanne, Degas, Gauguin, Manet, Toulouse-Lautrec, Van Gogh and Picasso, among others, greatly enhancing the museum's Impressionist and Post-Impressionist holdings. The Foundation now includes museums in Abu Dhabi, Berlin, Bilbao and Venice (which is named for Solomon's niece Peggy, another art-collecting magpie).

The building

Collection of art aside, it's the **structure** that dominates – it's not hard to theorize that the egomaniacal Wright engineered it that way. Most visitors find it difficult not to be impressed (or sidetracked) by the tiers of cream concrete overhead, an uplifting interior space designed so that the public could experience the spiral of the central rotunda from top to bottom. The circular galleries rise upward at a not-so-gentle slope, so you may prefer to start at the top of the museum and work your way down; most of the temporary exhibits are designed to be seen that way.

The collection

Magnificent **temporary exhibitions** take up most of the museum, but you'll always see plenty of **Kandinsky**'s exuberant work (most temporary shows are linked, albeit tenuously, to pieces in the permanent collection). The Level 3 annexe houses the permanent **Kandinsky at the Bauhaus** exhibit, where you'll find some of the best pieces, including the jarring *Komposition 8*.

The Level 2 annexe also contains a small permanent display from the **Thannhauser Collection**: it's almost overwhelming to immediately see **Picasso**'s haunting *Woman Ironing* (on the right as you enter the annexe). Next in line are works by **Van Gogh** including his vivid *Roadway with Underpass* and *Landscape with Snow*. Further around the room you'll find a **Gauguin**, *In the Vanilla Grove*; **Monet**'s *The Palazzo Ducale Seen from San Giorgio*; and **Cézanne**'s hazy *Bibémus* and the wonderful *Man with Crossed Arms*. Note, though, that even the permanent displays get moved around, so you may not see all of the above.

National Academy Museum

1083 Fifth Ave, at East 89th St • Wed–Sun 11am–6pm • $15 • ☎ 212 369 4880, ⓦ nationalacademy.org • Subway #4, #5, #6 to 86th St

The **National Academy Museum** acts as the official gallery for the National Academy of Design, founded in 1825 by a group of artists including Samuel Morse. Intended to ape London's prestigious Royal Academy, it is today based in the bow-fronted, Beaux Arts townhouse next to the Church of the Heavenly Rest. The house was substantially rebuilt by millionaire Archer Huntington in 1913 (Archer's father made a fortune in San Francisco overseeing early American railways), and in 1939 he donated the building to the Academy.

The museum is usually open to the public for three or four **shows** a year, starting with the Academy's Annual in the spring, featuring work selected from members of the Academy, a list that has included big names like **Richard Diebenkorn**, **Chuck Close**, **Robert Rauschenberg** and **Jasper Johns**. Each artist – famous, notorious or neither – is required to donate a picture to the place when they join. On alternate years, work is supplied by a juried invitational group of exclusively non-academicians. The rest of the year, the Academy hosts thematic exhibitions with work from its permanent collection. When the galleries are closed between shows (check the website before you go), you can still peruse the shop.

Cooper-Hewitt National Design Museum

2 East 91st St, at Fifth Ave • ☎ 212 849 8400, ⓦ cooperhewitt.org • Subway #6 to 96th St

Housed in an elegant mansion completed for millionaire industrialist **Andrew Carnegie** in 1902, the **Cooper-Hewitt National Design Museum** is expected to reopen in 2014 after a mammoth redevelopment project ("Re:Design"). Established in 1897 by the granddaughters of Peter Cooper (see p.89), the museum became part of the Smithsonian network in 1967. The expansion will include a new permanent exhibition dubbed **"What is Design?"** on the first floor – drawing on the museum's collection of 200,000 items – and two higher floors of temporary exhibits. These shows are almost always worth checking out and include a diverse roster of subjects from modern car design to high fashion. The nearby townhouses at 7–11 90th St host the elegant **National Design Library**. Check the website for opening times and prices.

Jewish Museum

1109 Fifth Ave, at East 92nd St • Mon, Tues, & Sat & Sun 11am–5.45pm, Thurs 11am–8pm; also Fri 11am–5.45pm March–Nov • $12, Sat free, Thurs 5–8pm pay what you wish • ☎ 212 423 3200, ⓦ thejewishmuseum.org • Subway #6 to 96th St

Given how Jewish culture has flourished in New York, it is fitting that the **Jewish Museum** is the largest museum of Judaica outside Israel. Housed in the French Gothic **Felix Warburg Mansion** (built for the famous Jewish banker in 1908), the top two floors house "Culture & Continuity: The Jewish Journey", a permanent exhibition that traces the development of Judaism from 1200 BC to the modern day. Pivotal events such as the Babylonian exile of 586 BC, the destruction of the Temple in 70 AD, and the development of the Jewish diaspora are highlighted with films and some rare artefacts, including ancient pottery, ageing Hanukkah lamps, Roman burial stones and precious Torahs. After tackling anti-Semitism and the establishment of Israel in 1948, the exhibition concludes with a thoughtful study of modern Jewish identity. The lower floors host temporary exhibits, usually of famous Jewish artists such as Man Ray. It's a short walk from here north to the next museum, but make a detour along East 97th Street to see the **St Nicolas Russian Orthodox Cathedral**, its onion domes and crosses a wonderfully incongruous slice of Moscow amid the East Side mansions.

Museum of the City of New York

1220 Fifth Ave, at East 103rd St • Daily 10am–6pm • $10; free tours Wed 2pm • ☎ 212 534 1672, ⓦ mcny.org • Subway #6 to 96th St

Housed in a grand neo-Georgian building purpose-built in 1930 (that also served as the posh high school in the cult TV series *Gossip Girl*), the **Museum of the City of New York** has been transformed by major renovations in recent years. Most of the stylish galleries feature temporary exhibits – subjects delve into all sorts of New York-themed topics, from affordable housing design and Currier & Ives prints (the museum has one of the world's largest collections) to World Fairs and the Gilded Age. The enlightening "Timescape" audiovisual presentation (25min; 15min and 45min past the hour) on the second floor, which tackles the history of the city from the Lenape Indians to the 9/11 attacks, is permanent, as is the **Activist New York** gallery, a thought-provoking journey through the city's most contentious protest movements, from defending the Quakers in the 1650s to ongoing debates on gay rights, park access and bike lanes.

North and east of here, the neighbourhood rather joltingly switches from blocks of quiet, moneyed apartment buildings to **El Barrio**, or **Spanish Harlem** (p.204).

Yorkville and around

Subway #4, #5 or #6 to 86th St

It's only in **Yorkville** that the Upper East Side displays minute traces of New York's European immigrant history: around 1900, this was a German–Hungarian neighbourhood that spilled out from East 79th to 96th streets between Lexington and the East River.

Lexington Avenue itself was only gentrified in the 1960s, as the western stretches of the Upper East Side increased in value, and money-savvy property developers rushed in to snap up real estate farther east. Fifty years later, the signs of its economic heyday are already long gone, and this is now one of the cheaper residential areas in the city. The proliferation of small apartments (as well as a generous number of hip restaurants and sports bars) means that the East 70s and 80s are home to a number of young, unattached and upwardly mobile professionals.

Amid all the DVD stores and fast-food joints, there are a few hints of the old neighbourhood, notably traditional German delicatessens and cafés: look for lauded sausage-maker **Schaller and Weber**, at 1654 Second Ave at East 86th Street (Mon–Fri 9am–6pm, Sat 8.30am–6pm), established in 1937; and **Heidelberg**, next door at no. 1648 (see p.316), which is one year older. **Orwasher's Handmade Bread**, at 308 East 78th St near Second Avenue (Mon–Sat 7.30am–7pm, Sun 9am–4pm), was founded in 1916 and claims to have invented raisin pumpernickel bread during World War II.

15

Gracie Mansion

East End Ave, at East 88th St • 45min tours Wed 10am, 11am, 1pm & 2pm • $7, reservations required: call ☎ 311 or ☎ 212 570 4751 • ⓦ nyc.gov • Subway #4, #5, #6 to 86th St

One of the reasons that riverside Carl Schurz Park, at the end of East 86th Street, is so exceptionally well maintained is the high-profile security that surrounds **Gracie Mansion**. Built in 1799 by Scottish-born merchant Archibald Gracie, it is one of the best-preserved Federal-style buildings in New York. Appropriated by the city in 1896 (in lieu of unpaid taxes), Gracie Mansion has been the official **residence of the mayor of New York City** since 1942, when Fiorello LaGuardia set up house here; the name's a misnomer, since it's more a large wood-frame house than a grand residence. The mansion was meticulously restored in 2002, but other than a few antiques and the bold murals in the dining room, the house itself isn't particularly compelling, and the **tours** are most interesting for the effusive guides and the stories associated with past mayors.

Current billionaire mayor **Michael Bloomberg** has opted not to live at Gracie Mansion (though he does hold meetings and functions here) – a far cry from the **Rudy Giuliani** era when, after an acrimonious split, he and his wife continued to live in the same home even when his new partner was visiting.

Mount Vernon Hotel Museum

421 East 61st St, between First and York aves • Tues–Sun 11am–4pm, June & July Tues until 9pm, closed Aug • $8; visits by guided tours only (provided on demand until 3.30pm) • ☎ 212 838 6878, ⓦ mvhm.org • Subway N, R, #4, #5, #6 to Lexington Ave/E 59th St

Close to the East River is the **Mount Vernon Hotel Museum and Garden**, a fine schist stone house squashed between modern tower blocks. Inside, you'll find a series of 1820s period rooms, meticulously restored since 1924 when the house was saved by the Colonial Dames of America (an association of women who can trace their ancestry back to colonial times). The Dames were attracted by a connection with Abigail Adams Smith (daughter of President John Adams), though recent research has revealed this to be rather tenuous; the property was indeed once part of an estate bought by Abigail and her husband in 1795 (when this area was lush countryside), but the family soon went bankrupt, and it was actually completed as a carriage house in 1799 by the new owner. It served as a hotel between 1826 and 1833 before reverting to a private residence.

Roosevelt Island

Roosevelt Island sits in the middle of the East River, an odd little corner of New York that's home to around thirteen thousand people. While the modern tower blocks and new-town layout can seem a little soulless, there is a languid, small-community vibe on the island that can be appealing – it also has a breezy promenade with fabulous views of Midtown, and a scintillating (and bargain) cable-car ride across the river.

ARRIVAL AND INFORMATION

Arrival A scenic aerial tramway near the Queensboro Bridge (E 60th St and Second Ave) connects Manhattan with Roosevelt Island (3min) every 15min, 6am–2am, Fri & Sat until 3.30am; every 7.5min during rush hour; $2.75 one-way or $2.50 with Metrocard; ⓣ212 832 4555, ⓦrioc.com. You can also take the F train here. The Roosevelt Island Bus ($0.25) loops from Tramway Plaza north to the new Octagon development and back, stopping along Main St.

Information Head to the Roosevelt Island Historical Society kiosk, situated across from the tramway station (ⓣ212 688 4836, ⓦrihs.us); usually open Thurs–Sun noon–5pm, though times vary.

Brief history

Only two miles long and no more than 800ft wide, the island was known as **Minnahannock** by the local Native Americans. In 1686, ownership passed to English farmer Robert Blackwell, who imaginatively renamed it **Blackwell Island**. In 1828, the city of New York snapped up the land for $32,000 and assigned it for use as a **quarantine site** for criminals, lunatics and smallpox victims; in 1843, Charles Dickens came to expose conditions of the chronically ill, insane and destitute who were crowded into the eight hospitals and asylums built here. By 1921, it was officially known as **Welfare Island**, but by the 1950s much of the island was deserted, forgotten and unloved. Forward-thinking city mayor John Lindsay enlisted architects John Burgee and Philip Johnson to demolish most of the old buildings and create a master plan for new residential living areas. Duly rechristened Roosevelt Island in 1973, the island received its first new inhabitants two years later. Today, locals are fiercely protective of their hidden enclave: to snag one of the cheap apartments here, you'll have to join the years-long official waiting list.

North island

Arriving via the tramway or subway, stroll north along Main Street to see the white clapboard **Blackwell House**, built in 1796 by James Blackwell; the exterior has been lovingly restored, but you usually can't go inside. From here you can take the bus or wander up the west promenade soaking up the views of the Upper East Side. At the north end of the island, **Octagon Tower** was built in 1839 as the admin centre of New York's first municipal asylum (most of it was demolished in the 1970s) and is now incorporated into the Octagon Development; you can take a peek at the magnificent domed lobby and spiral staircase inside. At the northern tip itself, **Lighthouse Park** affords excellent views of the upper reaches of the East River, and is also home to a 50ft-high Gothic lighthouse, dating back to 1872.

South island

The southern end of the island is encompassed by **Southpoint Park** and the **Franklin Roosevelt Four Freedoms Park** (Thurs–Sun 9am–5pm; free), designed by famed architect Louis Kahn in the 1970s but only completed in 2012. You can wander along the riverside path here to see a ghostly reminder of the island's past: the ruins of the **Smallpox Hospital**, completed in 1856 by architect James Renwick. Nearby, the **Strecker Laboratory**, the city's premier laboratory for bacteriological research when it opened in 1892, was restored in the early 1990s and houses subway electrical infrastructure.

The Upper West Side and Morningside Heights

While the Upper East Side has always been a privileged stronghold, the Upper West Side, its counterpart on the other side of Central Park, is the somewhat younger, vaguely hipper, but nonetheless affluent rival. A decade or two ago, the Upper West Side was the neighbourhood of choice for upwardly mobile dot-commers, and though those days seem long gone, young professionals and families with just-about-school-age-children still make up a sizeable part of the population. This isn't to say it lacks glamour; the lower stretches of Central Park West and Riverside Drive are quite fashionable, while the network of performing spaces at Lincoln Center makes the neighbourhood New York's de facto centre of culture.

As you move further north, gorgeous – and occasionally landmarked – blocks pop up in the 80s, 90s and 100s, especially off and along Riverside Drive and the West End. In general, though, the neighbourhood loses some of its lustre along the way, culminating in **Morningside Heights**, home to **Columbia University** at the edge of Harlem, as well as the monolithic **Cathedral of St John the Divine**.

ARRIVAL AND DEPARTURE

By subway The #1,#2, and #3 lines run up Broadway the length of the Upper West Side and Morningside Heights, with the #1 stopping locally every six or so blocks; the B and C trace the path up and down Central Park West.

The Upper West Side

North of 59th Street, Midtown West morphs into the largely residential **Upper West Side**, though the area around Lincoln Center is quite commercial. The neighbourhood stretches alongside Central Park, running west from the park to the Hudson River, and north from Columbus Circle at 59th Street to 110th Street and the beginning of Morningside Heights. Its main artery is **Broadway** and its twin pinnacles of prosperity are the historic apartment houses of **Central Park West** and **Riverside Drive**. In between is a chequerboard of modern high-rise buildings, old brownstone, gourmet markets, flashy boutiques and family restaurants.

Brief history

Like practically every other neighbourhood in the city, the Upper West Side was once farmland. That began to change in 1879, when the opening of the Ninth Avenue elevated train made the open space west of Central Park more accessible to city residents, who mainly still lived downtown. Cheap tenements began to pop up, and the New York Central Railroad line, which transported livestock to the 60th Street stockyards, went in about a year later, adding the smell of farm animals to what was already a sensory overload. Between 59th and 65th streets, the neighbourhood became home to more warehouses than anything else, and the district had the early makings of a soulless slum.

One diamond in the rough, though, was the **Dakota Building** on 72nd Street, built in 1884. Slowly, other townhouses and high-class living quarters rose around it, displacing some of the hulking warehouses. Ten years later, as Manhattan began to grow north in earnest, the confluence of Eighth Avenue, Broadway and 59th Street became a hotbed of excitement. Concerts were held at the Majestic Playhouse on Broadway and 60th Street, theatres showcased popular vaudeville acts and quality watering-holes multiplied. By the 1920s, theatres for all types of entertainment (some more risqué than others) lined the Ninth Avenue train circuit. By 1929, shopping had taken over as the neighbourhood's main attraction, and the area has hardly looked back since.

Columbus Circle

Intersection of Broadway, Central Park West and 59th St • Subway A, B, C, D, #1 to 59th St-Columbus Circle

Columbus Circle is a roundabout, a rarity in Manhattan. It's also a pedestrian's worst navigation nightmare – be careful crossing the street. Amid the hum of traffic it's easy to overlook Columbus himself, a **statue** of whom stands uncomfortably atop a lone column in the centre island. Sit on the steps below and you can check out some striking nearby architecture.

Time Warner Center

10 Columbus Circle • Mon–Sat 10am–9pm, Sun 11am–7pm, restaurant hours may vary from these • Subway A, B, C, D, #1 to 59th St-Columbus Circle

The glitzy **Time Warner Center**, a massive, multi-million-dollar home for companies like CNN and Warner Books, finally opened in February 2004 after a highly publicized and problematic construction that included worker deaths and an on-site fire. The business

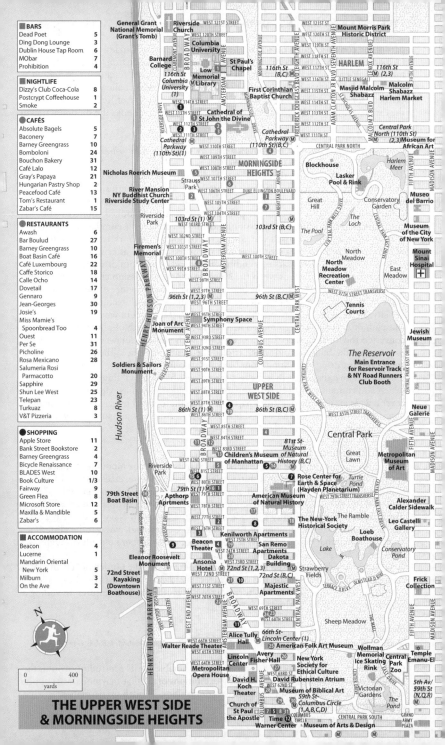

THE UPPER WEST SIDE & MORNINGSIDE HEIGHTS

part of the complex squats on top of the Shops at Columbus Circle (ⓦshopsatcolumbuscircle.com), a multistorey mall where, aside from some 45 or so mostly high-end shops, you'll find a couple of the city's priciest restaurants, including *Per Se*, run by Thomas Keller (see p.317). If your budget doesn't allow for a few hundred per head for dinner, you can kill some time – and still try some of Keller's creations – at the casual, third-floor *Bouchon Bakery* (see p.287), which overlooks the shopping ruckus.

Museum of Arts and Design

2 Columbus Circle • Tues–Sun 11am–6pm, Thurs & Fri till 9pm • $15; pay what you wish Thurs after 6pm • ☎ 212 299 7777,
ⓦ madmuseum.org • Subway A, B, C, D, #1 to 59th St-Columbus Circle

The oddball, vaguely Venetian building of white marble capped by lollipop columns and portholes that once loomed over Columbus Circle's southern side (at no. 2) was originally constructed as a museum showplace for Huntington Hartford's private art collection, opening its doors to the public in 1964. As a misjudged counter to his contemporaries' funding of Expressionist art, however, the museum lasted only five years, while the building itself was considered by some New York residents to be one of the city's grand follies, a sentiment that resonated for years afterwards.

Despite this, and after years of standing empty and falling into disrepair, preservationists were furious when the **Museum of Arts and Design** chose the place for the relocation of its collection. The battle was fought over whether or not the museum's practical needs should take precedence over the building's architectural importance to the city. In the end, with lawsuits flying all around, the museum won its case. The Museum of Arts and Design moved in after $90 million worth of renovations had converted the former gallery into a sleek tower with random cutaways that allow light to penetrate the building and which tripled the exhibition space. The eclectic collection, featuring everything from blown-glass objets d'art to contemporary jewellery, is now displayed to full effect spread over half the building's twelve floors, which also contain a small theatre and artist-in-residence studios. Changing exhibits cover a wide array of media (from paper to porcelain to metal to glass) and are often accompanied by lectures and workshops. A modern American restaurant, *Robert*, occupies the top floor and offers extravagant views.

Around Columbus Circle

Opposite Columbus Circle, on the park side, stands the **Maine Monument**, a large stone column with the prow of a ship jutting out from its base, erected in 1913 and dedicated to the 260 seamen who died when the battleship *Maine* inexplicably exploded in Havana Harbor in 1898, propelling forward the Spanish-American War. The boat was built over nearly a decade's time in the Brooklyn Navy Yard (see p.217). Across the street, at the junction of Broadway and Central Park West, is the glittering **Trump International Hotel**, which is responsible for the **Unisphere** outside, though it's not a patch on the one out in Flushing Meadows (see p.245).

For aesthetic relief, go west a few blocks and contemplate the **Church of St Paul the Apostle**, at Columbus Avenue and 60th Street (☎212 265 3495, ⓦstpaultheapostle .org), a beautiful Old Gothic structure housing Byzantine basilica features, including a high altar by Stanford White.

Museum of Biblical Art

1865 Broadway, at 61st St • Tues–Sun 10am–6pm • Free • ☎ 212 408 1500, ⓦ mobia.org • Subway A, B, C, D, #1 to 59th
St-Columbus Circle

Occupying the second floor of a corner building notable for its protruding atrium, the **Museum of Biblical Art** showcases rotating exhibitions of art that may not always appear directly religious but at least have spiritual connections. Though no permanent collection is on display, the museum is able to draw on the rare Bible collection that the the American Bible Society, headquartered in the same building, possesses.

New York Society for Ethical Culture

2 West 64th St, at Central Park West • ☎ 212 874 5210, ⓦ nysec.org • Subway #1 to 66th St-Lincoln Center

A few steps north of Columbus Circle is the **New York Society for Ethical Culture**, "a haven for those who want to share the high adventure of integrating ethical ideals into daily life". Founded in 1876 (though the building itself wasn't built until 1902), this distinguished organization also helped to found the NAACP (National Association for the Advancement of Colored People) and the ACLU (American Civil Liberties Union). It holds regular Sunday meetings and organizes occasional recitals and lectures on social responsibility, politics and other related topics.

American Folk Art Museum

2 Lincoln Square, Columbus Ave, at 66th St • ☎ 212 595 9533, ⓦ folkartmuseum.org • Tues–Sat noon to 7.30pm, Sun noon to 6pm • Free
• Subway #1 to 66th St-Lincoln Center

The **American Folk Art Museum**, once housed in an asymmetrical bronze building right next to MoMA (MoMA purchased the structure in 2010, when the Folk Art Museum went into default, and at press time, was planning to tear it down to pave the way for a new addition), occupies a smallish exhibit space across from Lincoln Center. What you'll see is somewhat unpredictable and rotates regularly, but the main holdings – which are lent out frequently for travelling exhibitions and to other spaces, like the South Street Seaport Museum (see p.55) – include an array of quilts, photos, carvings and unusual portraits by self-taught, or outsider, artists. Free music Fridays, at 5.30pm, is a draw.

Lincoln Center

Between 62nd and 66th sts, bordered by Amsterdam and Columbus aves and Broadway

16

Lincoln Center for the Performing Arts, an imposing group of six marble-and-glass buildings arranged around a large plaza, serves as the city's temple of high culture. Home to the world-class **Metropolitan Opera**, the **New York City Ballet** and the **New York Philharmonic**, as well as a host of other smaller companies, Lincoln Center is worth seeing even if you're not catching a performance; the best way is on an **organized tour** – otherwise you'll only be allowed to peek into the ornate lobbies of the buildings.

Not everything takes place in the concert halls; there's a sloped, grassy park atop the new *Lincoln* café-restaurant; an "urban grove", full of trees and benches, sits next to the David H. Koch Theater; and the celebrated **fountain**, a popular meeting spot at the centre of it all, offers *Bellagio*-style effects – designed by the folks who were also responsible for the flamboyant waterworks at the renowned Vegas mega-hotel.

Brief history

The Center is not, as most assume, named for President Abraham Lincoln; rather, it honours the name of the surrounding area in Manhattan's early times, probably named Lincoln for a tenant farmer who tilled the land here. Robert Moses came up with the idea of creating a cultural centre here in the 1950s as a way of "encouraging" the area's gentrification, one of his rare exercises in urban renewal that has been extremely successful. A number of architects worked on the plans, and the complex was finally built in the mid-1960s on a site that formerly held some of the city's poorest slums. In a case of life imitating art imitating life, once the slums were emptied and their residents moved to ghettos farther uptown, the deserted area became a movie set: before construction began in 1960, the run-down buildings served as the open-air location for *West Side Story*, which was based on the stage musical set here.

INFORMATION AND TOURS | **LINCOLN CENTER**

Access The fountain, between 63rd and 64th sts, is a good meeting spot, and the Atrium, 61 W 62nd St (see Tours below) serves as the visitor center (Mon–Fri 8am–10pm, Sat & Sun 9am–10pm).

Subway #1 to 66th St-Lincoln Center or A, B, C, D, to 59th St-Columbus Circle.
Information and events Contact Lincoln Center Information (☎ 212 875 5000, ⓦ lc.lincolncenter.org) for

WHAT'S IN A NAME?

Famous buildings and institutions, not to mention roads, bridges and more, undergo name changes for various reasons: company transformations (Citicorp to Citigroup), the choice to honour a public figure (the Queensboro Bridge – already also known as the 59th Street Bridge – has become the Ed Koch Queensboro Bridge, in honour of the ex-mayor) or, most commonly, money (the case at the David H. Koch Theater). A few of the more noteworthy instances:

OLD NAME	CURRENT NAME	WHY?
Museum of Radio & Television	Paley Center for Arts	William Paley, an early CEO of CBS, founded the museum
New York State Theater	David H. Koch Theater	Billionaire energy mogul who made $100 million donation to Lincoln Center
New York General Post Office	James Farley Building	Democratic politician who was also US Postmaster General
New York Public Library main building	Stephen A. Schwarzmann Building	Investment banker who donated $100 million for renovation and expansion
Triborough Bridge	Robert F. Kennedy Bridge	New York senator and US attorney general

16

specifics on scheduled entertainment at the Lincoln Center, which is often free (for example, there's an Autumn Crafts Fair in early September, folk and jazz bands at lunchtime, Thursday-evening concerts in the Atrium and dazzling fountain and light displays every evening in the summer). In addition, Lincoln Center hosts a variety of affordable summertime events, including July's Midsummer Night Swing and August's multicultural Out of Doors festival.

Tours Tours leave from the airy, pleasant David Rubinstein Atrium, on Broadway between 62nd and 63rd streets, and take in the main part of the Center (2–5 tours daily 10.30am–4.30pm, 60–90min; $17, ages 6–12 $8; ☎ 212 875 5350). Be warned that tours can get booked up and times vary each day (phone ahead to be sure of a place), and note that some focus more on art and architecture; whichever kind you take, you'll likely get to peek in on some rehearsals. The Atrium also hosts free music Thursdays (7.30pm). Backstage tours of the Met are available too: Sept–June Mon–Thurs 3pm, Sun 10.30am & 1.30pm; reservations required; $20; ☎ 212 769 7028.

The David H. Koch Theater

20 Lincoln Center Plaza, Lincoln Center • ☎ 212 870 5570 for ticket information • Subway #1 to 66th St-Lincoln Center

Philip Johnson's spare and elegant **David H. Koch Theater**, on the south side of Lincoln Center Plaza, is home to the New York City Ballet (including its famed annual performances of the *Nutcracker* in December). Its enormous foyer is ringed with balconies embellished with delicate bronze grilles and boasts an imposing, four-storey ceiling finished in gold leaf; the auditorium itself, a flashy jewel-box, feels fitting for the high-art performances. Speaking of art, an enormous *Numbers* by Jasper Johns lords it over one of the landings and deserves a look. The ballet season runs from late November to February and early April to June.

Avery Fisher Hall

10 Lincoln Center Plaza, Lincoln Center • ☎ 212 875 5030 for performance information • Subway #1 to 66th St-Lincoln Center

Opposite David H. Koch Theater on the north side of Lincoln Center Plaza, **Avery Fisher Hall** was the first of the three major buildings to be completed. Johnson had a hand in this one, too; he was called in to refashion the interior after its acoustics were found to be below par, and worked in collaboration with sound expert Cyril Harris on the project. Untouched during the renovations that marked the Center's fiftieth anniversary, the hall is set to be dramatically overhauled in upcoming years – though probably not before 2017. The Philharmonic performs here from late September into June, while **Mostly Mozart**, the country's first and most popular indoor summer chamber-music series, takes place in July and August.

The Metropolitan Opera House

30 Lincoln Center Plaza, Lincoln Center • See p.354 for tickets • Subway #1 to 66th St-Lincoln Center

In contrast to the surrounding Modernist starkness, Lincoln Center Plaza's focal point, the **Metropolitan Opera House** (aka "the Met"), is gushingly ornate and oozes opulence, with enormous crystal chandeliers – more sparkling than ever thanks to every stone being replaced – and swooping, red-carpeted staircases, designed for grand entrances in evening wear. Behind two of the high arched windows hang **murals by Marc Chagall**. The artist wanted stained glass, but at the time it was felt that glass wouldn't last long in an area still less than reverential toward the arts, so paintings were hung behind square-paned glass to give a similar effect. These days, they're covered for part of the day to protect them from the sun; the rest of the time they're best viewed from the plaza outside. The mural on the left, *Le Triomphe de la Musique*, is cast with a variety of well-known performers, while *Les Sources de la Musique* is reminiscent of Chagall's renowned scenery for the Met production of *The Magic Flute*: the god of music strums a lyre while a Tree of Life, Verdi and Wagner all float down the Hudson River.

Lincoln Center plazas

Two piazzas flank the Met. To the south there is **Damrosch Park**, a large space facing the Guggenheim Bandshell, where chairs are set up in the summer so you can catch free lunchtime concerts and various performances. To the north you will find the lovely, smaller **Hearst Plaza**, which has an infinity pool and the so-called **Illumination Lawn**, a grassy spot on the roof of a stylish café-restaurant. It also faces the **Vivian Beaumont Theater**, designed by Eero Saarinen in 1965 and home to the smaller **Mitzi E. Newhouse Theater** and **Claire Tow Theater**, allowing a Broadway, off-Broadway and off-off-Broadway venue to coexist under the same roof.

16

New York Public Library for the Performing Arts

40 Lincoln Center Plaza, Lincoln Center • Mon & Thurs noon–8pm, Tues, Wed, Fri & Sat noon–6pm • Free • ☎ 917 275 6975 or ☎ 212 870 1630, ⓦ nypl.org/lpa • Subway #1 to 66th St-Lincoln Center

The **New York Public Library for the Performing Arts** holds over eight million items (everything from performing-arts ephemera to scores and manuscripts), plus a museum that exhibits costumes, set designs and music scores; it hosts performances and screenings as well.

Alice Tully Hall, Walter Reade Theater and Juilliard School of Music

Broadway, at 65th St

Off of Lincoln Center Plaza stand a few more related structures, including **Alice Tully Hall**, a recital hall that houses the Chamber Music Society of Lincoln Center, and the **Walter E. Reade Theater**, which features foreign films and retrospectives and, together with the Avery Fisher and Alice Tully halls, hosts the annual New York Film Festival in September (see p.402). The celebrated **Juilliard School of Music** is in an adjacent building (see p.353).

Dante Park

The smallish **Dante Park**, an island on Broadway across from the main Lincoln Center Plaza, features a statue of its namesake; the American branch of the Dante Alighieri Society put it up in 1921 to commemorate the 600th anniversary of the writer's death. But the park's pièce de résistance is a piece of art dating from 1999: *Time Sculpture*, a bronze and stone geometric slab featuring a series of large clocks, was designed by Philip Johnson and dedicated to the patrons of Lincoln Center.

Central Park West

Central Park West stretches north from Columbus Circle to 110th Street along the western edge of the park. Home to some of the city's most architecturally distinguished apartment buildings, like the **Dakota** and **Majestic**, as well as the enormous **American Museum of Natural History**, it bustles with taxis and tour buses. In contrast, the sidestreets between Central Park West and Columbus Avenue in the upper 60s and 70s are quiet, tree-lined and filled with beautifully renovated brownstone, many of which are single-family homes.

Most of the monolithic, mansion-inspired apartment complexes in this area date from the early twentieth century and rim the edge of the park, hogging the best views. The southernmost of these is the **Hotel des Artistes**, at 1 West 67th St on Central Park West. It was built in 1917 especially for artists (hence the name), and was once the Manhattan address for the likes of Noël Coward, Norman Rockwell, Isadora Duncan and Alexander Woollcott. The building now consists of expensive apartments.

Four blocks north, between 71st and 72nd streets, you'll find the fittingly named **Majestic**. This gigantic, pale yellow, Art Deco landmark was thrown up in 1930 and is best known for its twin towers and avant-garde brickwork.

Dakota Building

1 West 72nd St, at Central Park West • Subway B, C to 72nd St

One of New York's more illustrious residences. the **Dakota Building** was a very early exercise in large housing co-operatives. The rather hoary story of its name is that when construction finished in 1884, its uptown location was considered as remote as the Dakota Territory by Manhattanites. Whatever the case, this grandiose hulk of German Renaissance masonry is undeniably impressive. Its turrets, gables and other odd details were all included for one reason: to persuade wealthy New Yorkers that life in an apartment could be just as luxurious as in a private house. For the most part, the developers succeeded: over the years, few of the residents here haven't had some sort of public renown, whether Lauren Bacall, Judy Garland or Leonard Bernstein; of course, it's best known as the home of the late John Lennon (see box, below).

16

> ### THE DEATH OF JOHN LENNON
>
> The Dakota Building, at 1 West 72nd St, is most famous as the former home of **John Lennon** – and present home of his widow, **Yoko Ono**, who owns a number of the building's apartments. It was outside the Dakota, on the night of December 8, 1980, that the ex-Beatle was murdered – shot by a man who professed to be one of his greatest admirers.
>
> His murderer, **Mark David Chapman**, had hung around outside the building all day, clutching a copy of his hero's latest album, *Double Fantasy*, and accosting Lennon for his autograph, which he received. This was nothing unusual: fans loitered outside the building and hustled for a glimpse of the singer. But when the couple returned from a late-night recording session, Chapman was still there, and he pumped five .38 bullets into Lennon as he walked through the Dakota's 72nd Street entrance. Lennon was picked up by the doorman and rushed to the hospital in a taxi, but he died on the way from blood loss. A distraught Yoko issued a statement immediately: "John loved and prayed for the human race. Please do the same for him." No one really knows the reasons behind Chapman's actions. Suffice it to say his obsession with Lennon had obviously unhinged him. Chapman was given a sentence of twenty years to life in prison; he has since been denied parole on seven separate occasions – Ono has sent a letter opposing his release each time, telling the parole board she wouldn't feel safe with Chapman walking the streets. (He's up again in 2014, but his chances of freedom seem unlikely.)
>
> Fans of Lennon may want to light a stick of incense across the road in **Strawberry Fields** (see p.153), a section of Central Park that has been restored and maintained in his memory through an endowment by Ono. Its trees and shrubs were donated by a number of countries as a gesture towards world peace. The gardens are pretty enough, if unspectacular, though it would take a hard-bitten cynic not to be a little bit moved by the **Imagine** mosaic on the pathway.

San Remo

145–146 Central Park West, at 74th St • Subway B, C to 72nd St

North of the Dakota Building is **San Remo**, another apartment complex, dating from 1930, which is one of the most significant components of the skyline here: its ornate twin towers, topped by columned, mock-Roman temples, are visible from most points in Central Park. Architecture aside, the residents' board is known for its snooty exclusiveness: they rejected Madonna as a buyer of a multi-million-dollar co-op, though her former boyfriend Warren Beatty did live here with Diane Keaton; Bono, Steve Martin, Stephen Spielberg and Demi Moore all have places too.

Central Park West–76th Historic District

A block north from San Remo is the **Central Park West–76th Historic District**, from 75th to 77th streets on Central Park West, and on 76th Street toward Columbus Avenue. It's home to a number of small, late nineteenth-century row houses, as well as the **Kenilworth Apartments**, at 151 Central Park West on 75th Street, notable for its mansard roof and carved limestone exterior.

The New-York Historical Society

170 Central Park West, at 77th St • Tues–Thurs & Sat 10am–6pm, Fri 10am–8pm, Sun 11am–5pm • $15, ages 5–13 $5; pay what you wish Fri 6–8pm • ☎ 212 873 3400, ⓦ nyhistory.org • Subway B, C to 81st St-Museum of Natural History

The sometimes-overlooked **New-York Historical Society** has greatly enhanced its appeal with a new renovation that has added, among other enticements, a soaring entryway, full of city artefacts; a museum within a museum, down in the basement and a cheery, upscale café-restaurant, *Caffè Storico*, that's open after museum hours for dinner (see p.318).

Start your visit off with a dramatic eighteen-minute film (narrated by Liev Schreiber) running through the history of the city, and then move on to the highlights of the permanent collection. Among the books, prints and portraits, as well as a research library with some two million manuscripts, are illustrations by **James Audubon**, the Harlem artist and naturalist who specialized in lovingly detailed paintings of birds: remarkably, the Historical Society holds all 433 existing original watercolours of Audubon's landmark *Birds of America*, though only a handful are shown at a time (except for a full exhibition in springtime) in order to preserve their condition. Elsewhere a broad cross-section of **nineteenth-century American painting** holds lots of portraiture and Hudson River School landscapes, most notably Thomas Cole's metaphorical *Course of Empire* series, though the sharp realism of Asher Brown Durand is also worth pausing over. The **Henry Luce Center**, on the top floor, contains cultural and historical odds-and-ends that help make the museum seem more about American, rather than New York history: advertising ephemera, political buttons and, above all, well over one hundred colourful Tiffany lamps. In the **library** are the original Louisiana Purchase document and the correspondence between Aaron Burr and Alexander Hamilton that led up to their deadly duel (see p.207), though the space is mainly geared toward researchers.

The **DiMenna Children's History Museum**, on the lower level, is an unusual mini-museum. It takes a unique approach by teaching history to children through the history of children (orphans, famous folk, notable New Yorkers); kids (it will probably be of most interest to those 8 to 10) can learn about the real-life Newsies in an interactive exhibit and thumb through books from an extensive library.

The American Museum of Natural History

Central Park West, between 77th and 81st sts, main entrance to museum on Central Park West at 79th St and to Rose Center on 81st St • Daily 10am–5.45pm, Rose Center open until 8.45pm on first Fri of month • Suggested admission $19, ages 2–12 $10.50, with additional cost for IMAX films, certain special exhibits and Hayden Planetarium shows ($33/$20.50 for an all-in pass) • ☎ 212 769 5100, ⓦ amnh .org • Subway B, C to 81st St-Museum of Natural History

The **American Museum of Natural History** is one of the best museums of its kind in the world, an enormous complex of buildings full of fossils, gems, taxidermy and other

16

BUTTERFLIES ARE NOT FREE

Half the year at the American Museum of Natural History (generally mid-Oct to May), the **Butterfly Conservatory** provides a welcome change from taxidermy and fossils. For an extra $6 (well worth it; note that it's a timed admission ticket), you get to step inside a vivarium – a hothouse environment – and watch colourful butterflies, from all over the world, flit about on plants, walls and, on occasion, you or your neighbour (don't brush them off if they do). It's humid and a bit smelly inside, but you soon forget any discomfort with the magic going on around you. You can even see pupae developing in a display case.

---

natural specimens. This elegant giant fills four blocks with a strange architectural melange of heavy Neoclassical and rustic Romanesque styles – it was built in several stages, the first of which was overseen by Central Park designer Calvert Vaux. Founded in 1869, it is one of the oldest natural-history museums in the world, with four floors of exhibition halls and some 30 million-plus items on display.

The entrance and second floor

The museum's vast marble front steps on Central Park West are a great place to read or soak up the sun. An appropriately haughty statue of museum co-founder Theodore Roosevelt looks out towards the park from his perch on horseback, flanked by a pair of Native Americans marching gamely alongside. This entrance (which opens onto the second floor) leaves you well positioned for a loop of the more interesting halls on that level: principally the **Hall of Asian Peoples** and **Hall of African Peoples**, both of which are filled with fascinating, often beautiful, art and artefacts, and backed up with informal commentary and indigenous music. The Hall of Asian Peoples begins with relics from Russia and Central Asia, moves on to pieces from Tibet – including a gorgeous re-creation of an ornate, gilded Tibetan Buddhist shrine – and then takes in China and Japan, with displays of some fantastic textiles, rugs, brass and jade ornaments; a Chinese bridal chair is topped with so many ornaments you wonder if it might just tip over when held aloft. The Hall of African Peoples displays ceremonial costumes, musical instruments and masks from all over the continent. Another highlight of this floor is the lower half of the **Hall of African Mammals**, a double-height room whose exhibits continue on to the third-floor balcony: don't miss the life-size family of elephants in the centre of the room (it's fairly difficult to do so).

The third and fourth floors

Once you're on the third floor, stop by the mildly creepy **Reptiles and Amphibians Hall**, filled with samples of almost any species in the category. A little less interesting is the **Eastern Woodlands and Plains Indians** exhibit, a rather pedestrian display of artefacts, clothing and the like.

The wildly popular **Dinosaur Exhibit**, the first stop for many, dominates the fourth floor. The museum houses the largest dinosaur collection in the world, with more than one hundred specimens on display. Here, you can touch fossils, watch robotic dinosaurs and walk on a transparent bridge over a 50ft-long Barosaurus spine. Interactive computer programs supplement the multi-level exhibits. The rest of the floor is given over to early vertebrates and mammals, from miniature camels to the largest known specimen of turtle.

The first floor

Downstairs on the first floor is the **Hall of Gems and Minerals**, which includes some strikingly beautiful crystals – not least the Star of India, the largest blue sapphire ever found. The enormous, double-height gallery dedicated to **Ocean Life** includes a 94ft-long (life-size) Blue Whale disconcertingly suspended from the ceiling. The **Hall of North American Mammals** has had a bit of work done to refresh the dark corridors, marble floors and illuminated diorama cases filled with stuffed specimens that have seen seventy years' worth of children on school trips. The greatest draw in this area, however, is the **Hall of Biodiversity**. It focuses on both the ecological and evolutionary aspects of biodiversity, with multimedia displays on everything from the changes humans have wrought on the environment (with examples of solutions brought about by local activists and community groups in all parts of the world) to a walkthrough of a simulated Central African rainforest. The **Lefrak Theater**, also located on this floor, presents some interesting nature-oriented IMAX films (there is an additional charge of $6).

The Rose Center for Earth and Space
Across from the Hall of Biodiversity is the **Rose Center for Earth and Space**, including the **Hall of Planet Earth**, a multimedia exploration of how the Earth works, with displays on a wide variety of subjects such as the formation of planets, underwater rock formation, plate tectonics and carbon dating. Items on display include a 2.7-billion-year-old specimen of a banded iron formation, volcanic ash from Mount Vesuvius and an earthquake monitoring system – a three-drum seismograph and colour screen work together to show real-time seismic activity from around the globe. The centrepiece of the room is the Dynamic Earth Globe, where visitors are able to watch the Earth go through its full rotation via satellite, getting as close as possible to the views astronauts see from outer space.

The Hall of Planet Earth links visitors to the rest of the Rose Center, which is made up of the **Hall of the Universe** and the **Hayden Planetarium**. The latter, an enormous sphere, 87ft in diameter, appears to be floating inside a huge cube above the 81st Street entrance. Inside are research facilities, classrooms and two theatres.

The state-of-the-art **Space Theater** uses a Zeiss projector to create sky shows with sources like the Hubble telescope and NASA laboratories. On the planetarium's second floor, the **Big Bang Theater** offers a multi-sensory re-creation of the "birth" of the universe: currently a half-hour movie entitled *Journey to the Stars*, narrated by Whoopi Goldberg. Outside the globe, the **Cosmic Pathway** is a sloping spiral walkway that takes you through thirteen billion years of cosmic evolution via a computerized timeline. It leads to the Hall of the Universe, which offers exhibits and interactive displays on the formation and evolution of the universe, the galaxy, stars and planets, including a mini-theatre where visitors can journey inside a black hole through computerized effects. There is even a display here entitled "The Search for Life" – examining the planetary systems on which life could exist – in case you hadn't questioned the meaning of existence enough by this point.

16

North on Broadway
Back on Broadway, at 72nd Street, tiny, triangular **Verdi Square** makes a fine place to take a break from the marvels of Lincoln Center. From the square, featuring a craggy statue in the likeness of the composer, you can fully appreciate the ornate balconies, round towers and cupolas of the **Ansonia Hotel** across the street (2109 Broadway, at West 73rd St). Never actually a hotel (it was planned as luxury apartments), the Ansonia was completed in 1904 and the dramatic Beaux Arts building is still the grande dame of the Upper West Side. It's been home to luminaries like Enrico Caruso, Arturo Toscanini, Lily Pons, Florenz Ziegfeld, Theodore Dreiser, Igor Stravinsky, Babe Ruth and, more recently, Angelina Jolie and Natalie Portman.

The enormous limestone **Apthorp Apartments** occupy an entire block from Broadway to West End Avenue, between 78th and 79th streets and were built in 1908 by William Waldorf Astor. The ornate iron gates of the former carriage entrance lead into a central courtyard with a large fountain visible from Broadway, though you won't be allowed to stroll in. The building, recently converted to condos from its former rent-stabilized self, is in a fair enough state now, though its fortunes have hiccuped over the years – it was used as the location for the crack factory in the 1991 movie *New Jack City*. The Upper West Side above 79th Street has seen a lot of changes in the last decade or so as the forces of gentrification have surged northward. One of the older establishments in the area is gourmet hub **Zabar's** (see p.385), at 2245 Broadway on 80th Street, which has been selling baked goods, cheese, caviar, gourmet coffee and tea – as well as an exhaustive collection of cooking gadgets – since 1934.

Children's Museum of Manhattan

212 West 83rd St, between Broadway and Amsterdam Ave • Tues–Fri & Sun 10am–5pm, Sat 10am–7pm, first Fri of the month 10am–8pm • $11, free first Fri of month 5–8pm • ☎ 212 721 1223, ⓦ cmom.org • Subway #1 to 86th St

Just off Broadway, the **Children's Museum of Manhattan** holds five floors of interactive exhibits that stimulate learning, in a fun, relaxed environment for kids (and babies) of all ages. Things rotate somewhat regularly, but a few permanent exhibits can be found: one centres on Dora and Diego-related amusements, and the other is the floor-wide PlayWorks area, where the younger set can occupy themselves with a talking dragon, fire truck and sand box, among other diversions.

Riverside Park

At the western edge of 72nd Street begins the four-mile stretch of **Riverside Park**. The entrance is marked by Penelope Jencks' pensive **Eleanor Roosevelt Monument** on the corner of 72nd Street and Riverside Drive, dedicated in 1996 by then First Lady Hillary Clinton. A less appealing local landmark is the new forest of skyscrapers overlooking the park from what used to be derelict shipping yards south of 72nd Street. This development, known as **Riverside South**, evolved – if that's the right word – from longtime plans to build something colloquially known as **Trump City** (who else but the billionaire developer?); at least the waterfront alongside has been preserved.

Riverside Park was conceived in the mid-nineteenth century as a way of attracting the middle class to the remote Upper West Side and covering the unappealing Hudson River Railway tracks that had been built along the Hudson in 1846. Though not as imposing or as spacious as Central Park, Riverside was designed by the same team: Frederick Law Olmsted and Calvert Vaux. Begun in 1873, the park took 25 years to finish; rock outcrops and informally arranged trees, shrubs and flowers surround its tree-lined main boulevards, and the overall effect is much the same today as it was then. The biggest changes to the park came in the 1960s, when Robert Moses widened it and added some of his usual concrete touches, including the rotunda at the **79th Street Boat Basin**. The basin is a delightful place for a break, with paths leading down to it located on either side of 79th Street at Riverside Drive (you'll hit Moses' rotunda first – keep going until you see water). Not on many visitors' itineraries, this is a small harbour and one of the city's most peaceful locations; a few hundred Manhattanites live on the water in houseboats, while others just moor their motorboats and sailboats. As well, there are summertime **kayak launches** from here (see p.394) and from a bit farther south, at 72nd Street.

The park continues along the water, punctuated by tennis courts, ball fields and a community garden (between 90th and 91st streets) before terminating just north of the General Grant National Memorial (see p.195).

Riverside Drive

The main artery of the Riverside Park neighbourhood is **Riverside Drive**: starting at West 72nd Street, it winds north, flanked by palatial townhouses and multistorey

---

RIVERSIDE DRIVE MONUMENTS

Riverside Drive is dotted with notable monuments: at West 89th Street, look for the **Soldiers and Sailors Monument** (1902), a marble memorial to the Civil War dead. Then there's the **Joan of Arc Monument** at West 93rd Street, which sits on top of a 1.6-acre cobblestone-and-grass park named Joan of Arc Island and is located in the middle of the Drive; it dates from 1915. You'll hit the **Firemen's Memorial** at West 100th Street, a stately frieze designed in 1913 with the statues of Courage and Duty on its ends. The most famous of Riverside Drive's monuments is **Grant's Tomb** (see p.195), further north.

apartment buildings, mostly thrown up in the early part of the twentieth century. In the 70s, especially, there is a concentration of lovely turn-of-the-twentieth-century townhouses, many with copper-trimmed mansard roofs and private terraces or roof gardens. Between 80th and 81st streets you will find a row of historic **landmark townhouses**: classic brownstones, they have bowed exteriors, bay windows and gabled roofs. You'll also find a number of other architectural surprises in this area, as many of the residences in the 80s between Riverside and West End have stained-glass windows as well as stone gargoyle faces leering from their facades.

There are more historic apartment buildings on Riverside Drive as you head north between 105th and 106th streets. What is now the **Riverside Study Center** (used by the shadowy Catholic sect Opus Dei) at 330 Riverside is a glorious five-storey Beaux Arts house built in 1900 – note the copper mansard roof, stone balconies and delicate iron scrollwork. The current headquarters of the **New York Buddhist Church** is at 331 Riverside Drive, though it was formerly the home of Marion "Rosebud" Davies, a 1930s actress most famous for her role as William Randolph Hearst's mistress.

The odd little building next door to no. 331 is also part of the church; it showcases a larger-than-life bronze statue of **Shinran Shonin** (1173–1262), the Japanese founder of the Jodo-Shinsu sect of Buddhism. The statue originally stood in Hiroshima and somehow survived the atomic explosion of August 1945. In 1955 it was brought to New York as a symbol of "lasting hope for world peace" and has been in this spot ever since. When it arrived, local lore had it that the statue was still radioactive, so in the 1950s and 1960s children were told to hold their breath as they went by. The Beaux Arts **River Mansion**, as 337 Riverside Drive is called, was home to **Duke Ellington** – and the stretch of West 106th Street between here and Central Park has been tagged Duke Ellington Boulevard in his honour.

16

Nicholas Roerich Museum

319 West 107th St, off Riverside Drive • Tues–Fri noon–5pm, Sat & Sun 2–5pm • Free , with suggested donation $5 • ☎ 212 864 7752, ⓦ roerich.org • Subway #1 to Cathedral Parkway-110th St

Near to Riverside Drive, in a manicured brownstone house, is the overlooked but appealing **Nicholas Roerich Museum**. It contains a small, weird and virtually unknown collection of original paintings by Nicholas Roerich, a Russian artist who lived in India and was influenced by religious mysticism; there are also some pieces by his son on display.

Strauss Park

Broadway, 106th St and West End Ave • Subway #1 to Cathedral Parkway-110th St

At the terminus of West End Avenue – itself running more or less parallel to Riverside Drive – is the small, triangular **Strauss Park**. The statue by Augustus Lukeman of a reclining woman gazing over a water basin was dedicated by Macy's founder Nathan Strauss to his brother and business partner, Isidor, and Isidor's wife, Ida, both of whom went down with the *Titanic* in 1912.

Morningside Heights

North of the Upper West Side, **Morningside Heights** stretches from 110th Street to 123rd Street, west to the Hudson River and east to Morningside Park, a small and rather unspectacular green space. The neighbourhood has a somewhat cool, college-town aura, a diverse mix of academics, professionals and working-class families who have banded together in the name of community preservation. Excepting the massive **Cathedral of St John the Divine** and **Columbia University**, there are few sights here per se, but it's worth ambling up here to get a sense of a close-knit neighbourhood, a feeling that the Upper West Side lost some time ago.

CATHEDRAL TOURS

Public **tours** of the Cathedral Church of Saint John the Divine are given Tuesday to Saturday at 11am (with additional tours in the afternoons), and Sunday at 1pm ($6) – meet at the Info Center, the blue booth right inside the main door. Access to the top of the cathedral was restricted for years due to the 2001 fire, but "vertical tours" have resumed. To clamber up spiral stone staircases to the roof, and be rewarded with a super view, call ☎ 212 932 7347 to make a reservation (Wed noon, Sat noon & 2pm; $15). Consider, too, visiting on a Monday around 1pm for the free organ recital.

The Cathedral Church of Saint John the Divine

1047 Amsterdam Ave, at 112th St • Mon–Sat 7.30am–6pm, Sun 7.30am–7pm • Free • ☎ 212 316 7540, ⓦ stjohndivine.org • Subway #1 to Cathedral Parkway-110th St

The **Cathedral Church of Saint John the Divine** rises out of its surroundings with a solid majesty – hardly surprising, since it is the largest Gothic-style cathedral in the world, if still unfinished. Indeed, its floor space – 600ft long by 320ft wide at the transepts – is big enough to swallow both the cathedrals of Notre Dame and Chartres whole.

This Episcopal church was conceived, in 1892, as a Romanesque monolith. When the architect in charge was replaced in 1911, the building's style shifted: it has ended up French Neo-Gothic. Work progressed well until the outbreak of war in 1939, and it wasn't until the late 1970s that it resumed. The church's problems aren't limited to timely construction, though: it declared bankruptcy in 1994, fraught with funding difficulties. Church members launched a massive international fundraising drive, which helped clear them from bankruptcy, but in 2001 church finances again became precarious following a fire that did significant damage to the cathedral. But don't let any of that put you off visiting – the church is one of New York's most impressive sights.

Though the structure appears finished at first glance, take a look up into one of its huge, incomplete towers, and you'll see how much there is left to do. Whether it ever gets done or not doesn't change the church's activity: St John's is very much a **community church**. It houses a soup kitchen and shelter for the homeless, sponsors AIDS awareness and health outreach initiatives, and has a gymnasium.

The interior

The **Portal of Paradise** at the cathedral's main entrance was completed in 1997, and is dazzlingly carved from limestone and painted with metallic oxide. Keep an eye out for the 32 biblical figures depicted (both male and female) and such startling images as a mushroom cloud rising apocalyptically over Manhattan. The portal is evidence of just how slow progress here really is: the carving took ten years. Only after entering the church does its staggering size become clear; the space is awe-inspiring, and definitely adds to the building's spiritual power. The interior shows the melding of the two architectural styles, particularly in the choir, where a heavy arcade of Romanesque columns rises to a high, Gothic vaulting; it is hoped the temporary dome will someday be replaced by a tall, delicate Gothic spire.

The open-minded, progressive nature of the church is readily visible throughout the cathedral building: note the intricately carved wood **Altar for Peace**, the **Poets Corner** (with the names of American poets carved into its stone-block floor), and an altar honouring AIDS victims. The amazing stained-glass windows include scenes from both the Bible and American history. All kinds of art, both religious and secular, grace the interior, from teak Siamese prayer chests to seventeenth-century tapestries, to a rare religious work by the late graffiti artist Keith Haring – his final finished piece.

The gardens

Outdoors, the cathedral's south side features the **Bestiary Gates**, their grilles adorned with animal imagery (celebrating the annual Blessing of the Animals ceremony held here on the Feast of St Francis), and a **Children's Sculpture Garden**, showcasing small bronze animal sculptures created by local schoolchildren. Afterwards, take a stroll through the cathedral yard.

Columbia University and around

The seven blocks between Broadway and Morningside Drive from 114th to 121st streets, with its main entrance at Broadway and 116th Street • Tours of the campus leave from the Visitor Center at the Low Memorial Library (Mon–Fri 11am & 3pm; free) • ☎ 212 854 4900, ⓦ columbia.edu • Subway #1 to 116th St-Columbia University

Ivy League-affiliated **Columbia University** is one of the most prestigious academic institutions in the country. Established in 1754, Columbia has a long and venerable history – it is the country's fifth-oldest institution of higher learning, it awarded the first MD degree in America, and the university sponsored groundbreaking atomic research in the 1940s. The Morningside Heights campus, modelled after the Athenian *agora* (or town square), was laid out by McKim, Mead, and White after the university moved here from midtown in 1897.

Amid the campus's Italian Renaissance-style structures, the domed and colonnaded **Low Memorial Library**, at 116th Street on Broadway, is a real stunner. Built in 1902, the Neoclassical structure is on the New York City Register of Historic Places and is a commanding sight. St Paul's Chapel, with its dome, stained glass and Guastavino tiling, is also worth poking around. Across Broadway sits women's-only **Barnard College**, one of the Seven Sisters' institutions and a part of Columbia University.

Running alongside the campus, Broadway is characterized by a lively bustle, with numerous inexpensive restaurants, bars and cafés, and a few bookstores. The former *West End* bar (2911 Broadway, at 113th Street) was the hangout of Jack Kerouac, Allen Ginsberg and the Beats in the 1950s; it still serves a student crowd, although it's now a Cuban restaurant.

16

Riverside Church

490 Riverside Drive, at 120th St • Daily 7am–10pm, Sun service 10.45am, hour-long tours follow service at 12.15pm • Free • ☎ 212 870 6700, ⓦ theriversidechurchny.org • Subway #1 to 116th St-Columbia University

Several blocks north and west of Columbia University, **Riverside Church** has a graceful French Gothic Revival tower, loosely modelled on the cathedral at Chartres. Like St John the Divine, it has become a community centre for the surrounding parish and puts on the odd musical and theatrical event. Twenty floors up, the **carillon** (the largest in the world, with 74 bells) has great views of Manhattan's skyline, New Jersey and beyond; however, tours up the tower have been suspended for a number of years – and that's unlikely to change soon (you can always call to be sure). Make sure to root around inside the body of the church, too: its open interior stands in stark contrast to the mystery of St John the Divine.

Grant's Tomb

Riverside Drive, at 122nd St • Thurs–Mon 9am–5pm, mausoleum open every other hour from 10am; free talks at 11.15am, 1.15pm & 3.15pm • ☎ 212 666 1640, ⓦ nps.gov/gegr • Subway #1 to 125th St-Columbia University

Up the block from Riverside Church is the General Grant National Memorial, better known as **Grant's Tomb**. This Greek-style memorial is the nation's largest mausoleum, home to the bodies of conquering Civil War hero (and blundering eighteenth US President) Ulysses S. Grant and his wife, in two black marble Napoleonic sarcophagi. The main floor has displays on the general's life and exploits.

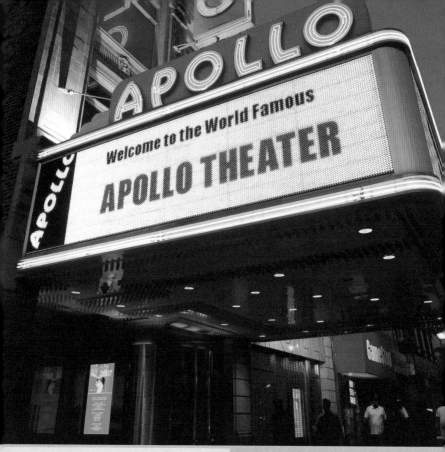

APOLLO THEATER, 125TH STREET

Harlem and north Manhattan

The most famous black community in America, Harlem has been the bedrock of African-American culture since the 1920s, when poets, activists and jazz blended in the Harlem Renaissance. Though it acquired a notoriety for street crime in the 1970s, it is now a neighbourhood on the rise, thanks to real estate and retail developments. Indeed, Harlem's streets are as safe as any other in New York, and the most pressing issue of the day is gentrification. Though most tourists still visit Harlem solely to see its wonderful gospel choirs on Sundays, you'll also find some fabulous West African and soul food restaurants, a vibrant local jazz scene and plenty of historic sights – some of the prettiest streets in the city are preserved here.

Further uptown is **Hamilton Heights**, a largely residential spot pepped up by an old Federal-style historic mansion and the campus of the City College of New York. Continuing north from there, you'll hit the Dominican stronghold of **Washington Heights**, while the northernmost tip of the island, known as **Inwood**, is home to **The Cloisters**, a museum-as-mock-medieval-monastery that holds the Met's superlative collection of medieval art. All the areas detailed below are generally safe for visitors, especially during the day when there are usually lots of people around – just take the usual precautions at night, and stick to the main thoroughfares. To get around at night by **taxi**, your best bet is to grab one of the many livery cabs cruising the main avenues (see p.26), and negotiate the fare in advance (around $20–25 to midtown).

INFORMATION

Tourist information Harlem's official information kiosk is inside the Studio Museum at 144 W 125th St (Mon–Fri noon–6pm, Sat & Sun 10am–6pm; ☎ 212 222 1014). You'll also find plenty of help at the Harlem Heritage Tourism and Cultural Center, at 104 Malcolm X Blvd, just south of West 116th Street (daily 10am–6pm; ☎ 212 280 7888, ⓦ harlemheritage.com); this is the office of local tour operator Neal Shoemaker (see p.30), who is a wealth of local knowledge. Of the websites that serve the neighbourhood, ⓦ harlemonestop.com has excellent listings and local information.

Harlem

Subway A, B, C, #1, #2 and #3 to 125th St

Practically speaking, **Harlem**'s sights are too spread out to amble between: they stretch over seventy blocks. You'll do best to make several trips if you want to see them all. It can also be helpful to take a **guided tour** (see p.30) to get acquainted with the area. In summer, be sure to check out **Harlem Week** (ⓦ harlemweek.com), a series of concerts and special events held in July and August.

Brief history

Although the Dutch founded the settlement of **Nieuw Haarlem** in 1658, naming it for a town in Holland, the area remained primarily farmland up until the mid-nineteenth century, when the New York and Harlem Railroad linked the area with Lower Manhattan. The suburb's new, fashionable brownstones attracted better-off immigrant families, mainly German Jews from the Lower East Side, but they failed to tempt the wealthy northwards. Black real-estate agents saw their chance: from the late 1890s they snapped up the empty houses for next to nothing, then rented them to the city's growing community of African-Americans.

Harlem's explosion of black culture quickly appeared in the 1920s, the musical and literary movement known as the **Harlem Renaissance** (see box, p.199). The Depression and postwar years were not kind to the area, however, and the Renaissance was followed by several decades of worsening economic conditions. In the 1960s and 1970s, drug lords such as **Frank Lucas** and **Nicky Barnes** made millions selling heroin; in the late 1980s, crack-cocaine devastated the neighbourhood.

In the late 1990s, things began to turn around. A plethora of urban and community grants were put into effect for commercial and retail development, housing and general urban renewal. That initial investment is paying off: Harlem's historic areas are well maintained and there seems to be construction everywhere you turn. The questions facing the community now are how to manage and control the area's development (particularly as Columbia University expands into older neighbourhoods), as well as how to reconcile it with the long-term poverty and unemployment still very much in evidence.

Up to 116th Street

Subway B, C to Cathedral Parkway, #2, #3 to Central Park North for 110th St • B, C, #2, #3 to 116th St

Harlem lies north of 110th Street and Central Park, and it's from here along any of Harlem's main north–south arteries to **116th Street** and 125th Street that the neighbourhood's recent

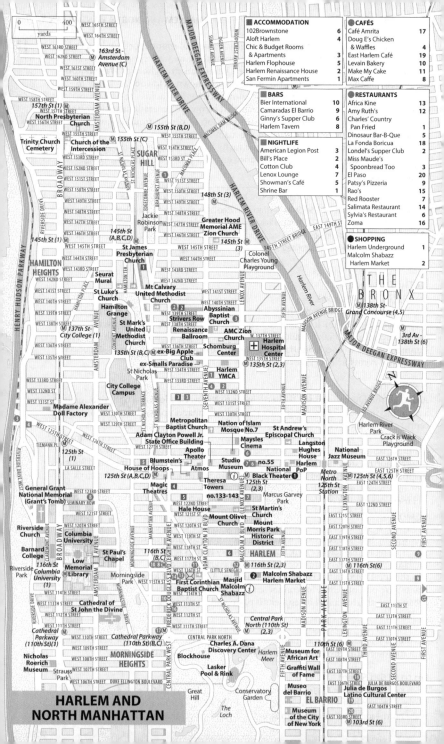

HARLEM AND NORTH MANHATTAN

ACCOMMODATION
102Brownstone	6
Aloft Harlem	4
Chic & Budget Rooms	
& Apartments	3
Harlem Flophouse	5
Harlem Renaissance House	2
San Fermin Apartments	1

BARS
Bier International	10
Camaradas El Barrio	9
Ginny's Supper Club	6
Harlem Tavern	8

NIGHTLIFE
American Legion Post	3
Bill's Place	2
Cotton Club	4
Lenox Lounge	7
Showman's Café	5
Shrine Bar	1

CAFÉS
Café Amrita	17
Doug E's Chicken	
& Waffles	4
East Harlem Café	19
Levain Bakery	10
Make My Cake	11
Max Caffe	8

RESTAURANTS
Africa Kine	13
Amy Ruth's	12
Charles' Country	
Pan Fried	1
Dinosaur Bar-B-Que	5
La Fonda Boricua	18
Londel's Supper Club	2
Miss Maude's	
Spoonbread Too	3
El Paso	20
Patsy's Pizzeria	15
Rao's	9
Red Rooster	7
Salimata Restaurant	14
Sylvia's Restaurant	6
Zoma	16

SHOPPING
Harlem Underground	1
Malcolm Shabazz	
Harlem Market	2

transformation is most in evidence. Sixth Avenue becomes Malcolm X Boulevard (though it's still known to most by its old name Lenox Ave), while Seventh Avenue becomes Adam Clayton Powell, Jr Boulevard (shortened to Powell Blvd here), a primarily residential strip of graceful brownstones. From Cathedral Parkway subway station wander up **Frederick Douglass Boulevard** (Eighth Ave) between 110th and 125th streets to see the most obvious signs of change, with new cafés, stores and bars replacing vacant lots; the new condo buildings around here have been dubbed Harlem's "Gold Coast".

At 116th Street, turn right – the stretch between Frederick Douglass and Malcolm X boulevards has become a hub for West African immigrants and is unofficially known as **Little Senegal** or Little West Africa. It's estimated that at least 40,000 Senegalese have settled in New York in the last few years, as well as smaller groups from Nigeria, Ivory Coast, Guinea and Mali. They've opened up shops, beauty parlours and restaurants here to create a thriving neighbourhood.

There are also some African-influenced buildings nearby, including the fanciful blue-and-white Moorish-style **First Corinthian Baptist Church** (usually locked; ☏212 864 5976), at 1912 Powell Blvd on West 116th Street. Originally built as the Regent Theater in 1912, this was one of America's earliest movie palaces before being transformed into a church in 1929.

Malcolm Shabazz Harlem Market

52 West 116th St, at Malcolm X Blvd • Daily 10am–8pm • Free • ☏ 212 987 8131 • Subway #2, #3, to 116th St

Just beyond Malcolm X Boulevard you'll see the bazaar-like **Malcolm Shabazz Harlem Market**, established in 1994 with help from the nearby mosque (see below), its entrance marked by colourful fake minarets. The market's offerings include T-shirts, jewellery, clothing and more, all with a distinctly Afro-centric flavour – it's worth stopping by, mostly since what's on sale here differs so much from the usual flea-market staples. Note that many stalls don't open until after lunch.

Masjid Malcolm Shabazz

102 West 116th St, at Malcolm X Blvd • Visits by appointment only • Free • ☏ 212 662 2200 • Subway #2, #3, to 116th St

At the junction of Malcolm X Boulevard and West 116th Street, look for the green onion dome of the **Masjid Malcolm Shabazz**, once the Nation of Islam's Temple No.7

THE HARLEM RENAISSANCE

The **Harlem Renaissance**, during which the talents of such icons as Billie Holiday, Paul Robeson and James Weldon Johnson took root and flowered, served as inspiration for generations of African-American musicians, writers and performers. In the 1920s, Manhattan's white residents began to notice Harlem's cultural offerings: after downtown went to bed, the sophisticated set drove north, where **jazz musicians** such as Duke Ellington, Count Basie and Cab Calloway played in packed venues like the Cotton Club, Savoy Ballroom, Apollo Theater and Smalls Paradise, and the liquor flowed freely, despite Prohibition. But the Harlem Renaissance wasn't just about music. It was also characterized by the rich body of **literature** produced by Johnson, Langston Hughes, Jean Toomer and Zora Neale Hurston, among many others – Hughes declared the movement to be over in 1931 after the death of noted African-American socialite and patron **A'Lelia Walker**.

Yet even before the Great Depression, it was hard to scrape out a living here, and the economic downturn of the 1930s drove out the middle class. It may be because evening revellers never stayed longer than the last drink that neither they, nor many histories of the period, recall the rampant **poverty** that went hand-in-hand with Harlem's raunchy, anything-goes nightlife.

One of the lasting legacies of this period, however, has been the neighbourhood's sense of **racial consciousness**. First evidenced during the 1920s and 1930s in the writings and speeches of men like Marcus Garvey, W.E.B. DuBois and Charles S. Johnson, the same spirit is still alive today in such larger-than-life firebrands as reverends Al Sharpton (whose National Action Network is based in Harlem) and Calvin Butts (influential minister of the Abyssinian Baptist Church).

17

and Malcolm X's base until his split with the Nation in 1964 (see box, p.210). After Malcolm's assassination in 1965, the mosque was firebombed then rebuilt with the dome you see today. The Nation of Islam later moved to 106 West 127th St, and the Shabazz mosque now serves an Orthodox Sunni community of predominantly African-American and Senegalese Muslims. Non-Muslims can **visit the mosque**, but you must email ✉ msmosque@aol.com in advance (name, reason to visit, preferred time) – do so and you'll get a rare insight into the American Muslim community.

Mount Morris Park Historic District
Subway #2, #3, to 125th St

The area around Malcolm X Boulevard between West 118th and 124th streets is known as the **Mount Morris Park Historic District**. Initially inhabited by white commuters, the area then became home to the city's second-largest neighbourhood of Eastern European Jewish immigrants (after the Lower East Side), and finally shifted to a primarily black neighbourhood in the 1920s. This series of complex demographic shifts has created a profusion of diverse religious structures, and has helped place the neighbourhood on the National Register of Historic Places. Today, it's an eminently desirable place to live – writer Maya Angelou lives on 120th Street – and the district has an active community-improvement association (☎ 212 369 4241, ⊛ mmpcia.org) that runs events and talks. It also holds the **Morris Park Annual Historic House Tour Open Day** in June, the best time to see inside the area's elegant homes.

One of the district's most interesting buildings is **Mount Olivet Baptist Church**, at 201 Malcolm X Blvd on West 120th Street, a Greco-Roman-style temple that was built as a synagogue in 1907 (the Baptists bought it in 1925). Compare its design with the sombre, bulky Romanesque Revival **St Martin's Episcopal Church**, at the southeast corner of Malcolm X Boulevard and West 122nd Street; completed in 1889, it's noted for the 42-bell carillon installed in the tower (rung on Sundays). Both buildings open only for services.

Marcus Garvey Park
West 120th and 124th sts, between Mount Morris Park West and Madison Ave • Daily 6am–dusk • Free • ⊛ nycgovparks.org • Subway #2, #3 to 125th St

Heading east along West 122nd Street from Malcolm X Boulevard brings you to **Marcus Garvey Park**, formerly Mount Morris Park; it takes its new name from the black leader of the 1920s. The park's most notable feature is an octagonal 47ft-high cast-iron **Mount Morris Fire Watchtower** built in 1857 on a peak in the centre, a unique example of the early-warning devices once found throughout the city and in operation till 1909.

125th Street and around
Subway A, B, C, D, #2, #3, #4, #5, #6 to 125th St

The stretch of **125th Street** between Broadway and Fifth Avenue is Harlem's main commercial drag. It's here that recent investment in the area is most obvious – note the presence of numerous chains, mobile-phone stores and fashion retailers like H&M. This was Malcolm X's beat in the 1950s and 1960s – he strolled and preached on 125th Street, and photos of him and his followers here have passed into legend.

Ex-President **Bill Clinton** – still much admired in Harlem – established his offices at 55 West 125th St just east of Malcolm X Boulevard in 2001, a move that in large part accelerated the current renaissance of the area.

National Jazz Museum
104 East 126th St, suite 2D • Mon–Fri 10am–4pm • Free • ⊛ jazzmuseuminharlem.org • Subway #4, #5, #6 to 125th St

Harlem – along with New Orleans – is one of the cradles of **jazz**. Duke Ellington, Thelonious Monk, Charlie Parker, Count Basie, John Coltrane and Billie Holiday all

CRACK IS WACK

Keith Haring fans should make the pilgrimage two blocks east of the National Jazz Museum to the subtly named **Crack is Wack Playground** (East 127th St and Second Ave), where the pop-artist painted the now-famous *Crack Is Wack* mural in 1986 on both sides of the handball court walls. Featuring Haring's signature cartoonish style and bright colours, the mural made a serious anti-drug statement at the height of the Harlem crack epidemic.

got their start here, yet there is surprisingly little to show for this musical heritage. The **National Jazz Museum** is a rare exception, though for now it is more of an organizational body than a conventional museum; the plan is to eventually open a full-scale jazz museum opposite the Apollo Theater on West 125th Street (the target is 2015), but for now its main function is to arrange jazz-related programmes, classes and live events (check the website). Aficionados should still check out the visitors' centre, which is chock-full of books, CDs, DVDs and a first-class exhibit of photos of jazz legends and venues on the walls – the enthusiastic volunteers are a mine of information, and you may also catch New Orleans pianist (and artistic director) Jonathan Batiste knocking out a tune. They also have a copy of the now legendary "**Great Day in Harlem**" photo, taken by Art Kane in 1958 and a one-time ensemble of all the era's top jazz musicians (Count Basie, Sonny Rollins and 55 others). Fans can visit the stoop where the shoot took place at 17 East 126th St. One block north, at 20 East 127th St, is **Langston Hughes House**, the faded 1869 brownstone where the lauded poet lived from 1948 till his death in 1967 (only a stencilled name on the window in the door marks the connection).

Studio Museum in Harlem

144 West 125th St, at Malcolm X Blvd • Thurs & Fri noon–9pm, Sat 10am–6pm, Sun noon–6pm • $7, free Sun • ☎ 212 864 4500, ⓦ studiomuseum.org • Subway #2, #3 to 125th St

The absorbing **Studio Museum in Harlem** has over 60,000 square feet of exhibition space dedicated to contemporary African-American painting, photography and sculpture. The permanent collection is displayed on a rotating basis and includes works by Harlem Renaissance-era photographer James Van Der Zee, as well as paintings and sculptures by postwar artists.

Adam Clayton Powell, Jr State Office Building

163 West 125th St, at Powell Blvd • Mon–Sat 10am–5pm • Free, photo ID required to enter • ☎ 212 961 4390 • Subway A, B, C, D, #2, #3 to 125th St

Looming over the middle of West 125th Street, the Brutalist **Adam Clayton Powell, Jr State Office Building** was commissioned in 1972 and built on the corner of Powell Boulevard (it's still Harlem's tallest building). The building was named in honour of Harlem's first black congressman (see box, below), and his 12ft-high bronze **statue** was unveiled here in 2005.

REVEREND ADAM CLAYTON POWELL, JR

In the 1930s, the **Reverend Adam Clayton Powell, Jr** (1908–1972) was instrumental in forcing Harlem's stores, most of which were white-owned and retained a white workforce, to begin employing the blacks whose patronage ensured the stores' survival. Later, he became the first African-American on the city council, then New York's first black congressional representative, during which time he sponsored the country's first minimum-wage law. His distinguished career came to an embittered end in 1967 when, amid strong rumours of the misuse of public funds, he was excluded from Congress by majority vote. This failed to diminish his standing in Harlem, where voters re-elected him: he sat until the year before his death, and there's a fitting memorial on the boulevard that today bears his name.

17

Theresa Towers

2090 Powell Blvd, at West 125th St • Closed to the public • Subway A, B, C, D, #2, #3 to 125th St

The tall, narrow **Theresa Towers** office building was until 1967 the Theresa Hotel. Designed by George and Edward Blum in 1913, it still stands out from the rest of West 125th Street, thanks to its gleaming white terracotta patterns topped with sunbursts. Not desegregated until 1940, the hotel became known as the "Waldorf of Harlem". Fidel Castro was a guest here in 1960 while on a visit to the United Nations, when he shunned midtown luxury in a popular political gesture.

Apollo Theater and around

253 West 125th St, at Frederick Douglass Blvd • ☎ 212 531 5300, ⓦ apollotheater.org • Subway A, B, C, D, #2, #3 to 125th St

Walk a little further west along 125th Street from the Powell Building and you reach the legendary **Apollo Theater**. Although it's not much to look at from the outside, from 1934 to the 1970s this venue was the centre of black entertainment in New York. Almost all the great figures of jazz and blues played here, along with singers, comedians and dancers; past winners of its famous **Amateur Night** (still running March–Oct Wed 7.30pm; tickets $20–32) have included Ella Fitzgerald, Billie Holiday, Luther Vandross, The Jackson Five, Sarah Vaughan and James Brown.

Yet the Apollo is not just a music venue; it's become the spiritual heart of black America, a place where locals and outsiders instinctively come together at important moments in history: when **James Brown**'s casket lay in state in the theatre in 2006, the queues to view it stretched for blocks, and when **Michael Jackson** died in 2009, fans gathered to celebrate his music outside – an official exhibit was arranged inside the theatre a few days later.

On the other side of the street, look out for the verdigris-stained pillars of **Blumstein's** department store at 230 West 125th St, the Art Nouveau landmark completed in 1923 and scene of Adam Clayton Powell, Jr's biggest victory against the whites-only hiring policy in 1934 (see box, p.201). Blumstein's itself is long gone, but the stores around here are well worth dipping into: **Atmos** (Mon–Sat 11am–8pm, Sun noon–7pm; ⓦ atmosnyc.com), at 203 West 125th St, has a cult following for its ultra-hip trainers, while **House of Hoops** (daily 10am–8pm) at 268 West 125th St is dedicated to all things basketball.

135th Street and around

Subway B, C, #2, #3 to 135th St

The blocks north of 125th Street contain little of interest until you reach **135th Street**, the historic heart of Harlem; though the commercial pulse of the neighbourhood has drifted south over the years, back in the 1920s and 1930s this was where most of the action took place. The junction of Powell Boulevard and West 135th Street was particularly important: legendary **jazz** clubs Small's Paradise and Big Apple faced each other on 135th Street, on the west side of Powell (see p.205). The streets nearby were also the haunt of ragtime composer **Scott Joplin**, who moved to Harlem around 1916, while Billie Holiday got her start on West 133rd Street, known as "**Jungle Alley**" in the 1930s, when it was lined with speakeasies.

TOURS OF THE APOLLO THEATER

You can tour the nation's temple of African-American culture, but you'll need to call in advance. Pre-arranged one-hour **guided tours** of the Apollo Theater are available for groups of 20 or more on Monday, Tuesday, Thursday & Friday at 11am, 1pm & 3pm; Wednesday at 11am; weekends at 11am & 1pm ($16 Mon–Fri, $18 Sat & Sun). Smaller groups should call Billy Mitchell, the tour director (☎ 212 531 5337), and he will try to add you to the next scheduled group.

17

Equally storied is **West 136th Street**, a block of narrow faux brownstones (with plaster facades) between Powell and Douglass completed in 1896; no. 108–110 was the home of African-American millionaire **A'Lelia Walker** (see p.199), where Harlem artists, writers and musicians gathered for all-night parties.

Continuing north on Powell, you'll see the forlorn-looking **Renaissance Ballroom** (see box, p.205) on the right between West 137th and 138th streets. Turn right on Odell Clark Place (138th St) for the Abyssinian Church – signs around here declaring "The Abyssinian Neighbourhood" usually mean the church owns property on that block.

Abyssinian Baptist Church

132 Odell Clark Place (formerly 138th St), at Powell Blvd • Tourists are welcome at the Sun 11am service only; 2hr 30min • Free •
⊙ 212 862 7474, ⓦ abyssinian.org • Subway B, C, #2, #3 to 135th St

Thousands of tourists visit the **Abyssinian Baptist Church** each year just to see and hear the gut-busting **choir** on Sunday (see box, below) – it's a magical experience, but remember that this is a religious service and not a show (no photos). The church was first incorporated in 1808 in what is now Tribeca (making it the second-oldest black church in the US). Its founders included a group of African-Americans living in New York, as well as some Ethiopian merchants, who were tired of segregated seating at Baptist churches (the church's name comes from the traditional name for Ethiopia). The Abyssinian started becoming the religious and political powerhouse that it is today in 1908, when the **Reverend Adam Clayton Powell, Sr** (1865–1953) was appointed pastor, moving the church to Harlem in 1920. Construction on the current Gothic and Tudor building was completed in 1923, and **Reverend Adam Clayton Powell, Jr** (see box, p.201) took over in 1937. He remained pastor until 1971, and for a while this was the largest Protestant congregation in the US.

Strivers' Row

West 138th and West 139th sts, between Powell Blvd and Frederick Douglass Blvd • Subway B, C, #2, #3 to 135th St

The three blocks known as **Strivers' Row** contain some of the finest row houses in Manhattan. A dignified Renaissance-derived strip that's an amalgam of simplicity and elegance, it was conceived during the 1890s housing boom by McKim, Mead, and White among others. Note the unusual rear service alleys of the houses, reached via iron-gated cross-streets (replete with the original "Walk your Horse" signs). At the end

---

SUNDAY GOSPEL AND HIP-HOP CHURCH

Harlem's uplifting **gospel music** has long enticed visitors and for good reason: both it and the entire revival-style Baptist experience can be mind-blowing. Gospel tours are big business; most are pricey, but they usually offer transport uptown and brunch after the service. If you don't feel like shelling out the cash, or if you're looking for a more authentic experience, you can also easily go it alone. The choir at the **Abyssinian Baptist Church** (Sun 11am only) is arguably the best in the city, but long queues of tourists (which can stretch around the block) make the experience, well, touristy (you'll need to get here at least 30min early). Another fairly popular option is the **Metropolitan Baptist Church**, at 151 West 128th St on Powell Blvd (Sun 11am; ⊙ 212 663 8990, ⓦ metropolitan-bc151.org). **Mount Neboh Baptist Church**, at 1883 Powell Blvd on West 114th St (Sun 8am & 11am; ⊙ 212 866 7880, ⓦ mountneboh.org), is much less of a circus; worship here is taken seriously and services are not designed as tourist attractions, but the congregation is very welcoming to nonmembers (you can also catch the choir rehearsing at 6.30pm on Tues). Wherever you go, dress accordingly: those wearing vests, flip-flops or shorts will not be allowed to enter.

For a quite different experience, the **Hip-Hop Church** currently meets at the Greater Hood Memorial AME Zion Church, at 160 West 146th St (Thurs 7pm; ⊙ 212 281 3130); once again, this is a serious place of worship, but with rappers and DJs supplying the music. Hip-hop pioneer **Kurtis Blow** is one of the founders.

17

of the nineteenth century, this came to be the desirable place for ambitious professionals within Harlem's burgeoning black community (starting with rail porters) to reside – hence its nickname.

Schomburg Center for Research in Black Culture

515 Malcolm X Blvd at West 135th St · Exhibitions Mon–Sat 10am–6pm; general research and reference division Tues–Thurs noon–8pm, Fri & Sat 10am–6pm; moving image and recorded sound division Tues–Sat 10am–6pm · Free · ☎ 212 491 2200, ⊛ nypl.org/locations/schomburg · Subway #2, #3 to 135th St

If you're interested in learning more about African-American history and culture, visit the **Schomburg Center for Research in Black Culture**, a member of the New York Public Library system. Primarily a **research library**, the main reason for a casual visit is to explore the superb temporary **exhibitions** here, held in three small galleries and covering a range of related African-American themes, such as the struggle to end segregation in US schools and the Emancipation Proclamation. With more time you can peruse the **general research library**, containing a wonderful array of African, Caribbean and African-American literature, as well as current periodicals, and the **movie archive**, a repository of black film, music and spoken-arts recordings. The centre is also the site of the ashes of renowned poet **Langston Hughes**, best known for penning *The Negro Speaks of Rivers*. That poem inspired Houston Conwill's terrazzo and brass "cosmogram" in the atrium beyond the main entrance; it's a mosaic built over a tributary of the Harlem River. Seven of Hughes' lines radiate out from a circle, and the last line, "My soul has grown deep like the rivers," located in a fish at the centre, marks where he is interred.

Originally a lending branch, the Division of Negro Literature, History and Prints was created in 1925 after the community began rallying for a library of its own. The collection grew dramatically, thanks to **Arthur Schomburg**, a black Puerto Rican nicknamed "The Sherlock Holmes of Black History" for his obsessive efforts to document black culture. Schomburg acquired over ten thousand manuscripts, photos and artefacts, and he sold them all to the NYPL for $10,000; he then worked as curator for the collection, sometimes using his own funds for upkeep, from 1932 until his death six years later. Since that time, the amassing of over ten million items has made the centre the world's top research facility for the study of black history and culture.

El Barrio

Subway #6 to 103rd St, 110th St or 116th St

East or **Spanish Harlem** extends from the affluence of the Upper East Side to East 132nd Street, and from the Harlem River as far west as Park Avenue. The neighbourhood has been a centre of New York's large **Puerto Rican** community since the 1950s, and is better known by locals as **El Barrio** – which simply means "the neighbourhood". Before World War II, this was actually **Italian Harlem**, a major Sicilian enclave: actor Al Pacino was born here in 1940, and *Rao's* restaurant (see p.320) – established in 1896 – and *Patsy's Pizzeria* which opened in 1933 still remain. Today the character of East Harlem is changing again, with a fast-growing Chinese community creating what some call Manhattan's second Chinatown.

Harlem's regeneration is gradually spilling over to El Barrio – optimistic estate agents have dubbed it "**SpaHa**" – and the southern and western sections, particularly along Lexington Avenue, can be fun to explore (especially for the street art and the food). Yet most of the neighbourhood remains characterized by blocks of low-rise, low-income housing, shabby bodegas and livery-cab services that give the area an intimidating atmosphere – it still has the highest violent crime rate in Manhattan and the highest jobless rate in the city. Until the 1970s, the hub of the area was **La Marqueta**, under the elevated Metro North railway tracks on Park Avenue between East 111th and 116th streets; originally a five-block street market of Hispanic products, it's now largely vacant

HARLEM'S HISTORIC JAZZ VENUES

Jazz remains a crucial part of Harlem's appeal, though most clubs today are small, intimate affairs – between the 1920s and 1960s, Harlem was home to some of the biggest nightspots in the city, many of which attracted hordes of white patrons from downtown as well as middle-class blacks.

The Abyssinian Development Corporation acquired the **Renaissance Ballroom**, at Powell Boulevard on West 138th Street, as a likely future home for the Classical Theater of Harlem, though plans are moving ahead very slowly. This tile-trimmed, square-and-diamond-shaped dance club once hosted Duke Ellington and Chick Webb in the 1920s. Nicknamed the "Rennie", it was a haven for middle-class blacks but has been abandoned since the 1970s.

The same corporation, in partnership with the city, has transformed another former club, **Small's Paradise** at 2294 Powell Blvd, on the southwest corner of Powell Boulevard and West 135th Street. This finial-topped brick building was built in 1925 and hosted a mixed black and white crowd from the beginning, when the club was known as "The Hottest Spot in Harlem"; Malcolm X worked here in 1943. Today, it's occupied by an *International House of Pancakes* and topped by the state-of-the-art Thurgood Marshall Academy High School, opened in 2004. On the other side of West 135th Street at 2300 Powell Blvd (now *Popeye's Chicken*), was the **Big Apple Restaurant and Jazz Club**, which is rumoured to be the birthplace of New York City's nickname. It's said that when jazzmen met on the road in the 1930s, they would call to each other, "See you at the Big Apple" as a sort of shorthand reference to the city. The term duly entered the vernacular after local journalists started using it and the city's tourism authorities adopted it in the 1970s.

Opened in the 1930s, **Minton's Playhouse**, at 206–210 West 118th St between St Nicholas and Powell, became the birthplace of **bebop**. In the 1940s, after finishing their sets at Harlem's clubs, Dizzy Gillespie, Charlie Parker, John Coltrane and other greats would gather at Minton's for late-night jam sessions that gave rise to the improvised jazz style – innovator **Thelonious Monk** was actually house pianist here for three years. Miles Davis called Minton's "the black jazz capital of the world". Shuttered in the 1970s, Minton's reopened as a low-key jazz venue in 2006, but closed again in 2010.

As for the **Cotton Club**, it was originally at West 142nd Street and Lenox Avenue in the 1920s, and was a segregated establishment – though most of the performers here were black, as was the staff, only whites were allowed to attend as guests. That building was demolished in 1958, but a new version reopened in Harlem in 1978 at 656 West 125th St, where it continues to put on a good jazz show at night as well as a Sunday gospel brunch.

in spite of repeated attempts to revitalize it. If you're looking for insight into New York's Latin culture, start at the **Museo del Barrio** (see p.206).

Taller Boricua

Julia de Burgos Latino Cultural Center, 1680 Lexington Ave at East 106th St • Tues, Wed, Fri, Sat noon–6pm, Thurs 1–7pm • Free •
☎ 212 831 4333, ⓦ tallerboricua.org • Subway #6 to 103rd St

To check out the contemporary art scene, stop by the **Taller Boricua** gallery inside the redbrick Julia de Burgos Latino Cultural Center; a popular **salsa** night also runs here on Wednesdays (5.30pm; ladies $10; men $10 before 6.30pm, $15 thereafter). The centre is named for the lauded Puerto Rican poet who died poverty-stricken in Harlem in 1953, a striking mosaic **mural** (created by Manny Vega in 2006) of whom is on the opposite corner of East 106th Street, part of the ongoing Hope Community project. You'll see *Nuyorican Poets Café* founder Pedro Pietri commemorated at East 104th Street and Lexington, as well as the awe-inspiring **Spirit of East Harlem** mural (1978).

Graffiti Wall of Fame

Park Ave and East 106th St • Subway #6 to 103rd St

Facing Park Avenue, the **Graffiti Wall of Fame** (on the west side of the railway viaduct) commemorates the exuberant street art that developed in New York in the 1970s. Featuring art from many of the city's best-known graffiti writers, the inner side of the

17

wall (with the best work) is actually located in the Central Park East 1 Elementary School playground, so the gates are sometimes locked during term – you'll have to ask at the school further along 106th Street for a closer look.

Museo del Barrio

1230 Fifth Ave, at East 104th St • Wed–Sat 11am–6pm • Suggested donation $9, free every third Sat of month and Wed 6–9pm • ☎ 212 831 7272, ⓦ elmuseo.org • Subway #6 to 103rd St

Literally translated as "the neighbourhood museum", the **Museo del Barrio** has two sections, both hosting temporary exhibits on various aspects of Puerto Rican and Latino culture. The permanent collection galleries display everything from the museum's rare **Taíno** artefacts, a pre-Columbian civilization that flourished in Puerto Rico and other Caribbean islands, to modern and conceptual art, while the other section hosts high-quality travelling exhibitions.

The galleries are relatively small, but there's also a decent **café** on site (selling duck, cheese and guava *empanadas, tamales* and rice pudding for around $3) and **El Teatro**, which shows Latin-influenced plays and movies (usually Wed 6.30pm; free). The museum also hosts concerts, poetry readings and other events, and is planning to offer local walking tours in the future – check the website for details.

Museum for African Art

1280 Fifth Ave at East 110th St • ⓦ africanart.org • Subway #2, #3 to Central Park North, #6 to 110th St

Delayed many times, the **Museum for African Art** should be open by 2014, the first museum building built on Museum Mile since the completion of the Guggenheim in 1959. Exhibits will showcase a wide range of genres, from Congolese urban art and North African jewellery to modern photography and ancient Nigerian artefacts.

Hamilton Heights and Sugar Hill

Subway #1 to 137th St, #1, A, B, C, D to 145th St

Much of West Harlem, between West 125th and 155th streets, and from St Nicholas Avenue to the Hudson River, is taken up by the area known as **Hamilton Heights**. Like Morningside Heights to the south, there's a blend of campus buildings (in this case, belonging to the City College of New York) and residences here, lightened by a sprinkle of slender parks on a bluff above Harlem. One stretch, the **Hamilton Heights Historic District**, bounded by Amsterdam and St Nicholas avenues from West 140th to 145th streets, contains florid row-houses in a variety of architectural styles, including Beaux Arts and Romanesque Revival. In the 1920s and 1930s, many affluent African-Americans began to migrate to the neighbourhood – as a result, the area between West 145th and 155th streets and Edgecombe and Amsterdam avenues became known as **Sugar Hill**. Today, it's another area of gorgeous townhouses, well worth exploring.

City College

160 Convent Ave, at West 138th St • Campus open daily; bookstore Mon–Thurs 9am–7pm, Fri 9am–3pm • ☎ 212 650 7000, ⓦ ccny.cuny.edu • Subway #1 to 137th St

Visitors wandering up from 125th Street and St Nicholas Avenue B or C subway station will be pleasantly surprised by **Convent Avenue** and the nearby grounds of **City**

LA GRANDE JATTE IN HARLEM

Harlem is littered with great street art, but if you see just one mural make it Eva Cockcroft's *Homage to Seurat: La Grande Jatte in Harlem* (1986), on West 142nd Street between Amsterdam Avenue and Hamilton Place. Beautifully restored in 2009, Cockcroft has replaced the French painter's demure Parisiens with African-American figures.

College. The rustic-feeling campus of Collegiate Gothic halls mantled with white terracotta fripperies occupies 35 acres along Convent Avenue, from West 131st Street to 141st Street. The most impressive section is the **North Campus Quadrangle** just before 140th Street, designed by the noted architect George Browne Post and completed in 1908. Nearby **Shepard Hall** (home to the School of Architecture), is the tallest and most striking building, soaring over the campus like a Gothic cathedral.

Founded downtown in 1847 (as the Free Academy of the City of New York), the college didn't charge tuition, and thus became the seat of higher learning for many of New York's poor, including polio-vaccine pioneer Jonas Salk, writer Mario Puzo and soldier-turned-statesman Colin Powell. The college has also produced an astounding ten Nobel laureates. Even though free education here came to an end in the 1970s, three-quarters of the students still come from minority backgrounds.

Hamilton Grange National Memorial
414 West 141st St, near Convent Ave • Visitor Center Wed–Sun 9am–5pm; ranger-guided tours at 10am, 11am, 1pm, 2pm and 4pm; self-guided tours noon–1pm and 3–4pm • Free • W nps.gov/hagr • Subway A, B, C, D to 145th St

Hamilton Heights' premier historical lure is the house of founding father Alexander Hamilton. Now the **Hamilton Grange National Memorial**, it stands in the northwest corner of St Nicholas Park, next to City College at West 141st Street. Completed in 1802, the Grange has bounced around the island a couple of times: it stood at its original site on 143rd Street until 1889, then was moved to 287 Convent Ave, in the shadow of the fiercely Romanesque St Luke's Church to which it was originally donated (Hamilton's statue remains here). In 2008, the 298-tonne structure was lifted (in one piece, no less) up and over the church's entryway to begin the journey to its new home. The National Parks Service completed a massive renovation project in 2011.

Washington Heights
Subway A, C, #1 to 168th St

The largely **Dominican** neighbourhood of **Washington Heights** encompasses most of the northern tip of Manhattan between West 155th and Dyckman streets (200th St). The neighbourhood is gradually becoming better known, thanks in part to local boy Lin-Manuel Miranda's hit Broadway musical *In the Heights*.

ALEXANDER HAMILTON
Alexander Hamilton's life is much more fascinating than his house. Born around 1755 on the island of Nevis in the British West Indies, he came to the American colonies in 1772. He was an early supporter of the Revolution, and his intelligence and enthusiasm quickly brought him to the attention of George Washington. Hamilton became the general's aide-de-camp, and rose quickly through military ranks. When Washington was elected President, he named Hamilton as the first Secretary of the Treasury. Hamilton, quick in both understanding and temper, tended to tackle problems head-on, a propensity that made him enemies as well as friends. He alienated both John Adams and Thomas Jefferson, and when Jefferson won the presidency in 1801, Hamilton was left out in the political cold. Temporarily abandoning politics, he moved away from the city to his grange (or farm) to tend his plantation and conduct a memorably sustained and vicious feud with **Aaron Burr**, who had beaten Hamilton's father-in-law in a Senate election.

Following a short tenure as Vice President under Jefferson, Burr ran for governor of New York; Hamilton strenuously opposed his candidacy and, after an exchange of extraordinarily bitter letters, the two men fought a **duel** in Weehawken, New Jersey (roughly where the Lincoln Tunnel now emerges), on July 11, 1804. When pistols were drawn, Hamilton honourably discharged his into the air, a happening possibly explained by the fact that his eldest son had been killed in a duel on the same field a few years earlier. Burr, evidently made of lesser stuff, aimed carefully and fatally wounded Hamilton. He remains one of two non-presidents to find his way onto US money (Benjamin Franklin's the other): you'll find his portrait on the $10 note.

17 From Sugar Hill, walk along St Nicolas Avenue, which eventually runs into Broadway some ten blocks north. This is the main drag of a once elegant, now mostly raggedy neighbourhood, though the gentrification of Harlem has also had an impact up here. It's worth coming for the food (see p.320) and for a couple of historic sights if you have time, though the area is probably best known as the stomping ground of New York's pioneer **graffiti** artists: **TAKI 183**, who started tagging in 1969 and lived on 183rd Street, is credited with sparking the craze after a *New York Times* article in 1971, while his inspiration was **Julio 204**, a Puerto Rican from 204th Street who had started a few years earlier.

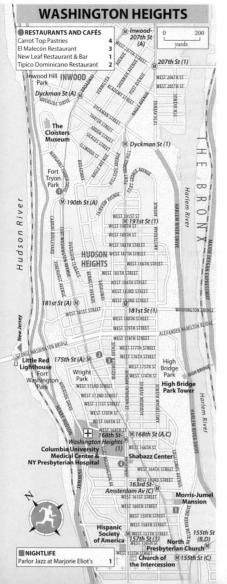

WASHINGTON HEIGHTS

RESTAURANTS AND CAFÉS
Carrot Top Pastries	4
El Malecón Restaurant	3
New Leaf Restaurant & Bar	1
Típico Dominicano Restaurant	2

NIGHTLIFE
Parlor Jazz at Marjorie Eliot's	1

Hispanic Society of America

613 West 155th St, at Broadway • Tues–Sat 10am–4.30pm, Sun 1–4pm, library closed Aug • Free, $10 donation suggested • ☎ 212 926 2234, ⓦ hispanicsociety.org • Subway C to 155th St, #1 to 157th St

One of the few sights worth visiting in Washington Heights is **Audubon Terrace**. Completed in 1908, this Acropolis of folly is what's left of a hopelessly optimistic attempt to glorify this area, when museums were dolled up as Beaux Arts temples.

There is only one museum left here, the **Hispanic Society of America** (most of the complex is occupied by Boricua College) but it makes the trip worthwhile. Founded in 1904 by Archer Huntington (whose home is now the National Academy, p.176), the Society owns one of the largest collections of Hispanic art outside Spain. The main, dimly lit gallery glows with the rosy hues of a Castilian palace, the first floor boasting Goya's *Duchess of Alba* in imperious pose as a Spanish *maja*. The adjacent Bancaja Gallery is a real treasure, containing fourteen giant murals by Joaquín Sorolla y Bastida (his *Vision of Spain* was commissioned specifically for the society in 1911). Upstairs there are galleries of painted tiles and ceramics, rare Spanish lustreware and Roman mosaics, but the paintings on the balcony above the main gallery take precedence: some classics from El Greco, including his *Holy Family*, and typically expressive portraits by Velázquez and Goya among them. Note also the equestrian statue of El Cid and limestone reliefs of Don Quixote in the courtyard outside, created by Huntington's wife Anna Hyatt in the 1920s.

Trinity Church Cemetery

West division entrance at 770 Riverside Drive, near West 153rd St; east division entrance West 155th St at Church of the Intercession • Daily 9am–4pm • ☎ 212 368 1600, ⓦ trinitywallstreet.org • Subway C to 155th St, #1 to 157th St

Just across West 155th Street from Audubon Terrace lies the **Trinity Church Cemetery**, its large, placid grounds dotted with some fanciful mausoleums and divided into two sections by Broadway. The eastern division contains the Celtic-cross monument to naturalist John James Audubon (near the church entrance on 155th St), and the tomb of former mayor Ed Koch, who died in 2013. Robber-baron John Jacob Astor is buried in the western division (as is his great-grandson, John Jacob Astor IV, who died on the *Titanic*), along with poet and Chelsea developer Clement Clark Moore, Alfred Tennyson Dickens, the son of Charles Dickens (who died suddenly on a visit to New York in 1912) and Eliza Jumel (see below). Ralph Ellison (author of *Invisible Man*), is interred in the mausoleum near the Riverside Drive entrance. Established in 1842, the site hasn't always been so tranquil: two large bronze slabs on the grounds mark the particularly bloody Battle of Fort Washington during the Revolutionary War.

The Morris–Jumel Mansion and around

65 Jumel Terrace, at West 160th St and Edgecombe Ave • Wed–Sun 10am–4pm • $5 • ☎ 212 923 8008, ⓦ morrisjumel.org • Subway C to 163rd St

Within easy walking distance of Audubon Terrace and the Trinity Church Cemetery is the **Morris–Jumel Mansion**. Another uptown surprise, this creaky old house somehow survived the urban renewal (or better, destruction) that occurred all around it, and is now one of the city's more successful museums, its proud Georgian outlines faced with a later Palladian portico. Built as a rural retreat in 1765 by Loyalist Colonel Roger Morris, the house served briefly as Washington's headquarters in 1776 before falling into the hands of the British. Wealthy wine merchant Stephen Jumel bought the derelict house in 1810 and refurbished it for his wife (and ex-mistress) Eliza, formerly a prostitute. New York society didn't take to such a past, but when Jumel died in 1832, Eliza married ex-Vice President Aaron Burr, twenty years her senior (he was 77), in the front parlour: the marriage lasted for six months before old Burr left, having gone through her inheritance, only to die on the day of their divorce. Eliza battled on to the age of 91, and on the second floor of the house you'll find her portrait, bedroom and boudoir, restored to circa 1820s. You can also see Burr's and Washington's bedrooms, the kitchen in the basement and the gold wings above the downstairs foyer doors, allegedly given to Eliza by Napoleon.

Just opposite the entrance to the mansion's grounds is the gorgeous block of **Sylvan Terrace**, a tiny cobblestone mews lined with yellow and green wooden houses built in 1882 – and seeming impossibly out of place just barely off the wide-open intersection of Amsterdam and St Nicholas avenues.

The Shabazz Center

3940 Broadway, at West 165th St • Tues–Sat 11am–6pm (Thurs till 8pm) • Free • ☎ 212 568 1341, ⓦ theshabazzcenter.net • Subway A, C, #1 to 168th St

Northwest of the Morris–Jumel Mansion is the **Audubon Ballroom**, scene of **Malcolm X**'s assassination in 1965 and now, after some controversy, a part of the huge Columbia-Presbyterian Hospital complex. Columbia restored a portion of the original ballroom facade during construction, and now the Malcolm X and Dr Betty Shabazz Memorial and Educational Center, or just **Shabazz Center**, commemorates the black leader with murals, events and film screenings. The first floor also contains illuminating touch-screen panels that highlight important phases of Malcolm's life, including interviews and videos of the man himself.

Little Red Lighthouse

Riverside Drive, at West 178th St • **Fort Washington Park** Daily sunrise–sunset • Free • ⓦ nycgovparks.org/parks/fortwashingtonpark • Subway A to 175th St

Blanketing much of the shoreline between Washington Heights and the Hudson River, **Fort Washington Park** is named after a Revolutionary War fort once located here

17

(now long gone), but best known today for the George Washington suspension bridge and the 40ft-high **Little Red Lighthouse** beneath it. The lighthouse is an incongruous structure, immortalized in Hildegarde Swift's classic 1942 children's book of the same name – the **Little Red Lighthouse Festival** every autumn includes a special guest reading of the book (and this is usually the only time you can go inside the lighthouse). Originally named Jeffrey's Hook Lighthouse, the current structure was completed in 1889 in Sandy Hook, New Jersey, and moved here in 1921 where it operated for another 26 years.

Highbridge Park

West 155 St and Dyckman St, Edgecombe Ave & Amsterdam Ave • Daily sunrise–sunset • Free • Ⓦ nycgovparks.org/parks/highbridgepark • Subway A to 175th St

Another New York green space given a makeover in recent years, **Highbridge Park** is best known for its iconic Romanesque High Bridge Water Tower (200ft), completed in 1872, and the **High Bridge** itself, a pedestrian-and-bicycle-only walkway that is expected to reopen in 2014 to connect with parkland in the Bronx. Part of the Old Croton Aqueduct, the 1450ft-long granite bridge served the city from 1848 until 1958, carrying nearly 100 million gallons of water a day at its peak.

The Cloisters Museum

99 Margaret Corbin Drive, Fort Tryon Park • Daily: March–Oct 10am–5.15pm; Nov–Feb 10am–4.45pm • Suggested donation $25, includes same-day admission to the Metropolitan Museum of Art • ☎ 212 923 3700, Ⓦ metmuseum.org • Subway A to 190th St-Fort Washington Ave, from where #M4 bus runs to the Cloisters (but can take 1hr 30min); a taxi from midtown will cost $25–30

The main reason visitors come this far uptown is to see **The Cloisters Museum**. It stands above the Hudson like some misplaced Renaissance palazzo-cum-monastery, and is home to the Met's collection of medieval tapestries, metalwork, paintings and sculpture. The museum opened in 1938, largely thanks to donations from **George Grey Barnard** and **John D. Rockefeller, Jr**, and though it looks authentic, it was designed by modern architect Charles Collens, who also did Riverside Church (see p.195), with

---

MALCOLM X

Born Malcolm Little in 1925, in Omaha, Nebraska, influential African-American Muslim minister and political activist **Malcolm X** spent much of his later life in New York. He had a rough childhood and after moving to Harlem in 1943 became a small-time crook. In 1946, he ended up in jail; by the time he was released in 1952, he had become a committed follower of Elijah Muhammad's **Nation of Islam**. Despite the name, orthodox Muslims consider the Nation to be a separate religion, with many differences from Islam (members believe, for example, that Allah came to Earth in the person of one W. D. Fard, and that racial intermarriage is forbidden). Malcolm rose quickly within the Nation, setting up temples in Boston and becoming minister of Temple Number Seven in Harlem in 1954. Tall, handsome and an enigmatic speaker, he soon became the public face of the group, speaking out against the inequalities and racism of the time. Yet by 1964, Malcolm had fallen out with the Nation's leaders, who were finding it difficult to control their star speaker; and Malcolm was becoming disillusioned with the Nation's unorthodox doctrine (not to mention Elijah Muhammad's alleged sex life). Malcolm converted to more orthodox Sunni Islam (adopting the name **El-Hajj Malik El-Shabazz**), and took a life-changing pilgrimage to Mecca in 1964 – seeing Muslims of all races praying together was especially enlightening.

Back in the US he started two new organizations – Muslim Mosque Inc, and the Organization of Afro-American Unity – but by now he was receiving regular death threats. He was finally gunned down on February 21, 1965, at a meeting in the Audubon Ballroom (see p.209). Three members of the Nation of Islam were eventually imprisoned for the murder (all three were subsequently released). Today, Malcolm X is considered one of the greatest and most influential African-Americans; his autobiography (co-written by Alex Haley) is still widely read, and he was portrayed by Denzel Washington in the lauded Spike Lee movie *Malcolm X* (1992).

portions of five medieval cloisters (basically, covered walkways and their enclosed courtyards) cleverly incorporated into the structure.

The collection

Once at the museum, start from the entrance hall and work counterclockwise: the collection is laid out in roughly chronological order. First off is the simplicity of the **Romanesque Hall** and the frescoed Spanish **Fuentidueña Chapel**, dominated by a huge, domed twelfth-century apse from Segovia that immediately induces a reverential hush. The hall and chapel form a corner on one of the prettiest of the cloisters, **St Guilhem**, which is ringed by Corinthian-style columns topped by carved capitals from late twelfth-century southern France. At the centre of the museum is the **Cuxa Cloister**, from the twelfth-century Benedictine monastery of Saint-Michel-de-Cuxa near Perpignan in the French Pyrenees; its Romanesque marble capitals are brilliantly carved with monkeys, eagles and lions, whose open mouths reveal half-eaten human legs.

The nearby **Unicorn Tapestries** (c.1495–1505, Flanders) are even more spectacular – brilliantly alive with colour, observation and Christian symbolism. The most famous is the seventh and last, where the slain unicorn has miraculously returned to life and is trapped in a circular pen. It isn't just the creature's resurrection that's mystifying – the entire sequence is shrouded in mystery: aside from the fact that they were designed in France and probably made in Brussels, little else is known for certain, even who the intended original recipients were (the most plausible claim is Anne of Brittany, wife of King Louis XII). As for the tapestries' allegorical meaning, the unicorn is said to represent both a husband captured in marriage and Christ risen again.

Most of the Met's medieval paintings are to be found downtown, but one important exception is Dutch master **Robert Campin**'s *Mérode Triptych*. This fifteenth-century oil painting depicts the Annunciation scene in a typical bourgeois Flemish home of the day, and is housed in its own antechamber next to the Boppard Room, outfitted with a chair, cupboard and other household articles from that period (though from different countries of origin). On the left of the altarpiece, the artist's patron and his wife gaze timidly through an open door; to the right, St Joseph works in his carpenter's shop. St Joseph was mocked in the literature of the day, which might account for his rather ridiculous appearance – making a mousetrap, a symbol of the way the Devil traps souls.

The lower level

On the lower level, a large **Gothic chapel** boasts a high vaulted ceiling and mid- to late fourteenth-century Austrian stained-glass windows, along with the monumental **sarcophagus of Ermengol VII**, Count of Urgell (Urgell is now in Catalunya, Spain), with its whole phalanx of (now sadly decapitated) family members and clerics carved in stone to send him off.

Also on the lower floor are two further cloisters to explore (one with a small café), along with the **Treasury**, crammed with spellbinding objects. As you amble around this part of the collection, try not to miss the *Belles Heures de Jean, Duc de Berry*, perhaps the greatest of all medieval Books of Hours; it was executed by the Limburg Brothers with dazzling miniatures of seasonal life and extensive border-work in gold leaf. Other highlights include the twelfth-century walrus tusk **Cloisters Cross**, believed to have been made by a craftsman known as Master Hugo for the now-ruined great abbey at Bury St Edmunds in England. It contains a mass of 92 tiny expressive characters from biblical stories, as well as what seem to be disturbing anti-Semitic inscriptions. The cross is one of the most controversial pieces in the collection; experts still debate its provenance and meaning, and the story of how one of England's greatest pieces of medieval art ended up here is equally hazy – the Met outbid the British Museum for the piece in 1963 (paying $600,000), but how the shady Croatian seller acquired it is unknown.

PROSPECT PARK

Brooklyn

"The Great Mistake." So ran local newspaper headlines when Brooklyn became a borough of New York in 1898. Then the fourth-largest city in the US, it began a century of labouring in the shadow of its taller but smaller brother across the East River, drawing hordes to the famous Coney Island beach – the closest white-sand strip to Manhattan – but generally not offering much in the way of high culture. No longer. The past decade or so, Brooklyn has become synonymous with artisanal food, handmade crafts, pop-up flea markets and numerous other trends. Its signature brownstone townhouses and tree-lined streets are complemented by top-rated restaurants, hip bars, standout museums, and galleries and performance spaces that present more daring work than you'll generally find in Manhattan. Feel free to holiday in Brooklyn, dipping into Manhattan as and when the mood strikes.

The most accessible district in the borough is pretty, elite **Brooklyn Heights**, a clutch of old mansions and townhouses abutting the East River directly opposite Lower Manhattan. A little north of here, the once-derelict warehouses of the area known as **Dumbo** have been converted to expensive apartments, art galleries and theatres overlooking a popular waterfront park space. Due south of the Heights lie **Boerum Hill**, **Cobble Hill** and **Carroll Gardens**, a trio of plush neighbourhoods with no real attractions but block after block of historic brownstones and some of the borough's best restaurants and cafés; the Brooklyn–Queens Expressway cuts them off from **Red Hook**, full of stone-block streets, warehouses-turned-artists'-studios and some limited waterfront attractions.

A mile or so southeast of BoCoCa (as some, though not the locals, refer to the area), **Prospect Park**, designed by Central Park creators Frederick Law Olmsted and Calvert Vaux, contains the usual ball fields and trails and is flanked by the first-rate Brooklyn Botanic Garden and Brooklyn Museum, plus the leafy **Park Slope** neighbourhood. North of the park, **Prospect Heights** leads into **Fort Greene**, where you'll find some of the most pristine residential blocks in the city along with the famous Brooklyn

18

CAFÉS	
Di Fara Pizza	3
Nathan's	9

RESTAURANTS	
Café Glechik	5
Gargiulo's	7
Primorski	8
Purple Yam	2
Randazzo's Clam Bar	4
Roberta's	1
Totonno Pizzeria	
Napolitano	6

ACCOMMODATION	
Akwaaba Mansion	1

Academy of Music performance complex. Fort Greene adjoins **Bedford-Stuyvesant**, the largest African-American community in New York, which in turn links to **Crown Heights**, home to a large Hasidic Jewish population.

Then there's coastal Brooklyn: start in polyglot **Bay Ridge** for a scenic bike ride along the water, and then visit **Coney Island**, the venerable seaside amusement district known for its rattletrap roller coaster, the Cyclone, and the New York Aquarium. Grab some *borscht* (beetroot soup) at the nearby Russian enclave of **Brighton Beach**.

Finally, anyone visiting New York for contemporary art (or, for that matter, vintage clothes) should head to gallery-dotted **Williamsburg**, just one stop on the L train from Manhattan's East Village and also a top choice for eating, drinking and live music. **Greenpoint**, north of Williamsburg on the border of Long Island City, houses the artsy overflow from Williamsburg but maintains a quieter feel, thanks to the Polish old guard still prevalent.

Brief history

In 1636, **Dutch colonists** bought farmland from the **Lenape Indians** amid the flat marshes in the southwestern corner of Long Island. The **Village of Breuckelen** received a charter from the Dutch West India Company in 1646. The town began to take on its present form in 1814 when Robert Fulton's steamship service linked Long Island with Manhattan and Brooklyn Heights was established as a leafy retreat for wealthier Manhattanites.

Brooklyn's **incorporation** into the City of New York in 1898 was a bitterly fought political battle. In the end it was decided by just 277 votes – a tiny percentage of the total 129,000 cast. By the early 1900s, Brooklyn had more than one million residents, many of them Jewish and Italian; in 1910, 35 percent of its population was foreign born (the proportion is similar today).

Even with the population boom, Brooklyn suffered in the twentieth century: its strong manufacturing and shipping sectors dwindled, and unemployment climbed steadily. By the 1980s, "white flight", provoked first by racism, then by drug-related crime and violence, had left previously desirable residential neighbourhoods vacant and impoverished.

With a citywide drop in crime beginning in the mid-1990s, however, middle-class families began restoring townhouses in Park Slope, Cobble Hill, Prospect Heights and Fort Greene, and young artists and professionals flooded Williamsburg, trends that have continued – and spread.

INFORMATION

Tourist information Your main sources for information on the borough – brochures, papers, books – are the Brooklyn Tourism and Visitors Center, 209 Joralemon St (Mon–Fri 10am–6pm, Sat & Sun 10am–4pm; ☎718 802 3846, ⓦ visitbrooklyn.org) in Downtown Brooklyn and the Brooklyn Historical Society (see p.218) in Brooklyn Heights.

Downtown Brooklyn and around

Spilling out from the foot of the Brooklyn and Manhattan bridges between Atlantic and Flatbush avenues, **Downtown Brooklyn** is a somewhat motley district of office buildings and commuter colleges. Aside from the Brooklyn Tourism and Visitors Center in Borough Hall (see above) and the underground New York Transit Museum, there's surprisingly little to see here. The neighbourhoods around downtown are a different story though.

To the east, **Fort Greene** has some of the city's most beautiful residential architecture. West of downtown is **Brooklyn Heights**, the borough's most prestigious neighbourhood. Northeast of the Heights is a historic sliver of land known as the Fulton Ferry District, which is adjacent to **Dumbo**, Brooklyn's answer to Tribeca, with its glossy mix of chichi design emporia, art galleries, waterfront parks, multimillion-dollar apartments and cool eateries. To start your trip in grand style, walk or bicycle here from Lower Manhattan over the Brooklyn Bridge (see p.61), and try to be on the Dumbo waterfront or the Brooklyn Heights promenade at sunset – the light is magical.

18

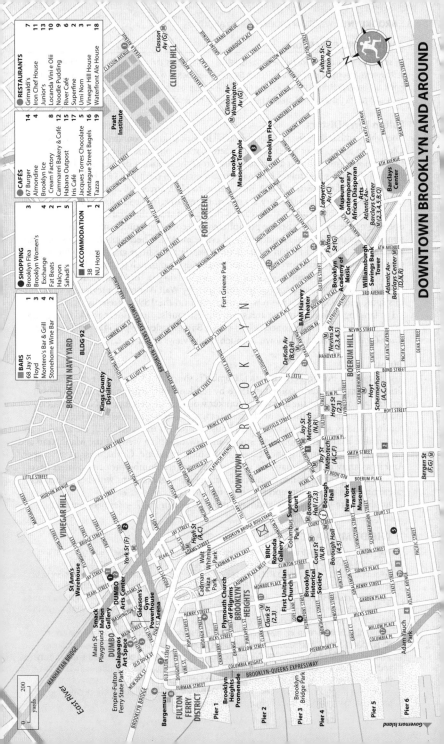

DOWNTOWN BROOKLYN AND AROUND

BARS		
68 Jay St		1
Floyd		3
Montero's Bar & Grill		4
Stonehome Wine Bar		2

SHOPPING		
Brooklyn Flea		1
Brooklyn Women's		3
Exchange		
Fat Beats		4
Halcyon		5
Sahadi's		2

CAFÉS		
67 Burger		3
Almondine		4
Brooklyn Ice		4
Cream Factory		
Cammareri Bakery & Café		1
Habana Outpost		5
Iris Café		14
Jacques Torres Chocolate		4
Montague Street Bagels		8
Tazza		12
		15
		17
		16
		19

● RESTAURANTS	
Grimaldi's	7
Iron Chef House	11
Junior's	13
Locanda Vini e Olii	10
Noodle Pudding	9
River Café	6
Superfine	2
Umi Nom	3
Vinegar Hill House	1
Waterfront Ale House	18

■ ACCOMMODATION	
3B	1
NU Hotel	2

18

ARRIVAL AND DEPARTURE

By subway The handiest stops for the business district in Downtown Brooklyn are Jay St-MetroTech on the A, C, F or R and Borough Hall via the #2, #3, #4 or #5. The A and C also run to the waterfront area, at High St, while the F goes there on York St. All these stops are close enough to walk to Brooklyn Heights, while the Clark St stop on the #2 and #3 lines is right in the heart of the Heights.

Fulton Ferry District

Though you'd hardly guess it today, this small historic district, bounded by the East River, Old Fulton Street, Front Street and Main Street, was at one time the busiest spot on the Brooklyn waterfront. If you do arrive **on foot** from the Brooklyn Bridge, take the first set of stairs off the bridge and follow Cadman Plaza West down the hill to Old Fulton Street on the west edge of the district. The A and C trains to High Street will also let you off at Cadman Plaza West, and the **ferry** is a pleasant alternative in the summer months (see p.27).

Named for **Robert Fulton**, the area was the hub of steamship traffic until the 1883 opening of the Brooklyn Bridge precipitated an economic slump only recently remedied by the booming residential real estate market. Check out the imposing **Eagle Warehouse**, at 28 Old Fulton St; its penthouse, with the huge glass clock-window, is one of Brooklyn's most coveted apartments (though no match for the $18 million penthouse triplex in Dumbo's Clock Tower, at 1 Main St). The headquarters of *The Brooklyn Eagle*, the newspaper edited for a time by **Walt Whitman**, previously stood on this spot, and its old press room was integrated into the 1893 warehouse.

The landing is flanked by the area's two biggest tourist attractions: an old coffee barge that hosts classical music concerts – so-called **BargeMusic** (see p.354) – and the ritzy *River Café*, at 1 Water St, known as much for its views as for its fare.

Dumbo

Just east of the Fulton Ferry District, **Dumbo** is short for Down Under the Manhattan Bridge Overpass, a term coined in 1978 by residents of the neighbourhood – mostly artists – who thought the awkward moniker would deter developers. No such luck: many of Dumbo's handsome brick factories have been transformed into luxury condominiums, joined by glass towers housing more of the same. Still, the area has an undeniable allure, its cobblestone streets and jaw-dropping views of the Manhattan and Brooklyn bridges forming one of New York's most dramatic, Gotham-esque cityscapes. And in a canny move to maintain the district's cachet, Dumbo property owners have lured some top-notch galleries and performing-arts organizations with below-market-rate rents; cool restaurants and bars have followed.

Dumbo's core – which was landmarked by the city in 2007 – lies between the

---

THE DUMBO ART SCENE

The local galleries and venues – even bookstores and record shops, which also get in on the act – populating Dumbo's lofts and warehouses provide an anchor and identity for the neighbourhood. The **Dumbo Arts Center**, established at 111 Front St, was the first nonprofit arts group in the area, and in addition to showcasing work in a gallery, it originated the **Dumbo Arts Festival**, a three-day affair in late September (see p.402). The second floor of the 111 Front Street building is home to ten or so galleries, most of which are open Wed–Sat/Sun noon–6pm; poke around to see lots of mixed media efforts.

A number of organizations have followed suit, including Galapagos Arts Space, 16 Main St (ⓦgalapagosartspace.com), which hosts cabaret, burlesque and other unusual performances; SmackMellon, 92 Plymouth St (ⓦsmackmellon.org), showing daring pieces by emerging artists; and PowerHouse Arena, 37 Main St (ⓦpowerhousearena.com), an art-publisher-cum-bookstore that holds readings, workshops and photography exhibitions. On the first Thursday of each month, the neighbourhood pieces together a **Gallery Walk** (5.30–8.30pm; check ⓦdumbo.is for participating venues), good for homing in on free receptions.

Brooklyn and Manhattan bridges, north of the Brooklyn–Queens Expressway. Water and Front streets are the main thoroughfares but any sidestreet is equally evocative, and the waterfront is the place to take your lunch or coffee and laze away a few hours.

Gleason's Gym

77 Front St, 2nd floor • Call ahead for details of Sat-night boxing events (usually monthly; $20) • ☎ 718 797 2872, ⓦ gleasonsgym.net • Subway A, C to High St, F to York St

To savour what's left of Dumbo's old-fashioned grit, head to **Gleason's Gym**, where tomorrow's prizefighters work out. Everyone from Jake LaMotta to Muhammad Ali has trained at Gleason's, first established in Manhattan in 1937; drop by to see people punch heavy bags or, if you're lucky, spar with each other ($10 spectator fee).

18

Brooklyn Bridge Park

Brooklyn waterfront, from Manhattan Bridge to Atlantic Ave • ⓦ brooklynbridgepark.org • Subway A, C to High St, F to York St, #2, #3 to Clark St

The redeveloped waterfront along Dumbo and Brooklyn Heights goes by the umbrella name of **Brooklyn Bridge Park**; it's a series of playgrounds, scenic viewpoints and reclaimed quays, and plays host to a variety of events and activities. Just east of the Brooklyn Bridge, Empire-Fulton Ferry State Park is the oldest section and boasts the restored Jane's Carousel (May to mid-Oct daily except Thurs 11am–7pm; mid-Oct to April Thurs–Sun 11am–6pm; $2). Adjacent to that is Main Street Lot, with a playground, large lawn and giant steps for picnicking.

On the other side of the Brooklyn Bridge, the piers beneath the Brooklyn Heights Esplanade hold all sorts of family fun. Pier One has a small play area and waterside promenade; in summertime, its "boathouse" offers free kayaking at weekends (sometimes available further up in Dumbo, too). Pier Six is more impressive, with a popular water park, climbing area and a ferry link to Governors Island. Elsewhere, there are green swaths, fishing spots, a bike path and, in summertime, a pop-up pool (between piers One and Two); an aggressive programming schedule features yoga, open-air movies and conservation tours, for a start.

Vinegar Hill

A few seemingly stray cobblestone blocks northeast from the heart of Dumbo make up **Vinegar Hill**, a historic district that took its name from Ireland's Battle of Vinegar Hill – it was developed in the early nineteenth century mainly to house Irish immigrants who worked at the Brooklyn Navy Yard. On a sunny day, don't miss dining outdoors at the *Vinegar Hill House* (see p.322).

Brooklyn Navy Yard

Brooklyn waterfront, from Manhattan Bridge to Williamsburg Bridge • BLDG 92 Visitor Center, 63 Flushing Ave at Carlton Ave • Wed–Sun noon–6pm • Free • ☎ 718 907 5992, ⓦ brooklynnavyyard.org • Turnstile Tours offers a variety of ways to see the yard, including regular "Past, Present and Future" hop-on, hop-off bus tours on Sat & Sun 2.30pm (2hr; $30) • Subway A, C to High St, F to York St

The industrial park of **Brooklyn Navy Yard** – nearly derelict save for some unglamorous city works usage since its decommissioning in the 1960s – has recently become not just a thriving business setting but an attraction in its own right. Anyone can visit the LEED-platinum-certified BLDG 92 to get acquainted with some Navy Yard history; a modular, energy-efficient glass structure is attached to an 1857 brick house originally built for the marine commandant and now a museum holding three floors', worth of exhibitions. Linger over models of well-known ships built at the yard, including the USS *Ohio*, *Maine* and *Missouri*, and hear oral history from the likes of historian Howard Zinn, who worked at the yards in his youth; however, to appreciate what the place was, and what it's become, it's essential to take one of the fascinating tours.

The most frequent of those, an overview called "Past, Present and Future" (others include World War II tours and kid detective tours), goes into great detail on the yard's former military importance – an astonishing 71,000 people worked here during World War II –

and its current redevelopment. Some three hundred businesses call the grounds home these days; tenants include a body armour manufacturer, the **Kings County Distillery** (a bourbon maker holed up in the redbrick Paymaster Building; tours Sat 2.30–5.30pm, every 20–30min; $8; kingscountydistillery.com) and Steiner Studios, where *Boardwalk Empire* is shot. One highlight is Dry Dock One, in which a visiting ship may or may not be docked; a viewing platform gives views out to the river and of various cranes hard at work.

Brooklyn Heights

18

Brooklyn Heights is one of New York City's most beautiful and historical neighbourhoods, and is the borough's most coveted place to live. Downtown bankers and financiers began building brownstone townhouses here in the early nineteenth century, while writers flocked to the Heights after the subway opened in 1908; W.H. Auden, Carson McCullers, Truman Capote, Tennessee Williams, Norman Mailer and Paul and Jane Bowles (pre-Morocco) all lived in the neighbourhood. Although many one-family brownstones were divided into apartments during the 1960s and 1970s and the streets now feel fairly cosmopolitan – if a bit frumpier than you'd expect given what it costs to live here – Brooklyn Heights today is in many ways not much different from how it was a hundred years ago.

The north edge, along Henry Street and Columbia Heights, is the oldest part of the neighbourhood, where blocks are lined with Federal-style brick buildings. The unassuming, well-maintained wooden structure at **24 Middagh St** (at the corner of Willow), erected in 1824, is the area's longest-standing house, though other examples from around the era can be found along Middagh and Willow.

Continue south on Henry to **Pierrepont Street**, studded with fine brownstone townhouses; it's a scenic stretch by which to reach the **Promenade**. At the corner of Pierrepont and Monroe Place, look in if you can on the neo-Gothic interior of the **First Unitarian Church**.

Plymouth Church of the Pilgrims

75 Hicks St, at Orange St • Mon–Fri 10am–4pm, services Sun 11am, tour follows (or by appointment) • Free • ☎ 718 624 4743, ⓦ plymouthchurch.org • Subway #2, #3 to Clark St, A, C to High St

---

WALT WHITMAN: BROOKLYN BOY

Though only sporadically celebrated during his lifetime, poet **Walt Whitman** (1819–1892) has moved to the pantheon of Great American Writers. And of the many places he lived, none was as influential as Brooklyn.

Born in Huntington, Long Island, Whitman moved to the borough at the age of 4, moving from place to place thanks to his family's precarious financial situation. His formal schooling ended at age 11, after which he began working as a typesetter's apprentice in what is now Downtown Brooklyn. Whitman went on to found his own paper, *The Long-Islander*, which he sold after only nine months, but it was enough experience to get him hired as editor of *The Brooklyn Eagle*.

During his two-year tenure at the *Eagle* – still published in Brooklyn Heights – he argued for the establishment of Fort Greene Park and fought for recognition of local artists. But most importantly, he gathered ideas for his magnum opus, *Leaves of Grass*, which he would begin to write in 1850. Whitman himself paid for the publication of the first edition in 1855, even helping with the typesetting to keep costs down. Predictably, he couldn't even sell the first run of 795 copies; when newspapers got around to reviewing it, many denounced it as obscene.

Undeterred, Whitman revised *Leaves* for the rest of his life, expanding the original twelve-poem booklet to a 400-page tome. These first lines of the penultimate poem, *Crossing Brooklyn Ferry*, capture Whitman's wide embrace of all humanity:

Crowds of men and women attired in the usual costumes, how curious you are to me!
On the ferry-boats the hundreds and hundreds that cross, returning home, are more curious to me than you suppose,
And you that shall cross from shore to shore years hence are more to me, and more in my meditations, than you might suppose.

The simple **Plymouth Church of the Pilgrims** (entrance on Orange St) went up in the mid-nineteenth century and became famous as the preaching base of **Henry Ward Beecher**, abolitionist and campaigner for women's rights. His fiery orations drew men like Horace Greeley and Abraham Lincoln, and Mark Twain based *Innocents Abroad* on travels with the church's social group. The building was also a stop on the Underground Railroad, where slaves were hidden on their way to freedom. Fitting then, that in 1963, Martin Luther King, Jr delivered an early version of his "I Have a Dream" speech here. Tours of the church, focusing on the history and architecture, can be arranged by calling in advance.

18

Brooklyn Historical Society

128 Pierrepont St, at Clinton St • Wed–Fri & Sun noon–5pm, Sat 10am–5pm; library Wed–Fri 1–5pm • $6, under 12 free • ☎ 718 222 4111, ⓦ brooklynhistory.org • Subway R to Court St, #2, #3, #4, #5 to Borough Hall

The **Brooklyn Historical Society** explores the borough's neighbourhoods, architecture, ecology and subcultures with changing exhibits. The second-floor library with its local history collection is an evocative highlight, and the Society publishes detailed neighbourhood guides to a handful of Brooklyn districts, for sale at the front desk.

The Promenade

Walk back west on any street between Clark and Remsen to reach the **Promenade** (more formally known as the Esplanade), a pedestrian path with terrific views of the Statue of Liberty, downtown Manhattan's skyscrapers and the Brooklyn Bridge. Below is the still-developing Brooklyn Bridge Park (see p.217).

Downtown Brooklyn

The core of **Downtown Brooklyn**, the business district in essence – an area bordered by (clockwise from north) Sands and Middagh streets, Flatbush Avenue, Atlantic Avenue and Court Street – reflects the borough's split personality. While it has touches of metropolitan grandeur and civic pride, for the most part it lacks Manhattan's sophistication, and despite recent investments – the new Barclays Center arena, various hotels and condos – ungainly office buildings and lack of night-time streetlife prevail.

The eastern edge of residential Brooklyn Heights is defined by **Cadman Plaza**, created after World War II when the city decided to move Brooklyn's elevated streetcars underground. Nowadays it hosts a farmers' market (Tues & Sat year-round, plus Thurs from April to mid-Dec, 8am–4pm). Just south of the plaza, at Court and Montague streets, stands the lovely, massive **State Supreme Court**, designed by the same architects responsible for the Empire State Building. Further south, the Greek-style **Borough Hall**, at 209 Joralemon St, looks tiny in comparison; it was erected in 1849, then topped with its odd cupolaed belfry near the end of the century. On the southern border, Atlantic Avenue (which is claimed by Boerum Hill and Brooklyn Heights as well to an extent) holds a number of antique shops and Middle Eastern food joints; it's also the site of September's boisterous Atlantic Antic street party.

New York Transit Museum

Two blocks south of Borough Hall, on Boerum Place, at Schermerhorn Street • Tues–Fri 10am–4pm, Sat & Sun 11am–5pm • $7, ages 3–17 $5 • ☎ 718 694 1600, ⓦ mta.info/mta/museum • Subway #2, #3, #4, #5 to Borough Hall, A, C, F, R to Jay St-MetroTech

The **New York Transit Museum** is housed underground in the refurbished Court Street shuttle station from the 1930s. Popular with kids (and school groups) for good reason, museum exhibits include maps, models and photographs that detail the evolution of the city's public transit system, along with antique turnstiles and some interactive displays of fuel technologies. The highlight for many is jumping on and off the various models of restored subway and tram cars in the lower level, though few parents will be able to resist the photo opportunity of placing their children in the driver's seat of one of the buses on the main floor.

18

Barclays Center

Atlantic Ave, at Flatbush Ave • ☏ 917 618 6700, ⓦ barclayscenter.com • Subway B, D, N, Q, R, #2, #3, #4, #5 to Atlantic Ave-Barclays Center

The anchor of the Atlantic Yards development, Bruce Ratner's vision for turning a smallish parcel of land into an arena and a sixteen-skyscraper subdivision (drawn-out protests and lawsuits, followed by years of sluggish economy, curtailed much of the plans), opened its doors in late 2012. Home to the Brooklyn Nets, previously owned by Ratner and then sold to Russian billionaire Mikhail Prokhorov – with a tiny share (since divested) held by rapper Jay-Z – the stadium brings the first professional major-league team to the borough since baseball's Dodgers left town some fifty-plus years ago. The New York Islanders, a pro hockey team, join the party in the 2015–16 season. Though controversial, Barclays is less of an eyesore than one might imagine: the rust-coloured, low-lying stadium swooping almost gracefully towards the busy intersection at which it lies.

Fort Greene

Cross over chaotic Flatbush Avenue, and Fulton Street will bring you into the heart of **Fort Greene**, a historically African-American neighbourhood that withstood the dark days of the 1970s and 80s better than most places in Brooklyn and is now quite prosperous. There are two main commercial drags – Dekalb and Lafayette avenues, which run roughly parallel to each other – but it's the blocks connecting them that hold the most historic and attractive buildings and townhouses.

Brooklyn Academy of Music

30 Lafayette Ave • ☏ 718 636 4100, ⓦ bam.org • Subway B, D, N, Q, R, #2, #3, #4, #5 to Atlantic Ave-Barclays Center, C to Lafayette Ave, G to Fulton St

The multipurpose **Brooklyn Academy of Music** marks the high-culture centre of the borough. At the corner of Ashland Place and Fulton Street is the BAM Harvey Theater, where most plays are staged, many with top-tier actors. The interior has been preserved in a state of glamorous pseudo-decay. Continue south on Ashland Place to reach BAM's main building – the 1908 opera house, with its colourful terracotta cornice and undulating glass canopy. BAM also hosts dance, classical music and film; the BAMkids film festival; and, in recent years, the New York City Opera, late of Lincoln Center. The swanky, glittering *BAMcafé*, on the second floor of the opera house, offers free live music – jazz, blues, R&B – Friday and Saturday nights from 9 or 9.30pm until late.

Williamsburgh Savings Bank Tower

1 Hanson Place • Subway B, D, N, Q, R #2, #3, #4, #5 to Atlantic Ave-Barclays Center, C to Lafayette Ave, G to Fulton St

Sharing the block with BAM is the **Williamsburgh Savings Bank Tower**, Brooklyn's second tallest building and its most iconic. Built in 1927 but only recently turned into luxury condos, it stands 512ft (34 storeys) tall and sports one of the biggest four-sided clocks in the world, each face measuring 27ft in diameter. In wintertime, it plays host to the Brooklyn Flea (see opposite).

Museum of Contemporary African Diasporan Arts

80 Hanson Place, at S Portland • Wed & Fri–Sat noon–7pm, Thurs noon–8pm, Sun noon–6pm • $5, under 12 free • ☏ 718 230 0492, ⓦ mocada.org • Subway B, D, N, Q, R, #2, #3, #4, #5 to Atlantic Ave-Barclays Center, C to Lafayette Ave, G to Fulton St, D, N, R to Pacific St

At the intersection of Hanson Place and South Portland Avenue, the **Museum of Contemporary African Diasporan Arts** makes its home. The gallery space is small, but the three multimedia exhibits mounted here every year are provocative, taking on issues like race, class and police violence. There's also a fine gift-shop.

South Portland Avenue

Heading north on **South Portland Avenue** from the Museum of Contemporary African Diasporan Arts you'll soon come to one of the prettiest blocks in all of New York City –

OUTER BOROUGHS ARCHITECTURE

Not all of New York's most dazzling residential architecture is in Manhattan; Brooklyn, in particular, has eye-catching blocks of Italianiate and neo-Gothic townhouses built in the mid-to-late 1800s sprinkled through its historic neighbourhoods. The following streets/areas in the outer boroughs are worth the trek to see:

45th Avenue between 21st and 23rd streets, Long Island City, Queens See p.241
Bed-Stuy historic district, Brooklyn See p.230
Grand Concourse, the Bronx See p.252

Middagh Street, Brooklyn Heights See p.218
South Portland Avenue, Fort Greene, Brooklyn See opposite

18

the stretch between Lafayette and DeKalb avenues, which is lined with stately townhouses with high stoops under a lush canopy of trees. The biannual Fort Greene House Tour in early May allows you to peek inside several residences, gardens and artists' studios ($25; ☎718 875 1855, ⓦhistoricfortgreene.org); note that it alternates with an equally worthwhile Clinton Hill House Tour (ⓦsctyclintonhill.tumblr.com), which covers the adjacent neighbourhood, also full of brownstone houses, gardens and the like.

The next block down, South Elliott Place, is landmarked on its east side, on which Spike Lee's production offices, Forty Acres and a Mule, as well as the super-narrow home at no. 37 – just thirteen feet wide – reside.

Fort Greene Park

South Portland Avenue comes to a dead-end at **Fort Greene Park**, designed by Frederick Law Olmsted and Calvert Vaux in 1867, and named after Revolutionary War general Nathaniel Greene. Seventy years later, Walt Whitman, as editor of *The Brooklyn Eagle*, urged that the space be turned into parkland, a "lung" for the growing borough. At the park's summit, the 148ft **Prison Ship Martyrs Monument** (1908) commemorates the estimated 11,500 Americans who died in the floating prison camps maintained by the British during the Revolutionary War. Sixteen squalid ships, rife with smallpox, were moored in old Wallabout Bay (just offshore from the Brooklyn Navy Yard). The bones of the dead, collected as they washed ashore for decades after, are housed in a small crypt at the base of the tower. Elsewhere, there are tennis courts, playgrounds, a weekend farmers' market and a nature path with labels of the wide variety of trees in the park.

Brooklyn Masonic Temple

317 Clermont St, at Lafayette Ave • ☎718 638 1256, ⓦ masonicboom.com • Subway G to Clinton-Washington aves

The 1909 **Brooklyn Masonic Temple** rises like a fortress from its surroundings on Clermont Street. Masons no longer meet here, but hipsters do, with indie bands and DJs playing in the renovated theatre. The concert hall also hosts Golden Gloves boxing events on occasion.

Brooklyn Flea

176 Lafayette Ave, between Clermont St and Vanderbilt Ave • April–Nov Sat 10am–5pm • ⓦ brooklynflea.com • Subway G to Clinton-Washington Aves

In a matter of a half-decade, the **Brooklyn Flea**, which features more than 250 vendors selling all manner of vintage goods, has grown from upstart to institution. Originated in the schoolyard opposite the Brooklyn Masonic Temple, it occupies a few other locations as well and has spawned a food-related offshoot, Smorgasburg (see p.235). Search the aisles for vintage and handmade finds, and enjoy treats from an army of food carts. A winter market takes place indoors at 1 Hanson Place (Sat & Sun 10am–5pm), and a Sunday market has started up in Williamsburg, at 27 North 6th St (also 10am–5pm).

South Brooklyn

The neighbourhoods of **Cobble Hill**, **Boerum Hill** and **Carroll Gardens**, along with the former industrial zone along the **Gowanus Canal** and the wharves of **Red Hook**, make up the area traditionally known as **South Brooklyn** – confusing, because geographically much of the borough is actually south of this area. Until 1894, however, this was the southern border of the city of Brooklyn, so the term has stuck. The most popular areas to visit here are Court and Smith streets, which run north–south through Cobble Hill and Carroll Gardens. They're lined with some of Brooklyn's best boutiques and places to dine; Smith Street in particular is chock-a-block with bars, restaurants and clothes

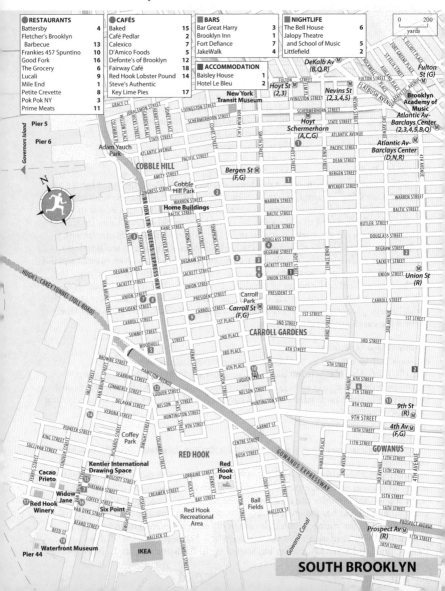

● RESTAURANTS	
Battersby	4
Fletcher's Brooklyn Barbecue	13
Frankies 457 Spuntino	10
Good Fork	16
The Grocery	6
Lucali	9
Mile End	1
Petite Crevette	8
Pok Pok NY	3
Prime Meats	11

● CAFÉS	
Baked	15
Café Pedlar	2
Calexico	7
D'Amico Foods	5
Defonte's of Brooklyn	12
Fairway Café	18
Red Hook Lobster Pound	14
Steve's Authentic Key Lime Pies	17

■ BARS	
Bar Great Harry	3
Brooklyn Inn	1
Fort Defiance	7
JakeWalk	4

■ ACCOMMODATION	
Baisley House	1
Hotel Le Bleu	2

■ NIGHTLIFE	
The Bell House	6
Jalopy Theatre and School of Music	5
Littlefield	2

shops. If industrial decay is more your style, don't miss the district of Red Hook, with its active art scene.

ARRIVAL AND DEPARTURE

By subway The F or G to Bergen St deposits you on the border between Cobble Hill and Carroll Gardens; the Carroll St stop on the same lines leaves you at the southern end of Carroll Gardens, closest to Gowanus and a bus ride (or long walk) to Red Hook. If you're walking here from Brooklyn Heights, simply continue south on Court St.

By bus No subway line goes out to Red Hook, but it's easy enough to reach by bus. Take the #B61 bus from Columbia St on the western edge of Carroll Gardens and Cobble Hill.

By water taxi New York Water Taxi (☎ 212 742 1969, ⊛ nywatertaxi.com) runs a free weekend ferry service from Pier 11 in Manhattan to Ikea, at the southern tip of Red Hook; boats leave and arrive every 40min (11am–8.40pm). During the week it's $5 (every 40min; 2–8pm).

Cobble Hill and Boerum Hill

Just south of Atlantic Avenue, the main east–west streets through **Cobble Hill** – Amity, Congress and Warren – are a mix of brownstones and redbrick row houses built between the 1840s and the 1880s. **Court Street** is the neighbourhood's main commercial artery, though the pickings here get a bit more interesting as you head further south toward Carroll Gardens; **Smith Street** caters to a slightly younger crowd, mostly because of its profusion of bars, skate shops and the like.

Over on Clinton Street, which runs parallel to Court, sits the idyllic little **Cobble Hill Park**. Along the park's southern border is a cobblestone alleyway – **Verandah Place**, a renovated mews built in the 1850s. Writer Thomas Wolfe lived in the basement at no. 40 in the 1930s and described the apartment in his novel *You Can't Go Home Again*: "Here, in winter, the walls… sweat continuously with clammy drops of water. Here, in summer, it is he who does the sweating." Living conditions weren't nearly so dismal in the nearby **Home Buildings**, a tidy row of redbrick cottages lining a pedestrian mews, Warren Place. Built in 1878 as utopian workers' housing, the 44 homes are each only eleven feet wide.

Meanwhile, the neighbourhood's literary attachments continue; Martin Amis lives on the block-long Strong Place, and Jonathan Lethem, noted former denizen of **Boerum Hill**, has written about both areas in his novels. Boerum Hill, to Cobble Hill's east, is less architecturally impressive than its neighbour, though it has its share of sober Greek Revival and Italianate buildings, developed around the same period.

Carroll Gardens

As you walk south along Court Street, Cobble Hill blends into **Carroll Gardens** around Degraw Street. Built as a middle- and upper-class community between 1869 and 1884, this part of South Brooklyn has been an Italian enclave since dockworkers arrived here in the early 1900s; **Al Capone** is said to have been married in 1918 at the Saint Mary Star of the Sea Church on Court Street. The area was later named for Charles Carroll, the only Roman Catholic to sign the Declaration of Independence.

Many of the neighbourhood's older Italian residents have moved out to Staten Island and New Jersey, but you'll still find a few classic *salumerias* and pastry shops alongside the hipper places (like *Momofuku Milk Bar*, right outside the south entrance of the Carroll Street subway stop) on Court and Smith streets, the area's arteries. Duck a few blocks south, turning on fourth Place, to find one of the more unusual residential alleys in the city, Dennet Place, its shortened doorways evoking something out of the Brothers Grimm.

West of the main blocks, across the Brooklyn–Queens Expressway (BQE) overpass, greet the **Columbia Street Waterfront District**, a perpetually up-and-coming district of shops and restaurants that forms the gateway to grittier Red Hook further south. Don't expect Brooklyn Heights esplanade, however; the waterfront here is still an active loading and unloading area for deep-sea container ships and cruise ships, with very limited public access.

Gowanus

The southeast edge of Carroll Gardens is defined by the **Gowanus Canal**, a name that inspires a bit of a shudder in older Brooklynites. Originally a wetlands area famous for its oysters, it became a fetid stillwater around 1870, thanks to sewers from Park Slope that drained here and oil refineries that sat along its banks. In 1999, however, city engineers finally repaired the drain pump so water could flow freely through the canal and into Gowanus Bay, and the canal now supports a surprising amount of marine life, including shrimp and oysters, as well as a growing art, restaurant and nightlife scene.

The **Gowanus Dredgers Canoe Club** (☎718 243 0849, ⓦgowanuscanal.org) runs free canoe tours of the canal on Wednesdays and Saturdays from April to October, starting at Second Street at Bond; walking and bike trips along the banks are an option for anyone still wary of the water. Across the canal, on the border with Park Slope, the hundred-year-old **Brooklyn Lyceum**, at 227 Fourth Ave (☎718 857 4816, ⓦbrooklynlyceum.com) was once Public Bath No. 7; after standing derelict for years, the Lyceum has been redesigned as a café-performance space-cultural centre.

Red Hook

Though only a half-mile from the Columbia Street Waterfront District, **Red Hook** feels oddly like the outskirts of a city in the Deep South, a place where hulking redbrick warehouses crumble along the waterfront while, inland, two- and three-storey apartment buildings share cobblestoned blocks with garden centres and car-repair shops. A handful of quirky stores, restaurants and cafés line the main strip, **Van Brunt Street**, where the service is almost universally relaxed and friendly – a community vibe that served Red Hook well when it was devastated by 2012's Hurricane Sandy; the look-out-for-one-another ethos helped immensely with the cleanup and with getting businesses back up and running.

Brief history

Settled by the Dutch in 1636, Red Hook got its name from the colour of the soil and the shape of the land, which forms a corner, or *hoek*, where the Upper New York Bay meets the Gowanus Bay. It eventually became one of the busiest and toughest shipping centres in the US, inspiring Hubert Selby's book *Last Exit to Brooklyn* and Arthur Miller's play *A View from the Bridge*. Some say that urban planner **Robert Moses** deliberately severed the notoriously crime-ridden neighbourhood from the rest of Brooklyn when he routed the Brooklyn–Queens Expressway down Hicks Street in 1954. In any case, by the 1960s, the increasing automation of the docking industry left longshoremen out of work and sent most of the freighters from Red Hook to bigger ports in New Jersey.

The waterfront and piers

Red Hook's waterfront is now a curious assemblage of abandoned and repurposed warehouses and parkland. From the end of Pier 41 Governors Island appears almost within wading distance and Lady Liberty seems to raise her torch just for you. Nearby, the **Waterfront Museum and Showboat Barge** (Thurs 4–8pm, Sat 1–5pm; donation requested; ☎718 624 4719, ⓦwaterfrontmuseum.org), at 290 Conover St at Pier 44, presents historical exhibits, art and occasional kid-friendly workshops and performances in a restored railroad barge moored off a small park at the end of Conover Street.

Adjacent **Fairway**, at 480–500 Van Brunt St, is Brooklyn's best mainstream supermarket; at the back is a waterfront café (see p.290). In the warehouse across the street from Fairway, the **Brooklyn Waterfront Artists Coalition (BWAC)**, at 499 Van Brunt St, holds three main group shows per year, on weekends (1–6pm) from mid-May to mid-June, from late July to mid-August and from late September to late October, as well as October's two-day Red Hook Film Festival (☎718 596 2506, ⓦbwac.org). The other gallery of note in the area is the **Kentler International Drawing Space**, at 353 Van

SMALL-BATCH BROOKLYN

There's no doubt that handcraft mania has swept Brooklyn, what with the Brooklyn Flea (see p.221) and Smorgasburg (see p.235) highlighting every product imaginable: pickles and pop tarts, handbags and hot sauce. In Red Hook, you can do a mini-trail of some of the more interesting local drink producers, who have taken advantage of the large industrial spaces to set up shop. The best-known, and oldest, such local maker is Six Point Brewery, 40 Van Dyke St (Wsixpoint.com; check the website to see if tours are running), which turns out some hop-heavy quaffs – Sweet Action and Righteous Ale are two of their top sellers to look out for in local bars and shops. Along the waterfront, the Red Hook Winery, Pier 41, Suite 325A (O347 689 2432, Wredhookwinery.com; daily 11am–5pm; tastings $5–12, weekend tours $15; call ahead for tours), has a tasting room fronting its winemaking facilities. They cultivate their grapes on the North Fork of Long Island, a region best known for its Merlots, Cabernet Francs and Sauvignon Blancs – all of which are featured here. A newer spot melds two great tastes: Cacao Prieto (O347 225 0310, Wcacaoprieto.com), a chocolatier that also distills whisky under the name Widow Jane (Wwidowjane.com) in a brick warehouse at 218 Conover St; tours available Thurs ($10). Leave with a bar of dark chocolate ($10), a bottle of smooth rye ($40) and a smile.

18

Brunt St, which as its name suggests displays fine works on paper (Thurs–Sun noon–5pm; O718 875 2098, Wkentlergallery.org).

Red Hook Ball Fields

There are a couple of good dining options in the neighbourhood (see p.290 & p.323), but if you're in Red Hook on a summer weekend it's a tradition to eat at the **Red Hook Recreational Area** (also called the **Red Hook Ball Fields**; May–Oct Sat & Sun 11am– early evening), at Clinton and Bay streets,. Surrounding a soccer pitch, a dozen or so food-stands dole out delicious tacos, *ceviche*, *tamales*, *pupusas*, *huaraches* and more. To reach the fields from Van Brunt, head east on Van Dyke Street.

Prospect Park and around

Where Brooklyn really surpasses itself is on Flatbush Avenue in the vicinity of **Grand Army Plaza** – an elegant, if congested, traffic circle around a stately memorial arch. The plaza faces the **Brooklyn Public Library** and the entrance to **Prospect Park**, and immediately east of it on Eastern Parkway, the **Brooklyn Museum** houses, among other things, an excellent ancient Egyptian trove and the **Brooklyn Botanic Garden**. The plaza also acts as a border to several very different neighbourhoods, including up-and-coming **Prospect Heights** and the serene, liberal bastion of **Park Slope**.

ARRIVAL AND DEPARTURE

By subway The #2 and #3 subway lines stop at Grand Army Plaza, while the Brooklyn Museum has its own stop just a few blocks further down the line. The B and Q trains to Prospect Park get you closest to the park's main attractions, and Park Slope's chief subway stops are the F to Seventh Ave/9th St and the R to Fourth Ave/Union St.

Grand Army Plaza

Central Park architects Frederick Law Olmsted and Calvert Vaux designed **Grand Army Plaza** in the 1860s and 1870s as an approach to Prospect Park, but it didn't take on its current grandeur until the end of that century. The 80ft-tall triumphal **Soldiers' and Sailors' Memorial Arch**, modelled on Paris's Arc de Triomphe and a tribute to the Union victory in the Civil War, was unveiled in 1892.

Saturday is by far the best day to visit, when dozens of farmers from New York and New Jersey set up stalls here at the city's second-largest **farmers' market** (Sat year-round 8am–4pm). At the height of summer, expect to find bounteous produce, meats, flowers, jams and pickles, along with occasional cooking demonstrations. The wintertime selection can be thin, but you can always get a crunchy apple, donut and steaming cup of cider.

Brooklyn Public Library

10 Grand Army Plaza • ☎ 718 230 2100, ⓦ brooklynpubliclibrary.org • Subway #2, #3 to Grand Army Plaza

On the east side of Grand Army Plaza, the central branch of the immense **Brooklyn Public Library** started in 1912 with the help of a $1.6 million donation from Andrew Carnegie and finally finished in 1941. Its entrance curves along with the roundabout; move up close to decipher the literary allusions of the gold figurines on the gate.

18

Prospect Park

☎ 718 965 8951, ⓦ prospectpark.org

Energized by their success with Central Park, Olmsted and Vaux landscaped **Prospect Park** in the early 1860s. Its 585 acres include a 60-acre lake on the east side, a 90-acre open meadow on the west, and a circular 3.35-mile park drive around the periphery, primarily reserved for runners, cyclists and rollerbladers (vehicular traffic is allowed during weekday rush hours only). Despite attractions that have sprung up over the

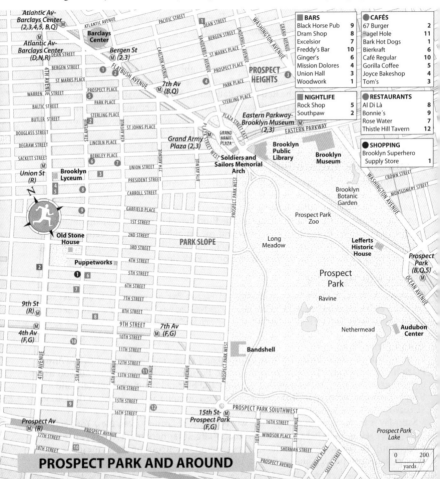

■ BARS	
Black Horse Pub	9
Dram Shop	8
Excelsior	7
Freddy's Bar	10
Ginger's	6
Mission Dolores	4
Union Hall	3
Woodwork	1

■ NIGHTLIFE	
Rock Shop	5
Southpaw	2

● CAFÉS	
67 Burger	2
Bagel Hole	11
Bark Hot Dogs	1
Bierkraft	6
Café Regular	10
Gorilla Coffee	5
Joyce Bakeshop	4
Tom's	3

● RESTAURANTS	
Al Di Là	8
Bonnie's	9
Rose Water	7
Thistle Hill Tavern	12

● SHOPPING	
Brooklyn Superhero Supply Store	1

PROSPECT PARK AND AROUND

years – the new Lakeside recreational development (not open at time of press, but with skating rinks and a return to the original Olmsted and Vaux lake-area design among its features), a tennis centre and the popular Celebrate Brooklyn outdoor music festival – Prospect Park remains for the most part remarkably bucolic.

For casual fun, head to the **Drummer's Grove** near the Parkside and Ocean Avenue entrance on the southeast corner of the park; the crowd that gathers on Sunday afternoons (April–Oct; 2pm) is no amateur circle – some very accomplished musicians have been jamming here for decades. The **Celebrate Brooklyn** concert series likewise draws top-notch musical and dance talent to its summer series of outdoor concerts, held at the **Bandshell**, just inside the 9th Street entrance at Prospect Park West ($3 donation requested; ☎718 683 5600, ⓦbricartsmedia.org); they also hold a few shows at Brooklyn Bridge Park (see p.217).

18

Audubon Center

In the Boathouse, close to the Lincoln Rd entrance at mid-park on the east side • April–Oct Thurs & Fri noon–4pm, also Pop-Up Audubon takes place April–Oct Sat & Sun noon–5pm, Nov & Dec Sat & Sun noon–4pm at various designated locations • Free • ☎ 718 287 3400 • Subway B, Q to Prospect Park

The **Audubon Center** serves as the park's main visitor centre as well as the trailhead for the park's four nature trails. Their programming has been cut back a bit due to budget constraints, but the new "Pop-Up Audubon" has begun to take over some of the slack: nature tours, ecological exhibitions and other activities will be on offer. Check the website for precise location details.

Prospect Park Zoo

450 Flatbush Ave, on eastern side of park • April–Oct Mon–Fri 10am–5pm, Sat & Sun 10am–5.30pm; Nov–March daily 10am–4.30pm • $8, 3–12 $5 • ☎ 718 399 7339, ⓦ prospectparkzoo.com • Subway B, Q to Prospect Park

The **Prospect Park Zoo**, run by the venerable Wildlife Conservation Society, showcases kangaroos, red pandas, poisonous frogs, peacocks, baboons and sundry other fauna in natural-looking habitats. It's a small-scale affair but likeable enough for those with kids in tow – little ones should especially enjoy milking cows in the Barn and Garden exhibit (mid-May to mid-Oct only), and watching the playful sea lions being fed.

Lefferts Historic House

Just south of Prospect Park Zoo, on eastern side of park • April, May, Oct & Nov Thurs–Sun noon–5pm; June & Sept Thurs–Sat noon–5pm; July–Aug noon–6pm; Dec & Feb–March Sat–Sun noon–4pm • $3 suggested donation • ☎ 718 789 2822 • Subway B, Q to Prospect Park

Tour guides at the **Lefferts Historic House**, an eighteenth-century Dutch farmhouse, use the place as a prop to talk (mostly to children) about what Brooklyn was like in the 1820s. Just south of the house stands a 1912 **carousel** (April, May, Sept & Oct Thurs–Sun noon–5pm; July & Aug Thurs–Sun noon–6pm; $2) with 51 hand-carved horses and other animals; it was originally installed at Coney Island.

Brooklyn Museum

200 Eastern Parkway • Wed 11am–6pm, Thurs 11am–10pm, Fri–Sun 11am–6pm, first Sat of every month (save Sept) until 11pm • Suggested donation $12 • ☎ 718 638 5000, ⓦ brooklynmuseum.org • Subway #2, #3 to Eastern Parkway

East of Grand Army Plaza and the Public Library stands the imposing **Brooklyn Museum**. Designed by McKim, Mead, and White, it's second only to the Metropolitan Museum of Art in terms of exhibit space in New York City, with five floors of galleries. The museum is best known for its distinguished store of Egyptian relics and a feminist art wing that includes Judy Chicago's groundbreaking 1970s installation, *The Dinner Party*. A regular schedule of talks, arts-and-crafts demonstrations and performances is best experienced via the free **First Saturdays** programme, held on the first Saturday evening of each month. On these nights, the museum stays open until 11pm (admission is free after 5pm), becoming a vast all-ages party with live music and dancing.

18

The collection

Just inside the front entrance stands a changing selection of a dozen bronze sculptures by Auguste Rodin. Elsewhere, exhibits are set up to showcase a cross-section of museum holdings, with some detailed African carvings and pencil drawings by artists such as Isamu Noguchi and Louise Nevelson.

The second floor is dedicated to the **Asian and Islamic galleries**, with pieces from China, Korea, India and Japan, as well as Ottoman Turkish and Qajar Persian textiles, mosaics, manuscripts and jewellery; however, it's undergoing extensive renovation and the galleries won't be viewable again until sometime in 2015.

The carved-stone *Brooklyn Black Head* of the Ptolemaic period, arguably the museum's crown jewel, is one of 1200 objects in the authoritative **Ancient Egyptian Art** collection – one of the largest outside of Egypt – on the third floor. Sarcophagi and sculptures are nicely complemented by small galleries of Assyrian, Sumerian and other ancient Middle Eastern art; keep an eye out for the exquisite "Coffin for an Ibis", with its astonishing detail. Those who don't spook easily may also enjoy the "Mummy Chamber", which features four Egyptian mummies plus a mummified cat. On the same floor, **European Paintings** presents works by Monet and a few other big names, though none is particularly essential viewing.

One flight up, most of the **Decorative Arts collection** is in six evocative period rooms, including a nineteenth-century Moorish smoking room from John D. Rockefeller's estate. It shares the floor with the Elizabeth A. Sackler Center for Feminist Art, the centrepiece of which is **The Dinner Party**, a massive triangular dinner table with custom-made china place settings for 39 famous women. Constructed in 1974–79 by artist Judy Chicago and hundreds of volunteers, it's an impressive and moving display, even if the explanatory timeline – or "herstory" – in the adjoining gallery feels a bit dated.

On the fifth floor, Georgia O'Keeffe's sensual *Brooklyn Bridge* opens the uneven "American Identities" permanent exhibition, which draws thematic connections among works in the museum's varied **Painting and Sculpture** collection. More interesting – in fact, one of the most diverting parts of the entire museum – is the **Visible Storage/Study Center** exhibit, basically a couple of thousand museum holdings not on display in the main museum. Besides paintings, more than a thousand objects of Americana are packed behind glass, including chairs, Tiffany lamps and a futuristic bicycle.

Brooklyn Botanic Garden

900 Washington Ave • March–Oct Tues–Fri 8am–6pm, Sat & Sun 10am–6pm; Nov–Feb Tues–Fri 8am–4.30pm, Sat 10am–4.30pm • $10, under 12 free, free Tues and Sat before noon, also free winter weekdays • ☎ 718 623 7200, ⓦ bbg.org • Subway #2, #3 to Eastern Parkway; #4, #5 to Franklin Ave

Located just behind the Brooklyn Museum, the **Brooklyn Botanic Garden** is one of the most enticing park spaces in the city. Plants from around the world occupy 22 gardens and exhibits spread over 52 acres, all sumptuous but not overmanicured. What you'll see depends largely on the season. Late March brings colour to Daffodil Hill, while April and May see the cherry trees blooming in the Japanese Garden, designed in 1914 and the oldest garden of its kind outside of Japan. The Rose Garden starts to flourish in the early summer, the elaborate water-lily ponds are at their best in mid-to-late summer and early autumn, and the autumnal colours in the Rock Garden are striking. A winter visit lets you enjoy the warmth of the Steinhardt Conservatory, filled with orchids, tropical plants, palms and one of the largest collections of bonsai trees in the West. One part that's not season-determinant is the Celebrity Path, a stone walkway that honours Brooklyn's famous sons and daughters. A garden shop stocks a wide array of exotic plants, bulbs and seeds, and the pleasant *Terrace Café* offers a farm-friendly array of snacks and lunches.

Park Slope

The western exits of Prospect Park leave you in **Park Slope**, a district of stately nineteenth-century brownstone townhouses inhabited since the 1970s by a notoriously liberal crew of urban pioneers; it's also in an eternal baby boom, and pushchairs jam the pavements.

The tree-lined blocks between Prospect Park West and Eighth Avenue from Union to 15th Street contain some of the finest Romanesque and Queen Anne residences in the US, helping this area earn the nickname "The Gold Coast of Brooklyn". Almost all the buildings were constructed in the 1880s and 1890s but they're hardly uniform, displaying a fine array of building materials (brick, brownstone and granite in various combinations) and details, from original gaslights to turrets and bay windows. Especially attractive blocks to seek out include Montgomery Place and Third Street, near the north end of the Slope and, just beyond the southern borders, Webster Place, between Sixth and Seventh avenues. **Seventh Avenue** is the Slope's traditional main drag, lined with all the essentials – florists and wine shops, cafés and boutiques – but it can lack a bit of excitement. These days you'll find a younger crowd, along with trendier shops, bars and restaurants, on **Fifth Avenue**.

Though outnumbered by straight couples, lesbians have flocked to Park Slope since the 1970s, and it's as gay-friendly a neighbourhood as you'll find in the city. The **Brooklyn Pride Festival & Parade**, a community-oriented, relatively noncommercial event, takes place every June; it includes a fun run, happy hour and night-time parade.

Old Stone House

Between Fourth and Fifth aves, and 3rd and 5th sts • Sat & Sun 11am–4pm • $3 suggested donation • ☎ 718 768 3195, ⓦ theoldstonehouse.org • Subway R to Union St–Fourth Ave

You can learn about the Slope's history at the **Old Stone House** in J.J. Byrne Park, famous as the site of one of the most dramatic skirmishes of the Battle of Brooklyn and the first headquarters of the Brooklyn Dodgers baseball team. The reconstructed building contains changing exhibits and a diorama of the house as it looked in its early days – it is, however, frequently rented out for parties or other events.

Prospect Heights

Just north of Grand Army Plaza, **Prospect Heights** has handsome and varied, late nineteenth-century residences that rival those of nearby Park Slope. You could spend a pleasant hour or so walking up and down its lovely side streets, but its main appeal will probably be its **food and drink** options, which are within easy walking distance of the Brooklyn Museum and the Brooklyn Botanic Garden; **Vanderbilt Avenue** is your best bet.

Green-Wood Cemetery

500 25th St, at Fifth Ave; another entrance on Fourth Ave, at 35th St; and weekend entrances on Fort Hamilton Parkway and Prospect Park West • Daily: May–Aug 7am–7pm; March–April, & Sept & Oct 7.45am–6pm; Nov–Feb 8am–5pm • Guided tram tours Wed and last Sun of the month 1pm, $15 • ⓦ green-wood.com • Subway R to 25th St

Southwest of Prospect Park – and a hardy walk from central Park Slope – is the famed **Green-Wood Cemetery**. Founded in 1838 and almost as large as Prospect Park at 478 acres, Green-Wood was very much *the* place to be buried in the nineteenth century. Interred here are politician and crusading newspaper editor Horace Greeley; famed preacher Henry Ward Beecher; William Marcy "Boss" Tweed, Democratic chief and scoundrel; glass-maker Louis Comfort Tiffany; and the entire Steinway clan of piano fame, at peace in a 119-room mausoleum. The bucolic grounds took a battering during Hurricane Sandy – around 300 trees were harmed or felled – and numerous gravestones suffered damage. You may hardly notice, though. Guided explorations of the site are held regularly via weekly trolley tours and full-moon "flashlight tours".

Ditmas Park and Midwood

South of Prospect Park, a few undervisited areas provide some fun exploration, assuming you have the time and aren't set on just seeing major parks and museums. **Ditmas Park** has the city's most attractive collection of stand-alone Victorian mansions, on the plot bordered by Stratford, Cortelyou, Marlborough and Albemarle; it feels as far removed from the city as you can get. After wandering up and down, hit Cortelyou Road for its burgeoning collection of cool restaurants and cafés (the Q train will get you there).

A bit further south, **Brooklyn College** is the most attractive part of **Midwood**, and you're free to walk around the manicured green of the small campus; free tours are also held at 10am and 3pm. The area's other claim to fame is as the home to *Di Fara's* (see p.290), which many consider to be the best pizzeria in the whole of New York City.

18

Central Brooklyn

The neighbourhoods within **Central Brooklyn** – most notably **Bedford-Stuyvesant** and **Crown Heights**, to the northeast and east of Prospect Park – are far rougher than those in South Brooklyn, but they are worth a look for their architecture and street culture. Predominantly African-American, Bed-Stuy, as it's called, is experiencing a real-estate rush on its brownstone houses, and Crown Heights, with its Hasidic Jewish and West Indian populations, may not be far behind. Keep in mind that while the area is generally safe during the daytime, there's still some street crime, so remain alert.

Bedford-Stuyvesant

Subway C to Norstrand Ave

Immediately east of Clinton Hill, **Bedford-Stuyvesant** is the nation's largest black community after Chicago's South Side, with more than 400,000 residents. It stretches north–south from Flushing to Atlantic avenues, and east as far as Saratoga; its main arteries include Bedford and Nostrand avenues and Fulton Street.

Originally two separate areas, the adjacent districts of Bedford and Stuyvesant were populated by both blacks and whites in the nineteenth century. During the Great Migration between 1910 and 1920, large numbers of southern African-Americans moved north and settled in this area. In the 1940s the white population began to leave, taking funding for many important community services with it. Economic decline continued for several decades, reaching an all-time low in the 1980s.

The poverty and neglect had an unintended upside: because few of its brownstones were razed in the name of economic development, the neighbourhood has the densest collection of pre-1900 homes in New York, attracting a fervent crowd of young fixer-uppers – both white and black – over the past decade.

Gothic, Victorian and other classic brownstones abound, especially inside the **Stuyvesant Heights Historic District**, which includes parts of MacDonough, Macon, Decatur, Bainbridge and Chauncey streets, primarily between Tompkins and Stuyvesant avenues. Outside the main historic section, make sure to swing by the landmark **Boys' High School**, at 832 Marcy Ave, on any wanderings; the Romanesque Revival pile saw the likes of Norman Mailer pass through its halls. The couple of blocks of row houses on Jefferson and Hancock streets between Nostrand and Tompkins are as dignified and radiant as any in the city.

Crown Heights

Subway #3 to Nostrand Ave

South of Bedford-Stuyvesant and east of Prospect Heights is thrumming **Crown Heights**, bounded by Atlantic Avenue and Empire Boulevard to the north and south, and Ralph and Washington avenues to the east and west. This community is home to the largest **West Indian** community in New York as well as an active, established population of about ten thousand **Hasidic Jews**, most of them belonging to the Russian Lubavitcher sect (in the mid-twentieth-century, roughly 75,000 Jews called the neighbourhood home).

Eastern Parkway, the large throughway that runs past the Brooklyn Museum, is the main traffic artery of Crown Heights, and landscaped walkways on either side of the path provide much-needed green space.

Over Labor Day weekend, Crown Heights hosts the annual **West Indian–American Day Parade and Carnival**, during which almost two million revellers dance, eat and applaud colourful floats and steel-drum outfits. The parade, which organizers claim is the biggest in the nation, runs west along Eastern Parkway from Rochester Avenue in Crown Heights to Grand Army Plaza (see Chapter 32, "Parades and festivals", for more information). To get a taste of West Indian culture and cuisine year-round, wander along Nostrand Avenue from the #3 train stop, where there's a string of dirt-cheap Caribbean snack joints – grab a "double" (fried bread wrapped around a chickpea mixture, topped off by pepper sauce) and take in the scene. Meanwhile, Franklin Avenue, to the west, has shown serious signs of gentrification in recent years, with some fancyish cafés, restaurants and shops setting down sticks between Lincoln Place and St Mark's Avenue.

18

Brooklyn Children's Museum

145 Brooklyn Ave, at St Mark's Ave • Tues–Sun 10am–5pm, extended hours third Thurs of month (when free 4–7pm) • $9 • ☎ 718 735 4400, ⊛ brooklynkids.org • Subway #3 to Kingston Ave, C to Kingston-Throop Ave

North of Eastern Parkway, the **Brooklyn Children's Museum** was the first museum of its kind, founded way back in 1899; a "green" renovation and expansion by Uruguayan architect Rafael Viñoly added solar panels and other energy-saving devices, doubled the space and gave the museum the chance to modernize its collection. Galleries hold hands-on exhibits concentrating on science, the environment, local neighbourhood life – which highlights various ethnic districts around Brooklyn – and much more; the "Water Wonders" play area and the live animals on display downstairs should especially thrill the younger set.

Wyckoff Farmhouse Museum

5816 Clarendon Rd, at Ralph Ave • Tues–Fri tours 1 & 3pm, Sat 11am, 1pm & 3pm, Sun (May–Oct only) 11am, 1pm & 3pm; grounds open 10am–4pm on tour days • $5, 10 and under $3 • ☎ 718 629 5400, ⊛ wyckoffassociation.org • Getting there requires some work, either by subway on the A or #4 to Utica Ave then the # B46 bus, then a nine-block walk, the #2/#5 to Newkirk, then # B8 bus to Beverley Rd at 59th St, or the #3 train to Sutter Ave-Rutland Rd then the # B47 bus to Clarendon Rd and Ralph Ave

The oldest house in the city is by no means an essential stop for casual visitors, but for those interested in architectural, colonial or borough history, it may be worth the trek – especially if coupled with a visit to Weeksville (see p.232) and Prospect Park's Lefferts Homestead (see p.227). The wooden saltbox structure, built by Pieter Claesen Wyckoff, dates back to around 1652, though renovations and additions are more circa mid-1800s. A guided tour takes in the cramped space – a family of thirteen resided in the original one-room house – and reimagines colonial times; docents do their best to evoke the customs and lifestyle. A new building is being added to the site to hold offices and displays, somewhat disrupting the bucolic integrity.

Coney Island and around

It's possible, in theory, to walk, rollerblade or bike almost the entire southern **coast** of Brooklyn. On occasion paths disappear, and you must share the service road off the highway with cars, but you'll never be on the highway itself. Even those of less sturdy stock will find this area – which stretches east from **Bay Ridge** through **Coney Island**, **Brighton Beach** and several smaller neighbourhoods all the way to maritime Sheepshead Bay – worth visiting for the breathtaking views, carnival amusements and varied cuisine. If you're not on a bike or similarly speedy transport, though, you'll do best to focus on Brighton Beach and adjacent Coney Island, which make an easy afternoon trip by subway.

18

WEEKSVILLE

In the shadow of a housing project on the eastern reaches of Crown Heights stands one of the most fascinating historical sights in Brooklyn – the remnants of the once-thriving town of **Weeksville**. Founded by African-American James Weeks in 1838 just eleven years after New York abolished slavery, Weeksville soon became a refuge for both escaped slaves from the South and free blacks fleeing racial violence in the North (a similar if smaller village, Carrsville, existed adjacent to it). By the 1860s it had its own schools and businesses, and had begun turning out some of the city's first black professionals. Weeksville flourished until the 1930s; by the 1950s all but four wood-frame cottages from the town had been destroyed. In the late 1960s efforts headed by a Pratt Institute history professor, James Hurley, led to the (re)discovery of the so-called Hunterfly Road Houses (the name of the former alley that ran by the homes), and activists petitioned the city to preserve them. Call in at the brand-new headquarters of **Weeksville Heritage Center**, 1698 Bergen St between Buffalo and Rochester aves (Tues–Fri 10am–4.30pm, tours Tues–Fri at 3pm; $5; ☎718 756 5250, ⓦweeksvillegardenparty.tumblr.com), to get oriented and join a tour of the three houses (one of which is a double house) that remain. They date back to the 1860s and are furnished in line with various periods of Weeksville's century-long existence. Tour guides do an admirable job filling in atmosphere with stories about Weeksville, gleaned from ongoing research, oral histories and archeological digs. It's a bit of a hike to get here; the closest subway is the A or C train to Utica Avenue, from where you'll walk four blocks south on Utica to Bergen, turn left and walk another couple of blocks.

ARRIVAL AND DEPARTURE

By subway The last few stops of the R train are in Bay Ridge. For Coney Island take the D, F, N or Q train to the last stop at Stillwell Ave. Brighton Beach is a B or Q ride away from the heart of the city, to the Brighton Beach stop, though it and Coney Island are walkable from each other.

Bay Ridge

In the farthest corner of southwest Brooklyn, this large, quiet neighbourhood is known for its ethnic mix (Chinese, Irish, Italians, Scandinavians and Lebanese) and good schools; senior citizens, many of them longtime residents, make up a large chunk of the population.

The main reason to visit Bay Ridge is to ride the **Shore Road Bike Path**, which offers a glorious ride along the bay, including views of the shimmering **Verrazano-Narrows Bridge** (built in 1964), which flashes its minimalist message across the entrance to New York Bay. At 4260ft, this slender, beautiful span was, until Britain's Humber Bridge opened in 1981, the world's longest. The bridge, which connects Brooklyn to Staten Island, is named for the first European explorer of New York Harbor, Giovanni da Verrazano. You can't pedal across it, unfortunately: urban planner Robert Moses vetoed the pedestrian/bicycle pathways that flanked the roadway in the original design for fear they'd lead to a rash of suicides.

To reach the bike path, get off the R train at Bay Ridge Avenue (locals know it as 69th St) and ride west toward the water (depending on where you're coming from, you can hop various buses, including the #B1, #B4, #B9 and express #B27 and #B37, to get near here). At the pier at street's end, a path leads south right along the water's edge; however, to see some of Bay Ridge's nicest homes, turn left before the water on Shore Road. Wind through Shore, Narrows and River roads between 75th and 83rd streets, where you'll see some Greek and Gothic Revival houses. Most distinctive is the **Gingerbread House**, at 8220 Narrows Ave on 83rd Street; the 1916 structure, done in a rare style known as Black Forest Art Nouveau, looks like a witch's backwoods lair, all piled-up stones and drooping eaves. It was put on the market a couple of years ago for $12 million – and taken off after about twelve months, without being sold.

US Army Garrison Fort Hamilton

101st Street and Fort Hamilton Parkway • Mon–Fri 10am–4pm, Sat 10am–2pm • Free • ☎718 630 4349, ⓦharbordefensemuseum.com • Subway R to Bay Ridge-95th St/Fourth Ave

A bit less pastoral than Bay Ridge's bike path but still worth a visit, the **US Army Garrison Fort Hamilton** is a historic military base that serves as home to the **Harbor Defense Museum**. The stone structure, which dates back to the 1830s (the garrison itself to sixty years before that), was once used to protect the fort from any possible rear attack. Artefacts and weapons – guns, mines, missiles, cannon – tell the official history of the defence of New York Harbor.

Coney Island

18

Accessible to anyone for the price of a subway ride, beachfront **Coney Island** has given working-class New Yorkers a holiday ever since a kerosene-lit carousel opened here in 1867. A series of fabulous amusement parks drew huge crowds on hot summer days over the years until the 1960s, when the area fell into slow decline, only to be adopted and repopularized by a hip crowd of historians and artists drawn to its retro charm in the 1990s. Some movements toward modernizing were in place, but Hurricane Sandy put a stop to most business, even shutting down venerable *Nathan's* (home of the "famous Coney Island hot dog" and the annual **Hot Dog Eating Contest** on July 4) indefinitely.

It's an enjoyable place to spend an afternoon or evening, despite – or perhaps because of – its seediness. Most rides and attractions are open daily only from late May to early September, with weekend hours in the spring and autumn. If you can, visit Coney Island on a Friday night during the season, when the beach is lit up by an impressive **fireworks** display; a walk along the famous **boardwalk**, where hip-hop blares from boom boxes and loudspeakers, and the language of choice is Spanish or Russian as often as English, is essential whenever you go. The raucous annual **Mermaid Parade** (ⓦconeyisland.com) in mid- to late June ranks as one of the oddest, glitziest small-town festivals in the country, where participants dress (barely) as mermaids, King Neptune and other sea-dwellers.

Luna Park, Wonder Wheel and Cyclone

Coney Island Boardwalk • Luna Park $29 for unlimited rides • ☎ 718 373 5862, ⓦ lunaparknyc.com • Subway D, F, N, Q to Coney Island-Stillwell Ave

The amusement park area, inland of the boardwalk, centres on the newly constructed **Luna Park**, which has a slightly incongruous modern look and feel. It does offer some unique, head-spinning (and stomach-churning) rides, like the Eclipse and the Air Race; time will tell if they gain classic status of the two most thrilling attractions in the vicinity. It has managed to incorporate one of those, the venerable **Cyclone** roller coaster (late March–Oct hours vary, weekends-only early and late in the season; $8; ☎718 265 2100), into its fold. A creaky wooden contraption more than 80 years old, it's not for the faint hearted – as you wait in the snaking line, you can actually see the cars lose contact with the metal rails at one point. Sit up front for the most terrifying view or in the back for an extra-strong sense of vertigo.

Less scary but still good fun, the **Wonder Wheel** (late March–Oct hours vary; $6; ☎718 372 2592, ⓦwonderwheel.com), is an official New York City landmark; the 1920 ride is the world's tallest Ferris wheel besides the London Eye. From the top you get panoramic views of Coney Island and the ocean. It's the signature ride in **Deno's Wonder Wheel Amusement Park**, with its kiddie park ($3 per ride) and handful of adult thrills.

MCU Park

Surf Ave between West 17th and 19th streets • Subway D, F, N, Q to Coney Island-Stillwell Ave

Another great summer attraction in Coney Island is **MCU Park**, the scenic oceanside baseball stadium that has helped lend a more prosperous air to the neighbourhood. The park is home to the **Brooklyn Cyclones** (see p.390), a New York Mets-affiliated minor-league team that draws a dedicated crowd. Seating is intimate, beer flows freely and tickets start at just $9.

Coney Island Museum

1208 Surf Ave • Thurs–Sun noon–6pm • 99¢ • ☎ 718 372 5159, ⓦ coneyisland.com/museum.shtml • Subway D, F, N, Q to Coney Island-Stillwell Ave

East of Stillwell Avenue, the nonprofit **Coney Island Museum** is one indoor destination you don't want to miss. You can tour relics of Coney Island past, hear a lecture on the beach's history or catch a night-time burlesque performance or film screening.

Sideshows by the Seashore

West 12th St at Surf Ave • Early June to Aug daily 1–8pm; late May and first half of Sept Fri, Sat & Sun 1–8pm • $10, under 12 $5 • ⓦ coneyisland.com/sideshow.shtml • Subway D, F, N, Q to Coney Island-Stillwell Ave

This 45-minute act, the modern incarnation of the long-running amusement park "freak show", features sword-swallowers, contortionists, fire-eaters, glass walkers and other skilful masochists. If you love what you see, sign up for ongoing classes to learn the skills.

New York Aquarium

Surf Ave and West 8th St • June–Aug Mon–Fri 10am–6pm, Sat & Sun 10am–7pm; Sept, Oct, April–May Mon–Fri 10am–5pm, Sat & Sun 10am–5.30pm; Nov–March daily 10am–4.30pm • $9.95 • ☎ 718 265 3474, ⓦ nyaquarium.com • Subway F, Q to West 8th St-NY Aquarium

On the boardwalk, east of the amusement park and halfway to Brighton Beach, sits the seashell-shaped New York Aquarium, a top-of-the-line operation run by the Wildlife Conservation Society, which also administers New York's four excellent zoos. It's had its ups and downs recently – the benefits of a large expansion and the thrill over the acquisition of the baby walrus Mitik, which was originally rescued off the coast of Alaska, were tempered by the water damage from Hurricane Sandy, which shut the place for more than half a year.

Even now, the museum is still only partially reopened, and won't be fully operational until 2016. Check out the indoor pools in Conservation Hall and Glovers Reef, where you'll see rays and piranha, and learn about coral and habitat protection. Outside folks crowd around the otter and penguin displays, and no doubt will too at the new shark exhibit, complete with glass tunnel – the better to see the creatures swim above you – meant to open in 2014. The sea lion show at the "Aquatheater" is slickly produced and several steps beyond most feeding demonstrations – it's guaranteed to delight the kids.

Brighton Beach

East along the boardwalk from Coney Island (and walkable from there), at Brooklyn's southernmost end, **Brighton Beach** was once an affluent seaside resort of its own. Often called Little Odessa, it is now home to the country's largest community of immigrants from Russia and the former Soviet states, who started relocating here in the 1970s. The eldest of them pack the boardwalk benches to soak up the sun and gossip.

Brighton Beach Avenue runs parallel to the boardwalk; the street is a bustling mixture of Russian souvenir shops and **food emporiums**. Sit-down food is also readily available at

---

BROOKLYN BEER

In 1900 nearly fifty breweries operated in Brooklyn, but the last of these, Schaefer and Rheingold, closed in 1976. For years after its founding in 1987, the **Brooklyn Brewery**, at 79 North 11th St (☎ 718 486 7422, ⓦ brooklynbrewery.com), was "Brooklyn" in name only – the founders had their beer produced upstate. But in 1996 the operation moved into its Williamsburg headquarters, reviving Brooklyn's brewing tradition and making Brooklyn Lager a very popular beverage citywide; it has gained rivals in recent years, namely Red Hook's SixPoint (see p.225) and Fort Greene's Kelso (made by Greenpoint Beer Works).

Hang out in its cafeteria-style beer hall (see p.340) or take a tour (Mon–Thurs 5–7pm, $8, reservation only; Sat 1, 2, 3, 4 & 5pm, Sun 1, 2, 3 & 4pm, free, no reservations). It's $5 for a beer; offerings may include seasonal brews you can't always find in stores and restaurants.

restaurants on the boardwalk, though you might want to wait until evening, when the **supper clubs** open up. These cavernous places offer a near-parody of a rowdy Russian night out, complete with lots of food, loud music, surreal floor shows and plenty of vodka.

Manhattan Beach, just east from Brighton Beach, offers a less-trammelled strip of sand and some pricey real estate to match.

Northern Brooklyn

Northeast of downtown and past Fort Greene are the neighbourhoods of **Williamsburg**, which is divided among artsy refugees from Manhattan and sections that are strongly Hasidic Jewish or Latino, and **Greenpoint**, a Polish stronghold that's in turn being inundated by artsy refugees from Williamsburg. While short on typical tourist attractions, these districts are long on atmosphere, whether you want to ogle tattooed twenty-somethings or immerse yourself in the sounds of Spanish, Yiddish or Polish.

18

ARRIVAL AND DEPARTURE

By subway The L train goes to Williamsburg, with Bedford Ave and Lorimer St the most convenient stops. Greenpoint is reachable by the G train to Greenpoint Ave, though it's easy to walk across McCarren Park from Williamsburg.

Williamsburg

Bedford Avenue is the heart of Williamsburg, where the blocks teem with a particular breed of self-consciously downmarket bohemian, decked out in vintage clothes and hopping from coffee shop to record store to nifty boutique.

While the densest concentration of activity is on Bedford, many of the more interesting spots are elsewhere, having gravitated towards cheaper rents. (Indeed, some would argue, with some validity, that the real hipsters have decamped to Bushwick or some other on-the-verge neighbourhood.) **Grand Street**, for one, is lined with some fine galleries and shops, and some of the formerly industrial spaces on **North Sixth Street** between Bedford and Wythe avenues are now filled with bars and design stores. **Metropolitan Avenue** also has some good bars and restaurants.

A prime culinary attraction is **Smorgasburg** (April to mid-Nov Sat 11am–6pm; ⓦsmorgasburg.com), a food market that's a spin-off of the Brooklyn Flea (see p.221); both it and the Williamsburg version of the Flea (Sun) are held in the same location, on the waterfront between North Sixth and Seventh streets – Smorgasburg moves to Dumbo on Sundays. Scores of vendors sell everything from delectable cold sesame noodles and *banh mi* to BLTs, with an emphasis on local, fresh and sustainable.

The few dozen galleries in the neighbourhood include the pioneering **Pierogi**, at 177 North 9th St between Bedford and Driggs, though its heyday is past, as well as its related space at 191 North 14th St, The Boiler; some of the city's best secondhand clothing shops are close by (see p.382). On the other end of the neighbourhood, next to the Williamsburg Bridge, the **Williamsburg Art and Historical Center**, at 135 Broadway on Bedford (Fri–Mon 1–6pm; ☎718 486 7372, ⓦwahcenter.net), displays local painting and sculpture in a vast gallery on the second floor of the imposing Kings County Savings Bank.

If you're interested in doing serious gallery-hopping in the neighbourhood, pick up the free monthly booklet *Wagmag* (ⓦwagmag.org) at any bookshop or gallery, or visit on the second Friday night of the month for **Williamsburg Every Second**, when many galleries stay open until 9 or 10pm and host performances and parties.

A bit more history oriented than any of the galleries but still in the same vein, the **City Reliquary**, 370 Metropolitan Ave at Havemeyer St (Thurs–Sun noon–6pm; $5 suggested donation; ⓦcityreliquary.org), displays a mishmash of NYC-related ephemera such as vintage postcards, seltzer bottles and Jackie Robinson memorabilia; the fact that it grew from an apartment window display to a museum speaks volumes about the 'hood. But the cutting-edge feel of Williamsburg has started to wear away: ultra-sleek high-rises have sprouted up, capitalizing on views like the one from tiny **Grand Ferry Park**; just south, the massive Domino's Sugar Factory is being converted into housing.

South-side Williamsburg, by contrast, seems frozen in time, especially in the vicinity of **Lee Avenue** and Bedford Avenue, which run parallel between Division Avenue and the Brooklyn–Queens Expressway. Here, kosher delicatessens line the streets and signs are written in Yiddish and Hebrew, thanks to the large population of **Hasidic Jews** in the area – a community presence since 1903, when the Williamsburg Bridge brought over many Jews from the cramped Lower East Side.

Greenpoint

Quiet **Greenpoint**, which hugs the northern border of the borough, has the distinction of being the childhood home of Mae West, the birthplace of the oft-ridiculed

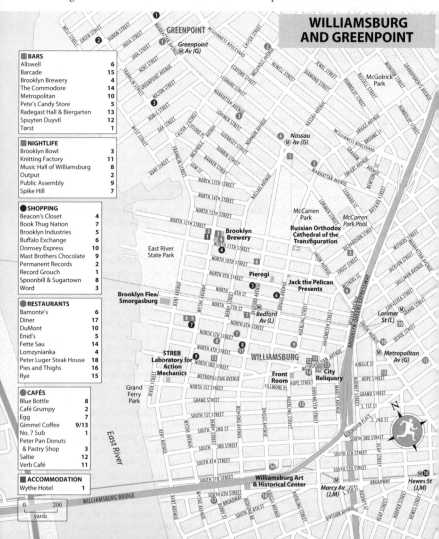

WILLIAMSBURG AND GREENPOINT

■ BARS

Allswell	6
Barcade	15
Brooklyn Brewery	4
The Commodore	14
Metropolitan	10
Pete's Candy Store	5
Radegast Hall & Biergarten	13
Spuyten Duyvil	12
Tørst	1

■ NIGHTLIFE

Brooklyn Bowl	3
Knitting Factory	11
Music Hall of Williamsburg	8
Output	2
Public Assembly	9
Spike Hill	7

● SHOPPING

Beacon's Closet	4
Book Thug Nation	7
Brooklyn Industries	5
Buffalo Exchange	6
Domsey Express	10
Mast Brothers Chocolate	9
Permanent Records	2
Record Grouch	1
Spoonbill & Sugartown	8
Word	3

● RESTAURANTS

Bamonte's	6
Diner	17
DuMont	10
Enid's	5
Fette Sau	14
Lomzynianka	4
Peter Luger Steak House	18
Pies and Thighs	16
Rye	15

● CAFÉS

Blue Bottle	8
Café Grumpy	2
Egg	7
Gimme! Coffee	9/13
No. 7 Sub	1
Peter Pan Donuts & Pastry Shop	3
Saltie	12
Verb Café	11

■ ACCOMMODATION

Wythe Hotel	1

Brooklynese accent and home to the largest Polish community in New York City; there's also a substantial Puerto Rican contingent. The relaxed, low-rise area has absorbed some of the artsy feel of Williamsburg to the south, but the younger residents haven't diluted the Polish character of the businesses along its tidy main strip, **Manhattan Avenue** (partly because they're establishing their own strip on **Franklin Street**, though to be fair there are a few cool spots mixed in on Manhattan).

While Greenpoint and neighbouring areas were originally known as Boswijck (later Bushwick), meaning "wooded district", the Industrial Revolution took the "green" out of Greenpoint, as the area became home to the "Black Arts" – printing, pottery, gas, glass and iron. In 1950, refineries caused a 17- to 30-million-gallon underground oil spill, larger than the Exxon Valdez disaster in Alaska, which spilled "only" eleven million gallons. It's not immediately visible except as an occasional slick on the surface of Newtown Creek, which separates Greenpoint from Queens, but it's very much on the minds of residents who fear the toxic effects of the residue. Cleanup is ongoing, but still has years to finish – if that's even possible at this point.

18

These things aside, Greenpoint merits a quick visit for its blend of Polish and hipster cultures and their respective cuisines. If you're coming from Williamsburg, take Driggs Avenue north past the **Russian Orthodox Cathedral of the Transfiguration**, at North 12th Street on Driggs, a New York City landmark whose five green-copper onion domes hover above the trees of **McCarren Park**. The park itself forms the unofficial line between Greenpoint and Williamsburg; in addition to tennis courts, playgrounds and dog runs, it contains a historic pool, which reopened in 2012.

Turn left on Manhattan Avenue and continue straight to get to the heart of Greenpoint. Along the way you'll find an assortment of Polish delis and bakeries, which spill over onto Nassau, where **Steve's Meat Market**, at 104 Nassau Ave between Leonard and Eckford (☎718 383 1780), claims to make the best *kielbasa* (spicy Polish sausage) in the US. Keep moving north on Manhattan and an air of isolation takes over, though there are an increasing number of cool cafés and restaurants in these parts. Wander down the narrow side-streets of Manhattan and you'll get a feel for the tight-knit local community – and how it is changing. *Café Grumpy*, 193 Meserole Ave, at Diamond, is a youth magnet (see p.292), while further towards the water, an assortment of bars and restaurants has sprouted up along Franklin Street and around Greenpoint Avenue.

Newtown Creek Nature Walk and Wastewater Treatment Plant

East end of Paidge Ave • Park daily sunrise–sunset • Subway G to Greenpoint Ave, then two blocks east to Provost St and about eight blocks north to Paidge Ave

On the banks of Newtown Creek, an unusual waterfront park offers splendid views and unmatched solitude. A walkway, formed like the hull of a ship (complete with portholes), snakes down to the water, along which are plantings, sculptures, benches and steps that go right down to creek level; look out and you'll see bridges to Queens, the occasional barge, giant mounds of trash – more mesmerizing than it sounds – and the Chrysler Building, among other skyline beauties. You can also catch sight of what's behind you: the bulbous silos (they call them "digester eggs") of the Newtown Creek Wastewater Treatment Plant, which has a visitor center, 329 Greenpoint Ave (by appointment ☎718 595 5140; they also run monthly tours of the eggs, along with a variety of educational programmes in the centre). As you descend back to the parking lot on your way back down the path, note how the walkway perfectly frames the Empire State Building.

Queens

With its ever-shifting ethnic composition and frankly utilitarian housing stock, Queens represents the "new" New York – the city as an international crossroads, the melting pot on full boil. The largest (in terms of physical size) of the boroughs, Queens is, in fact, the most diverse county in the US, with nearly half the 2.3 million residents foreign-born, and these hailing from 150 different countries. Not surprisingly, it's something of a culinary hotspot. Take the elevated #7 train to Woodside, Jackson Heights and Flushing and you can eat unassailably authentic versions of Thai catfish salad, Indian *vindaloo* and Colombian *arepas*, respectively. In Astoria you'll find Bosnian *burek* and Greek *spanikopita*, Brazilian *feijoada* and Egyptian braised lamb cheeks.

Culturally, the richest spot in Queens is **Long Island City**, where a cluster of galleries has cropped up around the contemporary art centre MoMA PS1, an affiliate of midtown's Museum of Modern Art. Farther out, **Flushing Meadows Corona Park** draws sports fans and families – the former to Citi Field, where the **New York Mets** play, and the USTA Billie Jean King National Tennis Center, home of late summer's **US Open Tennis Championships**, and the latter to the Queens Museum of Art, Queens Zoo and New York Hall of Science. At the southeast end of the borough (accessible via the A train), in **Jamaica Bay** and the **Rockaways**, lie parks and beaches that feel miles from the city; both areas were hit hard by Hurricane Sandy, and the Rockaways in particular have a way to go before rebuilding is complete.

INFORMATION

Tourist information For information on the borough and discounts at local merchants, contact Discover Queens (Mon–Fri 10am–6pm, Sat & Sun 11am–7pm; ☎718 592 2082, ⓦ queensnyc.com); the visitor centre is located at 90-15 Queens Blvd, in Elmhurst.

19

Long Island City and Astoria

Long Island City and **Astoria**, only a few minutes by subway from midtown Manhattan, rank as the hippest neighbourhoods in Queens. It can be a little unclear which is which, given that the whole area is technically Long Island City, with Astoria a self-designated neighbourhood within it. Practically speaking, though, most people think of Astoria as the part of Long Island City north of 36th Avenue, and Long Island City as the area south of the Queensboro Bridge and north of the Long Island Expressway. Astoria is far more residential and has more destination-type sights, like museums focusing on movie history and the sculptor Isamu Noguchi, though Long Island City does have some charming pockets among its largely industrial streets as well as cultural draws of its own.

ARRIVAL AND INFORMATION

By train/subway Edging the East River right across from the United Nations, Long Island City is a five-minute ride on the #7 train from Grand Central Terminal, well worth the trip if you're interested in cutting-edge art. For Astoria, the N and Q head north through the neighbourhood, and the R train stops at Steinway St.
By bus The #Q103 bus, which runs along Vernon Blvd, connects Long Island City with the Noguchi Museum and Socrates Sculpture Park in Astoria; the #Q104 and #66 buses connect major sights in the neighbourhoods as well.
Information The Greater Astoria Historical Society, at 35-20 Broadway (☎718 278 0700, ⓦ astorialic.org), organizes walking tours and screenings, and has books on the borough for sale.

Long Island City

If you've been to MoMA, your ticket stub from that institution gets you free entrance into the main attraction, **MoMA PS1**, while **SculptureCenter** and the **Fisher Landau Center for Art** also put on first-rate shows, as do a number of small galleries. The other cultural claim to local fame is as home to **Silvercup Studios**, the largest film and

NAVIGATING QUEENS

One reason many New Yorkers have no love for Queens is the deeply unsettling street-number system, which can leave you baffled on the corner of 30th Road and 30th Street. But the so-called "Philadelphia method" of addressing, applied borough-wide in the 1920s, does have an underlying logic. Basically, **streets** run north–south, while **avenues**, **roads** and **drives** run east–west. Avenue numbers get higher as you head south, while street numbers get higher as you head east (First Street is on the East River, and 180th is in Jamaica). And in Queens, addresses let you know right where you are: the digits before the hyphen indicate the cross-street: 20-78 33rd Street, for instance, is between 20th and 21st avenues.

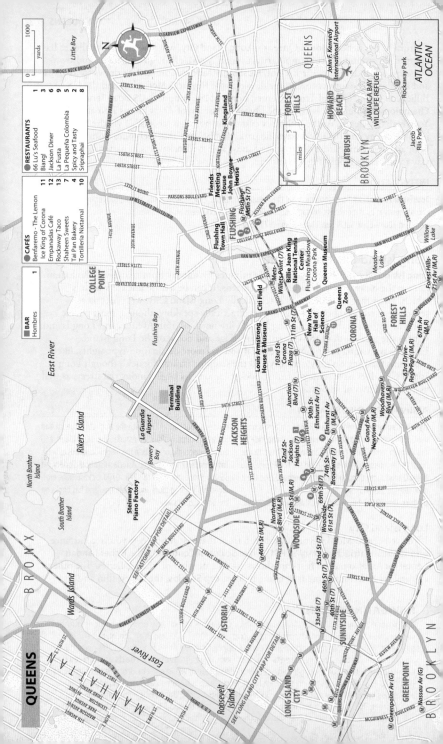

television production studio on the East Coast, which stretches out along 21st Street next to the Queensboro Bridge. *Sex and the City* (both movies included) and *The Sopranos* were shot here; *30 Rock* still is.

Despite the recent (and ongoing) construction of some massive high-rise condo buildings on the waterfront, there's a keen sense of community, which you can feel in the eating and drinking establishments in the **Hunters Point** neighbourhood along **Vernon Boulevard** between 46th and 51st avenues. Stroll two blocks west to get some eye-grabbing views of the United Nations and the east side of Manhattan from sylvan **Gantry Plaza State Park**.

MoMA PS1 Contemporary Art Center

22–25 Jackson Ave, at 46th Ave • Mon & Thurs–Sun noon–6pm • $10 suggested donation, free with MoMA ticket • ☎ 718 784 2084, Ⓦ momaps1.org • Subway #7 to 45th Road-Court Square, E, M to 23rd St-Ely Ave, G to Long Island City-Court Square

The renowned **MoMA PS1 Contemporary Art Center** occupies a hundred-room nineteenth-century brick schoolhouse. Founded in 1971, PS1 became affiliated with the **Museum of Modern Art** in 2000. It has no real permanent collection of its own, instead using its substantial space to mount sprawling thematic shows and retrospectives; however, one of the long-term installations, James Turrell's *Meeting*, is as surprising and provocative a piece as you'll find. The schoolroom-themed *M. Wells Dinette*, on the ground floor (museum admission not required), marks the city's most daring museum café (see p.292).

5 Pointz

45–46 Davis St • Ⓦ 5ptz.com • Subway #7 to 45th Road-Court Square, E, M to 23rd St-Ely Ave, G to Long Island City-Court Square

Across Jackson Avenue from PS1, the block-long warehouse complex known as **5 Pointz** is covered with graffiti art contributed by hundreds of artists over the course of a decade. It faces an uncertain future – indeed, recent reports have the place set to be razed for luxury apartments – so for the moment you can only stand in awe at the kaleidoscopic work (unless you want to contact the organization for a tour or permission to photograph the place).

Hunters Point Historic District and around

Near PS1, the **Hunters Point Historic District** centres on 45th Avenue between 21st and 23rd streets, with an immaculate string of late nineteenth-century row houses in the shadow of the **Citigroup Building**, which is the tallest building in the city outside of Manhattan. Past that tower and the Neoclassical **Long Island City Courthouse**, **SculptureCenter**, 44-19 Purves St (Mon & Thurs–Sun 11am–6pm; $5 suggested donation; ☎718 361 1750, Ⓦ sculpture-center.org), displays innovative work in a former trolley-repair shop that was cleverly renovated by architect Maya Lin.

Fisher Landau Center for Art

38-27 30th St, between 38th and 39th aves • Mon & Thurs–Sun noon–5pm • Free • ☎718 937 0727, Ⓦ flcart.org • N, Q to 39th Ave-31st St

In a bit of a no-man's land between the hearts of Astoria and Long Island City, the **Fisher Landau Center for Art** occupies a surprising cultural oasis near a spider's web of elevated trains and congested roads. You'll almost certainly have this airy space to yourself as you contemplate works by Jenny Holzer, Jasper Johns, Matthew Barney and Yinka Shonibare – or whatever other big names in contemporary art happen to be currently selected from real-estate heiress Emily Fisher Landau's thousand-item-plus personal collection.

Astoria

Northeast of Long Island City is **Astoria**, bounded on the north and west by the East River, to the south by 36th Avenue and to the east by 46th Street or thereabouts. The diverse neighbourhood is best known for being home to the largest concentration of

19

Greeks outside Greece, though many other groups are in abundance as well, including Moroccans, Egyptians, Bangladeshis, Bosnians and Brazilians; plenty of young professionals live here too in the 1930s brick apartment buildings and vinyl-sided row houses. The N trains from Manhattan run north through the middle of the neighbourhood, stopping at all of the major avenues, each of which forms its own community: 30th Avenue and Broadway are liveliest, with Greek coffee joints and nightclubs, discount department stores, butchers, fishmongers and ethnic restaurants of every type; a few cafés and restaurants on 34th and 35th avenues cater to **Kaufman Astoria Studios'** workers and visitors. The **Astoria Boulevard** stop will get you closest to one of New York's biggest and best beer gardens, *Bohemian Hall* (see p.341). Quieter Ditmars Boulevard is home to some of Astoria's oldest residents – the Italians predate the Greeks – and is near **Astoria Park**, which has beautiful views of Manhattan and a mammoth public pool.

Alternatively, you can take the R to Steinway Street, which accesses the east side of the neighbourhood; between 28th Avenue and Astoria Boulevard, Steinway is a strip of Egyptian- and Moroccan-run businesses, including a glut of **hookah cafés** where you can watch Arabic TV, sip tea and savour sweet apple tobacco.

Museum of the Moving Image

36-01 35th Ave, between 36th and 37th sts • Tues–Thurs 10.30am–5pm, Fri 10.30am–8pm, Sat & Sun 11.30am–7pm • $12, ages 3–18 $6, free Fri 4–8pm • ☎ 718 777 6888, ⓦ movingimage.us • Subway M, R to Steinway St, or N, Q to 36th Ave-31st St

Between 1920 and 1928, Astoria was the capital of America's **silent film industry**, and Paramount Pictures got its start at the present site of Kaufman Astoria Studios, drawing stars such as Rudolph Valentino and the Marx Brothers. Business dried up in the 1930s, when moviemakers were lured to Los Angeles by more reliable weather, but was rekindled in 1977 with the shooting of Sidney Lumet's *The Wiz*, and the studios are now extremely busy with everything from commercials to blockbusters. Part of the Kaufman Astoria complex is dedicated to the **Museum of the Moving Image**, which has reopened after a major expansion that added an adjacent three-storey building with a theatre and an education centre, plus a courtyard garden. A mirrored glass facade gives way to a white, angular entryway that feels not unlike a spacecraft (or at least a spacecraft of the popular imagination).

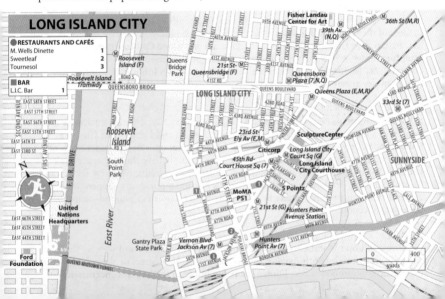

LONG ISLAND CITY

● RESTAURANTS AND CAFÉS
M. Wells Dinette — 1
Sweetleaf — 2
Tournesol — 3

■ BAR
L.I.C. Bar — 1

The museum's core collection, "Behind the Screen", is spread over two floors and contains more than 125,000 objects, including old movie cameras and special-effects equipment; early televisions; all kinds of costumes and props, including the chariot from *Ben Hur*; fascinating detailed sketches and set design models from *The Silence of the Lambs*; fan magazines, posters and enough *Star Wars* action figures to make an obsessed fan drool with envy; and movie stills and (psychologically) revealing black-and-white photos of famous actors and directors. There's a real focus on interactivity, too, as you have the opportunity to create a short animated film, make a soundtrack and see how live television is edited. If all this somehow fails to move you, you can always play a few rounds on the vintage arcade games near the end of the exhibit.

Sharing space on the third floor is a gallery for rotating exhibits and installations, while on the ground floor, the main theatre shows all sorts of cool film series, focusing on directors, claymation and nearly every other subject you might think of. Perhaps not surprisingly, the place can be swamped with school groups.

Noguchi Museum

19

9-01 33rd Rd • Wed–Fri 10am–5pm, Sat & Sun 11am–6pm • $10, under 12 free • ☎ 718 204 7088, ⓦ noguchi.org • Subway N, Q to Broadway (Queens) station; head west to Vernon Blvd, then south two blocks to 33rd Rd – about a 15min walk or a 5min ride on the #Q104 bus; #7 train to Vernon Blvd-Jackson Ave, then #Q103 bus

Off the beaten track but definitely worth the detour, the **Isamu Noguchi Garden Museum** is devoted to the works of Japanese-American abstract sculptor Isamu Noguchi (1904–88), who worked in Long Island City for many years and designed this museum at his studio site shortly before his death. At its centre is a garden filled with his stone sculptures, while the surrounding galleries include a special section on his design work. It's a place for quiet contemplation of the artist's sublime exercises in simplicity.

Socrates Sculpture Park

One block north of the Noguchi Museum; Broadway, at Vernon Blvd • Daily 10am–sunset • ☎ 718 956 1819, ⓦ socratessculpturepark.org

While you're out at the Noguchi Museum, it would be crazy not to stop in at **Socrates Sculpture Park**. The park was an abandoned landfill until 1986, when sculptor Mark di Suvero transformed it into an outdoor studio, with space for artists to build on a massive scale. The resulting works range from ingenious kinetic installations to bizarre structures that appear to be growing out of the lawn.

Sunnyside and Woodside

After Astoria, the E and R trains run north of **Sunnyside** and **Woodside**, historically Irish enclaves but now also home to many Asian and Latino immigrants. You're not

---

STEINWAY & SONS PIANO FACTORY

Astoria has a reputation as an international crossroads, but it boasts few international exports, with one notable exception: **Steinway pianos**. Founded in 1853 in Manhattan by German immigrant Henry Steinway, the company moved its factory to Astoria in the late nineteenth century and has been turning out the finest pianos in the world ever since (though only 3 percent of pianos are Steinways, 98 percent of recording artists use them). About two thousand Steinway grand pianos are built in New York every year, retailing from $40,000 to well over $100,000. They are said to be the most complex object on earth that's put together by hand, with 12,000 parts assembled over the course of nine months. See this fascinating process yourself on a free **guided tour** (Tues 9.30am, approx 2hr 30min, not offered July & Aug; call at least a few months ahead for reservations; ☎ 718 721 2600, ⓦ steinway.com). Take the N to Ditmars Boulevard, walk seven blocks east to 38th Street and then go three blocks north to 1 Steinway Place at 19th Avenue.

missing too much if you skip these neighbourhoods on your way to the more interesting **Jackson Heights**, though planning enthusiasts may want to see the **Sunnyside Gardens** development, a utopian working-class "garden city" built in 1924 with encouragement from Eleanor Roosevelt and Lewis Mumford.

ARRIVAL AND DEPARTURE

By train and subway For Sunnyside, take the #7 train to the 46th Street stop and walk north on 46th (the opposite direction from the Art Deco "Sunnyside" sign on Queens Boulevard). East of Sunnyside, the #7 train swings away from Queens Boulevard and heads up narrower Roosevelt Avenue.

Jackson Heights

Developed just after the construction of the elevated train in 1917, **Jackson Heights** was laid out as a unified district of tidy brick homes and apartment blocks with attractive garden courtyards (the term "**garden apartment**" was coined here), lending the area a cohesiveness that's rare in Queens. Walking tours of the **historic district** – including its private gardens – are offered during Historic Jackson Heights Weekend each June (ⓦjhbg.org). If you're not on a tour, take a stroll down 35th and 37th

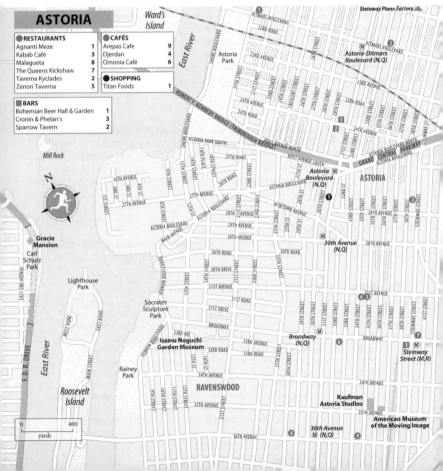

ASTORIA

● RESTAURANTS	
Agnanti Meze	1
Kabab Café	3
Malagueta	8
The Queens Kickshaw	7
Taverna Kyclades	2
Zenon Taverna	5

● CAFÉS	
Arepas Cafe	9
Djerdan	4
Omonia Café	6

● SHOPPING	
Titan Foods	1

■ BARS	
Bohemian Beer Hall & Garden	1
Cronin & Phelan's	3
Sparrow Tavern	2

avenues between 78th and 88th streets to get a feel for the architecture; the Towers, the Chateau and Linden Court are but a few of the attractive co-ops – with extravagant interior gardens – that pepper the place.

The neighbourhood is the most diverse in the city, with especially large concentrations of Latin American immigrants. Amble up **Roosevelt Avenue** and you'll find Argentinian steakhouses, Colombian street vendors selling treats such as *arepas* (savoury corn cakes) and Mexican bakeries displaying stacks of bread and pastries.

ARRIVAL AND DEPARTURE

By train and subway Get off at 74th St or 82nd St (or take the E, F or R to Roosevelt Ave) and you'll find yourself in central Jackson Heights.

Little India

Little India, along 74th Street between Roosevelt and 37th Avenue, is something of a contrast. This is the largest Indian community in New York, and South Asians from all over come here to find colourful saris, elaborate gold jewellery for weddings, groceries and music, and perhaps a pungent betel leaf from a street cart. The restaurants here far surpass the more quotidian fare on better-known East 6th Street in Manhattan: *Jackson Diner (*see p.326), is one of the more popular spots.

Corona and Flushing Meadows

East of Jackson Heights is gritty **Corona**, immortalized in Queens native Paul Simon's song *Me and Julio Down by the Schoolyard*. Once entirely Italian (*corona* is Italian for "crown"), the fast-growing neighbourhood is now mostly first- and second-generation immigrants from the Dominican Republic, Mexico, Ecuador and Colombia, and about a fifth of households live below the poverty line. It's also home to **Louis Armstrong House** and **Flushing Meadows–Corona Park**, home to the Mets' Citi Field and the USTA Billie Jean King National Tennis Center.

Louis Armstrong House Museum

34-56 107th St, between 34th and 37th avenues • Tues–Fri 10am–5pm, Sat & Sun noon–5pm • $10 • ☎718 478 8274, ⓦlouisarmstronghouse.org • Subway #7 to 103rd St-Corona Plaza, walk north on 104th St, turn right on 37th Ave and then left on 107th St

Opened as a museum in 2003, the great jazz artist's home has been preserved just as he and his wife, Lucille, left it. Armstrong, who lived here from 1943 until his death in 1971, made audio recordings of the day-to-day goings-on in the house, and these play inside, creating a ghostly atmosphere. Guided tours, which show off Armstrong's trumpets, furnishings and various other artefacts, start every hour on the hour (last one

---

THE WORLD COMES TO QUEENS

In late April 1939, as the US emerged from the Great Depression and war loomed, 1200 acres of the new Flushing Meadows–Corona Park became the stage for America's love affair with modernity. Drawing visitors from across the nation (and delegates from 62 others), the **1939–40 World's Fair** featured displays of technologies yet to be realized, including robotics and fluorescent lights. General Motors sponsored a "Futurama" ride through a utopian modern city, and New Yorkers saw broadcast television for the first time. The fair was a great success, and brought attention to this little-known borough. In part due to the reputation established by the expo, the United Nations briefly operated from here following World War II.

The **1964–65 World's Fair**, held in the same location, in many ways book-ended the era of jubilant optimism that the 1939 fair had opened. While technological and engineering advances such as lasers and computers thrilled 52 million fair-goers, the fair's tone – in the wake of President Kennedy's assassination – was markedly different. Many of the temporary structures stand around the park, either appropriated for other uses or left to decay.

begins at 4pm); the recently completed visitors' centre across the street holds much more of Armstrong's personal archives. Occasional concerts take place in the Japanese garden behind the house. If you'd like to learn more about Queens' substantial jazz history, you could pick up a map ($10) of the so-called **Queens Jazz Trail Tour** from Flushing Town Hall (see p.248); in addition to Dizzy Gillespie and Cannonball Adderley, who lived near Armstrong, such notables as Ella Fitzgerald, Count Basie, Lena Horne, Fats Waller and, briefly, Charles Mingus called the borough home.

Flushing Meadows–Corona Park

Between the Van Wyck Expressway and Grand Central Parkway, east of 111th St • Ⓦ nycgovparks.org • Subway #7 to Mets-Willets Point, then walk south past the tennis complex to the park; or head directly to the museums by getting off at the 111th St station and walking south on 111th St until you hit the park's northwest corner

Flushing Meadows–Corona Park is an enormous (1200-acre) swathe of green first laid out in the 1930s, and its few key attractions – a couple of interesting museums, a zoo, and some relics of the two World's Fairs held here (see box, p.245) – make for a good afternoon out, especially if you have children who need space to run around. There are also some spots for physical activity, including a par-3 golf course and the World Ice Arena (Mon–Fri 9am–5.15pm, Sat noon–4.45pm & 8–9.50pm, Sun noon–4.45pm; ☎718 760 9001, Ⓦworldice.com; $5 weekdays, $8 weekends, $5 skate rental), a large indoor skating facility. As well, if early plans come to pass, there will be a brand-new soccer stadium built here to house a nascent major-league soccer team, New York FC (see p.392).

For refreshment after seeing the park, visit the *Lemon Ice King of Corona* (see p.293).

Citi Field

123-01 Roosevelt Ave • Subway #7 to Mets-Willets Point

Citi Field replaced decrepit Shea Stadium as the home field of the **New York Mets** (see p.389) baseball team in April 2009. The new stadium seats 45,000 (10,000 fewer than Shea) and has an old-fashioned facade of brick, granite and cast stone, mimicking that of old Ebbets Field in Brooklyn, former home of the Brooklyn Dodgers, New York's previous National League franchise. The Mets have a loyal fan base, if for no other reason than that many Queens and Brooklyn residents can't stand the Yankees, though the team's recent woes – the closeness of the owners to the main figure (Bernie Madoff) in a pyramid scheme, and a somewhat extended rebuilding period – have alienated more than a few.

Billie Jean King National Tennis Center

Flushing Meadows–Corona Park • Subway #7 to Mets-Willets Point

Due south of the Citi Field stadium stands the US Tennis Association's **Billie Jean King National Tennis Center**, the largest public tennis facility in the world, with more than twenty indoor and outdoor courts. The main event, the US Open Tennis Championships (see p.393), takes place at the end of each summer. Tickets to the early matches are easy enough to come by; closer to the finals, you may have to buy from touts.

New York Hall of Science

47-01 111th St, at 46th Avenue • April–Aug Mon–Fri 9.30am–5pm, Sat & Sun 10am–6pm; Sept–March same hours except closed Mon • $11, 2–17 $8, free Sept–June Fri 2–5pm & Sun 10–11am, playground $4, mini-golf $6 • ☎718 699 0005, Ⓦnysci.org • Subway #7 to 111th St

A concrete and stained-glass structure retained from the 1964 World's Fair, the **New York Hall of Science** dazzles kids with interactive science exhibits. It's divided into around ten different sections, some of the best of which include "Mathematica" and "Seeing the Light" – puzzle at the Moebius Strip or how shadows are cast. Elsewhere, you can measure what percentage of your body is water and how fast you can throw a baseball; frequent demonstrations and video presentations take place, too. Outside are two more of the museum's highlights: a mini-golf course, under the shadow of two rockets; and a giant, fun Science Playground, with contraptions that function as both exhibits and playspaces. It's a must if you're there with children under the age of ten. The grounds of the hall serve as host to September's World Maker Faire, which anyone with a passing interest in invention should find their way to.

Queens Zoo

53-51 111th St • April–Oct Mon–Fri 10am–5pm, Sat & Sun 10am–5.30pm; Nov–March daily 10am–4.30pm • $8, 3–12 $5 • ☎718 271 1500, ⓦ queenszoo.com • Subway #7 to 111th

Adjacent to the New York Hall of Science, the **Queens Zoo** is not nearly as spectacular as those in Central Park and the Bronx, although it has transformed Buckminster Fuller's 1964 geodesic dome into a dizzying aviary, and some beautiful big animals – including bison, Shetland cattle and elk – roam the grounds.

Unisphere and New York Pavilion

East of the Queens Zoo, the **Unisphere** is a 140ft-high, stainless-steel globe that weighs 450 tonnes – probably the main reason why it was never moved after the 1964 fair. Robert Moses intended this park to be the "Versailles of America", but the severe, perfectly symmetrical pathways radiating out from the sphere, the anachronistic and often bizarrely ugly architecture, and the roaring Grand Central Parkway all feel more Eastern Bloc than French – particularly when you look south and see the rusting towers of Philip Johnson's 1964 **New York Pavilion**, now home to **Queens Theatre in the Park** (☎718 760 0064, ⓦqueenstheatre.org), which puts on music, dance and family-friendly programmes. Fortunately, the whole picture is softened a bit on sunny days, when the park swarms with kids on bikes and skateboards.

19

Queens Museum of Art

New York City Building, Flushing Meadows–Corona Park • Wed–Sun noon–6pm; guided tours Sun at 2, 3 & 4pm • Suggested donation $8 • ☎718 592 9700, ⓦ queensmuseum.org • Subway #7 to 111th St

Flushing Meadows–Corona Park's finest attraction is the **Queens Museum of Art**, housed right next to the Unisphere in a building from the 1939 fair that served briefly as the first home of the United Nations. The museum has just completed a renovation, which doubled its size; in the process a large glass facade was added, leading to a skylit atrium that has gobbled up the part of the building that the museum used to share with the World's Fair Skating Rink.

The one must-see item in the museum is the **Panorama of the City of New York**, a product of the 1964 fair. With a scale of one inch to one hundred feet, the 9300-square-foot panorama is the world's largest architectural model, incorporating 895,000 buildings, each hand-carved out of wood, as well as rivers, harbours, bridges and even tiny planes drifting in and out of the airports. The two other permanent exhibits of note in the museum are the collection of glassworks by **Louis Comfort Tiffany**, who established his design studios in Corona in the 1890s, and the relief map of New York's water-supply system, a wood-and-plaster model that dates back to the time of the 1939 World's Fair.

Flushing

Originally an early Quaker community, **Flushing** is most notable as the city's second Chinatown: more than two-thirds of the neighbourhood is Asian or Asian-American, a far greater proportion than in Manhattan's Chinatown. While it's not as architecturally quaint as its counterpart, it feels more authentic, and its bustling **restaurants** (see p.326) and shops cater almost exclusively to locals rather than tourists.

Main Street

Head north on **Main Street** from the subway station and you'll pass a couple of old Quaker landmarks, as well as a few other historical buildings. On the west side of Main Street between 39th and 38th avenues is **St George's Church**, an elegant 1854 Gothic landmark

THE QUAKER LEGACY

You may spot the occasional sign in the neighbourhood indicating your place on the Flushing Freedom Mile, which commemorates the neighbourhood's Quaker associations (along with a few other random historical events). Just across the street from the town hall is a shingle cottage, the **Flushing Quaker Meeting House**, at 137-16 Northern Blvd (☎718 358 9636), which dates from 1694, making it the oldest surviving house of worship in the city and the second-oldest Quaker institution in the country. It is open Sundays at 11am for services and noon & 2.30pm for 30-minute tours (free), on which you can also see the centuries-old cemetery (without headstones, as per Quaker tradition).

Flesh out the Quaker story with a quick visit to the **Kingsland Homestead**, at 145-35 37th Ave (Tues, Sat & Sun 2.30–4.30pm; $3; ☎718 939 0647, ⓦqueenshistoricalsociety.org), a small wooden farmhouse maintained by the Queens Historical Society. You can see the house from Bowne Street (which runs south from Northern Blvd), where it is set back in **Weeping Beech Park**. South of the park on Bowne Street, the 1661 Quaker-style **Bowne House** (☎718 359 0528, ⓦbownehouse.org) was the home of John Bowne, who helped Flushing acquire the tag "birthplace of religious freedom in America" by resisting discrimination at a time when the Dutch persecuted anyone who wasn't Calvinist; the gardens and parlour can be viewed on group tours.

19

with a tall central tower. Just around the corner from Main Street a few blocks north, Romanesque Revival **Flushing Town Hall**, at 137-35 Northern Blvd (daily noon–5pm; ☎718 463 7700, ⓦflushingtownhall.org), is now a cultural centre with a sophisticated calendar of musical performances; there's also an art gallery inside ($5 suggested donation).

Alternatively, you might head south from the Main Street subway station; at the first intersection, with 40th Road, a pavement counter, *Corner 28 Restaurant and Caterers* (full restaurant inside), serves succulent Peking duck to go, either on the bone or in a bun. More treats can be had at the nearby **Golden Mall**, at 41-28 Main St, such as hand-pulled noodles, dumplings and cumin-flavoured lamb. Veer off on Kissena Boulevard and you'll pass the stately **Free Synagogue of Flushing**, at no. 41–60 (☎718 961 0030, ⓦfreesynagogue.org), on your right. The oldest surviving Reform Jewish synagogue in the US, it looks like a small-town courthouse, but with brick additions and blue stained-glass windows.

Sri Mahā Vallabha Ganapati Devasthānam

45–57 Bowne St • Mon–Fri 8am–9pm, Sat & Sun 7.30am–9pm • Free • ☎718 460 8484, ⓦnyganeshtemple.org • Subway #7 to Flushing-Main St, take the #Q65 bus south from the Free Synagogue

The **Sri Mahā Vallabha Ganapati Devasthānam** is the most visually arresting of a handful of Eastern-religion temples in the neighbourhood south from the Free Synagogue (though the Buddhist Nichiren Shoshu Temple, at 42-32 Parsons Blvd, gives it a good run for the money). Also known as the **Ganesh Temple**, this grey building honours the elephant-headed Hindu god.

Jamaica Bay

Those who make it out to **Jamaica Bay** – what looks on the map like it might be part of Brooklyn but largely takes up the extreme southern edge of Queens – usually do so to get a bit of a nature break from urban life.

Jamaica Bay Wildlife Refuge

Gateway National Recreation Area • Daily: trails sunrise to sunset, visitor centre 8.30am–5pm • ☎718 318 4340, ⓦnps.gov/gate • Subway A to Broad Channel and walk half-mile north; bus #Q53 from Rockaway Park or Jackson Heights, #Q21 from Rockaway Park or Woodhaven

Jamaica Bay Wildlife Refuge is named for the Jameco Indians, whose territory this once was. Near Broad Channel on the largest of these islands, you can hike trails through the diverse habitats of more than 325 varieties of migrating **bird**; the main loop encircles the

West Pond, home to flocks of ducks and geese. A unit of the 26,607-acre Gateway National Recreation Area, which extends through coastal areas of Queens, Brooklyn, Staten Island and New Jersey, this is one of the most important urban wildlife areas in the United States – and an odd juxtaposition, where in-between glimpses of diving ibises and the like, you'll see giant jets taking off from JFK Airport, just minutes away.

The Rockaways

Subway A (rush hour) to Rockaway Park-Beach 116th St or the A to Broad Channel, where you transfer to the S (Rockaway Shuttle – all times of day), which also takes you to Rockaway Park-Beach 116th St; there are numerous other stops the length of the peninsula, depending on which part of the beach you wish to access

Partly enclosing Jamaica Bay, the spit of **Rockaway** stretches for ten miles southwest of Brooklyn, and holds the only places to surf in New York City. The eponymous beach, celebrated by the Ramones in song, runs along the shore from Beach 9th Street to Beach 149th Street. Unfortunately, few if any areas suffered more harm from October 2012's Hurricane Sandy, which laid waste to the beach, ripped up the boardwalk and damaged numerous homes and buildings, by flood, wind and fire. Residents were not deterred and the beach opened as usual for summer 2013; grab a snack at *Rockaway Taco* (see p.293) or one of the pop-up concession stands closer to the ocean and make your way to the sands.

19

Jacob Riis Park and Breezy Point

No subway access, so unless you've got a bike to take you from the end of the A line, take the #Q22 bus from Beach 116th St or the #Q35 from Flatbush Ave in Brooklyn – the latter is by far the faster option from Manhattan • ☎ 718 318 4300, ⓦ nyharborparks.org

The lovely sands of **Jacob Riis Park** on the western end of the Rockaway spit are quieter and more pristine (if certainly disturbed by Hurricane Sandy; see box, below) than the rest of the shore, because it's part of the Gateway NRA. This is widely considered to be New York City's best beach, and it features an in-need-of-renovation Art Deco bathhouse and an outdoor clock that have been New York City landmarks since the 1930s. At the westernmost tip of the peninsula, also beyond the reach of public transport but an easy bicycle ride from the end of the train line, the heavily Irish cooperative community of **Breezy Point** feels like a beach town imported from another state – come here to truly escape New York City.

HURRICANE SANDY

In 2012, Hurricane Sandy brought the city to a temporary halt. Ravaging the East Coast (with damages estimated at around $75 billion), the storm touched down in the New York City area late evening October 29 and proceeded to bring floods that surged nearly fourteen feet at their highest, near downtown Manhattan's Battery; winds reached up to 80 miles per hour. Bridges and tunnels shut; the subways stopped running; power was lost in various areas, including lower Manhattan below 34th Street, where in many places it took days to come back – a wander through the empty, darkened city streets was a surreal adventure. Almost every street in Brooklyn's Red Hook flooded; parts of Staten Island's Midland Beach area were turned to rubble. The worst of the damage, however, may well have been in the Rockaways, where days of waiting for power and other amenities people take for granted turned into weeks, or longer. Residents here, as elsewhere in low-lying areas, were told to evacuate prior to the hurricane, but most remained to see the storm through. In addition to the wreckage caused by flooding and wind – strong enough to rip off roofs and take out the Rockaway Beach boardwalk – a fire destroyed more than one hundred homes in the close-knit community of Breezy Point. Photos made the places look like war-torn neighbourhoods, and folks were still digging out of their homes months later. Travel to the area was made harder as the A train – the primary public transit link to the spit of land – was knocked out and not restored until summer 2013. Despite all this, the beaches in the area managed to open for the traditional start of the season, Memorial Day weekend; much work remains to be done, though. To donate or volunteer, contact an organization like New York Cares (ⓦ newyorkcares.org).

NEW YORK BOTANICAL GARDEN

The Bronx

"The Bronx?" wrote poet Ogden Nash in 1931. "No thonx!" Nash eventually recanted his two-line barb, but most New Yorkers hold similar feelings due to the borough's reputation for being tough and crime-ridden. Still, what is true in the South Bronx – which, despite a few signs of gentrification, remains one of the city's poorest areas – hardly applies to the whole of the Bronx, which harbours beautiful parks, posh neighbourhoods, a world-class botanic garden and zoo, and, of course, Yankee Stadium. With a unique landscape that ranges from greenery to high-rises, the Bronx is New York's only mainland borough, its hilly geography more like neighbouring Westchester County than Long Island and Manhattan. Sights are mostly spread far apart, save for the concentration around the Little Italy section of Belmont, which is within walking distance of the Bronx Zoo and the New York Botanical Garden.

INFORMATION

Tourist information Find out more about the borough from the Bronx Tourism Council (☎718 590 3518, ⓦilovethebronx.com) or the Bronx Council on the Arts (☎718 931 9500, ⓦbronxarts.org). BCA sponsors all sorts of events and series, as well as a tram (see below) that hits some of the top area sights.

Brief history

First settled in the seventeenth century by a Swedish landowner named **Jonas Bronck**, it became part of New York City in the late nineteenth century. For half a century, it was solidly working class and middle class, only taking a turn into serious poverty in the 1950s, when urban planner Robert Moses sliced the borough in half with the **Cross Bronx Expressway**, severing the South Bronx from its wealthier neighbours to the north. The South Bronx was literally left to burn in the 1970s, taking the reputation of the whole borough down with it, but it has been making a slow recovery in the years since, with substantial residential development over the past decade.

The South Bronx

When most people hear the words "the Bronx", they think of the **South Bronx**, the mostly residential, mostly impoverished area south of the Cross Bronx Expressway. It was here, on the streets of Hunts Point and other tough neighbourhoods of "the Boogie Down" – hip-hop's name for the borough – that rap, break-dancing and graffiti art were born in the late 1970s. Anyone interested in street culture should do a lot of random strolling, preferably by day, or take a **Birthplace of Hip-Hop Bus Tour** (☎212 714 3527, ⓦhushtours.com; $75), led by well-known scene insiders.

The main reason most people visit the South Bronx, though, is to see the New York **Yankees** play on their home field, the new **Yankee Stadium**, which replaced the legendary "House That Ruth Built" in 2009.

The area southeast of the stadium – mostly in the neighbourhoods of **Hunts Point** and **Mott Haven** – is also a locus of culture for the Bronx, with a handful of community-oriented art galleries and boutiques, and some small performance spaces. Mott Haven, especially, has interesting corners to poke around, with a couple of designated historic districts full of elegant apartments and brownstone, fanciful churches and antique shops. Hunts Point, meanwhile, is the home of the **New Fulton Fish Market**, formerly down in the South Street Seaport; the action takes place very early in the morning (pre-7am; ⓦnewfultonfishmarket.com).

Every first Wednesday of the month (except in Jan & Sept), the Bronx Council on the Arts (see above) sponsors a free **culture tram** touring some of the arts-oriented sights, starting at the Longwood Art Gallery at Hostos Community College, 450 Grand Concourse on 149th Street; trolleys leave at 5.30, 6.30 and 7.30pm.

Yankee Stadium

E 161st St, at River Ave • Game days and times vary, but take place April–Sept; tours noon–1.40pm every 20min, depending on whether it's game day ($20, under 15 $15) • ☎718 579 4531 for tours, ☎212 926 5337 box office, ⓦnewyork.yankees.mlb.com • Subway B, D, #4 to 161st St-Yankee Stadium

The (still relatively) new **Yankee Stadium** is home to the legendary **New York Yankees** baseball team (see box, p.253) and – appropriately, perhaps, given the team's gigantic payroll – is the most expensive stadium ever built in the US; estimates range from $1.5 billion up to $2 billion. The design of the 53,000-capacity, open-air park revives aspects of the 1923 stadium – "The House That (Babe) Ruth Built" – that were lost in subsequent renovations, such as the limestone and granite exterior facade, and includes a spot for Monument Park, where fans can find retired jersey numbers and plaques honouring famous Yankees.

The best way to see the stadium is, of course, to catch a game (see p.389), though diehards may want to take a guided tour, which offers access to Monument Park, the field, dugouts, press box and clubhouse when available.

The Grand Concourse

The aptly named **Grand Concourse**, east of Yankee Stadium, runs through a rather low-income area, though you wouldn't guess it from much of the street's architecture. In its southern reaches, the concourse is a magnificent wide boulevard marked by tree-lined medians and opulent Art Deco buildings that now house apartments, social-service organizations and retirement homes. Across from Yankee Stadium at 161st Street is the massive **Bronx County Courthouse and Borough Hall**, a 1933 construction that combines Neoclassical columns with Art Deco friezes and statuary. North of here stretches **Joyce Kilmer Park**, named for the woman who penned the lines "I think that I shall never see / A poem lovely as a tree…" A monument to Louis J. Heintz, who first proposed the Grand Concourse, and the white Lorelei Fountain (officially the Heinrich Heine

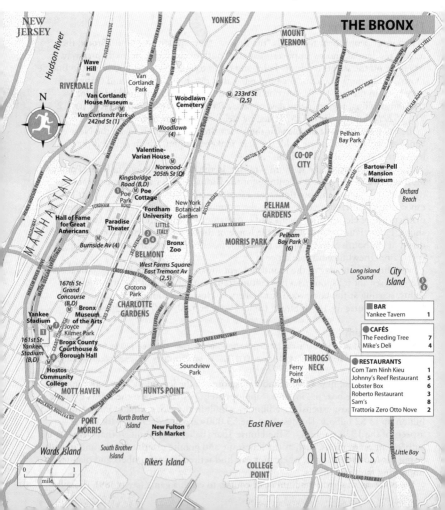

■ BAR	
Yankee Tavern	1

● CAFÉS	
The Feeding Tree	7
Mike's Deli	4

● RESTAURANTS	
Com Tam Ninh Kieu	1
Johnny's Reef Restaurant	5
Lobster Box	6
Roberto Restaurant	3
Sam's	8
Trattoria Zero Otto Nove	2

THE BRONX BOMBERS

The **Yankees**, who inspire love and loathing in New York (and mostly the latter outside the city), moved from north Manhattan to the Bronx in 1923. Leading the way was **George Herman "Babe" Ruth**, who had joined the team in 1920 (fleeced from the Boston Red Sox, still the team's arch-rivals). The original "Bronx Bomber", Ruth hit the stadium's first home run – and soon enough, Yankee Stadium was known as "**The House That Ruth Built**".

Playing alongside Ruth, **Lou Gehrig** earned the nickname "The Iron Horse" by playing in 2130 consecutive games (a record that stood for 56 years); the championships began to roll in, even more so when **Joe DiMaggio** joined Gehrig on the team after Ruth's retirement. **"Yogi" Berra**, **Mickey Mantle**, former single-season home run leader **Roger Maris**, **Reggie Jackson** and, more recently, **Mariano Rivera** were but a few other greats who also wore the famous Yankee pinstripes.

The Yankees won the World Series an amazing nineteen times between 1927 and 1962 and finished the twentieth century with three straight titles; after a nine-year gap, they returned to the top in 2009. With one of the highest payrolls in the major leagues – once routinely topping $200 million, though now in a new era of fiscal "restraint" – they're always a threat to do it again. For their devoted fans (and sworn enemies), they remain the team to beat.

Fountain, after the German poet) form a gracious backdrop for residents, who come here to take in the sun on benches and stroll at sunset.

More Art Deco and Art Moderne architecture proliferates in the central and northern stretches of the Concourse, with particularly scenic blocks right around 175th Street and 181st Street. A bit north, the 1929 **Paradise Theater**, at no. 2403 (☎718 933 3585, ⓦparadisetheater.net), hides an elaborate confection of chandeliers and filigree behind its landmarked facade; damaged by fire in late 2012, it's now been transformed into a megachurch.

20

Bronx Museum of the Arts

1040 Grand Concourse, at East 165th St • Thurs, Sat & Sun 11am–6pm, Fri 11am–8pm • Free, though donations accepted • ☎718 681 6000, ⓦbronxmuseum.org • Subway B, D to 167th St-Grand Concourse

The **Bronx Museum of the Arts** occupies a converted synagogue that was expanded and modernized by the renowned firm Arquitectonica in 2006; look for the jagged glass facade. Exhibits of contemporary art by Asian, Latino and African-American artists lie within, and eclectic performances are held on the first Friday evening of each month.

The Central Bronx

The **Central Bronx**, north of the Cross Bronx Expressway and south of Gun Hill Road, has neither the intense grit of the South Bronx nor the quiet ritz of the borough's extreme north. As in much of the Bronx, its inhabitants are working-class African-Americans, Puerto Ricans and Dominicans, though its historical centre is prestigious (and predominantly white) **Fordham University**, founded by Jesuits in 1841 and set on lush green lawns. Other points of interest include **Belmont**, better known as the Bronx's Little Italy, and verdant **Bronx Park**, home to the city's prized **Bronx Zoo** and **New York Botanical Garden**. Serious sightseers can seek out the **Poe Cottage** and the **Hall of Fame for Great Americans**.

ARRIVAL AND DEPARTURE

By train/bus Take the B, D or #4 train to Fordham Rd, then transfer to the eastbound #Bx12 for the short ride to Arthur Ave, or take the #2 train to Pelham and transfer to the #Bx12 bus headed west. Almost everything you'll want to see in Belmont lies on Arthur between Crescent Ave and East 187th St; from there, it's not far to both the zoo (to the east) and the botanical garden (directly to the north). Special express buses run up Madison Ave (#BxM11), heading straight to these two sights.

Belmont

Smack in the middle of the Bronx, and within easy walking distance of the Fordham University campus, the New York Botanical Garden and the Bronx Zoo, **Belmont** is home to one of New York's largest Italian-American communities, with its main thoroughfare, **Arthur Avenue**, offering a more authentic and low-key alternative to Little Italy in Manhattan.

The neighbourhood dates to the late nineteenth century, when Italian craftsmen building the Bronx Zoo settled here, and although Haitians, Mexicans and Albanians are just a few of the ethnic groups who also operate businesses on Arthur Avenue, the Italian community dominates, with daily Mass at **Our Lady of Mount Carmel Church**, at East 187th Street on Belmont Avenue, still held in Italian (a few days in Spanish as well). If your trip happily coincides with the **Ferragosto di Belmont**, on the second Sunday in September, you'll see residents turn out in their festive best to dance, eat, perform *commedia dell'arte* and compete in the annual cheese-carving contest.

Bronx Zoo

Bronx River Parkway, at Fordham Rd • April–Oct Mon–Fri 10am–5pm, Sat, Sun & holidays 10am–5.30pm; Nov–March daily 10am–4.30pm • $16.95, ages 3–12 $11.95; Wed by donation, parking $15, additional charges for some rides and exhibits • ☎ 718 367 1010 or 220 5103, ⓦ bronxzoo.org • Subway #2, #5 to West Farms Square-East Tremont Ave, then three blocks north to Asia Gate entrance; bus #BxM11 express ($5.50, MetroCard or exact change) from Madison Ave to Bronx River Gate B

One of the Bronx's main attractions, the **Bronx Zoo** is the largest urban wildlife park in the country. Opened in 1899, the zoo has significantly expanded from its small cluster of original buildings to reach 265 wooded acres harbouring nearly eighteen thousand creatures in natural-looking habitats. Check the website for daily feeding times and educational events, and try to come on a weekday to avoid large crowds.

The forty-acre **Wild Asia** exhibit (May–Oct; $4), where tigers, elephants and gaur (big cows) roam relatively freely, is one of the zoo's highlights, though don't expect to linger; the only way to see it is on a narrated twenty-minute, all-inclusive ride on the Bengali Express Monorail train. Also open only in warm weather is the **Children's Zoo** (April–Oct; $4), which allows kids to climb with lemurs, learn camouflage skills from tortoises and feed farm animals.

The innovative **Congo Gorilla Forest** (year-round; $5) houses more than four hundred African animals representing 55 species, including tiny colobus monkeys, mandrill baboons and the largest population of western gorillas in the country; some are quite playful and will show off to the crowd. **Madagascar!**, which has taken up residence in the converted Lion House, a 1903 Beaux Arts beauty, showcases lemurs, crocodiles,

---

FIVE FOOD STOPS ON ARTHUR AVENUE

There is no better part of the Bronx than Arthur Avenue to visit if you want to do a little eating tour. Venerable bakeries, family-friendly restaurants, gourmet delis that make their own sauces and sausages – all proliferate in this Italian food haven. A few favourites:

Calandra Cheese 2314 Arthur Ave. They don't have prepared foods, but there's no denying the creamy richness of their home-made ricotta and mozzarella cheeses – good enough to eat on their own.

Cosenza's Fish Market 2354 Arthur Ave. The market runs a pavement stand outside the shop in warm weather – the perfect stop for fresh clams ($5 for 6) or oysters ($1.50 a pop) on the half-shell.

DeLillo's Pastries 610 E 187th St, at Arthur Ave. This 90-year-old shop, which recently moved into sleek new digs, was once owned by author and native son Don

DeLillo's parents; the pastries, coffees and Italian ice cream are still spot on.

Madonia Brothers Bakery 2348 Arthur Ave. Arguably the best Italian bakery in the city; the olive bread, thick and chewy and studded with whole salty olives, is a knockout, and toothsome cannolis are filled on the spot.

Mike's Deli Near the back of Arthur Avenue Retail Market, 2344 Arthur Ave. Try their enormous focaccia sandwiches, from offerings with spicy *soppressata* and fresh mozzarella to eggplant *parmigiana*.

hissing cockroaches and the plump, reddish-orange tomato frog, among other rare species. Look also at the **Sea Bird Colony**, **World of Reptiles** and the **Himalayan Highlands**, home to endangered species like the red panda and the snow leopard.

In winter, many animals are kept in indoor enclosures without viewing areas, but the endangered Siberian tigers love a snowy day; if you visit the three-acre **Tiger Mountain** habitat at that time, it may just be you and these enormous cats, separated by a thin plate of glass.

New York Botanical Garden

2900 Southern Blvd, at Fordham Rd and Bronx River Parkway · Tues–Sun 10am–6pm, until 5pm mid-Jan to Feb · $25 all-access, 12 and under $10; $10 grounds-only, 12 and under $2, free Wed; parking $12 · ☎ 718 817 8700, 🌐 nybg.org · Subway B, D, #4 to Bedford Park, then a 20min walk; Metro-North Harlem Line to Botanical Garden Station

Adjacent to the zoo, just north of Fordham Road, is a quieter but equally worthwhile attraction: the lush, 250-acre **New York Botanical Garden** offers a lot of bang for the buck, especially in warm weather. The main entrance, on Kazimiroff Boulevard opposite Fordham University, is a short walk north from the zoo along Southern Boulevard, which changes to Kazimiroff Boulevard; the gates will be on your left.

The glittering glass **Enid A. Haupt Conservatory**, built when the park opened in 1891, acts as a dramatic entrance, magnificently showcasing rainforest, aquatic and desert ecosystems. It also houses a palm court with towering old trees and a fern forest, and hosts special exhibits like the popular orchid show in March/April and the always-crowded **Holiday Train Show**, a twinkling winter wonderland of miniature structures and model trains, which opens close to Thanksgiving and runs until mid-January (for which you should get an advance ticket).

To explore the garden, hop aboard the tram near the entrance, which – if taken straight through – wends around the park in about thirty minutes. You can get off at any of the half-dozen stops, depending on what strikes your fancy: cherry and lilac collections; daffodil hill; conifers; peonies; crabapples… the list goes on. Most of these plantings edge a fifty-acre core of native **forest**.

What you'll see is seasonally dependent. Nearly four thousand plants make up the **Peggy Rockefeller Rose Garden**, in bloom in late May/June and early September. The **Azalea Garden** peaks in late April and early May, with a shower of pinks and purples covering a tree-filled slope; fortunately, other colours last on these hills through summer and into autumn. The new Native Plant Garden focuses on species from the Northeast and is meant to have different flowers and ferns, among other flora, flourishing each season.

Kids can head to the **Everett Children's Adventure Garden**, twelve acres of plant and science exhibits and some mazes. Programmes let kids cook, taste and draw popular plants such as peppermint, chocolate and vanilla.

Poe Cottage

2640 Grand Concourse, at East Kingsbridge Rd · Sat 10am–4pm, Sun 1–5pm · $5 · ☎ 718 881 8900, 🌐 bronxhistoricalsociety.org · Subway B, D to Kingsbridge Rd

West of Fordham University is the **Edgar Allan Poe Cottage**, built in 1812. This white-clapboard anachronism on a twenty-first-century working-class Latino block was Edgar Allan Poe's rural home from 1846 to 1849, just before he died in Baltimore. It originally sat in a farmland setting on East Kingsbridge Road near East 192nd Street, but was moved to its current location, at the northern tip of **Poe Park**, when threatened with demolition. Never a particularly stable character and dogged by financial problems, Poe also had to contend with the death of his wife, Virginia, shortly after they moved in. In his gloom, he did manage to write the short, touching poem *Annabel Lee* (in homage to his wife) and other famous works, including *The Bells*, during his stay. The recently restored cottage displays several rooms as they were in Poe's time, as well as a small gallery of 1840s artwork; first stop before the actual house, though, is the new **visitor centre** in Poe Park, 2650 Grand Concourse at 192nd St (Tues–Sat 9am–5pm; rotating exhibitions on display), with its sharply angled roof meant to conjure the image of a raven.

Valentine-Varian House

3266 Bainbridge Ave, at East 208th St • Sat 10am–4pm, Sun 1–5pm • $5 • ☎ 718 881 8900, ⓦ bronxhistoricalsociety.org • Subway D to Norwood-205th St

The Bronx Historical Society also runs the **Valentine-Varian House** (otherwise known as the Museum of Bronx History), an eighteenth-century Georgian stone farmhouse that was occupied by the British during the American Revolution. Only recommended for serious history buffs, the museum stands in a small park and contains numerous old photographs that show just how rapidly the Bronx shifted from an agrarian landscape to an urban one.

Hall of Fame for Great Americans

2155 University Ave • Daily 10am–5pm • $2 suggested donation; tours ☎ 718 289 5910, ⓦ bcc.cuny.edu/halloffame • Subway #4 to Burnside Ave

On the picturesque campus of the Bronx Community College – formerly New York University's Bronx campus – stands the **Hall of Fame for Great Americans**, a 630ft-long open-air hilltop colonnade designed by the renowned architect Stanford White in 1900 and studded with bronze busts of the 98 honourees. Together they form a peculiar cast of characters, with world-famous figures like George Washington and Henry David Thoreau rubbing shoulders with virtual unknowns like steamboat builder James Buchanan Eads and dentist William Thomas Green Morton.

20

The North Bronx

The **North Bronx**, shorthand for the area above 225th Street in the west and Gun Hill Road in the east, is the northernmost area of the city; anyone who makes it up here usually wants to see the stately **Riverdale** neighbourhood and its incredible riverfront estate **Wave Hill**, the rolling hills of **Woodlawn Cemetery** and **Van Cortlandt Park**, or the ocean views from **City Island** and **Orchard Beach**.

ARRIVAL AND DEPARTURE

By train Getting up this way by public transport is not impossible – the Metro North Railroad is particularly useful in getting to Riverdale – but if you have access to a car, this is a good time to use it. Otherwise, it's best to visit particular groups of sights together, like Woodlawn Cemetery and Van Cortlandt Park, or City Island and Orchard Beach.

Woodlawn Cemetery

Entrances on Jerome Ave, at Bainbridge and on Webster Ave, at East 233rd St • Daily 8.30am–5pm; walking tours Sun 2pm $15–20 • Call for availability and reservations ☎ 718 920 1469; otherwise ☎ 718 920 0500, ⓦ thewoodlawncemetery.org • Subway #4 to Woodlawn, #2, #5 to 233rd St or Metro North Harlem Line railroad to Woodlawn

The venerable **Woodlawn Cemetery** is a huge place and a bucolic joy to walk around. Like Green-Wood in Brooklyn, it boasts a number of tombs and mausoleums that are memorable mainly for their gaudiness, although a few monuments stand out: Oliver Belmont, financier and horse dealer, rests in a Gothic fantasy modelled on the resting place of Leonardo da Vinci in Amboise, France; F.W. Woolworth built himself an Egyptian palace guarded by sphinxes; John H. Harbeck is interred in a (not-so) mini-cathedral with heavy bronze doors; and sculptor Patricia Cronin's 2002 marble *Memorial to a Marriage* depicts the artist and her partner, Deborah Kass, locked in a sleepy embrace. You can pick up a self-guided walking tour map at the main gates and security booths to locate the many famous individuals buried here, including Herman Melville, Irving Berlin, Elizabeth Cady Stanton,

Joseph Pulitzer, Fiorello LaGuardia, Robert Moses, Celia Cruz, Miles Davis and Duke Ellington.

Van Cortlandt Park

Between Broadway and Jerome Ave • ⓦ nycgovparks.org • Subway #1 to 242nd St or #4 to Woodlawn

Immediately west of Woodlawn Cemetery across Jerome Avenue lies vast **Van Cortlandt Park**, a forested and hilly all-purpose recreation space. Apart from the pleasure of hiking and running through its woods or watching a cricket game on the parade ground, the park only holds a few scattered sights, like a nature centre, a house museum (see below) and also the country's oldest public golf course (see p.395).

Van Cortlandt House Museum

242nd St, at Broadway • Tues–Fri 10am–3pm, Sat & Sun 11am–4pm • $5, Wed free • ☎ 718 543 3344, ⓦ ncsdny.org • Subway #1 to 242nd St or #4 to Woodlawn

The **Van Cortlandt House Museum**, nestled in Van Cortlandt Park's southwestern corner, is the best thing on the grounds. This is the Bronx's oldest building, an authentically restored Georgian structure built in 1748, complete with a historically accurate herb garden. New York City's archives were buried for safekeeping on the hills above, and it was in this house that George Washington slept before marching to victory in Manhattan in 1783.

Wave Hill

249th St, at Independence Ave • Mid-March to Oct Tues–Sun 9am–5.30pm; Nov to mid-March 9am–4.30pm • $8, Sat 9am–noon & all day Tues free (May–June & Sept–Oct free 9am–noon); free garden/greenhouse tours from Perkins Visitor Center Sun at 2pm; free gallery tours Tues & Sat 1pm • ☎ 718 549 3200, ⓦ wavehill.org • Metro North Hudson Line to Riverdale Station, walk up 254th St three blocks, turn right on Independence Ave and proceed two blocks

The spectacular country estate of **Wave Hill**, in the moneyed district of Riverdale, offers one of the city's best escapes from the urban grind, with lush exotic gardens, greenhouses, an art gallery, several easy but varied nature trails and rolling lawns dotted with Adirondack chairs overlooking the Hudson River and dramatic Palisades.

At various times home to Teddy Roosevelt (as a child), Arturo Toscanini and Mark Twain, the Wave Hill house was built in 1843 by jurist William Lewis Morris, but credit for the site's astounding beauty goes to George W. Perkins, a partner at J.P. Morgan, who linked the house's property with that of the adjacent villa (now called the Glyndor House) in the early twentieth century and landscaped the grounds with an artistry rivalling that of Central Park creator Frederick Law Olmsted. The Perkins family donated the estate to the city in 1960; a recent restoration fixed up parts of the facade and interior stairs, among other upgrades. The busy events calendar includes everything from classical music concerts and family art classes to beekeeping workshops; check the website for details.

City Island

Take subway #6 to Pelham Bay Park (the end of the line), then transfer to the #Bx29 bus, which runs over a short causeway to and from the mainland. On the first Friday of the month, from 5.30 to 9.30pm, a tram (free; ☎ 718 885 9100, ⓦ cityislandchamber.org) runs from the subway station around the island and back, via Pelham Bay Park

On the far east side of the Bronx, 230-acre **City Island** juts into Long Island Sound and has the feel of a seaside New England town (the population is around five thousand), albeit one with a bit of urban grit.

There are a few quirky shops along the main strip (City Island Avenue), and a quaint museum just off it, the **City Island Nautical Museum**, at 190 Fordham St (Sat & Sun 1–5pm or by appointment; donation; ☎ 718 885 0008, ⓦ cityislandmuseum.org), which touts all of the island's claims to fame – the yachts that won the America's Cup from 1958 to 1987 were built here, for instance – and often hosts interesting lectures

---

THE BRONX'S PHANTOM THEME PARK

Pelham Bay Park looks to the west over **Co-op City**, a seemingly endless tract of middle-class housing that is one of the Bronx's bleaker icons. Few residents know that their homes stand on New York's great, lost amusement park: **Freedomland**.

Built in the shape of the United States, the 205-acre park opened in 1960 with entertainments based on American history: the Great Fire of 1871 raged in Chicago, gunfights blazed in the Old Southwest, and earthquakes rocked San Francisco. Reporters loved Freedomland because it inspired such headlines as "Stagecoach Wreck Injures 10 in the Bronx". But the public was not so enthralled. Park developers blamed competition from the 1964 World's Fair in Flushing, though the expo had barely begun when Freedomland declared bankruptcy late in the year. By 1965, Co-op City was in progress: Freedomland had vanished without a trace.

---

by local historians. One of the most evocatively sited burial grounds you'll see anywhere, **Pelham Cemetery**, is a short walk away.

Most people come for the waterfront **restaurants** though: the food may not be particularly creative, but seaside dining is a treat. To avoid crowds, come on a weekday, when the fish is also fresher. Try the venerable *Lobster Box* (see p.327), at 34 City Island Ave, for old-school seafood, or, just down the road at the fishing piers, the charmingly downscale *Johnny's Reef Restaurant* (see p.327), at 2 City Island Ave.

Pelham Bay Park and Orchard Beach

Subway #6 to Pelham Bay Park station • In summer, buses #Bx5 and #Bx12 run from the station to Orchard Beach; on the first Friday of the month, from 5.30 to 9.30pm, a tram (free; ☎ 718 885 9100, ⓦ cityislandchamber.org) runs from the station around the island and back, via Pelham Bay Park; parking is $6 summer weekdays, $8 weekends

The wide crescent of **Orchard Beach**, the easternmost part of expansive **Pelham Bay Park**, marks one of the few really pleasant additions the "master builder" Robert Moses made to the city. Just turn right after the causeway, and then follow the path along the water. The beach and boardwalk pulse constantly during summertime; a once grand, and now decrepit, bathhouse pavilion offers some architectural interest; and a nature centre organizes walks, birdwatching and other events.

At the northern end of the boardwalk, a sign for the **Kazimiroff Nature Trail** points the way into a wildlife preserve named for Theodore Kazimiroff, co-founder of the Bronx County Historical Society and an amateur naturalist who helped stop these wetlands from being turned into landfill. The network of trails, which wind through 189 acres of meadow, forest and marsh, is serene and peaceful – a stark contrast with the rest of Pelham Bay Park, now crisscrossed by highways.

Bartow-Pell Mansion Museum

895 Shore Rd, Pelham Bay Park • Wed, Sat & Sun noon–4pm, guided tours hourly beginning 12.15pm, gardens daily 8.30am–dusk • $5 for museum, grounds free • ☎ 718 885 1461, ⓦ bartowpellmansionmuseum.org • Westchester Bee-Line bus #45 runs from Pelham Bay Park subway; on the first Friday of the month, from 5.30 to 8.30pm, a free tram (☎ 718 885 9100, ⓦ cityislandchamber.org) runs from Pelham Bay Park subway station to the mansion

The Greek Revival **Bartow-Pell Mansion Museum** is a national landmark worth seeing for its beautifully furnished interior, which gives a glimpse of how the other half lived in the 1800s (Mayor LaGuardia wisely commandeered the place for his summer office in 1936); the lavish gardens overlook Long Island Sound.

Staten Island

The free ride across the harbour to Staten Island is one of the highlights of New York, but is there any point in getting off the ferry? Roughly triangular, Staten Island is almost 14 miles long and 7.5 miles wide, making it more than twice the size of Manhattan. Primarily a collection of sleepy suburban communities, culturally Staten Island has more in common with New Jersey than with the other four boroughs – most tourists promptly hop on the next boat back to the big city. Yet it would be a mistake to dismiss the "forgotten borough" so readily; its leafy streets harbour some real gems, not least a fabulous Chinese garden, a Tibetan gallery and an authentic colonial village, as well as some excellent Sri Lankan restaurants and plenty of parks and beaches that seem a million miles away from the hectic streets of Manhattan.

21

ARRIVAL AND INFORMATION

By ferry The free Staten Island ferry (☎718 727 2508, ⓦsiferry.com) departs from the Whitehall Ferry Terminal (subway #1 to South Ferry; R to Whitehall St; #4, #5 to Bowling Green). Departures every 15–20min during rush hours (7–9am & 5–7pm), every 30min throughout the rest of the day and evenings, and every hour late at night (the ferry runs 24hr). On weekends, boats run every 30min from Manhattan, but slightly less frequently on the return trip.

By train The Staten Island Railway (SIR; 24hr; ⓦmta.info) runs from the ferry terminal (St George) to Tottenville at the southern end of the island; you can use your MetroCard, but the fare ($2.50 with MetroCard; otherwise $2.75) is only payable at St George, Tompkinsville and Ballpark (free otherwise).

By bus Given the limited scope of the railway, you'll need to take a bus (ⓦmta.info) to fully explore Staten Island; you can use your MetroCard to pay ($2.50; express bus $6). Bus maps are available at the ferry terminal in St George; the main bus station is just outside. Take #S40 for Snug Harbor; #S51 for Alice Austen House and Fort Wadsworth; #S74 for Historic Richmond Town and Jacques Marchais Museum of Tibetan Art. Most services operate every 20–30min Mon–Sat, and less frequently Sun.

Information For more information on Staten Island events and attractions, or to download free maps, visit ⓦstatenislandarts.org or ⓦvisitstatenisland.com.

St George and around

Passengers disembark the ferry on the northeast corner of the island, in the town of **St George**, Staten Island's "Downtown" district, home to most of the borough government offices and law courts. While it's no waterfront paradise, with views blocked by high-rises and the town cut off from the harbour by large roads, it does boast a handful of mildly appealing attractions.

Borough Hall

10 Richmond Terrace • Mon–Fri 9am–5pm • Free • ☎718 816 2000, ⓦstatenislandusa.com • SIR to St George

The 1906 French Renaissance **Borough Hall**, straight ahead as you walk out of the ferry terminal, has a marble lobby adorned with vivid WPA murals illustrating the island's history (enter at the back on Stuyvesant Place). Local artist Frederick Charles Stahr completed the thirteen murals in the late 1930s, beginning with Verrazano's "discovery" of Staten Island in 1524 and ending with the construction of the Bayonne Bridge (1928–31). The hall still houses the Borough President's Office and other civic offices.

Snug Harbor Cultural Center

1000 Richmond Terrace • **Visitor Center** Wed–Sun noon–5pm • Free • ☎718 448 2500, ⓦsnug-harbor.org • Bus #S40

In contrast to the more urban area around the ferry terminal, the atmosphere of the **Snug Harbor Cultural Center**, in nearby New Brighton, is one of bucolic calm, with museums, gardens and galleries spread over 83 rolling acres.

The campus functioned as an affluent retirement community for "aged, decrepit and worn-out sailors" from 1833 to 1976 (thanks to wealthy benefactor Robert Randall), before being renovated for public use, with its 28 remaining buildings ranging in style from grand Greek Revival halls to sophisticated Italianate buildings. The oldest structure is the beautifully restored Main Hall (Building C), which functions as the **Visitor Center**. Inside, you'll find temporary art exhibitions and a small display on the history of the site; you can also get a free map here. At the back of the visitor centre, you can walk through to the **Newhouse Center for Contemporary Art**, a showcase for local artists (same hours; $5, or

---

FERRIS FANTASY?

In 2012, plans were announced to build a 625ft-high Ferris wheel, aka the **New York Wheel**, potentially the largest in the world (though Dubai – where else? – is already planning to top this), on the northeast waterfront of Staten Island, near the ferry terminal and home of the Staten Island Yankees. The $500 million mega-project includes a huge outlet mall and 200-room hotel; completion is slated for 2015, but don't hold your breath.

$8 with Chinese Garden). By 2014 the **National Lighthouse Museum** (ⓦlighthouse museum.org) is aiming to open in Building 11 – check the website for the latest.

Staten Island Botanical Garden

Daily dawn to dusk • Free • ☎ 718 273 8200 • Bus #S40

Most of the Snug Harbor grounds are given over to the **Staten Island Botanical Garden**. This 53-acre sanctuary includes a section of flowers catering to butterflies and an antique rose garden, but the real gem is the **Chinese Scholar's Garden** (Tues–Sun: mid-March–Oct 10am–5pm; Nov–mid-March 10am–4pm; $5, or $8 with art galleries). This one-acre complex of Ming Dynasty-style, pagoda-roofed halls, artfully planted courtyards, bamboo groves and goldfish ponds was completed in 1999 by artists from Suzhou, China.

Staten Island Museum

Buildings A & B • Mon–Fri 11am–5pm, Sat 10am–5pm, Sun noon–5pm • $3 • ☎ 718 727 1135, ⓦ statenislandmuseum.org • Bus #S40

By 2014 the venerable **Staten Island Museum** should have been relocated from St George

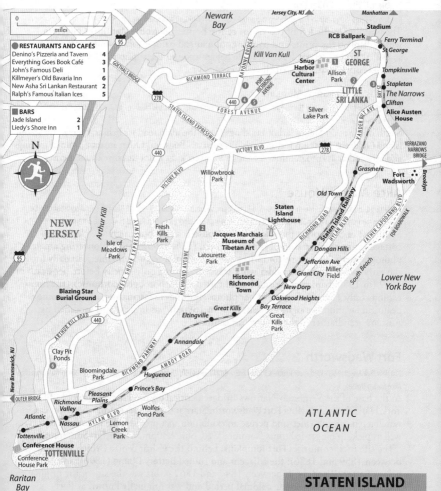

RESTAURANTS AND CAFÉS

Denino's Pizzeria and Tavern	4
Everything Goes Book Café	3
John's Famous Deli	1
Killmeyer's Old Bavaria Inn	6
New Asha Sri Lankan Restaurant	2
Ralph's Famous Italian Ices	5

BARS

Jade Island	2
Liedy's Shore Inn	1

STATEN ISLAND

21

LITTLE SRI LANKA

New York's Little Sri Lanka lies in the Tompkinsville neighbourhood of Staten Island (centred along Victory Blvd), a short, stiff walk from the ferry terminal – it's one of the largest Sri Lankan communities outside of Sri Lanka itself. Try the cheap hoppers (noodles) and curries at *New Asha* (see p.327), or peruse the local grocery shops for Ceylon teas, chutneys, spices, sweets and other delicacies.

---

to restored buildings on the Snug Harbor campus (to the right of the visitor centre), with a major exhibition on Staten Island across three centuries, contemporary art and paintings from the Hudson River School (Jasper Cropsey and Edward Moran among them). A life-size replica of a mastodon skeleton will dominate the lobby, along with the museum's extensive collection of rare, local fossils. Check the website for the latest information.

Noble Maritime Collection

Building D • Thurs–Sun 1–5pm • Free, donation suggested • ☎ 718 447 6490, ⓦ noblemaritime.org • Bus #S40

The building to the left of the visitor centre houses the **Noble Maritime Collection**, which displays the prints and paintings of nautical painter John Noble (1913–1983), as well as his houseboat studio (Noble began to build the studio in New York Harbor in 1941, out of parts of boats he salvaged).

Staten Island Children's Museum

Building M • Tues–Sun: June–Aug 10am–5pm; Sept–May noon–5pm • $6 for adults and children • ☎ 718 273 2060, ⓦ statenislandkids .org • Bus #S40

South of the main Snug Harbor buildings (from the main road it's behind them), the **Staten Island Children's Museum** features exhibits such as "Bugs and Other Insects", animal feedings and arts-and-crafts programmes – enough to divert kids, if not utterly enthral them.

Alice Austen House

2 Hylan Blvd, at Edgewater St • March–Dec Tues–Sun 11am–5pm; suggested donation $3 • ☎ 718 816 4506, ⓦ aliceausten.org • Bus #S51 from the ferry dock to Hylan Blvd and Bay St (15min), then walk one block east down the hill toward the waterfront

Southeast of St George, the **Alice Austen House** is a tiny but enigmatic clapboard cottage facing the Verrazano Narrows. Austen (1866–1952) was a pioneering amateur photographer whose work comprises one of the finest records of American daily life in the early twentieth century. Her work was rediscovered only shortly before her death in 1952 (in 1950, bankrupt, she'd been admitted to the borough poorhouse). The house exhibits only a small selection of her photos, but they're fascinating, and the home's beautiful location is a sight in itself; built in 1690, it was bought and modified by Austen's grandfather in the nineteenth century.

Fort Wadsworth

210 New York Ave (Bay St) • Wed–Sun 10am–4.30pm • Free • ☎ 718 354 4500, ⓦ nps.gov/gate • Bus #S51 (or 15–20min walk from the Alice Austen House)

At the base of the Verrazano-Narrows Bridge, a critical position for the defence of New York Harbor, sits sprawling **Fort Wadsworth**. Start at the **visitor centre**, where you can watch a ten-minute video and peruse an exhibition that provides the historical context, as well as pick up ranger-led tours (summer Wed–Sun 2.30pm; winter Fri–Sun 2pm; free).

The site itself comprises **Fort Tompkins**, behind the visitor centre (which was built between 1859 and 1876); the adjacent and ruined **Battery Duane** (1896); and far below, **Battery Weed**, built between 1847 and 1862 – this was the site of the original fort, which dates back to the colonial period and was originally known as Fort

Richmond. You can't go inside any of these fortifications unless you take the tour, and the real star is the view from the **overlook** above Battery Weed – the panorama of the harbour, Manhattan and the Verrazano Bridge is mesmerizing.

South of here is the more upscale neighbourhood of **South Beach** (also accessible via bus #S51), known for its 2.5-mile **FDR Boardwalk**, a great place to jog or rollerblade.

Jacques Marchais Museum of Tibetan Art

338 Lighthouse Ave • March–Nov Wed–Sun 1–5pm; Dec–Feb Fri–Sun 1–5pm; closed Jan • $6 • ☎ 718 987 3500, ⓦ tibetanmuseum.org • Bus #S74 (ask to be let off at Lighthouse Ave, then hike about 10min up the steep hill); a cab from the ferry terminal is $16–20

In the centre of Staten Island's residential heartland, the **Jacques Marchais Museum of Tibetan Art** is an unlikely treasure. Despite being christened Jacques, Marchais (1887–1948) was actually female. Starting in the 1920s, she became a successful art dealer, and used her income to indulge a passion for Tibetan art (though she never visited Tibet herself). Eventually, she assembled about three thousand pieces, and between 1943 and 1947 built this small fieldstone complex, which clutches onto the steep hillside much like monasteries in Tibet. One building houses the museum gift shop and a small gallery, and the other, designed to resemble a *gompa*, or temple, displays changing exhibits and a small fraction of the collection, including religious sculptures, *thangka* paintings, a rare Bhutanese sand *mandala* and a 250-year-old carved-wood *stupa*. In October, monks in maroon robes perform ritual ceremonies at the annual Tibetan Festival, and food and crafts are sold.

Historic Richmond Town

441 Clarke Ave • July & Aug Wed–Sun 11am–5pm; Sept–June Wed–Sun 1–5pm • $8, children 4–11 $5; free Fri 1–5pm • Free guided tours Wed–Fri 2.30pm, Sat & Sun 2pm & 3.30pm • ☎ 718 351 1611, ⓦ historicrichmondtown.org • Bus #S74

Spread out along the main Richmond Road at Arthur Kill Road, a short walk west and south from the Tibetan museum, lies **Historic Richmond Town**. Home to the Staten Island Historical Society, it's an open-air museum of around 27 historic buildings; at its core is the old village of Richmond, centre of the island's government until 1898 (when St George started to take over), as well as clapboard houses transported from other parts of the island.

The **visitor centre**, housed in the stately courthouse and built in 1837, is home to a gift shop, maps and small exhibitions about the site. Opposite lies the **Historical Museum**, which contains exhibits about the history of Staten Island, while in the streets nearby there are around fifteen restored buildings you can go inside (including the 1696 Dutch-style **Voorlezer's House**, the nation's oldest existing school building) – at weekends and during peak months, these are often staffed by costumed volunteers who use traditional techniques to make wooden water buckets and weld tin, all carried off to surprisingly picturesque and un-gimmicky effect.

Conference House

298 Satterlee St, at Hylan Blvd • Guided 1hr tours roughly every 20min, April to mid-Dec Fri–Sun 1–4pm • Free • ☎ 718 984 6046, ⓦ conferencehouse.org • SIR to Tottenville or bus #S74 from Historic Richmond Town

At the far southern end of the island, in the quiet seaside neighbourhood known as **Tottenville**, the **Conference House** is a fine rubble-stone manor built by English Captain Christopher Billopp around 1680. Other than its age (ancient by American standards), its claim to fame is acting as host to the failed **peace conference** in 1776 during the American Revolution; the American delegation was led by Benjamin Franklin and John Adams, the British by Admiral Richard Howe. The nearby **visitor centre** lays out the history of the site, while guided tours take you inside the house for a peek at period furnishings and the original kitchen, which has been restored to working order. The surrounding grounds are occupied by the lovely 267-acre **Conference House Park**.

THE ALGONQUIN

Accommodation

Accommodation in New York eats up the lion's share of most travellers' budgets. Many hotels in the city charge more than $200 a night; $400–500 in high season can be common – these are pre-tax rates (see opposite). It is certainly possible to get a safe, clean room for less than that, but it's almost always easier to find a place to splurge on than it is to find a real bargain (although coming at less busy times of the year helps). There are a handful of hostels with dorms for the young or budget-minded. Other moderately priced options include bed and breakfasts, which basically entail staying in somebody's spare room with all the amenities of a private apartment. These rooms go for approximately $150 and up for a double and can be booked through an agency (see p.273).

Keep in mind that even though there are thousands of guest rooms, sometimes there still aren't enough to go around. Most properties have a steady parade of occupants and as a result show some wear and tear. Unless you're checking into a new or luxury hotel – and sometimes even then – don't be surprised to occasionally see chipped furniture and scuffs on the wall. That said, there is a difference between continuous use and unsanitary conditions; if you feel your room is dirty or unsafe, don't hesitate to talk to the management.

BOOKING AND INFORMATION

22

Reservations Make these as far in advance as you can: although it is possible to get good last-minute deals, you may also get a special deal for an advance purchase (usually at least two weeks). And, at certain times of the year (May, Sept & Oct as well as the weeks leading up to Christmas and New Year), you're likely to find everything chock-full if you wait until just before your trip. There are three ways to book a room: directly through the hotel (by phone or through its website), on a travel website or through a travel agent. Whichever way you choose, enquire about discounts: business hotels downtown reduce prices on weekends; special offers may be available; and months like January, February, July and August tend to give better deals.

Taxes Hotels will nearly always quote you the price of a room before tax. Taxes will add 14.75 percent to your bill, plus $3.50 per night in "occupancy tax" and room fees.

Tipping Expected at upmarket hotels (and some others too) – tip the bellhop a few bucks if you're going to let him carry your bags to your room, and leave something for the cleaning staff too ($2–5 per day, depending on the type of place).

HOTELS

While midtown Manhattan, with its proximity to the main tourist sights, still dominates the **hotel** landscape, many of the hipper hotels to appear in recent years have done so in Chelsea and the Meatpacking District, NoMad, Tribeca, the Lower East Side and even across the water in Williamsburg. The Upper West or Upper East sides should do if your taste runs more to Central Park and the high culture of museums and Lincoln Center, though you won't have as much choice. The following selection of hotels runs the gamut from the city's cheapest to most luxurious. Unless noted, the prices quoted at the end of each listing represent the expected price of the hotel's cheapest double room, excluding all taxes, during the high season when rates are at a premium; note, though, that there's hardly such a thing as a fixed room price. "Published" rates may be quite different from advance online reservations, and figures quoted to you can change on a daily basis, depending on availability.

FINANCIAL DISTRICT

★ **Andaz Wall Street** 75 Wall St ☎ 212 590 1234, ⓦ andaz.com; subway #2, #3, #4, #5 to Wall St; map p.43. Spacious, stylish rooms right on Wall Street, with a host of generous extras: 24hr tea and coffee (posh Italian espresso no less) in the lobby, free wine daily 6–8pm, free wi-fi and free snacks and soft drinks at any time. $418

TRIBECA AND SOHO

Cosmopolitan 95 W Broadway, at Chambers St ☎ 212 566 1900, ⓦ cosmohotel.com; subway A, C, #1, #2, #3 to Chambers St; map p.64. A great Tribeca location plus smart, well-maintained rooms and relatively low prices make the *Cosmopolitan* a good deal. $379

★ **Crosby Street Hotel** 79 Crosby St, between Spring and Prince sts ☎ 212 226 6400, ⓦ firmdalehotels.com; subway N, R to Prince St, #6 to Spring St; map p.64. It's very expensive, but you get bright and spacious rooms set around a courtyard on the edge of trendy Soho, with fluffy towels, luxurious bathrooms, floor-to-ceiling windows and contemporary sculpture and art splashed all over the hotel. Get a room on the higher floors for spectacular views.

English afternoon tea ($34) is served all day in the tranquil drawing room. $680

The James 27 Grand St, at Thompson St ☎ 212 465 2000, ⓦ jameshotels.com; subway A, C, E, J, N, Q, R, Z, #1, #6 to Canal St; map p.64. Another pricey but exquisite boutique, just north of Canal St, featuring panoramic views from the stylish rooms and all the extras; iPod stations, free wi-fi (and use of Mac computers), snacks and drinks, and rooftop pool and bar. $498

The Mercer 147 Mercer St, at Prince St ☎ 212 966 6060, ⓦ mercerhotel.com; subway N, R to Prince St; map p.64. Housed in a Romanesque Revival building in Soho, *Mercer* has been one of the top accommodation choices of visiting celebs such as Leonardo DiCaprio since it opened in 1998. The loft studios also have massive 90-square-foot bathrooms, with over-sized tubs and walk-in showers for splashing around, and the concierge can arrange private training or massage virtually around the clock. Free access to local gyms. $595

★ **Smyth Tribeca** 85 West Broadway, between Warren and Chambers sts ☎ 212 587 7000, ⓦ thompsonhotels .com; subway A, C, #1, #2, #3 to Chambers St; map p.64.

22

One of the best boutiques in this part of town, with plush, contemporary design and furnishings with Classical and Art Deco touches; iPod docking station, plasma TV and large bathroom (with Kiehl products) included. **$413**

Soho Grand 310 W Broadway, between Canal and Grand sts ☎ 212 965 3000, ⍇ sohogrand.com; subway A, C, E to Canal St; map p.64. In a great location at the edge of Soho, this place draws guests of the model/actor variety. The stylish, chocolate-hued rooms have personality to match, while cast-iron staircases with vault lights, a glass elevator shaft and 20ft ceilings lend the common areas an industrial yet inviting feel. There's also a sharp-looking bar, restaurant and hidden outdoor terrace. **$479**

Tribeca Grand 2 Sixth Ave, between White and Walker sts ☎ 212 519 6600, ⍇ tribecagrand.com; subway #1 to Franklin St; map p.64. Craving anonymity, the *Tribeca Grand* is unlabelled and tucked behind a brick facade. Inside, the striking *Church Lounge* beckons with a warm glow (it's a great space in which to hang out). Rooms are fashionably understated, though bathrooms boast phones and TVs, and the staff are extra attentive. Off-season weekends can be several hundred dollars cheaper. **$489**

LOWER EAST SIDE AND EAST VILLAGE

★ **Blue Moon** 100 Orchard St, between Delancey and Broome sts ☎ 212 533 9080, ⍇ bluemoon-nyc.com; subway F to Delancey St, J, M, Z to Essex St; map p.83. Lower East Side tenement transformed into a luxurious boutique, with rooms named after 1930s and 1940s celebrities and decked out with period iron-frame beds and the odd antique – rooms on the 6th, 7th and 8th floors also come with fabulous views across the city. Continental breakfast, iPod docks and wi-fi included. **$275**

Bowery Hotel 335 Bowery, at E 3rd St ☎ 212 505 9100, ⍇ theboweryhotel.com; subway #6 to Bleecker St; map p.88. This fabulous boutique property oozes sophistication and tempts guests with countless amenities, including iPod docks, DVD players, floor-to-ceiling windows, marble tubs with a view and a cool lounge bar. All this luxury comes at a price though. **$525**

Hotel 91 91 E Broadway ☎ 646 438 6600, ⍇ hotel91 .com; subway F to East Broadway; map p.83. Funky Lower East Side boutique, with a slightly Asian theme – orchids grace every room, and a statue of Buddha sits in the lobby. Rooms are compact but well equipped, with LCD TVs and plush marble bathrooms – this is a real bargain for this area, but ask for a room away from the Manhattan Bridge if you're a light sleeper. Free wi-fi. **$220**

WEST VILLAGE

Larchmont 27 W 11th St, between Fifth and Sixth aves ☎ 212 989 9333, ⍇ larchmonthotel.com; subway F, L to 14th St; map pp.96–97. A budget hotel, in a terrific location on a tree-lined street in Greenwich Village. Rooms

are small but homely and clean (with TV and a/c). A robe and slippers are thoughtfully provided so you can traipse down the hall to the shared bath. Includes continental breakfast. **$119**

Washington Square 103 Waverly Place, at Washington Square Park ☎ 212 777 9515, ⍇ washingtonsquarehotel .com; subway A, B, C, D, E, F, M to W 4th St; map pp.96–97. In the heart of Greenwich Village, this hotel is quite close to the area's many nightlife options. Don't be deceived by the posh-looking lobby – the rooms are surprisingly plain for the price (though rates are significantly cut in August). The Art Deco "Deluxe" rooms have a bit more character and continental breakfast is included. **$592**

CHELSEA AND THE MEATPACKING DISTRICT

Chelsea Lodge 318 W 20th St, between Eighth and Ninth aves ☎ 212 243 4499, ⍇ chelsealodge.com; subway C, E to 23rd St; map p.107. The *Lodge* is a gem of a place: a converted boarding house with Early American/ Sportsman decor. Standard rooms, which offer in-room showers and sinks (there's a shared toilet down the hall) are a little snug for two, but the few deluxe rooms are great value and have full bathrooms. A three-day cancellation policy applies. **$169**

★ **Chelsea Pines Inn** 317 W 14th St, between Eighth and Ninth aves ☎ 212 929 1023 or ☎ 888 546 2700, ⍇ chelseapinesinn.com; subway A, C, E to 14th St; map p.107. Housed in an old brownstone on the Greenwich Village/Chelsea border, this super-friendly hotel offers a personalized experience and has clean, comfortable, "shabby chic" rooms, all done with a movie motif and recently renovated. Long popular with a gay and lesbian clientele. Best to book in advance. **$289**

Comfort Inn Chelsea 18 W 25th St, between Sixth Ave and Broadway ☎ 212 645 3990, ⍇ comfortinn.com; subway F, M to 23rd St; map p.107. The *Comfort Inn Chelsea* is a solid chain hotel with good prices and clean, albeit smallish, rooms. Near Madison Square Park, it's equidistant from downtown and midtown. Off-season rates drop significantly. **$269**

Gansevoort 18 Ninth Ave, at W 13th St ☎ 212 206 6700, ⍇ hotelgansevoort.com; subway A, C, E to 14th St, L to Eighth Ave; map p.107. When cobblestone streets in the Meatpacking District were torn up was made room for this sleek hotel, preservationists were horrified, but the neighbourhood seems to have benefited. Rooms, in muted tones, are stylish, with top-notch electronics, but you're really paying for the 360-degree views, the full spa, the heated rooftop pool (one of very few in the city) and the scene. **$545**

Hotel Americano 518 W 27th St, between Tenth and Eleventh aves ☎ 212 216 0000, ⍇ hotel-americano .com; subway #1 to 28th St; map p.107. The first venture outside of Mexico by renowned boutique developers Grupo Habita, the eye-catching *Americano* sits right on the High Line, with 56 rooms and a sleek, modern style all of its own. Some evidence: Japanese-style platform beds, showers that look out onto the skyline and separate elevators for guest use and public use. **$395**

The Standard 848 Washington St, at W 13th St ☎ 212 645 4646, ⓦ standardhotels.com; subway A, C, E to 14th St, L to Eighth Ave; map p.107. With the High Line running under it, fabulous views from its rooms and a bevy of exclusive food and nightlife options nearby, André Balazs' *Standard Hotel* is just about too hip for its own good. There's a clean, Modernist feel to the decor. **$555**

UNION SQUARE, GRAMERCY AND THE FLATIRON DISTRICT

★ **Ace** 20 W 29th St, at Broadway ☎ 212 679 2222, ⓦ acehotel.com; subway N, R to 28th St; map p.114. Capturing the spirit of old New York yet fully modern, the *Ace Hotel* has set a new standard for bohemian chic. A whole host of different room styles are on offer (including bunks), with muted tones, artwork and the odd retro-style fridge or guitar that can make it feel even more expensive than it is. In a short time, it's also established itself as a restaurant hotbed, with the *Breslin*, *No. 7 Sub* and *John Dory Oyster Bar* all on the premises (see p.284). **$499**

Carlton 88 Madison Ave ☎ 212 532 4100, ⓦ carltonhotelny.com; subway #6 to 28th St; map p.114. A smartly located, Beaux Arts building entered by a stylish if unflashy portal, the *Carlton* offers roomy quarters outfitted in cream-and-tan-striped wallpaper and mahogany furnishings. Beds are all fluffiness, and the casual, if somewhat pricey, seafood restaurant offers superb service. **$420**

Gershwin 7 E 27th St, between Fifth and Madison aves ☎ 212 545 8000, ⓦ gershwinhotel.com; subway N, R to 28th St; map p.114. This hotel is a bit playful with its Pop Art exterior and public spaces, though rooms are pretty straightforward affairs. **$309**

Giraffe 365 Park Ave S, at 26th St ☎ 212 685 7700, ⓦ hotelgiraffe.com; subway #6 to 28th St; map p.114. The tall and slender *Giraffe* is similar in tone and amenities to sister hotels *Library* (see p.268) and *Casablanca* (see p.270), but these rooms invoke the sleek Art Moderne style

of the 1920s and 1930s. Prices include complimentary breakfast, afternoon wine and cheese, and a 24hr espresso bar. **$413**

Gramercy Park 2 Lexington Ave, at E 21st St ☎ 212 920 3300, ⓦ gramercyparkhotel.com; subway #6 to 23rd St; map p.114. The Ian Schrager Group (enlisting the help of artist Julian Schnabel) renovated the once-bohemian *Gramercy Park* into a very different property: the grand entrance got a red carpet and a chandelier, but also reclaimed lumber, modern artworks and strange light fixtures. Rooms are similarly eclectic, bold and luxurious. It's also in a lovely location – guests get a key to the adjacent private park (see p.115). **$675**

Herald Square 19 W 31st St, between Fifth Ave and Broadway ☎ 212 279 4017, ⓦ heraldsquarehotel.com; subway N, R to 28th St; map p.114. The original home of *Life* magazine, *Herald Square* still features Philip Martiny's sculpted cherub *Winged Life* over its Beaux Arts doorway. The inside is clean but somewhat soulless and without much in the way of extras, though rates are pretty unbeatable; if possible, see a few rooms on arrival – there's quite a variety. **$259**

Hotel 17 225 E 17th St, between Second and Third aves ☎ 212 475 2845, ⓦ hotel17ny.com; subway L, N, Q, R, #4, #5, #6 to 14th St-Union Square; map p.114. 17 rooms come with basic amenities; many share bathrooms. The hotel itself is neat and nicely situated on a pleasant tree-lined street just minutes from Union Square and the East Village. **$149**

Hotel 31 120 E 31st St, between Park and Lexington aves ☎ 212 685 3060, ⓦ hotel31.com; subway #6 to 28th St; map p.114. An affordable Murray Hill option run by the folks who own *Hotel 17*. The sixty rooms are clean (some share bathrooms) and the location is quiet. **$149**

King and Grove New York 29 E 29th St, between Park and Madison aves ☎ 212 689 1900, ⓦ kingandgrove .com; subway #6 to 28th St; map p.114. This hotel has changed hands a few times recently; its bright, colourful (if rather small) rooms are a surprise after the dark woods of the lobby. **$389**

★ **NoMad** 1170 Broadway, at W 28th St ☎ 212 796 1500, ⓦ thenomadhotel.com; subway #6 to 28th St; map p.114. A competitor for the same crowd as the nearby *Ace* (see above), with a celebrated on-site restaurant (see p.309), the welcoming *NoMad* offers stylish, spacious rooms with damask patterns, Iranian rugs, clawfoot tubs, king-size beds and a mishmash of tasteful art on the walls – different in each space. A definite cut above. **$425**

Roger 131 Madison Ave, at E 31st St ☎ 212 448 7000, ⓦ therogernewyork.com; subway #6 to 33rd St; map p.114. The former *Roger Williams* has undergone a very modern luxury transformation; the lobby and rooms, some of which come with views of the Empire State from their terraces, have comfort and style to spare. **$519**

TOP 5 LUXURY HOTELS

Mark Upper East Side. See p.272
Morgans Midtown East. See p.269
The Plaza Midtown East. See p.269
Sherry-Netherland Upper East Side. See p.272
Waldorf-Astoria Midtown East. See p.269

22

22

MIDTOWN EAST: 32ND TO 59TH STREETS

70 Park Avenue Hotel 70 Park Ave, at 38th St ☎212 973 2400, ⓦ70parkave.com; subway #4, #5, #6, #7 to 42nd St-Grand Central; map p.123. This classy boutique hotel is adorned with re-creations of classical friezes and frescoes, and original lighting and furnishing design featuring rich woods and muted earth tones. Extras include 24hr fitness centre (and in-room spa services), flat-screen TVs, wi-fi and a nightly wine reception (5–6pm). Pet-friendly. **$469**

Affinia Shelburne 303 Lexington Ave, between E 37th and 38th sts ☎212 689 5200, ⓦaffinia.com; subway #6 to 33rd St; map p.123. Luxurious hotel in the most elegant part of Murray Hill. All the freshly decorated rooms (basically suites) have kitchenettes, and there's a separate restaurant downstairs, *Rare*, that specializes in gourmet burgers (and provides room service). There's also a buzzing bar scene – with the requisite great views – on the seasonal roof terrace. **$399**

★ **Algonquin** 59 W 44th St, between Fifth and Sixth aves ☎212 840 6800, ⓦalgonquinhotel.com; subway B, D, F, M, #7 to 42nd St-Bryant Park; map p.123. New York's oldest continuously operated hotel and one of the city's famed literary hangouts (see p.125) has retained its old-club atmosphere and decor from the days of the Round Table, though the rooms have been refurbished to handsome effect (large flat-screens, refreshed carpets and bedding, bursts of colour, free wireless). Ask about summer and weekend specials. **$519**

Bryant Park Hotel 40 W 40th St, between Fifth and Sixth aves ☎212 869 0100, ⓦbryantparkhotel.com; subway B, D, F, M, #7 to 42nd St-Bryant Park; map p.123. This hotel – in the old American Radiator Building, a striking black-and-gold mix of Gothic and Art Deco architecture – shows off its edgy attitude in its stylish contemporary rooms, luxurious 70-seat film-screening room, and vaulted *Cellar Bar*, which is always filled with media types. **$490**

Chambers Hotel 15 W 56th St, between Fifth and Sixth aves ☎212 974 5656, ⓦchambershotel.com; subway F to 57th St; map p.123. Designed by architect David Rockwell, *Chambers* is well-placed for Central Park and MoMA visits, though you can just sit and admire the 500 original works of art in its gallery-sized hallways. The modern, tasteful rooms approximate a New York apartment, as do the mezzanine-level lounge spaces. A *Momofuku* (see p.280 & 303) offspring, *Má Pêche*, is the on-site restaurant. Good off-season deals. **$495**

Comfort Inn Manhattan 42 W 35th St, between Fifth and Sixth aves ☎212 947 0200, ⓦcomfortinn manhattan.com; subway B, D, F, M, N, Q, R to 34th St-Herald Square; map p.123. The best things about this hotel are the free, deluxe continental breakfast, complimentary wi-fi and cheery, good-value rooms. The management, though, can be less than helpful; it's not always possible to see a room before you decide to bunk down. **$289**

Dylan 52 E 41st St, between Park and Madison aves ☎212 338 0500, ⓦdylanhotel.com; subway #4, #5, #6, #7 to Grand Central-42nd St; map p.123. Classy and clever, *Dylan*'s rooms have been attentively designed (the 11ft ceilings make them look quite large) and bathrooms are clad in Italian marble. If you're looking to splurge, book the Alchemy Suite, a Gothic-style bedchamber with a vaulted ceiling and stained-glass windows. **$430**

Fitzpatrick Manhattan 687 Lexington Ave, between E 56th and 57th sts ☎212 355 0100, ⓦfitzpatrickhotels .com; subway #4, #5, #6, N, R to 59th St-Lexington Ave; map p.123. This handsome Irish-themed hotel, with fewer than one hundred rooms, is perfectly situated for visits to midtown stores, Upper East Side museums and Central Park. A hearty Irish breakfast ($21) is served all day. There's another branch right by Grand Central. **$419**

Iroquois 49 W 44th St, between Fifth and Sixth aves ☎212 840 3080, ⓦiroquoisny.com; subway B, D, F, M, #7 to 42nd St-Bryant Park; map p.123. Once a haven for rock bands, this elegant, reinvented boutique hotel has comfortable, tasteful rooms with Italian-marble baths and mahogany and suede headboards. The lounge is named for actor James Dean, resident at the hotel from 1951 to 1953 (room no. 803). **$529**

Jolly Madison Towers 22 E 38th St, at Madison Ave ☎212 802 0600, ⓦjollymadison.com; subway #4, #5, #6, #7 to Grand Central-42nd St; map p.123. This NYC outpost of the leading Italian chain offers restful, fairly spacious rooms fitted with handcrafted furnishings and Venetian glass, all at reasonable prices. **$299**

Lexington 511 Lexington Ave, at E 48th St ☎212 755 4400, ⓦlexingtonhotelnyc.com; subway #6 to 51st St; map p.123. Just renovated, and nicer than you might expect from a former Radisson, with an uplifting lobby, bright rooms, fully kitted-out fitness centre and capable concierge. **$400**

Library 299 Madison Ave, between E 41st and E 42nd sts (entry on E 41st St) ☎212 983 4500, ⓦlibraryhotel .com; subway #4, #5, #6, #7 to Grand Central-42nd St; map p.123. The *Library*'s concept, one of New York hostelry's quirkier, has each floor devoted to one of the ten major categories of the Dewey Decimal System. Coloured in shades of brown and cream, the rooms come in petite-size (can sleep two, but very snug) and deluxe (a bit more breathing room, though still average-size), but are nicely appointed with big bathrooms. There's a wine-and-cheese get-together every weekday evening. Lots of special deals advertised on the website too. **$380**

★ **Mansfield** 12 W 44th St, between Fifth and Sixth aves ☎212 277 8700, ⓦmansfieldhotel.com; subway B, D, F, M to 42nd St; map p.123. One of the nicest little hotels in the city, the *Mansfield* manages to be both grand and intimate. A clubby library lounge and an inviting bar – with live jazz during the week – lend the place an affable air, conducive to simply wandering around. Rooms are trim and nicely appointed, and there's complimentary continental breakfast and all-day cappuccino. **$399**

★ **The Metro** 45 W 35th St, between Fifth and Sixth aves ☎ 212 947 2500, ⓦ hotelmetronyc.com; subway B, D, F, M to 34th St-Herald Square; map p.123. A very stylish hotel, with some minimal Hollywood theming, a delightful seasonal rooftop, clean, understated rooms and free continental breakfast. There's also free wi-fi, a fitness room and a nice restaurant, the *Metro Grill*. **$329**

Morgans 237 Madison Ave, between E 37th and E 38th sts ☎ 212 686 0300, ⓦ morganshotel.com; subway #6 to 33rd St; map p.123. Its debut now nearly thirty years gone, *Morgans* is still one of the chicest places to lay your head in town. Rooms, with maple panelling, neutral tones and checkerboard accents, are soothing, with specially commissioned black-and-white photos by the late Robert Mapplethorpe. **$469**

★ **The Plaza** Fifth Ave at Central Park South ☎ 212 759 3000, ⓦ theplazany.com; subway N, R to Fifth Ave-59th St; map p.123. *The Plaza* has come back from its hiatus and transformation, which turned part of it into apartments, looking better than ever. The grand tradition of the hotel is still there in the Baccarat chandeliers (in the rooms too) and 24-carat-gold fixtures, but now there are flat-screen TVs and iPads, wireless control panels to dim the lights and summon the floor butler, along with every other amenity you can imagine. Needless to say, service is impeccable. **$875**

★ **Pod** 230 E 51st St, between Second and Third aves ☎ 212 355 0300, ⓦ thepodhotel.com; subway #6 to 51st St; map p.123. This pleasant hotel is one of the best deals in midtown. All 370 pods (solo, double, bunk, queen and "double double", all reminiscent of a colourful ship's quarters) come with a/c, iPod docks, free wi-fi and flat-screen TVs, though single and bunk rooms share bathrooms. The open-air roof-deck bar is a bonus, with stunning views. There's another location at 145 E 39th St. **$255**

Roger Smith 501 Lexington Ave, at E 47th St ☎ 212 755 1400, ⓦ rogersmith.com; subway #6 to 51st St; map p.123. Stylish and helpful, with inviting rooms (including plenty of suites) individually decorated in contemporary, whimsical American style, and bold, colourful artwork on display in the public spaces. In summary, lots of personality. **$369**

Shoreham 33 W 55th St, between Fifth and Sixth aves ☎ 212 247 6700, ⓦ shorehamhotel.com; subway F to 57th St; map p.123. The *Shoreham* is done up, or rather, down, in minimalist chic: a cool white marble lobby, polished steel columns and clean room designs

(necessary for the smallish spaces in the standard rooms) emphasize the fact. There's a lively scene in the sleek bar downstairs. **$439**

Stanford 43 W 32nd St, between Broadway and Fifth Ave ☎ 212 563 1500, ⓦ hotelstanford.com; subway B, D, F, M, N, Q, R to 34th St-Herald Square; map p.123. A clean, moderately priced hotel on the block known as Koreatown. The rooms are a tad small, but attractive and very quiet. Free continental breakfast, jazz performances in the second-floor *1986 Est. Wine Bar & Lounge*, and efficient, friendly staff. **$289**

The Strand 33 W 37th St, between Fifth and Sixth aves ☎ 212 448 1024, ⓦ thestrandnyc.com; subway B, D, F, M, N, Q, R to 34th St-Herald Square; map p.123. The rooms, some of which have views of the Empire State Building, are fresh and comfortable and the vintage black-and-white photos striking, but it's the soothing lobby and lovely roof-deck bar that help the hotel stand out. **$439**

Waldorf-Astoria 301 Park Ave, at E 50th St ☎ 212 355 3000, ⓦ waldorfnewyork.com; subway #6 to 51st St; map p.123. One of the city's first grand hotels (see p.122), the *Waldorf* has been restored to its 1930s glory and is a wonderful place to stay, if you can afford it (or someone else is paying). It's no wonder this is a favourite pick for presidents and visiting heads of state – the spacious accommodation features the latest electronic gadgets, triple sheeting and marble baths. At least drop by for a drink at the legendary mahogany bar downstairs, a peek at one of the opulent banquet halls or a treatment at the full-service spa. **$539**

Warwick 65 W 54th St, at Sixth Ave ☎ 212 247 2700, ⓦ warwickhotelny.com; subway F to 57th St; map p.123. Legendary newspaperman William Randolph Hearst commissioned the hotel in 1926, and stars of the 1950s and 1960s – including Cary Grant, Rock Hudson, the Beatles, Elvis Presley and JFK – stayed here as a matter of course. Although the hotel has lost its showbiz cachet, the elegant lobby, restaurant and cocktail lounge still make it a pleasant place to stay. The staff are helpful and quite friendly. **$450**

Wyndham Midtown 45 205 E 45th St, off Third Ave ☎ 212 867 5100, ⓦ wyndham.com; subway #4, #5, #6, #7 to 42nd St-Grand Central; map p.123. This sleek, beige-toned spot is a serene midtown oasis. Rooms are bright and airy (more than half are suites), with modern

---

ROOMS WITH VIEWS

Hilton Times Square See p.270
Ink48 See p.270
JW Marriott Essex House See p.270
Mandarin Oriental See p.272
The Standard See p.267

22

touches and a handful of fun eccentricities (a tiny TV in the bathroom, hideaway cabinets and compartments). **$399**

MIDTOWN WEST: 30TH TO 59TH STREETS

★ **414** 414 W 46th St, between Ninth and Tenth aves ☎212 399 0006, ⊕414hotel.com; subway C, E to 50th St; map p.141. Popular with Europeans but welcoming to all, this guesthouse, which has larger-than-ordinary rooms across two townhouses, makes a nice camp a bit removed from Times Square's bustle. The courtyard garden is a wonderful place to enjoy your morning coffee. **$250**

Affinia Manhattan 371 Seventh Ave, at W 31st St ☎212 563 1800, ⊕affinia.com; subway #1, #2, #3 to 34th St-Penn Station; map p.141. This large hotel is housed in a 1929 building opposite Penn Station and Madison Square Garden; a recent redesign by the Rockwell Group has brought a more artistic flair to the place, as well as added rooms – they still have numerous suites with kitchenettes but also petite queens. Though it's a bustling address, the elegant lobby, in-room spa service and pillow menu all help foster relaxation. **$339**

Ameritania Hotel 230 W 54th St, at Broadway ☎212 247 5000, ⊕ameritanianyc.com; subway B, D, E to Seventh Ave; map p.141. With sleek, angular furnishings, soaring columns and a bold colour palette, this offbeat hotel is one of the cooler-looking options in the city. Rooms have ample though not extravagant amenities; deluxe rooms (only a little pricier than the standard ones) feature marble baths. **$359**

Casablanca 147 W 43rd St, between Sixth Ave and Broadway ☎212 869 1212, ⊕casablancahotel.com; subway B, D, F, M, #1, #2, #3, #7 to 42nd St; map p.141. Geometric Moorish tiles, inlaid wood and *Rick's Café* (free continental breakfasts and 24hr coffee) are all here in this small, themed hotel along with daily wine-and-cheese reception (5–8pm; free) and complimentary gym passes. While the decor is 1940s Morocco, the rooms all have up-to-date amenities (DVD, wi-fi, etc). **$396**

★ **Distrikt** 342 W 40th St, between Eighth and Ninth aves ☎212 706 6100, ⊕distrikthotel.com; subway A, C, E to 42nd St-Port Authority; map p.141. With a city neighbourhood theme – subtle in the decor, more obvious in having floors named "Chelsea", "the Village", etc – the welcoming *Distrikt* has rooms done in classy muted browns and beiges, with black and white accents; choose one of the upper floors ("Harlem") for the best views. The street is on the insalubrious side. **$399**

Edison 228 W 47th St, between Broadway and Eighth Ave ☎212 840 5000, ⊕edisonhotelnyc.com; subway N, Q, R to 49th St or #1 to 50th St; map p.141. The most striking thing about the 1000-room *Edison* is its beautifully restored Art Deco lobby. The rooms, while not fancy, are clean and recently renovated; the prices are reasonable for midtown; and a classic coffee shop (see p.285) provides a

taste of old NYC. If you want a big hotel right on Broadway, look no further. **$265**

★ **Grace** 125 W 45th St, between Sixth and Seventh aves ☎212 354 2323, ⊕grace.room-matehotels.com; subway B, D, F, M to 42nd St-Bryant Park; map p.141. You won't find many hotels like this one, with a lobby that more closely resembles a concession stand; a tiny glassed-in pool overlooked by a louche loungey bar; different retro wallpaper on each floor; and ultra modern (and pet-friendly) rooms, with platform beds and, in some rooms, bunks (great if you've got a small group). **$359**

Hampton Inn Manhattan-Times Square North 851 Eighth Ave, between W 51st and 52nd sts ☎212 581 4100, ⊕hamptoninn.com; subway C, E to 50th St; map p.141. While the facade has absolutely zero character, the hotel warms up slightly inside. Decent-sized rooms with space to sit are decorated in maroon, brown and gold, with free in-room internet access, coffee-makers and movie channels. **$419**

Hilton Times Square 234 W 42nd St, between Seventh and Eighth aves ☎ 212 840 8222, ⊕hilton.com; subway A, C, E to 42nd St-Port Authority or N, Q, R, S, #1, #2, #3, #7 to Times Square-42nd St; map p.141. This gorgeous property is housed in a 44-storey tower, with awesome views in all directions. The neutral-toned rooms are especially good size for a Manhattan hotel, freshly done up with attractive furnishings and rather large-screen TVs. Ask about packages or specials. **$459**

Hudson 356 W 58th St, between Eighth and Ninth aves ☎ 212 554 6000, ⊕hudsonhotel.com; subway A, B, D, C, #1 to 59th St-Columbus Circle; map p.141. Once you get past the *Hudson*'s chartreuse-lit stairs and space-shuttle-esque bar, the wood-panelled rooms are surprisingly tasteful (though minuscule), and there's the added cache of a library and sky terrace. Rates are lower during the week than on weekends. **$419**

★ **Ink48** 653 Eleventh Ave, between 47th and 48th sts ☎212 757 0088, ⊕ink48.com; subway C, E to 50th St; map p.141. On a strip of car-related businesses (petrol stations, dealers, repair shops), this old printing press has been remade into a dashing hotel; all the spacious rooms face out, many to the Hudson, for splendid views (try to get a corner room on one of the upper floors if possible), and have modern decor, (typically) king beds and lofty ceilings. The rooftop bar, *Press Lounge* (see p.337), is a real plus, as is the full-treatment spa. Dog-friendly. **$519**

JW Marriott Essex House 160 Central Park S, between Sixth and Seventh aves ☎212 247 0300, ⊕marriott.com; subway F, N, Q, R to 57th St; map p.141. Formerly known as simply *Essex House* (then the Jumeirah Essex House), this beautiful hotel was restored to its original Art Deco splendour with a $90 million renovation a few years back. The best rooms have spectacular Central Park views, and despite the attentive service and marble lobby, the atmosphere is quite relaxed. $579

Le Parker Meridien 119 W 56th St, between Sixth and Seventh aves ☎212 245 5000, ⓦparkermeridien.com; subway F, N, Q, R to 57th St; map p.141. This hotel maintains a shiny, clean veneer, with comfortably modern, spacious rooms (and lots of them), a huge fitness centre, rooftop swimming pool and 24hr room service. The *Burger Joint* (see p.312), tucked away in a corner of the lobby, is a fun place for a bite to eat. $539

Mayfair 242 W 49th St, between Broadway and Eighth Ave ☎ 212 586 0300, ⓦmayfairnewyork.com; subway C, E, #1 to 50th St or N, R to 49th St; map p.141. This boutique-style hotel, across the street from the St Malachy Actors' Chapel, has toile-papered rooms and a charming, old-fashioned feel. A nice touch is the preponderance of historic photographs on loan from the Museum of the City of New York (see p.178). $300

Michelangelo 152 W 51st St, between Sixth and Seventh aves ☎212 765 1900, ⓦmichelangelohotel .com; subway N, R to 49th St, #1 to 50th St, B, D, E to Seventh Ave; map p.141. A veritable palazzo on Broadway, this hotel, part of an Italian chain, features acres of marble. While no expense is spared in the luxurious "standard" rooms, suites come in Art Deco, Empire or Country French – take your pick. Make sure to check out the special internet rates. $569

Millennium Broadway 145 W 44th St, between Broadway and Sixth Ave ☎212 768 4400, ⓦmillenniumhotels.com; subway N, Q, R, #1, #2, #3, #7 to Times Square-42nd St; map p.141. Black marble and modern Italian wall-to-ceiling artwork dominate the *Millennium Broadway* lobby; the sleek lines continue in the beautiful off-white and neutral-tone bedrooms. $419

Muse 130 W 46th St, between Sixth and Seventh aves ☎212 485 2400, ⓦthemusehotel.com; subway B, D, F, M to 47–50th sts-Rockefeller Center; map p.141. A small hotel in the centre of the Times Square area, *The Muse* is popular with Europeans. The slightly dark and oddly decorated lobby contrasts with the airy rooms, done in bold black-and-white patterns. $539

New York Marriott Marquis 1535 Broadway, at W 45th St ☎212 398 1900, ⓦmarriott.com; subway N, Q, R, #1, #2, #3 to Times Square-42nd St; map p.141. It's worth dropping by here even if you love to gawk at the split-level atrium and ride the glass elevators to New York's only revolving bar and restaurant. The enormous hotel, decked out in lots of marble, is well designed for conference or convention guests; many rooms come equipped with sofabeds. $404

Night Hotel Times Square 157 W 47th St, between Sixth and Seventh aves ☎212 768 3700, ⓦnighthoteltimessquare.com; subway B, D, F, M to 47–50th sts-Rockefeller Center; map p.141. The

TOP 5 BOUTIQUE HOTELS

Ace Flatiron District See p.267
Blue Moon Lower East Side. See p.266
Mansfield Midtown East. See p.268
NoMad Flatiron District. See p.267
Wythe Williamsburg. See p.273

colourful, funky lobby, filled with distinctive chandeliers and fish-filled aquaria, gives way to more restrained rooms that are relatively good value for the area. $363

Novotel 226 W 52nd St, at Broadway ☎212 315 0100, ⓦnovotel.com; subway #1 to 50th St; B, D, E to Seventh Ave, N, Q, R to 49th St; map p.141. This international chain hotel is large enough to offer a decent range of facilities while small enough (though not approaching boutique size) to cultivate some character. The look is casual but sleek, featuring uncluttered wood with blue accents. $405

Paramount 235 W 46th St, between Broadway and Eighth Ave ☎212 764 5500, ⓦnycparamount.com; subway A, C, E to 42nd St-Port Authority, N, Q, R, S, #1, #2, #3, #7 to Times Square-42nd St; map p.141. Theatrical both inside and out, this historic boutique spot has a flashy lobby full of modern art and textured touches; some rooms seem closet sized, but are designed with enough pizzazz to at least keep your stay in style. $359

Park Savoy 158 W 58th St, between Sixth and Seventh aves ☎212 245 5755, ⓦparksavoyhotelny.com; subway F, N, Q, R to 57th St; map p.141. Despite a somewhat chilly desk staff, the cosy rooms of the *Park Savoy*, just a block from Central Park, represent great value for the area. $195

Salisbury 123 W 57th St, between Sixth and Seventh aves ☎212 246 1300, ⓦnycsalisbury.com; subway F, N, R to 57th St; map p.141. Good service, large (somewhat old-fashioned) rooms, most with kitchenettes. The proximity to Central Park and Carnegie Hall is the attraction here. $339

The Time 224 W 49th St, between Broadway and Eighth Ave ☎212 246 5252, ⓦthetimeny.com; subway C, E, #1 to 50th St; N, R to 49th St; map p.141. *Tempus fugit* – and everything here reminds you of this, from the waist-level clock in the lobby to the hallways bedecked with Roman numerals. Smallish, cheerful rooms are decked out with Bose sound systems, ergonomic workstations and LCD screens. $349

Westin New York at Times Square 270 W 43rd St, at Eighth Ave ☎212 201 2700, ⓦwestinny.com; subway A, C, E to 42nd St-Port Authority, N, Q, R, S, #1, #2, #3, #7 to Times Square-42nd St; map p.141. The outsized copper-and-blue-glass high-rise seems a little out of place – it was designed by Miami architects – but it's nonetheless been a welcome addition to the Times Square scene since

22

22

its debut more than a decade ago. The generous, high-tech (though you pay for wi-fi) rooms have comfortable beds and sweeping views, while bathrooms come equipped with five-speed double shower-heads. **$539**

UPPER EAST SIDE

Franklin 164 E 87th St, between Lexington and Third aves ☎ 212 369 1000, ⊛ franklinhotel.com; subway #4, #5, #6 to 86th St; map p.169. An apparent contradiction: how can one establishment win kudos as both "sexiest hotel" and "best bed and breakfast"? In any case, the quiet residential location makes up for its distance to the heart of the city, and the cheery rooms and bathrooms fitted with Bulgari bath products prove very relaxing. **$324**

★ **Mark** 25 E 77th St, at Madison Ave ☎ 212 744 4300, ⊛ themarkhotel.com; subway #6 to 77th St; map p.169. This hotel really lives up to its claims of sophistication and elegance. The lobby is decked out in Biedermeier furniture and sleek Italian lighting, and there's a pervasive sense of refinement in the plush guest rooms, restaurant and invitingly dark bar. **$695**

Pierre 2 E 61st St, at Fifth Ave ☎ 212 940 8101, ⊛ tajhotels.com; subway N, R to 59th St; map p.169. The *Pierre* still drips with luxury, its rooms offering views of Central Park, iPod docks and DVD players, though it's not quite the palace it was when Salvador Dalí used to stay. If the surreal prices prohibit a stay, afternoon tea in the glorious frescoed *Rotunda* is highly recommended. **$645**

Sherry-Netherland 781 Fifth Ave, at E 59th St ☎ 212 355 2800, ⊛ sherrynetherland.com; subway N, R to 59th St; map p.169. If a large sum of money ever comes your way, rent a whole floor here and live-in permanently (many of the guests do) – the stunning views of Central Park are worth it. The lobby is splendidly ornate; service is excellent; and room service is by renowned restaurateur Harry Cipriani. **$649**

Surrey 20 E 76th St, at Madison Ave ☎ 212 288 3700, ⊛ thesurrey.com; subway #6 to 77th St; map p.169. Just steps from "Museum Mile", this plush hotel has hosted guests since 1926, but the interior is a showcase for contemporary design; standard "salons" (rooms) have been beautifully furnished with ornate carpets, hand-crafted wardrobes and modern desks. Has a spa and rooftop garden. **$695**

UPPER WEST SIDE

Beacon 2130 Broadway, at W 75th St ☎ 212 787 1100, ⊛ beaconhotel.com; subway #1, #2, #3 to 72nd St; map p.183. The *Beacon* is perfectly situated for strolling the gourmet markets and museums of the Upper West Side. While the rooms are comfortable and reasonably sized (with kitchenettes – and plenty of suites, making them

quite family friendly), they probably won't win any style awards. **$325**

Lucerne 201 W 79th St, at Amsterdam Ave ☎ 212 875 1000, ⊛ thelucernehotel.com; subway #1 to 79th St, B, C to 81st St; map p.183. This beautifully restored 1904 brownstone, with its extravagant Baroque terracotta entrance, charming rooms and accommodating staff, is just a block from the Museum of Natural History (see p.189) and close to the liveliest stretches of Broadway and Columbus Avenue. **$361**

Mandarin Oriental New York 80 Columbus Circle, at W 60th St ☎ 212 805 8800, ⊛ mandarinoriental.com/newyork; subway A, B, C, D, #1 to 59th St-Columbus Circle; map p.184. The pampering is on a par with the astronomical rates at this entertainment-industry favourite. A plush palace of spacious, handsome rooms complete with Frette linens and floor-to-ceiling windows, the hotel offers spectacular views from the 35th floor *Lobby Lounge* (open to all) – if those from your room aren't spectacular enough. **$955**

★ **Milburn** 242 W 76th St, between Broadway and West End ☎ 212 362 1006, ⊛ milburnhotel.com; subway #1 to 79th St; map p.183. Once past the classic-feel lobby, the rooms and suites (all with kitchenettes) are a little less showy but are on the large side for the neighbourhood. And the presence of a library of children's books and game consoles makes this welcoming and well-situated hotel great for families; free continental breakfasts and wi-fi, too. **$249**

On the Ave 2178 Broadway, at W 77th St ☎ 212 362 1100, ⊛ ontheave-nyc.com; subway #1 to 79th St; map p.183. The just-renovated *On the Ave* aims for a modern look and feel – which it achieves with its stainless-steel sinks and minimalist baths, though the furniture might be another matter. Nevertheless, it's clean and comfortable, rooms are decently sized, there are two upper-floor balconies for guests to use and discounts are sometimes available. **$350**

HARLEM AND NORTH MANHATTAN

102Brownstone 102 W 118th St, between Malcolm X and Powell blvds ☎ 212 662 4223, ⊛ 102brownstone .com; subway #2, #3 to 116th St; map p.198. Choice of elegant studio apartments (with kitchens) or suites, all with a romantic Victorian theme but equipped with wi-fi, free local phone and cable TV – it's a real bargain and only a short subway ride from Times Square. **$200**

★ **Aloft Harlem** 2296 Frederick Douglass Blvd ☎ 212 749 4000, ⊛ aloftharlem.com; subway A, B, C, D to 125th St; map p.198. First hotel to open in Harlem since the early 1960s, with a bright, stylish interior, high-tech amenities (a pair of iMacs for use, in addition to free wi-fi all over), contemporary decor and airy loft-inspired rooms with large showers and platform beds. **$279**

BROOKLYN

Le Bleu 370 Fourth Ave, between 4th and 5th sts, Gowanus ☎718 625 1500, ⓦhotellebleu.com; subway F, G, R to Fourth Ave-9th St; map p.215. If you can ignore the disjunctive positioning of this modern glass stack right next to a Staples megastore, *Le Bleu* has a lot of things going for it: a boutique feel, with fewer than fifty rooms; bright, airy quarters, many with terraces and balconies; reasonable rates; and proximity to Prospect Park and Carroll Gardens, as well as good views of Manhattan. **$249**

NU Hotel 85 Smith St, at Atlantic Ave, Boerum Hill ☎718 852 8585, ⓦnuhotelbrooklyn.com; subway F, G to Bergen St, A, C, G to Hoyt-Schermerhorn sts; map p.222.

Cool, bright rooms, some with hand-painted murals by local artists, in one of the few convenient Brooklyn hotels that's not a depressing chain. Though on a high-traffic thoroughfare, it's close to some of the nicest walking neighbourhoods around. **$289**

★ **Wythe** 80 Wythe Ave, at N 11th St, Williamsburg ☎718 460 8000, ⓦwythehotel.com; subway L to Bedford St; map p.236. This old factory has been smartly converted into a chic boutique hotel; various industrial touches have been preserved and emphasized, whether exposed brick or floor-to-ceiling warehouse-style windows. "Baby queens" offer a good deal, though you may want to pay extra for more space and the Brooklyn or Manhattan-side views from higher floors. **$200**

22

HOSTELS

Hostels are just about the only option for backpackers in New York. While they can vary greatly in quality, most are fine as long as you don't mind sleeping in a bunk bed and sharing a room with strangers (though if you're travelling in a group of four or six you can often book a room for yourselves). Some hostels are affiliated with organizations that require you to be a member in order to stay, so be sure to ask when calling for a reservation. For hostels that do not participate in the larger budget-travel community, always ask about safety, security and locker availability before checking in and bunking down. Expect to pay $50–70 for a dorm bed, two to three times as much for a private double; note that prices change seasonally (not always in line with the high seasons listed at the start of this chapter).

American Dream 168 E 24th St, between Third and Lexington aves ☎212 260 9779, ⓦamericandreamhostel.com; map p.114. A great location helps make this clean, hospitable hostel a good option for a short-term budget stay; complimentary wi-fi and continental breakfast. Prices increase on weekends. Dorms **$59**, private rooms for singles **$85**, doubles **$110**

Chelsea International Hostel 251 W 20th St, between Seventh and Eighth aves ☎212 647 0010, ⓦchelseahostel.com; subway C, E to 23rd St; map p.107. A smart choice located in the heart of Chelsea. The shared dorms are clean and rudimentary, or you can book a private double (or quad) room. All guests must leave a $10 key deposit. No curfew; passport required. Dorms **$68**, doubles **$155**

Equity Point New York @ Times Square 206 W 41st St, between Seventh and Eighth aves ☎212 703 8600, ⓦequity-point.com; subway A, C, E to 42nd St-Port Authority or N, Q, R, S, #1, #2, #3, #7 to Times Square-42nd St; map p.141. A brightly coloured lobby and rooms makes this hostel, right in the middle of the madness, a decent low-cost option. Rooms come with high-speed internet access and free continental breakfasts. Dorms **$70**, doubles **$280**

Vanderbilt YMCA 224 E 47th St, between Second and Third aves ☎212 912 2500, ⓦymcanyc.org/vanderbilt; subway S, #4, #5, #6, #7 to 42nd St-Grand Central; map p.123. Smaller and quieter than most of the hostels listed here, and neatly placed in midtown Manhattan, only five minutes' walk from Grand Central. Swimming pool, gym and launderette on the premises. All rooms have a/c and shared bathrooms. Singles **$125**, doubles **$150**

BED AND BREAKFASTS AND APARTMENTS

Staying at a **bed and breakfast** can be a nice way of visiting New York at an affordable price. But don't go looking for B&Bs on the streets: most rooms – except for a few that we've found off the beaten track (listed below) – are let out via official agencies, which all recommend making your reservations as far in advance as possible. Rates tend to start from about $150 for a double, and upwards of $200 a night for a studio apartment. B&Bs are also a good bet in the outer boroughs, especially in Brooklyn, where there are quite a few attractive townhouse options to choose from. It's worth looking on ⓦnewyork.craigslist.org or, more reliably, a site like ⓦvrbo.com, ⓦflipkey.com or ⓦairbnb.com for deals on vacation apartments that homeowners let for short- or long-term stays; these can be quite good value.

B&B AGENCIES

Affordable New York City ☎212 533 4001, ⓦaffordablenyc.com. Detailed descriptions are provided by this established network of 120 properties (B&Bs and

apartments) around the city. B&B accommodation $95–120 (shared bathroom) and $135–165 (private bathroom); studios $170–250 and one-bedrooms $175–300. Four- and five-night minimums; for apartments, cash and

22

travellers' cheques only. Very customer-oriented and personable staff.

City Lights Bed & Breakfast ☎212 737 7049, ⓦcitylightsbandb.com. There are more than 400 carefully screened B&Bs (and short-term apartment rentals) on this agency's books, with many of the hosts involved in theatre and the arts. B&B doubles are $105–250; apartments cost $135–600 and up per night depending on size. Two- or three-night minimum stay.

CitySonnet ☎212 614 3034, ⓦcitysonnet.com. This small, personalized, artist-run B&B/short-term apartment agency offers accommodation all over the city, but specializes in Greenwich Village, where the company is based. Singles start at $125 and doubles go up to $250. Five-night mininum stay.

Colby International 21 Park Ave, Eccleston Park, Prescot L34 2QY, UK ☎0151 292 2910, ⓦcolby international.com. Guaranteed accommodation can be arranged from the UK. Book at least a fortnight ahead in high season for these excellent-value apartments (studios to 3 bedrooms $200–450) and B&B singles ($100–110) and doubles ($130).

MANHATTAN B&BS AND GUESTHOUSES

Chic & Budget Rooms & Apartments 269 W 131st St, between Frederick Douglass and Powell blvds ☎917 464 3528, ⓦchicandbudget.com; subway A, B, C to 135th St; map p.198. This is an umbrella organization for four rental apartments and two guesthouses, all in Harlem and offering exceptional value; most of the year rooms rent for well under $200 (minimum 3 days), and come with modern, smart amenities, though located in historic brownstones. $115

★ **East Village Bed and Coffee** 110 Ave C, between E 7th and E 8th sts ☎917 816 0071, ⓦbedandcoffee .com; subway L to First Ave, F to Lower East Side-Second Ave; map p.88. Unusual location in the East Village/Alphabet City, in one of the most cutting-edge neighbourhoods in the city, with cheap, cosy rooms (shared bathrooms), friendly owners, kitchens, free wi-fi and computers, and a tranquil garden. On the downside, it's a long walk to the subway (and there's no breakfast). No sign

– look for the red door. $140

Harlem Flophouse 242 W 123rd St, between Powell and Frederick Douglass blvds ☎212 662 0678, ⓦharlemflophouse.com; subway A, B, C, #2, #3 to 125th St; map p.198. This hip, beautiful, artist-owned 1890s brownstone has just four rooms each with sinks, and two shared bathrooms with antique clawfoot tubs. Charming, but it's an old building and dimly lit throughout; not to everyone's taste. $100

Harlem Renaissance House 237 W 139th St, between Powell and Frederick Douglass blvds ☎212 226 1590, ⓦharlemrenaissancehouse.com; subway B, C, #2, #3 to 135th St; map p.198. Located on historic Strivers' Row, this friendly B&B occupies an 1891 Italianate townhouse with just three rooms equipped with bathroom, wi-fi, cable TV and iPod docks – continental breakfast included. Gay-friendly. $103

Inn at Irving Place 56 Irving Place, at E 17th St ☎212 533 4600, ⓦinnatirving.com; subway L, N, Q, R, #4, #5, #6 to 14th St-Union Square; map p.114. Frequented by celebrities, this handsome pair of 1834 brownstones rank as one of the most exclusive guesthouses in the city. The twelve rooms and "residences" are each named for a famous architect, designer or actor and all have different rates. The *Inn* also offers five-course high teas for $40 per person (see p.283). $415

Inn on 23rd St 131 W 23rd St, between Sixth and Seventh aves ☎212 463 0330, ⓦinnon23rd.com; subway F, M, #1 to 23rd St; map p.107. This family-run B&B is adorned with heirlooms and comfortable furniture in a series of themed rooms. Individually decorated spaces feature lots of exposed brick and the odd quirk, from skylight (in the appropriately titled Skylight Room) to Asian-styled knickknacks and wallpapering (the Bamboo Room). $429

Jones Street Guesthouse 31 Jones St, between Bleecker and West 4th sts ⓦjonesstreetguesthouse .com; subway A, B, C, D, E, F, M to West 4th St, #1 to Christopher St; map pp.96–97. Rare B&B in the heart of the West Village, just off Bleecker; two nicely renovated en-suite rooms, spotlessly clean, with friendly owners in the apartments above – closest you'll get to "living like a

---

APARTMENT SWAPPING

If you're coming to New York for more than a few nights and you happen to own a place in your home city/country, the least expensive and most authentic accommodation option by far is **apartment swapping**. You'd be amazed at the number of New Yorkers who would like to get out of the city for a few days or weeks; what's more, your humble Dublin or Seattle flat may seem spacious and exotic to a Manhattanite. Don't be afraid to play up your dwelling's positive features – the mountain view or medieval church that you take for granted may be just what your swap-partner's doctor ordered – and to ask for pictures and references of the potential swap in return. One of the most reputable exchange organizations is **Home Exchange** (☎310 798 3864, or ☎1 800 877 8723, ⓦhomeexchange.com).

local". Breakfast is courtesy of a voucher at nearby café *Doma*. Free wi-fi. $220

★ **Room in Soho Loft** 153 Lafayette St, between Grand and Howard sts ☎212 965 3000, listing at ⓦbedandbreakfast.com; subway N, R, #6 to Canal St; map p.64. In a great location at the edge of vibrant Soho, these unique, quirky (and cheap) loft apartments, above a gallery managed by the owners, are a great way to experience the neighbourhood; two en-suite seventh-floor rooms (walk-up only) and two fifth-floor rooms with shared bathroom. Kitchen included. $287

San Fermin Apartments 195 Edgecombe Ave, between 142nd and 145th sts ☎917 940 2682, ⓦsanferminapartmentsny.com; subway A, B, C, D to 145th St; map p.198. Set in a lovely 1910 brownstone in Sugar Hill (Harlem), this guesthouse features three comfortable en-suite doubles, and three doubles with shared bath, all dressed in a cool contemporary style. Free wi-fi and small kitchen included. $180

BROOKLYN B&BS AND GUESTHOUSES

3B 136 Lawrence St, Downtown ☎347 762 2632, ⓦ3bbrooklyn.com; subway A, C, F, R to Jay St-MetroTech; map p.215. It may not be an old brownstone on a leafy street, but this co-operative bed and breakfast wins plaudits for breaking new ground. Four options (two queen rooms, a two-bed suite and one dorm-style room with four bunks), with shared bathroom and high ceilings, in an apartment run by the residents of the other apartments in this building. Dorm $60, double $150, suite $180

Akwaaba Mansion 347 MacDonough St, at Stuyvesant Ave, Bedford-Stuyvesant ☎718 455 5958, ⓦakwaaba .com; subway A, C to Utica Ave; map p.213. A New York landmark, this Victorian mansion is one of a kind, featuring Afrocentric details like Daffodil rag dolls and Adrinkra fabrics. A tearoom, sunny porch and Southern-style breakfast will make anyone feel right at home. In case you were wondering, the Ghanaian name translates as "welcome". $185

Baisley House 294 Hoyt St, between Union and Sackett sts, Carroll Gardens ☎718 935 1959; subway F, G to Carroll St; map p.222. Another charming Victorian brownstone, this one dates from 1865. Just three rooms (single, small double and large double), all with shared bathrooms. There's a two-night minimum stay. $150

22

CAFÉ GITANE

Cafés, bakeries and snacks

Travellers will be hard-pressed to find an area of New York that doesn't offer something in the way of light bites: breads, pastries, pizzas, sandwiches, bagels, meats, cheeses, juices, ice creams and vegetarian goodies are among the many options available. Every neighbourhood has several favourite haunts; this chapter details establishments good for breakfast, lunch, snacks and coffee pit-stops – though a decent number offer full dinner menus too. If you're in the mood for a larger, sit-down affair, see Chapter 24, "Restaurants". New York's cafés and bakeries have been greatly influenced by the city's diverse ethnic populations – Italian and French outfits proliferate, not to mention Greek, Israeli and practically every other style. Many of the more long-established cafés are in downtown Manhattan, perfect for lingering or just resting up between sights.

One trend in the past half-decade has been the arrival of innovative **mobile food trucks**, a cut or three above your average kebab van (see p.286). New York also has a number of **coffee houses** and **tearooms** providing fresh coffee, tea, juices, pastries and light snacks. There are **coffee shops** or **diners** on just about every block that serve cheap, decent breakfast specials. And plenty of attention has been devoted in recent years to perfecting **sandwich, pizza, burger, hot dog, taco, donut, dumpling** and **empanada** variations – if you can think of it, no matter how unusual, it's probably already been done here.

THE FINANCIAL DISTRICT AND CITY HALL PARK

BAKERIES AND CAFÉS

Financier Patisserie 62 Stone St and several other locations in Manhattan ☎ 212 344 5600; subway #2, #3 to Wall St; map p.43. High-quality French pastry shop known for its luscious cakes and macaroons ($2.50–2.75) – a mini *"financier"* (French almond cake baked in the shape of a gold bar) is given with each coffee. Mon–Fri 7am–8pm, Sat 8.30am–6.30pm.

SANDWICHES AND SNACKS

Burger Burger 77 Pearl St, at Stone St ☎ 212 269 9100; subway R to Whitehall St; map p.43. One of the few downtown snack-stops open on Sundays, this small takeaway joint knocks out some of the best burgers in town; the classic Angus beef burger is $9.50, but the Chili Cheese ($11.50) and New Yorker ($12) are real treats.

Mon–Wed 11am–10pm, Thurs & Fri 10am–10pm, Sat & Sun noon–9pm.

Crêpes du Nord 17 S William St ☎ 646 422 9500; subway #2, #3 to Wall St; map p.43. Serves tasty French and Scandinavian crêpes with local sustainable produce from the *Smorgas Chef* (p.296) farm in the Catskills; think smoked salmon, scrambled eggs and dill *crème* ($11) or blueberries and ice cream ($9). Mon–Sat 11am–10pm, Sun 11am–9pm.

Leo's Bagels 3 Hanover Square, at Stone St ☎ 212 785 7828; subway #2, #3 to Wall St; map p.43. Get your bagel fix at this popular local joint, with the hand-rolled, chewy main event going for $1.15 (add $2.50 for huge dollops of cream cheese and various spreads). Also does salads, soups and sandwiches. Mon–Fri 6am–6pm, Sat & Sun 7am–5pm.

TRIBECA AND SOHO

BAKERIES AND CAFÉS

Balthazar Bakery 80 Spring St, between Crosby St and Broadway ☎ 212 965 1785; subway #6 to Spring St; map p.64. This bakery has wonderful breads (including a Valrhona dark chocolate loaf for $10) and pastries of all sorts (from $2 for the madeleines). They also serve great home-made fizzy lemonade ($3.50), sandwiches (from $9), and hefty slices of cake ($7.50). Mon–Fri 7.30am–8pm, Sat & Sun 8am–8pm.

Chobani SoHo 150 Prince St ☎ 646 998 3800; subway N, R to Prince St; map p.64. Hamdi Ulukaya's wildly popular Greek yogurt company opened a retail outlet in Soho in 2012, selling delectable combinations such as fig and walnut, and cucumber and olive oil ($4 for half-bowl; $5.50 for full). Sun–Thurs 8am–9pm, Fri & Sat 8am–10pm.

★ **Dominique Ansel Bakery** 189 Spring St, between Thompson and Sullivans sts ☎ 212 219 2773; subway C, E to Spring St; map p.64. The bakery responsible for the "Cronut" craze that swept NYC in 2013; hundreds still line

up two hours before opening to get their hands on the fried, flaky (and trademarked) delight that's a cross between a donut and a croissant ($5), though the buttery DKA ("Dominique's Kouign Amann") is just as addictive. Mon–Sat 8am–7pm, Sun 9am–7pm.

Once Upon a Tart 135 Sullivan St, between Houston and Prince sts ☎ 212 387 8869; subway C, E to Spring St; map p.64. A good place for a light lunch (sandwiches $8.75) or for real French-style tarts (pecan, chocolate and pumpkin among them, from $6.15). The interior is a bit cramped but intimate and oh-so-quaint. Also plenty of options for vegetarians (vegetable tarts from $6.50). Mon–Fri 8am–7pm, Sat 9am–7pm, Sun 9am–6pm.

SANDWICHES AND SNACKS

★ **Hampton Chutney** 68 Prince St, at Crosby St ☎ 212 226 9996; subway N, R to Prince St; map p.64. Don't let the name deceive you: this place is all about *dosas* and *uttapas* (from $7.95), traditional South Indian fare, albeit with plenty of American ingredients. Orders are spiced up with a choice of fresh, home-made chutneys: coriander, curry, mango, tomato or peanut. Daily 11am–9pm.

CHINATOWN

BAKERIES AND CAFÉS

Fay Da Bakery 83 Mott St, at Canal St ☎ 212 791 3884; subway J, N, Q, R, Z and #6 to Canal St; map p.71.

ROUGH GUIDE FAVOURITES

Bagels See p.280
Coffee (and tea) See p.278
Mini chains See p.284
Pizza by the slice See p.281
Street food See p.286

23

TOP 5 COFFEE SHOPS

Coffee is big business in New York, and there are loads of places to find baristas elegantly swirling a leaf on the top of a latte. The following pour the best cups in the city:

Blue Bottle Williamsburg, Brooklyn; also High Line, Tribeca and Chelsea. See p.292
Café Grumpy Greenpoint, Brooklyn; also Park Slope, Chelsea and Lower East Side. See p.292

Gorilla Coffee Park Slope, Brooklyn. See p.290
Mud East Village. See p.280
Stumptown Coffee Roasters Flatiron District. See p.283

23

Chinatown is littered with Hong Kong-style bakeries, but this is one of the best. Try the hot dog-like sausage or pork floss buns ($1.50), egg custard tarts (*dan tat* in Cantonese; $1) and the fresh mango or green-tea *mochi* rice balls ($1.25). Daily 7am–8.30pm.

Ten Ren's Tea Time 79 Mott St ☏ 212 732 7178; subway J, N, Q, R, Z and #6 to Canal St; map p.71. Modern Chinese teashop owned by the famous Taiwanese tea importers down the street, serving all the classic varieties plus tapioca, pearl and bubble teas (from $3.50–4). Sun–Thurs 11am–11pm, Fri & Sat 11am–midnight.

SANDWICHES AND SNACKS

Chinatown Ice Cream Factory 65 Bayard St, between Mott and Elizabeth sts ☏ 212 608 4170; subway J, N, Q, R, Z and #6 to Canal St; map p.71. An essential after-dinner stop, though the wondrously unusual flavours are good any time. Specialities include black sesame, taro, green tea, ginger, almond cookie and lychee (from $3.99 for one scoop, $6.50 for two). Daily 11am–11pm.

Fong Inn Too 46 Mott St, between Bayard and Pell sts; subway J, N, Q, R, Z and #6 to Canal St; map p.71. This basic shop sells two delicious main dishes, primarily to the line of eager takeaway customers: fried radish (or "turnip")

cake ($1.50) and silky soft soybean pudding, served piping hot with sweet syrup ($1–2.25). Daily 7am–9pm.

Hop Shing Restaurant 9 Chatham Square ☏ 212 267 0220; subway J, N, Q, R, Z and #6 to Canal St; map p.71. Offers bargain $1.90 dim sum, but it's their baked goods that really set them apart from other Chinatown diners; try the pineapple buns (*bo lo baau*) and roast pork buns (*char siu bao*), just $0.90 per bun. Sun–Thurs 7am–9.30pm, Fri & Sat 7am–10.30pm.

★ **Laoshan Shandong Guotie** 106 Mosco St, between Mulberry and Mott sts ☏ 212 693 1060; subway J, N, Q, R, Z and #6 to Canal St; map p.71. Identified simply by a "Fried Dumpling" sign in English, this hole-in-the-wall specializes in pan-fried pork dumplings characteristic of northern China, with the absolute bargain price of $1 for five. Squeeze onto a bench inside or take away. Daily 8am–9pm.

★ **Xi'an Famous Foods** 67 Bayard St, between Mott and Elizabeth sts; subway J, N, Q, R, Z and #6 to Canal St; map p.71. Delicious specialities from northwest China: hand-pulled noodles with chili oil and cumin-spiked lamb ($6–7) and savoury cumin lamb burger ($3), chunks of succulent lamb stuffed into pitta bread. Other locations in East Village, Midtown East and Flushing, Queens. Sun–Thurs 11.30am–9pm, Fri & Sat 11.30am–9.30pm.

LITTLE ITALY AND NOLITA

BAKERIES AND CAFÉS

Bread 20 Spring St, between Mott and Elizabeth sts ☏ 212 334 1015; subway #6 to Spring St; map p.71. Stylish café specializing in creative baguette and panini sandwiches ($11–14) packed with high-quality meats and cheeses; highlights include the fresh sardines and tuna, and aged Italian salami. Mon–Wed 9.30am–midnight, Thurs & Fri 9.30am–1am, Sat 10.30am–1am, Sun 10.30am–midnight.

Café Gitane 242 Mott St, between Prince and Houston sts ☏ 212 334 9552; subway N, R to Prince St; map p.71. Come here for a bowl of delicious *café crème* ($4). For those looking for a bite to eat, zesty Moroccan-influenced food is also on offer (couscous is $14). Chock-full of posers, but still one of the best cafés around. Sun–Thurs 8.30am–midnight, Fri & Sat 8.30am–12.30am.

★ **Ceci-Cela** 55 Spring St, between Mulberry and Lafayette sts ☏ 212 274 9179; subway #6 to Spring St;

map p.71. Cute French patisserie with a stand-up counter and bench as well as tables in the back. The croissants ($2) and *pain au chocolat* ($2.50) are divine, as are the brie baguettes (from $3.75–5). Mon–Thurs 6.30am–8pm, Fri 6.30am–9pm, Sat 7am–9pm, Sun 7am–8pm.

Eileen's Special Cheesecake 17 Cleveland Place, at Kenmare St ☏ 212 966 5585; subway #6 to Spring St; map p.71. Eileen Avezzano has battled *Junior's* in Brooklyn (p.322) for title of best cheesecake in the city since 1973; her version is light and fluffy (whipped) with a graham cracker base. Minis for $4, whole cakes from $12.50. Mon–Fri 9am–9pm, Sat & Sun 10am–7pm.

Ferrara Café 195 Grand St, at Mulberry St ☏ 212 226 6150; subway #6 to Spring St; map p.71. The best known and most traditional of Little Italy's coffee houses, this neighbourhood landmark has been around since 1892. Try the New York cheesecake, hand-dipped chocolate cannoli (pastries $4–5.75) or the gelato served on the street

($4.50). Outdoor seating is available in warmer weather. Daily 8.30am–11.30pm, Fri & Sat until midnight.

SANDWICHES AND SNACKS

★ **Parm** 248 Mulberry St, between Prince and Spring sts ☎212 993 7189; subway N, R to Prince St; map p.71. Sensational sandwiches from the lauded team at *Torrisi* (p.300) – try their Turkey Hero ($12) and Saratoga Club ($14). Sun–Wed 11am–11pm, Thurs–Sat 11am–midnight.

Prince Street Pizza 27 Prince St, between Mott and Elizabeth sts ☎ 212 966 4100; subway N, R to Prince St; map p.71. When the original Ray's closed in 2012 this pizza joint took up the tradition, with its game-changing, utterly addictive SoHo Square ($3.75), topped with mozzarella and "secret sauce". Daily 11am–midnight.

★ **Rice to Riches** 37 Spring St, between Mott and Mulberry sts ☎212 274 0008; subway #6 to Spring St; map p.71. Rice pudding made hip and utterly irresistible, served up in this funky space in a variety of sweet flavours, from peanut butter and choc chip to mango and cinnamon. Bowls start at $7. There are a few tables inside. Sun–Thurs 11am–11pm, Fri & Sat 11am–1am.

Saigon Vietnamese Sandwich 369 Broome St, between Mott and Elizabeth sts ☎212 219 8341; subway #6 to Spring St; map p.71. One of the best makers of Vietnamese sandwiches (known as *bánh mì*) in the city. The classic is made with a large chunk of French bread, and stuffed with grilled pork, sausage and thinly sliced pickled vegetables, all for just $4.50. Daily 7am–7pm.

THE LOWER EAST SIDE

23

BAKERIES AND CAFÉS

Kossar's 367 Grand St, at Essex St ☎212 473 4810; subway F, J, M, Z to Delancey St-Essex St; map p.83. This generations-old kosher treasure serves, bar none, the city's best *bialys* ($0.90), a flattened savoury dough traditionally topped with onion or garlic; the bagels ($1) aren't far behind. Mon–Thurs 6am–7pm, Fri 6am–5pm.

★ **Sugar Sweet Sunshine** 126 Rivington St, between Essex and Norfolk sts ☎212 995 1960; subway F, J, M, Z to Delancey St-Essex St; map p.83. Pudding lovers will be in serious danger at this fabulous bakery, established by two ex-employees of *Magnolia* (see p.282). Choose shots ($2.50) or cups ($5) of banana, choc chip or pumpkin puddings, as well as delectable cupcakes ($1.75) and other treats. Mon–Thurs 8am–10pm, Fri 8am–11pm, Sat 10am–11pm, Sun 10am–7pm.

Yonah Schimmel Knish Bakery 137 E Houston St, between Forsyth and Eldridge sts ☎212 477 2858; subway F to Lower East Side-Second Ave; map p.83. The fine *knishes* ($3.50–5), rounds of vegetable-, cheese- or potato-and-meat-stuffed dough, are baked fresh on the premises at this 1910 store, as are the wonderful bagels. Sun–Thurs 9am–7pm, Fri & Sat 9am–9pm.

SANDWICHES AND SNACKS

Cheeky Sandwiches 35 Orchard St, between Hester and Canal sts ☎ 212 555 5555; subway B, D to Grand St, F, J, M, Z to Delancey St-Essex St; map p.83. Visit tiny *Cheeky's* (look for the blue shutters) for fried chicken and gravy between buttermilk scones ($6.50) – they also do a classic New Orleans-style Po' Boy sandwich ($8.50). Sun–Thurs 8am–9pm, Fri & Sat 8am–midnight.

Doughnut Plant 379 Grand St, between Essex and Clinton sts ☎212 505 3700; subway F, J, M, Z to Delancey St-Essex St; map p.107. Also in *Chelsea Hotel*, at 220 W 23rd St; map p.107. Serious (and seriously delicious) donuts ($2.75–3.25); be sure to sample the

seasonal flavours and glazes, including chestnut cake, pumpkin and passion fruit. Cash only. Daily 6.30am–8pm.

Il Laboratorio del Gelato 188 Ludlow St, at E Houston St ☎212 343 9922; subway F to Lower East Side-Second Ave; map p.83. This shrine to cream and sugar (with an espresso bar) serves up over 48 flavours, including basil, lavender and avocado (scoops $4.75–6.75). Mon–Thurs 7.30am–10pm, Fri 7.30am–midnight, Sat 10am–midnight, Sun 10am–10pm.

Mikey's Burger 134 Ludlow St, between Rivington and Stanton sts ☎212 979 9211; subway F, J, M, Z to Delancey St-Essex St; map p.83. Michael Huynh's burger bar offers four types of 6oz burgers on potato rolls, including a beef burger with mustard seeds and corned beef hash ($6.50), an Asian-accented BLT ($7.50) and a lamb burger ($7.50). Cheese fries ($5) and shakes (try sesame; $6) make a fitting accompaniment. Sun–Thurs 11am–2am, Fri & Sat 11am–4am.

Pop Karma 95 Orchard St, between Delancey and Broome sts ☎917 675 7450; subway F, J, M, Z to Delancey St-Essex St; map p.83. Artisanal popcorn store, using organic corn and crazy flavours such as "zen cheddar", Mediterranean and "masala" (Indian spices). Bags $2–7.25. Daily 11am–8pm.

★ **Russ & Daughters** 179 E Houston St, between Allen and Orchard sts ☎212 475 4880; subway F to Lower East Side-Second Ave; map p.83. The original Manhattan gourmet shop, it was set up in 1914 to sate the appetites of homesick immigrant Jews with smoked fish, and now sells caviar, *halvah*, pickled vegetables, fine cheese and amazing hand-rolled bagels (regular from $2.75); try the "Super Heebster": whitefish and baked salmon salad with wasabi roe on a bagel ($10.95). Mon–Fri 8am–8pm, Sat 9am–7pm, Sun 8am–5.30pm.

★ **Vanessa's Dumpling House** 118A Eldridge St, between Grand and Broome sts ☎ 212 625 8008; subway B, D to Grand St; map p.83. This always-busy Chinese

TOP 5 BAGELS

Theories abound as to the **origin of the modern bagel**. Most likely, it is a derivative of the pretzel, with the word "bagel" coming from the German *biegen*, "to bend." Whatever their birthplace, it is certain that bagels have become a New York institution.

Until the 1950s, bagels were still handmade by Eastern European Jewish immigrants in cellars scattered around New York's Lower East Side. Modern-day bagels are softer and have a smaller hole than their ancestors – the hole made them easy to carry on a long stick to hawk on street corners. Their curiously chewy texture is a result of being boiled before they are baked. They are most traditionally (and famously) served with cream cheese and lox (smoked salmon).

Though bagels are now an American dietary staple, New Yorkers would say only a few places serve the real thing. Below is a list of some of the city's better bagelsmiths.

Absolute Bagels Upper West Side. See p.288
Bagel Hole Park Slope. See p.290
Ess-A-Bagel Midtown East. See p.284

Kossar's Lower East Side. See p.279
Russ & Daughters Lower East Side. See p.279

23

canteen, established by Beijing-native Vanessa Weng in 1999, knocks out various combinations of steamed or fried pork, shrimp and vegetable dumplings at the bargain price of $1 for four. Daily 7.30am–10.30pm, Sun until 10pm.

THE EAST VILLAGE

BAKERIES AND CAFÉS

★ **Big Gay Ice Cream Shop** 125 E 7th St, between First Ave and Avenue A ☎212 254 3500; subway L to First Ave; map p.88. The utterly addictive ice cream here has cheekily named flavours including the "salty pimp" (vanilla, *dulce de leche*, sea salt and chocolate dip) and the "gobbler" (pumpkin butter, maple syrup and pie pieces). Winter: Mon–Thurs 4–11pm, Fri–Sun 1–11pm; summer Sun–Thurs noon–11pm, Fri & Sat noon–midnight.

De Robertis 176 First Ave, between E 10th and E 11th sts ☎212 674 7137; subway L to First Ave; map p.88. Traditional Italian bakery/café that's been around since 1904. The Old New York vibe is so good that the establishment has been featured in multiple Woody Allen flicks. Try the mini amaretto cheesecake ($3.95), home-made ices (crushed ice flavoured with syrup) and cannoli (all from $3.75). Mon noon–11pm, Tues–Thurs 9am–11pm, Fri & Sat 9am–midnight, Sun 10am–10pm.

★ **Momofuku Milk Bar** 251 E 13th St at Second Ave ☎212 254 3500; subway L to Third Ave; map p.88. David Chang's bakery (opposite his *Ssäm Bar*) sells a host of sweet treats: thick cereal shakes ($6), crack pie (oat crust and buttery filling; $5.25) and compost cookies (pretzels, coffee and choc chips; $1.85). Daily 9am–midnight.

Mud 307 E 9th St between Second and First aves ☎212 228 9074; subway L to First or Third Ave; map p.88. A local favourite for its intensely strong fair-trade coffee (from $2.50), which is also sold from orange trucks around town (check for one at Astor Place). You can sit for hours at the café tables or in the back garden and enjoy the good veggie fare as well as rocking tunes. Hosts performances and art shows on occasion. Mon–Fri 8am–midnight, Sat & Sun 9am–midnight.

Spot Dessert Bar 13 St Mark's Place, between Second and Third aves ☎212 677 5670; subway #6 to Astor Place; map p.88. Celebrated chef Pichet Ong has concocted some irresistible treats for this basement café, decked out in a vaguely East Asian rustic style: "tapas" puddings might come with sesame pear, persimmon or chocolate banana ($8.75), while cupcakes ($2.75) and cookies ($2) are equally inventive. Sun–Wed noon–midnight, Thurs–Sat noon–1am.

Veniero's Pasticceria & Café 342 E 11th St, between First and Second aves ☎212 674 7070; subway L to First Ave, #6 to Astor Place; map p.88. An East Village bakery and neighbourhood institution since 1894, *Veniero's* desserts and decor are fabulously over the top. The ricotta cheesecake ($3.50) and cannoli ($2.75) are top-notch, and the home-made gelato (one scoop $1.65) is some of the best in the city. Sun–Thurs 8am–midnight, Fri & Sat 8am–1am.

SANDWICHES AND SNACKS

★ **Artichoke** 328 E 14th St between First and Second aves ☎212 228 2004, subway L to First Ave, map p.88. Fabulous late-night pizza slices to take away, with just four choices: sumptuous cheese-laden Sicilian ($4), Margarita ($4), crab ($4.50) or the trademark artichoke-spinach, topped with a super-creamy sauce ($4.50). Daily 10am–5am.

Crif Dogs 113 St Mark's Place, between First Ave and Ave A ☎212 614 2728; subway #6 to Astor Place; map p.88. Hot-dog aficionados swear by these naturally-smoked, shiny wieners bursting with flavour ($2.75), enjoyed Philly-steak style, smothered in cheese ($4), or the Chihuahua, topped with avocado and bacon ($4.50). Sun–Thurs noon–2am, Fri & Sat noon–4am.

Dos Toros Taqueria 137 Fourth Ave, between 13th and 14th sts ☎212 677 7300; subway #4, #5, #6 to Union

Square; map p.88. This authentic, reasonably priced Tex-Mex takeaway (with a few benches inside) attracts plenty of students and long lines at lunchtime. Opt for burritos ($8.04), tacos ($3.90) or quesadillas ($6.67) stuffed with *carne asada* (steak), *carnitas* (pork) or *pollo asado* (grilled chicken). Mon 11.30am–10.30pm, Tues–Fri 11.30am–11pm, Sat noon–11pm, Sun noon–10.30pm.

Liquiteria 170 Second Ave, at E 11th St ☎ 212 358 0300; subway #6 to Astor Place; map p.88. The smoothies here are by far the best in Manhattan (try the "Orangasm" with mango and strawberries; $6.50). There are over 30 combos, and loads of supplement shots. You can also get delicious, healthy lunches such as oatmeal with fresh fruit ($5.50) or organic peanut butter and jelly sandwiches ($4.60). Mon–Fri 7am–9pm, Sat & Sun 8am–9pm.

Mamoun's Falafel 22 St Mark's Place, between Second and Third aves; subway #6 to Astor Place; map p.88. This tiny takeaway (with a few seats inside) is the best place for cheap, wholesome falafel and *baba ganoush* in the city, with filling veggie plates for $5 (sandwiches $3), kebabs from $11.50 (plates) and convenient late-night hours. Mon–Wed 11am–4am, Thurs–Sun 11am–5am.

★ **Mile End Sandwich Shop** 53 Bond St, between Lafayette St and the Bowery ☎ 212 529 2990; subway #6 to Bleecker St; map p.88. Montreal-inspired Jewish deli specializing in freshly made Jewish comfort food; expect lots of curing, smoking, pickling and baking. Favourites include the classic hot pastrami sandwich ($12)

and the breakfast burger ($9). Daily 10am–6pm.

Otafuku 236 E 9th St, between Second and Third aves ☎ 212 353 8503; subway #6 to Astor Place; map p.88. Excellent Japanese hole-in-the-wall, serving generous octopus *takoyaki* balls ($6), various types of scrumptious *okonomiyaki* (savoury pancake; $8) and pan-fried noodles ($7). Sun–Thurs 1–10pm, Fri & Sat noon–11pm.

Pommes Frites 123 Second Ave, between E 7th St and St Mark's Place ☎ 212 674 1234; subway #6 to Astor Place; map p.88. Not the best fries in the city, but the gooey, Belgian-style toppings ($1.50 extra) make all the difference; try the rosemary garlic mayo or curry ketchup. Fries portions range from $4.50 to $7.75. Sun–Thurs 11.30am–1am, Fri & Sat 11.30am–3.30am.

★ **Porchetta** 110 E 7th St, between First Ave and Ave A ☎ 212 777 2151; subway #6 to Astor Place; map p.88. This tiny takeaway shop (with a few stools and counter inside) has developed a loyal following for its luscious Tuscan *porchetta* sandwiches ($12): thick slabs of roasted, seasoned pork in a ciabatta roll. Sun–Thurs 11.30am–10pm, Fri & Sat 11.30am–11pm.

This Little Piggy Had Roast Beef 149 First Ave at 9th St ☎ 212 253 1500; subway #6 to Astor Place; map p.88. This takeaway place specializes in glorious roast beef sandwiches on a roll, *au jus* with Cheez Whiz ($5.50), or on a hero loaf with fresh mozzarella and gravy ($9.50). Add hand-cut fries for $4. Sun–Thurs 11am–2am, Fri & Sat 11am–5am.

THE WEST VILLAGE

BAKERIES AND CAFÉS

Cafe Dante 79 MacDougal St, between Bleecker and Houston sts ☎ 212 982 5275; subway A, B, C, D, E, F, M to W 4th St; map pp.96–97. A morning stopoff for many locals since 1915. It's often jammed with NYU students and professors sipping cappuccinos, espressos and *caffè alfredo* with ice cream (coffee from $3.15, hot plates from $6). Sun–Thurs 10am–2am, Fri & Sat 10am–3am.

★ **Caffe Reggio** 119 MacDougal St, between Bleecker

and W 3rd sts ☎ 212 475 9557; subway A, B, C, D, E, F, M to W 4th St; map pp.96–97. Another historic Village coffee house, this time dating back to 1927, embellished with all sorts of Italian antiques, paintings and sculpture. Tennessee Williams sipped espresso here (now $2.75) and scenes from *Godfather II* were filmed inside. Mon–Thurs 8am–3am, Fri & Sat 8am–4.30am, Sun 9am–3am.

Doma na rohu 27 Morton St, at Seventh Ave ☎ 212 929 4339; subway #1 to Christopher St; map pp.96–97. A

23

TOP 5 PIZZA BY THE SLICE

New Yorkers are passionate about their **pizza**, but that's where agreement on the topic largely ends. There are many strongly held opinions when it comes to defining a good slice, and one man's mozzarella epiphany is often his neighbour's tasteless cardboard triangle. New York-style pizza was pioneered by Italian immigrants in the early 1900s: Gennaro Lombardi's pizzeria (see p.300) opened in 1905 and three of his staff went on to found *Totonno's* (see p.324) in 1924, *John's Pizzeria* (p.306) in 1929 and *Patsy's* in 1933. Characterized by its wide, thin slices (often eaten folded in half) and thin hand-tossed crust, aficionados claim that the flavour of New York pizza crust is due to the purity of the city tap water used to make the dough.

Here are some places to sample New York's countless pizza possibilities.

Artichoke East Village. See opposite
Di Fara Pizza Midwood, Brooklyn. See p.290

Joe's Pizza West Village. See p.282
Patsy's Pizza East Harlem. See p.320
Prince Street Pizza Nolita. See p.279

corner window, good coffee, a linger-all-day vibe, good food (sandwiches from $9), and beer and wine of the old Austro-Hungarian Empire make this a neighbourhood favourite. Mon–Fri 7am–midnight, Sat & Sun 9am–1am.

Magnolia Bakery 401 Bleecker St, at W 11th St ☎ 212 462 2572; subway #1 to Christopher St; map pp.96–97. There are lots of baked goods on offer here, but everyone comes for the heavenly and deservedly famous multicoloured cupcakes (celebrated in both *Sex and the City* and *Saturday Night Live*); $3.25–3.50 each. Queues can stretch around the block. Sun–Thurs 9am–11.30pm, Fri & Sat 9am–12.30am.

SANDWICHES AND SNACKS

Cones 272 Bleecker St, between Seventh Ave and Morton St ☎ 212 414 1795; subway #1 to Christopher St; map pp.96–97. Wonderful *gelati* by two Argentine brothers. Flavours like tiramisu and rich chocolate attract long queues, especially on warm summer nights (scoops from $4.36–7.12 for waffle cones). Daily 1pm–11pm, Fri & Sat until midnight.

Faicco's Pork Store 260 Bleecker St, between Morton and Leroy sts ☎ 212 243 1974; subway A, B, C, D, E, F, M to W 4th St; map pp.96–97. This old-school Italian butcher serves some of the best-value sandwiches in the city – huge rolls of ham, sausage, and chicken cutlet with aged provolone ($7.50–12). Add a tangy prosciutto ball for $1.50. Tues–Fri 8.30am–6pm, Sat 8am–6pm, Sun 9am–2pm.

Gray's Papaya 402 Sixth Ave at 8th St ☎ 212 260 3532; subway A, B, C, D, E, F, M to W 4th St; map pp.96–97. For a real New York experience, grab a crispy hot dog ($1.95) at this standing-room-only chain, the more established rival of *Papaya Dog* down the road. The "papaya" refers to the fresh tropical fruit drinks ($1.45) also sold here (gimmicky, but delicious). Open 24hr.

Joe's Pizza 7 Carmine St at Sixth Ave ☎ 212 366 1182; subway A, B, C, D, E, F, M to W 4th St; map pp.96–97. Classic New York pizza to go ($2.75) since 1975; nothing fancy, just thin-crust slices, with cheese that tastes like cheese and a rich tomato base – add pepperoni for some bite ($3.50). Daily 10am–4am.

Murray's Cheese Bar 264 Bleecker St, between Cornelia and Morton sts ☎ 646 476 8882; subway A, B, C, D, E, F, M to W 4th St; map pp.96–97. Just down the block from the famous cheese shop, sample buffalo cheese curds ($10), hominy grits with three cheeses ($10) and the gut-busting sensation that is Murray's cheeseburger ($17). Mon & Tues 5–10pm, Wed–Fri 5pm–midnight, Sat 10am–2.30pm & 5pm–midnight, Sun 10am–2.30pm & 5–10pm.

★ **Num Pang** 21 E 12th St at University Place ☎ 212 255 3271; subway N, Q, R, L, #4, #5, #6 to Union Square; map pp.96–97. Superb Cambodian-style sandwiches served on freshly toasted semolina-flour baguettes with chilli mayo and house-made pickles; try the pulled Duroc pork ($8.25) or peppercorn catfish ($8.50). Mon–Sat 11am–10pm, Sun noon–9pm.

Oatmeals 120 W 3rd St, between MacDougal St and Sixth Ave ☎ 646 360 3570; subway A, B, C, D, E, F, M to W 4th St; map pp.96–97. Porridge gets the Village treatment in this tiny shop, selling a variety of delicious steel-cut oatmeal in three sizes ($4–$6.25); sweet-morning classics like the peanut butter banana, or a more savoury treat like fig and gorgonzola. Mon–Fri 7am–6pm, Sat & Sun 8am–6pm.

Peanut Butter & Company 240 Sullivan St, between Bleecker and W 3rd Sts ☎ 212 677 3995; subway A, B, C, D, E, F, M to W 4th St; map pp.96–97. Peanut butter in ways you never imagined. Try the "Elvis" – a grilled peanut butter and honey sandwich with bananas ($7.50), or the slightly more adventurous "Pregnant Lady", made with pickles ($6.25). Sandwiches are $5–8. Sun–Thurs 11am–9pm, Fri & Sat 11am–10pm.

Taco Shop 166 W 4th St, between Cornelia and Jones sts ☎ 212 675 1955; subway A, B, C, D, E, F, M to W 4th St; map pp.96–97. Authentic Mexican tacos stuffed with tender cuts of meat and succulent vegetables for just $2.95 (try the beef *barbacoa* taco, made with seasoned short rib); margaritas are $7 (Mon–Fri 3–7pm and Sun 10am–4pm, three tacos and a soft drink is just $12). Sun–Thurs noon–midnight, Fri & Sat noon–2am.

Two Boots to Go West 201 W 11th St, at Seventh Ave ☎ 212 633 9096; subway #1, #2, #3 to 14th St; map pp.96–97. Great thin-crust pizzas with a cornmeal dusting and Cajun flavour. Try a small "Newman" (*sopressata*, sweet sausage and ricotta; $9.95) or the "Earth Mother" (vegetable Sicilian; $9.95). Mon–Wed 11am–midnight, Thurs 11am–1am, Fri & Sat 11am–2am, Sun noon–midnight.

CHELSEA

BAKERIES AND CAFÉS

Amy's Bread 75 Ninth Ave, between W 15th and W 16th sts ☎ 212 462 4338, subway A, C, E, L to 14th St; map p.107. Also 672 Ninth Ave, between 46th and 47th sts; map p.141. Launched by *ex-Bouley* pastry chef Amy Scherber in 1992. You can find Amy's breads in fine stores citywide. The grilled-cheese sandwiches ($6.95), made with chipotle peppers, are some of the best in the city.

Mon–Fri 7.30am–8pm, Sat 8am–8pm, Sun 8am–7pm.

Billy's Bakery 184 Ninth Ave, between W 21st and W 22nd sts ☎ 212 647 9956; subway C, E to 23rd St; map p.107. Opened by a former employee of *Magnolia Bakery*, though the rustic farmhouse interior is far less crowded and the cupcakes cheaper and just as scrumptious (there are a few other locations as well). Other highlights include a tangy Key Lime Pie. Mon–Thurs 8.30am–11pm, Fri & Sat

8.30am–12.30am, Sun 9am–11pm.

Eleni's Cookies 75 Ninth Ave, between W 15th and W 16th sts ☎ 1 888 435 3647; subway A, C, E, L to 14th St; map p.107. This bright, pink-hued store in Chelsea Market is super-moist cupcake and cookie heaven; the "Everything Cookie" (combining cranberries, walnuts and coconut) is virtually a meal in itself. It's also a great place for gifts. Mon–Fri 9am–8pm, Sat 9am–7pm, Sun 10am–7pm.

Empire Cake 112 Eighth Ave, between W 15th and W 16th sts ☎ 212 242 5858; subway A, C, E, L to 14th St; map p.107. Delectable cupcakes, cookies and takes on old-time favourites like snowballs (cake with custard, covered in icing and rolled in coconut flakes). Mon–Wed 8am–10pm, Thurs 8am–11pm, Fri 8am–midnight, Sat 10am–midnight, Sun 11am–10pm.

Sullivan Street Bakery 236 Ninth Ave, between W 24th and W 25th sts ☎ 212 929 5900; subway C, E to 23rd St; map p.107. A lovely array of freshly-made crusty breads is on display here, though there are also panini (goat cheese and beetroot, peach and roast pork; $10–13) and, best of all, *pizze* (crisp and cheeseless; $3.50–4/slice). Daily 7.30am–9pm.

SANDWICHES AND SNACKS

Kofoo 334 Eighth Ave, between W 26th and W 27th sts ☎ 212 675 5277; subway C, E to 23rd St; map p.107. Tiny, cheery shopfront for quick Korean takeaway snacks, notably variations on *kim-bob* – in essence, a sushi roll with fillings (cooked) other than raw fish. There's wild mushroom, *kimchiee* and barbecue chicken, among other possibilities. Mon–Sat 11am–10pm.

Lobster Place 75 Ninth Ave, between 15th and 16th sts ☎ 212 255 5672; subway A, C, E to 14th St; map p.107. A serious expansion has given this Chelsea Market fishmonger not just more space but a full-on bar-restaurant addition, the *Cull & Pistol*, which specializes in oysters and whole lobster. They've also ramped up takeaway options, adding oyster po' boys ($10.95) and belly clam sandwiches ($14.95) to their already sterling renditions of chowder, fresh sushi and lobster rolls. Great for a picnic meal on the High Line. Mon–Sat 9.30am–9pm, Sun 10am–8pm.

★ **Rocket Pig** 463 W 24th St, between W Ninth and Tenth aves ☎ 212 645 5660; subway C, E to 23rd St; map p.107. They do one thing – well, maybe there are a couple of small diversions, which can all be overlooked – a messy, smoked pork sandwich ($14), whose accoutrements (red onion jam, for one) help make it one of the city's newest signature sandwiches. Mon–Sat 11am–6pm.

23

UNION SQUARE, GRAMERCY PARK AND THE FLATIRON DISTRICT

BAKERIES AND CAFÉS

★ **Breads Bakery** 18 E 16 th St, between Broadway and Fifth Ave ☎ 212 633 2253; subway L, N, Q, R, #4, #5, #6 to 14th St-Union Square; map p.114. This newcomer, by way of Denmark and Israel, is already one of the city's best; you can't go wrong with the sandwiches or quiches, and the breads are out of this world, but make sure to top off whatever you get with a flaky, melt-in-the-mouth *rugelach* ($1.50 each). Mon–Fri 7am–7pm, Sat & Sun 8am–7pm.

The City Bakery 3 W 18th St, between Fifth and Sixth aves ☎ 212 366 1414; subway F, M to 14th St; map p.114. A good place to come for a filling lunch. Try the tortilla pie or the idiosyncratic pretzel croissant for heavy snacking; sweet tooths, meanwhile, should not miss out on the hot chocolate complete with home-made marshmallow, so thick you might need a fork. In February, or "hot chocolate month", there's a new, often strange flavour available each day. Mon–Fri 7.30am–7pm, Sat 8am–7pm, Sun 10am–6pm.

Lady Mendl's 56 Irving Place, at E 17th St, in the *Inn at Irving Place* (see p.274) ☎ 212 533 4466; subway L, N, Q, R, #4, #5, #6 to 14th St-Union Square; map p.114. Classic English high teas are the stock-in-trade of this small inn set in a handsome pair of brownstones. As per tradition, their five-course menus are served in the afternoon, complete with silver service and a tower of sandwiches ($40/person). Make reservations. Mon–Fri 3pm & 5pm, Sat & Sun noon, 2.30pm & 5pm.

★ **Stumptown Coffee Roasters** 20 W 29th St, between Broadway and Fifth Ave, in the *Ace Hotel* (see p.267) ☎ 212 679 2222; subway N, R to 28th St; map p.114. One of the country's most celebrated coffee roasters brings its product to a hip new hotel; you'll have your latte methodically made by dandified baristas and can drink it in the columned lobby (also a workspace/bar). Cash only. Mon–Fri 6am–8pm, Sat & Sun 7am–8pm.

SANDWICHES AND SNACKS

Beecher's 900 Broadway, at 20th St ☎ 212 466 3340; subway N, R to 19th St; map p.114. A multipurpose food establishment, though centred around their handmade cheeses (some of which are made on site – you can watch the process). There's a café and cheese counter, or you can descend to their cave-like bar-restaurant for more than just a soup or grilled sandwich. Mon–Sat 8am–8pm, Sun 11am–8pm; cellar Mon–Wed & Sun 11.30am–11pm, Thurs & Fri 11.30–midnight, Sat 5pm–midnight, Sun 5pm–11pm.

Defonte's of Brooklyn 261 Third Ave, at E 21st St ☎ 212 614 1500; subway #6 to 23rd St; map p.114. Main location 379 Columbia St, Red Hook; map p.222. The ninety-year-old Brooklyn original is a weathered classic on an obscure Red Hook corner by the Brooklyn–Queens Expressway; easier to hit this outpost near Gramercy, where the huge roast pork or roast beef sandwiches (add fried eggplant, fresh mozzarella and the special "hot salad") are just as toothsome ($8.95–10.95). Mon–Fri 9.30am–8pm, Sat 9.30am–6pm, Sun 10am–5pm.

23

Dogmatic 26 E 17th St, between Broadway and Fifth Ave ☎ 212 414 0600; subway L, N, Q, R, #4, #5, #6 to 14th St-Union Square; map p.114. A bright, hypermodern shopfront with innovative seating for innovative snack food – baguettes are hollowed and cooked on prongs, then stuffed with your choice of designer sausage and sauce (such as truffle Gruyère and mint yogurt); hot dogs are $5.50, the few sides on offer are $2.95–3.95. Mon–Fri 11am–9pm, Sat & Sun noon–7pm.

★ **Eisenberg's Sandwich Shop** 174 Fifth Ave, at W 22nd St ☎ 212 675 5096; subway N, R to 23rd St; map p.114. A colourful luncheonette, this shop has been serving Reubens (hot corned beef and Swiss cheese sandwiches; $10), tuna sandwiches ($7.25), matzoh-ball soup ($4) and old-fashioned fountain sodas at a well-worn counter since 1930. Mon–Fri 6.30am–8pm, Sat 9am–6pm, Sun 9am–5pm.

★ **No. 7 Sub** 1177 Broadway, between W 28th and W 29th sts, in the *Ace Hotel* ☎ 212 532 1680; subway N, R to 28th St; map p.114. Also 1 W 59th St, at Fifth Ave, in *Plaza Hotel* (see p.123) and 931 Manhattan Ave, Greenpoint, map p.236. Part of the dazzling array of food options available at the *Ace Hotel* (see p.267), this sandwich

vendor deals up esoteric combinations that aren't done justice by their lists of ingredients (sample: broccoli, lychee *muchim*, ricotta *salata*, pine nuts). The menu changes, but you should do well whatever you choose ($9–13). Mon–Fri 11am–7pm, Sat 11am–4pm.

Roomali 97 Lexington Ave, at E 27th St ☎ 212 679 8900; subway #6 to 28th St; map p.114. Quick, inexpensive ($5–6) and tasty Indian *roti* wraps – vegetarian and chicken mainly – with just the right amount of spice. Mon–Sat noon–11pm, Sun 1–11pm.

★ **Shake Shack** Madison Square Park, near E 23rd St and Madison Ave ☎ 212 889 6600; subway N, R to 23rd St; map p.114. Also 154 E 86th St, between Lexington and Third aves (map p.169) and multiple other locations. Danny Meyer's leafy food kiosk in the centre of Madison Square Park has proved wildly popular since opening in 2004 (there are now offshoots on the Upper East and West sides, in the Theater District, Downtown Brooklyn and Citi Field), with assorted office workers, tourists and foodies lining up for the perfectly grilled burgers and frozen-custard shakes. You can also buy beer and wine to sip outside, with nearly every item around $7 or less. Daily 11am–11pm.

MIDTOWN EAST

BAKERIES AND CAFÉS

Buttercup Bake Shop 973 Second Ave, between E 51st and E 52nd sts ☎ 212 350 4144; subway #6 to 51st St; map p.123. This *Magnolia Bakery* offshoot is similarly known for its 1950s-style comfort sweets, especially the moist cupcakes ($2.75 each) and banana pudding. Mon–Wed 8am–9pm, Thurs & Fri 8am–10pm, Sat 10am–10pm, Sun 10am–7pm.

Culture Espresso 72 W 38th St, between Fifth and Sixth aves ☎ 212 302 0200; subway B, D, F, M, #7 to 42nd St-Bryant Park; map p.123. A bit of an oasis among all the tall office buildings (though it is on the ground floor of one): a comfortable spot for excellent espressos, cappuccinos and the like, as well as baked goods and tasty, if small, sandwiches ($8–10). Daily 7am–7pm.

Ess-a-Bagel 831 Third Ave, at E 51st St ☎ 212 980 1010; subway #6 to 51st St; map p.123. Neighbourhood

residents swear by this shop, filled with all the lox, whitefish salad and cream cheese you could possibly want. Go early, as the tables fill up quickly. Mon–Fri 6am–9pm, Sat & Sun 6am–5pm.

Food Hall at the Plaza 1 W 58th St, Concourse Level of *The Plaza* ☎ 212 986 9260; subway N, Q, R to Fifth Ave-59th St; map p.123. If you're looking for wide variety in a sumptuous setting, head to the lower level of this venerable hotel, where outlets of *No. 7 Sub* (see above), *Luke's Lobster* (see p.302) and *FP Patisserie* (see p.287) *by François Payard*, among others, have set up shop; there's also a food hall (daily 11am–10pm) within the food hall, in which celebrity chef Todd English offers separate spots for raw shellfish, wood-fired pizza and grilled meats. Mon–Sat 8am–9.30pm, Sun 11am–6pm.

La Maison du Chocolat 30 Rockefeller Concourse, W 49th St between Fifth and Sixth aves and several other locations ☎ 212 265 9404; subway B, D, F, M to 47–50th St-Rockefeller Center; map p.123. The French vibe here is palpable: the original *Maison* is in Paris. The two hot chocolates on the menu (and two iced in summer; all $8–10) are so thick you'll need a spoon to eat them, but they're not as sweet as you might expect. Other treats are similarly expensive. Mon–Fri 9.30am–7pm, Sat 10am–7pm, Sun noon–6pm.

★ **Lucid Café** 311 Lexington Ave, at 38th St ☎ 212 867 3490; subway #4, #5, #6, #7 to 42nd St-Grand Central; map p.123. You'd do well to grab one of the two window seats and enjoy a strong shot of espresso ($2.75)

FIVE RELIABLE MINI-CHAINS

Forget Starbucks and McD's – New York's booming culinary sector has spawned its own mini-chains, from pizza and hot dogs to cupcakes and coffee. Some favourites:

Amy's Bread See p.282
Jacques Torres See p.289
Shake Shack See above
Num Pang See p.282
Xi'an Famous Foods See p.278

or a flat white ($4) alongside a buttery croissant at this tiny, charming spot. Mon–Fri 7am–6pm, Sat 8am–6pm, Sun 9am–3pm.

SANDWICHES AND SNACKS

Algonquin Hotel Lobby 59 W 44th St, between Fifth and Sixth aves ☎212 840 6800; subway B, D, F, M to 42nd St; map p.123. The archetypal American interpretation of the English drawing room, located in the airy, attractive lobby of the hotel of the same name (see p.268), and reeking of faux nineteenth-century robber-baron splendour. A light menu becomes available late morning, and cocktails go until late at night. Daily 11.30am–12.45am.

Black Shack Burger 320 Lexington Ave, between E 38th and E 39th sts ☎212 213 0042; subway #4, #5, #6, #7 to Grand Central-42nd St S; map p.123. In a brick and wood room below street-level, patties come grilled with a good char ($6.25–7.25). Service is a bit slow, but cheerful staff and the milkshakes ($6) and beers on offer ($6) make up for this. Daily 11am–10pm.

Food Gallery 32 11 W 32nd St, between Fifth and Sixth aves ☎212 967 1678; subway B, D, F, M, N, Q, R to 34th St-Herald Square; map p.123. Bright, sleek Asian food court in the middle of Koreatown, where you can sample ramen, spicy stews, stir fries, *kim-bob* – even rotisserie chicken – at the various counters. Mon–Sat 11am–midnight, Sun 11am–11pm.

Onya 143 E 47th St, between Third and Lexington aves ☎212 715 0460; subway #6 to 51st St; map p.123. Join the procession for lunchtime udon, where you'll start at the tempura station (good for accompaniment or dunked in the broth; choose two for $2) and then order your soup ($7–10) – though rice bowls and a few other options are on the menu. The cheerful back-room is a fine place for slurping them down. Mon–Sat 11am–3pm & 5–9.15pm.

Pampano Taqueria 805 Third Ave, between 49th and 50th sts ☎212 751 5275; subway #6 to 51st St; map p.123. In a below-street-level atrium of an anonymous office building, this small stand (connected to an upscale Mexican restaurant, whose entrance is on 49th) dishes out small but tasty tacos ($3.25) as well as more filling burritos ($8.50) and home-made guacamole ($2.50, with chips). Find a seat, listen to the waterfall on the wall and the lunchtime piano player, while sitting beneath the skylight – you may forget you're in midtown. Mon–Fri 11.30am–3pm.

23

MIDTOWN WEST

BAKERIES AND CAFÉS

Cupcake Café 545 Ninth Ave, between W 40th and W 41st sts ☎212 269 9975, or ☎465 1530; subway A, C, E to 42nd St-Port Authority; map p.141. The coffee and exquisitely decorated cupcakes ($3 each) are impeccable at this shabby-chic café. Mon–Sat 8am–7pm, Sun 9am–7pm.

Little Pie Company 424 W 43rd St, between Ninth and Tenth aves ☎212 736 4780; subway A, C, E to 42nd St-Port Authority; map p.141. True to its name, the *Little Pie Company* serves pies to die for. The peach-raspberry, available only in summer, has earned quite a passionate following, while the apple-walnut and three-berry varieties are always popular. Mon–Fri 8am–8pm, Sat 10am–8pm, Sun 10am–6pm.

Poseidon Bakery 629 Ninth Ave, between W 44th and W 45th sts ☎212 757 6173; subway A, C, E to 42nd St-Port Authority; map p.141. Known best for the phyllo dough hand-rolled on the premises and supplied to many of the city's restaurants, *Poseidon* also sells decadent *baklava*, strudel, cookies, spinach-and-meat pies and assorted other sweet Greek pastries. Tues–Sat 9am–7pm.

SANDWICHES AND SNACKS

★ **Café Edison** 228 W 47th St, between Broadway and Eighth Ave ☎212 840 5000; subway C, E, #1 to 50th St; map p.141. You might get a little attitude with the service at this old-style coffee shop tucked inside the Art Deco *Hotel Edison* (see p.270), but that's just part of the gruff charm. It

manages to be a favourite with theatre-types in any case – and the tasty soups (matzoh ball, mushroom barley, etc) and brisket sandwiches more than make up for it. Mon–Sat 6am–9.30pm, Sun 6am–7.30pm.

★ **Café Forant** 449 W 51st St, between Ninth and Tenth aves ☎212 245 4214; subway C, E to 50th St; map p.141. Cafés don't come friendlier than this quiet neighbourhood spot, hidden down an infrequently trafficked street in Hell's Kitchen. The brunch food is stellar, the sandwiches and salads fresh, the coffee is strong and the price is right; you can eat well for around $15 or so. Cash only. Tues–Sun 10am–4pm.

Gazala's Place 709 Ninth Ave, between W 48th and W 49th sts; another location at 380 Columbus Ave on the Upper West Side ☎212 245 0709; subway C, E to 50th St; map p.141. Supposedly the only Druze (a Middle Eastern sect) restaurant in the States – besides the outpost on the UWS – *Gazala's* serves a full lunch and dinner menu but is best-known for its *bourekas* (giant savoury pastries stuffed with cheese and other items; selection changes; around $9). Daily 11am–11pm.

Maison 1700 Broadway, at W 53rd St ☎212 757 2233; subway B, D, E to Seventh Ave; map p.141. This is a good place to linger over a coffee or a meal – a rarity in midtown. The menu offers a range of burgers, soups, salads, pastas and average French-tinged brasserie standards (stick with the simpler items on the menu), most running at $12–22; there's also a three-course prix-fixe lunch for $22.50. Large outdoor seating area. Daily 24hr.

23

FOOD TRUCKS OF NEW YORK

In the last ten years, the **food truck** has become a key fixture on New York streets, with thousands licensed by the city, ranging from tiny carts to full-size RVs. Many of these have deviated from the standard kebab/falafel/halal-chicken-with-rice format; at their best, they are convenient, relatively cheap and super tasty – no overboiled hot dogs here. Most have websites (check out ⓦnycfoodtrucks.org), though Twitter is the best way to keep track of their varying locations and opening times. Note, too, that the schedule is constantly changing; if you want a go-to spot with lots of variety, hit 47th Street between Park and Madison aves; there's always a line of trucks there.

Bìàn Dâng Midtown, Financial District and Dumbo ⓦ biandangnyc.com or ⓦ twitter.com/biandangnyc. Go for the Taiwanese-style fried chicken over rice with pork sauce ($8) and expect to have leftovers; handmade steamed pork dumplings ($4) are pretty tasty, too. Usually 11am or 11.30am until mid-afternoon.

Big D's Grub Midtown and Chelsea ⓦ bigdsgrub .com. Like a number of other trucks, they've hybridized Korean food with Mexican, offering tacos (3 for $7) and, more unusual, sub sandwiches ($8). But it's the addictive seasoned fries that keep you coming back.

Biryani Cart W 46th St and Sixth Ave ⓦ biryani cart.com. This is actually one of those doling up grilled meat over rice ($6), but it stands out as fresh and full of flavour, plus there are unusual options like shrimp or salmon over rice, and *kati* rolls.

Calexico Cart Prince and Wooster sts, and Worth Square in Madison Square Park ⓦ calexicocart.com. Simple cart managed by three Californian brothers, specializing in delicious *carne asada* tacos ($4) and burritos ($9) – luscious chopped steak stuffed into maize tacos with zesty salsa. There's also their Carroll Gardens restaurant (see p.289); another one has opened in Greenpoint. Mon–Fri 11.30am–4pm.

Cinnamon Snail Flatiron District and Midtown ⓦ cinnamonsnail.com. A much-needed (and delicious) vegan lunch truck, perhaps more expensive than most other carts (sandwiches approaching, if not at, $10), but where else will you find Creole-grilled tofu sandwiches or breakfast cashew-oat waffles?

Nuchas Union Square, Midtown and elsewhere ☏ 917 544 2653, ⓦ nuchas.com. Vendors of the perfect portable street food, the *empanada*, *Nuchas* doles out versions steps above average – choose from tasty fillings like slow-braised short rib or portobello and spinach.

★ **NY Dosas** Washington Square South at Sullivan St, West Village ⓦ twitter.com/nydosas. Thiru Kumar is one of New York's best-loved street vendors, cooking up spicy South Indian vegan food and filling *dosas* at his tiny cart; basic *sadha dosas* are $4, while the tasty *masala dosa* is $5. Mon–Sat 11am–4pm.

★ **Taim Mobile** Flatiron District, Soho and Financial District ⓦ taimmobile.com. A vegetarian's delight, with platters or sandwiches of creamy hummus and crisp falafel (sandwiches around $6, platters $11), accompanied by exotic smoothies. Mon–Fri from 11am, lunch and dinner.

Treats Truck Multiple locations, including Midtown and Upper West Side ⓦ treatstruck.com. If you're in the mood for a delicious fresh cookie ($1–2), brownie ($2.50–3.25) or other sweet to top off your street-food tour, track down the *Treats Truck* – location changes daily.

Wafels and Dinges Various locations, including East Village, Midtown and Central Park ☏ 1 866 429 7329, ⓦ wafelsanddinges.com or ⓦ twitter.com/ waffletruck. Belgian-themed waffle truck, offering crispy waffles (from $5) and *dinges* (toppings) like Belgian chocolate fudge for $1. Open most days from 8am until 10pm (1am Fri & Sat).

★ **Margon** 136 W 46th St, between Sixth and Seventh aves ☏ 212 354 5013; subway B, D, F, M to 47–50th sts-Rockefeller Center, N, Q, R to 49th St; map p.141. This narrow Cuban lunch counter is nearly always packed, but the jostling is worth it; savoury Cuban sandwiches ($9 with rice and beans), garlicky *pernil* (Wed special, $8.75) and, best of all, brightly seasoned octopus salad ($10) top the choices. Mon–Sat 7am–5pm.

Steak 'n Shake Signature 1695 Broadway, at W 52nd St ☏ 212 247 6584; subway B, D, E to Seventh Ave; map p.141. The first New York location of a beloved Midwestern chain (reputedly the late Roger Ebert's favourite), *Steak 'n Shake* does fresh, surprisingly inexpensive burgers that all come with an order of fries (the cheapest, the "original", is around $4); the Frisco melt is also a winner ($6). Daily 10am–midnight.

THE UPPER EAST SIDE

BAKERIES AND CAFÉS

★ **Café Sabarsky** In the Neue Galerie, 1048 Fifth Ave, at E 86th St ☏ 212 288 0665; subway #4, #5, #6 to 86th St; map p.169. Sumptuous decor that harkens back to Old Vienna fills the handsome parlour of the former Vanderbilt mansion. The menu reads like that of an upscale Central

European Kaffeehaus; it includes superb pastries, like Linzertorte and strudels ($9), and small sandwiches ($14–16), many made with cured meats. Mon & Wed 9am–6pm, Thurs–Sun 9am–9pm.

★ **FP Pâtisserie** 1293 Third Ave, at E 74th St ☎ 212 717 5252; subway #6 to 77th St; map p.169. Nice-born François Payard serves up the most beautiful ice-cream display you'll ever see, along with tempting éclairs, *macarons* ($2.50), a range of sandwiches ($14–15) and heavenly *croque monsieur* ($14) – there's a small coffee bar and "salón de thé" at the back. Mon–Sat 7.30am–8pm, Sun 9am–6pm.

Maison Kayser 1294 Third Ave, at E 74th St ☎ 212 744 3100; subway #6 to 77th St; map p.169. Just opposite *FP*, friendly competition is provided by Parisien boulanger Eric Kayser, with a similar range of tempting pastries, but a bigger sit-down menu of French classics, from quiche Lorraine ($13) and *tartines* ($14–16) to fabulous salads ($14–20) and foie gras ($19). Daily 7am–11pm.

Maison Ladurée 864 Madison Ave, between E 70th and E 71th sts ☎ 646 558 3157; subway #6 to 68th St; map p.169. The current fad for *macarons* in New York has been driven by the likes of this posh French bakery, founded in Paris in 1862 (the sweet treats also featured in *Gossip Girl*), with the delicate main event coming in a wide range of flavours ($2.80 or $26/box) – the salted caramel is hard to resist. Expect long lines in the afternoon. Mon–Sat 9am–7pm, Sun 10am–6pm.

Neil's Coffee Shop 961 Lexington Ave at E 70th St ☎ 212 628 7474; subway #6 to 68th St; map p.169. Classic neighbourhood Greek-owned diner, with gruff service, old bar stools and booths, hearty breakfasts (from $6.95), beer ($4.75) and cheap coffee ($1.75, with refills). You probably won't spend much more than $10. Popular with Hunter College staff and students. Mon–Fri 6am–9pm, Sat 7am–9pm, Sun 8am–7pm.

Serendipity 3 225 E 60th St, between Second and Third aves ☎ 212 838 3531; subway N, R, #4, #5, #6 to 59th St; map p.169. Adorned with Tiffany lamps, this long-established café and ice-cream parlour has been a favourite spot for sweet-sixteen parties and first dates since 1954. The "frrrozen" hot chocolate is out of this world ($8.95) and the wealth of ice-cream sundae offerings ($9.50) a real treat. Sun–Thurs 11.30am–midnight, Fri 11.30am–1am, Sat 11.30am–2am.

SANDWICHES AND SNACKS

Alice's Tea Cup 156 E 64th St, at Lexington Ave ☎ 212 486 9200; subway F to 63rd St; map p.169. *Alice's* offers mammoth afternoon teas "all day, every day" (from $22–25). The place also does a brisk business with its menu of crêpes, egg dishes and light and tasty sandwiches ($9–14). Cupcakes are great, too, and there are (naturally) over 95 tea varieties on sale for you to take home. Other branches at 102 W 73rd St and 220 E 81st St. Daily 8am–8pm.

Mitchel London Foods 22A E 65th St, between Fifth and Madison aves ☎ 212 737 2850; subway F to 63rd St; map p.169. The goods from caterer/restaurateur Mr London are justifiably praised. Try the salmon Niçoise salad ($9.75) or turkey and manchego cheese sandwiches ($8.50), with one of their unbelievably rich brownies ($3.75) for dessert. Mon–Fri 8.30am–8pm, Sat 10am–7pm, Sun noon–7pm.

Tal Bagels 333 E 86th St, between First and Second aves ☎ 212 427 6811; subway #4, #5, #6 to 86th St; map p.169. The bagels ($1.10; cream cheese from $2.75) may be a little too chewy, but the spread selection at this family institution is to die for, especially the smoked whitefish ($8.95). Don't let the queues scare you; they move fast. Daily 5.30am–10pm, Sun until 8pm.

THE UPPER WEST SIDE AND MORNINGSIDE HEIGHTS

BAKERIES AND CAFÉS

Bomboloni 187 Columbus Ave, between W 68th and W 69th sts ☎ 212 877 3080; subway #1 to 66th St, B, C to 72nd St; map.183. Light-as-air Italian donuts – well, the fillings perhaps aren't quite as light, be they marshmallow cream, Nutella or blood orange – are $2 a pop and make excellent sweet accompaniments to an afternoon coffee. There are also more substantial panini and salads for those in search of a meal. Mon–Thurs & Sun 7.30–10pm, Fri & Sat 7.30am–midnight.

Bouchon Bakery Ten Columbus Circle, Third Floor, Time Warner Center ☎ 212 823 9366; subway A, B, C, D, #1 to 59th St-Columbus Circle; map p.183. Also One Rockefeller Plaza, 49th St, between Fifth and Sixth aves; map p.123. At this Thomas Keller café, you can get something to go from the counter or sit at a table and stare through the windows onto the corner of Central Park, grazing on a ham-and-cheese

sandwich, croissant or decadent pastry. Mon–Wed & Sun 11.30am–7pm, Thurs–Sat 11.30am–8pm; takeaway hours start earlier.

Café Lalo 201 W 83rd St, between Amsterdam Ave and Broadway ☎ 212 496 6031; subway #1 to 86th St; map p.183. Reminiscent of Paris, down to the cramped tables and inconsistent service. Try the "shirred" eggs (made fluffy with a cappuccino machine) with all sorts of herbs and other add-ins ($7–14), or the wonderful Belgian waffles ($14). Great desserts too. Mon–Thurs 8am–2am, Fri 8am–4am, Sat 9am–4am, Sun 9am–2am.

★ **Hungarian Pastry Shop** 1030 Amsterdam Ave, between W 110th and W 111th sts ☎ 212 866 4230; subway #1 to 110th St; map p.183. This simple, no-frills coffee house is a favourite with Columbia University affiliates. You can sip your espresso and read Proust all day if you like (madeleines, anyone?); the only problem is

23

choosing between the pastries, cookies and cakes, all made on the premises. Mon–Fri 7.30am–11.30pm, Sat 8.30am–11.30pm, Sun 8.30am–10.30pm.

Max Caffé 1262 Amsterdam Ave, between 122nd and 123rd sts ☎212 531 1210; map p.198. Comfy, tin-ceilinged hangout for Columbia and other area students, who come to linger over coffee on the couches or show up for beer and wine at happy hour (Wed & Fri 5–7pm). Daily 8am–12.30am.

SANDWICHES AND SNACKS

★ **Absolute Bagels** 2788 Broadway between W 107th and W 108th sts ☎212 932 2052; subway #1 to 110th St-Cathedral Parkway; map p.183. This tiny Thai-run shop bakes hot, fresh, chewy bagels that some claim are the best in the city. After trying one with cream cheese and lox, you might find it hard to disagree. Daily 6am–9pm.

Baconery 911 Columbus Ave, between 105th and 106th sts ☎917 675 3385; subway #1 to 103rd St; map p.183. Pig lovers (of the meat, more than the animal, that is) rejoice; there's bacon in everything at this small café. Toasted sandwiches ($5.99–9.99) range from the expected (with egg and cheese) to the unusual (with avocado; with *sriracha* hot sauce and cucumber); the chocolate, bacon and peanut butter cookies ($2.99) are sinfully delicious. Daily 8am–8pm.

★ **Barney Greengrass** 541 Amsterdam Ave, between W 86th and W 87th sts ☎212 724 4707; subway #1 to 86th St; map p.183. The "sturgeon king" is an Upper West Side fixture; the deli (and restaurant) have been around seemingly since time began (or at least a hundred years). The smoked-salmon section is a particular treat. Deli Tues–Sun 8am–6pm, restaurant Tues–Fri 8.30am–4pm, Sat & Sun 8.30am–5pm.

Gray's Papaya 2090 Broadway, at W 72nd St ☎212 799 0243; subway #1, #2, #3 to 72nd St; map p.183. This popular hot-dog joint is an NYC institution, famous for its long-running "Recession Special": two dogs and a drink for $4.50. Daily 24hr.

Peacefood Cafe 460 Amsterdam Ave, at 82nd St ☎212 362 2266; subway #1 to 79th St, B, C to 81 St; map p.183. Also 41 E 11th St, map p.88. A friendly stop to pick up some tasty vegan baked goods, or to linger and make a full meal of it: go for an array of roasted veg ($6.95–11.95), fried seitan panini ($12.95) or cheeseless pizza ($12.95), perhaps washed down with a gingerade ($4). Daily 10am–10pm.

Tom's Restaurant 2880 Broadway, at 112th St ☎212 864 6137; subway #1 to 110th St; map p.183. The greasy-spoon diner – celebrated in song by Suzanne Vega and whose exterior doubled for *Monk's* in *Seinfeld* – is no great shakes food-wise, but the prices almost make up for the quality. Often filled with Columbia University students who come for the great breakfast deals (under $6) on weekday mornings. Mon–Thurs & Sun 6am–1.30am, Fri & Sat 24hr.

Zabar's Café 2245 Broadway, at W 80th St ☎212 787 2000; subway #1 to 79th St; map p.183. Adjacent to the famed Upper West Side gourmet shop (see p.385), this small spot is always crowded with locals and tourists. Best for the cheap, freshly prepared bagel-and-lox sandwiches, but everything's tasty: scones, panini, sandwiches, soup, coffee drinks, frozen yogurt and smoothies. Mon–Fri 7am–7pm, Sat 7.30am–7pm, Sun 8am–6pm.

HARLEM AND NORTH MANHATTAN

BAKERIES AND CAFÉS

Café Amrita 301 W 110th St, between Manhattan Ave and Frederick Douglass Blvd ☎212 222 0683; subway B, C to Cathedral Parkway; map p.198. If your ramble through Central Park leaves you at its northwest corner, sink into a leather chair at this friendly half-bar, half-café for an excellent coffee, beer or martini. Unusually, no wi-fi and no computers allowed. Mon–Fri 7am–9pm, Sat & Sun 8am–9pm.

Carrot Top Pastries 3931 Broadway, between W 164th and W 165th sts ☎212 927 4800; subway A, C, #1 to 168th St; map p.198. It's worth making the trip up here for the freshly baked tins of carrot, blueberry and chocolate-chip muffins ($1.65), but the small café also serves cheap breakfasts (from $2.50) and decent sandwiches (from $5.95). Mon–Sat 6am–9pm, Sun 7am–6pm.

East Harlem Café 1651 Lexington Ave, at E 104th St ☎212 996 2080; subway #6 to 103rd St; map p.198. Chilled-out coffee shop epitomizing the area's "SpaHa" pretensions, full of comfy sofas, Latino art and engrossed laptop users enjoying the superb hot drinks ($1.35) and pastries ($1.75). Mon–Fri 7.30am–7pm, Sat & Sun 9am–5pm.

★ **Levain Bakery** 2167 Frederick Douglass Blvd, between W 116th and W 117th sts ☎646 455 0952; subway B, C to 116th St; map p.198. Harlem outpost of the Upper West Side favourite, with their raspberry-filled *bomboloncini*, baguettes and massive, chunky cookies centre stage (try the dark-chocolate peanut butter chip; $4). Mon–Sat 8am–7pm, Sun 9am–7pm.

Make My Cake 121 St Nicholas Ave at W 116th St ☎212 932 0833; subway #2, #3 to 116th St; map p.198. Generously sized chocolate and red velvet cupcakes ($3.50) lead the offerings at this smart bakery. The shop opened in 1996, but its baking secrets date back to 1940s Mississippi. Mon–Thurs 8am–8pm, Fri 8am–9pm, Sat 9am–9pm, Sun 9am–7pm.

SANDWICHES AND SNACKS

Doug E's Chicken & Waffles 2245 Powell Blvd at W 132nd St ☎212 368 4371; subway #2, #3 to 135th St; map p.198. Classic Harlem fast food from seminal rapper Doug E Fresh – basic plates of chicken and waffles are $8, and there's also curry chicken, jerk chicken and rice 'n peas. Tues–Thurs noon–8pm, Fri & Sat noon–4am, Sun noon–8pm.

23

BROOKLYN

FULTON FERRY DISTRICT AND DUMBO

★ **Almondine** 85 Water St, near Main St ☎ 718 797 5026; subway A, C to High St, F to York St; map p.215. Excellent patisserie, run by a former *Le Bernardin* pastry chef with chocolatier Jacques Torres (see below), that churns out all kinds of buttery, flaky treats, as well as sandwiches on crusty baguettes ($7–8), soups and quiches. Mon–Sat 7am–7pm, Sun 10am–6pm.

Brooklyn Ice Cream Factory 1 Water St, at the Fulton Ferry pier ☎ 718 246 3963; subway A, C to High St; map p.215. Also 97 Commercial St, at Manhattan Ave, Greenpoint; map p.236. An old fireboat house contains the perfect reward for the walk across the Brooklyn Bridge: super-rich ice cream ($4 a scoop) with toppings created by the pastry chef at the neighbouring *River Café*. Daily noon–10pm.

Jacques Torres Chocolate 66 Water St, Dumbo ☎ 718 875 1269. Subway A, C to High St or F to York St; map p.215. This French-born chocolatier left Le *Cirque* in 2000 to open his first solo venture; since then, he's expanded to other locations in Soho, Rockefeller Center and elsewhere. Best-known for his super-thick hot chocolate and handmade creations, from chocolate crunch puffs to champagne truffles. Mon–Sat 9am–8pm, Sun 10am–6pm.

BROOKLYN HEIGHTS

★ **Iris Café** 20 Columbia Place, between Joralemon and State sts ☎ 718 722 7395; subway #2, #3, #4, #5 to Borough Hall, R to Court St; map p.215. This wonderful neighbourhood café, a bit off the main beat (unless you're walking down to Brooklyn Bridge Park), brews up powerful caffeinated drinks and fashions tasty baked goods and unusual sandwiches; they've also started full-on dinner service (mains $17–22). Mon & Tues 8am–4pm, Wed–Sun 8am–10pm.

Montague Street Bagels 108 Montague St, at Hicks St ☎ 718 237 2512; subway #2, #3 to Clark St, R to Court St, #2, #3, #4, #5 to Borough Hall; map p.215. Brisk service and fantastic, doughy bagels make this the perfect place to grab a snack before heading down to the Esplanade and parking yourself on a bench. Daily 24hr.

Tazza 311 Henry St, at Atlantic Ave ☎ 718 243 0487; subway #4, #5 to Borough Hall; map p.215. Right on the border with Cobble Hill, this likeable *enoteca* serves Italian wines by the glass, espresso, sweets culled from the city's best bakeries and decent panini – try the fig and ricotta ($4.95). Ample pavement seating in warm weather. Mon–Fri 7am–10pm, Sat & Sun 8am–10pm.

FORT GREENE

67 Burger 67 Lafayette St, at Fulton St ☎ 718 797 7150; subway C, G to Lafayette Ave-Fulton St; map p.222. Also 234 Flatbush Ave, at Bergen St, Park Slope; map p.226. Juicy burgers (unadorned varieties starting at $6.75), full of

flavour – though if the patty's not enough for you, feel free to add *jalapeños*, blue cheese, pesto or any number of other toppings – served in a clean, bright setting, with outdoor seating looking out on a main strip. Mon–Thurs & Sun 11.30am–10pm, Fri & Sat 11.30am–11pm.

Cammareri Bakery & Café 1 S Elliott Place, at Dekalb ☎ 718 852 8582; subway C, G to Lafayette Ave-Fulton St; map p.215. A corner perch looking out on Fort Greene Park seems the perfect setting for enjoying some strong coffee (from the *Gimme! Coffee* folks; p.292) and tasty baked goods, whether black-bottomed cupcakes, ciabatta sandwiches or a crusty, sesame-dotted loaf of bread. If the name sounds familiar, the original *Cammareri's* lent its name to *Moonstruck*. Mon–Fri 7.30am–6pm, Sat & Sun 8.30am–6pm.

Habana Outpost 757 Fulton St, at S Portland Ave ☎ 718 858 9500; subway C, G to Lafayette Ave-Fulton St; map p.215. The seasonal Brooklyn branch of the ever-popular Nolita institution, *Café Habana* wears its green credentials on its sleeve: the place is solar-powered and holds a weekend market on its outdoor dining patio with an emphasis on recycled products. Opt for a burrito ($8.75 –10) or *quesadilla* ($6–8) with a side of sweet plantains ($3.50) and an ear of corn slathered with mayo, cheese and lime ($3). Mid-April–Oct Mon–Fri noon–midnight, Sat & Sun 11am–midnight.

COBBLE HILL AND CARROLL GARDENS

Café Pedlar 210 Court St, between Warren and Wyckoff sts ☎ 718 855 7129; subway F, G to Bergen St; map p.222. Simply but elegantly adorned hangout for excellent coffee and baked goods; hard to get a table or bench spot sometimes, but nearby Cobble Hill Park makes a fine picnic setting. Daily 7am–7pm.

Calexico 122 Union St, between Hicks and Columbia sts, another location in Greenpoint ☎ 718 488 8226; subway F, G to Carroll St; map p.222. A small Mexican joint that started off as a Soho street cart; the *carne asada* is super tasty, whether in a taco or one of the miraculous rolled *quesadillas*. Mon–Sat 11.30am–11pm, Sun 11.30am–10pm.

D'Amico Foods 309 Court St, between Sackett and Degraw sts ☎ 718 875 5403; subway F, G to Carroll St; map p.222. Old-school coffee purveyors (since 1948), with a small seating area in the back to sip espresso and listen to the long-time regulars hold court. Mon–Sat 10am–5pm.

RED HOOK

For all the below, take the F, G to Smith-9th St, then the #B61 bus to Van Brunt St, or the F, G to Carroll St, then walk west to Van Brunt and turn left (south); about 20–25min total.

23

23

★ **Baked** 359 Van Brunt St, at Dikeman St ☎ 718 222 0345; map p.222. Relaxed neighbourhood café that's justly celebrated for its cookies, cakes, muffins, Rice Krispie treats, granola and marshmallows, all made on the premises but found in cafés and shops throughout the Northeast. Mon–Fri 7am–7pm, Sat & Sun 8am–7pm.

Fairway Café 480–500 Van Brunt St, at Reed St ☎ 718 694 6868; map p.222. You'll have to thread your way through the mammoth gourmet supermarket to get here, but it's well worth it for the wallet-friendly sandwiches (notably, a $10 lobster roll), salads and hot main dishes, which you can eat on the back deck overlooking the water. Daily 8am–9pm.

★ **Red Hook Lobster Pound** 284 Van Brunt St, between Visitation Place and Verona St ☎ 718 858 7650; map p.222. The *Pound* does delectable lobster rolls ($16), filled with fresh, plump chunks of lobster meat – the perfect snack on a warm spring or summer day – not to mention lobster mac & cheese ($10) and a number of other treats. They also run a food truck (find on Twitter @lobstertruckny). Hours change seasonally, but generally April–Nov Tues–Thurs & Sun noon–8pm, Fri & Sat noon–10pm; Dec–March Fri & Sat noon–9pm, Sun noon–8pm.

Steve's Authentic Key Lime Pies Pier 40, 185 Van Dyke St, at Ferris St ☎ 718 858 5333, ⊛ twitter.com/keylimepie; map p.222. Tucked away on the Red Hook waterfront, this beloved shop – recently moved to a much bigger location – dishes up some of the tastiest Key Lime pies in the Northeast ($5 for individual tarts). Hours vary, roughly Mon–Fri 9am–5pm, Sat & Sun 10am–6pm.

PARK SLOPE AND PROSPECT HEIGHTS

Bagel Hole 400 Seventh Ave, between 12th and 13th sts ☎ 718 788 4014; subway F, G to Seventh Ave; map p.226. The name works two ways, both to reference the hole in the bagel and that this place is basically the size of a hole in the wall. That doesn't stop them from churning out cheap crisp-chewy bagels as good as any in the city. Mon–Fri 7am–6pm, Sat 7am–5pm, Sun 7am–4pm.

★ **Bark Hot Dogs** 474 Bergen St, between Fifth Ave and Flatbush ☎ 718 789 1939; subway #2, #3 to Bergen St; map p.226. If you want to feel good about your hot-dog consumption, this is the place: an artisanal wiener shack where almost everything is home-made or locally sourced, recyclable and, most important, tasty (dogs are $4.25–7; extra toppings $0.75; sides $4); there are good local draught beers, too ($6). Mon–Thurs noon–11pm, Fri noon–midnight, Sat 11am–midnight, Sun 11am–10pm.

Bierkraft 191 Fifth Ave, between Union St and Berkeley Place ☎ 718 230 7600, ⊛ bierkraft.com; subway R to Union St; p.226. Though the speciality is beer, this is not a bar – just an unparalleled place for craft brews to go, either by the bottle or to fill up your growler

(see p.329). Oh, and the sandwiches (like the pastrami-spiced brisket, $11) happen to be among the best in town. Tuesday tastings (7pm) are a perfect time to show up. Mon–Sat noon–11pm, Sun noon–8pm.

★ **Café Regular** 318 11th St, at Fifth Ave ☎ 718 768 4170; subway F, G, R to Fourth Ave-9th St; map p.226. Excellent coffee and pastries in a tiny, Eurocentric café that feels a little hidden off the main drag. Daily 7am–5pm.

Gorilla Coffee 97 Fifth Ave, at Park Place ☎ 718 230 3244; subway #2, #3 to Bergen St; map p.226. Punk-rock outpost serving some of the best java in the neighbourhood, with strong, fresh drip coffee and expert espresso drinks topped off with perfect *crema*. Mon–Sat 7am–9pm, Sun 8am–9pm.

Joyce Bakeshop 646 Vanderbilt Ave, at Park Place ☎ 718 623 7470; subway B, Q to Seventh Ave or #2, #3 to Grand Army Plaza; map p.226. Friendly spot on Prospect Heights' burgeoning main strip with fresh-baked sweet and savoury scones, muffins, tarts and croissants. Mon–Fri 7.30am–7.30pm, Sat & Sun 9am–6pm.

Tom's 782 Washington Ave, at Sterling Place ☎ 718 636 9738; subway #2, #3 to Grand Army Plaza or Eastern Parkway; map p.226. A Brooklyn institution located a few blocks from the Brooklyn Museum, with great pancakes, lots of typical diner favourites and old-fashioned fountain drinks like lime rickeys and egg creams. Best, though, is an amiable vibe that makes first-timers feel like regulars; expect to wait in line for weekend brunch. Daily 7am–4pm.

MIDWOOD

Di Fara Pizza 1424 Ave J ☎ 718 258 1367; subway Q to Ave J; map p.213. It might be hard to fathom a piece of pizza worth $5 (not including toppings; whole pizzas are a much better deal starting at $25) plus what can be up to an hour's wait, yet neither deters people making the pilgrimage to the consensus best slice in the city. Go early. Wed–Sun noon–4.30pm & 6.30–9pm.

CONEY ISLAND

Nathan's 1310 Surf Ave, at Stillwell Ave ☎ 718 946 2705; subway D, F, N, Q to Coney Island-Stillwell Ave; map p.213. Right there when you get off the subway, this is the home of the "famous Coney Island hot dog". Serving since 1916 (though interrupted for half a year due to Hurricane Sandy damage), *Nathan's* holds a nationally televised annual Hot Dog Eating Contest on July 4. Other food items served up include fresh clams. Daily 8am–2am.

WILLIAMSBURG AND GREENPOINT

★ **Blue Bottle** 160 Berry St, between Fourth and Fifth sts ☎ 718 387 4160, ⊛ bluebottlecoffee.com; subway L to Bedford Ave; map p.236. The original New

23

York outpost (other spots have opened up in Chelsea and Tribeca, among other locales) of a well-known and well-regarded San Francisco roaster. Walk in to see a cross between a café and a lab, where the java used for iced coffee drips in giant bulbous tubes; filters are immaculately lined up to make individual cups of coffee to order; and a working roastery fills the spacious back. Mon–Fri 7am–7pm, Sat & Sun 8am–7pm.

★ **Café Grumpy** 193 Meserole Ave, at Diamond St ☎ 718 349 7623; subway G to Greenpoint Ave; map p.236. Also in Chelsea, Lower East Side and Park Slope. Spacious Greenpoint outpost for the artsy set, with exposed brick walls and lots of light; coffee is treated almost religiously here, each kind is lovingly described and each cup is expertly made to order. There's granola, pastries and pre-made vegetarian sandwiches too. Mon–Fri 7am–7.30pm, Sat & Sun 7.30am–7.30pm.

★ **Egg** 135 North 5th St, between Bedford Ave and Berry St ☎ 718 302 5151; subway L to Bedford Ave; map p.236. Delicious Southern-style breakfasts, including biscuits and gravy (a scone covered in white gravy; $11), though the sandwiches (ham and pimento cheese for $12, duck and duck-liver pâté $14) are good choices as well. The dinner menu (Wed–Sun only) showcases belt-breaking comfort food like fried chicken ($14/$18), andouille sausage and beans ($14) and toasted pound cake topped with lemon custard and vanilla ice cream ($6). Mon–Fri 7am–6pm, Sat & Sun 8am–6pm.

Gimme! Coffee 495 Lorimer St, between Grand and Powers sts ☎ 718 388 7771; subway L to Lorimer St, G to Metropolitan Ave; map p.236. Also 107 Roebling St, at

N 6th St; map p.236. This coffee haven is not your typical lounge-about-all-day Williamsburg café, but a bright, narrow spot to pick up a shot of espresso or cup of the house roast and kick-start your next few hours. A refreshing antidote. Daily 7am–8pm.

★ **Peter Pan Donut & Pastry Shop** 727 Manhattan Ave, between Norman and Meserole aves ☎ 718 389 3676; subway G to Nassau Avemap p.236. Totally old-school shop, with swivel stools at a curving, formica counter, where you can enjoy airy, delectable crullers, chocolate-cake donuts, or around twenty other varieties. Sit with a coffee and think about past times. Mon–Fri 4.30am–8pm, Sat & Sun 4.30am–7pm (donuts at 8am).

Saltie 378 Metropolitan Ave, near Havemeyer St ☎ 212 387 4777; subway L to Metropolitan Ave, G to Broadway; map p.236. Tiny shop with a short menu of unusual – and unusually delicious – sandwiches; the Scuttlebutt (with hard-boiled egg, feta, black olives and capers, among other ingredients) is likely the richest vegetarian sandwich you'll ever encounter. Most dishes $9–10. Daily 10am–6pm.

Verb Café 218 Bedford Ave, at 5th St ☎ 718 599 0977; subway L to Bedford Ave; map p.236. Wedged between a bookstore and a record shop, *Verb* was one of the first bohemian spots on Bedford, and still anchors the scene with an appropriately lackadaisical vibe, strong coffee, pastries, peanut-butter-and-banana sandwiches and a reliably kickin' alt-rock soundtrack. Mon–Thurs 7am–9pm, Fri 7am–11.30pm, Sat 7.30am–11.30pm, Sun 7.30am–7pm.

QUEENS

ASTORIA AND LONG ISLAND CITY

Arepas Cafe 33-07 36th Ave, at 33rd St, Astoria ☎ 718 937 3835; subway N, Q to 36th Ave; map p.244. A casual, friendly spot for *arepas* – a kind of thick corn cake stuffed like a pitta, with everything from shredded beef with plaintain and cheese to saucy shrimp. Mon–Thurs & Sun 11am–10pm, Fri & Sat 11am–midnight.

Djerdan 34-04 31st Ave, at 34th St, Astoria ☎ 718 721 2694; subway N, Q to Broadway or 30th Ave; map p.244. Cheap and filling *burek* – savoury meat, spinach or cheese pies, which go for $4.75 a slice – is the speciality of this simple Balkan eatery, and a tasty alternative to pizza. Try the "special" version, drizzled with garlicky yogurt. Daily 8am–11pm.

★ **M. Wells Dinette** 22-25 Jackson Ave, between 46th Rd and 46th Ave, in MoMA PS1, Long Island City ☎ 718 786 1800; subway G, #7 to Court Square; E, M to Court Square-Ely; map p.242. Cheekily modelled on a classroom (MoMA PS1's building used to be a school), *M. Wells Dinette* sets itself apart from every school-lunch cafeteria and museum café you may have once known. The

menu changes, but expect dishes like foie gras and oats, braised tongue with tarragon and other daring, cholesterol-rich exercises. Go with a friend or two, order enough to share and walk it off in the neighbourhood afterwards. Mon & Thurs–Sun noon to 6pm.

Omonia Café 32-20 Broadway, at 33rd St, Astoria ☎ 718 274 6650; subway N, Q to Broadway; map p.244. Broadway's liveliest café is still a stronghold for Greek men poring over Hellenic newspapers during the day, but after dinner the international crowd is younger and more upbeat. Make sure to order a thick wedge of flaky, buttery, sticky-sweet *baklava*, the best of the desserts here. Daily 7am–3am.

Sweetleaf 10-93 Jackson Ave, at 49th Ave and 11th St, Long Island City ☎ 917 832 6726; subway #7 to Vernon Blvd-Jackson Ave; map p.242. With its original pressed-tin details, home-made pastries and caffeinated offerings from cult coffee-roasters, this is a great neighbourhood pit-stop – or a prime place to while away a few afternoon hours. Mon–Fri 7am–7pm, Sat 8am–7pm, Sun 9am–6pm.

JACKSON HEIGHTS AND CORONA

Benfaremo – The Lemon Ice King of Corona 52-02 108th St, Corona ☎718 699 5133; subway #7 to 111th St – take a left at 108th St, then walk ten blocks; map p.240. Renowned Italian ice-cream purveyor that feels very old school – and has, in fact, been around for seventy years. Lemon is the classic flavour, but there's mango, coconut, even licorice and peanut butter ($1.50 for small); toffee apples are on sale too. Daily 10am–11pm or midnight, depending on crowds and weather.

★ **Empanadas Café** 56-27 Van Doren St, at 108th St, Corona ☎718 592 7288; subway #7 to 111th St – take a left at 108th St, then walk fifteen blocks; map p.240. There's no better place in the city to get a Latin American meat pie than this celebrated place; they're all tasty, especially the beef and cheese, and there's a sweet one that comes with Nutella and sliced bananas. Nothing costs more than $2. Daily 7am–10pm.

Shaheen Sweets 72-09 Broadway, Jackson Heights ☎1 800 648 4233; subway E, F, M, R, #7 to Roosevelt Ave-74th St – walk northwest along Broadway; map p.240. Stashed inside *Dera Restaurant* is this tidy sweets counter offering treats from the Indian subcontinent like *gulabjam*, sweet dough balls soaked in syrup, and *kheer*, a type of rice pudding. Daily 9am–7pm.

★ **Tortilleria Nixtamal** 104–05 47th Ave, between 104th and 105th sts, Corona ☎718 699 2434; subway #7 to 103rd St-Corona, from where it's a six-block walk; map p.240. Impeccable tacos – try *carnitas* ($2.50), *al pastor* and *pescado* (each $3) at the least – as well as platters, tasty *pozole* soup ($6.50) and *tamales* ($3). You can also buy products from the shopfront part of the restaurant (earlier hours than what are listed here). May–mid-Sept Mon–Wed 11am–6pm, Thurs–Sat 11am–10pm; mid-Sept–April Mon–Thurs 11am–6pm, Fri & Sat 11am–9pm.

FLUSHING

Tai Pan Bakery 37-25 Main St, between 37th and 38th sts ☎718 461 8668 or ☎1 888 1111; subway #7 to Main St-Flushing; walk two blocks north on Main St; map p.240. Snag a tray and a pair of tongs and get to work assembling your own Chinese carb feast from among the vast assortment of sweet (pineapple) and savoury (roasted pork) buns, sugary donuts and custard tarts in this chaotic and popular spot. There are a few hard-won tables. Daily 7am–8pm.

THE ROCKAWAYS

Rockaway Taco 95-19 Rockaway Beach Blvd ☎347 213 7466; map p.240. This little shack was a food trailblazer in the area a few years back; it's become a popular, reliable stop for good-weather food like fish or *chorizo* tacos ($3) and sweet fruit juices. Mon–Wed 11am–8pm, Thurs–Sun 9am–8pm.

THE BRONX

The Feeding Tree 892 Gerard Ave, at 161st St ☎718 293 5025; subway B, D, #4 to 161st St-Yankee Stadium; map p.252. Spicy jerk shrimp and chicken, curry goat stew and other Jamaican specialities come with rice and beans, mixed vegetables and sweet plantains at this friendly, no-frills fixture near Yankee Stadium (lunch specials start at $4.99, most dishes $6.50–13). Mon–Sat 7am–10pm, Sun noon–8pm.

Mike's Deli 2344 Arthur Ave, between 186th St and Crescent Ave ☎718 295 5033; subway B, D to Fordham Rd; map p.252. Tucked in the back of the Arthur Avenue Retail Market, there's usually a queue of folks waiting for overstuffed Italian sandwiches like eggplant parm or *porchetta* (for a twist try the "Paula Deen", with prosciutto, spicy *sopressata*, radicchio, fresh mozzarella, sun-dried tomatoes and truffle butter; $9/$12 on roll/hero). Mon–Sat 6am–6pm.

STATEN ISLAND

Everything Goes Book Café 208 Bay St ☎718 273 3675; SIR to Tompkinsville; map p.261. Alternative café and bookshop, a short walk from the ferry along Bay Street (with internet at 10 cents per minute and free wi-fi). Serves hummus plates ($3.50) and has a huge selection of teas (from $1.50). Tues–Thurs 10.30am–6.30pm, Fri & Sat 10.30am–10pm, Sun noon–5pm.

John's Famous Deli 15 Innis St and Nicholas Ave, Port Richmond ☎718 815 9100; take #S46 bus; map p.261. Justly lauded as producing the best hot roast-beef sandwiches in the state ($7.75), dripping with onions, mozzarella and gravy. Mon–Sat 6am–6pm.

★ **Ralph's Famous Italian Ices** 501 Port Richmond Ave, at Catherine St ☎718 273 3675; take #S44 bus; map p.261. In business since 1928, this beloved takeaway place has spawned numerous franchises. Its unusual and wide selection of "water ices", a sweetened frozen dessert made with fruit or other flavourings (such as honeydew, root beer and blueberry; from $1.75), similar to sorbet (not flavoured ice), have won many a heart and taste bud. Tends to open during the summer months only – call ahead.

23

LOMBARDI'S PIZZA

Restaurants

A large part of visiting New York City is experiencing not just the array of food but also the culture of dining. As a port city, New York has long received the best foodstuffs from around the globe and, as a major immigration gateway, it continues to attract chefs who know how to cook all the world's cuisines properly, even exceptionally, as well as populations who know the real thing. Then there are the "foodies", locals who make it their business to seek out the best, most unique and newest dining establishments in the city, and aren't shy about sharing the fruits of their labours. This chapter includes restaurants that offer everything from fried chicken to foie gras (and sometimes both), though bear in mind that New York's culinary scene is extremely dynamic – even the most food-obsessed locals have a hard time keeping up.

Restaurants are always opening and closing, trends change quickly and the establishment *du jour* can change in the blink of an eye; gastronomes and those on the prowl for something new turn to magazines like *Time Out New York* or *New York*, or The *New York Times*' Wednesday "Dining Out" section for reviews on the latest hotspots. More serious foodies look to sites like ⓦchowhound.com, ⓦeater.com, ⓦseriouseats.com, ⓦgrubstreet.com and *Village Voice*'s "Fork in the Road" blog (ⓦblogs .villagevoice.com/forkintheroad), or localized neighbourhood blogs for opinions and leads on sizzling new chefs and gourmet hotspots. For visitors, the most important aspect of exploring the city's diverse culinary landscape, though, is having a sense of adventure – eating is one of the great joys of being in New York, and it would be a shame to waste time on the familiar.

THE FINANCIAL DISTRICT

Although the neighbourhood is slowly becoming more residential, eating options in the Financial District remain geared to the great daily tide of commuters coming in and out of the city, a strange mix of takeaway feeding troughs, kebab stalls and overpriced power-lunch spots. New Yorkers tend to deem this part of town a culinary wasteland; we've included places that prove the exception to that rule. The best areas are Stone Street, Front Street and the newer places around Battery Park City; for cheap eats consider the cluster of halal kebab vans in Zuccotti Park. Note also that FiDi was the Manhattan neighbourhood most affected by Hurricane Sandy, with many restaurants remaining closed well into 2013 – some may never reopen.

AMERICAN AND CONTINENTAL

Blue Smoke 255 Vesey St, between West St and North End Ave ☎212 889 2005, ⓦbluesmoke.com/blue; subway #2, #3 to Wall St, J, Z to Broad St; map p.43. Authentic Southern barbecue courtesy of pitmaster Kenny Callaghan and the Danny Meyer empire, with perfectly smoked black pepper sausage ($10.95) and classics such as North Carolina pulled pork, smoked over hickory and apple wood ($18.95). Sun–Thurs 11.30am–10pm, Fri & Sat 11.30am–11pm.

★ **Bridge Café** 279 Water St, at Dover St ☎212 227 3344, ⓦbridgecafenyc.com; subway #4, #5, #6 to Brooklyn Bridge; map p.43. You wouldn't guess from this café-restaurant's up-to-the-minute interior that it is the city's oldest surviving tavern, opening in 1847 (the building, which is even older, was severely damaged by Hurricane Sandy). The crab cakes are excellent, as is the list of microbrew beers. Main dishes $23–34. Sun & Mon 11.45am–10pm, Tues–Thurs 11.45am–11pm, Fri 11.45am–midnight, Sat 5pm–midnight.

Delmonico's 56 Beaver St, at William St ☎212 509 1144,

24

WORLD CUISINES AND EATING SCENES

There's barely a country in the world whose gastronomy isn't ably represented somewhere in the city (especially in the outer boroughs), and you should try to experiment as much as possible – soul food in Harlem, Dominican in Washington Heights, Greek in Astoria and scores more.

Chinese In New York, it's almost as ubiquitous as American cooking – everything from familiar Cantonese to seafood-heavy Fujian cuisine to the chilli-spiked flavours of the Sichuan style. Don't just confine yourself to Manhattan's Chinatown; check out Main Street in Flushing, Queens, and Sunset Park, in Brooklyn.

Contemporary Asian Whether it's Nobu Matsuhisa's *Nobu* (see p.297), David Chang's *Momofuku* mini-empire (see p.303) or Zak Pelaccio's Malaysian-style joints, Asian food in the city goes far beyond standards like sushi and *kimchee*. The villages have plenty of fusion spots; find traditional Korean in Manhattan's Koreatown or Flushing, Queens; Malaysian in Chinatown; and Japanese pretty much everywhere, but especially around East Ninth Street.

Farm to table The farm-to-table movement – an emphasis on fresh ingredients, local food sourcing and sustainability – was pioneered by restaurants like *Blue Hill* (see p.305), in the West Village. These days, Williamsburg and South Brooklyn carry the torch as much as anywhere.

Italian Thin-crust pizza and red-sauce pasta joints abound, so do upscale places serving *crudo*, head cheese and *porchetta*. For old-school spots, hit Belmont in the Bronx; otherwise, the East and West villages, and Flatiron District are probably your best bets.

Jewish/Eastern European Jewish food is still largely associated with the Lower East Side, home to good delis and appetizing stores and a few traditional restaurants; it holds much in common with the filling fare of Russian and Polish food, found mainly in the East Village and Brooklyn's Greenpoint and Brighton Beach.

TOP 5 QUINTESSENTIAL NEW YORK

Amy Ruth's Harlem. See p.319
Katz's Deli Lower East Side. See p.302
Lombardi's Little Italy. See p.300
Oyster Bar Midtown East. See p.310
Peter Luger Steak House Williamsburg, Brooklyn. See p.325

24

ⓦdelmonicosrestaurantgroup.com; subway #2, #3 to Wall St; map p.44. Patrons tend to come to this 1837 landmark steakhouse for its historic charms, murals and classic dishes: the Delmonico Steak (boneless ribeye; $46), Lobster Newburg (created in 1876; $49) and Baked Alaska (created in 1867; $12). Cheaper fare is available in the bar. Mon–Fri 11.30am–10pm, Sat 5–10pm.

Harry's Café & Steak 1 Hanover Square, at Pearl St ☎212 785 9200, ⓦharrysnyc.com; subway #2, #3 to Wall St; map p.44. Housed in the basement of historic India House since 1972, and traditionally the haunt of Wall Street deal-makers. Order pastas (from $19.50), sandwiches ($13.50–26), martinis ($14) or the lauded porterhouse steaks ($46.50) while soaking up the "Gilded Age" atmosphere, immortalized in novels such as Tom Wolfe's *Bonfire of the Vanities* and Brett Easton Ellis's *American Psycho*. Mains $13–32. Mon–Fri 11.30am–midnight, Sat 11am–midnight (bar till 2am).

The Paris Café 119 South St ☎212 240 9797, ⓦtheparistavern.com; subway A, C, J, Z, #2, #3, #4, #5 to Fulton St; map p.44. Established in 1873, this old-fashioned restaurant (more Irish pub than French bistro) has played host to a panoply of luminaries, but was completely renovated after Hurricane Sandy shut it down for almost a year. The decent draught Guinness, pub-food menu and sports on TV still pull in a lively crowd; try the shepherd's pie or fish and chips (mains $12–17). Daily 11.30am–4am.

Southwest NY 301 South End Ave, at Albany St ☎212 945 0528, ⓦsouthwestny.com; subway R, #1 to Rector St; map p.44. This purveyor of contemporary American Southwest cuisine makes a pleasant change in this part of town, with a bright, cosy interior and tempting menu of

tacos ($14), burgers from $11 and mains such as *habanero* chicken sausage and cedar-planked salmon ($16–26). Mon–Fri 11.30am–11pm, Sat & Sun 10am–11pm.

FRENCH

Brasserie Les Halles 15 John St, between Broadway and Nassau St ☎212 285 8585, ⓦleshalles.net/brasserie; subway A, C, J, M, Z, #2, #3, #4, #5 to Fulton St; map p.44. One of two *Les Halles* in New York (the other in the Flatiron District), this French bistro serves "French Beef, American Style". The Rive Gauche fantasy of celebrity chef Anthony Bourdain, the meat-heavy menu also includes dishes like escargots in garlic butter and duck confit shepherd's pie. Most dinner dishes range $19–23; the steak frites ($21) is a great deal. Daily 7am–midnight.

ITALIAN

Acqua at Peck Slip 21 Peck Slip, at Water St ☎212 349 4433, ⓦacquarestaurantnyc.com; subway A, C, J, Z, #2, #3, #4, #5 to Fulton St; map p.44. Most authentic Italian food downtown, served in a bright, exposed-brick dining room; home-made, local and Italian ingredients make for excellent pastas ($14–20) and pizzas ($14–18). Close to South Street Seaport, but not touristy. Daily noon–midnight.

Adrienne's Pizzabar 54 Stone St ☎212 248 3838, ⓦadriennespizzabar.com; subway #2, #3 to Wall St; map p.44. One of the better restaurants downtown, with outdoor seating in summer. The food is fantastic; "nonna-style" square pizzas ($18.50) come in innovative combinations, but the crumbled sausage topping is especially tasty, and all the cheeses are high quality (regular pizza from $12). Mon–Sat 11.30am–midnight, Sun 11.30am–10pm.

SCANDINAVIAN

Smorgas Chef Downtown 53 Stone St ☎212 422 3500, ⓦsmorgas.com; subway #2, #3 to Wall St; map p.44. Established by Norwegian master chef Morten Sohlberg, this smart restaurant dishes out traditional dishes such as Swedish meatballs with lingonberry preserve and Icelandic cod (mains $19–24). The outdoor tables (summer only) and old-world feel enhance the European ambience. Mon–Sat 11am–11pm, Sun 11am–10pm.

TRIBECA

AMERICAN AND CONTINENTAL

Bubby's 120 Hudson St, between Franklin and N Moore sts ☎212 219 0666, ⓦbubbys.com; subway #1 to Franklin St; map p.64. A relaxed place serving American comfort food, like matzoh-ball soup ($10) and meatloaf with gravy and mash ($18). It's the pies, though, that really pull in the crowds – try a slice of the Key Lime ($8). The weekend brunch menu is very popular (9am–4pm). Open

24hr (closed Mon midnight–Tues 7am).

City Hall 131 Duane St, between Church St and W Broadway ☎212 227 7777, ⓦcityhallnewyork.com; subway A, C, #1, #2, #3 to Chambers St; map p.64. With a nod towards old-time New York City, *City Hall* is all class, serving amazing steaks and always-fresh oysters. Mains average $24–39 for dinner. Mon–Thurs noon–10pm, Fri noon–11pm, Sat 10am–3pm & 5–11pm.

TOP 5 BURGERS

Corner Bistro West Village. See p.305
Diner Williamsburg, Brooklyn. See p.324
Minetta Tavern West Village. See p.305
Shake Shack Flatiron District. See p.284
Txikito Chelsea. See p.308

Harrison 355 Greenwich St, at Harrison St ☎212 274 9310, ⓦtheharrison.com/harrison.php; subway #1 to Franklin St; map p.64. The posh Tribeca version of an upstate country inn, with a smart cherry-wood dining room and a contemporary American menu that includes potato-wrapped trout, and roasted quail; don't skip the crispy Brussels sprouts ($8). The desserts are also a must-try, such as the ice cream brownie sandwich ($10). Most dinner dishes range $21–28. Mon–Thurs 5.30–10.30pm, Fri & Sat 5.30–11pm, Sun 5–10pm.

Tribeca Grill 375 Greenwich St, at Franklin St ☎212 941 3900, ⓦmyriadrestaurantgroup.com; subway #1 to Franklin St; map p.64. The *Grill* is part-owned by Robert De Niro, but it's really the food – fine American cooking with Asian and Italian accents – that takes centre stage. The setting is nice, too: an airy, brick-walled eating area in a 1905 warehouse, around a central *Tiffany* bar. Main dishes range $22 to $39 (for the steak). Mon–Thurs 11.30am–10.30pm, Fri 11.30am–11.30pm, Sat 5.30–11.30pm, Sun 11.30am–3.30pm & 5.30–10pm.

AUSTRIAN/GERMAN

Blaue Gans 139 Duane St, between Church St and W Broadway ☎212 571 8880, ⓦkg-ny.com/blaue-gans; subway A, C, #1, #2, #3 to Chambers St; map p.64. Poster-filled walls and a long bar made of zinc add personality to this bright Austro-German restaurant, with tasty schnitzels, goulash and fresh fish (main dishes $15–20) the highlights of Chef Kurt Gutenbrunner's menu. The beer selection includes some unusual – and tasty – German draughts. Daily 11am–midnight (bar open until 2am).

FRENCH AND BELGIAN

Bouley 163 Duane St, at Hudson St ☎212 964 2525, ⓦdavidbouley.com; subway #1, #2, #3 to Chambers St; map p.64. Contemporary French food made from the freshest ingredients by celebrated chef David Bouley. Popular with celebs, the dinner prices are fairly steep (main

dishes $46–53); soften the blow by opting for one of the prix-fixe lunch options (from $55). Mon–Sat 11.30am–3pm & 5–11.30pm.

★ **Corton** 239 West Broadway, between Walker and White sts ☎212 219 2777, ⓦcortonnyc.com; subway #1 to Franklin St; map p.64. Mesmerizing modern French cuisine prepared by Paul Liebrandt, one of America's up-and-coming chefs. He serves a mind-bending tasting menu ($155), featuring delicacies such as foie gras with apple, scallop and truffles, and wild duckling in honey and turnip gelée. Tues–Sat 5.30–10pm.

Petite Abeille 134 W Broadway, between Duane and Thomas sts ☎212 791 1360, ⓦpetiteabeille.com; subway #1, #2, #3 to Chambers St; map p.64. Tintin comic books cover the walls at this nice little Belgian chain restaurant. It's notable for its 2lb pots of PEI mussels ($21.75), *pommes frites* ($5) and Belgian beer ($7); on Wed the mussels are all-you-can-eat ($27, plus one beer). Sun & Mon 9am–10pm, Tues–Fri 9am–11pm, Sat 8am–11pm.

ITALIAN

★ **Locanda Verde** 377 Greenwich St, at N Moore St ☎212 925 3797, ⓦlocandaverdenyc.com; subway #1 to Franklin St; map p.64. This casual Italian *taverna* is a showcase for star chef Andrew Carmellini's exceptional creations; try the *porchetta* sandwich ($17), spiced glazed duck ($29) or his fabulous pastas ($17–20). Mon–Fri 7–11am, 11.30am–3pm & 5.30–11pm, Sat & Sun 8am–3pm & 5.30–11pm.

JAPANESE

Nobu 105 Hudson St, at Franklin St ☎212 219 0500, ⓦnoburestaurants.com; subway #1 to Franklin St; map p.64. Nobu Matsuhisa's lavish woodland decor complements his superlative Japanese cuisine. Try the black cod with miso ($32) and chilled sake served in a hollow bamboo trunk from $55 (most dishes range $17–$32). Reservations are hard to get; if you can't get in, try the adjacent *Next Door Nobu*. Mon–Fri 11.45am–2.15pm & 5.45–10.15pm, Sat & Sun 5.45–10.15pm.

SOUTH ASIAN

Pakistan Tea House 176 Church St, at Reade St ☎212 240 9800; subway A, C to Chambers St; map p.64. Great, cheap Pakistani tandooris, baltis and curries. The staff will also create made-to-order flatbreads. Meat curries $6.99–7.99, *daal* from $5.99. Daily 10am–4am.

SOHO

AMERICAN AND CONTINENTAL

Aquagrill 210 Spring St, at Sixth Ave ☎212 274 0505, ⓦaquagrill.com; subway C, E to Spring St; map p.64. The expensive seafood at this cosy Soho spot is incredibly fresh. Russian Osetra caviar chimes in at $155 per ounce, or try the

grilled yellowfin tuna for a comparative bargain $28. The excellent raw bar and Sunday brunch dishes are cheaper ($16.50–$25). Mon–Thurs noon–3pm & 6–11pm, Fri noon–3pm & 6pm–midnight, Sat noon–4pm & 6pm–midnight, Sun noon–4pm & 6–10.30pm.

24

Cupping Room Café 359 W Broadway, between Broome and Grand sts ☎212 925 2898, ⓦ cuppingroomcafe .com; subway A, C, E to Canal St; map p.64. Snuggle in at this affordable American bistro for comfort food, but avoid visiting on weekends – the brunch queue can stretch around the block. Good bets are the vast choice of salads (from $14.95) or the juicy half-pound ground sirloin burger ($13.95). Live music on Wed–Sat nights. Mon–Thurs 7.30am–midnight, Fri 7.30am–2am, Sat 8am–2am, Sun 8am–midnight.

★ **The Dutch** 131 Sullivan St, at Prince St ☎212 677 6200, ⓦ thedutchnyc.com; subway C, E to Spring St; map p.64. Andrew Carmellini has shaken up the Soho scene with his latest American bistro, with locally sourced produce and seasonal salads accompanying steaks, shellfish, hefty sandwiches, flavourful chilli, fried chicken and freshly baked pies (dinner mains $19–34). Mon–Wed 11.30am–3pm & 5.30–11pm, Thurs & Fri 11.30am–3pm & 5.30pm–1am, Sat 10am–3pm & 5.30pm–1am, Sun 10am–3pm & 5.30–11pm.

Lure Fishbar 142 Mercer St at Prince St ☎212 431 7676, ⓦ lurefishbar.tumblr.com; subway N, R to Prince St; map p.64. Stylish basement seafood restaurant and sushi bar, with everything from steamed red snapper ($29) and crispy calamari ($14), to lobster rolls ($29) and clam chowder ($13) on the menu. Mon–Thurs 11.30am–11pm, Fri & Sat 11.30am–midnight, Sun 11.30am–10pm.

Mercer Kitchen Mercer Hotel, 99 Prince St, at Mercer St ☎212 966 5454, ⓦ themercerkitchen.com; subway N, R to Prince St; map p.64. This café and dimly lit cellar restaurant entices hotel guests and scenesters alike with its casual modern American creations and wood-burning oven; think raw tuna and wasabi pizza, fine steaks, burgers and slow-cooked salmon. With most dishes ranging from $21 to $24, this is one of the cheaper members of the Jean-Georges stable, and a good choice for Sunday brunch. Mon–Thurs 7am–midnight, Fri & Sat 7am–1am, Sun 7am–11pm.

Spring Street Natural Restaurant 62 Spring St, at Lafayette St ☎212 966 0290, ⓦ springstreetnatural .com; subway #6 to Spring St; map p.64. Though not wholly vegetarian, this restaurant serves up freshly prepared health-food in a large, airy space. Try the "Mayan" eggs ($11), served with tortillas, black beans and guacamole, for brunch. Mains $17–24. Mon–Thurs 9am–11.30pm, Fri 9am–12.30am, Sat 10.30am–12.30am, Sun 10.30am–11.30pm.

ASIAN

★ **Blue Ribbon Sushi** 119 Sullivan St, between Prince and Spring sts ☎212 343 0404, ⓦ blueribbonrestaurants .com; subway C, E to Spring St; map p.64. Widely considered one of the best sushi restaurants in New York, with fish flown in daily from Japan and sushi master Toshi

Ueki at the helm. Sip cold sake and feast on the outstanding oysters at the raw bar. Sushi platters from $25.50. Daily noon–2am.

Kelley and Ping 127 Greene St, between Prince and Houston sts ☎212 228 1212, ⓦ kelleyandping.com; subway N, R to Prince St; map p.64. Sleek pan-Asian tearoom and restaurant that serves tasty bowls of Thai and Malaysian curry ($13–14) and other dishes at moderate prices ($14–18). Dark wood cases filled with Thai herbs and cooking ingredients add to the informal, streetmarket-esque ambience. Daily 11.30am–5pm & 5.30–11pm.

Omen 113 Thompson St, between Prince and Spring sts ☎212 925 8923; subway C, E to Spring St; map p.64. Traditional Kyoto eatery with beautiful crockery and menus made from rice paper. Though named for its famous udon noodle soup ($20), it also serves some of the best sushi in the area (mixed sashimi platter; $36.50), with a rotating seasonal menu and an extensive sake list. Daily 6pm–midnight.

FRENCH

Balthazar 80 Spring St, between Crosby St and Broadway ☎212 965 1414, ⓦ balthazarny.com; subway #6 to Spring St; map p.64. Keith McNally's bistro is still one of the hottest restaurants in town. The tastefully ornate Parisian decor keeps your eyes busy until the food arrives; then all you can do is savour the fresh oysters ($21 half-dozen), duck shepherd's pie ($26) and *moules frites* ($22), as well as exquisite pastries. Main dishes $19–36. Mon–Thurs 7.30am–midnight, Fri 7.30am–1am, Sat 8am–1am, Sun 8am–midnight.

★ **L'Ecole** 462 Broadway, at Grand St ☎212 219 3300, ⓦ lecolenyc.com; subway N, Q, R to Canal St; map p.64. Students of the French Culinary Institute serve up affordable French delights – even the bread basket deserves reverence. Book in advance. The prix-fixe dinner menu is $39.50 per person for three courses (Mon–Sat 5.30–7pm & 8–9.45pm); it's $30 for lunch (three courses, Mon–Fri 12.30–2pm); and $24 for weekend brunch (Sat noon–3pm & Sun 11.30am–4pm).

Raoul's 180 Prince St, between Sullivan and Thompson sts ☎212 966 3518, ⓦ raouls.com; subway C, E to Spring St; map p.64. Sexy French bistro seemingly lifted from Paris (the founders actually arrived from Alsace in the 1970s). The food, especially the steak *au poivre* with frites ($39), is wonderful, if pricey – the service is great too. Reservations recommended. Daily 5pm–1am.

MEXICAN

Dos Caminos 475 W Broadway, at Houston St ☎212 277 4300, ⓦ doscaminos.com; subway #1 to Houston St; map p.64. Real-deal Tex-Mex served with style – try the table-side guacamole ($14) or red snapper *ceviche* ($11). Brunch should set you back

$13–18 per dish, while dinner dishes range between $15.50 and $26. Mon–Wed 11.30am–10pm, Thurs 11.30am–10.30pm, Fri 11.30am–11.30pm, Sat 11am–11.30pm, Sun 11am–10pm.

CHINATOWN

If you're after authentic (not to mention cheap) Chinese or Southeast Asian food, head for Chinatown, where the chaotic streets are lined with dumpling houses and roast-duck window displays. Weekends are especially busy, as New Yorkers come to this neighbourhood for dim sum. Walk down Eldridge Street and you'll see authentic Fujianese fish-ball shops, while Vietnamese food dominates Baxter Street.

CHINESE

Famous Sichuan 10 Pell St ☎212 233 3888, ⓦfamoussichuannewyork.com; subway J, N, Q, R, Z and #6 to Canal St; map p.71. Specializing in spicy Sichuan food, with all the classics; fiery bean curd Sichuan style (*mapo doufu*), sautéed string beans, hotpot, fragrant tea-smoked duck and *dan dan* noodles. Most dishes range $11–18. Lunch special sets are just $5.95. Daily 11am–1pm.

Great N.Y. Noodletown 28 Bowery, at Bayard St ☎212 349 0923, ⓦgreatnynoodletown.com; subway J, N, Q, R, Z and #6 to Canal St; map p.71. *Noodletown* is best during soft-shell crab season (May–Aug), when the crustaceans are crispy, salty and delicious (priced seasonally). The Cantonese-style roast meats, *lo mein* (noodles; $5.25) and soups ($4.95) are good year-round (try the baby pig on rice for $8.50). Daily 9am–3.30am.

Joe's Shanghai 9 Pell St, between Bowery and Mott St ☎212 233 8888, ⓦjoeshanghairestaurants.com; subway J, N, Q, R, Z and #6 to Canal St; map p.71. Probably Chinatown's most famous restaurant, this is really a temple to American-Chinese cuisine (think General Tso's chicken) rather than explicitly Shanghai food, though the classic "soup dumplings" (*xiao long bao*) for $4.95 and seafood dishes ($13.95–25.95) are pretty authentic. Daily 11am–11pm.

Nom Wah Tea Parlor 13 Doyers St ☎212 962 6047, ⓦnomwah.com; subway J, N, Q, R, Z and #6 to Canal St; map p.71. Dating back to 1920 but spruced up in 2010, this elegant and old-fashioned dim sum place offers a select menu of tasty snacks, from taro and shrimp dumplings ($3.50–3.75) to salt and pepper shrimp ($7.95) and their original egg roll ($3.95). Sun–Thurs 10.30am–9pm, Fri & Sat 10.30am–10pm.

Peking Duck House 28 Mott St, between Chatham Square and Pell St ☎212 227 1810, ⓦpeking duckhousenyc.com; subway J, N, Q, R, Z and #6 to Canal St; map p.71. This chic and shiny-clean eatery dishes up – you guessed it – duck; the crispy fried birds are carved tableside ($48; or served as part of a special dinner for $31 per person, minimum of 4 people). Slightly pricier than the competition, but worth it. Sun–Thurs 11.30am–10.30pm, Fri & Sat 11.45am–11pm.

Ping's Seafood 22 Mott St, between Chatham Square and Pell St ☎212 602 9988, ⓦpingsnyc.com; subway J, N, Q, R, Z and #6 to Canal Street; map p.71. While this Hong Kong-style seafood restaurant is good any time, it's most enjoyable on weekends for dim sum, when carts of tasty, bite-sized delicacies ($2.50–5) whir by every thirty seconds. Offers superb bang for your buck (most mains average $8–14). Mon–Thurs 10.30am–11pm, Fri 10.30am–11.30pm, Sat 9am–11.30pm, Sun 9am–11pm.

Red Egg 202 Centre St at Hester St ☎212 966 1123, ⓦredeggnyc.com; subway J, N, Q, R, Z and #6 to Canal St; map p.71. Modern restaurant serving high-quality American-Chinese favourites (think crispy garlic chicken, orange flavoured beef; $13–14) and excellent dim sum; the delicious snacks are made to order and served throughout the day ($2.75–5 per order). Don't miss the exquisite coconut pudding served in a coconut shell (serves two; $6.50). Mon–Fri 9am–11pm, Sat & Sun 10am–11pm.

★ **Tasty Hand-Pulled Noodle** 1 Doyers St, at Bowery ☎212 791 1817, ⓦtastyhandpullednoodles.com; subway J, N, Q, R, Z and #6 to Canal St; map p.71. Freshly made, hand-pulled noodles made to order – choose from seven different types, then opt for pan-fried ($5.50–7.50) or boiled noodles ($4.50–7) with pork, fish, beef, chicken, shrimp and several other combos. They also do excellent dumplings (from $2.55 for six). Daily 10.30am–10.30pm.

SOUTHEAST ASIAN

Bo Ky 80 Bayard St, at Mott St ☎212 406 2292; subway J, N, Q, R, Z and #6 to Canal Street; map p.71. The inexpensive noodle soups ($4–5) are good value at this cramped Chinese–Vietnamese eatery. The house speciality is a big bowl of rice noodles with shrimp, fish or duck. Daily 8am–10pm.

★ **New Malaysia** Chinatown Arcade, 46–48 Bowery, between Bayard and Canal sts ☎212 964 0284; subway J, N, Q, R, Z and #6 to Canal St; map p.71. Tucked away in a dingy arcade, this is one of the best Malaysian restaurants in town, with perfect *roti canai* ($3.95), *laksas* ($7.25) and crunchy satay sauce (main dishes $11–15). Daily 11am–10.30pm.

Sanur 18 Doyers St, at Pell St ☎212 267 0088; subway J, N, Q, R, Z and #6 to Canal St; map p.71. Don't be put off by the shabby exterior; this Indonesian hole-in-the-wall serves knockout curry with noodles from just $5.25, and breakfast *nasi lemak* for $2.50 (fragrant rice served with anchovies, peanuts, egg and curry). There's a larger restaurant in the basement. Tues–Sun 8am–10pm.

24

LITTLE ITALY AND NOLITA

Mulberry Street is Little Italy's main drag, and though often crowded with weekend tourists, the mostly Southern Italian eateries and carnival-like atmosphere can make for an entertaining dinner or dessert excursion. It's best not to have high culinary hopes for the neighbourhood, however: Little Italy's many red-sauce restaurants are fair, but not great. In contrast, Nolita is notable for its popular cutting-edge restaurants, which are often packed to the gills with aspiring fashionistas and film-industry hipsters.

AMERICAN

★ **Mac Bar** 54 Prince St, between Lafayette and Mulberry sts ☎ 212 226 0211, ⓦ macbar.net; subway N, R to Prince St; #6 to Spring St; map p.71. Celebration of macaroni and cheese, with offerings starting at the classic ($5.99), moving on to the mac stroganoff ($7.25), mac lobsta' ($8.99) and the mac quack ($7.99, with duck confit). Daily 11am–11pm.

BRAZILIAN

Bar Bossa 232 Elizabeth St, between Prince and Houston sts ☎ 212 625 2340; subway #6 to Spring St; map p.71. The great ambience at this Brazilian café (spot the tiny altar to Pelé), complements the extremely yummy food, including ginger-tomato soup, outstanding seafood stew and a very rich Guinness chocolate cake (main dishes $14, sandwiches $11). Daily 11am–midnight.

CUBAN

Café Habana 17 Prince St, at Elizabeth St ☎ 212 625 2001, ⓦ cafehabana.com; subway N, R to Prince St; map p.71. Small and always crowded, this Cuban–Latin American restaurant features some of the best skirt steak ($15.50) and fried plantains ($3.25) this side of Havana. They also have a takeaway counter next door (daily 11am–11pm) that serves great café con leche and sandwiches/burritos ($7.50–9.50). Daily 9am–midnight.

ITALIAN

Angelo's 146 Mulberry St, between Hester and Grand sts ☎ 212 966 1277, ⓦ angelosofmulberryst.com; subway N, R, #6 to Canal St; map p.71. Little Italy's red-sauce restaurants cater firmly to tourists these days, but this 1902 Neapolitan classic is the best place to get a sense of the area's original style, flavours and home-made pastas ($23–27). Mains range $26–33. Tues–Thurs & Sun noon–11.30pm, Fri noon–midnight, Sat noon–12.30am.

Emilio's Ballato 55 E Houston, between Mulberry and Mott sts ☎ 212 274 8881; subway B, D, F, M to Broadway-Lafayette St; map p.71. Serving some of the best Italian cuisine in the area, Emilio Vitolo's joint has a low-key, clubby atmosphere (popular with celebs), a spicy *penne arrabbiata*, tasty spaghetti *vongole* and veal chops so tender they melt in your mouth. Dishes average $16–26. Mon–Fri noon–11pm, Sat 4pm–midnight, Sun 4–11pm.

★ **Lombardi's** 32 Spring St, at Mott St ☎ 212 941 7994, ⓦ firstpizza.com; subway #6 to Spring St; map p.71. The oldest pizzeria in Manhattan (since 1905), *Lombardi's* still serves some of the best pizzas in town (original large $20.50), with the justly famous white clam pizza US$28; no slices though. There's open-air dining upstairs. Sun–Thurs 11.30am–11pm, Fri & Sat 11.30am–midnight.

★ **Peasant** 194 Elizabeth St, between Prince and Spring sts ☎ 212 965 9511, ⓦ peasantnyc.com; subway N, R to Prince St, J, M, Z to Bowery, #6 to Spring St; map p.71. A bit of a hangout after hours for city chefs, paying homage to Frank De Carlo's beautifully crafted Italian food such as *porchetta arrosto* (roasted suckling pig; $29), sumptuous pastas ($22–28) and brick-oven-fired pizzas ($14). Tues–Thurs 6–11pm, Fri & Sat 6–11.30pm, Sun 6–10.30pm.

Torrisi Italian Specialties 250 Mulberry St, between Prince and Spring sts ☎ 212 965 0955, ⓦ torrisinyc .com; subway #6 to Spring St; map p.71. This acclaimed nouveau Italian has upped its prices radically in the last few years, but it's still worth a splurge (no reservations; $75 prix-fixe menu); items could include sheep's-milk *gnocchi*, monkfish with pepper *marinara* and dirty duck *ragù* (lots of duck liver and brandy makes it "dirty"). Mon–Thurs 5.30–11pm, Fri–Sun noon–2pm & 5.30–11pm.

Vincent's Clam Bar 119 Mott St, at Hester St ☎ 212 226 8133; subway J, N, Q, R, Z, #6 to Canal St; map p.71. Another Little Italy mainstay since 1904 that serves fresh, cheap and spicy seafood dishes – clams, mussels and squid – with its famous sweet, medium or hot pepper *marinara* sauces (lunch plates $8.95–10.95; dinner $16–18). Sun–Thurs 11.30am–1am, Fri & Sat 11.30am–2am.

SOUTHEAST ASIAN

★ **Nyonya** 199 Grand St, between Mott and Mulberry sts ☎ 212 334 3669, ⓦ ilovenyonya.com; subway B, D to Grand St; map p.71. The food at this Malaysian restaurant is superb, and comes at wallet-friendly prices. Try the *roti canai* (crispy, light bread with curry), mango chicken, *mee goreng* (fried noodles) and *nasi lemak*, a Malaysian favourite of coconut rice and curry chicken or beef *rendang* (most dishes range $12–14). Sun–Thurs 11am–11.30pm, Fri & Sat 11am–midnight.

★ **Pho Bang** 157 Mott St, between Grand and Broome sts ☎ 212 966 3797; subway B, D to Grand St, J, Z, #6 to Canal St; map p.71. One of the most popular

Vietnamese restaurants in the city, often packed with diners at weekends. The main event is *pho*, Vietnamese beef noodle soup (from $6.25), which comes in several

varieties, though the crispy spring rolls ($4.75 for four) and chicken curry with French baguette ($6.75) are also excellent. Daily 10am–10pm.

THE LOWER EAST SIDE

The trendy Lower East Side, once dominated by immigrant tenements and sweatshops, has turned into something of a culinary destination, with Stanton, Rivington and Clinton streets as the main thoroughfares. You'll find some inviting gastronomic highlights here, such as *Mission Chinese* and *WD-50*, which have garnered dedicated fans for their sophisticated and unusual menus. There are also some terrific little Latin *comedores*, along with some stalwart old-time joints selling Jewish and Eastern European delicacies.

AMERICAN AND CONTINENTAL

★ **Georgia's Eastside Barbeque** 192 Orchard St, at Houston St ☎212 253 6280, ⓦgeorgiaseastsidebbq .com; subway F to Lower East Side-Second Ave; map p.83. Not smoked but equally mouthwatering oven-roasted, slow-cooked ribs ($19), tender pulled pork ($15), crunchy fried chicken ($15) and fried catfish sandwich ($9). Cash only. Mon 1–11pm, Tues–Sat noon–11pm, Sun 3–10pm.

Meatball Shop 84 Stanton St, at Allen St ☎212 982 8895, ⓦthemeatballshop.com; subway F to Second Ave; map p.83. The main event is served in sets of four with bread for $7 – choose your meatball (beef, pork, chicken, veg) and the sauce (tomato, pesto, spicy, parmesan, mushroom). Sun–Thurs noon–2am, Fri & Sat noon–4am.

Schiller's Liquor Bar 131 Rivington St, at Norfolk St ☎212 260 4555, ⓦschillersny.com; subway F to Delancey St, J, M, Z to Essex St; map p.83. This Keith McNally gem, made up to look like a Prohibition-era speakeasy, offers eclectic American and Continental dishes, including steak frites, seared salmon and pork chops smothered in sautéed onions (dinner mains $16–24). Mon–Thurs 11am–1am, Fri 11am–3am, Sat 10am–3am, Sun 10am–midnight.

★ **Shopsin's** Stall 16, Essex St Market, 120 Essex St (no phone), ⓦshopsins.com; subway F to Delancey St, J, M, Z to Essex St; map p.83. Something of a New York institution, Kenny Shopsin ran his famously idiosyncratic diner in the West Village for years (no mobile phones or parties larger than four), but was forced into this tiny space (two tables and counter top) by high rents. His addictive (and numerous) creations – like peanut-butter-filled pancakes – have a loyal following (filling plates average $14–22). Wed–Sat 9am–2pm, Sun 10am–2pm.

Stanton Social 99 Stanton St, between Ludlow and Orchard sts ☎212 995 0099, ⓦthestantonsocial.com; subway F to Lower East Side-Second Ave; map p.83. Chandeliers, lizard-skin banquettes and retro booths draw a young, cool crowd to this 1940s-inspired restaurant-cum-lounge bar. The tapas-style small plates here are designed for sharing: try the zesty red-snapper tacos with mango salsa or Thai spiced baby back ribs (sliders $5–9; dishes $13–21). Mon–Fri 5pm–1am, Sat 11.30am–1am, Sun

11.30am–11pm.

WD-50 50 Clinton St, between Rivington and Stanton sts ☎212 477 2900, ⓦwd-50.com; subway F to Delancey St, J, M, Z to Essex St; map p.83. Though the buzz has died somewhat, celebrated chef Wylie DuFresne still pulls in the crowds with his experimental New American cuisine; think pigtail and artichokes with olive oil jam and hazelnut, and popcorn soup with shrimp. Choose a twelve course ($155) or five-course ($90) tasting menu, or try two items at the bar for $25 ($15 per addition). Daily 6–10pm.

CHINESE

Congee Village 100 Allen St, between Delancey and Broome sts ☎212 941 1818, ⓦcongeevillagerestaurants .com; subway F to Delancey St, J, M, Z to Essex St; map p.83. As you exit the rear of the Tenement Museum you'll see this Cantonese restaurant, a shrine to the eponymous fragrant, soupy rice dish served in numerous varieties ($2.50–8.25) and a wide range of other Hong Kong favourites for $9–11. Sun–Thurs 10.30am–12.30am, Fri & Sat 10.30am–2am.

★ **Mission Chinese Food** 154 Orchard St, between Rivington and Stanton sts ☎212 529 8800, ⓦmissionchinesefood.com/ny; subway F to Lower East Side-Second Ave; map p.83. Cultish San Francisco Chinese fusion joint with a menu of small dishes like *char siu* pig ear terrine ($9) and tea-poached chilled greens ($6.50), and large dishes like staff favourite thrice-cooked bacon and spicy *mapo* tofu (both $12.50). Oh, and there's free beer while you wait for a table. Daily noon–3pm & 5.30pm–midnight.

DOMINICAN

Cibao Restaurant 72 Clinton St, at Rivington St ☎212 228 0873; subway F to Delancey St, J, M, Z to Essex St; map p.83. *El Cibao* is the best of a slew of Dominican restaurants on the Lower East Side. The fare is hearty and inexpensive; the rice and beans ($6.50) and huge sandwiches, particularly the Cubano ($5.50), are bargains. Cash only. Sun–Thurs 8am–9pm, Fri & Sat 8am–10pm.

JEWISH

Katz's Deli 205 E Houston St, at Ludlow St ☎212 254 2246, ⓦkatzsdelicatessen.com; subway F to Lower

24

East Side-Second Ave; map p.83. Jewish stalwart (opened in 1888), Katz's overstuffed pastrami or corned beef sandwiches should keep you going for about a week (sandwiches $15.45–16.75). The egg creams are also delicious ($3.75). Famous faux-gasm scene from *When Harry Met Sally* was shot here. Mon–Wed 8am–10.45pm, Thurs 8am–2.45am, Fri 8am–Sun 10.45pm, Sat open 24hr.

Sammy's Roumanian Steakhouse 157 Chrystie St, at Delancey St ☎ 212 673 0330; subway B, D to Grand St, Z to Bowery, F to Lower East Side-Second Ave; map p.83. This basement Jewish steakhouse offers much more than many customers are prepared for, including schmaltzy songs, delicious-but-heartburn-inducing food (complete with home-made *rugelach* and egg creams for dessert), and vodka chilled in blocks of ice. "Broilings" (huge meat plates) range from $19.95–39.95. Sun–Thurs 4–9.30pm, Fri & Sat 4–11pm.

THAI

Pok Pok Phat Thai 137 Rivington St, between Suffolk and Norfolk sts ☎ 212 447 1299, ⓦ pokpok phatthai.com/home; subway F to Delancey St, J, M, Z to Essex St; map p.83. Pad thai specialist (the original hails from Portland, Oregon), with a fabulous regular version ($9.50), nicely accompanied by *Pok Pok* Som drinking vinegars in various fruity flavours ($4.50). Daily noon–11pm.

THE EAST VILLAGE

Over time, the East Village's mix of radicals, professionals and immigrants has produced one of the most potent dining scenes in the city. The range of culinary options makes dining in this neighbourhood a real pleasure: you can peruse menus on Indian Row; sample dishes at the handful of Polish or Ukrainian eateries; or hit one of the numerous Japanese ramen bars around East 9th Street. The American and Continental dining scene here is equally enticing.

AMERICAN AND CONTINENTAL

★ **Acme** 9 Great Jones St, between Lafayette St and Broadway ☎ 212 203 2121, ⓦ acmenyc.com; subway #6 to Bleecker St; map p.88. Mads Refslund (from Copenhagen's *Noma*, no less), has shaken up this old Cajun spot with a Nordic-influenced "soil" section featuring salt-baked beetroot and carrots cooked with pine, and a sea/land section of dishes such as lamb shank ($29) or grilled Arctic char with cabbage, buttermilk and horseradish ($26). Mon–Fri 6pm–midnight, Sat & Sun 11am–3pm & 6pm–midnight.

DBGB Kitchen & Bar 299 Bowery, at E Houston St ☎ 212 933 5300, ⓦ dbgb.com/nyc; subway #6 to Bleecker St; map p.88. Popular outpost of the Daniel Boulud empire, blending huge mirrors, rustic tables and modern styling – it's US diner meets French brasserie, where sausages are a speciality (14 types, from Tunisian spicy lamb to Vermont cheese; $9–15), though the burgers ($14–19) and house-made foie gras ($13–23) are equally good. Mon noon–3pm & 5–11pm, Tues–Thurs noon–3pm & 5.30pm–midnight, Fri noon–3pm & 5.30pm–1am, Sat 11am–3pm & 5pm–1am, Sun 11am–3pm & 5–11pm.

★ **Graffiti Food & Wine Bar** 244 E 10th St, between First and Second aves ☎ 212 677 0695, ⓦ graffitinyc .com; subway #6 to Astor Place; map p.88. Pastry chef Jehangir Mehta cooks up a fusion of Chinese, American and Indian flavours in this artsy space, with just four tables and courses ranging $7–15: pickled ginger scallops and cumin eggplant buns grace the menu. Tues & Sun 5.30–10.30pm, Wed–Sat 5.30–11.45pm.

Luke's Lobster 93 E 7th St, between First Ave and Avenue A ☎ 212 387 8487, ⓦ lukeslobster.com; subway #6 to Astor Place; map p.88. Maine lobsters come to the East Village; this small place (just 8 stools inside) offers classic lobster rolls ($17), crab rolls ($14), shrimp rolls ($10) and thick chowders ($8). Sun–Thurs 11am–10pm, Fri & Sat 11am–11pm.

Mighty Quinn's Barbeque 103 Second Ave, at E 6th St ☎ 212 677 3733, ⓦ mightyquinnsbbq.com; subway L to Third Ave; map p.88. Texas and Carolinas-inspired slow-smoked barbecue, with a no-nonsense menu of lip-smacking brisket ($8.50), pulled pork ($7.25) and ribs ($8), accompanied by burnt-end baked beans (from $3). Sun–Thurs 11.30am–11pm, Fri & Sat 11.30am–midnight.

Peels 325 Bowery, at E 2nd St ☎ 646 602 7015, ⓦ peelsnyc.com; subway #6 to Bleecker St; map p.88. Celeb sightings abound at this popular brunch spot; it's justly renowned for its biscuits (a bit like British scones; $3), airy, bright upstairs section and street seating but all the food is good, from the shrimp and grits ($13.25) to the biscuits and gravy ($12.50). Daily 7.30am–midnight.

Prune 54 E 1st St, between First and Second aves ☎ 212 677 6221, ⓦ prunerestaurant.com; subway F to Lower East Side-Second Ave; map p.88. This Mediterranean-influenced American bistro still delivers one of the city's most exciting dining experiences, serving dishes like sweetbreads wrapped in bacon, wild striped bass with cockles, and ricotta ice cream with salted caramel chunks (dinner dishes range $23–32). Mon–Fri 11.30am–3.30pm & 5.30–11pm, Sat & Sun 10am–3.30pm & 5.30–11pm.

Sarita's Mac & Cheese 345 E 12th St, between Second and First aves ☎ 212 358 7912, ⓦ smacnyc.com; subway L to First Ave; map p.88. Indulge your macaroni and cheese cravings at this no-frills joint, with twelve

24

creative varieties on offer, blending cheddar, Gruyère, brie and goat's cheese with herbs and meats. Pick your portion sizes: nosh, major munch or mongo ($4.75–19). Sun–Thurs 11am–11pm, Fri & Sat 11am–1am.

★ **Saxon & Parole** 316 Bowery, at Bleecker St ⓣ212 254 0350, ⓦsaxonandparole.com; subway #6 to Bleecker St; map p.88. Named in honour of two NY racehorses kept in stables that once lined this stretch of the Bowery, this modern American grill is decked out in a rustic barn-like style (check the horse blankets on shelves) but it's the food that really impresses: tea-smoked mussels, horseradish-whipped potatoes and whisky jelly with steaks, washed down with a celery gimlet. The "s'mores" dessert (warm chocolate pudding, graham cracker, lemon marshmallow and whisky-barrel smoke; $10), deserves its own section. Mains $20–30. Mon–Thurs 5pm–11pm, Fri 5pm–midnight, Sat 10am–3.30pm & 5pm–midnight, Sun 10am–3.30pm & 5–10pm.

EAST ASIAN

Dok Suni 119 First Ave, between E 7th and St Mark's Place ⓣ212 477 9506; subway #6 to Astor Place; map p.88. Hip around the edges with great prices to boot, this is a fine bet (and longtime local favourite) for Korean home cooking, including *bibimbop*, *bulgogi* and *kimchee* rice. Main dishes $12.95–30, cash only. Mon 4.30–11pm, Tues–Fri 4.30pm–midnight, Sat noon–midnight, Sun noon–11pm.

Jeepney 201 First Ave, between E 13th and E 12th sts ⓣ212 533 4121, ⓦjeepneynyc.com; subway L to First Ave; map p.88. Creative, hip Filipino food from the folks behind lauded *Maharlika* down the avenue; think *longganisa* hot dogs ($8), spicy Filipino bangers and mash ($16), an incredible burger ($17) and really special cocktails (the spray of absinthe is a nice touch). Daily 4–11pm.

★ **Momofuku Noodle Bar** 171 First Ave, between E 10th and E 11th sts ⓣ212 387 8487, ⓦmomofuku.com; subway #6 to Astor Place; map p.88. Celebrated chef David Chang's first restaurant, where his most simple creations are still the best: silky steamed pork buns, laced with hoisin sauce and pickled cucumbers ($10), or steaming bowls of chicken and pork ramen noodles ($12–16). Mon–Thurs noon–4.30pm & 5.30–11pm, Fri noon–4.30pm & 5.30pm–2am, Sat noon–4pm & 5.30pm–2am, Sun noon–4pm & 5.30–11pm.

Tsampa 212 E 9th St, between Third and Second aves ⓣ212 614 3226; subway #6 to Astor Place; map p.88. Absorb the Buddhist vibes at this Tibetan restaurant, adorned with prayer flags and giant images of the Dalai Lama. Vegetarians have plenty to choose from, with lots of fresh greens, barley soup, various noodles and *momo* (Tibetan dumplings), though there are also several meat dishes. All main dishes are $11.95 (vegetarian), $12.95 (chicken) or $14.95 (seafood). Daily 5–11.30pm.

FRENCH

Le Philosophe 55 Bond St, between Lafayette St and Bowery ⓣ212 388 0038, ⓦlephilosophe.us; subway #6 to Bleecker St; map p.88. Fashionable French bistro helmed by *ex-Jean Georges* chef Matthew Aita, with classics such as duck *à l'orange* ($27) and roast chicken ($24); lunch is cheaper (main $13–22), and there's a bargain two-course prix fixe ($18). Sun–Wed 11.30am–3pm & 5.30–11pm, Thurs–Sat 11.30am–3pm & 5.30pm–1am.

INDIAN

Brick Lane Curry House 343 E 6th St, between First and Second aves ⓣ212 979 2900, ⓦbricklanecurryhouse.com; subway #6 to Astor Place; map p.88. Smack in the heart of Curry Row, and one of the best Indian restaurants in Manhattan, thanks to its wide selection of Brit-Indian favourites, including a tasty *bhaji* ($7), baltis (from $15) and some fiery *phaal* curries ($15–21). Sun–Thurs noon–11pm, Fri & Sat noon–1am.

Haveli 100 Second Ave, between E 5th and E 6th sts ⓣ212 982 0533, ⓦhavelinyc.com; subway #6 to Astor Place; map p.88. Far superior to most of its neighbours on E 6th St (with the notable exception of *Brick Lane*), this roomy Indian restaurant serves creative and well-executed classics (curries $10.95–13.95). Daily noon–midnight.

24

ITALIAN

Frank 88 Second Ave, between E 5th and E 6th sts ⓣ212 420 0202, ⓦfrankrestaurant.com; subway F to Lower East Side-Second Ave, #6 to Astor Place; map p.88. A tiny neighbourhood favourite, where basic, traditional American–Italian dishes like seared salmon ($15.95) and black linguini with calamari ($19.95) are served at communal tables. Cash only. Mon–Thurs 10.30am–1am, Fri & Sat 10.30am–2am, Sun 10.30am–midnight.

★ **Il Posto Accanto** 190 E 2nd St, between aves A and B ⓣ212 228 0977, ⓦilpostoaccanto.com; subway F to Lower East Side-Second Ave; map p.88. Nab a spot at a high wooden table at this small, intimate wine bar serving a vast array of Italian reds by the glass. You can easily make a meal from the excellent small plates of pasta ($11–14), panini ($8–10) and the like. Can get crowded, like its popular parent restaurant next door (*Il Bagatto*). Mon 5.30pm–3am, Tues–Fri noon–3am, Sat & Sun noon–3.30pm & 5.30pm–3am.

Motorino 349 E 12th St, near First Ave ⓣ212 777 2644, ⓦmotorinopizza.com; subway L to First Ave; map p.88. Another strong claim to serve the best pizza in the city, Mathieu Palombino's mouthwatering creations include the tongue-tingling *stracciatella* pizza (basil, olive oil and sea salt) and the cherry-stone clams masterpiece (pizzas $9–18). Sun–Thurs 11am–midnight, Fri & Sat 11am–1am.

24

JAPANESE

Curry-Ya 214 E 10th St, between First and Second aves ☎866 602 8779, ⓦnycurry-ya.com; subway #6 to Astor Place; map p.88. Grab a stool at the marble-top bar at this narrow, slick Japanese curry house for its nine types of freshly made, mouthwatering curry, from slightly sweet classic Japanese to organic chicken and seasonal vegetable ($8–15). Daily noon–11pm.

Hasaki 210 E 9th St, at Stuyvesant St ☎212 473 3327, ⓦhasakinyc.com; subway #6 to Astor Place; map p.88. Some of the best sushi in the city is served at this popular but mellow downstairs cubbyhole. Sit at the bar and the chefs will try to tempt you with a variety of improvised dishes not found on the menu (five pieces from $23). No reservations. Mon & Tues 5.30–11pm, Wed & Thurs noon–3pm & 5.30–11pm, Fri noon–3pm & 5.30–11.30pm, Sat 1–4pm & 5.30–11.30pm, Sun 1–4pm & 5.30–11.30pm.

★ **Ippudo** 65 Fourth Ave, between E 9th and E 10th sts ☎212 388 0088, ⓦippudony.com; subway #6 to Astor Place; map p.88. The first overseas outpost of Fukuoka-based "ramen king" Shigemi Kawahara, this popular Japanese ramen shop offers steaming bowls of classic *tonkotsu*-style noodles for $17 in booths and at communal wooden tables, as well as tasty pork buns and roast chicken appetizers. Be prepared for a long wait at weekends (no reservations). Mon–Thurs 11am–3.30pm & 5–11.30pm, Fri & Sat 11am–3.30pm & 5–12.30pm, Sun 11am–10.30pm.

Kenka 25 St Marks Place, between Third and Second aves ☎212 254 6363; subway #6 to Astor Place; map p.88. Heart of the *izakaya* scene in the East Village and a real slice of Shinjuku (in Tokyo), popular with Asian students (no English at the entrance, but menus are bilingual). The theme is early twentieth-century Japan; sit on wooden benches and order small plates of Japanese snacks from the huge menu ($5-6), and from the massive selection of quality sake. Sun–Tues 6–10.30pm, Wed & Thurs 6–11pm, Fri & Sat 6–11.30pm.

Robataya NY 231 E 9th St, between Second and Third aves ☎212 979 9674, ⓦrobataya-ny.com; subway #6 to Astor Place; map p.88. *The* place to experience *robatayaki*-style cuisine (the sister retaurant is in Roppongi, Tokyo); choose your fresh ingredients first, then watch as the chef cooks them in front of you, before delivering it to your table via a long paddle. Order vegetables ($5–7) and meats from $6–15. Wed & Thurs noon–2.30pm & 6–10.45pm, Fri & Sat noon–3pm & 6–11.45pm, Sun 6–10.45pm.

LATIN AMERICAN

Caracas Arepa Bar 93 1/2 E 7th, at 1st Ave ☎212 529 2314, ⓦcaracasarepabar.com; subway #6 to Astor Place; map p.88. Delicious Venezuelan home-made *arepas* ($6.50–8) served in a tiny cafeteria – there's a small takeaway place next door (both tend to get swamped at the weekend). Choose from various cheeses to shredded beef and *chorizo* fillings. Daily noon–11pm.

Hecho en Dumbo 354 Bowery between Great Jones and E 4th sts ☎212 937 4245, ⓦhechoendumbo. com; subway #6 to Astor Place; map p.88. This authentic Mexican diner migrated across the East River in 2010, but it still knocks out wonderful small plates ($9–14) and Mexico City contemporary cuisine such as house-cured beef, lamb shank confit and an innovative selection of tacos, *sopes* and burritos ($9–18). Mon–Thurs 5.30pm–11pm, Fri 5.30pm–midnight, Sat 11.30am–4pm & 5.30pm–midnight, Sun 11.30am–4pm & 5.30–11pm.

UKRAINIAN

★ **Veselka** 144 Second Ave, corner of E 9th St ☎212 228 9682, ⓦveselka.com; subway #6 to Astor Place; map p.88. This always-crowded Ukrainian diner has been an East Village institution since 1954, offering fine home-made hot *borscht* (and cold in summer) from $4.75, *kielbasa* sausage ($16.95), veal goulash ($17.95) and *pierogi* ($6.95 for four). Daily 24hr.

VEGETARIAN

Angelica Kitchen 300 E 12th St, between First and Second aves ☎212 228 2909, ⓦangelickitchen.com; subway L to First Ave; map p.88. Vegetarian macrobiotic restaurant with various daily specials at a decent price. Patronized by a colourful downtown crowd and serving some of the best veggie food in Manhattan. Main dishes $9.50–15. Cash only. Daily 11.30am–10.30pm.

B & H Dairy 127 Second Ave, between E 7th St and St Mark's Place ☎212 50 8065; subway #6 to Astor Place; map p.88. A tiny kosher vegetarian luncheonette since the 1950s, serving home-made soup (try the *pierogi*; $9.50) and absolutely divine *challah* French toast ($6.50). You can also create your own juice combinations (carrot–beetroot, for example). Daily 7.30am–11pm.

THE WEST VILLAGE

Restaurants in the West Village cater to the neighbourhood's many and varied residents – everyone from students to celebrities – so the culinary scene is fairly diverse. You'll find loads of takeaway spots and places with prix-fixe meals around New York University. Farther west, dining rooms get snazzier, menus more interesting and prices higher, particularly beyond Seventh Avenue, where there's a preponderance of French and Italian bistros.

AMERICAN AND CONTINENTAL

★ **Blue Hill** 75 Washington Place, between MacDougal and 6th sts ☎212 539 1776, ⓦbluehillfarm.com; subway A, B, C, D, E, F, M to W 4th St; map pp.96–97. One of the better restaurants in the West Village, lauded for the rustic American and New England fare, including cauliflower steak (a thick wedge of roast cauliflower; $32), and milk-fed pig with red cabbage and beetroot ($35), using seasonal upstate ingredients. Don't miss the rich chocolate bread pudding ($12). Mon–Sat 5.30–11pm, Sun 5.30–10pm.

Corner Bistro 331 W 4th St, at Jane St ☎ 212 242 9502, ⓦ cornerbistrony.com; subway A, C, E, L to 14th St; map pp.96–97. There's been a pub on this spot since at least the 1870s, but this classic dive incarnation dates from 1961 with cavernous cubicles, paper plates and maybe the best burger in town ($6.75). It's a long-standing haunt for West Village literary and artsy types, with a mix of locals and die-hard fans queuing up nightly for excellent and inexpensive food. Mon–Sat 11.30am–4am, Sun noon–4am.

Gotham Bar & Grill 12 E 12th St, between Fifth Ave and University Place ☎ 212 620 4020, ⓦ gothambarandgrill.com; subway L, N, Q, R, #4, #5, #6 to Union Square; map pp.96–97. Generally reckoned to be one of the city's best New American restaurants; if you don't want to splurge on a full meal, at least go for a drink at the bar, where you can watch the beautiful patrons drift in. Seasonal menu features Niman Ranch pork, miso cod, Maine lobster and more (dinner dishes range $20–48). Mon–Thurs noon–2.15pm & 5.30–10pm, Fri noon–2.15pm & 5.30–11pm, Sat 5–11pm, Sun 5–10pm.

★ **The Marrow** 99 Bank St, at Greenwich St ☎ 212 428 6000, ⓦ themarrownyc.com; subway A, C, E to 14th St; map pp.96–97. Contemporary German and Italian restaurant from celebrity chef Harold Dieterle (first *Top Chef* winner). Feast on pan-fried duck schnitzel ($31), juniper-braised lamb neck ($23) or some hand-cut fettuccini with sage sausage ($12). Daily Mon–Thurs 5–11pm, Fri 5–11.30pm, Sat 11am–2.30pm & 5–11.30pm, Sun 11am–2.30pm & 5–10pm.

★ **Mary's Fish Camp** 64 Charles St, at W 4th St ☎ 646 486 2185, ⓦ marysfishcamp.com; subway #1 to Christopher St; map pp.96–97. Lobster rolls, bouillabaisse and grilled whole fish adorn the menu at this small, noisy West Village spot. Go early, as they don't accept reservations and the queue lasts into the night. Definitely one of the best seafood spots in the whole city – you can almost smell the salty air. Dinner dishes $18–26. Mon–Sat noon–3pm & 6–11pm.

★ **Minetta Tavern** 113 MacDougal St, at Minetta Lane ☎ 212 475 3850, ⓦ minettatavernny.com; subway A, B, C, D, E, F, M to W 4th St; map pp.96–97. This classic restaurant from 1937 is loaded with atmosphere, with old photos on the walls and mural-clad dining room beyond the bar. It was revamped in 2008 by the McNally stable, and now serves fine French and New American cuisine; the Black Label Burger ($26) is one of the city's best, while weekend brunch involves delicacies such as slow-baked ham in hay ($22) and smoked salmon *latkes* ($22). Excellent service. Mon–Fri noon–2.30pm & 5.30pm–1am, Sat & Sun 11am–3pm & 5.30pm–1am.

The Spotted Pig 314 W 11th St, at Greenwich St ☎ 212 620 0393, ⓦ thespottedpig.com; subway #1 to Christopher St; map pp.96–97. New York's best gastropub, courtesy of British chef April Bloomfield. The menu is several steps above ordinary bar food – think crispy pig's ear salad with lemon caper dressing ($15) or smoked haddock chowder ($16) – and the wine list is excellent. Mon–Fri noon–3pm & 5.30pm–2am, Sat & Sun 11am–3pm & 5.30pm–2am.

ASIAN

Baoguette 120 Christopher St, between Bleecker and Bedford sts ☎ 212 929 0877, ⓦ baoguette.com; subway #1 to Christopher St; map pp.96–97. Tiny modern diner specializing in richly flavoured Vietnamese *bánh mì* sandwiches for $6.50 – they also do a great spicy catfish version ($8), plus noodles and rice plates (from $8). Mon–Sat 11.30am–11pm, Sun noon–10pm.

★ **Red Farm** 529 Hudson St, between W 10th and Charles sts ☎ 212 792 9700 ⓦ redfarmnyc.com; subway #1 to Christopher St; map pp.96–97. Local and seasonal produce drive this mega-popular contemporary Chinese joint, with playful dim sum creations like the "pac man" shrimp dumplings ($12.50 for four), and delectable mains such as the crisp-skin smoked chicken ($25). No reservations – go early or be prepared to wait. Daily 9am–2am.

Tomoe Sushi 172 Thompson St, between Bleecker and Houston sts ☎ 212 777 9346, ⓦ tomoesushi.com; subway #1 to Houston St; map pp.96–97. The nightly queues may look daunting, but there's a good reason to join them: this is some of the best, freshest sushi in Manhattan, and it's affordable to boot (sushi lunch set $17.75; fish dishes $10–14). There are some seasonal dishes (like a soft-shell crab roll) on the menu, but the fresh fish on offer is what draws the crowds. AMEX and cash only. Mon 5–11pm, Tues–Sat 1–3pm & 5–11pm, Sun 5–10pm.

AUSTRIAN

Wallsé 344 W 11th St, at Washington St ☎ 212 352 2300, ⓦ kg-ny.com/wallse; subway #1 to Christopher St; map pp.96–97. The Austrian fare offered here has been updated for the twenty-first century by chef Kurt Gutenbrunner, and the formal dining room is adorned with Julian Schnabel canvases. The uniquely crafted menu features light-as-air schnitzel, frothy Riesling sauces and fantastic strudels, and the wine list includes some rare vintages. Dinner dishes $27–38. Mon–Sat 5.30–11pm, Sun 11am–2.30pm & 5.30–11pm.

CARIBBEAN

Miss Lily's 132 W Houston St, at Sullivan St ☎ 646 588 5375, ⓦ misslilysnyc.com; subway #1 to Houston St;

24

map pp.96–97. Friendly servers dish out all the favourites at this super-hip Jamaican-style diner – codfish fritters ($9), curry goat ($23) and jerk chicken ($21) – while reggae and ska tracks create a beach-shack vibe. Mon–Wed 6pm–midnight, Thurs & Fri 6pm–1am, Sat 11am–5pm & 6pm–1am, Sun 11am–5pm & 6pm–midnight.

FRENCH

★ **Buvette** 42 Grove St, between Bleecker and Bedford sts ☎212 243 9579, ⊛ilovebuvette.com; subway A, B, C, D, E, F, M to W 4th St; #1 to Christopher St; map pp.96–97. Exquisite but casual and reasonably priced French restaurant, serving the best egg breakfasts in the city ($12), tempting small plates like salted butter and anchovies ($7) and beautifully crafted classics like *coq au vin* and *cassoulet* (both $15). Sit in the garden if it's warm enough. No reservations. Mon–Fri 8am–2am, Sat & Sun 10am–2am.

Cornelia Street Café 29 Cornelia St, between Bleecker and W 4th St ☎212 989 9319, ⊛corneliastreetcafe .com; subway #1 to Christopher St; map pp.96–97. As much American diner as French café, there is no more comfortable restaurant in NYC. The pastas, salads and weekend brunch offerings are great, and the prices aren't bad either (dinner dishes $15–24). Downstairs is a cabaret featuring jazz, poetry and performance art. Sun–Thurs 10am–midnight, Fri & Sat 10am–1am.

Tartine 253 W 11th St at W 4th St ☎212 229 2611; subway #1 to Christopher St; map pp.96–97. The French creations are worth lining up for at this tiny byo bistro; try the *quiche du jour* ($9.95), *bouchée à la reine* (chicken pot pie; $18) and the custard-filled tarts ($7). Cash only. Mon–Sat 9am–4pm & 5.30–10.30pm, Sun 10am–4pm & 5–10pm.

ITALIAN

★ **Babbo** 110 Waverly Place, between MacDougal St and Sixth Ave ☎212 777 0303, ⊛babbonyc.com; subway A, B, C, D, E, F, M to W 4th St; #1 to Christopher St; map pp.96–97. Originally a coach house, this Mario Batali establishment is deservedly touted as one of the best Italian restaurants in the city. Try the "mint love-letters" (ravioli) with spicy lamb sausage ($20) or goose-liver ravioli ($24), or go for one of the expensive tasting menus ($80–90). Reservations are hard to get (you can book up to one month in advance), so just show up early and either eat at the bar or try for one of the tables along the window they save for walk-in customers (they don't take reservations for those). Mon 5.30–11.15pm, Tues–Sat 11.30am–1.30pm & 5.30–11.15pm, Sun 5–10.45pm.

John's Pizzeria 278 Bleecker St, between Sixth and Seventh aves ☎212 243 1680, ⊛johnsbrickovenpizza .com; subway A, B, C, D, E, F, M to W 4th St, #1 to Christopher St; map pp.96–97. True, this is another tourist bottle-neck, but the worn-wooden booths, bright

neon-red sign and ramshackle floors are dripping with atmosphere. *Lombardi's* graduate John Sasso opened up here in 1929 – his coal-fired brick oven is still knocking super-thin crust, sweet tomato sauce and blistered, gooey cheese pizzas ($14.50–16.50, no slices; cash only). Be prepared to wait in line for a table. Mon–Thurs 11.30am–11.30pm, Fri 11.30am–midnight, Sat 11.30am–12.30pm, Sun noon–11.30pm.

★ **Kesté Pizza & Vino** 271 Bleecker St, between Jones and Cornelia sts ☎212 243 1500, ⊛kestepizzeria.com; subway A, B, C, D, E, F, M to W 4th St; #1 to Christopher St; map pp.96–97. One of the newest pizzerias on the block, stirring things up with its Neapolitan-designed wood-fired oven and its perfect pizzas; try the original Mast'nicola (*lardo*, pecorino romano and basil; $9) or lip-smacking Pizza del Papa (butternut squash cream, smoked mozzarella and artichoke; $19). No reservations. Mon–Sat noon–3.30pm & 5–11pm, Sun noon–3.30pm & 5–10pm.

MEXICAN

★ **Empellón Taqueria** 230 W 4th St, at W 10th St; ☎212 367 0999, ⊛empellon.com/taqueria; subway A, B, C, D, E, F, M to W 4th St; map pp.96–97. Mexican tacos with creative flair from Alex Stupak (a *WD-50* alum); think tacos stuffed with short-rib pastrami ($18; main $27) or fish tempura ($12; main $18). The prix-fixe lunch menus are good deals: $20 for two courses or $25 for three. Even the salsas ($3) come infused with mashed pumpkin seeds and smoked cashews. Sun–Wed 11.45am–3pm & 5.30–11pm, Thurs–Sat 11.45am–3pm & 5.30pm–midnight.

MIDDLE EASTERN

Moustache 90 Bedford St, between Grove and Barrow sts ☎212 229 2220, ⊛moustachepitza.com; subway #1 to Christopher St; map pp.96–97. A small, cheap spot specializing in "pitzas" (pizzas of pitta bread and eclectic toppings) for $10–13; also offers great hummus, chickpea and spinach salad ($6), and bargain lamb ribs ($16). Daily noon–midnight.

SPANISH

Sevilla 62 Charles St, at W 4th St ☎212 929 3189, ⊛sevillarestaurantandbar.com; subway #1 to Christopher St; map pp.96–97. A Village favourite since 1941, *Sevilla* is dark, fragrant (from garlic), and serves good, moderately priced food ($15–30). Try the garlic soup, the fried calamari and the large pitchers of strong *sangría*. Mon–Thurs noon–midnight, Fri & Sat noon–1am, Sun 1pm–midnight.

Tertulia 359 Sixth Ave, at Washington Place ☎646 559 9909, ⊛tertulianyc.com; subway A, B, C, D, E, F, M to W 4th St; map pp.96–97. Chef Seamus Mullen's Asturias *sidrerías*-inspired vision of Spanish cooking thoroughly deserves the plaudits, with a spread of tapas (black and white anchovies with sheep's-milk cheese, or smoked pig cheek with quail egg; $6–12) and small plates to share ($11–18); the crispy Brussels sprouts with pork belly is a masterpiece.

Mon–Thurs 9.30am–3pm & 5.30–11pm, ·Fri 9.30am–3pm & 5.30pm–midnight, Sat 11.30am–3.30pm & 5.30pm–midnight, Sun 11.30am–3.30pm & 5.30–11pm.

CHELSEA

West Chelsea is one of the more vibrant foodie havens in the city, with some excellent Spanish, Italian and New American spots that have sprouted along Ninth and Tenth avenues; with the advent of the High Line, it's only getting busier. The rest of the neighbourhood has something for everyone, whether it's a retro diner, an old-school steakhouse or wallet-friendly ethnic eats.

AMERICAN AND CONTINENTAL

Cafeteria 119 Seventh Ave, at W 17th St ☎ 212 414 1717, ⓦ cafeteriagroup.com; subway #1 to 18th St; map p.107. Don't let the name fool you: *Cafeteria* may be open 24 hours and serve great chicken-fried steak ($18), meatloaf ($16) and macaroni and cheese ($9), but it's nothing like a truck stop. Expect a smart all-white interior, gold-rimmed mirrors and a fashionable clientele. Daily 24hr.

Colicchio & Sons 85 Tenth Ave, at W 15th St ☎ 212 400 6699, ⓦ craftrestauransinc.com; subway A, C, E to 14th St, L to Eighth Ave; map p.107. Celebrity chef Tom Colicchio strikes again, offering a menu of complex combinations (eg butter-poached oysters with celery-root pasta and caviar; four-course dinner $82) in a somewhat overwrought dining area – though with attentive service. The *Tap Room* in the front, where an excellent-value prix fixe lunch ($25) and more casual dinner are served, has a warmer vibe. Tap Room Mon–Thurs noon–2.30pm & 5.30–10pm, Fri noon–2.30pm & 5.30–11pm, Sat 11am–2.30pm & 5–11pm, Sun 11.30am–2.30pm & 5–9pm; dining room Mon–Thurs & Sun 6–10pm, Fri 5.30-11pm, Sat 5–11pm, Sun 5–9pm.

★ **Cookshop** 156 Tenth Ave, at W 20th St ☎ 212 924 4440, ⓦ cookshopny.com; subway C, E to 23rd St; map p.107. Part of the Marc Meyer stable, with ever-busy street-side tables and a menu of seasonal, contemporary American fare – dishes change frequently, but might include pheasant pasta, grilled rabbit from the Hudson Valley and Vermont lamb shoulder (most $25–32); interesting brunch options too ($12–18), and a Meatless Mondays $38 four-course prix fixe. Mon–Fri 7.30am–4pm & 5.30–11pm, Sat 10am–4pm & 5.30–11pm, Sun 10am–4pm & 5.30–10.30pm.

The Old Homestead 56 Ninth Ave, between W 14th and 15th sts ☎ 212 242 9040, ⓦ theoldhomestead steakhouse.com; subway A, C, E to 14th St, L to Eighth Ave; map p.107. Steak. Period. But really gorgeous steak, served in an almost comically old-fashioned walnut dining-room by waiters in black vests. Expensive (most cuts are $40–52; a handful of main dishes $25–38) but portions are huge; there's a burger menu at lunch (starting at $15) if you want to keep things modest. Mon–Thurs noon–10.30pm, Fri noon–11.30pm, Sat 1–11.30pm, Sun 1–9.30pm.

Red Cat 227 Tenth Ave, between W 23rd and 24th sts ☎ 212 242 0199, ⓦ theredcat.com; subway C, E to 23rd St; map p.107. Superb service, a fine American–Mediterranean kitchen and a warm atmosphere all make for a memorable dining experience at *Red Cat*. It's a big local favourite and popular for dates – book ahead. Mains $23–41. Mon 5–11pm, Tues–Thurs noon–2.30pm & 5–11pm, Fri & Sat noon–2.30pm & 5pm–midnight, Sun 5–10pm.

FRENCH

★ **La Lunchonette** 130 Tenth Ave, at W 18th St ☎ 212 675 0342; subway A, C, E to 14th St, L to Eighth Ave; map p.107. Even though it's tucked away in a remote corner of Chelsea, this understated little restaurant is always packed with loyal patrons. The classic French-country menu (with reasonable wines to match) features favourites like lamb sausage with sautéed apples ($21), skate wing ($21), steak *au poivre* ($29), though the speciality is slow-cooked *cassoulet* (not always available). Mon–Thurs & Sun noon–3.30pm & 5.30–11pm, Fri & Sat noon–3.30pm & 5.30–11.30pm.

Paradou 8 Little W 12th St, between Greenwich and Washington sts ☎ 212 463 8345, ⓦ paradounyc.com; subway A, C, E to 14th St, L to Eighth Ave; map p.107. This underrated Provençal-style Meatpacking District bistro is a far better (and more authentic) option than some of the more touristy places in the area. Great wines by the glass (actually glass-and-a-half; $12–17) and relatively digestible prices for the food ($19–32 mains; prix-fixe menus available too). Wed–Thurs 6–11pm, Fri 6pm–midnight, Sat 11am–midnight, Sun 11am–7pm.

ITALIAN

Bottino 246 Tenth Ave, between W 24th and 25th sts ☎ 212 206 6766, ⓦ bottinonyc.com; subway C, E to 23rd St; map p.107. This popular Chelsea restuarant attracts the in-crowd looking for authentic Tuscan food served in a slick, downtown atmosphere. Pastas average $18, meaty main dishes $22–30. Also has a to-go adjunct that's quite crowded at lunchtime. Mon 6–11pm, Tues–Sat noon–3.30pm & 6–11pm, Sun 5.30–10pm.

Co. 230 Ninth Ave, at W 24th St ☎ 212 243 1105, ⓦ co-pane.com; subway C, E to 23rd St; map p.107.

24

Fashionable spot, one of the new wave of pizzerias in town. Start with some crostini ($5) and an escarole salad ($10), then share a few of the oddly shaped pizzas, like leek and sausage ($19), meatball ($18) or a classic margherita ($15). Mon 5–11pm, Tues–Sat 11.30am–11pm, Sun 11am–10pm.

LATIN AMERICAN

La Taza de Oro 96 Eighth Ave, between W 14th and 15th sts ☎ 212 243 9946; subway A, C, E to 14th St, L to Eighth Ave; map p.107. Come to this neighbourhood stalwart for a tasty, cheap and filling Puerto Rican meal. Specials change daily, but are always served with a heap of rice and beans (and most under $10). Don't miss the delicious *café con leche*. Mon–Sat 6am–10.30pm.

Rocking Horse 182 Eighth Ave, between W 19th and 20th sts ☎ 212 463 9511, ⓦ rockinghorsecafe.com; subway C, E to 23rd St, #1 to 18th St; map p.107. Wash down inventive Mexican cuisine (like *mixiote*, a chilli pork stew; $19.95) with deliciously potent *mojitos* and margaritas ($10–13) from the bar. Mon–Thurs noon–11pm, Fri noon–midnight, Sat 11am–midnight, Sun 11am–11pm.

SPANISH

El Quijote 226 W 23rd St, between Seventh and Eighth aves ☎ 212 929 1855; subway C, E, #1 to 23rd St; map p.107. *El Quijote* has changed very little over its long history (it needed only a minimal makeover when it

appeared in the 1996 film *I Shot Andy Warhol*, though the movie was set in 1968). It still serves decent seafood and fried meats ($16.95–35.95), but the bland paella should be avoided; go more for the old-school feel and the atmosphere than anything else. Mon–Thurs & Sun noon–midnight, Fri & Sat noon–1am.

★ **La Nacional** 239 W 14th St, between Seventh and Eighth aves ☎ 212 243 9308; subway A, C, E, #1, #2, #3 to 14th St; L to Eighth Ave; map p.107. Home of the Spanish Benevolent Society, *La Nacional* retains the feel of a club (witness the regulars hanging in an anteroom drinking beers and watching *futbol*) while being open to all comers. Try *croquetas* ($8), shrimp with garlic sauce ($9) and top-notch paella ($22). Mon–Wed noon–10pm, Thurs–Sun noon–11pm.

Txikito 240 Ninth Ave, between W 24th and 25th sts ☎ 212 242 4730, ⓦ txikitonyc.com; subway C, E to 23rd St; map p.107. The rough-hewn interior of this Basque tapas-bar-cum-restaurant feels a little like the inside of a wooden ship – albeit one that serves its passengers crispy beef tongue ($16), octopus carpaccio ($15), an occasional special of suckling pig ($30) and, at lunch, one of the more original burgers in town ($11), a smoky treat. The crisp fries with spicy cod roe mayonnaise ($7) should accompany any order. Mon 5–11pm, Tues–Thurs noon–3pm & 5–11pm, Fri 11am–3pm & 5pm–midnight, Sat 11.30am–3.30pm & 5pm–midnight, Sun 11.30am–3.30pm & 5–11pm.

UNION SQUARE, GRAMERCY PARK AND THE FLATIRON DISTRICT

These neighbourhoods are heavily trafficked, and are therefore prime spots for restaurants. Some of the city's best dining establishments are in this part of town, the finest of which have come to help define New American cuisine – especially as practiced by restaurateur Danny Meyer. There are also plenty of places to grab a cheap meal.

AMERICAN AND CONTINENTAL

Blue Water Grill 31 Union Square W, at 16th St ☎ 212 675 9500, ⓦ bluewatergrillnyc.com; subway L, N, Q, R, #4, #5, #6 to 14th St-Union Square; map p.114. All-round high-quality seafood restaurant. It's hard to go wrong here, whether you choose the grilled fish, caviar or delicacies from the raw bar. Prices are commensurately high (main dishes $25–39). Mon 11.30am–10pm, Tues–Thurs 11.30am–11pm, Fri 11.30am–midnight, Sat 10.30am–midnight, Sun 10.30am–10pm.

Craft 43 E 19th St, between Broadway and Park Ave S ☎ 212 780 0880, ⓦ craftrestaurantsinc.com; subway N, R, #6 to 23rd St; map p.114. The buzz has mostly come and gone at celebrity chef Tom Colicchio's signature restaurant, making this a relatively relaxed place for some of New York's most inventive food. Popular dishes include roast sweetbreads or foie gras (when available), diver scallops ($32) and tasty, roasted wild mushroom sides ($12–16). Everything is à la carte (save the $130 tasting menu), so expect to spend $100 or more per person. Mon–

Thurs & Sun 5.30–10pm, Fri & Sat 5.30–11pm.

★ **Gramercy Tavern** 42 E 20th St, between Broadway and Park Ave S ☎ 212 477 0777, ⓦ gramercytavern .com; subway N, R, #6 to 23rd St; map p.114. The neo-colonial decor, exquisite New American cuisine and perfect service make for a memorable meal. The seasonal tasting menus are well worth the steep prices ($116 for six courses; otherwise, $88 for starter and main à la carte), but you can also drop in for a drink and more casual meal in the lively front room (entrees – vegetarian lasagne, crispy duck leg and the like – $18–24). Main room Mon–Thurs noon–2pm & 5.30–10pm, Fri noon–2pm & 5.30–11pm, Sat 5.30–11pm, Sun 5.30–10pm; Tavern Mon–Thurs & Sun noon–11pm, Fri & Sat noon–midnight.

Hill Country 30 W 26th St, between Broadway and Sixth Ave ☎ 212 255 4544, ⓦ hillcountryny.com; subway N, R to 28th St, F to 23rd St; map p.114. Some of the most authentic Texas barbecue in the city, with huge servings of moist, fatty brisket and beer-can game hen, as well as peppery sausage brought in from Kreuz Market near

Austin. Grab a table, then order your meats (priced by the pound) and sides (such as macaroni and cheese) from the counters. Daily noon–2am, though kitchen closes 10pm Sun–Wed, 11pm Thurs and midnight Fri & Sat.

NoMad *NoMad* hotel, 1170 Broadway, at 28th St ☎212 796 1500 or ☎347 472 5660, ⓦthenomadhotel.com; subway N, R to 28th St; map p.114. The dining area in this fashionable hotel rambles through a glassy atrium, dark bar and clubby parlour room. When a triumphal roast chicken for two, stuffed with foie gras, black truffle and brioche ($79), gets carried through, it's reason to pause, wherever you are. Mon–Thurs 5.30–10.30pm, Fri & Sat 5.30–11pm, Sun 5.30–10pm.

Pure Food & Wine 54 Irving Place, between E 17th and 18th sts ☎212 477 1010, ⓦoneluckyduck.com/pages/purefoodandwine; subway L, N, Q, R, #4, #5, #6 to 14th St-Union Square; map p.114. Elegant raw-food restaurant, where food is never heated to more than 118 degrees Fahrenheit. Prepare for goat-cheese-stuffed squash blossom, corn and cashew *tamales* and zucchini *lasagne*, though the desserts are the real standouts; first courses $14–20, main dishes $20–26, desserts $15. Table tasting menus also available ($69). Daily noon–4pm & 5.30–11pm.

Union Square Café 21 E 16th St, between Fifth Ave and Union Square W ☎212 243 4020, ⓦunionsquarecafe.com; subway L, N, Q, R, #4, #5, #6 to 14th St-Union Square; map p.114. Choice California-style dining (with an Italian bent) in a classy but comfortable atmosphere. The creative menu changes regularly, though count on some Roman-style preparations of pastas and meat. Meals aren't cheap (main dishes $28–35). Mon–Thurs noon–2.15pm & 5.30–9.45pm, Fri noon–2.15pm & 5.30–10.45pm, Sat 11am–2.15pm & 5.30–10.45pm, Sun 11am–2.15pm & 5.30–9.45pm.

ASIAN

★ 15 East 15 E 15th St, between Fifth Ave and Broadway ☎212 647 0015, ⓦ15eastrestaurant.com; subway L, N, Q, R, #4, #5, #6 to 14th St-Union Square; map p.114. The attention given to both cooked dishes like slow-poached octopus ($15) and lobster and *uni* risotto ($32), and the fresh sushi and sashimi (chef's selection $60–90) help elevate this stylish Japanese restaurant to the upper echelons. Mon–Fri noon–1.45pm & 6–10.30pm, Sat noon–1.45pm & 6–10.30pm.

Jaiya Thai 396 Third Ave, at E 28th St ☎212 889 1330, ⓦjaiya.com; subway #6 to 28th St; map p.114. The food at this affordable restaurant is red hot and delicious. Don't let the bland decor deceive you – when the menu says "medium spicy", expect to get your head blown off. Spice-averse palates can aim for tamer but decent pad thai ($9.95–13.95). Mon–Thurs & Sun 11am–11pm, Fri & Sat 11.30am–midnight.

INDIAN

Madras Mahal 104 Lexington Ave, between E 27th and 28th sts ☎212 684 4010, ⓦmadrasmahalnyc.com; subway #6 to 28th St; map p.114. A kosher vegetarian's dream, but everyone else will like it too. Curries are around $10, though the South Indian specialities, like *dosas* ($7.95–8.95) and *idli* ($4.95–5.95) are the better bets. Mon–Thurs & Sun noon–10.30pm, Fri & Sat noon–10.30pm.

ITALIAN

I Trulli Enoteca and Ristorante 122 E 27th St, between Lexington and Park aves ☎212 481 7372, ⓦitrulli.com; subway #6 to 28th St; map p.114. Choose between the lovely restaurant, which features robust dishes like *orecchiette* (ear-shaped pasta) with rabbit *ragù* ($21) and roasted rack of lamb with potato pie ($38), and the wine bar, with its cheeses, cured meats and a handful of fresh pasta dishes. Mon–Thurs noon–3pm & 5.30–10.30pm, Fri noon–3pm & 5.30–11pm, Sat 5–11pm, Sun 3–10pm; wine bar Mon–Thurs 3–10.30pm, Fri 3–11pm, Sat 4–11.30pm & Sun 3–10pm.

★ Maialino *Gramercy Park Hotel*, 2 Lexington Ave ☎212 777 2410, ⓦmaialinonyc.com; subway #6 to 23rd St; map p.114. If a place can be both rustic and refined, Danny Meyer's attractive Roman trattoria, which looks out on Gramercy Park, is it. Much of the focus is on the hog (which gives the place its name) – there's excellent cured *salumi* ($9–17), pasta with *guanciale* ($17) or suckling pig *ragù* ($23) and, as a sometimes special, roast suckling pig – but everything's well prepared and desserts are exceptional. Reservations essential. Mon–Thurs 7.30–10am, noon–2pm & 5.30–10.30pm, Fri 7.30–10am, noon–2pm & 5.30–11pm, Sat 10am–2pm & 5.30–11pm, Sun 10am–2pm & 5.30–10.30pm.

SPANISH AND PORTUGUESE

★ Aldea 31 W 17th St, between Fifth and Sixth aves ☎212 675 7223, ⓦaldearestaurant.com; subway F, M to 14th St; map p.114. In a cool, relaxed dining room, Portuguese-accented dishes come exquisitely prepared and full of flavour. For this kind of refined seasonal cooking – say, duck confit with crisped duck skin and *chorizo*, or sea-salted cod with poached egg and ramps – prices are high but not too high (main dishes $27–36) and a three-course prix-fixe lunch ($25) seals the deal. Mon 11.30am–2pm & 5.30–10pm, Tues–Thurs 11.30am–2pm & 5.30–11pm, Fri 11.30am–2pm & 5.30pm–midnight, Sat 5.30pm–midnight.

Casa Mono 52 Irving Place, at E 17th St ☎212 253 2773, ⓦcasamononyc.com; subway L, N, Q, R, #4, #5, #6 to 14th St-Union Square; map p.114. This eclectic tapas bar both challenges and enchants the palate with such dishes as pumpkin and goat cheese *croquetas* ($9) and mussels with cava and *chorizo* sausage ($15). The adjacent

24

and sherry-heavy *Bar Jamón* (see p.335) on 125 E 17th St is open until 2am daily. Daily noon–midnight.

TURKISH

Turkish Kitchen 386 Third Ave, between 27th and 28th sts ☎ 212 679 6633, ⓦ turkishkitchen.com; subway #6 to 28th St; map p.114. Ruby-red walls and balconies lend a suitably exotic backdrop to this excellent Turkish restaurant, with dishes such as tender lamb kebabs and *tavuk pirzola* (chicken stuffed with green peppers and creamy cheese) starting at around $17. Mon–Fri noon–11pm, Sat 5.30–11pm, Sun 11am–3pm & 5.30–10.30pm.

MIDTOWN EAST

Catering mostly to weekday office crowds, Midtown East overflows with restaurants, some nondescript and overpriced, but some excellent too: a lot of Asian entries plus timeworn favourites such as the *Oyster Bar* in Grand Central Terminal or the classy and refined *Aquavit* and *Four Seasons*.

AMERICAN AND CONTINENTAL

'21' Club 21 W 52nd St, between Fifth and Sixth aves ☎ 212 582 7200, ⓦ 21club.com; subway E, M to Fifth Ave-53rd St; map p.123. This is one of New York's most enduring institutions – the city's Old Boys come here to meet and eat. There's a dress code, so wear a jacket and tie. Three-course early dinner prix-fixe menus are $42 in the Bar Room, which is a pretty good deal, considering some of the more elaborate dishes (ahi tuna, mixed grill) go for $40 and up on their own. Bar room Mon 5.30–10pm, Tues–Thurs noon–2.30pm & 5.30–10pm, Fri noon–2.30pm & 5.30–11pm, Sat 5.30–11pm; upstairs Tues–Sat 5.30–10pm.

★ Aquavit 65 E 55th St, between Madison and Park aves ☎ 212 307 7311, ⓦ aquavit.org; subway E, M to Fifth Ave-53rd St; map p.123. Go for a blowout in the main dining room ($85 for four courses, or $135 tasting menu, though dishes also à la carte) or relax over some Swedish meatballs and a variety of the namesake drink in the bar-lounge of this renowned Scandinavian restaurant. Exquisite fish dishes abound – silky gravlax, herring every which way, smoked Arctic char and the like – alongside a few meatier choices, like veal tartare or roasted pheasant. Reserve well ahead. Mon–Fri 11.45am–2.30pm & 5.30–10.30pm, Sat 5.30–10.30pm.

db Bistro Moderne *City Club Hotel*, 55 W 44th St, between Fifth and Sixth aves ☎ 212 391 2400, ⓦ danielnyc.com/dbbistro.html; subway B, D, F, M to 42nd St-Bryant Park, #7 to Fifth Ave-Bryant Park; map p.123. Famous chef-owner Daniel Boulud made things more affordable here than his other culinary shrines – except the casual *DBGB* (see p.302) – though you'll still spend a pretty penny to eat dishes like the signature $32 burger, with foie gras, black truffle and short-rib meat. Mon 7–10am, noon–2.30pm & 5–10pm, Tues–Fri 7–10am, noon–2.30pm & 5–11pm, Sat 8am–2.30pm & 5–11pm, Sun 8am–2.30pm & 5–10pm.

Four Seasons 99 E 52nd St, between Lexington and Park aves ☎ 212 754 9494, ⓦ fourseasonsrestaurant .com; subway E, M to Lexington Ave-53rd St; #6 to 51st St; map p.123. The face of New York's fine dining for decades, this timeless Philip Johnson-designed restaurant delivers on every front. If you can't stomach the grotesque prices on the French-influenced American menu (main dishes $48–68, though a somewhat more palatable prix-fixe is available), go for a cocktail and peek at the famous pool room. Housed in the Seagram Building, it is much stuffier than other top restaurants in the city. Grill Room Mon–Fri noon–1.45pm & 5–9.30pm; Pool Room Mon–Fri noon–2.30pm & 5–9.30pm, Sat 5–10pm.

The Modern 9 W 53rd St, inside the Museum of Modern Art ☎ 212 333 1220, ⓦ themodernnyc.com; subway E, M to Fifth Ave-53rd St; map p.123. The highly praised *Modern* seems elegant without trying too hard. Fresh, seasonal ingredients are artfully combined to yield unexpected but wholly delicious dishes. *Chorizo*-crusted codfish with white cocoa-bean purée, and a sturgeon and sauerkraut tart are just two of the unlikely options. Set meals start at $98 (considerably less at lunch); the bar room has slightly less expensive dining (eg spicy steak tartare $16, house-made sausage $18). Mon–Thurs noon–2pm & 5–10.30pm, Fri noon–2pm & 5.30–10.30pm, Sat 5–10.30pm, bar room only on Sun 11.30am–9.30pm.

★ Oyster Bar Lower level, Grand Central Terminal, at E 42nd St and Park Ave ☎ 212 490 6650, ⓦ oysterbarny .com; subway #4, #5, #6, #7 to 42nd St-Grand Central; map p.123. This wonderfully distinctive place is down in the vaulted dungeons of Grand Central (and, like the terminal, just celebrated its one hundredth birthday). Midtown office-workers who pour in for lunch come to choose from a staggering menu – she-crab bisque ($6.95), steamed Maine lobster (priced by the pound) and sweet Kumamoto oysters ($3.25 each) top the list. Prices are moderate to expensive; you can eat more cheaply at the counter or just enjoy a chowder and beer while taking in the atmosphere. Mon–Sat 11.30am–9.30pm.

Quality Meats 57 W 58th St, between Fifth and Sixth aves ☎ 212 371 7777, ⓦ qualitymeatsnyc.com; subway F to 57th St, N, R to Fifth Ave; map p.123. The front doors give the impression you're stepping into a meat locker – and you are, in a sense. Top-notch beef (double rib steak $55/person); in contrast to many steakhouses, the appetizers and sides are well done, too. Mon–Wed 11.30am–3pm & 5–10.30pm, Thurs & Fri 11.30am–3pm & 5–11.30pm, Sat 5–11.30pm, Sun 5–10pm, bar open daily till 1am.

24

Smith and Wollensky 797 Third Ave, at E 49th St ☎212 753 1530, ⓦsmithandwollensky.com; subway #6 to 51st St; map p.123. Grand, if clubby, steakhouse, where long-serving waiters wheel out choice cuts of aged beef ($45–54) – New York sirloin and porterhouse are ever popular. If you prefer a more relaxed setting, hit the casual grill around the corner, which serves similar cuts at cheaper prices, plus a giant burger ($17.50). Daily 11.45am–11pm, Wollensky's Grill daily 11.30am–2am.

ASIAN

★ **Arirang** 32 W 32nd St, between Fifth and Sixth aves ☎212 967 5088, ⓦkoreanrestaurantnyc.com; subway B, D, F, M, N, Q, R to 34th St-Herald Square; map p.123. Somewhat hard to find – and up three flights of stairs (or an elevator) – but it's worth seeking out for the chicken soups – with handmade dough flakes ($9.99) or ginseng ($18.99); seafood pancake ($13.99); and, if you're with two or three friends, chicken casserole ($54.99). Daily 10am–midnight.

Cho Dang Gol 55 W 35th St, between Fifth and Sixth aves ☎212 695 8222, ⓦchodanggolny.com; subway B, D, F, M, N, Q, R to 34th St-Herald Square; map p.123. Korean restaurants proliferate on 32nd Street between Fifth and Sixth; this one, a little off the beaten path, specializes in home-made tofu – on its own, in pancakes, soups and porridges. There's more, though, like simmered pork belly served as part of a spicy lettuce wrap ($38.95), meant to be shared. Daily 11.30am–10.30pm.

Hatsuhana 17 E 48th St, between Fifth and Madison aves ☎212 355 3345, ⓦhatsuhana.com; subway #6 to 51st St; map p.123. Also on Park Ave. *Hatsuhana* was one of the first restaurants to introduce sushi to New York many moons ago, and it's still going strong. Despite the spartan decor, this place is not cheap; sushi dinners start at $27.50. Mon–Fri 11.45am–2.45pm & 5.30–10pm, Sat 5–10pm.

Hide-Chan Ramen 248 E 52nd St, between Second and Third aves ☎2121800; subway #6 to 51st St; map p.123. Looking for top-notch noodle soups in a sit-down restaurant with a bit more atmosphere than most? *Hide-Chan* does the trick, while also offering one of the better restaurant happy hours around ($3 pork buns, $2

Sapporos). Mon–Thurs 11.30am–1am, Fri & Sat 11.30am–4am, Sun 4–10pm.

Menkui Tei 58 W 56 St, between Fifth and Sixth aves ☎212 707 8702; subway F to 57th St; map p.123. Primarily a noodle shop – their porky *hakata* ramen is one of the better such efforts in town – they also do admirable plates: things like *katsu don* and curry rice, in a narrow, bustling setting. Mon–Fri 11.30am–11pm, Sat & Sun 11.30am–9pm.

NY Kom Tang 32 W 32nd St, between Broadway and Fifth Ave ☎212 947 8482; subway B, D, F, M, N, Q, R to 34th St-Herald Square; map p.123. There's fresh sushi or sashimi ($21.95–39.95) and excellent grill-it-yourself barbecue (*kalbi* $24.99), but the rich, bountiful soups are the stars – everything from oxtail ($13.95) to young chicken with ginseng ($19.95). Good lunch deals. Mon–Sat 24hr.

Szechuan Gourmet 21 W 39th St, between Fifth and Sixth aves ☎212 921 0233, ⓦszechuangourmetnyc .com; subway B, D, F, M to 42nd St-Bryant Park; map p.123. Szechuan cuisine done right, in dishes like spicy *dan dan* noodles ($5.95), braised lamb with chilli ($15.95) and double-cooked pork belly with leeks ($13.95). The lunch specials are a steal. Daily 11.30am–10pm.

Wu Liang Ye 36 W 48th St, between Fifth and Sixth aves ☎212 398 2308; subway B, D, F, M to 47th–50th sts-Rockefeller Center; map p.123. Up a flight of stairs in a brownstone – a nice relief from the hubbub below – diners sit around tables sharing orders of *mapo* tofu ($14.95), wok-roasted prawns with salt and pepper ($25.95) and tea-smoked duck ($21.95). Most of the well-spiced Szechuan food has a fiery buzz to it. Mon–Fri 11.30am–10pm, Sat & Sun noon–10pm.

FRENCH

La Bonne Soupe 48 W 55th St, between Fifth and Sixth aves ☎212 586 7650, ⓦlabonnesoupe.com; subway F to 57th St, E, M to Fifth Ave-53rd St; map p.123. This friendly bistro, spread over two levels, makes a good post-museum or pre-Carnegie Hall stop; tasty burgers ($14.95) and soups ($19.95 as a meal with bread, salad, dessert and a drink) are highlights of an extensive menu. Mon–Thurs 11.30am–11pm, Fri & Sat 11.30am–11.30pm, Sun 11.30am–10.30pm.

★ **La Grenouille** 3 E 52nd St, between Fifth and Madison aves ☎212 752 1495, ⓦla-grenouille.com; subway E, M to Fifth Ave-53rd St; map p.123. The haute French cuisine here has melted hearts and tantalized palates since 1962. All the classics (seared foie gras, sautéed frog legs, etc) are done to perfection, the room is welcoming and the service is beyond gracious. Its prix-fixe lunch is $52–67 though can be ordered à la carte; dinner is $104 without wine ($72 if you make it in before 6pm); jacket required downstairs. Tues–Sat noon–2.30pm & 5–10.30pm.

24

> **TOP 5 VEGETARIAN (OR VEGETARIAN-FRIENDLY) RESTAURANTS**
> **Angelica Kitchen** East Village. See p.304
> **Cho Dang Gol** Koreatown. See p.311
> **Madras Mahal** Gramercy Park. See p.309
> **Peacefood Cafe** Upper West Side.
> See p.288
> **Pure Food and Wine** Union Square.
> See p.309

TOP 5 HAUTE CUISINE
Bouley Tribeca. See p.297
Corton Tribeca. See p.297
Daniel Upper East Side. See p.315
Le Bernardin Midtown West. See p.313
Per Se Upper West Side. See p.317

ITALIAN
Caffé Linda 149 E 49th St between Lexington and Third aves ☎646 497 1818, ⓦcaffelinda.com; subway #6 to 51st St; map p.123. One of the better casual Italians in a neighbourhood awash in mediocre restaurants. It's unpretentious, with well-prepared pastas ($16–21), meat and seafood dishes ($19–30) and good panini at lunchtime. Mon–Fri 11am–10.30pm, Sat & Sun 5–10.30pm.

Naples 45 MetLife Building (p.134), 200 Park Ave, at E 45th St ☎212 972 7000; subway #4, #5, #6, #7 to Grand Central-42nd St; map p.123. The Neapolitan pizzas at this place are bursting with flavour (toppings include fennel sausage, roast vegetables and prosciutto di Parma) and come with just the right amount of wood-burning-oven char (individual pizzas $16.95–19.50). Also does fish, chicken, steak and pasta specialities ($18–32). Mon–Fri 7.30am–10pm.

JEWISH
2nd Avenue Deli 162 E 33rd St, between Lexington and Third aves ☎212 689 9000, ⓦ2ndavedeli.com; subway #6 to 33rd St; map p.123. This reincarnation of a downtown family-run Jewish institution may no longer be on Second Avenue, but the stuffed cabbage ($25.95), pastrami sandwich ($15.95) and matzoh-ball soup ($7.50) are all as tasty as ever. It may seem expensive, but meaty sandwiches ($13.95–24.95) can often feed two – or at least provide leftovers. Daily 6am–midnight.

MIDTOWN WEST

It's safe to say that more overpriced tourist joints exist in Midtown West – especially right around Times Square – than elsewhere in the city. On the other hand, a thriving restaurant scene exists over on Ninth Avenue in Hell's Kitchen – and even further west of that. Elsewhere, Restaurant Row (West 46th St, between Eighth and Ninth aves) is a frequent stopover for theatre-goers seeking a late-night meal, and if you choose carefully, good options can be found closer to the action.

AFGHAN
Ariana Afghan Kebab 787 Ninth Ave, between West 52nd and 53rd sts ☎212 262 2323, ⓦariananyc.com; subway C, E to 50th St; map p.141. A casual neighbourhood restaurant serving inexpensive kebabs (chicken, lamb, fish and beef; $14–15) and vegetarian meals like eggplant curry ($12). Daily 11.30am–10.30pm.

AMERICAN AND CONTINENTAL
The Burger Joint 119 W 56th St between Sixth and Seventh aves, in *Le Parker Meridien* ☎212 708 7414, ⓦburgerjointny.com; subway F, N, Q, R to 57th St; map p.141. Though the secret has long been out on this greasy hamburger stand incongruously located in a swish Midtown hotel, it still makes for good fun, good value and, most important, good eating. You might have to wait for a table. Mon–Thurs & Sun 11am–11.30pm, Fri & Sat 11am–midnight.

Joe Allen 326 W 46th St between Eighth and Ninth aves ☎212 581 6464, ⓦjoeallenrestaurant.com; subway A, C, E to 42nd St-Port Authority; map p.141. Working to a tried-and-true formula of reliable, modestly priced fare served on checked tablecloths in an old-fashioned barroom atmosphere, *Joe Allen* has been a favourite of pre- and post-theatre goers for ages. You can't go wrong with a burger ($13.50) or sautéed calf's liver ($21). Mon, Tues & Thurs noon–11.45pm, Wed & Sun 11.30am–11.45pm, Fri noon–midnight, Sat 11.30am–midnight.

West Bank Café 407 W 42nd St, at Ninth Ave ☎212 695 6909; subway A, C, E, N, Q, R, #1, #2, #3, #7 to 42nd St-Times Square; map p.141. The menu here features mostly straightforward American dishes (grilled salmon $22, pork chop $24), with a few Italian pastas thrown in for good measure ($17–20). It's very popular with theatre people, especially after performances. Mon–Thurs & Sun 10.30am–midnight, Fri & Sat 10.30am–12.30am.

ASIAN
Go! Go! Curry 273 W 38th St, between Seventh and Eighth aves ☎212 730 5555, ⓦgogocurryusa-ny.com; subway A, C, E, #7 to 42nd St-Port Authority, N, Q, R, #1, #2, #3 to Times Square-42nd St; see p.141. Perhaps more appropriate for lunch or a quick dinner, this quirky hole in the wall slings up delicious and cheap Japanese *katsu* in a thick curry sauce, with all kinds of toppings. It also serves as a temple to former Yankee baseballer Hideki Matsui (who wore #55, hence the opening times). Daily 10.55am–9.55pm.

Inakaya 231 W 40th St, between Seventh and Eighth aves ☎212 354 2195, ⓦinakayany.com; subway A, C, E, #7 to 42nd St-Port Authority, N, Q, R, #1, #2, #3 to Times Square-42nd St; map p.141. The setting is a bit theatrical and the prices a bit inflated – par for the area – but there's no denying the freshness and flavour of the sushi and grilled meat, seafood and veg. A *bento* box at lunch ($25–35) offers a nice sampling. Mon–Fri 11.30am–2pm & 5–11pm, Sat & Sun 5–11pm.

Pam Real Thai 404 W 49th St, between Ninth and Tenth aves ☎212 333 7500, ⍈pamrealthaifood.com; subway C, E to 50th St; map p.141. Of the number of Thai restaurants in this part of Hell's Kitchen, *Pam* has won a following for its spicy (but not overwhelmingly so) food, good prices and some slightly unusual dishes (say, anchovy rice or fermented fish kidneys). Better to stick with a *larb* (salad with minced meat, $6.95) and one of the curries ($10–13). Cash only. Daily 11.30am–11.30pm.

Pure Thai Cookhouse 766 Ninth Ave, between 51st and 52nd sts ☎212 581 0999, ⍈purethaishophouse.com; subway C, E to 50th St; map p.141. Wok-induced smoke fills the air at this rough-hewn Thai spot, which does excellent stir-fries and noodles, some a bit more daring than elsewhere (crab and pork dry noodles, $12; chilli turmeric with beef, $12). Mon–Thurs noon–10.30pm, Fri & Sat noon–11.30pm, Sun noon–10pm.

Sugiyama 251 W 55th St, between Broadway and Eighth Ave ☎212 956 0670, ⍈sugiyama-nyc.com; subway A, B, C, D, #1 to 59th St–Columbus Circle, N, R to 57th St or B, D, E to 7th Ave; map p.141. Though you may want to take out a loan before dining at this superb Japanese restaurant, especially if you have a thing for Wagyu beef, you're guaranteed an exquisite experience, from the enchanting *kaiseki* (chef's choice) dinners ($98 and up, though three- and five-course dinners can go for $32 or $65) to the regal service. Tues–Sat 5.30–11.45pm, last seating 10.15pm.

Totto Ramen 366 W 52nd St, between Eighth and Ninth aves ☎212 582 0082, ⍈tottoramen.com; subway C, E to 50th St; map p.141. A bit of a surprise on a somewhat desolate block – though the whole area is picking up as a foodie haven – *Totto Ramen* is a narrow spot (with mainly counter seating) to slurp up delicious bowls of pliant noodles and hearty broth, preferably with spicy sesame oil ($9.50–15; additional toppings extra). Bonus: watch the folks behind the counter periodically apply a blowtorch to colour the *char siu* pork. Mon–Sat noon–midnight, Sun 4–11pm.

★ **Yakitori Totto** 251 W 55th St (second floor), between Broadway and Eighth Ave ☎212 245 4555, ⍈tottonyc.com; subway A, B, C, D, #1 to 59th St–Columbus Circle, N, Q, R to 57th St or B, D, E to Seventh Ave; map p.141. This popular hideaway is perfect for late-night snacking – though by that time you may miss out on some of the more esoteric grilled skewers (soft knee bone and rare thigh, anyone?). Chicken heart, skirt steak and chicken thigh with spring onions all burst with flavour; a fistful of skewers (most $3–5 each) along with some sides and a cold Sapporo draught make a nice meal. Mon–Thurs 11.30am–2pm & 5.30pm–midnight, Fri 11.30am–2pm & 5.30pm–midnight, Sat 5.30pm–1am, Sun 5.30–11pm.

FRENCH

Aureole One Bryant Park/135 W 42nd St, at Sixth Ave ☎212 319 1660, ⍈charliepalmer.com; subway B, D, F, M to 42nd St–Bryant Park; map p.141. Unbelievably tasty and inventive French-accented American food. The prix-fixe options start at $89 per head, or $118 for the five-course tasting menu. Stop by for the show-stopping desserts (like poached pineapple in sweet wine), a pre-theatre dinner ($55; 5–6pm), or the more affordable lunch special ($36) or Sunday Bar Room beef for two ($49/person). Mon–Thurs 11.45am–2.15pm & 5–10pm, Fri 11.45am–2.15pm & 5–11pm, Sat 5–11pm, Sun 5–10pm.

Chez Napoleon 365 W 50th St, between Eighth and Ninth aves ☎212 265 6980, ⍈cheznapoleon.com; subway C, E to 50th St; map p.141. One of several authentic Gallic restaurants that sprang up in this area during World War II, when it was a hangout for French soldiers. A friendly, family-run bistro, it's stuck in a time warp in a good way. There's a $32 three-course dinner or you can go for classics like *boeuf bourguignon* ($25) or *sole meunière* ($28); the wines are decent and well priced. Mon–Fri noon–2pm & 5–9.30pm, Sat 5–9.30pm.

★ **Le Bernardin** 155 W 51st St, between Sixth and Seventh aves ☎212 554 1515, ⍈le-bernardin.com; subway N, R to 49th St, B, D, E to Seventh Ave, #1 to 50th St; map p.141. The most reviewed seafood restaurant in the United States, serving incomparable new angles on traditional Brittany fish dishes in elegant surroundings. This is one dinner you'll never forget – marinated *hamachi*, sautéed langoustine, crispy bass with *shishitos* – especially once the bill arrives ($127 prix fixe; $147 for tasting menu). Mon–Thurs noon–2.30pm & 5.15–10.30pm, Fri noon–2.30pm & 5.15–11pm, Sat 5.15–11pm.

ITALIAN

Becco 355 W 46th St, between Eighth and Ninth aves ☎212 397 7597, ⍈becco-nyc.com; subway A, C, E, #7 to 42nd St–Port Authority; map p.141. Catering to the pre-theatre crowd, *Becco* is most notable for its $23 *Sinfonia di Paste*: the all-you-can-eat dinner with a choice of three pasta-and-sauce combinations; there's also a good-value $25 wine menu. Mon noon–3pm & 5–10pm, Tues noon–3pm & 4.30pm–midnight, Wed & Sat 11.30am–2.30pm & 4pm–midnight, Thurs noon–3pm & 5–10pm, Fri 11.30am–3pm & 5pm–midnight, Sun noon–midnight.

Don Antonio by Starita 309 W 50th St, between Eighth and Ninth aves ☎646 719 1043, ⍈donantoniopizza.com; subway C, E to 50th St; map p.141. The progeny of two celebrated Neopolitan pizza mavens, busy *Don Antonio* showcases a few different styles of pie; its signature, the Montanara Starita ($12), is light, smoky and chewy – and comes by way of the deep fryer and the brick oven. Traditional margheritas ($12) share the menu with items like the pistachio and sausage speciality pie ($21), in which a

24

TOP 5 PIZZA

Grimaldi's DUMBO, Brooklyn. See p.320
Kesté West Village. See p.306
John's Pizzeria West Village. See p.306
Lombardi's Little Italy. See p.300
Totonno's Coney Island. See p.324

---

pistachio pesto stands in as the sauce, and filled *pizzes* ($13–19). Mon–Thurs 11.30am–11pm, Fri & Sat 11.30am–midnight, Sun 11.30am–10.30pm.

Esca 402 W 43rd St, at Ninth Ave ☎ 212 564 7272, ⍟ esca-nyc.com; subway A, C, E to 42nd St-Port Authority; map p.141. Co-owned by Mario Batali, but more the baby of chef and co-owner Dave Pasternack, whose passion for fresh fish – and preparations that showcase it – is evident. Lots of *crudo* ($18–20) and whole fish grilled or salt-baked (main dishes $30–38). Mon noon–2.30pm & 5–10.30pm, Tues–Sat noon–2.30pm & 5–11.30pm, Sun 4.30–10.30pm.

Trattoria dell'Arte 900 Seventh Ave, at W 57th St ☎ 212 245 9800, ⍟ trattoriadellarte.com; subway N, R to 57th St; map p.141. Great, wafer-thin crispy pizzas (around $30–38 for a large one), decent and imaginative pasta dishes from around $24, flashy items like the veal chop ($48) and snapper *livornese* ($32), and a mouthwatering antipasto bar – all eagerly patronized by an elegant, out-to-be-seen crowd. Mon–Sat 11.45am–midnight, Sun 11am–10.30pm.

JEWISH AND RUSSIAN

Carnegie Deli 854 Seventh Ave, between W 54th and 55th sts ☎ 212 757 2245, ⍟ carnegiedeli.com; subway B, D, E to Seventh Ave; map p.301. With the demise of the *Stage Deli*, this famous Jewish deli has Midtown's pastrami-loving tourist crowd more or less to itself. It lays claim to the most generously stuffed sandwiches in the city served by the rudest of waiters. It trades mainly on its reputation as an essential experience; go if you must, but you're probably better off at *Katz's* (see p.301) or *2nd Avenue Deli* (p.312). Daily 6.30am–4am.

Petrossian 182 W 58th St, at Seventh Ave ☎ 212 245 2214, ⍟ petrossian.com; subway A, B, C, D, #1 to 59th St-Columbus Circle, N, Q, R to 57th St; map p.141. Pink granite and etched mirrors set the mood at this decadent Art Deco establishment, where champagne and caviar are the norm. If you want to head down a more affordable route, go with the $42 prix-fixe dinner and just pretend. Mon–Thurs 11.30am–3pm & 5–11.30pm, Fri & Sat 11.30am–3pm & 5.30–11pm, Sun 11.30am–3pm & 5–11pm.

Russian Tea Room 150 W 57th St, between Sixth and Seventh aves ☎ 212 581 7100, ⍟ russiantearoomnyc.com; subway F, N, Q, R to 57th St; map p.141. In its third incarnation, the restaurant has nowhere near the cachet of the original, but it still pulls folks in – the stroganoff ($39) and the chicken Kiev ($38) are faves. With appetizers $20–35 and main dishes $38–48, you'll need plenty of dough. Mon–Fri 7am–11.30pm, Sat & Sun 11am–11.30pm.

Samovar 256 W 52nd St, between Eighth and Ninth aves ☎ 212 757 0168, ⍟ russiansamovar.com; subway C, E to 50th St; map p.141. Each dish here is about $10 cheaper than its counterpart at the *Tea Room*, the vodka flows freely and there's live music most nights in this convivial hangout – which also owns the distinction of having been co-founded by the late Russian exile Joseph Brodsky. Daily noon–3am.

LATIN AMERICAN

Churrascaria Plataforma 316 W 49th St, between Eighth and Ninth aves ☎ 212 245 0505, ⍟ churrascariaplataforma.com; subway C, E, #1 to 50th St; map p.141. Meat (the fare of choice) is served in this huge, open Brazilian dining room by waiters carrying swords stabbed with succulent slabs of grilled pork, chicken and lots of beef. The $62.95 prix fixe (your only option) covers all of these various grilled meats and more. Don't miss the addictive *caipirinhas* (Brazil's national drink). Mon & Sun noon–11pm, Tues–Sat noon–midnight.

Hell's Kitchen 679 Ninth Ave, between W 46th and 47th sts ☎ 212 977 1588, ⍟ hellskitchen-nyc.com; subway C, E to 50th St; map p.141. Lively atmosphere aided and abetted by more than half a dozen flavours of frozen margarita and nouveau renderings of Mexican cuisine. Favourites include tuna *tostadas* ($14) to start, tamarind-rubbed sirloin ($32) as a main and caramelized banana *empanadas* ($7) to finish off with. Sun & Mon 5–11pm, Tues & Wed 11.30am–3pm & 5–11pm, Thurs & Fri 11.30am–3pm & 5pm–midnight, Sat 5pm–midnight.

THE UPPER EAST SIDE

Upper East Side restaurants mostly exist to serve a discriminating mixture of Park Avenue matrons and young professionals, and the cuisine here is much like that of the rest of Manhattan: a middling mixture of Asian, standard American, Italian and especially posh French restaurants. New Yorkers and visitors alike rarely come up here solely for the food, but since there are so many museums and sights in the neighbourhood you're likely to need a place to eat, at least for lunch.

AMERICAN AND CONTINENTAL

E.A.T. 1064 Madison Ave, between E 80th and E 81st sts ☎ 212 772 0022, ⍟ elizabar.com; subway #6 to 77th St; map p.169. Owned by restaurateur and gourmet grocer Eli Zabar, *E.A.T.* is pricey and crowded (main dishes $18–35) but the food is excellent, notably the soups ($10–12), salads

($16), and sandwiches (from $16); the mozzarella, basil and tomato fillings are fresh and heavenly. The takeaway counter and bakery is a bit cheaper. Daily 7am–10pm.

★ **Flex Mussels** 174 E 82nd St, between Third and Lexington aves ☎ 212 717 7772, ⊕ flexmusselsny.com; subway #4, #5, #6 to 86th St; map p.169. Mussels fresh from Prince Edward Island (Canada) take centre stage here, with plates with various sauces ranging $19.50–25. Make a point of trying the special hand-cut fries ($6). Mon–Thurs 5.30–11pm, Fri 5.30–11.30pm, Sat 5–11.30pm, Sun 5–10pm.

JG Melon Restaurant 1291 Third Ave, at E 74th St ☎ 212 650 1310; subway #6 to 77th St; map p.169. One of the few old-school bars on the Upper East Side, but best known for its juicy burgers ($9.75–10.50) and crispy waffle-cut fries. Sun–Thurs 11.30am–3am, Fri & Sat 11.30am–4am.

Kings' Carriage House 251 E 82nd St, between Second and Third aves ☎ 212 734 5490, ⊕ kingscarriagehouse .com; subway #4, #5, #6 to 86th St; map p.169. You'll feel as if you've been transported to the countryside at this romantic, converted carriage-house. With rustic American/French cuisine (such as foie gras flan and pheasant pot pie), it's a fine place for a meal or afternoon tea (daily 3–5pm; $24.95); prix-fixe meals only: $18.95 for lunch to $49 for dinner. Daily noon–10pm.

Pastrami Queen 1125 Lexington Ave, at E 78th St ☎ 212 734 1500, ⊕ pastramiqueen.com; subway #6 to 77th St; map p.169. This friendly diner has been knocking out giant hot pastrami sandwiches ($15.95) since 1956, as well as corned beef and a host of Jewish kosher classics (matzoh-ball soups) and desserts ($7–9). Daily 10am–11pm.

★ **Penrose** 1590 Second Ave, between E 82nd and E 83rd sts ☎ 212 203 2751, ⊕ penrosebar.com; subway #4, #5, #6 to 86th St; map p.169. This popular new gastropub makes an excellent lunch diversion from Museum Mile; highlights include the mighty Pat La Frieda Penrose burger, worth every morsel at $12, and the beer-battered and fried Irish sausages with smoky sauce ($6). Mon–Thurs 3pm–4am, Fri 1pm–4am, Sat & Sun 11am–4am.

ASIAN

Donguri 309 E 83rd St, between First and Second aves ☎ 212 737 5656, ⊕ itoen.com/donguri; subway #4, #5, #6 to 86th St; map p.169. Sushi lovers won't want to miss this little five-table spot featuring some of the best sashimi sets in town (from $18), as well as superb shrimp tempura ($26) and soba noodles (from $12). Reservations are highly recommended. Tues–Sun 5.30–9.30pm.

Naruto Ramen 1596 Third Ave, between E 89th and E 90th sts ☎ 212 289 7803, ⊕ narutoterakawa.com; subway #4, #5, #6 to 86th St; map p.169. Tiny Japanese

noodle shop, cooking up excellent bowls of ramen ($9) with pork, miso or curry, fried rice ($8) and Japanese curry ($9.50). Daily noon–10.45pm.

Pig Heaven 1540 Second Ave, between E 80th and E 81st sts ☎ 212 744 4333, ⊕ pigheavennyc.com; subway #6 to 77th St; map p.169. Good-value Chinese-American restaurant, with Taiwanese, Cantonese and Szechuan influences. The accent, not surprisingly, is on pork; dumplings, spare ribs, BBQ suckling pig and so on, but everything else is good too (main dishes average $14–15). Sun–Thurs noon–11.15pm, Fri & Sat noon–1.15am.

CZECH

Hospoda 321 E 73rd St, between First and Second aves ☎ 212 861 1038, ⊕ hospodanyc.com; subway #6 to 77th St; map p.169. Stylish Prague-based Czech gastropub serving specialities from Bohemia, Austria and Bavaria (along with more typical American dishes using seasonal ingredients): think fried egg bread, smoked Prague-style ham, rainbow trout and duck leg confit with red cabbage and potato dumplings (mains $18–38). The bar serves four types of Pilsner Urquell on draft – the same beer but with different degrees of foamy head, to bring out subtle flavours ($22 for tasting or $5–7 single, happy hour daily 4–7pm). Mon–Sat 4pm–midnight, Sun noon–11pm.

FRENCH

Café Boulud 20 E 76th St, between Madison and Fifth aves ☎ 212 772 2600, ⊕ cafeboulud.com/nyc; subway #6 to 77th St; map p.169. The muted but elegant interior of chef Daniel Boulud's second Manhattan restaurant is an exceedingly pleasant place to savour his sublime concoctions (case in point: venison terrine with lingonberry compote). Main dishes $17–45. Mon–Thurs 7–10am, noon–2.30pm & 5.45–10.30pm, Fri 7–10am, noon–2.30pm & 5.45–11pm, Sat 7–10am, noon–2.30pm & 5.30–11pm, Sun 8–11am, noon–3pm & 5.45–10.30pm.

★ **Daniel** 60 E 65th St, between Madison and Park aves ☎ 212 288 0033, ⊕ danielnyc.com; subway #6 to 68th St; map p.169. Expensive gourmet fare from chef Boulud (again) – think black sea bass in Syrah sauce and "quartet of pig provençale". Prix-fixe dinners only from $116; there's even an elaborate, seasonal, vegetarian version (same price). One of the best French restaurants in New York City (jacket required for men). Mon–Sat 5.30–11pm.

Jojo 160 E 64th St, between Lexington and Third aves ☎ 212 223 5656, ⊕ jojorestaurantnyc.com; subway F to Lexington Ave-63rd St; map p.169. Lavish townhouse restaurant created by feted French chef Jean-Georges Vongerichten, serving excellent French fusion cuisine with the freshest ingredients – one of the few top French places

24

open for lunch (prix fixe $32). Main dishes $21–49. Mon–Thurs noon–2.30pm & 5.30–10.30pm, Fri & Sat noon–2.30pm & 5.30–11pm, Sun noon–2.30pm & 5.30–10pm.

GERMAN

Heidelberg 1648 Second Ave, between E 85th and E 86th sts ☎212 628 2332, ⓦheidelbergrestaurant.com; subway #4, #5, #6 to 86th St; map p.169. The atmosphere here is *Mittel*-European kitsch, with gingerbread trim and waitresses in Alpine goatherd costumes. The food is the real deal, featuring excellent liver-dumpling soup, *Bauernfrühstück* omelettes, and pancakes, both sweet and potato (most dishes $19–28). And they serve *Weissbier* the right way, too – in 2-litre, boot-shaped glasses. Mon–Thurs 11.30am–11pm, Fri & Sat 11.30am–midnight, Sun noon–11pm.

ITALIAN

Ottomanelli's 86th St Café 1626 York Ave, between E 85th and E 86th sts ☎212 772 0080, ⓦnycotto.com; subway #6 to 77th St; map p.169. The Ottomanelli food empire dates back to 1900, and this old-school Italian diner is a real gem, with pizzas (from $7.95), juicy steak burgers ($8.95) and excellent pastas ($12.95). Daily 11am–10pm.

Paola's 1295 Madison Ave at E 92nd St ☎212 794 1890, ⓦpaolasrestaurant.com; subway #6 at 96th St; map p.169. One of the neighbourhood's better Italian restaurants, with fresh and tasty pastas ($20–24) – the *bolognese* is especially tasty. Sun & Mon 11am–4pm & 5–10pm, Tues–Sat 11am–4pm & 5–11pm.

MEXICAN

Cascabel Taqueria 1538 Second Ave, at E 80th St ☎212 717 7800, ⓦnyctacos.com; subway #6 to 77th St; map p.169. Funky taco shop offering two fresh corn tacos for $8.50, with fillings *like chorizo*, fish, shrimp and *carnitas* (plus veggie choices). Also does bigger chicken plates ($12.50) and delicious *churros* (two for $1). Great salsas.

Sun–Thurs 11am–midnight, Fri & Sat 11am–1am.

Maya 1191 First Ave, between E 64th and E 65th sts ☎212 585 1818, ⓦrichardsandoval.com/mayany; subway #6 to 68th St, F to 63rd St; map p.169. Excellent, high-end Mexican dishes are served in a large, colourful and noisy dining room. The rock shrimp *ceviche*, chicken *mole* and grilled dorado fillet make this one of the best restaurants in the Upper East Side – and among the best Mexican spots in the whole city. Main dishes $23–32. Mon–Thurs 11am–3pm & 5–10pm, Fri 11am–3pm & 5–11pm, Sat 5–11pm, Sun 5–10pm.

PERSIAN

Persepolis 1407 Second Ave, between E 73th and E 74th sts ☎212 535 1100, ⓦpersepolisnyc.com; subway #6 to 77th St; map p.169. One of the few places in New York for Persian food, this is also one of the best. Aromas of rose, cherry and cardamom fill the dining room (as well as a painting of the owner, a former goalkeeper, with his Tehran-based team Persepolis F.C.). Main dishes range $16–28. Daily noon–11.30pm.

TURKISH

Beyoglu 1431 Third Ave, at E 81st St ☎212 650 0850; subway #4, #5, #6 to 86th St; map p.169. The place to go for mouthwatering meze (the Turkish version of appetizers) for $5.50–7.50; the doner kebabs and fish specials are superb as well ($14.50–16). Loud (the second floor is quieter), reasonably priced, and definitely filling. Daily noon–11.30pm.

VEGETARIAN

Candle Café 1307 Third Ave, at E 75th St ☎212 472 0970, ⓦcandlecafe.com; subway #6 to 77th St; map p.169. This vegan favourite does its best to dress up all that tofu and seitan, often with surprising results. Salads are a standout, as are the soups and juices from the "farmacy". Moderately priced (main dishes $16–20). Mon–Sat 11.30am–10.30pm, Sun 11.30am–9.30pm.

THE UPPER WEST SIDE AND MORNINGSIDE HEIGHTS

The Upper West Side is yuppie-residential, with the cuisine on offer tailored to local tastes: generous burger joints, coffee shops and Latin American-influenced lounges, but also an increasing number of ambitious restaurants, especially around Lincoln Center, the Museum of Natural History and Columbia University.

AFRICAN

Awash 947 Amsterdam Ave, between 106th and 107th sts ☎212 961 1416, ⓦawashny.com; subway #1 to 103rd St; map p.183. Ethiopian expats flock to this brightly coloured restaurant offering sumptuous vegetarian and meat combo platters ($15–19). Dig in with your hands, but lay off the too-sweet honey wine. Also in downtown and Brooklyn. Daily 12.30–10.30pm.

AMERICAN AND CONTINENTAL

Boat Basin Café W 79th St, at the Hudson River with access through Riverside Park ☎212 496 5542, ⓦboatbasincafe.com; subway #1 to 79th St; map p.183. An outdoor restaurant, the *Boat Basin* is only open seasonally. The informal tables are covered in red-and-white-checked cloths, and the food is standard – mostly burgers and sandwiches ($9.25–16.95), with the odd outlier – but inexpensive considering the prime location.

24

On weekend afternoons a violin trio adds to the pleasant ambience. Usually April–Oct Mon–Wed noon–11pm, Thurs & Fri noon–11.30pm, Sat 11am–11.30pm, Sun 11am–10pm, weather permitting.

Boathouse Café Central Park Lake, at W 72nd St entrance ☎ 212 517 2233, ⓦ thecentralparkboathouse .com; subway B, C to 72nd St; map p.183. A peaceful retreat after a hard day's trudging around the Fifth Avenue museums. You get great views of the famous Central Park skyline and decent American/Continental cuisine, but at somewhat steep prices – say, branzino with spring vegetables ($28) and seared rack of lamb ($42). April–Nov Mon–Fri noon–4pm & 5.30–9.30pm, Sat & Sun 9.30am–4pm & 6–9.30pm.

Dovetail 103 W 77th St ☎ 212 362 3800, ⓦ dovetailnyc .com; subway B, C to 81st St-Museum of Natural History; map p.183. A rare Michelin-starred (and deservedly so) restaurant in this area, with bold, fresh, market-driven dishes like Brussels sprouts salad ($18), scallops with asparagus, crayfish and bacon ($42) and guinea hen with root vegetables ($42); menus are seasonal. Special set meals for Fri lunch and Sun "suppa"; there's even a speacial night (Mon) celebrating vegetables ($58 for four courses). Mon–Thurs 5.30–10pm, Fri & Sat 5.30–10.30pm, Sun 11.30am–2.30pm & 5.30–10.30pm.

Miss Mamie's Spoonbread Too 336 W 110th St, between Columbus and Manhattan aves ☎ 212 865 6744, ⓦ spoonbreadinc.com/miss_mamies.htm; subway B, C to Cathedral Parkway-110th St; map p.183. Excellent soul-food restaurant with a 1950s-themed interior, addictive North Carolina ribs ($15.95) and some of the best fried chicken ($13.95) in the city (allegedly the favourite of ex-President Clinton). Mon–Thurs noon–10pm, Fri & Sat noon–11pm, Sun 11am–9.30pm.

Ouest 2315 Broadway, between W 83rd and 84th sts ☎ 212 580 8700, ⓦ ouestny.com; subway #1 to 86th St; map p.183. This New American restaurant has earned a loyal following for its exceptional gourmet comfort-food, such as stewed tripe with wine and pancetta ($27) and squab with chive risotto ($35); there's also a $38 three-course pre-theatre menu (every day except Sat; get there by 6pm). Mon & Tues 5.30–9.30pm, Wed & Thurs 5.30–10pm, Fri 5.30–11pm, Sat 5–11pm, Sun 11am–2pm & 5–9pm.

Per Se 1 Central Park W, 10 Columbus Circle, Time Warner Center ☎ 212 823 9335, ⓦ perseny.com; subway A, B, C, D, #1 to 59th St-Columbus Circle; map p.183. The $300 nine-course prix fixe is a series of small plates that seek to transcend the standard dining experience; whimsical ideas along the lines of "Pearls and oysters", which pairs oysters with tapioca and caviar, should give you some idea – and it all works. Menu changes regularly; reservations accepted only by phone two months prior to the day, and

jackets are required for men. Mon–Thurs 5.30–10pm, Fri–Sun 11.30am–1.30pm & 5.30–10pm.

★ **Telepan** 72 W 69th St, between Columbus Ave and Central Park West ☎ 212 580 4300, ⓦ telepan-ny.com; subway #1 to 66th St, B, C to 72nd St; map p.183. One of the surer-footed spots in the neighbourhood, with an emphasis on market-fresh ingredients (especially vegetables) and comforting dishes, like scallop and sea urchin stew ($27). A celebrated burger, with French fries exploding out of an onion-ring mountain, is available at lunch (3 courses for $32). Brunch (again, $32 for baked goods plus two courses) is another good time to go. Mon 5–10pm, Tues 5–10.30pm, Wed & Thurs 11.30am–2.30pm & 5–10.30pm, Fri 11.30am–2.30pm & 5–11.30pm, Sat 11am–2.30pm & 5–11.30pm, Sun 11am–3pm & 5–10pm.

ASIAN

Josie's 300 Amsterdam Ave, at 74th St ☎ 212 769 1212, ⓦ josiesnyc.com; subway #1, #2, #3 to 72nd St; map p.183. Fresh, tasty veggie-friendly dishes with an Asian twist, as well as organic chicken and wild seafood. Mon–Thurs noon–10pm, Fri noon–11.30pm, Sat 10am–11.30pm, Sun 10am–10.30pm.

Sapphire 1845 Broadway, between W 60th and 61st sts ☎ 212 245 4444, ⓦ sapphireny.com; subway A, B, C, D, #1 to 59th St-Columbus Circle; map p.183. Capable Indian restaurant conveniently located near the Time Warner Center and Lincoln Center; most curries and tandoori meals are around $19–21. Mon–Thurs 11.45am–2.45pm & 5–10.30pm, Fri & Sat 11.45am–2.45pm & 5–11pm, Sun 5–10.30pm.

Shun Lee West 43 W 65th St, at Columbus Ave ☎ 212 595 8895, ⓦ shunleewest.com; subway #1 to 66th St; map p.183. This venerable local institution – conveniently across the street from Lincoln Center – has top-notch Chinese food; steer yourself towards the menu's many seafood delicacies ($30–37). The service and table settings are strictly formal (though attached is a café with dim sum) but you should feel free to dress casually. Another location exists over in Midtown East. Mon–Sat noon–midnight, Sun 11.30am–10.30pm.

FRENCH

Bar Boulud 1900 Broadway, between 63rd and 64th sts ☎ 212 595 0303, ⓦ danielnyc.com/barboulud.html; subway A, B, C, D, #1 to 59th St-Columbus Circle, or #1 to 66th St-Lincoln Center; map p.183. One of superstar chef Daniel Boulud's restaurants, particularly worthwhile are the house-made pâtés, terrines and charcuterie that comprise the most original part of the menu. There's also an excellent and extensive Rhone wine list. Right next door is the Mediterranean-inspired *Boulud Sud*, another winner. Mon–Thurs noon–2.30pm & 5–11pm, Fri

24

noon–2.30pm & 5pm–midnight, Sat 11am–4pm & 5pm–midnight, Sun 11am–4pm & 5–10pm, open later Mon–Sat on theatre nights.

Café Luxembourg 200 W 70th St, between Amsterdam and West End aves ☎212 873 7411, ⓦcafeluxembourg.com; subway #1, #2, #3 to 72nd St; map p.183. Popular Lincoln Center-area bistro that packs in a slightly sniffy crowd to enjoy first-rate, contemporary French food. Main dishes (roasted Arctic char, steak frites) run $26–36, while the brasserie menu (sandwiches, salads, burgers, *moules frites*) is a bit cheaper. Mon & Tues 8am–11pm, Wed–Fri 8am–midnight, Sat 9am–midnight, Sun 9am–11pm.

Jean-Georges *Trump International Hotel*, 1 Central Park W, between W 60th and 61st sts ☎212 299 3900, ⓦjean-georgesrestaurant.com; subway A, B, C, D, #1 to 59th St-Columbus Circle; map p.183. French fare at its finest, crafted by star chef Jean-Georges Vongerichten. The gracious service is a throwback to another, more genteel, era. With meals starting at $118 (tasting menus from $198), it's definitely the place for a special occasion; for the price-conscious, the $38 two-course lunchtime is a good bet, or adjourn to the front-room *Nougatine* for more reasonable meals in a somewhat casual (still refined) setting. The wine list includes bottles ranging from $40 all the way to $12,000. Mon–Thurs noon–2.30pm & 5.30–11pm, Fri & Sat noon–2.30pm & 5.15–11pm.

Picholine 35 W 64th St, between Broadway and Central Park W ☎212 724 8585, ⓦpicholinenyc.com; subway #1 to 66th St; map p.183. Right near Lincoln Center, this pricey French favourite executes Gallic fare with flair. The Scottish game, when available, is a treat (menus are seasonal; $98 for three-course prix fixe, a bit less pre- or post-theatre) and the cheese plate is to die for ($20). A terrific spot for a celebratory dinner. Tues–Thurs 5–10pm, Fri & Sat 5–11pm, Sun 5–9pm.

ITALIAN

Caffè Storico 170 Central Park West, at 77th St ☎212 873 3400, ⓦnyhistory.org/dine; subway B, C to 81st St-Museum of Natural History; map p.183. The onsite dining locale for the New-York Historical Society (p.189), cheery *Storico* offers serious-minded Italian fare; pastas run $16–22, mains (*cioppino*, veal *milanese*) $22–33. Slip in for a coffee or panini during a daytime visit, or come for the bargain Sunday prix fixe ($28 for three courses). Tues–Sun 11am–10pm.

Gennaro 665 Amsterdam Ave, between W 92nd and 93rd sts ☎212 665 5348, ⓦgennaronyc.com; subway #1, #2, #3 to 96th St; map p.183. A bustling spot for moderately priced favourites like warm potato, mushroom and goat cheese tart ($11.95) and braised lamb shank in red wine ($19), accompanied by reasonable Italian wines.

Save room for dessert. Cash only. Mon–Thurs 5–10.30pm, Fri & Sat 5–11pm.

★ **Salumeria Rosi Parmacotto** 283 Amsterdam Ave, between 73rd and 74th sts ☎212 877 4801, ⓦsalumeriarosi.com; subway #1, #2, #3 to 72nd St; map p.183. On your left as you enter is a deli counter with a dizzying array of gorgeous cured meats; on your right, the slender dining room, whose mirrored wall and ceiling are partially covered by a food-contoured plaster relief map of Italy. Order lots of small plates: a selection of that *salumi* ($6–9 each, sampling $18–27) and some cheeses ($8 each, sampling $17); crisp Brussels sprouts ($12); a pasta or two ($14–15). For takeaway, the *porchetta calabrese* sandwich ($14) is a no-brainer. Mon–Fri noon–10/11pm, Sat & Sun 11am–10pm.

V&T Pizzeria 1024 Amsterdam Ave, between W 110th and 111th sts ☎212 663 1708 or ☎666 8051, ⓦvtpizzeriarestaurant.com; subway #1 to 110th St; map p.183. Checked tablecloths, old-world paintings and a low-key feel are the hallmarks of this pizzeria near Columbia University, with predictably college-aged patrons. There's plenty more than just pizza ($18 for large with one topping), like pastas ($11–15) and classic Italian dishes with veal, chicken and shrimp (mostly $15–22). Mon & Sun 11.30am–11pm, Tues–Sat 11.30am–midnight.

LATIN AMERICAN

Calle Ocho In the *Excelsior Hotel*, 45 W 81st St, between Central Park West and Columbus Ave ☎212 873 5025, ⓦcalleochonyc.com; subway B, C to 81st St or #1 to 79th St; map p.183. Very tasty Latino fare, including *ceviche* (there's a wide selection priced $13–18) and *chimichurri* steak ($28) with yucca fries, served in an immaculately designed restaurant with a lively lounge. The *mojitos* ($10) are as tasty and potent as any in the city. Mon–Thurs 6–10.30pm, Fri 6–11.30pm, Sat noon–3pm & 5–11.30pm, Sun noon–3.30pm & 5–10pm.

MEXICAN

Rosa Mexicano 61 Columbus Ave, between W 62nd and 63rd sts ☎212 977 7700, ⓦrosamexicano.com; subway A, B, C, D, #1 to 59th St-Columbus Circle; map p.183. Right across from Lincoln Center, it's the perfect location for a post-opera meal. Try the guacamole ($14 per order), which is mashed at your table, and their signature pomegranate margaritas ($11.50). Mon–Thurs & Sun 11.30am–11pm, Fri & Sat 11.30am–12.30am.

MIDDLE EASTERN

Turkuaz 2637 Broadway, at W 100th St ☎212 665 9541, ⓦturkuazrestaurant.com; subway #1, #2, #3 to 96th St; map p.183. Sip a glass of raki in *Turkuaz's* cavernous dining room and linger over such Turkish delicacies as vine leaves stuffed with grilled salmon cubes ($16.95); there are some vegetarian options too. Bellydancing on weekend nights at

9.30pm. Mon–Thurs noon–11pm, Fri & Sat noon–midnight, Sun 11am–11pm.

HARLEM

While visitors to Harlem will find plenty of cheap Caribbean and West African restaurants, it would be unthinkable not to try the soul food for which the area is justifiably famous. Whether it's ribs or fried chicken and waffles you're craving, you simply can't go wrong.

AFRICAN

★ **Africa Kine** 256 W 116th St between Douglass and Powell blvds ☎212 666 9400, ⓦafricakine.com; subway B, C to 116th St; map p.198. Best place on the Little Senegal strip to try authentic West African and Senegalese dishes, such as lamb curry, lamb and peanut butter stew and spicy fish with okra, served with heaps of rice, all for around $10 at lunch ($11–15 dinner). There's also a small takeaway counter on the first floor. Daily 12.30pm–2am.

Salimata Restaurant 2132 Frederick Douglass Blvd, between 115th and 116th sts ☎212 280 6980; subway B, C to 116th St; map p.198. Basic Guinean canteen catering primarily to West African expats, with rich, meaty soups and aromatic stews from around $10–15 (cash only). Daily 1pm–3.30am.

Zoma 2084 Frederick Douglass Blvd, at W 113th St ☎212 662 0620, ⓦzomanyc.com; subway B, C to 116th St; map p.198. One of the sleekest places around, delivering solid Ethiopian food in minimalist digs at low prices. The combination platters are your best bet: here the veggie combo goes for $24.59 and is big enough to share. Meat eaters should try the *doro wat*, or long-simmered chicken in spices (most main dishes $17–21; cash and AMEX only). Mon–Fri 5–11pm, Sat & Sun noon–11pm.

CAJUN, SOUL FOOD AND BARBECUE

★ **Amy Ruth's** 113 W 116th St, between Malcolm X and Powell blvds ☎212 280 8779, ⓦamyruthsharlem.com; subway #2, #3 to 116th St; map p.198. The barbecue chicken ($13.95), named in honour of President Obama, is more than enough reason to visit this small, casual family restaurant, but waffles breakfasts (from $7.95) and desserts (think peach cobbler and banana pudding; $5) are equally enticing. Mon 11.30am–11pm, Tues–Thurs 8.30am–11pm, Fri 8.30am–5.30am, Sat 7.30am–5.30am, Sun 7.30am–11pm.

Charles' Country Pan Fried 2841 Frederick Douglass Blvd, between W 151st and W 152nd sts ☎212 281 1800; subway B, D to 155th St; map p.198. Fried chicken, barbecue chicken breast and smothered chicken leg are the specialities at this tiny Harlem spot, but the filling macaroni and cheese, collard greens and candied yams are equally good. Two pieces with two sides costs just $9.50, but there's an open lunch buffet for $10.99 ($15.16 for dinner and all day at weekends). Mon–Thurs 11am–11pm, Fri & Sat 11am–1am, Sun 11am–8pm.

★ **Dinosaur Bar-B-Que** 700 W 125th St, at Twelfth Ave ☎212 694 1777, ⓦdinosaurbarbque.com; subway #1 to 125th St; map p.198. This convivial joint, an outpost of the original (in Syracuse, NY, of all places) is especially known for its pit-smoked chicken wings ($6.95 for six) and pork ribs ($10.50). Live blues every Sat from 10pm onwards. Mon–Thurs 11.30am–11pm, Fri & Sat 11.30am–midnight, Sun noon–10pm.

Londel's Supper Club 2620 Frederick Douglass Blvd, between W 139th and W 140th sts ☎212 234 6114, ⓦlondelsrestaurant.com; subway B, C to 135th St; map p.198. A little soul food, a little Cajun, a little Southern-fried food. This is an attractive, down-home place where you can eat jumbo fried shrimp ($24.95) or more common treats such as Southern fried chicken and waffles ($13.95); either way, follow it up with some sweet-potato pie. Sunday brunch $22.95. Jazz and R&B on Fri and Sat evenings at 8pm and 10pm. Tues–Sat 5–11pm, Sun 11am–5pm.

Miss Maude's Spoonbread Too 547 Malcolm X Blvd, between W 137th and W 138th sts ☎212 996 0660, ⓦspoonbreadinc.com/miss_maudes.htm; subway #2, #3 to 135th St; map p.198. Some of the best soul-food in Harlem – Norma Jean Darden's generations-old family recipes include succulent ribs ($14.95), Louisiana catfish ($15.95) and fried chicken ($12.95). Mon–Thurs noon–9.30pm, Fri & Sat noon–10.30pm, Sun 11am–9.30pm.

★ **Red Rooster** 310 Malcolm X Blvd, between W 125th and W 126th sts ☎212 792 9001, ⓦredroosterharlem .com; subway #2, #3 to 125th St; map p.198. Marcus Samuelsson's restaurant offers a sophisticated take on Southern comfort food. Sandwiches are $15–17, while mains such as lamb and sweet potato hash are $18–29 (lunch is cheaper). Leave room for the Rooster mud pie ($11). Mon–Thurs 11.30am–3pm & 5.30–10.30pm, Fri 11.30am–3pm & 5.30–11.30pm, Sat 10am–3pm & 5–11.30pm, Sun 10am–3pm & 5–10pm.

Sylvia's Restaurant 328 Malcolm X Blvd, between W 126th and W 127th sts ☎212 996 0660, ⓦsylviasrestaurant.com; subway #2, #3 to 125th St; map p.198. Established in 1962, this is the best-known Southern soul-food restaurant in Harlem – so famous that Sylvia Woods started her own food line (the matron died in 2012). While the BBQ ribs ($17.95) are exceptional and the candied yams ($4.50) are justly celebrated, *Sylvia's* has become a bit of a tourist trap – try to avoid Sundays when tour groups arrive for the Gospel Brunch. Mon–Sat 8am–10.30pm, Sun 11am–8pm.

24

EL BARRIO (EAST HARLEM)

El Barrio sees far fewer visitors than Harlem, but its restaurants are definitely worth a try; Puerto Rican and Latino cuisines dominate, though the strip along Lexington Avenue around East 106th Street is developing a more varied scene.

El Paso 1643 Lexington Ave at E 104th St ☎212 831 9831, ⓦelpasony.com; subway #6 to 103rd St; map p.198. One of three authentic Mexican restaurants managed by a couple of chefs from Puebla – this is the newest and smartest venue, with fabulous tacos from $9 (for three), larger enchiladas ($12–13) and a range of regional Mexican dishes ($14–24) like *carnitas estilo Michoacan* (pork in tequila). Daily 11am–11pm.

La Fonda Boricua 169 E 106th St, between Lexington and Third aves ☎212 410 7292, ⓦfondaboricua.com; subway #6 to 103rd St; map p.198. Authentic Puerto Rican diner, where huge plates of rich meat stews, roast pork, rice and beans rarely top $8. Daily 11am–10pm.

Patsy's Pizzeria 2287 First Ave, between E 117th and E 118th sts ☎212 534 9783, ⓦthepatsyspizza .com; subway #6 to 116th St; map p.198. Opened by Pasquale "Patsy" Lancieri in 1933, this is one of the last vestiges of Italian Harlem, churning out paper-thin pizza slices ($1.75; pizzas from $12) from its coal-burning brick oven; Patsy learnt his trade at *Lombardi's*, but it was here that he "invented" the pizza slice concept. Daily 11am–11pm.

Rao's 455 E 114th St, between First and Pleasant aves ☎212 722 6709, ⓦraos.com; subway #6 at 116th St; map p.198. Founded in 1896 and the most authentic Italian (Neapolitan) dining experience in the city. To be honest, you are unlikely to ever eat a meal here (it's only got 10 tables "owned" by regulars, and one seating a night), but it's worth soaking up the ambience at the tiny bar – who knows, a table may become available (wearing a suit will help). Cash only, and remember it's "ray-o's". Mon–Fri 7–11pm.

WASHINGTON HEIGHTS

24

Northern Manhattan is the best place on the island to try authentic Dominican food, and you can often eat like a king for just a few dollars.

El Malecón Restaurant 4141 Broadway, between W 175th & W 176th sts ☎212 927 3812; subway A to 175th St; map p.208. This old-school Cuban joint is best known for its glistening spit-roasted chicken, but aromatic *asopaos* (soupy rice), plantains and puddings are just as good – all for less than $15. Sun–Thurs 7am–1.30am, Fri & Sat 7am–2am.

New Leaf Restaurant & Bar 1 Margaret Corbin Drive, Fort Tryon Park ☎212 568 5323, ⓦnewleafrestaurant .com; subway A to 190th St; map p.208. An airy, renovated 1930s building with views of Fort Tryon Park, offering fresh, American cuisine like sirloin burger and fries ($16), mostly to visitors coming from the nearby Cloisters. Tues–Thurs noon–3.30pm & 6–9pm, Fri noon–3.30pm & 6–10pm, Sat 11am–3.30pm & 6–10pm, Sun 11am–3.30pm & 5.30–9pm.

Típico Dominicano Restaurant 4172 Broadway at W 177th St ☎212 781 3900; subway #1 to 181st St, A to 175th St; map p.208. Smart, lively Dominican restaurant serving huge *paella típica Dominicana* ($18.95), *mofongo* (mashed plantains with pork) and plenty of stews, beans and rice – most dishes are under $10. Open 24hr.

BROOKLYN

Over the past decade-plus Brooklyn has turned into a seriously food-centric borough, with dozens of innovative restaurants cropping up everywhere in gentrified or rapidly gentrifying neighbourhoods like Park Slope, Carroll Gardens, Fort Greene, Williamsburg, even out in Bushwick and Ditmas Park. Eateries here tend to be more relaxed and cheaper than comparable spots in Manhattan, though there are plenty of places where you can splurge if you want to. Local and organic foods dominate the most progressive menus. Ethnic restaurants flourish in other parts of the borough, from long-established Polish spots in Greenpoint (itself with a burgeoning trendy scene) to Russian in Brighton Beach.

FULTON FERRY DISTRICT AND DUMBO

Grimaldi's 1 Front St, at Old Fulton St ☎718 858 4300, ⓦgrimaldisnyc.com; subway A, C to Brooklyn Bridge-High St; map p.215. Though this age-old fave has moved up the street from cramped quarters, the place still draws crowds for its delicious, thin and crispy pizza – but your chances have improved to avoid a long line. Cash only. Mon–Thurs 11.30am–10.45pm, Fri 11.30am–11.45pm,

Sat noon–11.45pm, Sun noon–10.45pm.

River Café 1 Water St, between Furman and Old Fulton sts ☎718 522 5200, ⓦrivercafe.com; subway A, C to Brooklyn Bridge-High St; map p.215. You can get better food for the price (or even much cheaper) in New York, but *River Café* is more about the romantic atmosphere and spectacular views of the Brooklyn Bridge. The prix-fixe dinner, with dishes like foie gras two ways and rack of lamb

CLOCKWISE FROM TOP LEFT *KATZ'S DELI* (P.301); *SCHILLER'S LIQUOR BAR* (P.301); *JUNIOR'S* (P.322); *LOMBARDI'S* (P.300) >

24

with house-made *merguez* sausage, costs $100 per person for three courses, and it's $135 for a six-course tasting menu, excluding wine. There's also a prix-fixe Sunday brunch ($55). Lunch (Mon–Sat) is à la carte and still pricey. Mon–Fri noon–3pm & 5.30–11pm, Sat & Sun 11.30am–2.30pm & 5.30–11pm.

Superfine 126 Front St, between Jay and Pearl sts ☎718 243 9005; subway F to York St; map p.215. *Superfine*'s ever-changing menu has a fresh, Mediterranean bent, with big salads (shrimp, calamari), pork chops and pasta ($13–24), while Sunday brunch skews Southwestern: *huevos rancheros* with New Mexican green chillies ($10) is a nod to the chef's roots. The bar is a cool hangout; there's a free pool table too. Tues–Sun 11.30am–3pm & 6–11pm; bar remains open from opening time until 2am weekdays, 4am weekends.

★ **Vinegar Hill House** 72 Hudson Ave, between Front and Water sts ☎718 522 1018, ⓦvinegarhillhouse.com; subway F to York St; map p.215. As charming and inviting a restaurant as you'll find, with exposed wood, pressed-tin ceilings, friendly service and a small, well-edited menu of farm-fresh dishes (lamb neck, rabbit leg and the like); there's a hideaway room downstairs, great for a small party, and the sourdough pancake ($10) at brunch is a singular achievement in the pancake world. Mon–Thurs 6–11pm, Fri 6–11.30pm, Sat 11am–3.30pm & 6–11.30pm, Sun 11am–3.30pm & 5.30–11pm.

BROOKLYN HEIGHTS

Iron Chef House 92 Clark St, between Henry St and Monroe Place ☎718 858 8517, ⓦironchefhouseny.net; subway #2, #3 to Clark St or #4, #5 to Borough Hall; map p.215. Fresh, tasty and artfully presented sushi, served by doting waiters, are this unassuming joint's hallmarks. Try the yellowtail collar (a frequent special) and some fancy rolls, or go all out with the house love-boat (feeds at least two). Daily 11am–3pm & 4.30–11pm.

Noodle Pudding 38 Henry St, at Middagh St ☎718 625 3737; subway #2, #3 to Clark St, A, C to High St-Brooklyn Bridge; map p.215. It can get quite busy and the service can be spotty, but it's great-value Italian in a neighbourhood somewhat lacking in options. The bread with spicy olive oil is addictive, the pastas well executed and the wine ridiculously cheap (if you opt for the quite-drinkable $4/glass, $15/bottle house tipple). Cash only. Tues–Thurs 5.30–10.30pm, Fri & Sat 5.30–11pm, Sun 5–10pm.

Waterfront Ale House 155 Atlantic Ave, between Clinton and Henry sts ☎718 522 3794, ⓦwaterfront alehouse.com; subway R to Court St, #2, #3, #4, #5 to Borough Hall, F, G to Bergen St; map p.215. This inexpensive pub serves good spicy chicken-wings ($10.95), chilli (including a venison version, $16.95) and

burgers ($11.95 and up), to go with a dozen or so unusual draught beers. Mon–Thurs 11.30am–11pm, Fri 11.30am–11.30pm, Sat noon–11.30pm, Sun noon–11pm.

DOWNTOWN BROOKLYN

Junior's 386 Flatbush Ave, at DeKalb Ave ☎718 852 5257, ⓦjuniorscheesecake.com; subway B, Q, R to DeKalb Ave; map p.215. Lit up like a Vegas casino, *Junior's* offers everything from chopped-liver sandwiches to ribs to a full cocktail bar; servings are mammoth. It relies on its scene and reputation as much as anything, though it's still good fun, and the cheesecake is plenty worthy. Mon–Thurs 6.30am–midnight, Fri & Sat 6.30am–1am.

FORT GREENE

Locanda Vini e Olii 129 Gates Ave, at Cambridge Place ☎718 622 9202, ⓦlocandavinieolii.com; subway C, G to Clinton-Washington aves; map p.215. Gorgeous, inventive Italian fare served in a restored pharmacy, all gleaming dark wood and glass. Rabbit terrine, fluffy *gnocchi*, even beef tongue in parsley sauce may pop up on the menu. Very affordable (pasta $15 or so, grilled/roasted meat and fish $20–27) and worth the walk to the far reaches of Fort Greene (aka Clinton Hill). Reservations recommended. Tues–Thurs & Sun 5.30–10.30pm, Fri & Sat 5.30–11.30pm.

Umi Nom 433 DeKalb Ave, at Classon Ave ☎718 789 8806, ⓦuminom.com; subway G to Classon Ave; map p.215. Southeast Asian small plates from a classically trained chef, who has settled in a bit of a removed location near Pratt. The room is warm and lively; go with friends and order to share. The roasted clams ($11), sautéed sausage ($11.50), pork belly *adobo* ($12) and greens ($9) should provide a nice starting point. Mon–Fri 6–11pm, Sat 12.30–3.30pm & 6–11pm.

BOERUM HILL, CARROLL GARDENS AND GOWANUS

Battersby 255 Smith St, between Douglass and Degraw sts; subway F, G to Carroll St; map p.222. This narrow slip of a place, with but a handful of tables, limited reservations (just for the tasting menu, and usually made a month in advance; otherwise, first come, first served) and constantly changing market-driven fare, has set the local foodie world ablaze. If you get in, consider yourself lucky and let them guide you – tasting dishes may be made up more or less on the spot. Mon–Sat 5.30–11pm, Sun 5.30–10pm.

Fletcher's Brooklyn Barbecue 433 Third Ave, between 7th and 8th sts ☎347 763 2680, ⓦfletchersbklyn.com; subway R to Union St; map p.222. Part of a citywide barbecue insurgence, as well as a burgeoning restaurant row on Third Avenue, *Fletcher's* does barbecue justice. The ribs are meaty and juicy; even a quarter-rack ($12) feels somewhat substantial. Mix and match with *char siu* ($7 for 1/4 pound) and brisket ($6 for 1/4 pound) and pair with baked beans ($4/$6) and house-made pickles ($3/$5). Sun–Thurs 11.30am–10pm or sold out, Fri & Sat 11.30am–11pm or sold out.

Frankies 457 Spuntino 457 Court St, at Luquer St ☎718 403 0033, ⊛frankiesspuntino.com; subway F, G to Carroll St; map p.222. Co-chefs Frank and Frank revive and refine Italian-American favourites on the south side of Carroll Gardens. Home-made pastas ($15–19) are the way to go, coupled with a fresh salad of seasonal greens and a few crostini; add an order of meatballs ($13) if you think it won't be enough. Enjoy your meal on the breezy garden patio out back. Mon–Thurs & Sun 11am–11pm, Fri & Sat 11am–midnight.

The Grocery 288 Smith St, between Sackett and Union sts ☎718 596 3335, ⊛thegroceryrestaurant.com; subway F, G to Carroll St; map p.222. Among the first serious restaurants that kick-started the area's gourmet aspirations, *Grocery* still chugs away with its emphasis on seasonal ingredients combined in simple but satisfying ways (venison with sweet and sour onions, for instance). Reservations recommended, though the garden is unreserved. Tues–Thurs 5.30–10pm, Fri 5.30–11pm, Sat 5–11pm.

Lucali 575 Henry St, at Carroll St ☎718 858 4086. Subway F, G to Carroll St; map p.222. Add this to to the list of pizzerias whose devotees claim it as the best in town. Located in a converted old-fashioned candy store, *Lucali* only serves pies ($24; minimal topping choices, $4 each) and *calzones* ($10), it's frequently hard to get a seat, but the product is a knockout. Cash only. Mon & Wed–Sun 6–10pm.

Mile End 97A Hoyt St, between Pacific St and Atlantic Ave ☎718 852 7510, ⊛mileenddeli.com; subway F, G to Bergen St or A, C, G to Hoyt-Schermerhorn; map p.222. In a short time, this Montréal-style deli has become a fixture, attracting long lunch lines for its *poutine* (fries with curds and gravy; $8/12) and smoked-meat sandwich: piled on rye bread with a smear of mustard, this peppery morsel is the Canadian version of a Jewish classic ($14). Breakfast and dinner are no slouch, either; they do standards bagels and lox ($11) and brisket ($22) proud – not to mention a Sunday-night Chinese set menu ($35). Mon & Tues 8am–4pm, Wed–Sat 8am–4pm & 6–11pm, Sun 10am–4pm & 6–10pm.

★ **Petite Crevette** 144 Union St, at Hicks St ☎718 855 2632; subway F, G to Carroll St; map p.222. The cosy, casual *Petite Crevette* employs a rather straightforward approach to fish and seafood: you pick it, they grill or sauté or do whatever to it, you eat every bite. Corn-crab chowder and soft-shell crabs (when in season) are standouts; alcohol is BYO. Mon & Sun 5–11pm, Tues–Sat noon–3pm & 5–11pm.

★ **Pok Pok NY** 127 Columbia St, between Kane and Degraw sts ☎718 923 9322, ⊛pokpokny.com; map p.222. Portland chef Andy Ricker has set NYC abuzz with his showcase of authentic flavours from northern Thailand (from where he frequently brings back ingredients). While most go crazy over the sticky wings ($13.95), don't miss out on the pork ribs with mustard greens ($13.25), seafood crêpe ($14.50) or spicy eggplant salad ($14.95). Get a bunch of dishes to share and accompany them with Southeast Asian beers or exotic cocktails (including one with the Thai firewater, Mekhong). No reservations, and it gets crowded; there's also an LES offshoot that specializes just in pad thai (see p.302). Daily 5.30–10.30pm.

★ **Prime Meats** 465 Court St, at Luquer St ☎718 254 0327, ⊛frankspm.com; subway F, G to Carroll St; map p.222. Frequently packed, this sibling of *Frankie's* (see opposite) serves up excellent steaks ($30, or as a special, a *côte de boeuf* for two), burgers ($18) and handcrafted sausages in a room that feels decades old. For lunch or brunch, content yourself with a breakfast sandwich ($6.50), mushrooms and eggs with bratwurst ($13) or a hearty lunchtime sandwich. No reservations. Mon–Wed 11am–midnight, Thurs & Fri 11am–1am, Sat 8am–1am, Sun 8am–midnight.

RED HOOK

★ **Good Fork** 391 Van Brunt St, between Coffey and Van Dyke sts ☎718 643 6636, ⊛goodfork.com; subway F, G to Smith-9th St, then bus #61; map p.222. Though it feels very much a neighbourhood restaurant, this sliver of a place with exposed brick and thrift-store decor turns out terrific fare with a focus on local ingredients that's worth travelling for. The changing menu is New American with Asian flourishes, as per the delectable dumplings ($9) and Korean-style grilled skirt steak with *kimchee* rice and a fried egg ($24). Tues–Fri 5.30–10.30pm, Sat 10am–3pm & 5.30–10.30pm, Sun 10am–3pm & 5.30–10pm.

PARK SLOPE AND PROSPECT HEIGHTS

★ **Al Di Là** 248 Fifth Ave, at Carroll St ☎718 783 4565, ⊛aldilatrattoria.com; subway R to Union St-Fourth Ave; map p.226. Venetian country cooking at its finest at this husband-and-wife-run trattoria. Standouts include beet and ricotta ravioli ($12), a delicate *malfatti* (spinach *gnocchi*; $15), the daily risotto and braised rabbit with polenta ($26). Early or late, expect at least a 45min wait (they don't take reservations); they've opened up a wine bar around the corner, where you can wait if you like. Mon–Thurs noon–3pm & 6–10.30pm, Fri noon–3pm & 6–11pm, Sat 11am–3.30pm & 5.30–11pm, Sun 11am–3.30pm & 5–10pm.

Bonnie's 278 Fifth Ave, at 1st St ☎718 369 9527, ⊛bonniesgrill.com; subway R to Union St-Fourth Ave; map p.226. Casual, fun-loving diner that's great for its

24

juicy, Cajun-spiced burgers ($11.95) and bottled beer list. As the owners are natives of western New York, *Bonnie's* also serves up big plates of sticky Buffalo chicken wings ($8.95 small order). Mon–Thurs & Sun noon–11pm, Fri & Sat noon–midnight.

Rose Water 787 Union St, at Sixth Ave ☎718 783 3800, ⓦrosewaterrestaurant.com; subway R to Union St-Fourth Ave; map p.226. Intimate Mediterranean–American bistro, serving excellent seasonal dishes with flavourful accents (say, roast lamb with fiddlehead ferns, $27), including an excellent-value three-course market-menu dinner Mon–Thurs for $28. Excellent brunch too. Mon–Fri 5.30–11pm, Sat & Sun 9.30am–3pm & 5.30–11pm.

Thistle Hill Tavern 441 Seventh Ave, at 15th St ☎347 599 1262, ⓦthistlehilltavern.com; subway F to Seventh Ave; map p.226. As good for families as it is for date night, the *Thistle Hill* complements fish & chips and burgers with more ambitious fare, like a seared bass swimming in nectar-like mushroom broth ($23) or spring vegetable ravioli ($16). Finish with strawberry pie, a deep-fried delight ($8). Mon–Fri 5pm–midnight, Sat & Sun 11am–midnight, bar nightly until 1am.

DITMAS PARK

★ **Purple Yam** 1314 Cortelyou Rd ☎718 940 8188, ⓦpurpleyamnyc.com; subway Q to Cortelyou Rd; map p.213. After years running a restaurant down in Soho, the husband-and-wife owners (head chef and host too) have decamped to up-and-coming Ditmas Park, which has received the homestyle Filipino cooking and friendly prices as if a piece to a missing puzzle. The porky *sisig* ($15) and *lechon* ($19) are musts, and the *adobo* ($16) and daily *kimchee* ($4) are not far behind. Finish it off with coconut *buko* pie ($7). Mon–Fri 5.30–10.30pm, Sat 11am–3.30pm & 5.30–11pm, Sun noon–3.30pm & 5.30–10pm.

CONEY ISLAND

Gargiulo's 2911 W 15th St, between Surf and Mermaid aves ☎718 266 4891, ⓦgargiulos.com; subway D, F, N, Q to Coney Island-Stillwell Ave; map p.213. A gigantic, noisy, century-old family-run Coney Island restaurant famed for its large portions of hearty Neapolitan food. Most pasta dishes are $11–19, most meat and seafood dishes $16–31. Mon, Wed & Thurs noon–10.30pm, Fri & Sat noon–11.30pm, Sun noon–9.30pm.

★ **Totonno's Pizzeria Napolitano** 1524 Neptune Ave, between 15th and 16th sts ☎718 372 8606, ⓦtotonnos.com; subway D, F, N, Q to Coney Island-Stillwell Ave; map p.213. The coal-oven-fired pizzas at this ancient (circa 1924), no-frills spot inspire devotion among pizza lovers for their sweet, fresh mozzarella and crispy crust. The basic starts at $19.50; add on toppings from there – you can't really go wrong. No slices; cash only. Wed–Sun noon–8pm.

BRIGHTON BEACH AND SHEEPSHEAD BAY

Café Glechik 3159 Coney Island Ave, between Brighton Beach Ave and 10th St ☎718 616 0766, ⓦglechik.com; subway B, Q to Brighton Beach; map p.213. A refreshingly down-to-earth place, this Ukrainian restaurant is known for its dumplings – *pelmeni* and *vareniki* ($6–9) – as well as its excellent soups (*borscht*, chicken with *pelmeni* both $6.60) and stews ($12.50–21.50). Don't forget an order of garlicky fries (included with entrees). Cash only. Mon–Thurs & Sun 11am–11pm, Fri & Sat 11am–midnight.

Primorski 282 Brighton Beach Ave, between 2nd and 3rd sts ☎718 891 3111, ⓦprimorski.net; subway B, Q to Brighton Beach; map p.213. One of the best of Brighton Beach's Russian hangouts, with a huge menu of authentic Russian dishes, including blintzes, stuffed cabbage and chicken Kiev. All sorts of banquet and couples deals are on offer; you could drop by for the $6.99 prix-fixe lunch, but then you'd miss the live dance music that takes place every evening. Daily 11am–10pm/midnight.

★ **Randazzo's Clam Bar** 2017 Emmons Ave, Sheepshead Bay ☎718 615 0010, ⓦrandazzosclambar .com; subway B, Q to Sheepshead Bay, then Voorhees Ave to Ocean Ave, turn right and walk to Emmons Ave, take a left – a 10min walk; map p.213. All kinds of old-school pasta dishes and Italian preparations of fish and seafood, along with briny, fresh clams – walk it off afterward along the marina. The family-owned place traces its history back nearly a hundred years, so you know they're doing something right. Mon–Thurs & Sun 11am–11pm, Fri & Sat 11am–midnight.

WILLIAMSBURG AND BUSHWICK

Bamonte's 32 Withers St, at Union Ave ☎718 384 8831; subway L to Lorimer St, G to Metropolitan Ave; map p.236. Red-sauce restaurants abound in NYC, but this is one of the legends, which has served traditional Italian-American dishes like *linguine* with clam sauce ($16.50) since 1900. Mon, Wed & Thurs noon–9.45pm, Fri & Sat noon–11pm, Sun 1–10pm.

Diner 85 Broadway, at Berry St ☎718 486 3077, ⓦdinernyc.com; subway L to Bedford Ave, J, M, Z to Marcy Ave; map p.236. This groovy restaurant in a Pullman diner-car has a tiny, changing menu of American grub (burgers and steaks, roasted chicken and fish, fantastic fries), along with a dozen varieties of champagne. Next door they've opened up the market-cum-restaurant *Marlow and Sons*, which does fresh oysters, chicken-under-a-brick and elegant cocktails. Mon–Thurs 11am–midnight, Fri 11am–1am, Sat 10am–1am, Sun 10am–midnight.

DuMont 432 Union Ave, at Devoe St ☎718 486 7717, ⓦdumontrestaurant.com; subway L to Lorimer St, G to Metropolitan Ave; map p.236. This bistro's sensitive restoration of the old-timey space is matched by the

24

well-edited menu. Try the signature salad of *haricots verts*, pecans, Danish blue cheese and bacon ($12) followed by a burger ($14). Mon–Thurs & Sun 11am–11pm, Fri & Sat 11am–midnight.

Fette Sau 345 Metropolitan Ave, at Havemeyer St ☎718 963 3404, ⊛fettesaubbq.com; subway L to Bedford Ave, G to Metropolitan Ave; map p.236. The industrial-chic vibe (it's in an old garage) of this barbecue specialist seems fitting for the neighbourhood. Order your meat by the pound (beef brisket, pork shoulder or pork belly $16), tack on a couple of sides (burnt-end baked beans $5.25) and wash it all down with a microbrew ($6 pints). Mon–Fri 5pm–2am, Sat & Sun noon–2am.

★ **Peter Luger Steak House** 178 Broadway, at Driggs Ave ☎718 387 7400, ⊛peterluger.com; subway J, M, Z to Marcy Ave; map p.236. Catering to carnivores since 1887, *Peter Luger* may just be the city's finest steakhouse. The service is surly and the decor plain, but the porterhouse steak – the only cut served – is divine (roughly $50/person). Old-school sides like creamed spinach are just a distraction, though don't pass on the bacon starter ($3.95/slice); the lunchtime burger (not available at dinner; only $12) is a great deal. Cash only; reservations required. Mon–Thurs 11.45am–9.45pm, Fri & Sat 11.45am–10.45pm, Sun 12.45–9.45pm.

★ **Pies and Thighs** 166 S 4th St, at Driggs Ave ☎347 529 6090, ⊛piesnthighs.com; subway J, M, Z to Marcy Ave; map p.236. This one-time underground institution has found a bright corner location in which to serve its Southern-style food: great chicken biscuits (a scone with a fried chicken filling; $6), expertly fried chicken ($13 with a side) and a changing rotation of pies (slice $4.50–5.50; sour cherry and bourbon pecan are a few favourites). Mon–Fri 9am–4am & 5pm–midnight, Sat & Sun 10am–4pm & 5pm–midnight.

Roberta's 261 Moore St ☎718 417 1118, ⊛robertaspizza.com; subway L to Morgan Ave; map

p.213. Charmingly ramshackle, this pizza joint, located in a bit of a nowheresville, draws huge crowds (expect a wait) for killer pies – speck and egg, Wu-Tang Clam and so on – well-executed pastas, salads and entrees, and an extensive drinks menu. It also has a "hidden" restaurant, *Blanca* (☎347 799 2807, ⊛blancanyc.com), which offers a $180 tasting menu for dinner Wed–Sat; reservations a month in advance. Mon–Fri 11am–midnight, Sat & Sun 10am–midnight.

Rye 247 S 1st St, between Roebling and Metropolitan aves ☎718 281 8047, ⊛ryerestaurant.com; subway J, M, Z to Marcy Ave; map p.236. The retro speakeasy feel seems totally natural in the dark wood and pressed-tin setting. A straightforward menu offers house smoked salmon ($15), meatloaf sandwich ($15), ribeye for two ($2.50 per oz) – but there's nothing simple about the cocktails, expertly and attentively made. The happy hour deal ($5 Old Fashioneds, $5 cheeseburgers) is, quite simply, one of the best deals going. Mon–Thurs 5.30–1am (dinner until 11pm), Fri 5.30pm–2am (dinner until midnight), Sat 11am–3.30pm & 6pm–2am (dinner until midnight), Sun 11am–1am (dinner until 10.30pm).

GREENPOINT

Enids 560 Manhattan Ave ☎718 349 3859, ⊛enids.net; subway G to Nassau Ave; map p.236. As much a bar and daytime hangout as a restaurant, *Enids* attracts a youthful audience for its loud rock soundtrack, popular brunch and casual sandwich-oriented, Southern-influenced menu. Daily 10am–11pm (til 2 or 4am in summer).

Lomzynianka 646 Manhattan Ave ☎718 389 9439, ⊛lomzynianka.com; subway G to Nassau Ave; map p.236. The service isn't the quickest, but the prices are astonishingly low (dinner plates $5.50 and up) at this congenial Polish restaurant. Both kinds of *borscht* – white and red – are must-trys; if you want to play it safe with your main dish, the hearty *kielbasa* is quite good. Daily noon–9pm.

24

QUEENS

The most ethnically diverse of all the boroughs, Queens offers some of the city's best opportunities to sample a wealth of authentic foreign flavours, from Bosnian and Greek to Brazilian and Colombian to Szechuan and Thai. Most places listed here are easily accessible by subway.

LONG ISLAND CITY AND ASTORIA

★ **Agnanti Meze** 19-06 Ditmars Blvd, Astoria ☎718 545 4554, ⊛agnantimeze.com; subway N, Q to Astoria-Ditmars Blvd; map p.244. Specializing in Greek meze – small plates for snacking – this restaurant overlooks Astoria Park. Don't miss the "specialties from Constantinople" section of the menu, with goodies like *bekri*-meze, wine-soaked cubes of tender meat. Daily noon–11pm.

Kabab Café 25-12 Steinway St, Astoria ☎718 728 9858; subway N, Q to Astoria Blvd; map p.244. The culinary highlight of Steinway Street's "Little Egypt", this

tiny, velvet-swathed den is the domain of Chef Ali, who lavishes patrons with traditional Middle Eastern goodies (smoky *baba ganoush*, lighter-than-air falafel) as well as his own creations – don't miss the honey-glazed duck. Ask the prices of off-the-menu specials if you're on a budget – they can be quite high. Tues–Sun 1–5pm & 6–10pm.

Malagueta 25-35 36th Ave, Astoria ☎718 937 4821, ⊛malaguetany.com; subway N, Q to 36th Ave; map p.244. Refined (but reasonably priced) Brazilian cuisine served in a simple, whitewashed corner space. If you want to spice up the *moqueca de camarão* (shrimp in coconut milk; $17), ask for a side of hot *molho* sauce. Come on Saturday for *feijoada* ($18), Brazil's national dish, a black-bean clay-pot stew served with collard greens and rice. Tues–Thurs 11.30am–10pm, Fri 11.30am–11pm, Sat 1–11pm, Sun 1–10pm.

The Queens Kickshaw 40-17 Broadway, between Steinway and 41st St, Astoria ☎718 937 4821, ⓦthequeenskickshaw.com; subway E, M to Steinway; map p.244. They specialize in gourmet grilled cheese sandwiches ($8–10), but there's also a full menu for each meal of the day, small-batch beers (and *kombucha* and cider) on draught and a pleasant vibe that makes it a community hangout for coffee lingerers as well. Mon–Fri 7.30am–1am, Sat & Sun 9am–1am.

Taverna Kyclades 33-07 Ditmars Blvd, Astoria ☎718 545 8666, ⓦtavernakyclades.com; subway N, Q to Astoria-Ditmars Blvd; map p.244. Friendly, popular Greek *taverna* specializing in seafood. Start with a selection of dips, including the garlic-yogurt-cucumber *tzatziki* ($5.50 on own, $9.95 as part of a trio), then move on to grilled calamari ($13.95) or sardines ($14.95). Dessert, a traditional Greek custard, is on the house. Mon–Thurs noon–11pm, Fri & Sat noon–11.30pm, Sun noon–10.30pm.

Tournesol 50-12 Vernon Blvd, Long Island City ☎718 472 4355, ⓦtournesolnyc.com; subway #7 to Vernon Blvd; map p.242. Warm French bistro in Hunters Point, steps from the Vernon Blvd #7 stop and an easy walk from MoMA PS1. Staples like steak frites ($18.50) and tarragon *escargots* ($9.50) are reliably good, the wine list is small but well chosen, and brunch is very tasty. Mon 5.30–11pm, Tues–Thurs 11.30am–3pm & 5.30–11pm, Fri 11.30am–3pm & 5.30–11.30pm, Sat 11am–3.30pm & 5.30–11.30pm, Sun 11am–3.30pm & 5–10pm.

★ Zenon Taverna 34-10 31st Ave, between 34 and 35th sts, Astoria ☎718 956 0133, ⓦzenontaverna .com; subway N, Q to 30th Ave, R, M to Steinway St; map p.244. Charred octopus ($14.95), grilled meatballs ($8.95) and *taramasalata* ($6.50) get your meal off on the right foot at this super-friendly Greek-Cypriot tavern; whole grilled bass ($25.95) or one of the lamb specials ($18.95–22.50) keeps it heading in the right direction. Daily noon–11pm.

SUNNYSIDE AND WOODSIDE

Sripraphai 64-13 39th Ave, Woodside ☎718 899 9599, ⓦsripraphairestaurant.com; subway #7 to 69th St or M, R to 65th St; map p.240. Truly authentic Thai food that puts anything in Manhattan to shame – sweet, sour, (very) spicy and cheap. Try the "drunken" noodles with beef and basil ($9.50) or a whole steamed striped bass with ginger, chilli and lime ($23), along with staples like papaya salad ($7.50) and hot-and-sour lemongrass soup ($5/$9.50). An outdoor patio is open in the summer. Mon, Tues & Thurs–Sun 11.30am–9.30pm.

JACKSON HEIGHTS

Jackson Diner 37-47 74th St, between 37th and Roosevelt aves ☎718 672 1232, ⓦjacksondiner.com; subway E, F, M, R to Roosevelt Ave, #7 to 74th St-Broadway; map p.240. The best-known Jackson Heights Indian restaurant, with outstanding versions of classics like tandoori chicken ($9.95) and goat curry ($11.95). Cash only. Mon–Thurs & Sun 11.30am–10pm, Fri & Sat 11.30am–10.30pm.

La Fusta 80-32 Baxter Ave, Elmhurst ☎718 429 8222, ⓦlafustanewyork.com; subway #7 to 82nd St-Jackson Heights; map p.240. The longest-running Argentinian restaurant in the city, and a welcome alternative to the usual steakhouse experience. The *parillada*'s the thing; go for the mixed grill, a mountain of short ribs, skirt steak, sweetbreads and various sausages, washed down with plenty of Malbec. Mon–Fri 11am–11.30pm, Sat 11am–midnight, Sun 2–11pm.

La Pequeña Colombia 83-27 Roosevelt Ave, at 84th St ☎718 478 8700, ⓦpequenacolombia.com; subway #7 to 82nd St-Jackson Heights; map p.240. Literally "Little Colombia", this simple spot doles out inexpensive but filling *empanadas* and *arepas* along with a gut-busting "Mountain Platter" – ground beef and rice with fried egg, rice, pork rind and plantains ($11). Try the fruit drinks, such as *maracuya* (passion fruit) or *guanabana* (soursop). Mon–Thurs 11am–11pm, Fri & Sat 9am–midnight, Sun 9am–11pm.

FLUSHING

66 Lu's Seafood 38-18 Prince St ☎718 321 0904; subway #7 to Main St-Flushing; map p.240. Bright Taiwanese spot that attracts a mostly local crowd. The special menus hold some real treats – try the clams with basil ($12.95) and sea bass with dried-bean-curd sauce ($22.95) – though many swear by the crispy pork chop over rice ($7); ask for help with recommendations. The ice-cold beer on tap pairs well with the food. Daily 11am–4am.

Biang! 41-10 Main St ☎718 888 7713, ⓦbiang-nyc .com; subway #7 to Main St-Flushing; map p.240. This sit-down Chinese restaurant from the *Xi'an Famous Foods* people (see p.278) expands on their tasty formula real treats – yes, there's cumin and chilli lamb noodles, but also skewers, stewed lamb ribs and a beer and *soju* cocktail list. Mon–Thurs & Sun 11.30am–11pm, Fri & Sat 11.30am–midnight.

Spicy and Tasty 39-07 Prince St ☎718 359 1601; subway #7 to Main St-Flushing; map p.240. Tea-smoked duck ($12.95) is the signature dish at this Sichuan specialist, regarded by many as the finest in NYC; prepare yourself for plenty of spicy noodle dishes as well. Daily 11.30am–10.30pm.

24

THE BRONX

In the Bronx, and the whole of the city, Belmont is the place to taste old-school Italian-American "red sauce" cuisine, while City Island's family establishments specialize in freshly caught seafood, best enjoyed on warm summer evenings when the waterside dining is at its most scenic.

SOUTH BRONX

Sam's 596–598 Grand Concourse, at 150th St ☎ 718 665 5341; subway #2, #4, #5 to 149th St-Grand Concourse; map p.252. About a 10min walk from Yankee Stadium, *Sam's* makes for a tasty, cheap pre-game meal, whether you want American soul food or Caribbean standards. Tues, Wed & Sun 11am–8pm, Thurs & Fri 11am–11pm.

BEDFORD PARK AND BELMONT

Com Tam Ninh Kieu 2641 Jerome Ave ☎ 718 365 2680; subway B, D, #4 to Kingsbridge Rd; map p.252. A convenient stop if you're close to the Poe Cottage, Fordham or the Botanical Garden (though Belmont's Little Italy isn't far away either), this small, casual Vietnamese joint has excellent renditions of *pho, bun, bánh mì* and other inexpensive specialities. Daily 8.30am–8.30pm.

Roberto Restaurant 603 Crescent Ave, between Arthur Ave and Hughes St ☎ 718 733 9503, ⓦ robertos .roberto089.com; subway B, D to 182nd-183rd sts; map p.252. Not quite so stuck in a time warp as other Belmont favourites, *Roberto* is renowned for its rich pastas, served with style on giant platters or, sometimes, baked in foil. Chef's specials are usually the way to go; main dishes (most $21–36) are big enough to share. Mon–Thurs noon– 2.30pm & 4.30–10pm, Fri & Sat noon–2.30pm & 4.30–11pm.

Trattoria Zero Otto Nove 2357 Arthur Ave, between 186th and 187th sts ☎ 718 220 1027, ⓦ 089bx .roberto089.com; subway B, D to 182nd-183rd sts; map p.252. In the comfort of an atmospheric, soaring back room, fine brick-oven pizzas ($10.95–17.95) and pastas ($17.95– 24.95; try the *al forno*) are served up to a crowd that spans generations. Tues–Thurs noon–2.30pm & 4.30–10pm, Fri & Sat noon–2.30pm & 4.30–11pm, Sun 1–9pm.

CITY ISLAND

Johnny's Reef Restaurant 2 City Island Ave ☎ 718 885 2086, ⓦ johnnysreefrestaurant.com; subway #6 to Pelham Bay Park, then #Bx29 bus; map p.252. Bustling joint at the end of the road; eat on a picnic table by the water and watch the gulls fly round. Start with clams on the half-shell ($5 for half-dozen), move on to something steamed or fried – the fried scallops are a good bet ($12) – and pair it with a cold beer. March–Nov: Mon–Thurs & Sun 11am–midnight, Fri & Sat 11am–1am.

Lobster Box 34 City Island Ave, at Rochelle St ☎ 718 885 1952, ⓦ lobsterboxrestaurant.com; subway #6 to Pelham Bay Park, then #Bx29 bus; map p.252. Don't mess around with appetizers or sides at this City Island old-timer at the south end of the island – lobster fried, grilled or steamed is the choice (market price) – though the raw bar is awfully tempting. Mon–Thurs & Sun noon–11pm, Fri & Sat noon–midnight.

24

STATEN ISLAND

Staten Island is a bit of a hike, but a nice break from the city; food here is not a major attraction, though it does do Sri Lankan cuisine particularly well, and has its own pizza legend in *Denino's*.

Denino's Pizzeria & Tavern 524 Port Richmond Ave, at Hooker Place ☎ 718 442 9401, ⓦ deninos.com; take bus #S44; map p.261. A Staten Island favourite since 1937, serving pizza with a slightly thicker, chewier crust than most brick-oven joints in the city (from $14.50). *Ralph's Famous Italian Ices* (see p.293) is right across the street, making dessert a no-brainer. Cash only. Sun–Thurs 11.30am–11pm, Sat & Sun 11.30am–midnight.

Killmeyer's Old Bavaria Inn 4254 Arthur Kill Rd, at Sharrotts Rd ☎ 718 984 1202, ⓦ killmeyers.com; take bus #S74; map p.261. A full-tilt German beer garden near

the south end of the island, complete with schnitzel, *sauerbraten* and giant steins of beer, and live oompah music outside on the weekends. Main dishes ($15.50–24) are large enough to feed two. Mon–Thurs 11am– midnight, Fri & Sat 11am–2am, Sun noon–midnight.

New Asha Sri Lankan Restaurant 322 Victory Blvd, at Cebra Ave ☎ 718 420 0649; take bus #S48, #S61 or #S66; map p.261. Head here for no-frills paper plates heaped with veggie *roti*, spicy chicken, curries and *idlis*, all for less than $10. Sun–Thurs 10am–10pm, Fri & Sat 9am–11pm.

HAPPY ENDING LOUNGE

Drinking

The bar scene in New York City is eclectic, with a vast range of places to drink and prices to suit most pockets. At the top end are the glamorous bars that most people associate with shows like *Sex and the City*: rooftop showcases like *230 Fifth* and venerable *King Cole Bar & Salon*, home of the Bloody Mary. At the other end of the spectrum are classic dives like *Subway Inn*, but there's plenty in-between, from *enotecas* and modern speakeasies to hookah bars and Irish pubs. Bars generally open their doors at noon and close them in the early hours of the morning – 4am at the latest, when they have to close by law (clubs can stay open later). Unless it's happy hour, in a basic bar in Manhattan you'll pay around $5–6 for a draught beer or house wine and a bit more for a standard cocktail. At the most-fashionable spots, fancy cocktails can start at around $15. Wherever you go, you'll be expected to tip a buck (perhaps more at pricier joints) per drink.

The most obvious drink choice is typically beer. You'll see the usual American standards – Budweiser, Sam Adams, etc – alongside such European staples as Stella Artois and Heineken pretty much everywhere. Bars with bigger selections often feature real ales on tap and **microbrews** from across the country (see box, below).

Wine demands a better-filled wallet than beer does. When in a restaurant or bar, expect a hundred-percent mark-up (at least) on the cost of a bottle. **Cocktails** are also big business in New York, with the current fad for highly experimental blending driving a slew of boutique lounge bars south of 14th Street. There are a couple of points of potential confusion for overseas visitors when it comes to **liquor**. Bear in mind that whether you ask for a drink "on the rocks" or not, you'll most likely get it poured into a glass filled with ice; if you don't want it like this ask for it "straight up". Also, American shots are approximately double the size of British and European shots.

When **buying your own liquor or wine**, you'll need to find a special wine or liquor store – supermarkets, bodegas (corner stores) and some pharmacies only sell beer and a limited amount of (poor) wine. You must be over 21 to buy or consume alcohol in a bar or restaurant, and it's against the law to drink alcohol on the street. Note that some bars insist you **show photo ID** to get in (even if you look well over 21), so make sure you carry some. Also by law, all NYC bars must serve **nonalcoholic drinks**, though you shouldn't expect to pay less for them; sodas, juices and sparkling waters often sell for the same price as beer.

THE FINANCIAL DISTRICT

Dead Rabbit 30 Water St, between Broad St and Coenties Slip ☎646 422 7906, ⓦdeadrabbitnyc.com; subway R to Whitehall St; map p.43. Wall Street newcomer in a gorgeous old space, with a menu of classic cocktails ($12), bottled punches ($10), highballs ($11), wine, beer and a vast range of whisky; bar menu features fish & chips, stews and meat pies. Tap Room daily 11am–4am; parlor Mon–Wed 5pm–2am, Thurs–Sat 5pm–3am.

★**Jeremy's Alehouse** 228 Front St, at Peck Slip ☎212 964 3537, ⓦjeremysalehouse.com; subway #2, #3, #4, #5, A, C, J, Z to Fulton St; map p.43. Unpretentious neighbourhood bar with bras and ties hanging from the rafters (donated by happy patrons), serving well-priced pints of beer from $4.75 (served in styrofoam cups) and excellent burgers ($5.75). Happy hour Mon–Fri 4–6pm. The fried clams ($9.95) also get rave reviews. Mon–Fri

---

GROWLERS AND THE CRAFT BEER REVOLUTION

Since the 1990s America has been undergoing a craft beer brewing renaissance, with generally small breweries knocking out limited batches of hoppy, tasty ales in a variety of styles. All over New York you'll see beer shops that cater to "**growlers**", refillable half-gallon glass or ceramic jugs that you can take home. The modern growler was introduced by a Wyoming brewer in 1989: you can buy them in any beer shop and some pubs for around $5–7 (or $15–18 full of beer).

Bridge and Tunnel ⓦbridgeandtunnelbrewery .com. Look out for this small batch specialist of beers like *dunkelweizen* (a dark, German wheat) and Tiger Eyes, a toasty brown ale with hints of hazelnut.

Bronx Brewery 856 E 136th St, Port Morris (South Bronx), ⓦthebronxbrewery.com. Visit the tasting rooms to sample Bronx pale ale and Bronx Black pale ale.

Brooklyn Brewery The king of NYC beer offers a fine range of ales in all styles (see p.340).

Chelsea Brewing Co. Chelsea Piers, Pier 59 ⓦchelseabrewingco.com. Manhattan's largest micro brewery, its beers served at the sports bar on site. Mon–Wed noon–midnight, Thurs–Sun midnight–2am.

Coney Island Brewing Co. 3008 W 12th St at Surf Ave, Coney Island, ⓦconeyislandbrewingcompany .blogspot.com. Visit the tasting room, just off the boardwalk.

Greenpoint Beer Works 529 Waverly Ave, Clinton Hill (Brooklyn), ⓦkelsoofbrooklyn.com. This brewery crafts the **Kelso of Brooklyn** beer brands and Heartland Brewery brand ales.

Rockaway Brewing Co 5-01 46th Ave at 5th St, Long Island City, ⓦrockawaybrewco.com. Queens-based brewer of mellow English ales and chocolatey stouts. Visit their facility to fill your growler (Fri 3–8pm, Sat & Sun 11am–4pm).

SingleCut Beersmiths 19-33 37th St, between 19th and 20th aves, Astoria (Queens) ⓦsinglecut beer.com. Lager specialist; pop in Thurs 5–10pm, Fri 5–11pm, Sat 1–11pm, Sun 1–8pm, to sip a pint in the tap room.

Sixpoint Craft Ales ⓦsixpoint.com. Popular Brooklyn brand – check the website for details of tours of their Red Hook brewery (see p.225).

25

8am–midnight, Sat 10am–midnight, Sun noon–midnight.

The Porterhouse at Fraunces Tavern 58 Pearl St, between Broad and Water sts ☎212 968 1776, ⓦfraucestavern.com; subway R to Whitehall St; map p.43. Below the Fraunces Tavern Museum lies an outpost of Dublin's Porterhouse Brewing Company – restaurant to the right, and bars to the left. Raise a pint of tangy Oyster Stout or Porterhouse Red (US$8) to George Washington, a regular in the 1780s (flights of three brews US$10). Happy hour Mon–Fri 4–7pm. Daily 11am–2.30am.

Ulysses 95 Pearl St/58 Stone St ☎212 482 0400, ⓦulyssesnyc.com; subway R to Whitehall St, #2, #3 to Wall St; map p.43. This Irish pub anchors the burgeoning

TOP 5 OUTDOOR DRINKING

Bohemian Hall & Beer Garden Astoria, Queens. See p.341
La Birreria (Eataly) Flatiron District. See p.335
Radegast Hall Williamsburg, Brooklyn. See p.341
Sweet & Vicious Nolita. See opposite
Governors Beach Club Governors Island. See p.344

Stone Street scene, though it still primarily caters to an after-work Wall Street crowd. Decent Guinness and pub food, including plenty of roasts; one of the few pubs open down here on Sundays. Daily 11am–4am.

TRIBECA AND SOHO

Bubble Lounge 228 W Broadway, between Franklin and White sts ☎212 431 3433, ⓦbubblelounge.com; subway #1 to Franklin St; map p.64. Swanky place to pop a cork or two. There's a long list of over 300 champagnes and other fizz, but beware the skyrocketing tabs (by-the-glass from $20, magnums from $180). Mon–Wed 5pm–1am, Thurs 5pm–2am, Fri & Sat 5pm–4am.

Café Noir 32 Grand St, at Thompson St ☎212 431 7910, ⓦcafenoirny.com; subway N, R to Prince St, #6 to Spring St; map p.64. This tapas bar with a Moroccan theme can be lots of fun: opt for the pitchers of *mojitos*, *sangría* or margaritas, nibble the tapas (the bigger plates are nothing special) and soak up the DJ sessions and the live samba on Mondays. Sun–Wed noon–2am, Thurs–Sat noon–4am.

★ **Ear Inn** 326 Spring St, between Washington and Greenwich sts ☎212 226 9060, ⓦearinn.com; subway C, E to Spring St, #1 to Houston St; map p.64. "Ear" as in "Bar" with half the neon "B" blacked out. This historic pub, a stone's throw from the Hudson River, opened in 1890. Its creaky (and some claim, haunted) interior is as cosy as a Cornish inn, with a good mix of beers on tap (US$6.50) and basic, reasonably priced American food. Free, old-school jazz every Sun 8–11pm. Daily noon–4am.

Fanelli Café 94 Prince St, at Mercer St ☎212 226 9412; subway N, R to Prince St; map p.64. Established in 1922 (the building dates from 1853), informal *Fanelli* is a favourite destination of the not-too-hip after-work crowd, with a small dining room at the back (mains $11–15). Daily 10am–2am, Thurs–Sat until 4am.

THE BAR SCENE

New York's watering holes are much more interesting below 14th Street than above. Some of the best establishments are located in the **East Village**, the **West Village**, **Nolita**, **Soho** and the western reaches of the **Lower East Side**. There's a decent mix of **midtown** drinking spots, though bars here tend to be geared to tourists and an after-hours office crowd and, consequently, can be pricey and rather dull (there are a few notable exceptions). The **Upper East Side** is home to quite a few raucous sports and Irish bars, while the **Upper West Side** has a serviceable array of bars, although most tend to cater to Columbia University students and more of a clean-cut yuppie crowd. Farther uptown, the bars of **Harlem**, while not numerous, offer some of the city's most affordable jazz in a relaxed environment (see p.347).

Check out the scene in the outer boroughs if you can, where bars range in feel from neighbourly to über hip. **Williamsburg** is an easy ride from Manhattan on the L train and the best place if you're short of time. Other areas to try are **Park Slope** and the collective of **Boerum Hill**, **Cobble Hill** and **Carroll Gardens**, especially along Smith Street; head out to **Fort Greene** or **Prospect Heights** if this still feels too tame. The listings in this chapter are grouped, approximately, according to the chapter divisions outlined in the Guide. Bear in mind that many places double as bar and restaurant, and you may therefore find them listed not here but in the previous chapter (and that you can have full meals at many of the spots listed in this chapter). For ease of reference, however, all specifically **gay and lesbian bars** are gathered together in Chapter 28, "Gay New York".

Kenn's Broome Street Bar 363 W Broadway at Broome St ☎212 784 6650, ⓦnyc-bar.com; subway A, C, E to Canal St; map p.64. Set in an ageing 1825 Federal-style house, this comfortable bar offers over eighteen beers (eight draughts), from Harpoon Winter Warm to Flying Dog Pale Ale (they also have Stella on tap), as well as decent burgers. Sun–Thurs 11am–1.30am, Fri & Sat 11am–2.30am.

M1-5 Lounge 52 Walker St, between Church St and Broadway ☎212 965 1701, ⓦm1-5.com; subway N, Q, R to Canal St; map p.64. Ultra-hip lounge bar, with a decent range of beers, wines and cocktails to accompany the sleek design and good food. Live music and DJs set the scene. Mon–Fri 4pm–4am, Sat 7pm–4am.

Puffy's Tavern 81 Hudson St, at Harrison St ☎212 766 9159, ⓦpuffystavernnyc.com; subway #1 to Franklin St; map p.64. Far from being P. Diddy's hangout, this small dive serves cheap booze without a single ounce of attitude, rare in this area. Weekly darts league, and five large flat-screen TVs show sports events. Daily 11.30am–4am.

The Room 144 Sullivan St, between Houston and Prince sts ☎212 477 2102, ⓦtheotheroom.com; subway C, E to Spring St; map p.64. Dark, cosy two-room bar with exposed brick walls and comfortable couches. No spirits, but an impressive array of domestic and international wines and beers. Daily 5pm–4am.

Toad Hall 57 Grand St, between W Broadway and Wooster St ☎212 431 8145; subway A, C, E to Canal St; map p.64. With a pool table, good service and excellent bar snacks, this stylish alehouse is a little less hip and a little more of a local hangout than some of its neighbours. Daily noon–4am.

CHINATOWN, LITTLE ITALY AND NOLITA

Mulberry Street Bar 176-1/2 Mulberry St, between Broome and Grand sts ☎212 226 9345; subway J, Z to Bowery, #6 to Canal St; map p.71. Though it looks like a back-room hangout from *The Sopranos*, this is actually a friendly local bar and restaurant open to all (plenty of mob movies have been filmed here). The wooden bar, tile floor and pressed-tin roof have barely changed since it opened in 1908. Pints from US$6, happy hour daily 3–7pm. Mon–Sat 11am–4am, Sun noon–4am.

Pravda 281 Lafayette St, between Prince and Houston sts ☎212 226 4944, ⓦpravdany.com; subway N, R to Prince St; map p.71. This chic Soviet Russian caviar bar serves over seventy stiff vodka drinks, from cocktails like "Leninade" ($14) to shots from $10, as well as blinis (from $11) for snacking. Now that its heyday has passed, there are fewer crowds, and hence a more relaxed vibe, but it's still a great place. Try the coconut vodka. Mon–Wed 5pm–1am, Thurs 5pm–2am, Fri & Sat 5pm–3am, Sun 6pm–1am.

Sweet & Vicious 5 Spring St, between Bowery and Elizabeth St ☎212 334 7915, ⓦsweetandviciousnyc .com; subway J, Z to Bowery; map p.71. *Sweet & Vicious* is the epitome of rustic chic, with exposed brick, lots of wood and antique chandeliers. The back garden is just as cosy as the inside bar. Daily 3pm–4am.

THE LOWER EAST SIDE

Back Room 102 Norfolk St, between Delancey and Rivington sts ☎212 677 9489; subway F to Delancey St, J, M, Z to Essex St; map p.83. With a hidden, back-alley entrance, this former speakeasy was reputedly once a haunt of gangster Meyer Lansky; cocktails are still served in teacups. To find it, walk down the metal steps (look for the "Toyco" sign) and through to the back of the building. Tues–Sat 7.30am–4am.

Barramundi 67 Clinton St, between Stanton and Rivington sts ☎212 529 6900, ⓦbarramundiny.com; subway F to Delancey St, J, M, Z to Essex St; map p.83. The infused vodka, decent beers, red-leather booths, tree-trunk tables and mounted deer's head attract an early-thirties crowd to this affable bar (there's no Australian connection, despite the name). To sample the swanky *2nd Floor on Clinton* lounge, walk to the back and push the buzzer next to the door marked "private". Daily 6pm–4am.

Barrio Chino 253 Broome St, at Orchard St ☎212 228 6710, ⓦbarriochinonyc.com; subway B, D to Canal St; map p.83. Don't be confused by the Chinese lanterns or drink umbrellas here – the owner's speciality is tequila, and there are a dozen brands to choose from. Shots are served with a traditional *sangría* chaser, made from a blend of tomato, orange and lime juices. Mon 5.30pm–1am, Tues–Thurs & Sun 11.30am–1am, Fri & Sat 11.30am–2am.

The Delancey 168 Delancey St, at Clinton St ☎212 254 9920, ⓦthedelancey.com; subway F to Delancey St, J, M, Z to Essex St; map p.83. Williamsburg hipsters meet Lower East Side chic at this bar and rock club, with a rooftop lounge in summer. Things can get frisky in the basement, which pulsates with live music. Daily 5pm–4am.

Experimental Cocktail Club 191 Chrystie St, between Stanton and Rivington sts; no phone, ⓦexperimentalcocktailclubny.com; subway J, Z to Bowery; map p.83. First US outpost of the lauded Parisian

TOP 5 HISTORIC PUBS

Ear Inn Tribeca. See opposite
Fanelli Café Soho. See opposite
McSorley's Old Ale House East Village. See p.333
Pete's Tavern Gramercy Park. See p.335
Subway Inn Upper East Side. See p.337

25

cocktail den (there's also one in London), featuring fourteen drinks from talented mixologist Nicholas de Soto (plus one beer and bar snacks supplied by *The Fat Radish*). Can get rowdy at weekends, when French expats descend *en masse*. Daily 6pm–4am.

Libation 137 Ludlow St, between Stanton and Rivington sts ☎866 216 1263, ⓦlibationnyc.com; subway F to Delancey St, J, M, Z to Essex St; map p.83. A sexy lounge spanning two floors. It's a bit eclectic, with

$12–14 cocktails, an American-style tapas menu and DJs spinning '80s, hip-hop and everything in between. Mon–Fri 5pm–4am, Sat & Sun noon–4am.

Magician 118 Rivington St, between Essex and Norfolk sts ☎212 673 7881; subway F to Delancey St, J, M, Z to Essex St; map p.83. Usually quiet during the week, the brightly lit back-room with large round tables is usually packed at the weekends, when the jukebox throws out plenty of 1980s indie music. Cash only. Daily 5pm–4am.

THE EAST VILLAGE

★ **7B** 108 Ave B, at E 7th St ☎212 473 8840; subway L to First Ave; map p.88. Opened as a Polish catering hall in 1935 ("Vazac's"), and also known as the *Horseshoe Bar*, this quintessential East Village hangout has often been used as the sleazy set in films and commercials. It features deliberately mental bartenders, cheap pitchers of beer and one of the best punk and rock 'n' roll jukeboxes in the East Village. Daily noon–4am.

★ **Alphabet City Beer Co** 96 Ave C, between E 6th and 7th sts ☎646 422 7103, ⓦabcbeer.co; subway #6 to Astor Place; map p.88. This bar and retail hybrid allows you to quaff the quality ales and ciders ($6), many local, from a communal table before filling your growler (p.329) or grabbing a take-out bottle or two. Sun–Thurs noon–midnight, Fri & Sat noon–2am.

Angel's Share 8 Stuyvesant St, between E 9th St and Third Ave ☎212 777 5415; subway #6 to Astor Place; map p.88. This serene, candlelit haven is a great date spot, kept deliberately romantic by the entry rules – parties larger than four will not be admitted. The cocktails are reputed to be some of the best in the city. Can be hard to find: walk into the Village Yokocho complex, up the stairs to the *Gyu-ya* restaurant and look for the unmarked door on the left. Daily 6pm–2.30am, Thurs until 2am.

Bar Veloce 175 Second Ave, between E 11th and E 12th sts ☎212 260 3200, ⓦbarveloce.com; subway L to Third Ave; map p.88. Stylish Italian wine bar fit for the Mod Squad, with excellent hors d'oeuvres and a fine wine list. Daily noon–3am.

★ **Booker & Dax** 207 Second Ave, at E 13th St ☎212 254 3500, ⓦmomofuku.com/new-york/booker-and-dax; subway #6 to Bleecker St; map p.88. Hip but laid-back cocktail bar from the *Momofuku* team, offering expertly crafted Manhattans and plenty of creative bar theatrics: drinks made with hot pokers ("friend of the devil") and plenty of liquid nitrogen knocking around. Sun–Thurs 6pm–2am, Fri & Sat 6pm–3am.

Bourgeois Pig 111 E 7th St, between First Ave and Ave A ☎212 475 2246, ⓦbourgeoispigny.com; subway L to First Ave, #6 to Astor Place; map p.88. The decadent Versailles theme at this funky wine bar, replete with wall-sized mirrors, chandeliers and crimson satin couches, is backed by an extensive cocktail menu (from $13; using just wines,

beers and champagne), including bubbly served in silver punch bowls. Daily 5pm–2am, Fri & Sat until 3am.

Burp Castle 41 E 7th St, between Second and Third aves ☎212 982 4756, ⓦburpcastlenyc.wordpress.com; subway #6 to Astor Place; map p.88. Delightfully weird place: the bartenders wear monks' habits, choral music is piped in and you are encouraged to speak in tones below a whisper. Oh, and there are over 550 different types of beer (12 on tap). Mon–Fri 5pm–4am, Sat & Sun 4pm–4am.

Cozy Café Hookah Lounge 43 E 1st St, between First and Second aves ☎212 475 0177, ⓦcozycafenyc.com; subway F to Lower East Side-Second Ave; map p.88. Comfortable sofas and soft pillows make this subterranean Middle Eastern hookah bar all the more relaxing. Belly dancers Fri & Sat nights. Cash only. Mon–Thurs & Sun 2.30pm–2.30am, Fri & Sat 3pm–4am.

★ **d.b.a.** 41 First Ave, between E 2nd and E 3rd sts ☎212 475 5097, ⓦdrinkgoodstuff.com; subway F to Lower East Side-Second Ave; map p.88. A beer-lover's paradise, *d.b.a.* has at least sixty bottled beers, fifteen brews on tap and an authentic hand-pump. Garden seating (with a small smoking section) is available in summer. Daily 1pm–4am.

Decibel 240 E 9th St, between Second and Third aves ☎212 979 2733, ⓦsakebardecibel.com; subway #6 to Astor Place; map p.88. A rocking atmosphere (with good tunes) pervades this beautifully decorated underground sake bar. The inevitable wait for a wooden table will be worth it, guaranteed. Daily 6pm–3am, Sun until 1am.

Gin Palace 95 Avenue A, at E 6th St ☎212 614 6818, ⓦginpalaceny.com; subway #6 to Astor Place; map p.88. This newish bar is a sort of steampunk take on a Victorian English pub; order gin and tonic on tap ($7), or one of the elaborate gin cocktails ($11), paired with a Scotch egg or two ($3). Daily 6pm–2am.

TOP 5 ROOFTOP BARS

230 Fifth Union Square. See p.335
The Delancey Lower East Side. See p.331
Press Lounge Midtown West. See p.337
Roof Garden Café, The Met Upper East Side. See p.337
VU Bar See p.336

Grassroots Tavern 20 St Mark's Place, between Second and Third aves ☎ 212 475 9443; subway #6 to Astor Place; map p.88. This wonderful, roomy underground den has dirt-cheap pitchers (from $7), free popcorn, an extended happy hour and at least three of the manager's pets roaming around at all hours of the day or night. Daily 4pm–4am.

Hi Fi 169 Ave A, between E 10th and E 11th sts ☎ 212 420 8392, ⓦ thehifibar.com; subway L to Third Ave; map p.88. Formerly a live music venue, this spot has been stripped of its stage, but features an mp3 jukebox with over 19,000 albums. Great-looking hipster boys and girls pack this place, drinking hard pretty much every night of the week. Mon–Thurs 4pm–4am, Fri–Sun 3pm–4am.

KGB Bar 85 E 4th St, at Second Ave ☎ 212 505 3360, ⓦ kgbbar.com; subway F to Lower East Side-Second Ave; #6 to Astor Place; map p.88. On the second floor, this dark bar is set in what was the HQ of the Ukrainian Communist Party in the 1930s. Better known now for its marquee literary readings and the Kraine Theater in the basement (see p.353). Daily 7pm–4am.

★ **The Lobby Bar** *Bowery Hotel*, 335 Bowery at E 3rd St ☎ 212 505 9100, ⓦ theboweryhotel.com; subway #6 to Bleecker St; map p.88. Perhaps the most lavish hotel bar in the city, adorned with thick Persian rugs, velvet sofas and wood panelling – a bit like one of those decadent clubs on the Upper East Side, but open to the public. Daily 5pm–2am, Thurs–Sat until 4am.

Manitoba's 99 Ave B, between E 6th and E 7th sts ☎ 212 982 2511, ⓦ manitobas.com; subway L to First Ave, #6 to Astor Place; map p.88. Run by Dick Manitoba, lead singer of the punk group The Dictators, the kicking jukebox and rough-and-tumble vibe at this spot make it a favourite among East Villagers who really just like to drink. Daily 2pm–4am.

McSorley's Old Ale House 15 E 7th St, between Second and Third aves ☎ 212 473 9148; subway #6 to Astor Place; map p.88. Yes, it's often full of tourists and NYU students, but this sawdust-strewn bar opened in 1854 – it's the oldest pub in NYC. Today, it only pours its own ale – light or dark (you get two small glasses with every order; US$5). Try the turkey sandwich with raw onion (add mustard); it's one of the best bar snacks in the city (US$4). Mon–Sat 11am–1am, Sun 1pm–1am.

Pouring Ribbons 225 Ave B, between 13th and 14th sts ☎ 917 656 6788, ⓦ pouringribbons.com; subway L to 1st Ave; map p.88. The somewhat unusual door policy – which does guarantee you a seat inside – is worth braving to sip expertly made cocktails ($14) from a cool second-floor perch. Tasty snacks provided by Beecher's (see p.283) round things out. Daily 6pm–2am.

★ **Proletariat** 102 St Mark's Place, between Ave A and First Ave ☎ 212 777 2017, ⓦ proletariatny.com; subway #6 to Astor Place; map p.88. Small, boutique alehouse (just 12 bar stools), serving all sorts of rare and unusual brews from a rotating list of 11 drafts – drinks are pricier (top brands $10–11) than the average around here, but aficionados will appreciate the selection. Daily 5pm–2am.

Third Man 116 Ave C, at E 8th St ☎ 212 598 1040, ⓦ louis649.com; subway L to First Ave, #6 to Astor Place; map p.88. This homage to Orson Welles' 1949 masterpiece looks the part, with stylish, dimly-lit digs and cocktails named after the main characters ($12). Daily 6pm–4am.

Wayland 700 E 9th St at Ave C ☎ 212 777 7022, ⓦ thewaylandnyc.com; subway L to First Ave, #6 to Astor Place; map p.88. Another rustic-chic cocktail bar on Ave C, with some dazzling blends and creations from apple-pie moonshine with apple-spice bitters ($12), to Fernet Branca and home-made citrus-infused cola on tap ($7). Snack on chicken liver and bacon on toast ($9) while you sip. Daily 5pm–4am.

★ **Zum Schneider** 107 Ave C, at E 7th St ☎ 212 598 1098, ⓦ zumschneider.com; subway #6 to Astor Place; map p.88. A German beer-hall (and indoor garden) with a mega-list of brews and *wursts* from the Fatherland. It can be a bit packed with frat-boy types; in the early evening, though, the old-world vibe is sublime. Mon–Thurs 5pm–2am, Fri 4pm–4am, Sat 1pm–4am, Sun 1pm–midnight.

THE WEST VILLAGE

★ **124 Old Rabbit Club** 124 MacDougal St, at Minetta Lane ☎ 212 691 8845; subway A, B, C, D, E, F, M to W 4th St; map pp.96–97. Best re-creation of a speakeasy in the Village, with over seventy beers to choose from, a cosy, cavern-like space and decent bar food. To get in, walk down the steps to the black door and press the buzzer. Sun–Thurs 6pm–2am, Fri–Sat 6pm–4am.

★ **55 Bar** 55 Christopher St, between Sixth and Seventh aves ☎ 212 929 9883, ⓦ 55bar.com; subway #1 to Christopher St; map pp.96–97. A gem of an underground dive-bar that's been around since 1919, with a great jukebox, congenial clientele and live jazz and blues music seven nights a week (including guitarist Mike Stern; sets $10). Daily 3pm–3am.

Amélie 22 W 8th St, between Fifth Ave and MacDougal St ☎ 212 533 2962, ⓦ ameliewinebar.com; subway A, B, C, D, E, F, M to W 4th St; map pp.96–97. Modern French-themed wine bar, with vintage theatre seats in the up-front lounge, a lacquered red bar and quieter tables at the back. Mon–Thurs 5pm–midnight, Fri 5pm–2am, Sat 2pm–2am, Sun 11am–midnight.

Blind Tiger Ale House 281 Bleecker St, at Jones St; ☎ 212 462 4682, ⓦ blindtigeralehouse.com; subway A, B, C, D, E, F, M to W 4th St, #1 to Christopher St; map pp.96–97. This wood-panelled pub is the home of serious ale connoisseurs, with 28 rotating draughts (primarily US microbrews such as Sixpoint and Smuttynose for around $6.50), a couple of casks and loads of bottled beers – they

25

SPORTS BARS

The sports bar is something of an institution in the US, and New York is certainly no exception – as in the rest of the country, they specialize in televising live sports events, typically the domestic big four: baseball, basketball, football (American) and ice hockey. In New York you'll also find plenty of bars showing live soccer games (typically Premier League) and even rugby and Aussie Rules.

The Australian 20 W 38th St, between Fifth and Sixth aves ☎212 869 8601, ⓦtheaustraliannyc.com; subway B, D, F, M to 42nd St-Bryant Park; map p.123. Major Aussie hangout, showing all Australian Rules and Rugby League games live (and on replay), plus plenty of US sports as well. Sun–Wed 11.30am–midnight, Thurs 11.30am–2am, Fri & Sat 11.30am–4am.

Black Horse Pub 568 Fifth Ave, at 16th St ☎718 788 1975, ⓦblackhorsebar.com; subway R to Prospect Ave; map p.226. The British ownership of the place shows up in the grub (bangers and mash, curry chips) as well as the attention to whatever Premier League (and other) game might be on; expect a crowd for big matches. Mon–Thurs & Sun noon–2am, Fri & Sat noon–4am, earlier during game days.

Football Factory 6 W 33rd St, between Fifth Ave and Broadway ☎212 967 7792, ⓦfootballfactoryny.com; subway B, D, F, M, N, Q, R to 34th St-Herald Square; map p.123. Possibly the top spot in Manhattan to watch

soccer; many of the world's top clubs have ardent fan groups that show up here regularly for games. Mon–Fri 11am–4am, Sat 7am–4am, Sun 8am–4am.

Smithfield 215 W 28th St, between Seventh and Eighth aves ☎212 564 2172, ⓦsmithfieldnyc.com; subway #1 to 28th St; map p.107. The major soccer rival to *Football Factory*, dedicated to all things football with the bonus of decent craft beers on tap; FC Barcelona players and Sir Alex Ferguson have all stopped by for drinks. Mon–Fri 11am–3.30am, Sat & Sun 9am–3.30am.

Woodwork 583 Vanderbilt Ave, at Dean St, Brooklyn ☎718 857 5777, ⓦwoodworkbk.com; subway C to Clinton–Washington Aves, B, Q to Seventh Ave, #2, #3 to Grand Army Plaza; map p.226. Not your average sports bar, with some elegant food choices, small batch bourbons, a rustic decor and fidelity to the "beautiful game". Mon–Fri noon–2am, Sat & Sun game time until 4am.

also serve cheese plates from *Murray's* (see p.385). The prime location means it tends to get packed. Daily 11.30am–4am.

Fat Black Pussycat 130 W 3rd St, between Sixth Ave and MacDougal St ☎212 533 4790, ⓦthefatblackpussycat.com; subway A, B, C, D, E, F, M to W 4th St; map pp.96–97. This lively pub is an NYU favourite, with popular happy hours (Sun–Fri 4–8pm), plenty of cosy wooden booths, darts and billiards. The pub's original location on MacDougal St is where Bob Dylan allegedly wrote *Blowin' in the Wind*. Daily 1pm–4am.

Jane Ballroom *Jane Hotel,* 113 Jane St, between Washington and West sts ☎212 924 6700, ⓦthejanenyc.com; subway A, C, E to 14th St; map pp.96–97. Gorgeous hotel bar, with opulent furnishings that make it look like a stately home (with a disco ball). Head up to the balcony for the best celebrity-watching. Can be tough to get in at weekends, thanks to a very discriminatory door policy (all-male groups can forget it). Mon, Tues & Sun 5pm–2am, Wed–Sat 5pm–4am.

Kettle of Fish 59 Christopher St, at Seventh Ave ☎212 414 2278, ⓦkettleoffishnyc.com; subway #1 to Christopher St; map pp.96–97. This basement bar is a

great escape from the scene on Seventh Ave, with plenty of real ales (including Sixpoint), no-nonsense staff and a mix of sports fans, tourists and students. The original on MacDougal St was a legendary Beat hangout (the famous old sign is still here). Mon–Fri 3pm–4am, Sat & Sun 2pm–4am.

Orient Express 325 W 11th St, between Greenwich and Washington sts ☎212 691 8845, ⓦorientexpressnyc.com; subway #1 to Christopher St; map pp.96–97. This classy, old-fashioned cocktail bar is a tribute to the famous train, with beechwood panelling, faux train windows and a long list of creative drinks – the Agatha III (Plymouth Gin and lemon with house-made pear-sage soda; $14) is a winner. Sun & Mon 1pm–1am, Tues–Thurs 1pm–2am, Fri & Sat 1pm–4am.

White Horse Tavern 567 Hudson St, at W 11th St ☎212 243 9260; subway #1 to Christopher St; map pp.96–97. A Greenwich Village institution, which opened in 1880: Dylan Thomas supped his last here before being carted off to the hospital with alcohol poisoning (check out the portrait and plaque inside), while Norman Mailer and Hunter S. Thompson were also regulars. Daily 11am–3am.

CHELSEA AND THE MEATPACKING DISTRICT

★ **El Quinto Pino** 401 W 24th St at Ninth Ave ☎212 206 6900, ⓦelquintopinonyc.com; subway C, E to 23rd St; map p.107. There are relatively few seats in this elegant

tapas bar, so come early to nibble on pork cracklings ($6) and an uncanny sea-urchin sandwich ($15), paired with a good selection of Spanish wines. Mon–Thurs 5pm–midnight, Fri

PIER 66 AND THE FRYING PAN

It's more Cape Cod than Manhattan, but **Pier 66 Maritime** (ⓦpier66maritime.com) is a great place to kick off a summer evening in the city. This former railroad barge offers riverside drinking and dining, and access to the historic lightship **Frying Pan** (ⓦfryingpan.com) – salvaged from the bottom of Chesapeake Bay, you can explore the salty, shell-encrusted interior. The far end of the barge often doubles as space for live acts. You'll find *Pier 66* at W 26th St and Twelfth Ave (open May–Oct 11.30am–midnight), in Hudson River Park.

& Sat 5pm–1am, Sun 5–11pm.

Half King 505 W 23rd St, between Tenth and Eleventh aves ☎212 462 4300, ⓦthehalfking.com; subway C, E to 23rd St; map p.107. This popular Irish pub is owned by a small group of writers/artists and features good food (burgers $13–17, fish and chips $18) and regular literary events; they've been known to book some heavy hitters (see p.360). Mon–Fri 11am–4am, Sat & Sun 9am–4am.

Peter McManus Café 152 Seventh Ave, at 19th St ☎212 929 9691; subway #1 to 18th St; map p.107. Unlike many Irish pubs in the city, this is the real deal, moving to this location in 1936 and since appearing in episodes of *Seinfeld* and *Law & Order*. The worn oak bar

adds character, along with the tasty in-house McManus Ale and two old-style telephone booths inside. Mon–Sat 11am–4am, Sun noon–4am.

Tía Pol 205 Tenth Ave, between 22nd and 23rd sts ☎212 675 8805; subway C, E to 23rd St; map p.107. This popular tapas bar frequently fills up its narrow space – consider coming early if you want to miss the crowds. You can graze on bar snacks like *croquetas* ($4/$8) and fried chickpeas ($4) or construct a meal with heartier plates like octopus salad ($14) and shrimp *al ajillo* ($12); wash it all back with the easy-drinking house-made *sangria* ($9 glass). Mon 5.30–11pm, Tues–Thurs noon–11pm, Fri noon–midnight, Sat 11am–midnight, Sun 11am–10.30pm.

UNION SQUARE, GRAMERCY PARK AND THE FLATIRON DISTRICT

230 Fifth 230 Fifth Ave, at E 27th St ☎212 725 4300, ⓦ230-fifth.com; subway N, R, #6 to 23rd St; map p.114. Classy lounge bar and celebrity haunt, with the best views of midtown and the biggest roof garden in the city (14,000 square foot) – blankets handed out to drinkers and special heaters mean that the roof is open even in winter. Drinks and snacks are reasonably priced for this type of experience (martinis from $14, hot apple cider $12), and there is no cover. Note the dress code (no sneakers/trainers; shirt for men). Mon–Fri 4pm–4am, Sat & Sun 10am–4am.

Bar Jamón 125 E 17th St, at Irving Place ☎212 253 2773, ⓦcasamononyc.com; subway L, N, Q, R, #4, #5, #6 to 14th Street-Union Square; map p.114. A superb place to sip on sherry and nosh on Spanish tapas (most between $3 and $10). Be forewarned though: there are only fourteen stools. Mon–Fri 5pm–2am, Sat & Sun 2pm–2am.

La Birreria (Eataly), 200 Fifth Ave, at W 23rd St ☎212 937 8910, ⓦeatalyny.com/birreria; subway N, R, #6 to 23rd St; map p.114. A sprawling rooftop bar above the insanely popular Eataly market, *Birreria* is a modern twist on the beer garden – you'd expect nothing less than the handcrafted ales and home-made sausages considering the foodie haven below. It's a bit pricey ($7–10 a pint), but the Del Borgo Re Ale Extra is one of the tastier beers in the city. Reservations can be made for spots as long as your group will be dining . Sun–Wed 11.30am–10pm, Thurs–Sat 11.30am–11pm.

★ **Molly's** 287 Third Ave between E 22nd and E 23rd sts ☎212 889 3361, ⓦmollysshebeen.com; subway

#6 to 23rd St; map p.114. While the city veers from throwback cocktails and nouveaux speakeasies to local microbrew palaces, the friendly bartenders at *Molly's* are content to pour some of the best pints of Guinness around – sawdust floor included. Daily 11am–4am.

Old Town Bar 45 E 18th St, between Broadway and Park Ave S ☎212 529 6732, ⓦoldtownbar.com; subway L, N, Q, R, #4, #5, #6 to 14th Street-Union Square; map p.114. This atmospheric bar is popular with the after-work crowd. Opened in 1892, much of the creaking interior is original, including the rickety dumbwaiter and fine mahogany bar. Mon–Sat noon to 1am, Sun 3pm–midnight.

Pete's Tavern 129 E 18th St, at Irving Place ☎212 473 7676, ⓦpetestavern.com; subway L, N, Q, R, #4, #5, #6 to 14th Street-Union Square; map p.114. Open since 1864, this former speakeasy now trades unashamedly on its history, which has included such illustrious patrons as O. Henry. Daily 11am–2.30am; kitchen closes earlier.

Revival 129 E 15th St, between Irving Place and Third Ave ☎212 253 8061, ⓦrevivalbarnyc.com; subway L, N, Q, R, #4, #5, #6 to 14th Street-Union Square; map p.114. Walk down the stairs and into this friendly narrow bar with great outdoor seating in the backyard. Popular with fans waiting for concerts at Irving Plaza around the block. Mon–Thurs & Sun 4pm–2am, Fri & Sat 3.30pm–4am.

25

MIDTOWN EAST

Campbell Apartment Southwest balcony in Grand Central Terminal ☎212 953 0409; subway #4, #5, #6, #7 to 42nd St-Grand Central; map p.123. Once home to businessman John W. Campbell, who oversaw the construction of Grand Central, this majestic space – built to look like a Florentine palace – was sealed up for years. Now, after a snappy refit by designer Nina Campbell (no relation), it's one of New York's most distinctive cocktail bars. Go early and don't wear trainers (or a T-shirt, ripped jeans or baseball cap; in other words, look the part). Mon–Thurs noon–1am, Fri & Sat noon–2am, Sun noon to midnight.

King Cole Bar & Salon St Regis hotel, 2 E 55th St, between Fifth and Madison aves ☎212 753 4500, ⓦkingcolebar.com; subway E, M to Fifth Ave-53rd St; map p.123. The reputed home of the Bloody Mary has recently been refurbished and reborn as a bar-restaurant meant to evoke a 1920s jazz lounge. Fortunately, the grand Maxfield Parrish mural remains in its proper spot, right above the bar. Ask about the secret in the painting while sipping on a cocktail and sampling the refined menu. Mon–Sat 11.30am–1am, Sun noon–midnight.

Le Colonial 149 E 57th St, between Lexington and Third aves ☎212 752 0808, ⓦlecolonialnyc.com; subway N, Q, R, #6 to 59th St-Lexington Ave; map p.123. The upstairs bar of this Vietnamese restaurant is decked out in opulent Asian style, with red velvet chairs, teak tables and ageing photos of Saigon. Try the speciality cocktails; Le Colonial is a mix of gin, cassis and raspberry (average drinks $16). Mon–Thurs & Sun 4.30pm–11.30pm, Fri & Sat 4.30pm–midnight.

P.J. Clarke's 915 Third Ave, at E 55th St ☎212 317 1616, ⓦpjclarkes.com; subway #6 to 51st St, E, M to Lexington Ave-53rd St; map p.123. Friendly bartenders serve from a decent array of wines (twelve by the glass) and a moderate selection of beers at P.J. Clarke's, one of the city's most famous watering holes. The bar is casual, though there is a pricey restaurant out back as as well as a clandestine, members-only restaurant, Sidecar (though membership is free). There are other locations near Lincoln Center and Battery Park City. Daily 11.30am–4am.

Rattle N Hum 14 E 33rd St, between Madison and Fifth aves ☎212 481 1586, ⓦrattlenhumbarnyc.com; subway B, D, F, N, Q, R to 34th St, #6 to 33rd St; map p.123. With thirty-odd beers on draught and a few times that in bottles, this long, busy bar is a prime destination for craft-brew lovers. Mon–Wed & Sun 10.30am–2pm, Thurs–Sat 10.30am–4am.

Salvation Taco 145 E 39th St, between Lexington and Third aves ☎212 865 5800, ⓦsalvationtaco.com; subway #4, #5, #6, #7 to 42nd St-Grand Central; map p.123. Hard to know what to label it – café, restaurant, gastrocantina – but Salvation Taco, in all its garishly hued, folk-art aesthetic glory, is best treated as a bar where you can get some of the more intriguing south-of-the-border-influenced snacks anywhere on offer. Crispy pig ears ($7), ceviche with pork cracklings ($9) and lamb on naan "taco" ($6; we didn't specify which border!) pair up with similarly daring cocktails (most around $12). Daily 7am–2am.

VU Bar La Quinta Manhattan, 14/F, 17 W 32nd St, between Fifth and Sixth aves ☎212 991 8842; subway B, D, F, M, N, Q, R to 34th St-Herald Square; map p.123. One of the best-kept secrets in Manhattan offers a mesmerizing rooftop view of the Empire State Building, looming just to the north. Drinks only (most cocktails $10), but you can order Korean food from the takeaway menus if you get hungry. Mon–Thurs & Sun 5pm–1am, Fri & Sat 5pm–2am.

MIDTOWN WEST

Ardesia 510 W 52nd St, between Tenth and Eleventh aves ☎212 247 9191, ⓦardesia-ny.com; subway C, E to 50th St; map p.141. A sleek but comfortable Hell's Kitchen wine bar with a bold snack menu (home-made pretzels, quail-egg toast, house-cured meats) and diverse selection of vintages, about 25 or so of which are available by the glass (most $9–15). Mon–Wed 5pm–midnight, Thurs & Fri 5pm–2am, Sat 2pm–2am, Sun 2–11pm.

★ **Jimmy's Corner** 140 W 44th St, between Broadway and Sixth Ave ☎212 221 9510; subway B, D, F, M to 42nd St-Bryant Park, N, Q, R, #1, #2, #3 to Times Square-42nd St; map p.141. The walls of this long, narrow corridor of a bar, owned by ex-fighter/trainer Jimmy Glenn, are a virtual boxing hall of fame. You'd be hard pressed to find a more characterful dive anywhere in the city – or a better jazz/R&B jukebox. Mon–Fri 11am–4am, Sat noon–4pm, Sun 3pm–4am.

★ **Kashkaval** 856 Ninth Ave, between W 55th and W 56th sts ☎212 581 8282, ⓦkashkavalfoods.com; subway A, B, D, #1 to 59th St-Columbus Circle; map p.141. Tucked into the back of a cheese shop, this cosy wine bar serves up tasty bites, including excellent cheese and meat plates, cold meze (the beetroot skordalia is good) and an array of fondues. Daily 11am–midnight.

McCoy's 768 Ninth Ave, between W 50th and W 51st sts ☎212 957 8055, ⓦmccoyspubnyc.com; subway C, E to 50th St; map p.141. In a wasteland of faux Irish pubs full of blarney, this narrow, unpretentious bar is, ahem, the real McCoy. It dates back to the late 1800s; the Jameson's flows freely, as do the draughts, which include a house lager and ale; the jukebox has a small but well-curated selection; and happy hour is basically any time you arrive (save for 7–11pm). Daily 10am–4am.

P.J. Carney's 906 Seventh Ave, between W 57th and

W 58th sts ☎212 664 0056, ⓦpjcarneys.com; subway N, R to Seventh Ave-57th St; map p.141. Despite the historic pedigree (this small bar was established in 1927) and a straggle of loyal locals, *Carney's* is crammed most nights with tourists and sports fans. The beer and pub food isn't bad, though, and it beats a number of other area spots; consider for an afternoon pit-stop between midtown and the park. Mon–Sat 10.30am–4am, Sun noon–4am.

Press Lounge *Ink48 Hotel*, 16th floor, 653 Eleventh Ave at W 48th St ☎212 757 2224, ⓦthepresslounge.com; subway C, E to 50th St; map p.141. Spacious rooftop bar with a gasp-inducing panorama of midtown Manhattan and the Hudson River, which you can view while sipping a seasonal cocktail ($16). Over-21s only, and "casual elegant" dress code enforced. Mon, Tues & Sun 5pm–1am, Wed–Sat 5pm–2am.

★ **Rudy's** 627 Ninth Ave, between W 44th and W 45th sts ☎646 707 0890, ⓦrudysbarnyc.com; subway

A, C, E to 42nd St-Port Authority; map p.141. One of New York's cheapest, friendliest and liveliest bars, a favourite with local actors and musicians. *Rudy's* offers free hot dogs, a backyard that's great in summer and some of the cheapest pitchers of beer in the city ($7–16). Daily 8am–4am.

Russian Vodka Room 265 W 52nd St, between Broadway and Eighth Ave ☎212 307 5835, ⓦrussianvodkaroom.com; subway C, E, #1 to 50th St, N, R to 49th St; map p.141. They serve more than fifty different types of vodka here, as well as their own fruit-flavoured and sublime garlic-infused concoctions; there's also caviar and plenty of small plate choices (herring, pâté and the like). Under the dim lighting, office workers mingle with Russian and Eastern European expats; don't ask for a mixer with your shot, unless you want to attract a stare or a laugh. Mon–Thurs & Sun 4pm–2am, Fri & Sat 4pm–4am.

THE UPPER EAST SIDE

ABV 1504 Lexington Ave, at E 97th St ☎212 722 8959, ⓦabvny.com; subway #6 to 96th St; map p.169. On the fringes of East Harlem, this acts as an overflow for super-popular *Earl's* around the corner (p.169), with a larger, smarter space serving a similar range of small plates and quality beers, with live music every Monday. Mon–Thurs 5pm–midnight, Fri 4pm–1am, Sat 11am–1am, Sun 11am–midnight.

★ **Balcony Bar & Roof Garden Café** Metropolitan Museum of Art, 1000 Fifth Ave, at E 82nd St ☎212 535 7710, ⓦmetmuseum.org; subway #4, #5, #6 to 86th St; map p.169. It's hard to imagine a more romantic spot to sip a glass of wine and kick off the evening, whether in the *Roof Garden Café*, which has some of the best views in the city, or in the *Balcony Bar* overlooking the Great Hall. Roof Garden Café: May–Oct Tues–Thurs & Sun 10am–4.30pm, Fri & Sat 10am–8pm; Balcony Bar: Fri & Sat 4–8.30pm.

Bar Pléiades *The Surrey*, 20 E 76th St, between Fifth and Madison aves ☎212 772 2600, ⓦthesurrey.com; subway #6 to 77th St; map p.169. This stylish Art Deco hotel bar is an homage to Chanel, with black-and-white lacquered surfaces, quilted walls and leather banquettes; cocktails ($16–21) and pricey canapés from *Café Boulud* ($28). Daily noon–midnight.

★ **Bemelmans Bar** *Carlyle Hotel*, 35 E 76th St, at Madison Ave ☎212 744 1600, ⓦrosewoodhotels.com/

en/carlyle; subway #6 to 77th St; map p.169. This hotel bar oozes old-school New York class, with Ludwig Bemelman's exuberant murals plastered all around, live piano, white-jacketed waiters and an opulent gold-leaf ceiling. Daily 5.30pm–12.30am.

★ **Earl's Beer & Cheese** 1259 Park Ave, at E 97th St ☎212 289 1581, ⓦearlsny.com; subway #6 to 96th St; map p.169. Right up on the edge of East Harlem, this tiny bar boasts cool tunes, great food (lots of cheesy things) and a non-frat clientele – draft beers change daily from a roster of excellent microbrews. Mon & Tues 4pm–midnight, Wed & Thurs, Sun 11am–midnight, Fri & Sat 11am–2am.

Stir 1363 First Ave, at E 73rd St ☎212 744 7190, ⓦstirnyc.com; subway #6 to 77th St; map p.169. Funky lounge bar and popular date venue, with comfy sofas and seductive pillows making another stark contrast to the mainly sports-bar territory around here. It becomes more club-like later on, with plenty of dancing, and the bar food and cocktails (especially the margaritas) are excellent. Tues & Wed 5pm–1am, Thurs 5pm–2am, Fri 5pm–3am, Sat 5pm–4am.

Subway Inn 143 E 60th St, at Lexington Ave ☎212 223 8929; subway N, R, #4, #5, #6 to Lexington Ave-59th St; map p.169. This neighbourhood dive-bar, across from Bloomingdale's, has been serving customers since 1937 and is great for a late-afternoon beer. Mon–Fri 10am–4am, Sat & Sun 11am–4am.

THE UPPER WEST SIDE

Dead Poet 450 Amsterdam Ave, between W 81st and W 82nd sts ☎212 595 5670, ⓦthedeadpoet.com; subway #1 to 79th St; map p.183. You may be waxing poetic and then dropping dead if you stay for the duration of this sweet little bar's happy hour, usually involving $4–5

pints or $5 Bloody Marys and running all weekend – there's some sort of special drink deal every day of the week. The back room has armchairs, books and a pool table, and there's a full dinner menu. Mon–Sat 10am–4am, Sun noon–4am.

25

Ding Dong Lounge 929 Columbus Ave, between W 105th and W 106th sts ☎212 663 2600, ⓦdingdonglounge.com; subway B, C to 103rd St; map p.183. This punk bar with a DJ and occasional live bands attracts a vibrant mix of graduate students, neighbourhood Latinos and stragglers from the nearby youth hostel. Happy hour 4–8pm, with $4 draught beer and $5 cocktails. Daily 4pm–4am.

Dublin House Tap Room 225 W 79th St, between Broadway and Amsterdam Ave ☎212 874 9528, ⓦdublinhousenyc.com; subway #1 to 79th St; map p.183. Beneath the cool neon sign, this lively, sometimes-overcrowded Upper West Side Irish pub is the place to go before or after a gig at the Beacon Theatre. Mon–Sat 8am–4am, Sun noon–4am.

MObar *Mandarin Oriental*, 80 Columbus Circle, at W 60th St between Ninth Ave and Broadway ☎212 805

8800, ⓦmandarinoriental.com/newyork; subway A, B, C, D, #1 to 59th St-Columbus Circle; map p.183. On the 35th floor of the *Mandarin Oriental* (see p.272), this boîte is a cosy alternative to the hotel's main lobby lounge, with a shiny nickel bar and leather seating. Choose from more than twenty wines by the glass and a host of exotic cocktails that will surely put a dent in your wallet. Tues–Thurs 4pm–midnight, Fri & Sat 4pm–1am.

Prohibition 503 Columbus Ave, at W 84th St ☎212 579 3100, ⓦprohibition.net; subway B, C, #1 to 86th St; map p.183. Stylish bar and lounge with funky decor (check out the lamps suspended in wine bottles) and free live music every night (usually funk or jazz). The back room is always much quieter, the beer selection is good if unsurprising and the eclectic martinis are spectacular. Daily 5pm until about an hour after the last band ends (which can be anywhere from 1am to 2.30am).

HARLEM

Bier International 2099 Frederick Douglass Blvd, at W 113th St ☎212 280 0944, ⓦbierinternational.com; subway B, C, #2, #3 to 116th St; map p.198. Harlem's first beer garden is a fine effort, with eighteen top-notch draughts and over thirty bottled beers ($6–8) on offer, and plenty of space to enjoy those summer evenings. Mon 4pm–1am, Tues–Thurs 4pm–2am, Fri 4pm–4am, Sat noon–4am, Sun noon–1am.

Camaradas El Barrio 2241 First Ave, at E 115th St ☎212 348 2703, ⓦcamaradaselbarrio.com; subway #6 to 116th St; map p.198. Smart redbrick local bar in the heart of Spanish Harlem, with great Puerto Rican food and bottled beers from all over Latin America; expect the salsa to get louder as the night progresses.

Sun–Wed 3pm–1am, Thurs–Sat 3pm–2am.

★ **Ginny's Supper Club** 657 Malcolm X Blvd, at W 143rd St ☎ 212 283 945; subway #3 to 145th St; map p.198. Stylish bar and jazz venue (under *Red Rooster*), with live sets accompanied by punchy house cocktails ($13–14) and excellent soul food plates ($16). Mon, Tues & Sun noon–midnight, Wed & Thurs 2pm–2am, Fri & Sat 10am–4am.

★ **Harlem Tavern** 2153 Frederick Douglass Blvd, at W 116th St ☎212 866 4500, ⓦharlemtavern.com; subway B, C, #2, #3 to 116th St; map p.198. Restaurant, bar and enticing beer garden (excellent seasonal beer selection), with live jazz and weekend brunches ($14.95). Mon–Fri noon–2am, Sat & Sun 11am–2am.

BROOKLYN

FULTON FERRY DISTRICT AND DUMBO

68 Jay St 68 Jay St, at Water St ☎718 260 8207, ⓦ68jaystreetbar.net; subway F to York St; map p.215. A friendly neighbourhood bar with good happy-hour deals (daily 4–7pm), a rock soundtrack (plus free live, mainly country-influenced music Saturday nights) and a relaxed, vaguely arty vibe. Mon–Fri 2pm–2am, Sat 3pm–2am, Sun 4pm–midnight.

BROOKLYN HEIGHTS

Floyd 131 Atlantic Ave, between Clinton and Henry sts ☎718 858 5810, ⓦfloydny.com; subway F, G to Bergen St; R to Court St; #2, #3, #4, #5 to Borough Hall; map p.215. Decked out with antique couches and comfy leather chairs, the main draws here are the cheap draught beers, popular indoor bocce court and televised English Premier League games. Mon–Thurs 5pm–2am, Fri 4pm–4am, Sat & Sun noon to 4am.

Montero's Bar & Grill 73 Atlantic Ave, at Hicks St ☎646 729 4129; subway F, G to Bergen St, R to Court St, #2, #3, #4, #5 to Borough Hall; map p.215. Old-timey joint with a nautical theme (it used to be a sailors' hangout); there's a pool table, decent-priced drinks, karaoke on Thursdays & Fridays and an incredibly friendly bartender. Daily noon–4am.

FORT GREENE

Stonehome Wine Bar 87 Lafayette Ave, between S Portland Ave and S Elliot Place ☎718 624 9443, ⓦstonehomewinebar.com; subway C to Lafayette Ave, G to Fulton St; map p.215. Stylish wine bar with the added bonus of backyard patio, perfect for warm evenings. The bar itself is a gorgeous, curving cherry-wood masterpiece, and the carefully crafted wine list is impressively long (more than thirty are available by the glass). Mon & Sun 5–11pm, Tues–Sat 5pm–midnight.

25

BOERUM HILL AND CARROLL GARDENS

★ **Bar Great Harry** 280 Smith St, at Sackett St, Carroll Gardens ☏718 222 1103, ⓦbargreatharry.com; subway F, G to Carroll St; map p.222. Essential stop on any Carroll Gardens pub crawl, with a vast list of microbrews and select imports (20 on tap, 70 in bottles). Prices range from $5 to $8. Daily 2pm–4am (though can shut earlier).

Brooklyn Inn 148 Hoyt St, at Bergen St, Boerum Hill ☏718 522 2525; subway F, G to Bergen St, A, C, G to Hoyt-Schermerhorn; map p.222. Locals – and their dogs – gather at this convivial favourite with high ceilings, a solid wood bar imported from Germany in the 1870s and friendly staff. Great place for a daytime buzz or shooting pool in the back room. Mon–Thurs 4pm–4am, Fri 3pm–4am, Sat & Sun 2pm–4am.

Jakewalk 282 Smith St, at Sackett St, Carroll Gardens ☏347 599 0294, ⓦthejakewalk.com; subway F, G to Carroll St; map p.222. Neighbourhood wine bar decked out in orange and gold, with around fifteen wines by the glass (from $8) to sample (along with plenty of whiskys and speciality cocktails). Be sure to order a few of the 15 cheeses ($5 each; $24 for a board of three plus two cured-meat selections) to go with your drink, sourced from the gourmet cheese shop a few blocks down. Mon–Fri 5pm–2am, Sat & Sun 11am–2am.

RED HOOK

Fort Defiance 365 Van Brunt St, at Dikeman St ☏347 453 6672, ⓦfortdefiancebrooklyn.com; subway F, G to Smith-9th sts; map p.222. It bills itself as a "café-bar" and does offer restaurant-like full meals (eg pan-roasted snapper, $19), but what Fort Defiance does best is make lovingly prepared cocktails (though the well-curated wine list and strong coffee rate highly too), which honour storied classics from famous bars. Mon–Fri 10am–midnight (closes 3pm Tues), Sat & Sun 9am–midnight.

PARK SLOPE

Dram Shop 339 Ninth St, between Fifth and Sixth aves ☏718 788 1444, ⓦdramshopbrooklyn.com; subway F, G, R to Fourth Ave-Ninth St; map p.226. Popular spot for a few different generations of drinkers and sports watchers, who fill up the wooden booths and, in good weather, tiny outdoor area. The double-patty burger (with fries, $12) is

TOP 5 ACTIVITIES AT BROOKLYN BARS

Bocce (like boules) **at Floyd** See p.338
Karaoke at Montero's Bar & Grill See p.338
Shuffleboard at Dram Shop See above
Trivia at Pete's Candy Store See opposite
Video games at Barcade See opposite

addictive, and, perhaps best of all there's a shuffleboard table under the twin TVs. Mon–Fri 2pm–4am, Sat & Sun noon to 4am.

Freddy's Bar 627 Fifth Ave, between 17th and 18th sts ☏718 768 0131, ⓦfreddysbar.com; subway R to Prospect Ave; map p.226. After being pushed out of Prospect Heights thanks to the Atlantic Yards project, this vaunted hangout has been transplanted to the South Slope – its divey soul (and colourful decor) intact; live music, or some kind of performance, most nights. Daily noon–4am.

Mission Dolores 249 Fourth Ave, at Carroll St ☏347 457 5606, ⓦmissiondoloresbar.com; subway R to Union St-Fourth Ave; map p.226. Sister to *Bar Great Harry* (see above), this is another craft-beer-heavy drinking spot ($5–9 per pint) but with a boisterous outdoor area in a converted garage. Mon & Tues 4pm–2am, Wed, Thurs & Sun 2pm–2am, Fri & Sat 2pm–4am.

Union Hall 702 Union St, at Fifth Ave ☏718 638 4400, ⓦunionhallny.com; subway R to Union St-Fourth Ave; map p.226. Vast bar, restaurant and live music venue, with a library-like interior of bookshelves, fireplaces and sofas near the bar, and two wildly popular bocce courts (arrive early to get a game). The basement hosts bands three or four times a week – check out the website for the schedule. Mon–Fri 4pm–4am, Sat & Sun 1pm–4am.

WILLIAMSBURG AND GREENPOINT

Allswell 124 Bedford Ave, at N 10th St ☏347 799 2743, ⓦallswellnyc.com; subway L to Bedford Ave; map p.236. A bright, cheerful gastropub from an alum of the *Spotted Pig* (see p.305), where you can't go wrong at happy hour ($1 oysters; $14 for burger, fries and a beer). Mon–Wed & Sun 10am–midnight, Thurs–Sat 10am–3.30am.

Barcade 388 Union St, between Powers and Ainslie sts ☏718 302 6464, ⓦbarcadebrooklyn.com; subway L to Lorimer St, G to Metropolitan Ave; map p.236. This former metalwork shop is crammed with old-fashioned arcade games (think Donkey Kong), each of which takes the original 25 cents per game. The beers are good, too, with an excellent choice of 25 brews on tap. Mon–Thurs 4pm–4am, Fri 2pm–4am, Sat & Sun noon–4am.

Brooklyn Brewery 1 Brewers Row, 79 N 11th St ☏718 486 7422, ⓦbrooklynbrewery.com; subway L to Bedford Ave; map p.236. New York's best-known microbrewery (see p.234) where you can sample beers ($5) in a bar setting. Mon–Thurs 5–7pm (by reservation only), Fri 6–11pm, Sat noon–8pm, Sun noon–6pm.

★ **The Commodore** 366 Metropolitan Ave, at Havemeyer St ☏718 218 7632; subway L to Lorimer St; G to Metropolitan Ave; map p.236. Straight out of Williamsburg central casting: a retro-style rec-room vibe, better-than-expected bar food (fried chicken, grilled cheese and *poblano* sandwich, sautéed kale), inexpensive cocktails and pitchers, a hip, young crowd, a few old video games… and somehow it all works perfectly. Daily 4pm–4am, kitchen closes 11 or 11.30pm.

Pete's Candy Store 709 Lorimer St, between Frost and Richardson sts 718 302 3770, petescandystore .com; subway L to Lorimer St, G to Metropolitan Ave; map p.236. This terrific little spot was once a real candy store. There's free live music every night, a reading series, Scrabble and Bingo nights, pub quizzes and some well-poured cocktails. Mon–Wed & Sun 5pm–2am, Thurs–Sat 5pm–4am.

Radegast Hall and Biergarten 113 N 3rd St, at Berry St 718 963 3973, radegasthall.com; subway L to Bedford Ave; map p.236. This Austro-Hungarian spacious wooden beer-hall serves steins of foamy German brews. The dining room does great food and is popular with families, while the beer garden attracts serious boozers. Sun–Thurs noon–2am, Fri & Sat noon–4am.

Spuyten Duyvil 359 Metropolitan Ave, at Havemeyer St 718 963 4140, spuytenduyvilnyc.com; subway L to Lorimer St or Bedford Ave, G to Metropolitan Ave; map p.236. Beer lovers should make for this popular pub, stocking over one hundred bottled brands (mostly potent Belgian brews), six on tap, and a rotating selection of cask-pulled ales. Mon–Thurs 5pm–2am, Fri 5pm–4am, Sat noon–4am, Sun noon–2am.

★ **Tørst** 615 Manhattan Ave, between Nassau and Driggs aves; subway G to Nassau Ave; map p.236. A shiny new temple for beer drinkers, *Tørst* boasts reclaimed wood and a sleek metal bar, behind which 21 draughts sit hooked up to the "flux capacitor", which allows bartenders to monitor and adjust the gas and carbonation without descending to the kegs below. The results: flawless draughts, available in 8-oz or 14-oz pours. Settle in and sample a few; it may be a while before you want to leave. Mon–Wed & Sun noon–midnight, Thurs–Sat noon–2am.

QUEENS

ASTORIA

Bohemian Hall and Beer Garden 29-19 24th Ave, between 29th and 30th sts 718 274 4925, bohemianhall.com; subway N, Q to Astoria Blvd; map p.244. This hundred-year-old Czech bar is the real deal, catering to old-timers and serving a good selection of pilsners, among other offerings. Out back there's a large beer garden with picnic tables, trees, free-flowing pitchers, burgers and sausages, and a bandstand for polka groups. Great fun in good weather, and worth the trip. Mon–Thurs 5pm–1am, Fri 3pm–3am, Sat noon–3am, Sun noon–2am.

Cronin & Phelan's 38-14 Broadway, between 38th and Steinway sts 718 545 8999, croninandphelans .com; subway E, M to Steinway St; map p.244. Boisterous locals' watering hole with laughably cheap pub fare – enormous portions of shepherd's pie ($9.95), burger with fries ($7.50), 16-oz steak with sides ($18.95) – plus an outdoor area and the odd open-mic night. Mon–Sat

8am–4am, Sun 11am–4am.

Sparrow Tavern 24-01 29th St, at 24th ave 718 606 2260, thesparrowtavern.com; subway N, Q to Astoria Blvd; map p.244. A low-key, comfortably worn neighbourhood joint (as opposed to the *Beer Garden* across the street), *Sparrow* is perfect for whiling away some time with friends over a few craft brews and well-done dishes (tacos and burgers to lamb ribs). Daily noon–4am.

LONG ISLAND CITY

★ **L.I.C. Bar** 45-58 Vernon Blvd, at 46th Ave 718 786 5400, longislandcitybar.com; subway #7 to Vernon Blvd-Jackson Ave or 45th Rd-Courthouse Square, G to 21st St; map p.242. A friendly, atmospheric place for a beer, burger and some free live music (Mon, Wed, Sat & Sun); hunker down at the old wooden bar or in the pleasant outdoor garden. Mon–Thurs & Sun 4pm–2am, Fri & Sat 2pm–4am.

THE BRONX

Yankee Tavern 72 E 161st St, at Gerard Ave 718 292 6130; subway B, D, #4 to 161st St-Yankee Stadium; map p.252. Since 1923, this has been the "original sports bar". Everyone wears their pinstripes on their sleeves in this dive, and Yankees employees come to blow off steam (or celebrate). Hours vary, but generally daily 10am–2am.

STATEN ISLAND

Jade Island 2845 Richmond Ave, between Independence and Yukon aves 718 761 8080, jadeislandstaten.com; bus #S44, #S61; map p.261. Staten Island's sole tiki bar (cum Chinese restaurant) offers bamboo booths, blowfish lamps, rum cocktails in coconuts and girls in hula skirts. And you wanted to head straight back to Manhattan. Mon–Thurs 11.30am–11pm, Fri 11.30am–midnight, Sat 12.30pm–midnight, Sun 12.30–11pm.

Liedy's Shore Inn 748 Richmond Terrace, between Clinton and Lafayette aves 718 447 9240; bus #S40; map p.261. Staten Island's oldest pub was opened in 1905 by German immigrant Jacob Liedy – once popular with sailors, today it's convenient to Snug Harbor and retains a no-nonsense local bar vibe. Daily 11.30am–10pm, Fri & Sat until midnight.

Nightlife

As the city that never sleeps, New York is a global nightlife hotspot. Even confirmed early birds should try to stay out late at least a few times during their stay, as the city's legendary energy is most obvious when most other cities have bedded down for the night. Since the early 2000s, New York's live music scene has been undergoing a post-punk and garage-rock revival, fuelled by bands from the East Village, the Lower East Side and Williamsburg in Brooklyn. The city also continues to set the standard in jazz, especially in Harlem. Hip-hop also remains a vital part of the musical scene in New York – Mos Def, 50 Cent and Jay-Z are all based here, among many others – though clubs and larger venues are the best places to catch live sets.

NEW YORK BURLESQUE

In the last ten years burlesque shows and clubs have gained a cult following in New York (*Time Out* has a section dedicated to the genre), with feted local perfomers such as Sugar Shack Burlesque (ⓦsugarshackburlesque.com), Ruby Solitaire (ⓦrubysolitaire.com) and Calamity Chang (ⓦcalamitychang.com). Sometimes dubbed "neo-burlesque", performances can include anything from classic striptease and campy comedy acts to variety shows and extravagant mini-dramas. Though rarely suitable for children and usually involving nudity in some form, acts are more focused on the wildly exaggerated performance than just stripping. Most shows take place in various venues across the Lower East Side and East Village such as the **Slipper Room** (ⓦslipperroom.com). Check *Time Out* for the latest listings.

26

Whatever you're planning to do after dark, remember to **carry ID** at all times to prove you're over 21 – you're likely to be asked by every doorman. Note that some venues do not even allow under-21s to enter, let alone drink – call to check if you're concerned. Note also that although **smoking is illegal** at most clubs, you'll soon realize that in practice, this is only sporadically enforced (despite recent police crackdowns).

The sections that follow provide accounts of the pick of the city's venues, but it's a good idea to get up-to-date info once you hit the ground.

ESSENTIALS

Listings *Time Out New York* ($4.99) is pretty reliable. Otherwise, grab a freesheet like *the Village Voice* (ⓦvillagevoice.com) or *The Onion* (whose cultural listings are excellent; ⓦtheonion.com). These can be found on street corners in self-serve newspaper boxes, as well as in many music stores; all of them contain detailed listings for most scenes.

Tickets For most of the large venues listed, tickets are sold through Ticketmaster (ⓦticketmaster.com). For many mid-sized and small venues, try Ticketweb (ⓦticketweb.com).

LIVE MUSIC

New York has a vibrant **live music** scene, though, like the city, most places are eclectic when it comes to genres; the same place can feature rock, hip-hop, folk and Latin music on different nights, and though rock/indie often dominates, only jazz has a truly separate club culture (see p.346). New York's **rock scene** has leant heavily toward garage and pop/indie rock in the last decade, with newer, more eclectic bands like Holy Hail, Hooray for Earth, Sleigh Bells and Yeasayer adding to an established roster that includes Vampire Weekend, Interpol, The Strokes, The Rapture and the Yeah Yeah Yeahs. As for **venues**, rising rents have forced many smaller and medium-sized places to close or decamp to Brooklyn (especially Williamsburg) and New Jersey. Most of the best performance spaces are still in Manhattan, though; there's a large cluster of exceptionally good venues in the East Village and Lower East Side.

LARGE VENUES

⭐ **Barclays Center** 620 Atlantic Ave at Flatbush Ave, Brooklyn ☎917 618 6100, ⓦbarclayscenter.com; subway B, D, N, Q, R, #2, #3, #4, #5 to Atlantic Ave; map p.215. Brooklyn's brand-new big stage hosts the Nets (p.391) and major sports events, but is also gaining a rep for mega concerts from the likes of Jay-Z, Beyonce, Rihanna and The Killers.

⭐ **Hammerstein Ballroom** 311 W 34th St, between Eighth and Ninth aves ☎212 564 4882, ⓦmcstudios.com; subway A, C, E to 34th St; map p.141. This grand 1906 building has seen many incarnations: it's been an opera house, a vaudeville hall and a Masonic temple, and it now hosts indie and rock bands. Capacity is 3600, but the sound system and acoustics are of high enough quality that most seats are pretty good. Tickets $50 and up.

Madison Square Garden Seventh Ave, at W 32nd St ☎212 465 6741, ⓦthegarden.com; subway A, C, E, #1, #2, #3 to 34th St; map p.141. New York's principal big stage, the Garden hosts not only hockey and basketball games but also a good portion of the stadium rock and pop acts that visit the city. Seating capacity is 20,000-plus, so the arena's not exactly the most soulful place to see a band – but for big names, it's the handiest option.

Radio City Music Hall 1260 Sixth Ave, at W 50th St ☎212 247 4777, ⓦradiocity.com; subway B, D, F, M to 47–50th St; map p.123. Not the prime venue it once was; it occasionally hosts a terrific concert, but for the most part its schedule is clogged with cutesy tribute shows, schlocky musicals and, of course, the "Christmas Spectacular". The acoustics are flawless and the building itself does have a great sense of occasion (see p.127) – it seems to inspire the artists who play here to put on a memorable show.

26

BEACH, BOAT AND POOL PARTIES

Summer in New York means beer gardens, street fairs and outdoor parties: you'll find plenty of action on the water, with a variety of boats offering weekly events and waterside venues in Williamsburg and South Street Seaport. Even stately Governors Island gets a piece of the action, hosting some of the biggest dance parties and concerts of the summer.

Beekman Beer Garden Beach Club ⓦ beekman beergarden.com; subway A, C, J, #2, #3, #4, #5 to Fulton St; map p.43. Features live music and DJs most summer evenings (May–Oct). Take your passport/ID. Open daily from noon (weather permitting).

Grace Bar Grace Hotel, 125 W 45th St, at Sixth Ave ☏ 212 354 2323, ⓦ grace.room-matehotels.com; map p.270. Several of Manhattan's hotels hold posh pool parties in the summer, but this is one of the most accessible, with swim-up bar, decent DJs and entry a (relatively) bargain $35. Mon–Thurs 5pm– midnight, Fri & Sun 5pm–2am.

Governors Island and Governors Beach Club ⓦ governorsbeachclub.com. This genteel island

(see p.39) converts into club central on summer weekends, with parties arranged by the likes of *Mister Saturday Night* (see p.348).

Premier List Pier 40, corner of W Houston St and the West Side Hwy ⓦ premierlistnyc.com; subway #1 to Houston St. Arranges cruise parties (hip-hop, R&B, reggae) on the *Queen of Hearts* ($20–40). Fri & Sat 8pm–midnight.

Williamsburg Park N 12th St at Kent Ave, Williamsburg, Brooklyn ⓦ freewilliamsburg.com; subway L to Bedford Ave; map p.236. Major concerts (some free) in the park near the East River promoted by JellyNYC and Open Space Alliance.

MID-SIZED AND SMALL VENUES

MANHATTAN

Arlene's Grocery 95 Stanton St, between Ludlow and Orchard sts ☏ 212 473 9831, ⓦ arlenesgrocery.net; subway F to Lower East Side-Second Ave; map p.83. An intimate, erstwhile bodega (hence the name) that hosts nightly gigs by local, reliably good indie bands. Regularly patronized by musicians, talent scouts and open-minded rock fans. Go on Mon nights (free) after 10pm for punk and heavy-metal karaoke, when you can sing along with a live band. Tues–Thurs & Sun cover $8, Fri & Sat $10. Daily 6pm–4am.

The Bitter End 147 Bleecker St, between LaGuardia Place and Thompson St ☏ 212 673 7030, ⓦ bitterend .com; subway A, B, C, D, E, F, M to W 4th St; map pp.96– 97. Young MOR bands in an intimate club setting, mostly folky rockers in the Dylan mould since 1961, though Lady Gaga got started here in 2007. A catalogue of the famous people who've played the club is posted by the door – it's a pretty long list. Cover is usually $8–12, but some gigs are free; there is a two-drink minimum. Daily 7pm–1am, Mon, Fri & Sat until 4am.

★ **Bowery Ballroom** 6 Delancey St, at Bowery ☏ 212 533 2111, ⓦ boweryballroom.com; subway J, Z to Bowery, B, D to Grand St; map p.83. No attitude, stellar acoustics and even better views have earned this venue praise from both fans and bands. Major labels test their up-and-comers here, so it's a great place to catch the Next Big Thing of any genre. Most shows cost $15–35. Pay in cash at the *Mercury Lounge* box office (see opposite), at the door, or by credit card through Ticketweb. Daily from 7pm.

★ **Cake Shop** 152 Ludlow St, between Rivington and Stanton sts ☏ 212 253 0036, ⓦ cake-shop.com; subway F

to Delancey St, J, M, Z to Essex St; map p.83. This unassuming coffee shop and record store becomes one of the city's most cutting-edge venues for indie rock most nights; cover ranges $7–12. Daily 9am–2am, Fri & Sat until 4am.

City Winery 155 Varick St, at Vandam St ☏ 212 608 0555, ⓦ citywinery.com; subway #1 to Houston St, C, E to Spring St; map p.64. Since opening in a converted club space a few years ago, *City Winery* has put a fine roster of rock, folk and roots music performers on its stage; it has full dinner service (food is OK, nothing special) and wine is actually made on the premises. Tickets $12–50. Mon– Thurs & Sun 11.30am–3.30pm & 5pm–midnight, Fri 11.30am–3.30pm & 5pm–2am, Sat 5pm–2am.

High Line Ballroom 431 W 16th St, between Ninth and Tenth aves ☏ 212 414 5994, ⓦ highlineballroom.com; subway A, C, E to 14th St; map p.107. One of the newer venues in town, with table seating available (full dinner if you like) for shows – acts run from indie rock to hip-hop, reggae and big band (most tickets $15). There are DJ sets too. $10 minimum for table seating during shows. Daily 6pm–late.

Irving Plaza 17 Irving Place, at E 15th St ☏ 212 777 6800, ⓦ venue.irvingplaza.com; subway L, N, Q, R, #4, #5, #6 to Union Square; map p.114. Once home to Off-Broadway musicals (hence the dangling chandeliers and blood-red interior), *Irving Plaza* now features an impressive array of rock, electronic and techno acts. The main room has wildly divergent acoustics; stand toward the back on the ground floor for the truest mix of sound. Tickets usually range $20–50. See website for show times.

The Living Room 154 Ludlow St, between Stanton and Rivington sts ☏ 212 533 7235, ⓦ livingroomny.com; subway F to Delancey St, J, M, Z to Essex St; map p.83.

LATIN & BALLROOM DANCE NIGHTS AND VENUES

After Work Fridays at SOB's (see below). Lessons followed by live salsa bands from 8pm on Fridays, featuring not only Latin greats but newer acts as well. Cover $10–15. Fri from 5pm.

Baila Wednesdays at Solas 232 E 9th St, between Second and Third aves; subway #6 to Astor Place; map p.88. Mambo and salsa dancing to DJs 8.30pm–1am (classes at 8pm), with $5 cover. See ⓦsalsanewyork.com for a full list of weekly salsa events.

Dance Tango *Ukrainian East Village Restaurant*, 140 Second Ave, between E 8th and E 9th sts ☎212 614 328, ⓦdancetango.com; subway L to Third Ave; map p.88. Tango every Friday night, starting with lessons at 7.15pm (cover $12; $15 with lesson).

Salsa on Sundays at The Crystal Room Taino Towers, 240 E 123rd St, between Second and Third aves ⓦSalsa-On-Sunday.com; subway #4, #5, #6 to 125th St. First Sunday of the month 6–10pm ($10); usually live band plus DJ and an older Latino crowd.

Samba New York ☎917 684 9447, ⓦsambanewyork.com; map p.107. Centre for Brazilian samba culture in New York, offering shows and classes in drumming and dancing. Check the website for class times and events.

Swing 46 349 W 46th St, between Eighth and Ninth aves ☎212 262 9554, ⓦswing46.com; subway A, C, E to 42nd St; map p.141. Jazz and supper club offering live swing bands and even dance lessons (cover: Mon–Thurs & Sun $12, Fri & Sat $15). Daily 5pm–1am (lessons at 9pm).

26

Comfortable couches (hence the name) and a friendly bar make for a relaxed setting in which to hear local, low-key folk and acoustic rock – Nora Jones got her start in music here. Shows usually free (with $10 donation). Note that the location will have changed by 2014, check the website for the latest. Daily 4pm–2am, Fri & Sat until 4am.

Mercury Lounge 217 E Houston St, at Essex St ☎212 260 7400, ⓦmercuryloungenyc.com; subway F to Lower East Side-Second Ave; map p.83. Dark, Lower East Side mainstay featuring a mix of local, national and international rock and pop acts. It's owned by the same crew as the *Bowery Ballroom*, and is similarly used as a trial venue by major labels for up-and-coming artists. Tickets usually $8–15. Daily shows from 7pm.

Pianos 158 Ludlow St, between Stanton and Rivington sts ☎212 505 3733, ⓦpianosnyc.com; subway F to Delancey St, J, M, Z to Essex St; map p.83. There's no cover to get in the door at this converted piano factory (hence the name), but to get into the tiny back room – where the music is – you'll need to fork out extra at the weekend (Fri & Sat; $5–10). The sound system's a standout, and the endless roster of mostly rock bands (expect four choices nightly) means the place is usually packed. Drink prices are somewhat high, and the queue to get in habitually long. Daily 2pm–4am (live music daily at 8pm).

★ **(Le) Poisson Rouge** 158 Bleecker St, at Thompson St ☎212 505 3474, ⓦlepoissonrouge.com; subway A, B, C, D, E, F, M to W 4th St; map pp.96–97. Mix of live rock, folk, pop and electronica at 7pm ($10–15), with dance parties most weekends (Fri & Sat; often free). Daily 5pm–2am, Fri & Sat until 4am.

Postcrypt Coffeehouse 2098 Broadway at W 116th St, in the basement of St Paul's Chapel ⓦpostcrypt.virb .com; subway #1 to 116th St; map p.183. Venerable Columbia student-run folk venue, with hardly any seating but free music and cheap drinks; only 35 people can legally fit inside, making for exceptionally intimate shows. Fri & Sat 9pm–midnight when school's in session.

Rockwood Music Hall 196 Allen St, between Houston and Stanton sts ☎212 477 4155, ⓦrockwoodmusichall .com; subway F to Lower East Side-Second Ave; map p.83. Seven nights of live music draw hordes of locals to this tiny space. Though there are no bad seats, it's a good idea to come early – it's often packed. Tickets $5–20. Mon–Thurs 6pm–4am, Fri–Sun 5.30pm–4am.

SOB's (Sounds of Brazil) 204 Varick St, at W Houston ☎212 243 4940, ⓦsobs.com; subway #1 to Houston St; map p.64. Premier place to hear hip-hop, Brazilian, West Indian, Caribbean and World Music acts within the confines of Manhattan. Vibrant and danceable, with a high quality of music. Shows most nights; ticket prices vary according to the performer. Mon–Thurs hours vary depending on shows, Fri 5pm–4am, Sat 6.30pm–4am, Sun noon–4pm.

★ **Village Underground** 130 W 3rd St, at Sixth Ave ☎212 777 7745, ⓦthevillageunderground.com; subway A, B, C, D, E, F, M to W 4th St; map pp.96–97. Tiny basement performance space that is one of the most intimate and innovative clubs around. Monday is jam-session night, the house band (playing vintage rock and R&B, funk and reggae) holds court Wednesday through Friday, while Tuesday & Saturday are club nights (all from 8.30pm). Cover $10–15.

BROOKLYN

The Bell House 149 7th St, between Second and Third aves ☎718 643 6510, ⓦthebellhouseny.com; subway F, M, G, R to Fourth Ave-9th St; map p.222. A converted printing house on a bleak stretch in Gowanus provides the

26

setting for indie band performances and wacky events – cook-offs, Burt Reynolds film celebrations and so on. The front-room bar is a pleasantly spacious place to drink, with happy-hour specials. Shows usually $15–30. Daily 5pm–4am.

Brooklyn Bowl 61 Wythe Ave, between 11th and 12th sts, Williamsburg ☎718 963 3369, ⓦ brooklynbowl .com; subway L to Bedford Ave; map p.236. A converted warehouse with live concerts, DJ sets, karaoke, food by the Blue Ribbon group (of *Blue Ribbon Sushi* and *Blue Ribbon Bakery*) and . . . oh yeah, the purported main attraction: bowling (see p.394). Shows usually $5–15, with the odd big name a lot more. Mon–Thurs 6pm–2am, Fri 6pm–4am, Sat noon–4am, Sun noon–2am.

Jalopy Theatre and School of Music 315 Columbia St, at Woodhull St ☎718 395 3214, ⓦ jalopy.biz; subway F, G to Carroll St; map p.222. If you want to hear bluegrass, folk or the occasional hard-to-classify musician in a relaxed setting, this tiny instrument shop/venue will be just the ticket. Lessons and workshops as well. Most shows $5–15. Tues–Fri 2pm–2am, Sat & Sun noon–2am.

Knitting Factory 361 Metropolitan Ave, at Havemeyer St, Williamsburg ☎347 529 6696, ⓦ bk.knittingfactory .com; subway L to Bedford Ave, G, L to Metropolitan Ave; map p.236. This intimate showcase for indie rock and underground hip-hop moved to Brooklyn in 2009, but has maintained a loyal following and quality acts. Most tickets $5–15. Daily shows from 6pm or 7pm.

Littlefield 622 Degraw St, between Third and Fouth aves, Gowanus ☎718 855 3388, ⓦ littlefieldnyc.com; subway R to Union St; map p.222. Housed in an old warehouse, this art and performance space hosts a diverse line-up of bands from indie rock and hip-hop to jazz and reggae, as well as art exhibitions, literary events and film screenings. Wed–Sun 8pm–2am (plus Mon comedy nights).

★ **Music Hall of Williamsburg** 66 N 6th St, between Wythe and Kent aves, Williamsburg ☎718 486 5400, ⓦ musichallofwilliamsburg.com; subway L to Bedford Ave; map p.236. A large performance space with excellent acoustics, set in an old factory. One of Brooklyn's really great venues and another in the *Bowery Ballroom* stable – expect the same kind of acts. From 6pm until the opening band starts, all drinks are $3. Tickets $10–20. Daily shows between 6pm and 8pm.

★ **The Rock Shop** 249 Fourth Ave, between President and Carroll sts, Gowanus ☎718 230 5740, ⓦ therockshopny.com; subway R to Union St; map p.226. Brooklyn rock club featuring primarily up-and-coming bands, with a full bar and restaurant upstairs. Mon–Thurs 5pm–2am, Fri 5pm–4am, Sat noon–4am, Sun noon–1am.

Southpaw 125 Fifth Ave, between Sterling Place and St John's Place, Park Slope ☎718 230 0236, ⓦ spsounds .com; subway #2, #3 to Bergen St, D, R to Union St; map p.226. Brooklyn's premier live venue, with 5000 square feet of space and a wide range of acts and DJs from almost every genre. Admission varies but is rarely more than $10–12, while a cab from lower Manhattan costs around $15. Daily 8pm–2am, Fri & Sat until 4am.

Spike Hill 184 Bedford Ave, between N 6th and N 7th sts, Williamsburg ☎718 218 9737, ⓦ spikehillmusic .com; subway L to Bedford Ave; map p.236. Right in the centre of the main Billyburg strip, with everything from honky-tonk to local indie bands taking to the stage and a pub next door. Mon–Sat 6pm–1am, Sun 2.30pm–1am.

JAZZ AND BLUES

Jazz in New York has seen a major resurgence since the 1990s. You'll find the best clubs in the **West Village** and especially **Harlem**, where a host of small, intimate venues showcase a variety of local talent, from Hammond-organ players to Afro-beat performers. Midtown venues have also steadily been improving in quality and there are a few decent places in **Chelsea** and the **East Village**. Note that **Woody Allen** (with The Eddy Davis New Orleans Jazz Band) still plays jazz clarinet at *Café Carlyle* (see p.348), though this has turned into a bit of a tourist circus. To find out **who else is playing**, check the usual sources, notably the *Village Voice* (ⓦ villagevoice.com) and *Time Out New York* (ⓦ timeoutny.com); other good jazz rags are the monthlies *Hothouse* (ⓦ hothousejazz.com), a free magazine available at venues and hotels, and *DownBeat* (ⓦ downbeat.com). **Price** policies vary from club to club; the major places that attract famous performers charge a hefty cover ($20–50) and a minimum for food and drinks. Smaller venues (especially in Harlem) come cheaper; some have neither admission fee nor minimum drink charge.

PARLOUR JAZZ AT MARJORIE ELIOT'S

Something of a right of passage for local jazz fans, every Sunday (4–6pm; free), a jazz concert has taken place in the parlour of legendary singer Marjorie Eliot's home at 555 Edgecombe Ave (at W 160th St; buzz Apt #3F; map p.208). Marjorie started the concerts in her living room in 1992, as a way to cope with the premature death of her son Phil. Just buzz-in and join the small crowd sitting in front of Marjorie's piano (go early to get a good seat); halfway through you get served apple juice and cookies.

BOWL, SPIN AND PARTY

Even **bowling** has been turned into a glamorous, club-like experience in New York, where you're more likely to see high heels and cocktails than bowling shoes and Budweiser. If **table tennis** is more your thing, head to SPiN, Susan Sarandon's ping-pong club.

Bowlmor Lanes Times Square, 222 W 44th St between Seventh and Eighth aves ☎212 680 0012, ⓦbowlmor.com; subway A, C, E to 42nd St; map p.141. Offers seven plush, themed lounges in addition to fifty lanes. Bowl a few sets or just enjoy the cocktails and food cooked up by celebrity chef David Burke. Mon 1pm–1am, Tues–Thurs 1pm–midnight, Fri 1pm–3am, Sat 11am–3am, Sun 11am–midnight.

Lucky Strike Lanes 624–660 W 42nd St at Twelfth Ave ☎646 829 0170, ⓦbowlluckystrike.com; subway A, C, E to 42nd St; map p.141. This Hollywood-based operation has a similar bar/bowl combo, with lane-side food service, lounges and addictive mini-burgers. Mon–Wed & Sun noon–midnight, Thurs–Sat noon–4am.

SPiN 48 E 23rd St, near Park Ave ☎212 982 8802, ⓦnewyork.spingalactic.com; subway N, R, #6 to 23rd St; map p.114. Here you can play ping pong ($10–20/30min), try and spot owner Susan Sarandon, or eat and drink at the bar. Mon 11am–midnight, Tues & Wed 11am–1am, Thurs 11am–2am, Fri & Sat 11am–4am, Sun 11am–10pm.

26

HARLEM JAZZ VENUES

★ **American Legion Post (Col. Charles Young #398)** 248 W 132nd St, between Powell and Frederick Douglass blvds ☎212 283 9701; subway #2, #3 to W 135th St; map p.198. This veterans' club hosts one of the best deals in Harlem, the free Sunday-evening jam sessions that run 7pm–midnight; the headliner is Seleno Clarke on his classic Hammond B3 organ, but the home-cooked meals and cheap drinks are also worth sampling. You have to sign in at the door. Jazz nights also Wed, Thurs and every other Sat 8pm–midnight.

★ **Bill's Place** 148 W 133rd St, between Malcolm X and Powell Blvds ☎212 281 0777, ⓦbillsplaceharlem.com; subway #2, #3 to 135th St; map p.198. Showcase for local star saxophonist Bill Saxton, hosted in an old speakeasy on what was Jungle Alley; he performs Fridays and Saturdays only, at 9pm and 11pm (doors open 8.30pm; donation $20, BYOB).

Cotton Club 656 W 125th St, at Twelfth Ave ☎212 663 7980, ⓦcottonclub-newyork.com; subway #1 to 125th St; map p.198. No relation to the famous original (this version opened in 1977), it packs in the tourists nonetheless with the Cotton Club All Stars knocking out swing, blues and jazz classics. Saturday & Sunday afternoon shows (with buffet) are $42, and Monday is swing dance night ($25; food extra). Thurs–Sat from 8pm ($55, including buffet dinner).

Showman's Café 375 W 125th St, at Morningside Ave ☎212 864 8941; subway A, B, C, D to 125th St; map p.198. This small, long-established blues, jazz and gospel-music haunt (since 1942) is often packed with Harlemites and, increasingly, tourists – it also features a real Hammond B3 organ. Jazz shows Mon–Thurs 8.30pm, 10pm, 11.30pm, Fri & Sat 9.30pm, 11.30pm, 1.30am; two-drink minimum and $5 cover Fri & Sat. Mon–Sat 1pm–4am.

★ **Shrine Bar** 2271 Powell Blvd, between W 133rd and W 134th sts ☎212 690 7807, ⓦshrinenyc.com; subway B, #2, #3 to 135th St; map p.198. Named for Fela Kuti's legendary joint in Lagos, this cosy bar and performance space features African decor and walls lined with album sleeves. The focus here is on World Music (note the United World Music sign at the front) but the jazz open-mic sessions (Sun 1pm) are great fun. Shows start at 6pm most nights, and there's flavoursome Israeli and West African food from the owners. Daily 4pm–4am.

WEST VILLAGE JAZZ VENUES

Bar Next Door 129 MacDougal St, between W 3rd and W 4th sts ☎212 529 5945, ⓦlalanternacaffe.com; subway A, B, C, D, E, F, M to W 4th St; map pp.96–97. Great underground venue, with live sets. Cover $12. Mon–Thurs & Sun 6pm–2am, Fri & Sat 6pm–3am.

Blue Note 131 W 3rd St, between Sixth Ave and MacDougal St ☎212 475 8592, ⓦbluenote.net; subway A, B, C, D, E, F, M to W 4th St, #1 to Christopher St; map pp.96–97. Open since 1981 (and unrelated to the record label), this jazz institution regularly hosts top international performers, with the likes of Sarah Vaughan, Dizzy Gillespie and Oscar Peterson in past years. Tickets usually range $15–25. Daily 6pm–1am, Fri & Sat until 3am.

Smalls Jazz Club 183 W 10th St, at W 4th St ☎212 252 5091, ⓦsmallsjazzclub.com; subway #1 to Christopher St; map pp.96–97. This cosy jazz dive is all about the music, with an impressive roster of visiting artists and a cool audio archive online – listen to the performers first to decide which night to visit. Cover $10–20. Daily 4pm–4am.

Village Vanguard 178 Seventh Ave, between Perry and W 11th sts ☎212 255 4037, ⓦvillagevanguard.com; subway #1, #2, #3 to 14th St; map pp.96–97. An NYC jazz landmark since 1935 (Sonny Rollins' *A Night at the Village Vanguard* was recorded here in 1957), with a regular diet of big names. Cover $25 per set, plus a one-drink minimum. Daily 7.30pm–1am.

26

Zinc Bar 82 W 3rd St, between Thompson and Sullivan sts ☎212 477 8337, ⓦzincbar.com; subway A, B, C, D, E, F, M to W 4th St; map pp.96–97. Great jazz venue with strong drinks and a loyal bunch of regulars. The blackboard above the entrance announces the evening's featured band. Hosts both new talent and established greats, with an emphasis on Latin American rhythms. Cover $10 with a one-drink minimum (two at the tables). Mon–Fri 6pm–2.30am, Sat & Sun 6pm–3am.

OTHER JAZZ VENUES

★ **Birdland** 315 W 44th St, at Ninth Ave ☎212 581 3080, ⓦbirdlandjazz.com; subway A, C, E to 42nd St; map p.141. Not the original place where Charlie Parker played, but nonetheless an established supper club that hosts some big names. Sets nightly at 8.30pm and 11pm. Music charge of $20–50; at a table, you'll need to spend a minimum of $10 or more on food or drink, while at the bar, the cover includes your first drink. Daily 5pm–1am.

Café Carlyle Carlyle Hotel, 35 E 76th St, at Madison Ave ☎212 744 1600, ⓦrosewoodhotels.com/en/Carlyle; subway #6 to 77th St; map p.169. Woody Allen plays clarinet here most Mon nights Jan–June at 8.45pm (cover: general seating $145–195; bar seating $100 plus $25 drink minimum); add on dinner and this is essentially a very expensive way to see Allen up close, along with hordes of camera-wielding fans (photos are allowed). It's certainly an experience, but jazz fans might want to check out other nights ($25–85). Mon–Sat 6.30pm–midnight.

Iridium Jazz Club 1650 Broadway, at W 51st St ☎212 582 2121, ⓦtheiridium.com; subway #1 to 50th St; map p.141. Contemporary jazz performed seven nights a week amid Surrealist decor described as "Dolly meets Disney". The late godfather of electric guitar, Les Paul, regularly played here from 1996 to 2009, and the current weekly tribute (Mon) honours him. Cover $25–35, $15 food and drink minimum. Daily 8pm–midnight.

Jazz at Lincoln Center 33 W 60th St, at Columbus Circle ☎212 258 9800, ⓦjalc.org; subway #1, A, B, C, D to 59th St; map p.183. There are three different spaces at this venue, but the 140-seater Dizzy's Club Coca-Cola has the best shows, panoramic views and a speakeasy-style atmosphere – the food is great also. Cover varies, usually $20–35. Daily 6pm–1am, Fri & Sat until 2.30am.

Smoke 2751 Broadway, at W 106th St ☎212 864 6662, ⓦsmokejazz.com; subway #1 to 103rd St; map p.183. This Upper West Side joint is a real neighbourhood treat, with plush couches, lavish chandeliers and a retro feel. Sets start at 8pm, 10pm and 11.30am. Tickets usually $35 at weekends (Fri & Sat), free other nights. Mon–Fri 5pm–3am, Sat & Sun 11.30am–3am.

BLUES

B.B. King Blues Club & Grill 237 W 42nd St, between

TOP CLUB NIGHTS

In addition to the clubs reviewed in this section, New York hosts some innovative club nights in some unusual places – many events take place only a few times a year, organizers often rotate venues and there's always something new going on. Check Time Out New York on arrival for the latest; at the time of writing these nights guaranteed good times.

718 Sessions at Santos Party House (see opposite) ⓦdannykrivit.net. Legendary monthly tea dance from Danny Krivit (soul and house classics) and Angel Moraes. Sun 6pm–midnight ($20).

The Bunker at Public Assembly 70 N 6th St, Williamsburg, Brooklyn ☎718 384 4586; ⓦpublicassemblynyc.com; subway L to Bedford Ave; map p.236. Quarterly club nights with just 150 tickets, iconic DJs (electronica dominates), 8hr sets and no guestlist. Advance purchase required ($20). The Bunker also stages nights at the Bossa Nova Civic Club and Output (p.opposite). Club nights 10pm–6am.

Dig Deeper, Brooklyn ⓦ facebook.com/digdeepernyc. Monthly soul party in Brooklyn from Mr Robinson and DJ Honky. Venues and hours vary.

Karaoke Killed the Cat at Union Hall 702 Union St, Brooklyn ☎718 638 4400; ⓦkaraokekilledthecat.com, ⓦunionhallny.com; subway D, N, R to Union St; map p.226. Karaoke dance parties? Believe it – it works. Friday at midnight (free).

Mister Saturday Night ⓦmistersaturdaynight.com. Parties for cool kids featuring resident DJs Eamon Harkin and Justin Carter; venues vary, but their Mister Sunday party takes place at Gowanus Grove, 400 Carroll St, between Bond and Nevins in Brooklyn (May–Aug 3–9pm) – take D, N, R to Union St.

NY Night Train Soul Clap & Dance-Off ⓦnewyorknighttrain.com/soulclap. Wild soul all-nighter from DJ Jonathan Toubin, with a $100 dance contest in the middle. Cover just $7, usually at Brooklyn Bowl (see p.347) midnight–4am (check website for dates).

One Step Beyond at the Rose Center, Central Park West at W 79th St ☎212 769 5200; ⓦamnh.org/plan-your-visit/one-step-beyond; subway B, C to 81st St; map p.183. Monthly dance parties at the American Museum of Natural History's trippy space centre (advance tickets $25). Fri 9pm–1am.

Seventh and Eighth aves ☎212 997 4144, ⓦbbkingblues.com; subway #1, #2, #3, N, Q, R to Times Square-42nd St; map p.141. Yes, this is an unashamedly tourist experience, but adjust your expectations accordingly and it can be good fun: some big names in rock and blues play here, and the Harlem Gospel Choir buffet brunch ($40 in advance) on Sundays is always entertaining. Daily 11am–1am.

★ **Terra Blues** 149 Bleecker St, between Thompson St and LaGuardia Place ☎212 777 7776, ⓦterrablues .com; subway A, C, E to 42nd St; map pp.96–97. The last remaining exclusively blues club in the city offers acoustic blues from 7.30pm and electric blues after 10pm, seven nights a week for $10–20 cover; all the big national names play here, and there's an excellent house band. Mon–Thurs & Sun 7pm–2.30am, Fri & Sat 7pm–3.30am.

26

NIGHTCLUBS

New York's **nightclubs** have had a hard time over the last decade, with venues like *Pacha* shut down for months at a time after NYPD raids, and a small group of overpriced bottle-service clubs catering to the rich and famous. At the time of writing legendary Ibiza club **Space** (ⓦspaceibiza.com) and UK megaclub **Sankeys** (ⓦsankeysnyc.com) looked set to open massive outposts in New York – let's hope the authorities leave these alone. You'll find the action spread out across the city, with the Lower East Side, Tribeca, the East and West villages and even Brooklyn offering as many venues as the Meatpacking District, the city's premier, if slightly overrated, nightlife hub (Hell's Kitchen is emerging as the home of megaclubs). The really cutting-edge club nights are organized by outfits that tend to move around, such as **Blackmarket Membership** (ⓦblkmarketmembership.com; $20), **Turrbotax** (ⓦturrbotax.wordpress.com), **Verboten New York** (ⓦverbotennewyork.com) and the Victorian- and Rococo-themed events of **Dances of Vice** (ⓦdancesofvice.com). It's important to check up-to-date info with magazines like *Time Out New York*.

bOb Bar 233 Eldridge St, between Houston and Stanton sts ☎212 529 1807, ⓦbobbarnyc.com; subway F to Lower East Side-Second Ave; map p.83. This cosy bar turns into one of the best dance parties in town after midnight, with DJ Church spinning a mix of hip-hop, reggae and R&B. Club nights Tues & Thurs–Sat 7pm–4am.

★ **Cielo** 18 Little W 12th St, between Washington St and Ninth Ave ☎212 645 5700, ⓦcieloclub.com; subway L to Eighth Ave, A, C, E to 14th St; map p.236. Expect velvet rope-burn at this super-exclusive see-and-be-seen place: there's only room for 250 people. Though run by Nicolas Matar, a former DJ at Ibiza's legendary *Pacha* club, it's the Monday-night reggae and dub party Deep Space from François K that most people talk about. Best sound system in the city. Cover $20–25. Mon & Wed–Sat 10pm–4am.

★ **Output** 78 Wythe Ave, at N 12th St ☎212 645 5700, ⓦoutputclub.com; subway L to Bedford Ave; map p.107. The "official club of Williamsburg" opened with much fanfare in 2013, with a smallish, industrial warehouse space, big sound system and a focus on dancing, not posing. Lots of techno and ambient music. Cover $15–20 (advance). Wed–Sat 10pm–5am.

Pacha 618 W 46th St ☎212 209 7500, ⓦpachanyc .com; subway A, C, E to 42nd St; map p.141. The New York outpost of the chain of Ibiza superclubs. Sprawling over 30,000 square feet, and featuring a spine-tingling high-tech sound system, three floors, palm trees and mosaic mirrors, this is the place for a big, corporate club experience, and a generally nonlocal clientele – expect large, sweaty crowds. Cover $30–40. Fri & Sat 10pm–6am.

Pyramid Club 101 Ave A, between E 6th and 7th sts ☎212 228 4888, ⓦthepyramidclub.com; subway L to First Ave, #6 to Astor Place; map p.88. This small club has been an East Village standby for years. Sunday is open-mic night ($5–7), but it's the insanely popular 1980s dance parties (Thurs, Fri & Sat; $5–6) that are not to be missed. Tues & Sun 9pm–1am, Thurs & Sat 9pm–4am, Fri 10pm–4am.

Santos Party House 96 Lafayette St, between Canal and Walker sts ☎212 584 5492, ⓦsantospartyhouse .com; subway J, N, Q, R, Z, #6 to Canal St; map p.71. Two-storey club and art space, with wild hip-hop, Latin and house most Thurs–Sat; check the website for the current schedule. Cover usually $10–15. Daily 7pm–4am.

Sapphire Lounge 249 Eldridge St, at Houston St ☎212 777 5153, ⓦsapphirenyc.com; subway F to Lower East Side-Second Ave; map p.83. DJ bar and lounge, with an arty, sleazy, sexy vibe, created by the dark lights and enhanced by the moody Lower East Side regulars. The programming is inventive, offering music of almost every genre on different nights, from reggae to hip-hop to breakbeat – as a plus, it's open every night of the week, and the cover is usually minimal ($5). Daily 7pm–4am.

Sullivan Room 218 Sullivan St, between W 3rd St and Bleecker St ☎212 252 2151, ⓦsullivanroom.com; subway A, B, C, D, E, F, M to W 4th St; map pp.96–97. Hidden basement club for serious dancing, popular with students from nearby NYU – features Propaganda on Saturday nights. The only downside: two toilets for the whole place. Cover $10–30. Wed–Sun 10pm–5am.

Webster Hall 125 E 11th St, between Third and Fourth aves ☎212 353 1600, ⓦwebsterhall.com; subway N, Q, R, W, L, #4, #5, #6 to Union Square; map p.88. Four floors, a hip, young crowd and the big electro mash-ups (Fri & Sat) make this a solid bet for a good night out. Cover $10–30. Club nights Thurs–Sat 10pm–4am.

METROPOLITAN OPERA HOUSE

Performing arts and film

"Performing arts" is really an all-encompassing title for New York's legion of cultural offerings. While many travellers tend automatically to think of the glittery Broadway productions put on in and around Times Square, locals will inform you that such a heading also includes more experimental Off-Broadway theatre companies, as well as comedy clubs, cabarets, dance troupes and the opera, to name but a few of the city's options. The silver screen is just as important a part of New York's arts scene as its live performances. New York gets the first run of many foreign films as well as most American ones, often long before they open elsewhere. There's also a very healthy arthouse and revival scene.

ESSENTIALS

INFORMATION

Listings Listings for arts and film can be found in a number of places. The most useful sources are the clear and comprehensive listings in *Time Out New York* magazine (ⓦtimeoutny.com), the free *New York Press* (ⓦnypress .com) and the "Voice Choices" section of the free *Village Voice* (ⓦvillagevoice.com). Fancier events are usually touted in *New York* magazine's "Agenda" section (ⓦnymag .com); "Goings On About Town" in *The New Yorker* (ⓦnewyorker.com); and the Fri "Weekend" and Sun "Arts and Leisure" sections of *The New York Times* (ⓦnytimes .com); of course, these are also all available online. You'll find specific Broadway listings in the free *Official Broadway Theater Guide*, available at theatre and hotel lobbies. Information on arts events is available on websites such as ⓦnewyork.citysearch.com and ⓦnycgo.com. You can also check the useful sites ⓦnytheatre.com, ⓦbroadway.com, and ⓦoffbroadway.com for up-to-date info on both major Broadway shows and local theatre listings.

Prices Prices for live performances vary wildly: expect to shell out $150 or so for orchestra seats at the hottest Broadway shows, while Shakespeare is performed for free in Central Park every summer. Off-Broadway's best seats are cheaper than those on Broadway but can still be high ranging, from $30 all the way up to $100. Off-Off-Broadway tickets should rarely set you back more than $25.

TICKET AGENCIES

When **buying tickets**, always ask where your seats are located, as once you get to the theatre and find yourself in the last row of the balcony, it's too late (for most seating plans, check ⓦplaybill.com).

TKTSbooths Duffy Square, located at Broadway between 45th and 47th streets; South Street Seaport at the corner of Front and Water streets (near the rear of 199 Water St); 1 Metro Tech Center, Brooklyn ☎212 912 9770, ⓦtdf.org. Offers cut-rate, day-of-performance tickets for many Broadway and Off-Broadway shows. Expect to pay half the face value, plus a $2.50 service charge. Broadway booth: Mon, Thurs & Fri 3–8pm, Tues 2–8pm, Wed & Sat 10am–2pm (for matinees) & 3–8pm, Sun 11am–7pm; South St Seaport booth: Mon–Sat 11am–6pm, Sun 11am–4pm; Metro Tech Center: Mon–Sat 11am–6pm.

Telecharge ☎1 800 432 7250 or ☎212 239 6200, ⓦtelecharge.com.

Ticket Central Playwrights Horizon Theater, 416 W 42nd St, between Ninth and Tenth avenues ☎212 279 4200 or ☎564 1235, ⓦticketcentral.com or ⓦplaywrightshorizons.org. Sells tickets to many Off-Broadway theatres. Expect a $5–7 surcharge per ticket. Daily noon–8pm.

Ticketmaster ☎1 800 745 3000, ⓦticketmaster.com.

27

THEATRE

Theatre venues in the city are referred to as being "Broadway," "Off-Broadway" or "Off-Off-Broadway". These groupings don't necessarily mean a theatre's address is physically on or off Broadway; instead they tend to represent a descending order of ticket prices, production polish, elegance and comfort – as well as seating capacity. The majority of **Broadway** theatres are located in the blocks just east or west of Broadway (the avenue) between 41st and 53rd streets (see pp.144–145); if you're hitting any of those, it's the show, rather than the venue, that will dictate interest and attendance. Less glitzy is **Off-Broadway**, the best place to discover new talent and adventurous new American drama and musicals (most venues for which seat between 100 and 500). **Off-Off-Broadway** is the fringe of New York's theatre world; venues (often fewer than 100 seats) aren't bound by union regulations to use professional actors, and shows range from shoestring productions of the classics to outrageous performance art. Quality varies from execrable to electrifying; frankly, there's a lot more of the former than the latter, so use weekly reviews as your guide.

OFF-BROADWAY

Astor Place Theatre 434 Lafayette St, at Astor Place ☎212 254 4371, ⓦblueman.com; subway #6 to Astor Place, N, R to 8th St-NYU. Showcase for exciting work since the 1960s, when Sam Shepard's *The Unseen Hand* and *Forensic and the Navigators* had the playwright himself playing drums in the lobby. For the last twenty-plus years, however, the theatre has been the home of the comically absurd but very popular performance artists Blue Man Group.

Atlantic Theater Company 336 W 20th St, at Eighth Ave ☎212 645 8015, ⓦatlantictheater.org; subway C, E to 23rd St, #1 to 18th St. As you'd expect from a theatre founded by David Mamet and William H. Macy, this place is known for accessible, intelligent productions of modern

dramatic classics, with works by everyone from Harold Pinter to Martin McDonagh. The ATC has a second stage on 16th St, and performances may also take place at the Lucille Lortel Theatre (see p.352).

Barrow Street Theatre 27 Barrow St, at Seventh Ave S ☎212 243 6262, ⓦbarrowstreettheatre.com; subway A, B, C, D, E, F, M to W 4th St, #1 to Christopher St. This small theatre inside a landmark West Village building was once the long-term home of Off-Broadway favourite The Drama Dept. That company has been replaced by a more profit-minded organization, which is generating artistically excellent but more commercially viable productions.

Brooklyn Academy of Music 30 Lafayette Ave, Brooklyn ☎718 636 4100, ⓦbam.org; subway B, D, N,

27

Q, R, #2, #3, #4, #5 to Atlantic Ave-Barclays Center. Despite its name, Brooklyn Academy of Music (usually referred to as BAM) regularly presents theatrical productions on its three stages, often touring shows from Europe and Asia. Every autumn BAM puts on the Next Wave festival of large-scale performance art. Not so much Off-Broadway as Off-Manhattan, but well worth the trip.

Cherry Lane Theatre 38 Commerce St, between Bedford and Barrow sts ☏212 989 2020, ⓦcherrylanetheatre.org; subway #1 to Christopher St-Sheridan Square. A historic Village spot, its ties to theatre going back some ninety years. There's a main stage and smaller room, good places to see the odd revival and new works by up-and-comers.

Lincoln Center Broadway, at W 65th St ☏212 362 7600, ⓦlct.org; subway #1 to 66th St. Lincoln Center holds venues for all manner of audiences and dramatic productions on its campus. The Vivian Beaumont Theater qualifies technically as a Broadway theatre, though it and the Mitzi E. Newhouse Theater are great places to see stimulating new work by playwrights like Tom Stoppard and John Guare; the new Claire Tow Theater, meanwhile, focuses on relative unknowns.

Lucille Lortel Theatre 121 Christopher St, between Bleecker and Hudson sts ☏212 352 3101 (tickets) or ☏924 2817 (admin), ⓦlortel.org; subway #1 to Christopher St-Sheridan Square. This 60-year-old theatre hosts a few different companies, including classical reinterpreters Red Bull Theater, and puts on everything from family-friendly fare to oddball musical adaptations of supernatural novels. *The Threepenny Opera* and *Buried Child* made their Off-Broadway debuts here.

New World Stages 340 W 50th St, between Eighth and Ninth aves ☏212 239 6200 (tickets) or ☏646 871 1730 (admin), ⓦnewworldstages.com; subway C, E to 50th St. Five stages with good sightlines, ranging in size from 199 to 499 seats. Several productions that debuted here have grown into small-scale hits.

New York City Center 131 W 55th St, at Seventh Ave ☏212 581 1212, ⓦnycitycenter.org; subway B, D, E to Seventh Ave, F to 57th St, N, Q, R to 57th St-Seventh Ave. This large midtown venue is best known for its Encores! series. These readings and studio performances usually run for one weekend only, and are designed to revive long-forgotten or overlooked musicals, from Rodgers and Hart to modern dance. It's also home to the Manhattan Theatre Club (ⓦmanhattantheatreclub.com), which deals in serious new theatre featuring major American actors. Many productions eventually transfer to Broadway; see them here first, though prices aren't much cheaper.

Orpheum Theater 126 Second Ave, between 7th St and St Mark's Place ☏212 477 2477, ⓦorpheum-theater.com; subway #6 to Astor Place. One of the East

Village's biggest theatres, once known for hosting David Mamet and other influential new voices, but for the past twenty years as the home of the percussion group Stomp. Wheelchair-accessible.

Playwrights Horizons 416 W 42nd St, at Ninth Ave ☏212 564 1235 (admin) or ☏279 4200 (tickets), ⓦplaywrightshorizons.org; subway A, C, E, #7 to 42nd St-Port Authority; N, Q, R, S, #1, #2, #3 to Times Square-42nd St. This well-respected drama-centric space is located right by Times Square, though its mission remains the same as it was when it was founded in a YMCA in 1971 – championing works by undiscovered playwrights. They also get top-line actors.

The Public Theater 425 Lafayette St, Brooklyn ☏212 539 8500, ⓦpublictheater.org; subway #6 to Astor Place. Founded by Broadway legend Joe Papp as the Shakespeare Workshop, The Public Theater is the city's primary presenter of the Bard's plays. In the summer, it produces the free Shakespeare in the Park series at the open-air Delacorte Theater in Central Park (see p.155). For most of the year, though, this major Off-Broadway institution (with its fancy new lounge and redone facade) delivers thought-provoking and challenging productions from new, mostly American writers.

Signature Center 480 W 42nd St, between Ninth and Tenth aves ☏212 244 7529, ⓦsignaturetheatre.org; subway A, C, E to 42nd St-Port Authority, N, Q, R, S, #1, #2, #3, #7 to Times Square-42nd St. The Gehry-designed Signature Center, unveiled in 2012, showcases works on its three stages in conjunction with the Signature Theatre Company; playwrights-in-residence for the group have included Tony Kushner and Athol Fugard.

Westside Theatre 407 W 43rd St, between Ninth and Tenth aves ☏212 315 2244, ⓦwestsidetheatre.com; subway A, C, E to 42nd St. Two small theatres, known for productions of Shaw, Wilde and Pirandello. The downstairs one has wheelchair access.

OFF-OFF-BROADWAY AND PERFORMANCE-ART SPACES

Dixon Place 161A Chrystie St, between Rivington and Delancey sts ☏212 219 0736, ⓦdixonplace.org; subway B, D to Grand St, F to Second Ave, J to Bowery. Very popular small venue dedicated to experimental theatre, dance and literary readings.

The Drilling CompaNY 236 W 78th St, at Broadway ☏212 873 9050, ⓦdrillingcompany.org; subway B, C to 81st St. Home of Lower East Side performance group, formerly known as Ludlow Ten, that's best known for producing the summer-long Shakespeare in the Park(ing Lot) series of free performances at the Municipal Parking Lot at Broome and Ludlow.

The Flea 41 White St, at Church St ☏212 226 2407, ⓦtheflea.org; subway #1 to Franklin St, A, C, E, J, N, Q,

R, Z to Canal St. Cutting-edge drama space run by Jim Simpson, Sigourney Weaver's husband. The programme stretches from performance art and drama to acrobatics. Though many of the actors here are not professionals, the quality remains impressively high.

Franklin Furnace Archive 80 Hanson Place #301, at S Portland Ave, Brooklyn ☎718 398 7255, ⓦfranklinfurnace.org; subway A, C to Lafayette Ave, G to Fulton St; B, D, N, Q, R, #2, #3, #4, #5 to Atlantic Ave. An archive dedicated to installation work and performance art, the Franklin Furnace has launched the careers of performers as celebrated and notorious as Karen Finley and Eric Bogosian. Performances take place at various downtown locations – check the website or call for updated schedules.

Here 145 Sixth Ave, at Spring St ☎212 352 3101, ⓦhere.org; subway C, E to Spring St. A very open-minded, intriguing space supporting experimental fare from both new artists and established performers; it's where Eve Ensler's *Vagina Monologues* got its start. Puppetry and performance art are special strengths.

Kraine 85 E 4th St, between Second and Third aves ☎212 777 6088, ⓦhorsetrade.info; subway F to Second Ave. This 99-seat East Village theatre is home to twelve different residential companies and is mostly known for presenting unusual comedies. Another plus for this budget space is the raked seating, which makes for good sightlines. It's in the basement of the same building as artsy *KGB*, a bar known for its author readings (see p.333).

★ **La Mama E.T.C. (Experimental Theater Club)** 74A E 4th St, at Second Ave ☎212 475 7710, ⓦlamama .org; subway F to Second Ave. The mother of all Off-Off venues, founded fifty years ago. A real gem with three different auditoria, La Mama is known for politically and sexually charged material as well as visiting dance troupes from overseas. For raw amateur performances, check out The Galleria space a few blocks away.

New York Theatre Workshop 79 E 4th St, at Second Ave ☎212 460 5475, ⓦnytw.org; subway F to Second Ave. An eminent experimental workshop that often chooses cult hit shows and has presented plays by Tony

Kushner, Susan Sontag and Paul Rudnick; best known these days as the place the global musical mega-hit *Rent* was first shown to the public.

Performing Garage 33 Wooster St, at Grand St ☎212 966 9796, ⓦthewoostergroup.org; subway A, C, E to Canal St. The Wooster Group (early members include Willem Dafoe and the late Spalding Gray) perform regularly in this Soho space. Tickets are like gold dust, but the effort to find them is worth it.

★ **PS122** 150 First Ave, at 9th St ☎212 477 5829 or ☎212 352 3101, ⓦps122.org; subway #6 to Astor Place, L to First Ave, F to Second Ave. A converted school in the East Village that is perennially popular for its jam-packed schedule of revolutionary performance art, dance, one-person shows and wintertime COIL Festival in its two theatres. The building was undergoing a needed renovation at press, so make sure to call or check the website for the latest.

St Ann's Warehouse 29 Jay St, Brooklyn ☎718 254 8779, ⓦstannswarehouse.org; subway A, C to High St, F to York St. St Ann's is consistently impressive for both drama and music – there are Broadway try-outs here as well as big-name musicians looking for a more intimate venue. The theatre recently moved to a new warehouse in Dumbo, not too far from its old location.

Theater for the New City 155 First Ave, at 10th St ☎212 254 1109, ⓦtheaterforthenewcity.net; subway #6 to Astor Place, L to First Ave, F to Second Ave. This major performance venue is best known as the site where Sam Shepard's Pulitzer Prize-winning *Buried Child* premiered in 1978. It's still churning out fine drama through its emerging-playwrights programme. TNC also performs outdoors for free at a variety of venues throughout the summer and hosts the Lower East Side Festival of the Arts at the end of May.

Tribeca Performing Arts Center 199 Chambers St, at Greenwich St ☎212 220 1460, ⓦtribecapac.org; subway #1, #2, #3 to Chambers St. TriPac, as it's known, is owned by Manhattan Community College, a fact reflected in its programming: mostly high-end local theatre and dance groups, plus kids' workshops and multicultural events. It's also known for fine jazz performances.

CLASSICAL MUSIC AND OPERA

New Yorkers take their classical music and opera seriously. Long queues form for anything popular, many concerts sell out, and summer evenings can see a quarter of a million people turning up in Central Park for free performances by the **New York Philharmonic**. Tickets can be somewhat easier to come by for performances by the city's top-notch chamber-music ensembles. Since moving from Lincoln Center, the **New York City Opera** (ⓦnycopera.com) appears regularly at Brooklyn Academy of Music (see p.354), New York City Center (see opposite) and the occasional other venue around town.

OPERA VENUES

Dicapo Opera Theatre 184 E 76th St, between Lexington and Third aves ☎212 288 9438, ⓦdicapo .com; subway #6 to 77th St. A full season of performances

(Oct–April/May; $50) with a programme of child-friendly opera recitals as well (kids $12, adults $24).

Juilliard School 60 Lincoln Center Plaza, at 65th St ☎212 799 5000, ⓦjuilliard.edu; subway #1 to 66th St.

Located right next door to the Met (see below), Juilliard students often perform under the direction of a famous conductor, usually for low ticket prices.

Metropolitan Opera House Lincoln Center, Columbus Ave, at 64th St ☎ 212 362 6000, ⊛ metoperafamily.org; subway #1 to 66th St. More popularly known as the Met, New York's premier opera venue is home to the world-renowned Metropolitan Opera Company from Sept/early Oct to late April/early May. Tickets are expensive (up to $310) and can be well-nigh impossible to snag, though 175 standing-room tickets go on sale at 10am on day of performance ($17–35) and 200 "rush-tickets" for orchestra seats go on sale at 6pm ($25). The limit is one ticket per person, and the queue has been known to form at dawn.

CONCERT HALLS

92nd Street Y Kaufmann Concert Hall 1395 Lexington Ave, at 92nd St ☎ 212 415 5740, ⊛ 92y.org; subway #4, #5, #6 to 86th St, #6 to 96th St. This 85-year-old, wood-panelled space is especially welcoming since performers are usually available to chat or mingle with the audience after shows. Great line-up of chamber music and solo events.

Alice Tully Hall Lincoln Center, Broadway and W 65th St ☎ 212 671 4050 or ☎ 212 875 5788, ⊛ lc.lincolncenter .org; subway #1 to 66th St. A smaller Lincoln Center hall for the top chamber orchestras, string quartets and instrumentalists. The weekend chamber series is deservedly popular, though the crowd is composed almost exclusively of the 65-and-over set. Tickets for performances vary greatly, but mostly run in the $30–70 range.

Avery Fisher Hall Lincoln Center, Broadway and W 65th St ☎ 212 875 5030, ⊛ lc.lincolncenter.org or ⊛ nyphil.org; subway #1 to 66th St. The permanent home of the New York Philharmonic, with ticket prices in the range of $30–150. The open rehearsals (9.45am on the first day of new concert weeks, usually Wed or Thurs) are a great bargain; tickets are $18. Avery Fisher also hosts the very popular, annual Mostly Mozart Festival in Aug.

★ **Bargemusic** Fulton Ferry Landing, Brooklyn ☎ 718 624 4924, ⊛ bargemusic.org; subway A, C to High St, F to York St. Chamber music in a wonderful river setting on a moving barge below the Brooklyn Bridge. Tickets are $35–45, $15–25 for full-time students. Fri & Sat (sometimes Thurs too) 8pm, Sun 2pm.

Brooklyn Academy of Music 30 Lafayette Ave, Brooklyn ☎ 718 636 4100, ⊛ bam.org; subway #2, #3, #4, #5, N, R to Atlantic Ave-Barclays Center. The BAM Opera House is the perennial home of Philip Glass operatic premieres and Laurie Anderson performances. It also hosts a number of contemporary imports from European and Chinese companies, often with a large modern-dance component.

Carnegie Hall 154 W 57th St, at Seventh Ave ☎ 212 247 7800, ⊛ carnegiehall.org; subway N, Q, R to 57th St-Seventh Ave. The greatest names from all schools of music have performed here, from Tchaikovsky (who conducted the hall's inaugural concert) to Toscanini to Gershwin to Billie Holiday to, um, Lady Gaga. The tradition continues, and the stunning acoustics – said to be the best in the world – lure big-time performers at sky-high prices. Check the website for up-to-date

---

TOP 5 FREE SUMMER CONCERT SERIES

It's easy to think of fusty old churches (though those can add a bit of character to a performance) or glittering concert halls (with their attendant high-priced seats) as the places to go to hear serious-minded music. Perhaps true for the most part, but in summertime, a number of free outdoor events provide a salve for those opera or philharmonic fanatics looking to avoid paying an arm and a leg – and an easy introduction for those interested in seeing what all the fuss is about.

Bryant Park ☎ 212 768 4242, ⊛ bryantpark.org. Home to free Broadway and Off-Broadway musical performances during the summer (weekly at lunchtime; check schedules), as well as Fall Festival with music and dance.

Lincoln Center Out-of-Doors ☎ 212 875 5108, ⊛ lcoutofdoors.org. Hosts a varied selection of daily free performances of music and dance events on the plaza in Aug.

New York Grand Opera ☎ 212 245 8837, ⊛ newyorkgrandopera.org. Occasional Wed night performances at the Naumburg Bandshell; Verdi is the traditional composer of choice, but they've also done

works by Puccini and others.

New York Philharmonic's Concerts in the Park ☎ 212 875 5709, ⊛ nyphil.org. A series of concerts and fireworks displays that turns up all over the city and the outer boroughs in July. Similarly, there's the Met in the Parks series (☎ 212 362 6000, ⊛ metopera.org) in July & Aug.

Washington Square Music Festival ☎ 212 252 3621, ⊛ washingtonsquaremusicfestival.org. This series has run for more than fifty years, and it consists of chamber orchestra pieces and occasionally jazz performed outdoors every Tues at 8pm throughout July.

admission rates and schedules. To learn more about the building itself, head to the Rose Museum on the second floor or take a tour (see p.148).

Cathedral of St John the Divine 1047 Amsterdam Ave, at 112th St ☎212 316 7490, ⓦstjohndivine.org; subway B, C, #1 to 110th St. A magnificent Morningside Heights setting that hosts occasional classical and New Age performances. Also home to the Early Music Foundation (ⓦearlymusicny.org), which performs scores from the eleventh to the eighteenth centuries.

Lehman Center for the Performing Arts 250 Bedford Park Blvd, Bronx ☎718 960 8833, ⓦlehmancenter.org; subway D, #4 to Bedford Park. First-class concert hall that puts on an array of performances: modern ballet, gospel, funk, oldies and major international names.

Merkin Concert Hall 129 W 67th St, at Broadway ☎212 501 3330, ⓦmerkinconcerthall.org; subway #1 to 66th St. This intimate and adventurous venue in the Elaine Kaufman Cultural Center is a great place to hear

music of any kind: classical, jazz, Broadway, kid-friendly, etc. Hosts the wintertime Ecstatic Music Festival.

★ **Symphony Space** 2537 Broadway, at 95th St ☎212 864 5400, ⓦsymphonyspace.org; subway #1, #2, #3 to 96th St. The Symphony Space has a varied performance schedule, from "ground-breaking, style-crashing" new classical to jazz and even the odd rock event.

Town Hall 123 W 43rd St, between Sixth Ave and Broadway ☎212 840 2824, ⓦthe-townhall-nyc.org; subway B, D, F, M to 42nd St-Bryant Park; N, R, Q, #1, #2, #3, #7 to Times Square-42nd St. This midtown hall has an unusual history: it was designed by Stanford White (the mastermind of the original Madison Square Garden) and commissioned by suffragettes as a protest-friendly space. One of the egalitarian innovations in the design was the omission of any box seats in order to provide better acoustics and sightlines from every seat in the house. As for programming, it's got an eclectic policy – from Broadway celebrations and folk singers to Cole Porter tributes and whirling dervishes.

DANCE

Dance – especially experimental or avant-garde performance – is quite popular in New York. The city has five major **ballet companies**, dozens of **modern troupes** and untold thousands of **soloists**; all performances are listed in broadly the same periodicals and websites as music and theatre, though you might also want to pick up *Dance Magazine* (ⓦdancemagazine.com) for a closer look. The official dance season runs April–June and Sept–Jan. The following list takes in major dance venues in the city, though a lot of the smaller, more esoteric companies and solo dancers also perform at spaces like Dixon Place (see p.352) and PS122 (see p.353).

92nd Street Y Harkness Dance Center 1395 Lexington Ave, at 92nd St ☎212 415 5552, ⓦ92y.org; subway #4, #5, #6 to 86th St, #6 to 96th St. Hosts a variety of performances, including a free "Fridays at noon" series and a five-week late winter dance festival; Sun afternoon events are followed by a discussion period.

Brooklyn Academy of Music 30 Lafayette St, Brooklyn ☎718 636 4100, ⓦbam.org; subway B, D, N, Q, R, #2, #3, #4, #5 to Atlantic Ave-Barclays Center. America's oldest performing-arts academy is still one of the busiest and most daring dance producers in New York. In the autumn, BAM's Next Wave festival features the hottest international attractions in avant-garde dance and music, and each spring since 1977 it has hosted the annual Dance Africa Festival, America's largest showcase for African and African-American dance and culture.

Danspace Project St Mark's Church-in-the-Bowery, 131 E 10th St, at Second Ave ☎212 674 8112 or ☎1 866 811 4111, ⓦdanspaceproject.org; subway #6 to Astor Place. Experimental contemporary dance, with a season running Sept–June, in one of the more distinctive performance spaces around – an airy church that dates back more than 200 years (see p.91).

David H. Koch Theater Lincoln Center, 65th St at Columbus Ave ☎212 870 5570, ⓦlc.lincolncenter.org;

subway #1 to 66th St. Lincoln Center's other major ballet venue (see p.356) is home to the revered New York City Ballet (ⓦnycballet.com), which performs for an eight-week season each spring.

Joyce Theater 175 Eighth Ave, at 19th St ☎212 691 9740, ⓦjoyce.org; subway #1 to 18th St, C, E to 23rd St. The Joyce is one of the best-known downtown dance venues, hosting short seasons by a wide variety of acclaimed dance troupes such as Pilobolus, the Parsons Dance Company and Savion Glover's.

Juilliard Dance Division 155 W 65th St, at Broadway ☎212 799 5000, ⓦjuilliard.edu; subway #1 to 66th St. The dance division of the Juilliard School often holds free workshop performances (some fifteen public ones a year, at the Peter Jay Sharp Theater on Lincoln Center's campus), and each spring six students work with six composers to present a Composers and Choreographers concert.

★ **Lincoln Center plaza at Damrosch Park** 65th St at Columbus Ave ☎212 875 5766, ⓦlc.lincolncenter .org and ⓦmidsummernightswing.org; subway #1 to 66th St. A delightful open-air venue for the enormously popular Midsummer Night Swing, where each night you can learn a different dance style en masse (everything from polka to rockabilly) and watch a performance – all for $17. Tickets go on sale in Damrosch Park at 5.30pm the night of

TV-SHOW TAPINGS

If you want to experience American TV up close, you can pick up free tickets for various shows. For most shows you must be 16, sometimes 17 or 18 to be in the audience; if you're underage or travelling with children, call ahead.

MORNING SHOWS

Good Morning America ⓦ gma.yahoo.com. Show up at the Broadway entrance (at 44th St) around 6.45am or earlier for a shot at a standby ticket; you can also try ahead of time through the website.

Live with Kelly and Michael ☎ 212 456 7000, ⓦ dadt.com/live/get-tickets.html. Request online or send a postcard with your name, address and telephone number to "Live with Kelly and Michael" Tickets, PO Box 230-777 Ansonia Station, New York, NY 10023-0777. Include your preferred date(s) and number of tickets (limit 4). For standby, go to ABC at 67th St and Columbus Ave at around 7am Mon–Fri.

Today There's no way to get advance tickets; just show up at 49th Street, between Fifth and Sixth avenues, as early as possible. Unlike the rest of the morning shows, which run until 9am, *Today* ends at 10am.

LATE-NIGHT SHOWS

The Colbert Report ⓦ colbertnation.com. In theory you can book tickets on the website, but it's almost always sold out. For standby tickets, arrive by 4pm at the studio at 513 W 54th St, between Tenth and Eleventh avenues.

The Daily Show with Jon Stewart ☎ 212 586 2477, ⓦ thedailyshow.com/tickets. Again, a very hard ticket to secure. There's no point in showing up for standby tickets; as a last resort call to find out if there

are any cancellations.

Late Show with David Letterman ☎ 212 247 6497, ⓦ cbs.com/shows/late_show/tickets. The website has all the info; you can, if you like, request tickets in person at 1697 Broadway, between W 53rd and W 54th streets (Mon–Fri 9.30am–noon, Sat & Sun 10am–6pm). Standby tickets are available by calling the number above from 11am on the day you wish to attend. Shoots Mon–Thurs at 5.30pm, with an additional show Thurs at 8pm.

Saturday Night Live ☎ 212 664 3056, ⓦ nbc.com/tickets. It's tough to get tickets in advance; for each upcoming season (usually Oct–May), you must send an email, in Aug only, to ✉ snltickets@nbcuni.com – include all contact information. If selected, you'll get two tickets assigned randomly (you cannot fix the date). Alternatively, standby tickets are distributed at 7am on the 49th St side of 30 Rockefeller Plaza on Sat morning (some weeks are reruns; call ahead). You can opt for either the 8pm dress rehearsal or the 11.30pm live taping.

The Tonight Show with Jimmy Fallon After years in Leno's Los Angeles, *The Tonight Show* is back in New York City. At time of press, information was not available about getting tickets, but the show is filmed at 30 Rock, and that's where you'll likely be getting standby tickets. Look online for details of how to get tickets ahead of time for tapings.

the show (or pick them up earlier at Avery Fisher Hall; see p.186); the season runs June–July. Lessons begin at 6.30pm, music and dance at 7.30pm .

Metropolitan Opera House Lincoln Center, 65th St at Columbus Ave ☎ 212 362 6000, ⓦ metoperafamily.org; subway #1 to 66th St. Home of the renowned American Ballet Theater (ⓦ abt.org), which performs at the Opera House from mid-May into July. Prices for ballet at the Met range from as little as $20 up to $375 for the best seats at special performances (usually more like $175 tops); $20 standing-room tickets go on sale the morning of the performance.

New York City Center 131 W 55th St, at Seventh Ave ☎ 212 581 1212, ⓦ nycitycenter.org; subway B, D, E

to Seventh Ave, N, Q, R to 57th St-Seventh Ave, F to 57th St-Sixth Ave. This large, midtown venue hosts some of the most important troupes in modern dance, including the Paul Taylor Dance Company, the Alvin Ailey American Dance Theater and the American Ballet Theater; there's Sept–Oct's Fall for Dance Festival as well.

New York Live Arts 219 W 19th St, at Seventh Ave ☎ 212 924 0077, ⓦ newyorklivearts.org; subway #1 to 18th St. Home to the Bill T. Jones/Arnie Zane Dance Company, New York Live Arts (the former Dance Theater Workshop) has a midsize main stage and some smaller studios that host movement-based performances from numerous troupes throughout the year.

CABARET AND COMEDY

New York is one of America's **comedy** capitals, and there are several major clubs that feature professional performers, some of whom you'll recognize from television and film. There are also a good number of alternative comedy venues in downtown Manhattan that eschew the standard "comedy routine" fare for zanier "conceptual" comedy. Most mainstream clubs have shows every night, with two or more on weekends; it's usual to be charged a cover plus a two-drink minimum fee. **Cabaret** has cooled off a bit of late, but there are still a couple of top venues where you can see some truly amazing stuff from the likes of Woody Allen and KT Sullivan.

COMEDY CLUBS

Carolines on Broadway 1626 Broadway, at 49th St ☎ 212 757 4100, ⓦ carolines.com; subway #1 to 50th St, N, R to 49th St. *Carolines* books some of the best stand-up acts in town; this is where most of the biggest names perform. Also has a "supper lounge", *Comedy Nation*, downstairs. Cover $15–55 plus two-drink minimum.

Chicago City Limits Theater 318 W 53rd St, at Eighth Ave ☎ 212 888 5233, ⓦ chicagocitylimits.com; subway C, E to 50th St. The oldest improvisation theatre in New York. Cover $20 plus two-drink minimum.

Comedy Cellar 117 MacDougal St, at Bleecker St ☎ 212 254 3480, ⓦ comedycellar.com; subway A, B, C, D, E, F, M to W 4th St. Now in its fourth decade, this popular Greenwich Village comedy club is a good late-night hangout. Cover $12–24 plus two-drink minimum.

Comic Strip Live 1568 Second Ave, between 81st and 82nd sts ☎ 212 861 9386, ⓦ comicstriplive.com; subway #4, #5, #6 to 86th St. Famed showcase for stand-up comics and young singers going for the big time. Cover $15–25 plus two-drink minimum.

Dangerfield's 1118 First Ave, at 61st St ☎ 212 593 1650, ⓦ dangerfields.com; subway #4, #5, #6, N, R to 59th St. Vegas-style new-talent showcase founded in 1969 by the late Rodney Dangerfield, making it among the oldest – if not *the* oldest – continually running comedy club in the States. Cover $20 plus two-drink minimum, though discounts available online.

Gotham Comedy Club 208 W 23rd St, between Seventh and Eighth aves ☎ 212 367 9000, ⓦ gothamcomedyclub.com; subway C, E, #1 to 23rd St. A swanky comedy venue in Chelsea, highly respected by New York media types and those who scout up-and-coming comics. Cover $12–30 plus two-drink minimum.

Stand-Up New York 236 W 78th St, at Broadway ☎ 212 595 0850, ⓦ standupny.com; subway #1 to 79th St. Upper West Side all-ages forum for established comics, many of whom have appeared on Letterman and other late night shows; also has nights for up-and-comers. Cover $15–20 plus two-drink minimum – you're required to

arrive 30min before showtime, so call or check the website for the night's schedule before arriving.

★ **Upright Citizens Brigade Theatre** 307 W 26th St, between Eighth and Ninth aves ☎ 212 366 9176, ⓦ ucbtheatre.com; subway C, E to 23rd St, #1 to 28th St. Consistently hilarious sketch-based and improv comedy, seven nights a week. You can sometimes catch *Saturday Night Live* cast members (or ex-members) in the ensemble. Second location in East Village, at corner of E 3rd St and Ave A. Cover $5–10, though some late-night free shows too.

CABARET

Café Carlyle *Carlyle Hotel*, 35 E 76th St, at Madison Ave ☎ 212 744 1600, ⓦ rosewoodhotels.com; subway #1 to 77th St. This regal room is where Woody Allen plays clarinet every Mon, and divas like Judy Collins drop by for a week's residency. If you don't want to eat (the food's expensive and unexciting), standing at the bar is just as fun – though it's still a pricey night out. Cover $25–145, jacket required.

Don't Tell Mama 343 W 46th St, at Ninth Ave ☎ 212 757 0788, ⓦ donttellmamanyc.com; subway A, C, E to 42nd St-Port Authority. Lively and convivial Midtown West piano bar and cabaret featuring rising stars and singing waitresses. Cover free to $30 plus two-drink minimum.

Duplex 61 Christopher St, at Seventh Ave ☎ 212 255 5438, ⓦ theduplex.com; subway #1 to Christopher St. West Village cabaret popular with a boisterous crowd. Barbra Streisand and Lea Delaria have both performed here, and Off-Off-Broadway shows like *Nunsense* played here in their infancy. Has a rowdy piano bar downstairs and a cabaret room upstairs. Cover free to $20 plus two-drink minimum.

★ **Joe's Pub** 425 Lafayette St, between Astor Place and 4th St ☎ 212 539 8778, ⓦ publictheater.org; subway #6 to Astor Place, N, R to 8th St. The hipper, late-night arm of the Joseph Papp Public Theater, this is one of the sharpest and most popular music venues in the city, with a wide range of cabaret acts nightly. Tickets usually from $15, with a $12 food/two-drink minimum.

27

FILM

Despite rising costs that put a normal ticket at $14, New York is a movie-lover's dream. There are plenty of state-of-the-art **cinemas** all over the city; most are charmless multiscreen complexes, but they also have the advantages of superb sound, luxurious seating and perfect sightlines. For **listings**, your best bets are *Time Out New York* or *New York* magazine or freebies like the *Village Voice* (see p.28); otherwise check the local papers on Fri, when new reviews and schedules for the following week are published. For accurate showtimes, and to book a ticket in advance, call ☎ 212 777 3456 or check ⓦ fandango.com or ⓦ moviefone.com. We've highlighted our pick of New York's best cinemas below, divided into those showing first-run mainstream and indie fare, and the venues that specialize in revivals and more obscure and experimental flicks, though the list is by no means exhaustive.

27

FIRST-RUN MOVIES

AMC Empire 25 234 W 42nd St, at Eighth Ave ☎ 212 398 2597, ⊛ amctheatres.com; subway A, C, E to 42nd St-Port Authority, N, Q, R, #1, #2, #3, #7 to Times Square-42nd St. One of the few skyscraper multiplexes: 25 screens, all with stadium seating, soaring upward. Usually crowded on weekends, it offers a decent mix of mainstream and indie films.

AMC Loews Lincoln Square 13 & IMAX 1998 Broadway, at 68th St ☎ 212 336 5020, ⊛ amctheatres .com/lincolnsquare; subway #1 to 66th St. More and more mainstream films are being converted to IMAX technology and are being re-released on the huge screens here in high resolution just months after their original theatrical debuts. Worth checking out for sci-fi spectaculars, if nothing else. Oh, and the venue has twelve other first-run theatres besides, though it's often bedlam.

BAM Rose Cinemas 30 Lafayette Ave, at Ashland Place, Brooklyn ☎ 718 636 4133, ⊛ bam.org; subway C to Lafayette Ave, G to Fulton St, B, D, N, R, Q, #2, #3, #4, #5 to Atlantic Ave-Barclays Center. There are four screens at BAM's film site. The programme is mostly one or two current films mixed with a couple of classics or rarities; the year-round BAMcinématek series usually offers the most interesting choices.

Clearview's Ziegfeld 141 W 54th St, between Sixth and Seventh aves ☎ 212 765 7600, ⊛ clearviewcinemas .com; subway B, D, E to Seventh Ave, F to 57th St. Sitting on the site of the old Ziegfeld Follies (hence the name), this midtown movie palace with its massive screen (one of the biggest in the country) is the place locals come to for an old-fashioned cinema experience. Numerous film premieres also take place here.

Regal Battery Park Stadium 11 102 North End Ave ☎ 212 945 4370; subway #1, #2, #3 to Chambers St. One great reason to visit: its out-of-the-way siting makes this possibly the quietest multiplex around.

Regal Union Square 14 850 Broadway, at 13th St ☎ 212 253 6266; subway L, N, Q, R, #4, #5, #6 to 14th St-Union Square. Stadium-seating venue in a central location.

INDIES AND FOREIGN

Angelika Film Center 18 W Houston St, at Mercer St ☎ 212 995 2570, ⊛ angelikafilmcenter.com; subway B, D, F, M to Broadway-Lafayette. Six-screen arthouse venue with a rather overhyped reputation – screens are tiny, floors are hardly sloped and the subway tends to rumble by at inopportune moments, rattling the subterranean rooms. Still, it's one of the few surviving venues for smaller films in the city.

Cinema Village 22 E 12th St, between University and Fifth aves ☎ 212 924 3363, ⊛ cinemavillage .com; subway L, N, Q, R, #4, #5, #6 to 14th St-Union Square. A 50-year-old cinema with three screens (and limited seating) showing indie flicks and numerous documentaries.

FILM FESTIVALS AND SEASONAL SCREENINGS

There always seems to be some **film festival** or other running in New York. The granddaddy of them all, the **New York Film Festival** (⊛ filmlinc.com), starts at the end of September and runs for two weeks at the Lincoln Center. It's well worth catching if you're in town, though tickets for the most popular films can sell out very quickly. If you're determined to see something, watch the reviews in *The New York Times* each morning – when movies are panned, there's usually a cluster of people trying to sell off their tickets outside the cinema that night.

For info on the larger film festivals, see pp.398–403; below is a list of some of the smaller, but still worthwhile, festivals and seasonal screenings.

New York Jewish Film Festival at Lincoln Center ⊛ thejewishmuseum.org/nyjff; Jan.

Dance on Camera ⊛ dancefilms.org; late Jan.

New York International Children's Film Festival ⊛ gkids.com; March, though screenings on weekend mornings year-round.

Human Rights Watch International Film Festival ⊛ ff.hrw.org; June.

NewFest: The New York LGBT Film Festival ⊛ newfest.org; June.

Bryant Park Summer Film Festival ⊛ bryantpark.org; June–Aug; free. Outdoor screenings of old Hollywood favourites on Mon nights at sunset.

GenArt Film Festival ⊛ genart.org; June.

Asian American Film Festival ⊛ asiancinevision .org; July.

RiverFlicks for Grown-Ups at Hudson River Park ⊛ hudsonriverpark.org; July–Aug, Wed for adults, Fri for kids. Free screenings of box-office hits and cult crowd-pleasers.

Socrates Sculpture Garden Outdoor Cinema ⊛ socratessculpturepark.org; July–Aug. Free screenings of classics every Wed starting at sunset in Long Island City, Queens.

Margaret Mead Film & Video Festival ⊛ amnh .org; Oct or Nov. Anthropological films at the Museum of Natural History.

IFC Center 323 Sixth Ave, at W 3rd St ☎ 212 924 7771, ⓦ ifccenter.com; subway A, B, C, D, E, F, M to W 4th St. An independent with five screens, showing new indies, foreign and documentaries, and popular (weekend) midnight shows. Features a much larger screen and a better sound system than you'll find at most other arthouses.

Landmark Sunshine Cinema 143 E Houston St, at First Ave ☎ 212 260 7289, ⓦ landmarktheatres.com; subway F to Second Ave. When this former Yiddish vaudeville house opened as a cinema more than a decade ago, it quickly seized the Angelika's crown as the best place to see indie films, thanks to larger screens, better seating and its less-threadbare look.

Lincoln Plaza 1886 Broadway, at 62nd St ☎ 212 757 2280, ⓦ lincolnplazacinema.com; subway A, B, C, D, #1 to 59th St-Columbus Circle. This six-screen cinema is as close as the Upper West Side gets to an arthouse venue. While it plays an occasional smaller mainstream Hollywood picture, it's known for acclaimed foreign and independent films.

Nitehawk Cinema 136 Metropolitan Ave, between Berry St and Wythe Ave ☎ 718 384 3980, ⓦ nitehawkcinema.com; subway J, M to Marcy Ave, L to Bedford Ave, G to Metropolitan St-Lorimer Ave. It was only a matter of time until someone got the idea to combine a theatre and restaurant in Williamsburg. Sip on a draught beer ($6–7) and nibble on gourmet popcorn ($6–8), *haute* burgers ($12) or even a salami and cheese plate ($6–25) while catching a new indie or old (cult) classic in one of three small theatres.

Paris Theatre 4 W 58th St, at Fifth Ave ☎ 212 688 3800, ⓦ theparistheatre.com; subway F to 57th St, N, Q, R to 59th St/Fifth Ave. An old-fashioned cinema (there's even a balcony) that specializes in foreign films as well as well-reviewed mainstream fare.

The Quad 34 W 13th St, between Fifth and Sixth aves ☎ 212 255 2243, ⓦ quadcinema.com; subway F, L, M to 14th St, L, N, R, #4, #5, #6 to 14th St-Union Square. Shows a selection of indie movies – including numerous gay-themed flicks – that can be quite hard to find anywhere else.

REVIVALS

Anthology Film Archives 32 Second Ave, at 2nd St ☎ 212 505 5181, ⓦ anthologyfilmarchives.org; subway F to Second Ave. A bastion of experimental film-making. Programmes of mind-bending abstraction, East Village grunge flicks and auteur retrospectives all rub shoulders here.

Chelsea Classics at the Clearview Chelsea, 260 W 23rd St, between Seventh and Eighth aves ☎ 212 691 5519; subway C, E, #1 to 23rd St. Thurs (and the odd Sat) nights belong to campy classics (frequently starring dames like Joan Crawford, Bette Davis or Bette Midler). Introduced by the blonde "lady" with green streaks, Hedda Lettuce.

★ **Film Forum** 209 W Houston St, between Sixth and Seventh aves ☎ 212 727 8110, ⓦ filmforum.org; subway #1 to Houston St, A, B, C, D, E, F, M to W 4th St. The cosy three-screen Film Forum has an eccentric but famously popular programme of new independent movies, documentaries and foreign films, as well as a repertory programme specializing in silent comedy, camp classics and cult directors. All in all, one of the best alternative spaces in town.

The Museum of Modern Art 11 W 53rd St, at Fifth Ave ☎ 212 708 9400, ⓦ moma.org; subway E, M to Fifth Ave/53rd St. MoMA (see p.128) is famous among local cinephiles for its vast collection of films, exquisite programming and regular audience of cantankerous senior citizens. The movies themselves range from Hollywood screwball comedies to hand-painted Super 8.

Museum of the Moving Image 36-01 35th Ave, at 36th St, Astoria, Queens ☎ 718 777 6888, ⓦ movingimage.us; subway N to 36th Ave, G, R to 36th St. The AMMI is usually well worth a trip out to Queens, either for the pictures – which are often serious director retrospectives and silent films, with a strong emphasis on cinematographers – or for the cinema museum itself (see p.242).

Symphony Space 2537 Broadway, at 95th St ☎ 212 864 5400, ⓦ symphonyspace.org; subway #1, #2, #3 to 96th St. A varied and often surprising programme of festivals (including one for shorts), special directors' series and weekend double features.

★ **Walter Reade Theater** Lincoln Center, 165 W 65th St, at Broadway ☎ 212 875 5601, ⓦ filmlinc.com; subway #1 to 66th St. Programmed by the Film Society of Lincoln Center, the Walter Reade is simply the best place in town to see great films. This beautiful, modern theatre has perfect sightlines, a huge screen and impeccable acoustics. The emphasis is on foreign films and the great auteurs; it's also home to many of the city's festivals, including the New York Film Festival (see p.402) and New Directors, New Films (see p.399).

27

LITERARY EVENTS AND READINGS

New York has long been viewed as a literary hotspot , and the city's proliferation of competitive bookstores means that you can see someone performing wordy wonders any night of the week (see pp.374–376 and pp.398–403).

92nd Street Y Unterberg Poetry Center 1395 Lexington Ave, at 92nd St ☎ 212 415 5760, ⓦ 92y.org; subway #4, #5, #6 to 86th St, #6 to 96th St. Quite simply the definitive place to hear all your Booker, Pulitzer and

TOP 5 SPOTS FOR POETRY SLAMS

Poetry and story slamming is a literary version of freestyle rapping, in which performers take turns presenting stories and poems (often mostly or entirely improvised) on stage. At their best, slams can be thrilling, raw and very funny, not to mention competitive – many feature a judges' panel.

Bowery Poetry 308 Bowery, between Houston and Bleecker sts ☎212 614 0505; subway F to Second Ave, #6 to Bleecker St. For most of the week, this spot is *Duane Park*, an upscale burlesque club, but Sun and Mon nights, poetry takes centre stage; the founder, Bob Holman, used to run *Nuyorican* (see below).

Louder Arts Bar 13, 35 E 13th St, between Broadway and University Place ☎212 979 6677, ⓦbar13.com or ⓦlouderarts.com. On Mon nights (with some exceptions), this group puts on a poetry slam.

The Moth ⓦthemoth.org. Offbeat literary company that's known for its story slams – open-mic nights

where amateurs vie for a five-minute on-stage storytelling spot. They move around at venues such as the Village's *Bitter End*, Brooklyn's *Bell House* (see p.345), and *Housing Works Bookstore Café* (see p.374). There's also the yearly Moth Ball (Nov) done for charity.

Nuyorican Poets Café 236 E 3rd St, between aves B and C ☎212 780 9386, ⓦnuyorican.org; subway F to Second Ave. Known for its poetry slams, Alphabet City's *Nuyorican* remains one of the most vibrant performance spaces in town. There are also theatre and film-script readings.

Pete's Candy Store 709 Lorimer St, Williamsburg. See p.341

Nobel prize-winning favourites, as well as many other exciting new talents. Name almost any American literary great – from Tennessee Williams to Langston Hughes – and they've probably appeared here; expect the current line-up to have big headliners too. Additional programmes are held at 92Y Tribeca (200 Hudson St, at Canal St).

Barnes & Noble The city's numerous B&Ns host a surprisingly diverse range of readings almost every night of the week. The Union Square branch generally gets the highest-profile authors and events, though the Tribeca and Fifth Ave outposts compete too.

Half King 505 W 23rd St, between Tenth and Eleventh aves ☎212 462 4300, ⓦthehalfking.com; subway C, E to 23rd St. Popular bar (see p.335) owned by a cadre of writers and others; it's not surprising, then, that most Mon nights are devoted to free readings by a big-name contemporary author. On other occasions there's an

intriguing programme centred on great magazine writing read by a group of journalists. Check the calendar on the website for schedules.

KGB 85 E 4th St, at Second Ave ☎212 505 3360, ⓦkgbbar .com; subway F to Second Ave, #6 to Astor Place. Grubby but welcoming little bar that hosts free readings pretty much every night; expect to see top names and well-known local writers. Call or check the website for up-to-date schedules. The building also houses the Kraine Theater (see p.353).

Symphony Space 2537 Broadway, at 95th St ☎212 864 5400, ⓦsymphonyspace.org; subway #1, #2, #3 to 96th St. The highly acclaimed Selected Shorts series, in which actors read the short fiction of a variety of authors (everyone from James Joyce to David Sedaris), usually packs the Symphony Space theatre; Bloomsday on Broadway, a one-day celebration of Joyce's *Ulysses*, has been going on since 1981.

Gay New York

There are few places in America – indeed in the world – where gay culture thrives as it does in New York City. Open gays and lesbians are mainstream here – so much so that the city is one of the few places where Republican administrations avidly court gay voters. That acceptance makes it easy to find shops, bars, clubs, media, entertainment, social services and much more dedicated to the sizeable gay population. All of the city's alternative communities come together in major events like Pride Week in late June (Pride Month), which takes in a rally, Dyke March, Dyke Ball, Brooklyn Pride, Black Pride, innumerable parties and the infamous (if commercialized and sweltering) Lesbian & Gay Pride Parade (see p.400).

The largely liberal orientation of city politics has been generally beneficial to the gay community since the 1969 riots at the *Stonewall Bar* marked the onset of the gay-rights movement (see box, p.104); the state – with major vocal elements from the city – has helped lead the recent charge toward **marriage equality**. The New York State Supreme Court initially ruled gay marriage illegal in 2006; two years later, Governor David Patterson issued a directive that required state agencies to recognize same-sex marriages officiated elsewhere as valid in New York. He followed that with legislation to legalize such marriage in the city, which the State Assembly passed but the Senate voted down in late 2009. Patterson's successor, Andrew Cuomo, a strong supporter of the cause, was able to mount a successful drive for its passage in 2011 (and three-time mayor, Michael Bloomberg, was an outspoken proponent); helped by a few key Republican votes, the State Senate voiced its approval two days before the Pride Parade in June. The US Supreme Court's June 2013 decision in favor of marriage equality was greeted with jubilation outside the *Stonewall Inn* (see p.364) and elsewhere.

There are a few **neighbourhoods** where the gay community makes up the majority of the population. Chelsea (especially Eighth Ave between 14th and 23rd sts), the East Village/ Lower East Side, Hell's Kitchen and Brooklyn's Park Slope are the largest of these, and have all but replaced the West Village as gay New York's hub. A strong gay presence still lingers in the vicinity of Christopher Street in the West Village, but it's in Chelsea that gay male socializing is most ubiquitous and open. Lesbians will find large communities in laidback Park Slope and around East Houston Street. Other neighbourhoods with a strong gay and lesbian presence are Morningside Heights (Columbia University's college town), Queens' Astoria and Brooklyn's Prospect Heights (mainly residential), Dumbo and Williamsburg.

28

ESSENTIALS

Listings Several free weekly newspapers and magazines serve New York's gay community: *Gay City News* (ⓦ gaycitynews.com; actually a biweekly), *Next* (for men; ⓦ nextmagazine.com) and *GO* (for women; trans-friendly; ⓦ gomag.com). You'll find these at the LGBT Community Services Center (see below), at newspaper dispensers on streetcorners, bars, cafés, lesbian and gay bookstores, and occasionally at newsstands, where glossy national mags such as *Out*, *Metrosource* and others are also available. The listings in *Time Out New York* magazine are helpful as well. If you're looking for a date or just people to party with while you're here, post a personal (or respond to someone else's) on craigslist (free; ⓦ newyork.craigslist.org), the popular online message-board.

RESOURCES

The Audre Lorde Project 147 W 24th St, 3rd floor, Manhattan ☎ 212 463 0342 and 85 S Oxford St, Brooklyn ☎ 718 596 0342, ⓦ alp.org. Centre for LGBT people of non-Caucasian ethnicity, focused on the New York City area.

Gay Men's Health Crisis (GMHC) 446 W 33rd St, between Ninth and Tenth aves ☎ 212 367 1000, ⓦ gmhc.org. Despite the name, this incredible organization – the oldest and largest not-for-profit AIDS organization in the world – provides testing, information and referrals to everyone: gay, straight and transgender.

The Lesbian, Gay, Bisexual & Transgender Community Services Center 208 W 13th St, west of Seventh Ave ☎ 212 620 7310, ⓦ gaycenter.org. The Center houses well over a hundred groups and organizations, sponsors workshops, parties, movie nights, guest speakers, youth services, programmes for parents and lots more. Even the bulletin boards are fascinating.

SAGE: Senior Action in a Gay Environment 305 Seventh Ave, at 27th St, 15th floor ☎ 212 741 2247, ⓦ sageusa.org. Support and activities for gay seniors. Most activities take place at the LGBT Center, at 208 W 13th St (see above), where the group maintains another small office.

ACCOMMODATION

As well as the hotels reviewed below, check out *Chelsea Pines Inn* (see p.266), *Hotel 17* (see p.267), and *JW Marriott Essex House* (see p.270).

Colonial House Inn 318 W 22nd St, between Eighth and Ninth aves ☎ 212 243 9669, ⓦ colonialhouseinn .com; subway C, E to 23rd St; map p.107. You won't mind that this B&B is a little worn around the edges – its attractive design and contributions to the GMHC (see above) make for a feel-good experience. Only the deluxe rooms include en-suite bathrooms, while some rooms have refrigerators, fireplaces and sleep four. Continental breakfast included. **$130**

Incentra Village House 32 Eighth Ave, between W 12th and Jane sts ☎ 212 206 0007, ⓦ incentravillage.com; subway A, C, E to 14th St, L to Eighth Ave; map pp.96–97. Some of the dozen Early American-look studios in this residential neighbourhood townhouse come with kitchenettes and one has access to a private garden; there's a

suite too. Three-night cancellation policy and three-night minimum stay at weekends. **$269**

CAFÉS AND RESTAURANTS

Bluestockings 172 Allen St, between Stanton and Rivington sts ☎212 777 6028, ⊛bluestockings.com; subway F to Second Ave or Delancey St; map p.83. Fair Trade café and lefty bookstore that functions as an informal centre for the lesbian and bi community. Hosts Dyke Knitting Circle, as well as near-nightly readings, performances, meetings and screenings. Daily 11am–11pm.

Cafeteria 119 Seventh Ave, at W 17th St ☎212 414 1717, ⊛cafeteriagroup.com; subway #1 to 18th St; map p.107. See p.307.

Cowgirl 519 Hudson St, at W 10th St ☎212 633 1133, ⊛cowgirlnyc.com; subway #1 to Christopher St; map pp.96–97. Genial restaurant with a Texas/Western theme. It's big on burger-and-bbq offerings ($11.25–20.50), and hosts a sometimes lively bar scene among the kitschy decor. Mon–Thurs 11am–11pm, Fri 11am–midnight, Sat 10am–

midnight, Sun 10am–11pm; bar until 2am Fri & Sat.

East of Eighth 254 W 23rd St, between Seventh and Eighth aves ☎212 352 0075, ⊛eastofeighthny.com; subway C, E, #1 to 23rd St; map p.107. Excellent dishes with a variety of influences; crabcakes ($12), Southern-style pork chops ($19), pizzas and pastas ($12–18) sit alongside matzoh-ball soup ($7), Southeast Asian pot stickers ($10) and Oaxacan guacamole ($9). Mon–Fri noon–midnight, Sat 11am–12.30am, Sun 11am–10.30pm.

Manatus 340 Bleecker St, between Christopher and W 10th sts ☎212 989 7042, ⊛manatusnyc.com; subway #1 to Christopher St-Sheridan Square; map pp.96–97. Laidback and comfortable diner, with a comprehensive menu (omelettes $6–11, burger deluxe $10, sautéed chicken and fish dishes $15–25) on one of the Village's more active streets. Daily 24hr.

BARS

Gay men's bars cover the spectrum from relaxed pubs to hard-hitting clubs full of glamour and attitude. Most of the more-established places are in Greenwich Village and Chelsea, and along Avenue A in the East Village. Park Slope in Brooklyn and the East Village are the centres of the lesbian scene, while dyke bars and club nights can be found in Chelsea and along Hudson Street in the West Village as well. Williamsburg has become a major hotspot for young, hip, mixed LGBT club nights. Check local weeklies for current listings.

MAINLY FOR MEN

Barracuda 275 W 22nd St, between Seventh and Eighth aves ☎212 645 8613; subway C, E, #1 to 23rd St; map p.107. A favourite spot in New York's gay scene, and pretty laidback for Chelsea. Two-for-one happy hour 4–9pm during the week, crazy drag shows, karaoke nights and a look that changes several times a year. Daily 4pm–4am.

The Boiler Room 86 E 4th St, between First and Second aves ☎212 254 7536, ⊛boilerroomnyc.com; subway F to Second Ave; map p.88. Used to be one of the hottest bars in the city but now it's really just a local bar with a pool table. While still a good hangout (mostly gay but with some lesbian presence), don't expect any atmosphere; it's always got the look of a retiree's garage during the summer. Daily 4pm–4am.

Boxer's NYC 37 W 20th St, between Fifth and Sixth aves ☎212 255 5082, ⊛boxersnyc.com; subway F, M, R to 23rd St; map p.107. Also Boxers HK, 742 Ninth Ave, between 50th and 51st sts, map p.141. This fun sports bar is spread across two levels, with pool tables, TVs all over the place and brick-oven pizzas to soak up some of the beer; long happy hours and lots of drink specials. Mon–Fri 4pm–2am, Sat & Sun 1pm–2am.

★ **Brandy's Piano Bar** 235 E 84th St, between Second and Third aves ☎212 744 4949, ⊛brandyspianobar.com; subway #4, #5, #6 to 86th St; map p.169. Handsome

uptown cabaret/piano bar with a crazy, mixed and generally mature clientele. Definitely worth a visit; note there's a two-drink minimum during the nightly sets (which start at 9.30pm). Daily 4pm–3.30am.

The Eagle NYC 554 W 28th St, between Tenth and Eleventh aves ☎646 473 1866, ⊛eaglenyc.com; subway C, E to 23rd St, #1 to 28th St; map p.107. The place for leather-bar fans, with a super-cool industrial feel and bi-level, multi-room layout, plus an open roof terrace that's inevitably the most packed part of the bar. Dress code some nights. Mon–Thurs 10pm–4am, Fri–Sun 4pm–4am.

★ **Excelsior** 390 Fifth Ave, between 6th and 7th sts, Park Slope, Brooklyn ☎718 832 1599, ⊛excelsior brooklyn.com; subway F, G, R to Fourth Ave-9th St; map p.226. The amusingly versatile jukebox, friendly rather than overtly cruisey clientele and two outside spaces make this Brooklyn's best bar for gay men. Mon–Fri 6pm–4am, Sat & Sun 2pm–4am.

G Lounge 223 W 19th St, between Seventh and Eighth aves ☎212 929 1085, ⊛glounge.com; subway #1 to 18th St; map p.107. Nearly as stylish as its "guppie" clientele, this deservedly popular lounge features a different DJ every night of the week. Daily 4pm–4am.

GYM 167 Eighth Ave, between 18th and 19th sts ☎212 337 2439, ⊛gymsportsbar.com; subway A, C, E, L to 14th

28

St-Eighth Ave, #1 to 18th St; map p.107. Casual, friendly, non-sceney hangout that features large-screen TVs, video games, pool table and smokers' patio. A sports bar that's rare in that you can actually watch a game. Mon–Thurs 4pm–2am, Fri 4pm–4am, Sat 1pm–4am, Sun 1pm–2am.

Hombres 85–28 37th Ave, between 85th and 86th sts, Jackson Heights ☎ 718 930 0886, ⓦ hombreslounge .com; subway #7 to 82nd St-Jackson Heights; map p.240. Latin-leaning spot well out in Queens, but draws a crowd for happy hours and late-night DJ parties. Daily 5pm–4am.

Julius 159 W 10th St, at Waverly Place ☎ 212 243 1928, ⓦ juliusbarnyc.com; subway #1 to Christopher St-Sheridan Square; A, B, C, D, E, F, M to W 4th St; map pp.96–97. Its claim to being the oldest gay bar in the city gives it distinction; its divey feel, inexpensive burgers and lack of attitude give you the reasons to go. Mon–Thurs 11am–2am, Fri & Sat 11am–4am, Sun noon–3am.

★ **Marie's Crisis** 59 Grove St, between Seventh Ave S and Bleecker St; subway #1 to Christopher St-Sheridan Square; map pp.96–97. Well-known cabaret/piano bar popular with tourists and locals, straights and gays alike. Features old-time singing sessions nightly. Often packed, always fun. Daily 4pm–4am.

Metropolitan 559 Lorimer Ave, at Metropolitan Ave, Brooklyn ☎ 718 599 4444, ⓦ metropolitanbarny.com; subway L to Lorimer St, G to Metropolitan Ave; map p.236. Hipster hangout without (much) attitude helps it attract all types. Hosts an 80s night every other Saturday at 10pm (which follows "craft magic happy hour" 4–9pm). Daily 3pm–4am.

Phoenix 447 E 13th St, between Ave A and First Ave ☎ 212 477 9979, ⓦ phoenixbarnyc.com; subway L to First Ave; map p.88. This relaxed East Village pub is much loved by the so-not-scene boys who live there, and other guys who just want reasonably priced drinks and a fun crowd; things heat up for its crowded Friday-night party. Daily 4pm–4am.

Stonewall Inn 53 Christopher St, between Waverly Place and Seventh Ave S ☎ 212 488 2705, ⓦ thestonewallinnnyc.com; subway #1 to Christopher St-Sheridan Square, A, B, C, D, E, F, M to W 4th St; map pp.96–97. Yes, *that* Stonewall, site of the seminal 1969 riot, mostly refurbished and flying the pride flag like they own it – which, one could say, they do. Bingo, DJs, drag variety shows, male dancers and lesbian nights; call or check the website to see what's on. Daily 2pm–4am.

Therapy 348 W 52nd St, between Eighth and Ninth aves ☎ 212 397 1700, ⓦ therapy-nyc.com; subway C, E to 50th St; map p.141. Sleek bilevel bar/lounge geared to Midtowners and the post-work drinking crowd. DJ sets, drag shows and theme nights make up the weekly calendar; wash down bar snacks while imbibing signature cocktails that keep up the psychological motif like the Freudian Slip (citron vodka, lemonade and fresh ginger) and the Psychotic Episode (suffice to say it includes banana liqueur). Mon–Thurs & Sun 5pm–2am, Fri & Sat 5pm–4am.

Vlada 331 W 51st St, between Eighth and Ninth aves ☎ 212 974 8030, ⓦ vladabar.com; subway C, E to 50th St; map p.141. A somewhat posh Russian-themed bar, where vodka is the house speciality: the options, which can run to twenty or so, might include cherry, horseradish or pumpkin; they also offer a full menu, with Russian favourites *pelmeni* ($14) and chicken Kiev ($18). Daily 4pm–4am.

XES 157 W 24th St, between Sixth and Seventh aves ☎ 212 604 0212, ⓦ xesnyc.com; subway F, M, #1 to 23rd St; map p.107. A comfortable neighbourhood spot with karaoke nights (Wed & Sun, with the latter hosted by drag queen Hedda Lettuce), long happy hours and an outdoor patio. Mon & Tues 4pm–2am, Wed–Sun 4pm–4am.

MAINLY FOR WOMEN

★ **Cubbyhole** 281 W 12th St, at W 4th St ☎ 212 243 9041, ⓦ cubbyholebar.com; subway A, C, E, L to 14th St-Eighth Ave; map pp.96–97. This small, kitschy West Village dyke bar is worn-in and welcoming, and feels like it's been here forever (really just twenty or so years). An essential stopoff. Mon–Fri 4pm–4am, Sat & Sun 2pm–4am.

Ginger's 363 Fifth Ave, between 5th and 6th sts, Park Slope, Brooklyn ☎ 718 788 0924, ⓦ gingersbarbklyn .com; subway F, G, R to Fourth Ave-9th St; map p.226. The best girl bar in New York is this dark, laidback Park Slope joint with a pool table, outdoor space, dance and karaoke nights and plenty of convivial company. Mon–Fri 5pm–4am, Sat & Sun 2pm–4am.

Henrietta Hudson 438 Hudson St, at Morton St ☎ 212 924 3347, ⓦ henriettahudson.com; subway #1 to Houston St or Christopher St-Sheridan Square; map pp.96–97. Relaxed in the afternoon but brimming by night, especially on weekends, this is the top lesbian place in Manhattan. Weekly theme nights – karaoke, game night, DJs, etc. Mon & Tues 5pm–2am, Wed–Fri 4pm–4am, Sat & Sun 2pm–4am.

CLUBS

Gay and lesbian club nights in New York can be some of the most outrageous in the world; however, they can change time, venue and level of hipness with speed. Check *Time Out New York* magazine, *Next Magazine* (ⓦ nextmagazine.com) and *GO NYC* (ⓦ gomag.com) for up-to-date info.

Big Apple Ranch 39 W 19th St, fifth floor, between Fifth and Sixth aves ⓦ bigappleranch.com; subway F,

N, R to 23rd St; map p.114. Not a club per se, but a weekly country-and-western dance party, complete with lessons in two-step and line dancing. It's held in the Dance Manhattan dance studio. Cover $10. Sat only 8pm lessons, 9pm–1am open dancing.

The Monster 80 Grove St, at Sheridan Square ❶212 924 3558, ⓦmanhattan-monster.com; subway #1 to Christopher St; map pp.96–97. Large, campy bar with drag cabaret, piano and downstairs dancefloor. Very popular, especially with tourists, yet has a strong "neighbourhood" feel. Every night brings something else, from amateur and professional go-go boys to Latin

grooves and a Sunday tea dance (5.30pm). Usually no cover, but $6–8 when there is one. Mon–Fri 4pm–4am, Sat & Sun 2pm–4am.

Splash 50 W 17th St, between Fifth and Sixth aves ❶212 691 0073, ⓦsplashbar.com; subway F, M to 14th St; map p.114. Large (10,000 square feet), loud club with all the trimmings: smoke, lights and go-go boys on pedestals; there's also a basement lounge. Cover can be free to $20; it's cheaper the earlier you go, and great drink deals compensate as well. Daily 4pm–4am.

ARTS AND CULTURE

Center for Lesbian and Gay Studies CUNY Graduate Center, 365 Fifth Ave, between 34th and 35th sts ❶212 817 1955, ⓦweb.gc.cuny.edu/clags. Fascinating talks and seminars featuring academic luminaries. Particular attention is paid to international, transgender and disability studies.

Lesbian Herstory Archives 484 14th St, between Eighth Ave and Prospect Park West, Park Slope, Brooklyn ❶718 768 3953, ⓦlesbianherstoryarchives .org. Original materials on dyke life, mostly throughout the twentieth century. Old-school and inspiring. Open a few hours a day on a variable schedule, so call ahead or visit the website for times.

Leslie-Lohman Gay Art Foundation 26 Wooster St, between Grand and Canal sts ❶212 431 2609, ⓦleslielohman.org. The Foundation maintains an archive and permanent collection of lesbian and gay art, with galleries open to the public during shows. Tues–Sun noon–6pm.

MIX (New York Queer Experimental Film/Video

Festival) ❶212 742 8880, ⓦmixnyc.org. This celebrated annual festival, which takes place in November, offers politically radical and technically avant-garde films.

National Archive of LGBT History/The Pat Parker– Vito Russo Center Library LGBT Community Services Center (see p.362) ❶212 620 7310. Terrific, interesting archive of gay life in America, and a lending library with 12,000 titles. The archive is open Tues–Thurs 6–9pm, Fri & Sat 1–4pm.

NewFest ❶646 290 8136, ⓦnewfest.org. This not-to-be-missed annual film festival has both kicked off Pride Month in June and been held late July; check the website first. Expect celebrities, outrageous parties and an interesting array of flicks.

New York City Gay Men's Chorus ❶212 344 1777, ⓦnycgmc.org. Wildly popular gay men's choral group (with over 250 members) that has sung with Jesse Tyler Ferguson (of *Modern Family* fame) and other big names at major venues like Carnegie Hall. Call or check website for concert schedule and membership information.

28

SHOPS

If you're looking for books, club clothes or something a little more, um, funky, you should be able to find it at one of these specialized spots; the West Village and Chelsea have the greatest concentration of gay-oriented stores.

Babeland 94 Rivington St, between Orchard and Ludlow sts ❶212 375 1701; subway F to Delancey St; map p.83. Also 43 Mercer St, between Grand and Broome sts, ❶212 966 2120, ⓦbabeland.com, map p.64. Superlative, sophisticated feminist (and queer) sex-toy store, perhaps the best in the nation. Sex workshops fill up quickly. Mon–Wed & Sun noon–10pm, Thurs–Sat noon–11pm.

Nasty Pig 265A W 19th St, between Seventh and Eighth aves ❶212 691 6067, ⓦnastypig.com; subway #1 to 18th St; map p.107. Casual and sporty clothing and fetish store with a friendly attitude. Mon–Sat noon–9pm, Sun 1–9pm.

Nickel 77 Eighth Ave, at 14th St ❶212 242 3203, ⓦnickelspanyc.com; subway A, C, E, L to 14th St-Eighth Ave; map pp.96–97. Housed in an old bank building, this

men-only spa also sells hair and skincare products. Mon–Fri 11am–9pm, Sat & Sun 10am–9pm.

Rainbows and Triangles 192 Eighth Ave, between 19th and 20th sts ❶212 627 2166, ⓦrainbow sandtriangles.com; subway C, E to 23rd St; map p.107. A good source for fiction and nonfiction as well as coffee-table books; they even rent out a couple of apartments if you're looking for a place to stay. Mon–Sat 11am–10pm, Sun noon–9pm.

Universal Gear 140 Eighth Ave, between 16th and 17th sts ❶212 206 9119; ⓦuniversalgear.com; subway A, C, E, L to 14th St-Eighth Ave; map p.107. Also 715 Ninth Ave, between 48th and 49th sts; map p.141. Stylish garb for gays, with a huge underwear selection. Mon–Thurs & Sun 11am–10pm, Fri & Sat 11am–midnight.

Commercial galleries

Art, especially contemporary art, is huge in New York. The city remains at the centre of the global art market, with hundreds of dealers and over six hundred galleries, major auction houses such as Sotheby's, a highly successful public art programme and numerous high-profile art schools and colleges: the Pratt Institute, Parsons School of Design and NYU's Tisch School of the Arts among them. Though several other cities claim to have more innovative scenes – the 1950s and 1960s were really New York's creative heyday – plenty of artists continue to live here, from classical realist Jacob Collins and "relational" artists Maurizio Cattelan and Liam Gillick to well-known figures such as Maya Lin. New York is also the home of modern graffiti, with street artists such as Ellis Gallagher and Swoon leading the current scene.

Even if you have no intention of buying, many of the high-profile galleries are well worth a visit, as are some of the alternative spaces, run on a nonprofit basis and less commercial than mainstream galleries. Broadly speaking, Manhattan galleries fall into five main areas: the **Upper East Side**; **57th Street** between Sixth and Park avenues; **Soho** for established artists; **Chelsea** for most of the galleries (around three hundred) and up-and-coming artists; and **Tribeca** and the **Lower East Side** for more experimental displays. Some of the most vibrant gallery scenes in the city are to be found outside Manhattan, however, in **DUMBO** and **Williamsburg** (in Brooklyn) and the neighbourhood of **Long Island City** (Queens).

Listed below are some of the more interesting exhibition spaces in Manhattan and elsewhere. The best time to gallery-hop is on weekday afternoons; the absolute worst time is on Saturday, when out-of-towners flood into the city's trendier areas to do just that. Openings – usually free and easily identified by crowds of people drinking wine from plastic cups – are excellent times to view work, eavesdrop on art-world gossip and even eat free food.

INFORMATION

Several of the city's more exclusive galleries are invitation-only, but most accept walk-ins (although sometimes with a bit of attitude). Admission is almost always free; the galleries that do charge a fee are considered a bit tacky.

Check ⓦ oneartworld.com, ⓦ artdealers.org or the weekly *Time Out New York* for openings and listings of the major commercial galleries.

TRIBECA AND SOHO

Arts Projects International 434 Greenwich St, G/F, at Vestry St ☎ 212 343 2599, ⓦ artprojects.com; subway #1 to Canal St. Highly respected for showing leading contemporary artists from Asia, this gallery's engaging exhibits are mostly in print and have featured artists like Zheng Xuewu, Gwenn Thomas and Richard Tsao. Tues–Sat 11am–6pm.

★ **The Drawing Center** 35 Wooster St, between Grand and Broome sts ☎ 212 219 2166, ⓦ drawing center.org; subway A, C, E, N, R, Q to Canal St. Presents shows of contemporary and historical works on paper, from emerging artists to the sketches of the Great Masters. Charges admission of $5 (free Thurs 6–8pm). Wed–Sun noon–6pm, Thurs until 8pm.

Louis K. Meisel Gallery 141 Prince St, between Wooster St and West Broadway ☎ 212 677 1340, ⓦ meiselgallery.com; subway N, R to Prince St. Specializes in Photorealism – past shows have included

Richard Estes and Chuck Close – as well as Abstract Illusionism (owner Meisel claims to have invented both terms). Also exhibits saucy American pin-ups. July & Aug by appointment only; Sept–June Tues–Sat 10am–6pm.

OK Harris 383 W Broadway, between Spring and Broome sts ☎ 212 431 3600, ⓦ okharris.com; subway C, E to Spring St. Named for a mythical travelling gambler, OK is the gallery of Ivan Karp, a cigar-munching champion of Super-Realism. One of the first Soho galleries and, although not as influential as it once was, still worth a look. July Tues–Fri noon–5pm; closed Aug; Sept–June Tues–Sat 10am–6pm.

Team Gallery 83 Grand St, at Greene St ☎ 212 279 9219, ⓦ teamgal.com; subway A, C, E, N, R, Q to Canal St. Beautiful, voyeuristic and cutting-edge work by artists such as Tracey Emin and Genesis P-Orridge, and web artist Cory Arcangel, is shown here. Tues–Sat 10am–6pm, Sun noon–6pm.

ART TOURS

If you're short of time and don't want the hassle of navigating New York's gallery scene alone, a great way to see the best spaces in the city is through an art tour. Guides are usually insiders with excellent connections. Here are a couple of your best bets:

Art Entrée 48–18 Purves St, Queens ☎ 718 391 0011, ⓦ artentree.com. This excellent Long Island City-based company provides studio, gallery, museum, architecture and public art tours throughout NYC. Note that they're personalized, and therefore, expensive.

New York Gallery Tours 526 W 26th St, Manhattan ☎ 212 946 1548, ⓦ nygallerytours .com. First-rate tours of Lower East Side, Chelsea, Upper East Side and Soho galleries ($20) on most Saturdays.

29

THE EAST VILLAGE AND LOWER EAST SIDE

★ **Elizabeth Street Gallery** 209 Elizabeth St, between Prince and Spring sts ☎212 941 4800, ⓦelizabethstreetgallery.com; subway #6 to Spring St. This intriguing gallery specializes in antiques, sculpture and decorative objects, but the real highlight is the building itself – an 1850s New York City firehouse – and the adjacent garden, studded with romantic sculptures like a Florentine park. Mon–Fri noon–7pm, Sat noon–6pm.

Feature Inc 131 Allen St, between Delancey and Rivington sts, Lower East Side ☎212 675 7772, ⓦfeatureinc.com; subway F, J, M, Z to Delancey St-Essex St. This former Chicago gallery tends toward briefly exhibiting fairly cerebral modern artists (such as the controversial Richard Kern of "New York Girls" fame) rather than extensively highlighting a select few. Wed–Sun noon–6pm.

Frosch & Portmann 53 Stanton St, between Eldridge and Forsyth sts, Lower East Side ☎646 266 5994, ⓦfroschportmann.com; subway F to Second Ave. Extremely hip gallery curated by Swiss owner Eva Frosch, offering a line-up of young contemporary artists who tend to produce surreal or abstract work. Wed–Sun noon–6pm.

★ **Fuse Gallery** 93 Second Ave, between E 6th and E 5th sts, East Village ☎212 777 7988, ⓦfusegallerynyc .com; subway #6 to Astor Place, F to Second Ave. Funky, contemporary art at the back of the *Lit Lounge*; features up-and-coming artists such as Rick Froberg and Ellen Stagg. Wed–Sat 3–8pm.

Sperone Westwater 257 Bowery, between Houston and Stanton sts, Lower East Side ☎212 999 7337, ⓦsperonewestwater.com; subway F to Second Ave. Founded in Soho in 1975, Sperone Westwater moved to this new Norman Foster-designed building in 2010 and is overseen by art-world maven Angela Westwater. Expect a wide range of artists in all media, with a particular dedication to Arte Povera artists and Bruce Nauman. Tues–Sat 10am–6pm.

THE WEST VILLAGE

★ **Gavin Brown's Enterprise** 620 Greenwich St, at Leroy St ☎212 627 5258, ⓦgavinbrown.biz; subway #1 to Houston St. An ultra-hip space featuring the young, cool and fearless of the mixed-media art world; look out for the white building marked "The Whole World". Tues–Sat 10am–6pm.

CHELSEA

303 Gallery 547 W 21st St ☎212 255 1121, ⓦ303gallery.com; subway C, E to 23rd St. 303 Gallery shows works in a comprehensive range of media by fairly well-established contemporary artists. Tues–Sat 10am–6pm.

Allen Sheppard Gallery 530 W 25th St ☎212 989 9919, ⓦallensheppardgallery.com; subway C, E to 23rd St. One of the most interesting painter galleries in the district, this space exhibits great stuff from the likes of David Konigberg, Willy Lenski and Sonya Sklaroff. Tues–Sat noon–6pm.

Barbara Gladstone Gallery 515 W 24th St ☎212 206 7606, ⓦgladstonegallery.com; subway C, E to 23rd St. Paintings, sculpture and photography by hot contemporary artists like Matthew Barney and Rosemarie Trockel. Tues–Sat 10am–6pm.

Edward Thorp 210 Eleventh Ave, 6th floor, between W 24th and W 25th sts ☎212 691 6565, ⓦedwardthorpgallery.com; subway C, E to 23rd St. Mainstream contemporary American, South American and European painting and sculpture. Highlights of their roster include painter Matthew Blackwell and sculptor Deborah Butterfield. July Tues–Fri 11am–5pm; Aug by appointment only; Sept–June Tues–Sat 11am–6pm.

★ **Gagosian Gallery** 555 W 24th St ☎212 741 1111, ⓦgagosian.com; subway C, E to 23rd St. A stalwart fixture on the New York scene, the Gagosian features both modern and contemporary works, including pieces by artists such as Damien Hirst, David Salle, Eric Fischl and Richard Serra, and photographer Alec Soth. There's also a branch uptown, at 980 Madison Ave. Tues–Sat 10am–6pm.

Gemini G.E.L. at Joni Moisant Weyl 535 W 24th St, 3rd floor ☎212 249 3324, ⓦjoniweyl.com; subway #6 to 77th St. Etchings and contemporary graphics, with some vintage prints; has shown works by Roy Lichtenstein and Robert Rauschenberg. Tues–Sat 10am–6pm.

Greene Naftali Gallery 526 W 26th St, 8th floor ☎212 463 7770, ⓦgreenenaftaligallery.com; subway C, E to 23rd St. A wide-open, airy gallery noted for its top-notch large group shows and conceptual installations. Very cool stuff. Tues–Sat 10am–6pm.

Lehmann Maupin 540 W 26th St ☎212 255 2923, ⓦlehmannmaupin.com; subway C, E to 23rd St. Shows a range of established international and American contemporary artists working in a variety of media, among them Tracey Emin, Juergen Teller and Gilbert & George. Also showcases diverse new talent. Tues–Sat 10am–6pm.

Mary Boone Gallery 541 W 24th St ☎212 752 2929, ⓦmaryboonegallery.com; subway C, E to 23rd St. An extension of Boone's uptown gallery 745 Fifth Ave (see opposite), this Chelsea space has facilities for large-scale works and installations by the up-and-coming darlings of the art world. At least a couple of the artists nurtured by

Boone – David Salle and Julian Schnabel – have achieved superstar status. Tues–Sat 10am–6pm.

Matthew Marks Gallery 522 W 22nd St ☎212 243 0200, ⓦmatthewmarks.com; subway C, E to 23rd St. The centrepiece of Chelsea's art scene, Matthew Marks shows pieces by such well-known minimalist and abstract artists as Cy Twombly and Ellsworth Kelly. Also has nearby branches at 523 W 24th St and 526 W 22nd St. Tues–Sat 10am–6pm.

Paula Cooper 521 & 534 W 21st St ☎212 255 1105, ⓦpaulacoopergallery.com; subway C, E to 23rd St. An influential gallery that shows a wide range of contemporary painting, sculpture, drawings, prints and photographs, particularly minimalist and conceptual works, and even has a recording label, Dog w/a Bone. Tues–Sat 10am–6pm.

★ **Robert Miller** 524 W 26th St ☎212 366 4774, ⓦrobertmillergallery.com; subway C, E to 23rd St. Exceptional shows of twentieth-century artists (Lee Krasner, Joan Nelson and Bernar Venet, to name but a few) – this is one of New York's true big-gun galleries. Tues–Sat 10am–6pm (July Mon–Fri 10am–6pm, Aug by appointment only).

Sikkema Jenkins & Co 530 W 22nd St ☎212 929 2262, ⓦsikkemajenkinsco.com; subway C, E to 23rd St. This

TOP 5 PUBLIC WORKS OF ART 29

The Alamo East Village. See p.89
Atlas and Prometheus Midtown East. See p.126
Broken Kilometer Soho. See p.68
The Charging Bull Financial District. See p.50
Time Sculpture Upper West Side. See p.187

somewhat controversial space often features exhibits with a definite political slant. Recently, it's been focusing on drawings and illustration. Tues–Sat 10am–6pm.

Sonnabend 536 W 22nd St ☎212 627 1018, ⓦsonnabendgallery.com; subway C, E to 23rd St. A top gallery featuring painting, photography and video from contemporary American and European artists. Regular exhibitions from the likes of Robert Morris and Gilbert & George. Tues–Sat 10am–6pm.

★ **Zach Feuer** 548 W 22nd St ☎212 989 7700, ⓦzachfeuer.com; subway C, E to 23rd St. A relatively new and young power-broker in the Chelsea scene, Zach Feuer shows works by bold young artists in the mould of Dana Schutz. Tues–Sat 10am–6pm.

WEST 57TH STREET AND AROUND

Marlborough Gallery 40 W 57th St, between Fifth and Sixth aves ☎212 541 4900, ⓦmarlboroughgallery.com; subway F to 57th St, N, R to Fifth Ave-59th St. Specializing in famous American and European names, with sister galleries in Chelsea, London, Monaco and Madrid. The original London gallery was founded in 1947 to help foster artistic talents such as Henry Moore and Philip Guston. Mon–Sat 10am–5.30pm.

Mary Boone 745 Fifth Ave, between 58th and 57th sts, 4th floor ☎212 752 2929, ⓦmaryboonegallery.com; subway F to 57th St, N, R to Fifth Ave-59th St. Mary Boone was Leo Castelli's protégée, and her gallery specializes in installations, paintings and works by up-and-coming European and American artists, as well

as established artists already involved with the gallery. There's now also an interesting branch in Chelsea (see opposite). Tues–Fri 10am–6pm, Sat 10am–5pm.

★ **Pace Gallery** 32 E 57th St, 2nd floor, between Madison and Park aves ☎212 421 3292, ⓦthepacegallery.com; subway #5, #4, #6 to 59th St. This celebrated gallery exhibits works by most of the great modern American and European artists, from Picasso to Calder to Noguchi and Rothko. Also has a good collection of prints and African art. Chelsea satellites located at 534 W 25th St (☎212 929 7000), 510 W 25th St (☎212 255 4044) and 508 W 25th St (☎212 989 4258) specialize in edgier works and large installations. Tues–Fri 9.30am–6pm, Sat 10am–6pm; Chelsea galleries Tues–Sat 10am–6pm.

THE UPPER EAST SIDE

Leo Castelli 18 E 77th St, between Madison and Fifth aves ☎212 249 4470, ⓦcastelligallery.com; subway #6 to 77th St. One of the original dealer-collectors, Castelli

was instrumental in aiding the careers of Rauschenberg and Warhol, and this gallery offers big contemporary names at high prices. Tues–Sat 10am–6pm.

DUMBO, BROOKLYN HEIGHTS AND GOWANUS

BRIC Rotunda Gallery 33 Clinton St, Brooklyn Heights ☎718 875 4047, ⓦbricartsmedia.org; subway R, #2, #3 to Court St-Borough Hall. This mixed-media, not-for-profit exhibition space features work by Brooklyn-based contemporary artists. Tues–

Sat noon–6pm (during exhibitions only).

★ **DUMBO Arts Center** 111 Front St, Suite 212, DUMBO ☎718 694 0831, ⓦdumboartscenter.org; subway F to York St, A, C to High St. A huge warehouse space dedicated to showing innovative new group work in

29

TOP 5 ART MUSEUMS
Frick Collection See p.171
Guggenheim Museum See p.175
Metropolitan Museum of Art See p.157
Museum of Modern Art See p.128
Whitney Museum of American Art
See p.173

noon–5pm ($2 donation suggested).

Smack Mellon Gallery 92 Plymouth St, at Washington St, DUMBO ☎718 834 8761, ⓦsmackmellon.org; subway F to York St, A, C to High St. An interesting space that displays multidisciplinary, high-tech work by artists who have for the most part flown under the radar of art critics and spectators. Wed–Sun noon–6pm.

UrbanGlass 126 13th St, between Second and Third aves, Gowanus ☎718 625 3685, ⓦurbanglass.org; subway F, G to Fourth Ave. Small but amazing glass gallery attached to the studio of the same name. Tues–Fri 10am–6pm, Sat & Sun 10am–5pm.

five to six shows yearly. The self-proclaimed origin and centre of DUMBO's art scene. Wed–Sat noon–6pm, Sun

WILLIAMSBURG

★ **Front Room** 147 Roebling St, between Metropolitan Ave and Hope St ☎718 782 2556, ⓦfrontroom.org; subway L to Bedford Ave. One of the neighbourhood's best galleries and also a popular performance-art space. Best place to get a good first sense of the local scene. Fri–Sun 1–6pm.

Pierogi 177 N 9th St, between Bedford Ave and Driggs Ave ☎718 599 2144, ⓦpierogi2000.com; subway L to Bedford Ave. This former workshop mounts fascinating installations of various kinds. It is noted in the art world

for its travelling "flatfiles", a collection of folders containing the work of six hundred or so artists, stored clinically and provocatively in metal, sliding cabinets. Tues–Sun 11am–6pm.

WAH (Williamsburg Art and Historical) Center 135 Broadway, at Bedford Ave ☎718 486 6012, ⓦwahcenter.net; subway J, M, Z to Marcy Ave. Beautiful, fascinating multimedia arts centre, with a focus on painting and sculpture (see p.235). Wed–Fri 1–5pm, Sat & Sun noon–6pm.

ALTERNATIVE SPACES

The galleries listed previously (at least those in Manhattan) are part of a system designed to channel artists' work through the gallery spaces and, eventually, into the hands of collectors. While initial acceptance by a major gallery is an important rite of passage for an up-and-coming artist, it shouldn't be forgotten that this system's philosophy is based on making money for gallery owners, who normally receive fifty percent of the sale price. The galleries below provide a forum for the kind of risky and non-commercially viable art that many other galleries may not be able to afford to show.

Apex Art 291 Church St, between White and Walker sts ☎212 431 5270, ⓦapexart.org; subway N, Q, R to Canal St, #1 to Franklin St. A nonprofit exhibition space that invites dealers, artists, writers, critics and international art-world bodies to act as curators and mount idea-based shows, along with lectures and associated events. Tues–Sat 11am–6pm.

Art in General 79 Walker St, between Broadway and Lafayette St ☎212 219 0473, ⓦartingeneral.org; subway N, Q, R to Canal St. Founded in 1981, this exhibition space is devoted to the unconventional art of emerging artists. Past exhibits have featured Emily Roysdon's multimedia work and Romanian artist Ioana Nemes. Tues–Sat noon–6pm.

★ **Artists Space** 38 Greene St, at Grand St, 3rd floor ☎212 226 3970, ⓦartistsspace.org; subway A, C, E, N, R, Q to Canal St. One of the most respected alternative

spaces, with frequently changing theme-based exhibits, film screenings, videos, installations and events. In over thirty years of existence, Artists Space has presented the work of thousands of emerging artists. Wed–Sun noon–6pm.

★ **Here** 145 Sixth Ave, between Dominick and Spring sts ☎212 352 3101, ⓦhere.org; subway C to Spring St. Eclectic experimental art space, with a comfy lobby café and a range of multimedia galleries hosting new works by the likes of Karinne Keithley and Tina Satter. Opening times vary.

White Columns 320 W 13th St, entrance on Horatio St, between Hudson and W 4th sts ☎212 924 4212, ⓦwhitecolumns.org; subway A, C, E to 14th St. White Columns focuses on emerging artists, and is considered very influential. Check out the fascinating, ever-changing group shows. Tues–Sat noon–6pm.

BEACON'S CLOSET, BROOKLYN

Shopping

Retail junkies beware: shops are one of New York's killer attractions. The city is the undisputed commercial capital of America, especially in fashion. There are flagship stores for every major brand, both ubiquitous (H&M) and exclusive (Vera Wang), so you can stock up just as easily on a designer leather clutch as you can a pair of tennis socks. In between all the big names, you'll find dozens of quirky local boutiques, vintage (secondhand) stores and bazaars. The city also contains some of America's most famous department stores – Bloomingdale's and Macy's among them – as well as a roster of specialist book, music and comic stores. Finally, enticing markets – green, flea and crafts – are scattered throughout the five boroughs. We've sifted through the best that the city has to offer and presented our pick of Manhattan's retail wonders below.

30

INFORMATION

Opening hours Roughly Monday to Saturday 9am to 6pm in midtown Manhattan. Downtown shops (Soho, Tribeca, the East and West villages, the Lower East Side) tend to stay open later, at least until 8pm and sometimes until about midnight; bookstores especially are often open late. Most stores are open Sunday as well, but with abbreviated hours. Chinatown's shops and stalls are open all day, every day, while the stores that serve workers in the Financial District stick to nine-to-five office hours and are usually shuttered on Saturday and Sunday. These places excepted, expect retail establishments to be most crowded on weekends, especially in Soho and midtown.

Payment Credit cards are widely accepted: even the smallest shops usually take American Express, MasterCard and Visa. A total 8.875 percent sales tax (which includes 4 percent state tax) will be added to your bill for all purchases with one exception: clothing and footwear under $110 are exempt from the entire sales tax.

NEW YORK NOVELTY

New York is home to hundreds of unique, obscure and just plain crazy independent stores, though these are increasingly being pushed out to the outer boroughs. Details of specialist book and comics (see p.375) and record stores (see p.386) appear later in the chapter.

Exit 9 51 Ave A, between E 3rd and E 4th sts ☎212 228 0145, ⍟shopexit9.com; subway F to Lower East Side–Second Ave; map p.88. Kooky emporium of kitsch, stocking soaps, bags, cards and various other offbeat goodies – great for last-minute gifts. Mon–Fri noon–8pm, Sat 11am–8pm, Sun noon–7pm.

Kiosk 95 Spring St, between Broadway and Mercer St ☎212 941 9816, ⍟kioskkiosk.com; subway #6 to Spring St; map p.64. Quirky store, part art gallery, selling bizarre objects from around the world, and a themed section focusing on different countries. Expect anything from foam doggies and Obama stamps to genuine Shaker onion baskets. Blink and you'll miss the tiny entrance smothered with stickers (Sabon is on the right). Mon–Sat noon–7pm.

Little Lebowski Shop 215 Thompson St, between W 3rd and Bleecker St ☎212 388 1466, ⍟little lebowskishop.com; subway A, B, C, D, E, F, M to W 4th St; map pp.96–97. This wacky theme store has garnered a cult following with its cool retro T-shirts and tributes to the movie *The Big Lewboksi* (yes, the owner really does wander around in his dressing gown). Mon, Wed & Thurs noon–9pm, Fri & Sat noon–11pm, Sun noon–7pm.

Obscura Antiques and Oddities 207 Ave A, between E 12th and E 13th sts ☎212 505 9251, ⍟obscura antiques.com; subway L to First Ave; map p.88. This spooky East Village classic specializes in antiques, rare taxidermy and strange, freaky artefacts – owners Mike Zohn and Evan Michelson even have a show on the Discovery Channel (*Oddities*). Mon–Sat noon–8pm, Sun noon–7pm.

Posteritati 239 Centre St, between Broome and Grand sts ☎212 226 2207, ⍟posteritati.com; subway #6 to Spring St; map p.64. Vast selection of over nine thousand movie posters, from classics such as *20,000 Leagues Under the Sea* and *Goldfinger* to modern blockbusters like *Avatar*. Tues–Sat 11am–7pm, Sun noon–6pm.

Toy Tokyo Shop 91 Second Ave, between E 5th and E 6th sts ☎212 673 5424, ⍟toytokyo.com; subway #6 to Astor Place; map p.88. Dizzying ensemble of Asian toys and cult memorabilia, mostly from Japan: action figures, vintage robots, roto-plastic figures and wind-ups. Mon–Thurs & Sun 1–9pm, Fri & Sat 12.30–9.30pm.

★ **Village Chess Shop** 230 Thompson St, between W 3rd and Bleecker sts ☎212 475 8130, ⍟chess-shop .com; subway A, B, C, D, E, F, M to W 4th St; map p.96–97. Every kind of chess set for every kind of budget since 1972. Usually packed with people playing and contemplating their next move. Daily 24hr.

Yunhong Chopsticks Shop 50 Mott St, between Bayard and Pell sts ☎212 566 8828, ⍟happychopsticks .com; subway A, C, E, J, N, Q, R, Z, #1, #6 to Canal St; map p.71. The only US branch of this Beijing chopstick maker, with more than 200 different styles on offer, many hand-painted beauties made from mahogany, ebony and silver. Daily 10.30am–8pm.

ARTS AND CRAFTS

Brooklyn Women's Exchange 55 Pierrepont St, between Henry and Hicks sts, Brooklyn Heights ☎718 624 3435, ⍟brooklyn-womens-exchange.org; subway #2, #3 to Clark St; map p.215. A crafts co-operative that dates back 150 years, the Exchange offers lots of handmade toys, clothes, bedding and so forth. Tues–Fri 11am–6pm, Sat & Sun 11am–5pm.

Kate's Paperie 435 Broome St, between Broadway and Crosby St ☎212 941 9816, ⍟katespaperie.com; subway #6 to Spring St; map p.64. Any kind of paper you can imagine or want, including great handmade cards, albums and exotic notebooks. Mon–Wed 10am–7pm, Thurs–Sat 10am–8pm, Sun 11.30am–7pm.

La Sirena 27 E 3rd St, between the Bowery and Second Ave ☎212 780 9113, ⍟lasirenanyc.com; subway #6 to Bleecker St, F to Second Ave; map p.88. Mexican folk art

TOP 5 LATE-NIGHT STORES

Eataly food, see p.385
Forbidden Planet comics, see p.375
Generation Records music, see p.386
St Mark's Bookshop books, see p.374
Village Chess novelty shops, see opposite

store selling pieces direct from Mexico, everything from museum-quality items to brilliantly coloured, traditional marketplace merchandise like serapes, sombreros and religious icons. Daily noon–7pm.

Utrecht Art Supplies 237 W 23rd St, between Seventh and Eighth aves ☎212 675 8699, ⓦ utrechtart.com; subway C, E, #1 to 23rd St; map p.107. This brand has a forty-year hold on the NYC art market. It carries all manner of paints and brushes, printmaking supplies and drawing materials (charcoal to crayons), along with portfolios in which to carry the finished products. Mon–Fri 9am–6pm, Sat 10am–7pm, Sun 11am–6pm.

30

BEAUTY AND COSMETICS

All department stores stock the main brands of **beauty products** – as does Century 21, often at a *heavy* discount (see p.377) but if you're looking for hard-to-find cosmetics lines, here are the best options.

Aveda 140 Fifth Ave, at W 19th St ☎212 645 4797, ⓦ aveda.com; subway N, R to 23rd St; map p.114. New Agey cosmetics company specializing in plant-extract-based shampoos, conditioners and skincare – this store gives samples and often offers cheap(ish) facials. Mon–Wed 10am–8pm, Thurs–Sat 10am–9pm, Sun 11am–7pm.

C.O. Bigelow Pharmacy 414 Sixth Ave, between W 8th and W 9th sts ☎212 473 7324, ⓦ bigelowchemists .com; subway A, B, C, D, E, F, M to W 4th St, #1 to Christopher St; map pp.96–97. Established in 1882, C.O. Bigelow is one of the oldest pharmacies in the country – and that's exactly how it looks, with the original Victorian shopfittings still in place. Specializing in lesser-known and European beauty brands, this is the place to come for beauty and cosmetic items that you can't find elsewhere in the city. Mon–Fri 7.30am–9pm, Sat 8.30am–7pm, Sun 8.30am–5.30pm.

Kiehl's 109 Third Ave, between E 13th and E 14th sts ☎212 677 3171, ⓦ kiehls.com; subway L to Third Ave; map p.88. Decorated with aviation and motorcycle memorabilia, this 150-year-old pharmacy sells its own range of natural-ingredient-based classic creams, oils and so on. Known for giving out plenty of samples to customers, whether you're buying or not. Lots of celebs swear by this stuff, especially the patented Crème de Corps body lotion. Mon–Sat 10am–8pm, Sun 11am–6pm.

MAC 506 Broadway, between Spring and Broome sts ☎212 334 4641, ⓦ maccosmetics.com; subway #6 to Spring St; map p.64. Also 689 Fifth Ave, Times Square, and several other locations. MAC is known for both its high-quality, non-animal-tested cosmetics and its HIV/AIDS fundraising (pick up a Viva Glam lipstick to donate). Home of the famed Ruby Woo lipstick, popular with models and celebs. Daily 11am–7pm, Wed–Sat till 8pm.

MiN New York Apothecary & Atelier 117 Crosby St, between Houston and Prince sts ☎212 206 6366, ⓦ minnewyork.com; subway N, R to Prince St; map p.64. Stylish boutique offering a range of niche brands, fragrances and beauty products for both men and women. Mon & Sun noon–6pm, Tues–Sat 11am–7pm.

Ray's Beauty Supply 721 Eighth Ave, at W 45th St ☎800 253 0993, ⓦ raybeauty.com; subway A, C, E to 42nd St; map p.141. This ramshackle store supplies most of the city's hairdressers with their potions and props. Something of an "industry insider" place, but the public is welcome. The low prices make it worth a detour. Mon–Fri 9.30am–6pm, Sat 10.30am–5pm.

Ricky's 590 Broadway, between Houston and Prince sts ☎212 226 5552, ⓦ rickysnyc.com; subway N, R to Prince St; map p.64. Plus several other locations. New York's haven for the overdone, the brash and the OTT (think drag-diva favourites and plenty of lurid wigs). Stocks cool brands like Urban Decay and Tony & Tina as well as a house line of products. Mon–Sat 9am–10pm, Sun 10am–8pm.

★ **Sabon** 93 Spring St, between Broadway and Mercer St ☎212 925 0742, ⓦ sabonnyc.com; subway N, R to Prince St, #6 to Spring St; map p.64. Luxury body and bath fragrances, soaps and aromatic oils from Israel; friendly assistants help you try the products at the old-fashioned sink in the middle of the store. Jan–April Mon–Sat 10am–9pm, Sun 11am–8pm; May–Dec Mon–Sat 10am–10pm, Sun 11am–8.30pm.

Sephora 555 Broadway, between Prince and Spring sts ☎212 625 1309, ⓦ sephora.com; subway N, R to Prince St; map p.64. Also Times Square at 42nd St ☎212 737 4672. "Warehouse" of perfumes, make-up and body-care products all lined up alphabetically so everything's easy to find and you don't have to pester any salespeople. Call for additional locations. Mon–Sat 10am–9pm, Sun 11am–8pm.

Zitomer 969 Madison Ave, at E 76th St ☎212 737 5560, ⓦ zitomer.com; subway #6 to 77th St; map p.169. A venerable pharmacy that has transformed itself into a full-blown mini-department store, Zitomer serves the beauty and cosmetic needs of the Fifth Ave gentry. Stocked to the gills with every brand and item imaginable. Mon–Fri 9am–8pm, Sat 9am–7pm, Sun 10am–6pm.

BOOKS

New York is a paradise for book lovers. Despite the challenge of Amazon.com and the internet in general, there are still more independent **booksellers** here than in most other parts of America. Quick literary fixes can be easily taken care of, too – superstores like Barnes & Noble (ⓦ barnesandnoble.com) still have a presence in New York (for now).

GENERAL INTEREST AND NEW BOOKS

Bookbook 266 Bleecker St, between Sixth and Seventh aves ☎ 212 807 8655, ⓦ bookbooknyc.com; subway #1 to Christopher Place; map pp.96–97. The old Biography Bookshop was reincarnated here in 2010, with a decent roster of recent and backlist fiction, children's books, travel, history, drama, cookbooks, art and fashion titles. Mon–Thurs & Sun 11am–10pm, Fri & Sat 11am–11pm.

★ **Book Culture** 2915 Broadway at W 114th St ☎ 646 403 3000, ⓦ bookculture.com; subway #1 to Cathedral Parkway-110th St; map p.183. The newer main shop of the largest independent bookstore in the city (the first Book Culture, now mostly academic-oriented, remains at 536 W 112th St) boasts a fine selection of literary (especially international) fiction, children's books and much more. Mon–Fri 9am–11pm, Sat 10am–11pm, Sun 10am–10pm.

McNally Jackson 52 Prince St, between Mulberry and Lafayette sts ☎ 212 274 1160, ⓦ mcnallyjackson.com; subway N, R to Prince St; map p.71. This Canadian book chain has gained a foothold in the heart of Manhattan with its prime Soho location. Great service, and the staff here are friendly, too. Mon–Sat 10am–10pm, Sun 10am–9pm.

St Mark's Bookshop 31 Third Ave, at E 9th St ☎ 212 260 7853, ⓦ stmarksbookshop.com; subway #6 to Astor Place; map p.88. Founded in 1977, the best-known independent bookstore in the city offers a good selection of titles on contemporary art, politics, feminism, the environment and literary criticism, as well as more obscure subjects. Cool postcards, too, and stocked full of radical and art magazines. Mon–Sat 10am–midnight, Sun 11am–midnight.

Shakespeare & Co 939 Lexington Ave, between E 68th and E 69th sts ☎ 212 570 0201, ⓦ shakeandco.com (also 716 Broadway, at Washington Place ☎ 212 529 1330; subway #6 to 68th St; map p.169). New and used books, both paper and hardcover. Great for fiction and psychology. Mon–Fri 9am–8pm, Sat 10am–7pm, Sun 11am–6pm.

Three Lives & Co 154 W 10th St, at Waverly Place ☎ 212 741 2069, ⓦ threelives.com; subway A, B, C, D, E, F, M to W 4th St, #1 to Christopher St; map pp.96–97.

Excellent literary bookstore that has an especially good selection of works by and for women, as well as general titles. There's an excellent reading series in the autumn, which has previously hosted the likes of Maya Angelou and Peter Carey. Mon & Tues noon–8pm, Wed–Sat 11am–8.30pm, Sun noon–7pm.

★ **WORD** 126 Franklin St, at Milton St, Greenpoint ☎ 718 383 0096, ⓦ wordbrooklyn.com; subway G to Greenpoint Ave; map p.236. Beloved Brooklyn indie shop, with a beautifully curated range of paperback fiction (especially classics), cookbooks, cute cards and stationery and a full roster of literary events. Daily 10am–9pm.

SECONDHAND BOOKS

Argosy Bookstore 116 E 59th St, at Park Ave ☎ 212 753 4455, ⓦ argosybooks.com; subway #4, #5, #6 to 59th St-Lexington Ave; map p.123. Open since 1925 and unbeatable for rare books, Argosy also sells clearance books and titles of all kinds, though the shop's reputation means you may find mainstream works cheaper elsewhere. Mon–Fri 10am–6pm; Sept to mid-May also Sat 10am–5pm.

★ **Book Thug Nation** 100 N 3rd St, between Berry St and Wythe Ave, Williamsburg ⓦ bookthugnation.com; subway L to Bedford Ave; map p.236. Serious (but not as scary as it sounds) used bookstore and event space in Williamsburg, well worth a detour; the main focus is literary fiction (with one of the best used fiction sections in the city), film and philosophy. Daily noon–8pm.

Housing Works Used Books Café 126 Crosby St, between Houston and Prince sts ☎ 212 334 3324, ⓦ housingworks.org; subway B, D, F, M to Broadway-Lafayette, N, R to Prince St, #6 to Bleecker St; map p.64. Excellent selection of very cheap and secondhand books. With a small espresso and snack bar and comfy chairs, it's a great place to spend an afternoon. Proceeds benefit its own AIDS charity work. Mon–Fri 10am–9pm, Sat & Sun 10am–5pm.

Spoonbill & Sugartown 218 Bedford Ave, between N 5th and N 4th sts, Williamsburg ☎ 718 387 7322, ⓦ spoonbillbooks.com; subway L to Bedford Ave; map p.236. Specializing in used, rare and new books on

---

NEW YORK'S CLOSEST SHAVE

Tucked away between Nolita's fashion boutiques is a shop that looks like it's come straight off the set of *Sherlock Holmes*; the **New York Shaving Co**, 202B Elizabeth St, between Spring and Prince streets (☎ 212 334 9495, ⓦ nyshavingcompany.com; subway #6 to Spring St; map p.71), is an old-fashioned tribute to men's grooming; buy shaving kits, brushes, razors and cologne, or even a traditional shave ($30) from a real pro. Mon–Fri 11am–8pm, Sat 10am–8pm, Sun 11am–7pm.

BEST SPAS TO STEAM, SPLASH AND JUST HANG OUT

New York is crammed with all sorts of spas and steam baths from which to escape the hectic streets outside, from rooms caked in sea salt to Japanese-style retreats. These are some of the best places to relax for a few hours.

Bliss 568 Broadway, 2/F, between Houston and Prince sts ☎877 862 5477, ⓦblissworld.com; subway N, R to Prince St; map p.64. Top-notch spa with massage, facial, nail and wax services. There's a bevy of beauty potions to purchase, including the spa's own popular lotions and the full line of Crème de la Mer skin products. There are two other spas at 12 W 57th St between Fifth and Sixth aves, and inside the *W Hotel* at 541 Lexington Ave at 49th St (use the number above for an appointment at any location). Daily 9am–9pm.

★ **Jin Soon** 56 E 4th St, between Second Ave and the Bowery ☎212 473 2047, ⓦjinsoon.com; subway #6 to Astor Place; map p.88. Other branches at 23 Jones St in the West Village and 421 E 73rd St in the Upper East Side. Small, soothing Japanese hand-and-foot spa. It's great for mani- and pedicures. Mon–Sat 11am–8pm, Sun 11am–7pm.

Juvenex 25 W 32nd St, between Fifth Ave and Broadway ⓦjuvenexspa.com. Popular with Broadway performers and dancers. Access to tubs, sauna and steam for 90min is $65. Ladies only 7am–5pm, couples 5pm–7am (24hr).

Mermaid Spa 3703 Mermaid Ave, Brooklyn ⓦmermaidspany.com. Best Russian baths in the city; just $35 per visit. Daily 10am–10.30pm.

Peninsula Spa 700 Fifth Ave, at 55th St ⓦpeninsula.com. Ultra-luxurious spa in the *Peninsula Hotel*; packages at around $285, but you'll feel like royalty. Daily 8am–9.30pm.

Phyto Universe 715 Lexington Ave, at E 58th St (ⓦphytouniverse.com). Lush oasis from the French hair specialists (the focus here is on hair treatments, but it's a tranquil place to chill). Treatments from $160. Mon–Sat 10am–7pm.

Shibui Spa 377 Greenwich St ⓦthegreenwichhotel .com/spa. Another serene hotel spa, with a stylish Japanese theme, pool and lounge. Soaks in the baths from $75/30min. Daily 6am–10pm.

contemporary art, art history, architecture and various design fields. Daily 10am–10pm.

★ **Strand Bookstore** 828 Broadway, at E 12th St ☎212 473 1452, ⓦstrandbooks.com; subway N, R, Q, L, #4, #5, #6 to Union Square; map p.88. Yes, it's hot and crowded, and the staff seem to resent working here, but with "18 miles of books" and a stock of more than 2.5 million titles, this is the largest discount book operation in the city. There are recent review copies and new books for half-price in the basement; older books go for anything from 50¢. Mon–Sat 9.30am–10.30pm, Sun 11am–10.30pm.

SPECIAL-INTEREST BOOKSTORES
ART AND ARCHITECTURE
See also the excellent bookstores at the Met (p.157), MoMA (p.128) and New Museum of Contemporary Art (p.79).

MoMA Design Store 81 Spring St, at Crosby St ☎646 613 1367, ⓦmomastore.org; subway N, R to Prince St, #6 to Bleecker St; map p.64. Contemporary art books galore. Mon–Sat 10am–8pm, Sun 11am–7pm.

Unoppressive, Non-Imperialist Bargain Books 34 Carmine St, between Bleecker and Bedford sts ☎212 229 0079, ⓦunoppressivebooks.blogspot.com; subway A, B, C, D, E, F, M to W 4th St, #1 to Houston St; map pp.96–97. Arty overstock among a hotchpotch of travel guides, biographies, children's pop-up books and spiritual titles. Mon–Thurs & Sun 11am–10pm, Fri & Sat 11am–midnight.

COMICS AND SCI-FI
Forbidden Planet 832 Broadway, at E 13th St ☎212 473 1576, ⓦfpnyc.com; subway #4, #5, #6, L, N, R, Q to 14th St-Union Square; map p.88. Science fiction, fantasy, horror fiction, graphic novels and comics. Great for its large backlist of indie and underground comics, they also hawk T-shirts and the latest sci-fi toys and collectibles. Mon, Tues & Sun 9am–10pm, Wed–Sat 9am–midnight.

Jim Hanley's Universe 4 W 33rd St, between Fifth Ave and Broadway ☎212 268 7088, ⓦjhuniverse .com; subway B, D, F, M, N, Q, R to 34th St-Herald Square; map p.123. Offers mainstream issues from the big leagues (DC, Marvel) as well as graphic novels, manga, small pressings and collectibles. Authors, illustrators and comic-related media types (Neil Gaiman, Mr Tarantino, Guillermo Del Toro) have often stopped by to discuss their work. Staff are knowledgeable and try extra-hard to please. Mon, Tues & Sun 10am–9pm, Wed–Sat 9am–11pm.

St Mark's Comics 11 St Mark's Place, between Second and Third aves ☎212 598 9439, ⓦstmarkscomics.com; subway #6 to Astor Place; map p.88. Pilgrimage site for comic, manga and graphic-novel fans from all over the world, with plenty of rare memorabilia (T-shirts, action-figures) to enhance their huge stock of comics. Mon & Tues 10am–11pm, Wed 9am–1am, Thurs–Sat 10am–1am, Sun 11am–11pm.

30

30

CRIME AND MYSTERY

The Mysterious Bookshop 58 Warren St, at West Broadway ☎212 587 1011, ⓦmysteriousbookshop .com; subway #1, #2, #3 to Chambers St; map p.64. The founder of this store started the Mysterious Press (now owned by Warner Books). The shop sells mysteries of every kind, from classic detectives to just-published titles, and also trades in some first editions and "Sherlockiana". Mon–Sat 11am–7pm.

FOREIGN LANGUAGE

J. Levine Books & Judaica 5 W 30th St, between Fifth Ave and Broadway ☎212 695 6888, ⓦlevinejudaica .com; subway R, N to 28th St; map p.114. The best selection of Bibles, Torahs and Jewish texts in the city – a huge range of books in English. Mon–Wed 9am–6pm, Thurs 9am–7pm, Fri 9am–2pm, Sun 10am–5pm; closed Sun in July.

Kinokuniya Bookstore 1073 Sixth Ave, between W 40th and W 41st sts ☎212 869 1700, ⓦkinokuniya .com; subway B, D, F, M to 42nd St-Bryant Park; map p.141. The largest Japanese bookstore in New York, with English books on Japan, too. Mon–Sat 10am–8pm, Sun 11am–7.30pm.

Rizzoli 31 W 57th St, between Fifth and Sixth aves ☎212 759 2424, ⓦrizzoliusa.com; subway F to 57th St; map p.123. Manhattan branch of the prestigious Italian bookstore chain and publisher. They specialize in European publications, and have a good selection of foreign newspapers and magazines along with art books of all sorts. Mon–Fri 10am–7.30pm, Sat 10.30am–7pm, Sun 11am–7pm.

Russian Bookstore 21 174 Fifth Ave, between W 22nd and W 23rd sts ☎212 924 5477, ⓦrussianbookstore21 .com; subway N, R to 23rd St; map p.114. All books, all in Russian. For curiosity's sake, worth a trip even for a non-speaker (and they also have Russian titles in English). Mon–Sat 11am–6pm.

MISCELLANEOUS

Bluestockings 172 Allen St, between Stanton and Rivington sts ☎212 777 6028, ⓦbluestockings.com; subway F to Lower East Side-Second Ave; map p.83. New and used titles on queer and gender studies, global capitalism, feminism, police and prisons, democracy studies and black liberation. Cosy, well-stocked, collective-style store in what was once a dilapidated crack house; nice Fairtrade café, too. Daily 11am–11pm.

Center for Book Arts 28 W 27th St, in between Broadway and Sixth Ave, 3rd floor ☎212 481 0295, ⓦcenterforbookarts.org; subway N, R to 28th St; map p.114. Not so much a bookstore as a space dedicated to the art of bookmaking. Hosts regular readings and workshops – fascinating stuff. Mon–Fri 10am–6pm, Sat 10am–4pm.

Complete Traveller Antiquarian Bookstore 199 Madison Ave, at E 35th St ☎212 685 9007, ⓦctrarebooks.com; subway #6 to 33rd St; map p.123. An extensive collection of rare travel tomes, including the entire Baedekers series, WPA Guides, old books on NYC and maps galore. You can also find other (non-travel) first pressings and vintage children's books here. Mon–Fri 9.30am–6.30pm, Sat 10am–6pm, Sun noon–5pm.

Drama Bookshop 250 W 40th St, between Seventh and Eighth aves ☎212 944 0595, ⓦdramabookshop .com; subway A, C, E to 42nd St; map p.141. Theatre books, scripts and publications on all manner of drama-related subjects since 1917. Mon–Sat 11am–7pm, Thurs till 8pm, Sun noon–6pm.

Idlewild Books 12 W 19th St, between Fifth and Sixth aves ☎212 414 8888, ⓦidlewildbooks.com; subway N, R to 23rd St; map p.114. Travel book and world literature specialist, just the place to inspire your next trip; also carries a wide selection of books in French and Spanish. Mon–Thurs noon–7.30pm, Fri–Sun noon–6pm.

Kitchen Arts & Letters 1435 Lexington Ave, between E 93rd and E 94th sts ☎212 876 5550, ⓦkitchenartsandletters.com; subway #6 to 96th St; map p.169. Cookbooks and books about food; run by a former culinary editor. Mon 1–6pm, Tues–Fri 10am–6.30pm, Sat 11am–6pm (closed Sat July & Aug).

The Old Print Shop 150 Lexington Ave, between E 29th and E 30th sts ☎212 683 3951, ⓦoldprintshop .com; subway #6 to 28th St; map p.114. The place to find a great old map of a New York neighbourhood, a first-edition art book or a print from an old *Harper's Weekly*. June–Aug Mon–Thurs 9am–5pm, Fri 9am–4pm; Sept–May Tues–Fri 9am–5pm, Sat 9am–4pm.

Revolution Books 146 W 26th St, between Sixth and Seventh aves ☎212 691 3345, ⓦrevolutionbooksnyc .org; subway #1 to 28th St; map p.107. New York's major left-wing bookstore and contact point, with a wide range of political and cultural titles and periodicals. More significantly, a place for healthy discourse: almost every night, the store holds screenings, salons or other events (after official closing time). Daily noon–7pm.

DEPARTMENT STORES

Barneys, Bergdorf Goodman and Saks Fifth Avenue are among the world's most famous (and most beautiful) **department stores** – each of their buildings is a landmark in itself. In general, the status of department stores in America is not what it once was; the last decades of the twentieth century were particularly tough, as speciality outlets swallowed up business. The department stores that have survived this transition, especially those in New York, have tweaked their offerings to provide fewer essentials and more luxuries (Macy's is a rare exception). Many of these stores offer **in-house discount cards** for foreign visitors – ask at the information desk.

TOP 5 ICONIC NY STORES

Bloomingdale's department stores, see below
FAO Schwarz toys, see p.387
Kiehl's beauty products, see p.373
Strand Bookstore books, see p.375
Tiffany & Co jewellery, see p.379

Barneys New York 660 Madison Ave, at E 61st St ☎212 826 8900, ⓦbarneys.com; subway N, R to Fifth Ave-59th St; map p.123. Barneys has been considered the trendiest New York department store for well over a decade now, and shows no sign of weakening. It's a temple to designer fashion, and the best place to find cutting-edge labels or next season's hot item. The Co-op section, focusing on younger styles, was such a hit that the powers that be opened several standalone Barneys Co-op stores (see website for details). Mon–Fri 10am–8pm, Sat 10am–7pm, Sun 11am–6pm.

★ **Bergdorf Goodman** 754 and 745 Fifth Ave, at E 58th St ☎212 753 7300, ⓦbergdorfgoodman.com; subway F to 57th St, N, R to Fifth Ave-59th St; map p.123. This venerable department store caters to the city's wealthiest shoppers. Haute-couture designers and salons fill both buildings, one for men, one for women, and it's the fairer of the sexes that get to shop within the former Vanderbilt mansion on the east side of Fifth. Has exclusive rights to lines by Yves Saint Laurent and Chloé, among others. Mon–Fri 10am–8pm, Sat 10am–7pm, Sun noon–6pm.

Bloomingdale's Lexington Ave and E 59th St (officially 1000 Third Ave) ☎212 705 2000, ⓦbloomingdales .com; subway N, R, #4, #5, #6 to Lexington Ave-59th St; map p.123. Out-of-towners flock here for its famed "classiness", though local power-shoppers are more likely to view it as a bit of a frumpy has-been. It does still have the atmosphere of a large, bustling bazaar, packed with concessionaires offering perfumes and designer clothes. Mon, Tues & Thurs 10am–8.30pm, Wed, Fri & Sat 10am–10pm, Sun 11am–7pm.

Henri Bendel 712 Fifth Ave, between W 55th and W 56th sts ☎212 247 1100, ⓦhenribendel.com; subway N, R to Fifth Ave-59th St; map p.123. More gentle in its approach than the biggies, this store's refinement is thanks in part to its classic reuse of the Coty perfume building, with windows by René Lalique. There's an array of top-shelf fashion accessories, designer handbags and designer jewellery – with price tags certain to send your blood pressure soaring. The powder rooms appear designed for royalty. Mon–Sat 10am–8pm, Sun noon–7pm.

Jeffrey 449 W 14th St, between Ninth and Tenth aves ☎212 206 1272, ⓦjeffreynewyork.com; subway A, C, E to 14th St; map p.107. Opened in the 1990s, Jeffrey is a relative newcomer to New York's department-store scene. The all-white emporium sits set squat in the middle of the city's cutting-edge Meatpacking District, and features offerings from trend-setting lines like Boudicca and Tess Giberson. Mon–Wed & Fri 10am–8pm, Thurs 10am–9pm, Sat 10am–7pm, Sun 12.30–6pm.

Macy's 151 W 34th St, on Broadway at Herald Square ☎212 695 4400 or ☎1-800 289 6229, ⓦmacys.com; subway B, D, F, M, N, Q, R to 34th St-Herald Square; map p.141. With two buildings, two million square feet of floor space and ten floors (four for women's garments alone), Macy's is, quite simply, the largest department store in the world. Given its size, it's not the hotbed of top fashion it ought to be: most merchandise is of mediocre quality. One highlight is The Cellar, the housewares department in the basement, arguably the best in the city. If you're not American, head to the visitor centre to receive a ten-percent discount card (bring your passport). Mon–Sat 10am–9.30pm, Sun 11am–8.30pm.

Saks Fifth Avenue 611 Fifth Ave, at E 50th St ☎212 753 4000, ⓦsaksfifthavenue.com; subway E, M to Fifth Ave-53rd St, B, D, F, M to 47–50th St-Rockefeller Center; map p.123. Since 1924, the name Saks has been virtually synonymous with style. No less true today, the store has updated itself to carry the merchandise of all the big designers, while still retaining its reputation for quality. The ground floor can be a bit like Grand Central terminal as multiple salesgirls assault you with drive-by perfume sprays, but they stock top cosmetic lines (like Armani) that you can't find elsewhere in the city. Mon–Wed, Fri & Sat 10am–7pm, Thurs 10am–8pm, Sun noon–6pm.

DISCOUNT DEPARTMENT STORES

Century 21 22 Cortlandt St, between Broadway and Church St ☎212 227 9092, ⓦc21stores.com; subway R to Cortlandt St or Rector St, #1 to Rector St, #4, #5 to Wall St; map p.43. The granddaddy of designer discount department stores, where all the showrooms send their samples to be sold at the end of the season, usually at forty- to sixty-percent off retail prices – the richest pickings are in January and July. A limited number of dressing rooms, so buy what you want and return whatever doesn't fit. Mon–Wed 7.45am–9pm, Thurs & Fri 7.45am–9.30pm, Sat 10am–9pm, Sun 11am–8pm.

Loehmann's 101 Seventh Ave, between W 16th and W 17th sts ☎212 352 0856, ⓦloehmanns.com; subway #1 to 18th St; map p.107. New York's best-known department store for designer clothes at knockdown prices, especially glamorous evening wear. No refunds and no exchanges after thirty days. Mon–Sat 9am–9pm, Sun 11am–7pm.

30

ELECTRONIC AND VIDEO EQUIPMENT

Buying **electronic and video equipment** in New York can be a good deal, especially if you are visiting from Europe, where such merchandise is more expensive; make sure that appliances are compatible with your home country before handing over the cash. Tech-heads can brave the risky discount shopping on Sixth and Seventh avenues north of Times Square in the 50s for cameras, stereos and MP3 players, but it's much easier to head for the Apple stores (attractions in themselves), B&H or J&R, where merchandise is not only cheap but reliable as well.

30

★ **Apple Store** 103 Prince St, at Greene St ☎ 212 226 3126, ⓦ apple.com; subway N, R to Prince St; map p.64. Also at 767 Fifth Ave and 1981 Broadway; map p.123 & p.183 (and Grand Central Terminal). The original Apple gadget store in Manhattan gets extremely crowded, but the latest in laptops, iPads, iPhones and iPods are all here for as cheap as you'll get them anywhere – you can also play with the newest models. Head upstairs for technical support at the genius bar or sit in on one of the many tutorials in the theatre. Mon–Sat 9am–9pm, Sun 9am–7pm.

B&H Photo Video 420 Ninth Ave, between W 33rd and W 34th sts ☎ 212 444 6615 or ☎ 1 800 606 6969, ⓦ bhphotovideo.com; subway A, C, E to 34th St; map p.141. For film, cameras and speciality equipment; knowledgeable sales staff will take the time to guide you through a buying decision. Excellent used-goods section upstairs. Mon–Thurs 9am–7pm, Fri 9am–1pm, Sun 10am–6pm; closed Jewish holidays.

J&R Music and Computer World 15–23 Park Row, between Beekman and Ann sts ☎ 212 238 9000, ⓦ jr .com; subway N, R to City Hall, #2, #3 to Park Place,

#4, #5, #6 to Brooklyn Bridge-City Hall; map p.57. You'll find a good selection of stereo and computer equipment at this strip of stores down by City Hall, as well as home appliances and CDs. If you can plug it in, they sell it here – and often at the cheapest prices in the city. Mon–Wed 10am–7pm, Thurs & Fri 10am–7.30pm, Sat & Sun 11am–7pm.

Leica Store Soho 460 West Broadway, between Houston and Prince sts ☎ 212 475 7799, ⓦ leica-camera.com; subway C to Spring St; map p.64. This stylish showcase for the German camera-maker opened in 2013 with artsy photographic exhibits and special-edition cameras enhancing the usual selection of products. Daily 10am–7pm.

Microsoft Store Time Warner Center, 10 Columbus Circle ☎ 855 270 6581, ⓦ microsoftstore.com; subway A, B, C, D, #1 to 59th St-Columbus Circle; map p.183. Shrine dedicated to all the best Microsoft products, including the popular Surface, Windows 8 and Windows 8 PCs, Windows Phone and Xbox. Mon–Sat 10am–9pm, Sun 11am–7pm.

FASHION: ACCESSORIES

New York's massive fashion industry is supplemented by a host of accessory specialists, especially those selling jewellery (see opposite) and designer shades, but there are also stores dedicated to lingerie and mind-bogglingly expensive handbags.

Agent Provocateur 133 Mercer St, at Prince St ☎ 212 965 0229, ⓦ agentprovocateur.com; subway N, R to Prince St; map p.64. New York outpost of the saucy, sexy, luxury lingerie line, co-owned by Joe Corre, son of avant-garde designer Vivienne Westwood. Think frills, bows and lashings of lace. Mon–Sat 11am–7pm, Sun noon–6pm.

Alain Mikli Optique 575 Madison Ave, between E 56th and E 57th sts ☎ 212 751 6085, ⓦ mikli.com; subway N, Q, R to Fifth Ave-59th St; map p.123. The French king of eyewear. This is the only place to go for high-end fashionable frames. Mon–Wed & Fri 10am–6.30pm, Thurs 10am–7pm, Sat 10am–6pm, Sun noon–5pm (closed Sun July & Aug).

Flight 001 96 Greenwich Ave, at W 12th St ☎ 212 989 0001, ⓦ flight001.com; subway A, C, E to 14th St; map pp.96–97. The best place for bags in the city, from Mandarina Duck to Freitag, plus a stylish selection of travel accessories (alarm clocks, candles, speciality mini-toiletries) and books. Mon–Sat 11am–8pm, Sun noon–6pm.

Kate Spade 454 Broome St, at Mercer St ☎ 212 274 1991, ⓦ katespade.com; subway N, R to Prince St, #6 to

Spring St; map p.64. Boxy, high-quality fabric bags that were all the rage in the late 1990s. Get yourself one now that they're out of vogue. These days the store also sells dazzling shoes, beach towels and home accessories. Mon–Sat 10am–8.30pm, Sun 11am–7pm.

Robert Marc 551 Madison Ave, between E 55th and E 56th sts ☎ 212 319 2000, ⓦ robertmarc.com; subway E, M to Fifth Ave-53rd St; map p.123. Multiple other locations; check website. Exclusive New York distributor of frames by the likes of Lunor and Kirei Titan; also sells Retrospecs, restored antique eyewear from the 1890s to the 1940s. Very expensive. Mon–Wed & Fri 9.30am–6.30pm, Thurs 9.30am–7pm, Sat 10am–6pm, Sun noon–6pm.

Selima Optique 59 Wooster St, at Broome St ☎ 212 343 9490, ⓦ selimaoptique.com; subway A, C, E to Canal St; map p.64. Also 899 Madison, at E 72nd St; and 357 Bleecker St. Owner Selima Salaun stocks her own line of girly, groovy specs, alongside favourites from well-known designers like Dior and Kata. Mon–Sat 11am–8pm, Sun noon–6pm.

★ **Three Monkeys Eyewear** 35 Spring St, at Mott St ☎ 917 330 7377, 🌐 3monkeyseyewear.com; subway #6 to Spring St; map p.64. Hip sunglasses shop from Chilean eyewear maestro Jorge Pozo; all shapes and styles, from blue mirrors to thin metal frames. Mon–Thurs & Sun 11am–8pm, Fri & Sat 11am–9pm.

Victoria's Secret 591 Broadway at Houston St ☎ 212 219 3643, 🌐 victoriassecret.com; subway N, R to Prince St; map p.64. Also 115 Fifth Ave. The enduring appeal of the "world's most glamorous lingerie" is about quality, comfort and design, as much as their celebrity models. Mon–Sat 10am–8.30pm, Sun 11am–8.30pm.

FASHION: JEWELLERY

30

Few New York stores are as famous or iconic as **Tiffany & Co**, but there are plenty of alternative jewellery options in the city, from the hectic stalls in Diamond Row (see box, p.380) to the hip designers of Nolita. Craft and street markets are another important outlet for independent designers (see p.384).

Erica Weiner 173 Elizabeth St, between Kenmare and Spring sts ☎ 212 334 6383, 🌐 ericaweiner.com; subway #6 to Spring St; map p.71. Fashionable Brooklyn-born designer selling vintage-inspired jewellery; elegant rings, charm-laden necklaces and popular brass ginkgo-leaf earrings ($25). Daily noon–8pm.

Me & Ro 241 Elizabeth St, between Houston and Prince sts ☎ 917 237 9215, 🌐 meandrojewelry.com; subway B, D, F, M to Broadway–Lafayette; N, R to Prince St; map p.71. The hottest, most distinctive jeweller in Manhattan, with tasteful Modernist designs worth going out of your way for. Some items are quite expensive, but you can get really nice earrings here for a reasonable price. Mon–Sat 11am–7pm, Sun noon–6pm.

Swarovski Crystallized 499 Broadway, between Spring and Broome sts ☎ 212 966 3322, 🌐 swarovski-crystallized.com; subway F to Lower East Side-Second Ave; map p.64. Fashionable offshoot of the famed crystal-makers, with its specially designed jewellery collections and drawers of pick-your-own crystals enhanced with dazzling chandeliers, *Café Kristall* upstairs and the "Cascade", a glittering pillar of crystal that spills between the two floors. Mon–Sat 10am–9pm, Sun 11am–6pm.

Tiffany & Co 727 Fifth Ave, at E 57th St; subway N, R to Fifth Ave-59th St ☎ 212 755 8000, 🌐 tiffany.com; map p.123. Even if you're just window-shopping, Tiffany's is worth a perusal, its soothing green marble and weathered wood interior best described by Truman Capote's fictional Holly Golightly: "It calms me down right away. . . nothing very bad could happen to you there." Mon–Sat 10am–7pm, Sun noon–6pm.

FASHION: CLOTHING

New York is one of the major nerve centres of the global fashion industry, where you'll find boutiques for just about every major designer on the planet, with prices significantly lower than in European cities or Tokyo. We've divided this section into four categories: trendy labels and boutiques, where you can pick up local big names or one-offs; New York designers; discount stores, where you can snag big names at deep discounts; and vintage and thrift, including the increasingly popular (and browse-worthy) resale or consignment stores, where owners sell off last season's barely worn outfits.

NEW YORK DESIGNERS

Alexander Wang 103 Grand St, between Greene and Mercer sts ☎ 212 977 9683, 🌐 alexanderwang.com; subway N, R to Canal St; map p.64. One of the newest American designers to receive the Wintour/*Vogue* nod of approval. Casual men's and women's clothing from $250. Mon–Sat 11am–7pm, Sun noon–6pm.

Anna Sui 113 Greene St, at Prince St ☎ 212 941 8406, 🌐 annasui.com; subway N, R to Prince St; map p.64. Funky, thrift-store-inspired clothes for girly girls from the popular American designer. Mon–Sat 11.30am–7pm, Sun noon–6pm.

Calvin Klein 654 Madison Ave, at E 60th St ☎ 212 292 9000, 🌐 calvinklein.com; subway N, R to Fifth Ave-59th St; map p.169. Sleek, minimalist shirts and suits from the New York-based master of classic American fashion. Mon–Wed, Fri & Sat 10am–6pm, Thurs 10am–7pm, Sun noon–6pm.

Carolina Herrera 954 Madison Ave, at E 75th St ☎ 212 249 6552, 🌐 carolinaherrera.com; subway #6 to 77th St; map p.169. Posh Venezuelan designer based in New York since the 1980s, dressing First Ladies from Jacqueline Kennedy to Michelle Obama with refined, elegant styles. Mon–Sat 10am–6pm.

Diane von Fürstenberg (DVF) 874 Washington St, at W 14th St ☎ 646 486 4800, 🌐 dvf.com; subway A, C, E, L to Eighth Ave; map p.107. Belgian-born, ex-German princess now a NYC fashion powerhouse, best known for her iconic knitted-jersey wrap dress, sparkling party dresses and glittering clutches. Mon–Wed, Fri & Sat 11am–7pm, Thurs 11am–8pm, Sun noon–6pm.

DKNY 655 Madison Ave, at E 60th St ☎ 212 223 3569, 🌐 dkny.com; subway F to Lexington Ave-63rd St; map p.169. Also at 420 W Broadway, between Spring and Prince sts ☎ 646 613 1100. Donna Karan's younger, cheaper line has two concept-store locations in the city, selling accessories and homewares for the "DKNY lifestyle" alongside clothes. Mon–Sat 11am–8pm, Sun noon–7pm.

Donna Karan 819 Madison Ave, between E 69th and E 68th sts ☎1 866 240 4700, ⓦdonnakaran.com; subway #6 to 68th St; map p.169. The queen of New York fashion designs subtle clothes in understated shades guaranteed to flatter any figure. Mon–Wed, Fri & Sat 10am–6pm, Thurs 10am–7pm, Sun noon–5pm.

John Varvatos 122 Spring St, at Greene St ☎212 965 0700, ⓦjohnvarvatos.com; subway N, R to Prince St, #6 to Spring St; map p.64. Also at 315 Bowery, in the old CBGB space; map p.88. Boxy though flattering casual wear and suits, plus the American designer's highly successful line of leather Converse trainers. Mon–Sat 11am–7pm, Sun noon–6pm.

★ **Marc Jacobs** 163 Mercer St, between Houston and Prince sts ☎212 343 1490, ⓦmarcjacobs.com; subway N, R to Prince St; map p.64. Marc Jacobs rules the New York fashion world like a Cosmopolitan-sipping colossus. Women from all walks of life come here to blow the nest egg on his latest "it" bag or pair of boots. Check out his second line, Marc by Marc, at 403 Bleecker St, at 11th St (☎212 924 0026). Mon–Sat 11am–7pm, Sun noon–6pm.

Michael Kors 384 Bleecker St, at Perry St ☎212 242 0700, ⓦmichaelkors.com; subway #1 to Christopher St; map p.96–97. Classic American sportswear for women. Kors, a Long Island native, boosted his career by starring with Heidi Klum on *Project Runway*. Mon–Sat 10am–8pm, Sun 11am–7pm.

Patricia Field 306 Bowery, between Bleecker and E Houston sts ☎212 966 4066, ⓦpatriciafield.com; subway #6 to Bleecker St; map p.88. Touted as the founder of Manhattan's most inventive clothing store, Pat Field was one of the first NYC vendors of "punk chic"; her

recent renaissance came as the tour de force costumier behind Carrie Bradshaw's outfits in *Sex and the City*. This store has plenty of her wild designs at reasonable prices, as well as wacky accessories. Mon–Thurs 11am–8pm, Fri & Sat 11am–9pm, Sun 11am–7pm.

Polo Ralph Lauren 867 Madison Ave ☎212 606 2100 and **Polo Sport Ralph Lauren** 888 Madison Ave ☎212 434 8000, ⓦralphlauren.com; both between E 71st and E 72nd sts; subway #6 to 68th St; map p.169. The master of all things preppy: buy a blazer at the flagship and make like you're money. Mon–Wed 10am–7pm, Thurs 10am–8pm, Fri & Sat 10am–6pm, Sun noon–6pm.

Vera Wang 158 Mercer St, between Prince and Houston sts ☎212 382 2184, ⓦverawang.com; subway N, Q, R to Canal St; map p.64. The New York designer most synonomous with lavish wedding gowns, though this store highlights her equally celebrated ready-to-wear collection (991 Madison Ave is the place for brides-to-be). Mon–Sat 11am–7pm, Sun noon–6pm.

Vivienne Tam 40 Mercer St, at Grand St ☎212 966 2398, ⓦviviennetam.com; subway N, R, Q to Canal St; map p.64. Chinese-born, New York-based designer offering chic, stylish fashion inspired by Asian culture and modern design. Mon–Sat 11.30am–7pm, Sun noon–6pm.

TRENDY LABELS & BOUTIQUES

Abercrombie & Fitch 720 Fifth Ave, at W 56th St ☎212 306 0936, ⓦabercrombie.com; subway F to 57th St, N, Q, R to Fifth Ave-59th St; map p.123. Incredibly popular US casualware brand, targeted at young adults – prepare for long lines of shoppers outside the store (prices here are often half the price of its UK stores). Infamous for having bare-chested male models at the door. Mon–Sat 10am–8pm, Sun noon–6pm.

★ **Brooklyn Industries** 162 Bedford Ave, at N 8th St,

THE DIAMOND DISTRICT

The strip of 47th Street between Fifth and Sixth avenues is known as the Diamond District or "Diamond Row". At street level are dozens of retail shops and more than twenty specialist marts known as "exchanges" – combined, they sell more jewellery than any other area in the world. There are separate dealers for different gems, gold and silver – even dealers who will string your beads for you, appraisers and "findings" stores where you can pick up the basic makings of do-it-yourself jewellery, like chains and earring posts. Some jewellers trade only among themselves; some sell retail; and others do business by appointment only. Most shops are open Monday to Saturday 10am to 5.30pm, though a few close on Friday afternoon and Saturday for religious reasons, and the standard vacation time is from the end of June to the second week in July.

It is very important that you shop armed with some information. Research what you are looking for and be as particular as possible. If at all feasible, it's always better to go to someone who has been specifically recommended to you. For a listing of all the district's vendors, shopping tips and the "Buyers Bill of Rights", visit ⓦdiamonddistrict.org.

If you want to get your sparklies graded or appraised, try the Gemological Institute of America at 580 Fifth Ave, 2nd floor (Mon–Thurs 8am–5pm, Fri 8am–4pm; ☎212 221 5858, ⓦgia.edu), or the Universal Gemological Laboratory at 71 West 47th St, suite 204 (☎212 921 3324, ⓦuglinc.com).

Williamsburg ☎718 486 6464, ⓦbrooklynindustries
.com; subway L to Bedford Ave; map p.236. Also
multiple other locations in the city; see website.
Brooklyn chic in the form of hip vinyl bags and clothes
(T-shirts, jackets and trousers for men and women).
Founded by Lexy Funk in 1998, and still designer-owned.
Daily 10.30am–9pm.

Calypso St Barth's 407 Broome St, between Centre
and Lafayette sts ☎212 925 6200, ⓦcalypsostbarth
.com; subway #6 to Spring St; map p.64. Forget black;
colour is the name of the game at this outlet for the
major chain. Vibrant fashions imbued with a rich hippie
aesthetic – think string bikinis at $75 a pop. Mon–Sat
11am–7pm, Sun noon–7pm.

Forever 21 1540 Broadway ⓦforever21.com; map
p.88. The old Virgin Records space is now a behemoth
teenage-girl magnet, a freakishly large space featuring
floors of fashion and display cases dedicated to various
New York neighbourhoods – and it's open to 1am. Daily
9am–1am.

★ **Harlem Underground** 20 E 125th St, between
Fifth and Madison aves ☎212 987 9385; subway #4, #5,
#6 to 125th St; map p.198. Impress your friends with
apparel from this hot Harlem label; cool T-shirts for men
and women, featuring images from the world of hip-hop,
reggae (Bob Marley) and yes, even Barack Obama. Mon–
Sat 9am–6pm.

Intermix 1003 Madison Ave, at E 77th St ☎212 249
7858, ⓦintermixonline.com; subway #6 to 77th St;
map p.169. Also 125 Fifth Ave, at E 19th St ☎212 533
9720; and 98 Prince St, between Mercer and Greene sts
☎212 966 5303. Trendy boutiques for the working-girl
fashionista, and a flat-out fun place to shop. A wide
assortment of brands both high and low, and an admittedly
confusing merchandise layout – they're called "intermix"
for a reason. Mon–Sat 10am–7pm, Sun noon–6pm.

★ **Kirna Zabête** 96 Greene St, between Prince and
Spring sts ☎212 941 9656, ⓦkirnazabete.com; subway
N, R to Prince St; map p.64. The best of the downtown
shops, this is a concept store that stocks hand-picked
highlights from designers such as Jason Wu, Rick Owens and
Proenza Schouler. Mon–Sat 11am–7pm, Sun noon–6pm.

Pookie & Sebastian 1488 Second Ave, between E 77th
and E 78th sts ☎212 861 0550, ⓦpookieandsebastian
.com; subway F to Lexington Ave-63rd St; map p.169 .
Also 794 Lexington Ave, between E 61st and E 62nd sts.
Home of preppy chic, with girly clothes, cutesy tops,

designer denim, heaps of jewellery and assorted
accessories. You, too, could be a Pookie Girl. Mon–Wed
11am–8pm, Thurs–Sat 11am–9pm, Sun 11am–7pm.

Rag & Bone 119 Mercer St, between Grand and Canal
sts ☎212 219 2204, ⓦrag-bone.com; subway N, Q, R to
Canal St; map p.64. British expats Marcus Wainwright and
David Neville formed their label here in New York in 2002 to
design jeans, but today they sell children's clothes,
accessories and shoes as well as boho-chic fashions for men
and women. Mon–Sat 11am–8pm, Sun noon–7pm.

Scoop 1273–1277 Third Ave, at E 73rd St ☎212 535
5577, ⓦscoopnyc.com; subway #6 to 77th St. Also at
473–475 Broadway, between Broome and Grand sts;
and 430 W 14th St, at Washington St; map p.169. Every
season is cruise season at this lively fashion outpost for
youngish Upper East Side girls. There's a bit of a bubblegum,
Paris Hilton vibe to the place, but it's well stocked with the
latest designs from a dozen different labels, Zac Posen and
Rebecca Taylor among them. Mon–Fri 11am–8pm, Sat
11am–7pm, Sun noon–7pm.

Supreme 274 Lafayette St, between Houston and Prince
sts ☎212 966 7799, ⓦsupremenewyork.com; subway N,
R to Prince St; map p.64. Clothing and equipment for die-
hard skateboarders, hip-hop and modern punk fans, founded
here in 1994. Mon–Thurs 11.30am–7pm, Fri & Sat
11am–7.30pm, Sun noon–6pm.

Topshop 478 Broadway, at Broome St ☎212 966 9555,
ⓦus.topshop.com; subway N, R to Prince St, #6 to
Spring St; map p.64. Brits may be mildly amused, but
America's first Topshop attracted round-the-block lines
when it opened in 2009 (Top Girl herself Kate Moss cut the
ribbon). Regular collaborations with hip designers and
affordable prices keep the punters coming back. Mon–Sat
10am–9pm, Sun 11am–8pm.

Yumi Kim 105 Stanton St, at Ludlow St ☎212 420 5919,
ⓦyumikim.com; subway F to Delancey St, J, M, Z to Essex
St; map p.83. Downtown-chic clothing by New York-based
Kim Phan, whose silk printed dresses, vintage bodies and flirty
prints have been a big hit since launching in 2004 (everything
is 100-percent silk). Daily noon–7pm.

Zero 33 Bleecker St, at Mott St ☎212 925 3849,
ⓦzeromariacornejo.com; subway #6 to Bleecker St;
map p.88. Much-celebrated Chilean (but NYC-based)
designer Maria Cornejo's Noho boutique features the best
of her cutting-edge fashions, which tend toward a simple
colour palette and some unconventional cuts. Mon–Sat
11am–7pm, Sun 12.30–6.30pm.

FASHION: VINTAGE AND SECONDHAND STORES

Aside from the standout shops we've listed below, there's a heavy concentration of **secondhand and vintage stores** in
the Lower East Side, especially around Ludlow and Rivington streets. Don't be surprised to find a famous designer (or one
of their minions) rifling through the racks in this area – they're probably after inspiration for their next collection. Note also
that the **Salvation Army** operates three secondhand stores in the city, including the shop at 112th Fourth Ave, near Union
Square (see ⓦsalvationarmyusa.org).

30

DESIGNER STORES

We've listed the outlets for the major **designer labels** here – no big-name brand worth its cashmere would be without a Manhattan outpost, so the choice is enormous.

agnès b 13 E 16th St, between Fifth Ave and Broadway ☎ 212 741 2585, ⓦ usa.agnesb.com

Alexander McQueen 417 W 14th St, between Ninth and Tenth aves ☎ 212 645 1797, ⓦ alexandermcqueen.com

Burberry 131 Spring St, at Greene St ☎ 212 925 9300, ⓦ burberry.com

Chloé 850 Madison Ave, at E 70th St ☎ 212 717 8220, ⓦ chloe.com

Christian Dior 21 E 57th St, at Madison Ave ☎ 212 931 2950, ⓦ dior.com

Comme des Garçons 520 W 22nd St, at Tenth Ave ☎ 212 604 9200, ⓦ commedesgarcons.org

Dolce & Gabbana 825 Madison Ave, at E 69th St ☎ 212 249 4100, ⓦ dolcegabbana.com

Giorgio Armani 760 Madison Ave, at 65th St ☎ 212 988 9191, ⓦ giorgioarmani.com

Gucci 725 Fifth Ave, at 56th St ☎ 212 826 2600, ⓦ gucci.com

Marni 161 Mercer St, between Houston and Prince sts ☎ 212 343 3912, ⓦ marni.com

Miu Miu 100 Prince St, at Greene St ☎ 212 334 5156, ⓦ miumiu.com

Prada 575 Broadway, at Prince St ☎ 212 334 8888, ⓦ prada.com

Stella McCartney 112 Greene St, between Prince and Spring sts ☎ 212 255 1556, ⓦ stellamccartney.com

Versace 647 Fifth Ave, at E 52nd St ☎ 212 317 0224, ⓦ versace.com

Yves Saint Laurent 3 E 57th St at Fifth Ave ☎ 212 988 3821, ⓦ ysl.com.

★ **Amarcord** 252 Lafayette St, between Prince and Spring sts ☎ 212 431 4161, ⓦ amarcordvintagefashion .com; subway N, R to Prince St, #6 to Spring St; map p.64. Also 223 Bedford Ave, between N 4th and N 5th sts, Williamsburg (daily noon–8pm). This place is a real find. The owners make regular trips through their home country of Italy in search of discarded Dior, Gucci, Yves Saint Laurent and so forth from the 1940s onward. Things aren't too expensive, especially considering all the pieces are in mint condition. The Williamsburg store carries menswear. Mon–Sat noon–7.30pm, Sun noon–7pm.

Beacon's Closet 88 N 11th St, between Berry St and Wythe Ave, Williamsburg, Brooklyn ☎ 718 486 0816, ⓦ beaconscloset.com; subway L to Bedford Ave; map p.236. Also 10 W 13th St, between Fifth and Sixth aves, West Village (daily 11am–8pm). Vast 5500-square-foot used-clothing paradise, specializing in modern fashions and vintage attire. Mon–Fri 11am–9pm, Sat & Sun 11am–8pm.

★ **Buffalo Exchange** 332 E 11th St, at Second Ave ☎ 212 260 9340, ⓦ buffaloexchange.com; subway L to First Ave; map p.236. Also 504 Driggs Ave in Williamsburg. US clothes exchange that started in Arizona in the 1970s; bring in your former threads for a trade-in or cash on the spot. Designer jeans, and a surprisingly high quality of men's and women's clothes grace the store. Mon–Sat 11am–8pm, Sun noon–7pm.

Domsey Express 431 Broadway, at Hewes St, Williamsburg ☎ 718 384 6000; subway J, M to Hewes St; map p.236. This five-storey thrift store sells everything from boutique pieces to boot-camp salvage . . . by the pound! Plan to rifle ruthlessly; most of the offerings here are workaday basics from brands like Old Navy. Daily 9am–6pm.

★ **Edith Machinist** 104 Rivington St, at Ludlow St ☎ 212 979 9992; subway F to Delancey St, J, M, Z to Essex St; map p.83. Extremely popular with the trendy vintage set, this used-clothing emporium holds some amazing finds (particularly shoes) for those willing to sift through the massive stock. Tues–Sat noon–7pm, Sun noon–6pm.

Gabay's Outlet 225 First Ave, between E 13th and E 14th sts ☎ 212 254 3180, ⓦ gabaysoutlet.com; subway L to First Ave; map p.88. An East Village store crammed with remaindered merchandise (Marc Jacobs, YSL and the like) from midtown's department stores. Mon–Sat 10am–7pm, Sun 11am–7pm.

Housing Works Thrift Shop 143 W 17th St, between Sixth and Seventh aves ☎ 212 366 0820, ⓦ shophousingworks.com; subway #1 to 18th St; map p.107. Also 306 Columbus Ave, at W 75th St ☎ 212 579 7566; 202 E 77th St, at Third Ave ☎ 212 772 8461; 157 E 23rd St; 730–732 Ninth Ave; and several other locations. Upscale thrift stores where you can find secondhand designer pieces in very good condition. All proceeds benefit Housing Works, an AIDS social-service organization. Mon–Fri 10am–7pm, Sat 10am–6pm, Sun noon–5pm.

INA 21 Prince St, between Mott and Elizabeth sts ☎ 212 334 9048, ⓦ inanyc.com; subway N, R to Prince St; map p.71. Designer resale shop usually crammed with end-of-season, barely worn pieces by hot designers. Fair prices make it by far the best secondhand store in the city. The men's store is next door at 19 Prince St (☎ 212 334 2210; same hours). Mon–Sat noon–8pm, Sun noon–7pm.

Marmalade Vintage 174 Mott St, at Broome St ☎212 473 8070, Ⓦmarmaladevintage.com; subway J to Bowery, #6 to Spring St; map p.71. Fabulous vintage clothes from the 1940s to the 1990s, especially good for 1970s gear (including shoes and mink shawls). Prices are reasonable, and there are always some unique items. Mon–Sat 1.30–7.30pm.

Resurrection 217 Mott St, at Spring St ☎212 625 1374, Ⓦresurrectionvintage.com; subway #6 to Spring St; map p.71. Hands down the best high-end place for vintage clothing in the city, with first-class Pucci and Halston classics from the 60s to the 80s. The prices are high, but it's still worth it just to check out the Pucci gowns and python Dior jackets. Mon–Sat 11am–7pm, Sun noon–7pm.

Screaming Mimi's 382 Lafayette St, at E 4th St ☎212 677 6464, Ⓦscreamingmimis.com; subway #6 to Bleecker St or Astor Place; map p.88. One of the most well-established lower-end secondhand stores in Manhattan. Vintage clothes, including lingerie, bags, shoes and housewares, at reasonable prices. Mon–Sat noon–8pm, Sun 1–7pm.

Tokio 7 83 E 7th St, between First and Second aves ☎212 353 8443, Ⓦtokio7.net; subway #6 to Astor Place; map p.88. Attractive secondhand and vintage designer consignment items; known for its flashy, eccentric selection – think plenty of Gaultier, Moschino and McQueen – rather than boring, basic black. Daily noon–8pm.

What Comes Around Goes Around 351 W Broadway, between Broome and Grand sts ☎212 343 1225, Ⓦwhatgoesaroundnyc.com; subway A, C, E to Canal St; map p.64. Established and well-loved downtown vintage store. Popular with magazine stylists borrowing pieces for shoots. Mon–Sat 11am–8pm, Sun noon–7pm.

FASHION: SHOES

Most department stores carry two or more shoe salons – one for less-expensive brands and one for finer shoes. Barneys and Loehmann's are both known for their selection of high-end footwear, while the greatest concentration of bargain shoe shops is in the Village on West 8th Street, between University Place and Sixth Avenue, and on Broadway below West 8th Street.

Camper 125 Prince St, at Wooster St ☎212 358 1842, Ⓦcamper.com; subway N, R to Prince St; map p.64. Cult Spanish footwear with springy soles; some are based on eccentric takes on the bowling shoe. Mon–Sat 11am–8pm, Sun noon–6pm.

Jimmy Choo 645 Fifth Ave, at E 51st St ☎212 593 0800, Ⓦjimmychoo.com; subway E, M to Fifth Ave-53rd St; map p.123. Popular British designer has a huge Manhattan following for his high-heeled, high-priced, high-quality shoes. Mon–Fri 10am–7pm, Sat 10am–6pm, Sun noon–5pm.

John Fluevog 250 Mulberry St, at Prince St ☎212 431 4484, Ⓦfluevog.com; subway N, R to Prince St; map p.71. Innovative designs for a walk about town – most styles are casual but quirky, with buckles or brightly coloured detailing. Mon–Sat 11am–8pm, Sun noon–7pm.

Jutta Neumann 355 E 4th St, between aves C and D ☎212 982 7048, Ⓦjuttaneumann-newyork.com; subway F to Second Ave-Lower East Side; map p.88. Her custom-designed, super-comfy sandals are all the rage downtown, and she also sells popular leather handbags. Mon–Fri noon–7pm, Sat 1–6pm.

Kenneth Cole 610 Fifth Ave, at W 49th St ☎212 373 5800, Ⓦkennethcole.com; subway E, M to Fifth Ave-53rd St; map p.123. Classic and contemporary shoes and beautiful bags in excellent full-grain leather from another iconic NYC designer. Call for more locations. Mon–Sat 10am–8pm, Sun 11am–7pm.

Manolo Blahnik 31 W 54th St, at Fifth Ave ☎212 582 3007, Ⓦmanoloblahnik.com; subway E, M to Fifth Ave-53rd St; map p.123. World-famous strappy stilettos – good for height (of fashion), hell for feet. The Spanish designer is more popular than ever thanks to Carrie Bradshaw and company in *Sex and the City*. Mon–Fri 10.30am–6pm, Sat 10.30am–5.30pm, Sun noon–5pm.

Mooshoes 78 Orchard St ☎212 254 6512, Ⓦmooshoes.com; subway F to Delancey St, J, M, Z to Essex St; map p.83. All-vegan shoe and accessory store, "100 percent

---

SAMPLE SALES

At the beginning of each fashion season, designers' and manufacturers' showrooms are still full of leftover merchandise from the previous season. These pieces are removed via informal **sample sales**, which kick off in October and run through March, though there are usually a few in April and May. You'll always save at least fifty percent off the retail price, though you may not be able to try on the clothes and you can never return them. Always take plenty of cash with you; some sales will not accept credit cards. The best way to find out what sales are coming up is to check the current issues of *Time Out New York* and *New York* magazine (see p.28). You can also sign up for the free regular emails issued by Charlie Suisman's MUG (Ⓦmanhattanusersguide.com), Clothing Line (Ⓦclothingline.com) and Daily Candy (Ⓦdailycandy.com).

cruelty free". Numerous shoes, bags and other bits and pieces on sale. Mon–Sat 11.30am–7.30pm, Sun noon–6pm.

★ **Sigerson Morrison** 28 Prince St, at Mott St ☎212 219 3893, ⓦsigersonmorrison.com; subway N, R to Prince St; map p.71. Kari Sigerson and Miranda Morrison make timeless, simple and elegant shoes for women. A required pilgrimage for shoe worshippers. Daily 8am–6pm.

FLEA MARKETS AND CRAFT FAIRS

New York **flea markets** are good hunting grounds for vintage and outrageous clothes, collectibles, lingerie, jewellery and crafts; there's also any number of odd places – car parks, playgrounds or maybe just an extra-wide bit of pavement – where people set up to sell their wares, especially in spring and summer, as well as weekly street fairs (see ⓦnycstreetfairs.com). Note also that in December you'll find major Christmas gift and **craft markets** at Union Square (ⓦunionsquarenyc.org) and Bryant Park (ⓦtheholidayshopsatbryantpark.com).

Antiques Garage Flea Market 112 W 25th St, between Sixth and Seventh aves ⓦhellskitchenfleamarket.com; subway C, E, #1 to 23rd St; map p.107. Packed into a bi-level garage, over 100 vendors come to peddle all sorts of old knick-knacks, antique jewellery, framed items, toys, cigarette lighters and more. Sat & Sun 9am–5pm.

Brooklyn Flea 176 Lafayette Ave, between Clermont and Vanderbilt aves, Fort Greene (Sat); East River State Park, at N 7th St, Williamsburg (Sun) ☎212 243 5343, ⓦbrooklynflea.com; subway G to Clinton–Washington aves; C to Lafayette Ave (Sat), L to Bedford Ave (Sun); map pp.215 & 236. The "flea" epithet is a bit of a misnomer, as this is as much a high-quality outdoor arts and crafts fair as secondhand fair, with two hundred stalls and superb artisan food thrown in. During the winter (Dec–March), the market moves indoors – check the website for locations. For **Smorgasburg**, see p.235. Sat & Sun 10am–5pm.

Green Flea Columbus Ave, between W 76th and W 77th sts ☎212 239 3025, ⓦgreenfleamarkets.com; subway #1 to 79th St; map p.183. Two of the best and largest markets in the city: antiques and collectibles, desks and chests, textiles, vintage clothing, haberdashery and hot sauces, plus a farmers' market (Columbus location). Sun 10am–6pm, Nov–March till 5.30pm.

Hell's Kitchen Flea Market W 39th St, between Ninth and Tenth aves ☎212 243 5343, ⓦhellskitchen fleamarket.com; subway A, C, E to 42nd St; map p.141. This is the fastest-growing fair in New York, with 170 vendors selling regular and retro antiques, furniture, vintage clothes and bric-a-brac. Sat & Sun 9am–5pm.

Hester Street Fair Hester and Essex sts ⓦhesterstreetfair.com; subway F to East Broadway; map p.83. Hip flea and craft market best known for its artisanal food stalls, including *La Sonrisa empanadas*, *La Newyorkina* popsicles and *Luke's Lobster*. May–Oct Sat 10am–6pm.

Malcolm Shabazz Harlem Market 52 W 116th St, at Fifth Ave ☎212 987 8131; subway #2, #3 to 116th St; map p.198. Bazaar-like market, with an entrance marked by colourful fake minarets. A dazzling array of West African cloth, clothes, jewellery, masks, Ashanti dolls and beads. Also sells leather bags, music and Black Pride T-shirts. Daily 10am–8pm.

FOOD AND DRINK

Food is a New York obsession – hence the proliferation of gourmet groceries and speciality markets across the city. For general snacking and late-night munchies, there's usually a 24-hour corner shop (referred to as a "bodega" by residents) within a few blocks' walk of anywhere. Note that New York State's liquor-licensing laws mean that supermarkets and bodegas can only sell beer, and wine and spirits are only available in liquor stores. In either place, you'll need to be 21 to buy (and be able to prove it with a photo ID if asked).

★ **Agata & Valentina** 1505 First Ave, at E 79th St ☎212 452 0690, ⓦagatavalentina.com; subway #6 to 77th St; map p.169. The top gourmet grocer in town, with fresh pastas made on the premises, an enviable deli and cheese counter, a variety of pricey delicacies and an outstanding butcher. Daily 8am–9pm.

Alleva Dairy 188 Grand St, at Mulberry St ☎212 226 7990, ⓦallevadairy.com; subway J, Z, #6 to Canal St; map p.71. Oldest Italian *formaggiaio* (cheesemonger) and grocery in America. Makes its own smoked mozzarella, provolone and ricotta. Daily 8.30am–6pm, Sun till 3pm.

Barney Greengrass 541 Amsterdam Ave, between W 86th and W 87th sts ☎212 724 4707, ⓦbarney greengrass.com; subway #1 to 86th St; map p.183. "The Sturgeon King" is an Upper West Side smoked-fish institution, trading since 1908. You can sit down, or take your brunch makings to go. Tues–Sun 8.30am–5pm.

Chelsea Market 75 Ninth Ave, between W 15th and W 16th sts ☎212 243 6005, ⓦchelseamarket.com; subway A, C, E to 14th St; map p.107. A complex of eighteen former industrial buildings, among them the old Nabisco Cookie Factory. A true smorgasbord of stores, including *Amy's Bread*, Bowery Kitchen Supply, *Fat Witch Bakery*, *Morimoto*,

TOP 5 VINTAGE STORES

Amarcord Soho & Williamsburg, see p.382
Beacon's Closet Williamsburg & West Village, see p.382
Buffalo Exchange East Village & Williamsburg, see p.382
Edith Machinist Lower East Side, see p.382
Screaming Mimi's East Village, see p.383

Ronnybrook Dairy, Lobster Place and Manhattan Fruit Exchange. Mon–Sat 7am–9pm, Sun 8am–7pm.

Dean & Deluca 560 Broadway, between Prince and Spring sts ☎212 226 6800, ⓦdeandeluca.com; subway N, R to Prince St; map p.64. Second store at 1150 Madison Ave (at E 85th St). One of the original big neighbourhood food emporia. Beautiful quality fruit and veggies and top-notch prepared foods. Very chic, very Soho and not at all cheap. Mon–Fri 7am–8pm, Sat & Sun 8am–8pm.

Di Palo's Fine Foods 200 Grand St, at Mott St ☎212 226 1033, ⓦdipaloselects.com; subway B, D to Grand St; map p.71. Charming and authoritative family-run business since 1925 that sells some of the city's best ricotta, along with a fine selection of aged balsamic vinegars, oils and home-made pastas. Mon–Sat 9am–6.30pm, Sun 9am–4pm.

East Village Cheese Store 40 Third Ave, between E 9th and E 10th sts ☎212 477 2601; subway N, R to 8th St, #6 to Astor Place; map p.88. The city's most affordable source for cheese; its front-of-the-store bins sell pungent blocks and wedges of the stuff starting at just 50¢. Daily 8.30am–6.30pm.

★ **Eataly** 200 Fifth Ave, at W 23rd St ☎212 229 2560, ⓦeatalyny.com; subway N, R to 8th St, #6 to Astor Place; map p.114. This wildly popular Mario Batalli venture is part Italian café/restaurant complex, part food market, with an incredible range of wine, cheese, meat, breads and seafood, sourced locally or flown in from Italy. Market daily 10am–11pm.

Essex Street Market 120 Essex St, between Rivington and Delancey sts ☎212 388 0449, ⓦessexstreetmarket .com; subway F to Delancey St, J, M, Z to Essex St; map p.83. Here, a kosher fish market, Latino grocers, Saxelby Cheesemongers, Roni-Sue's Chocolates and a Chinese greenmarket all live under one roof, reflecting the diversity of the neighbourhood. Mon–Sat 8am–7pm, Sun 10am–6pm.

★ **Murray's Cheese Shop** 254 Bleecker St at Cornelia St ☎212 243 3289, ⓦmurrayscheese.com; subway A, B, C, D, E, F, M to W 4th St, #1 to Christopher St; map pp.96–97. More than three hundred fresh cheeses and excellent panini sandwiches, all served by a knowledgeable staff. Mon–Sat 8am–8pm, Sun 10am–7pm.

Porto Rico Importing Company 201 Bleecker St, between Sixth Ave and MacDougal St ☎212 477 5421,

ⓦportorico.com; subway A, B, C, D, E, F, M to W 4th St; map p.96–97. An astounding 110 coffees (their speciality) and 140 varieties of tea on offer. The house blends are almost as good as many of the more expensive coffees. Mon–Fri 8am–9pm, Sat 9am–9pm, Sun noon–7pm.

Sahadi's 187 Atlantic Ave, between Clinton and Court sts, Brooklyn Heights ☎718 624 4550, ⓦsahadis.com; subway #4, #5 to Borough Hall; map p.215. Fully stocked Middle Eastern grocery store selling everything from Iranian pistachios to creamy home-made hummus since 1948. Mon–Sat 9am–7pm.

Titan Foods 25-56 31st St, between Astoria Blvd and 30th Ave, Queens ☎718 626 7771, ⓦtitanfood.com; subway N to Astoria Blvd; map p.244. Olympic-sized store for comestible Greek goods, including imported feta cheese, yogurt and stuffed vine leaves. Mon–Sat 8am–9pm, Sun 9am–8pm.

Warehouse Wines and Spirits 735 Broadway, between W 8th St and Waverly Place ☎212 982 7770, ⓦwarehousewinesandspirits.com; subway #6 to Astor Place; map p.88. The top place to get a buzz for your buck, with a wide selection and frequent reductions on popular lines; cava and prosecco for $5–7, decent reds and whites for under $10. Mon–Sat 9am–6pm.

Zabar's 2245 Broadway, at W 80th St ☎212 787 2000, ⓦzabars.com; subway #1 to 79th St; map p.183. Zabar's is still the city's pre-eminent gourmet shop. Choose from an astonishing variety of cheeses, olives, meats, salads, freshly baked breads and croissants and prepared dishes. Upstairs, shop for shiny kitchen and household implements. Avoid weekend afternoons, when the tour buses pull up outside and turn the modest-sized store into Dante's seventh circle of hell. Mon–Fri 8am–7.30pm, Sat 8am–8pm, Sun 9am–6pm.

SWEET TREATS

Dylan's Candy Bar 1011 Third Ave, at E 60th St ☎646 735 0078, ⓦdylanscandybar.com; subway N, Q, R to Lexington Ave/59th St; map p.123. Dylan Lauren's iconic New York sweet store, with giant multicoloured lolly pops, chocolate fountain, Belgian hot chocolate and all sorts of old-fashioned candy. Expensive but fun. Mon–Thurs 10am–9pm, Fri & Sat 10am–11pm, Sun 11am–9pm.

Economy Candy 108 Rivington St, between Essex and Ludlow sts ☎212 254 832, ⓦeconomycandy.com; subway F to Delancey St, J, M, Z to Essex St; map p.83. A sweet shop on the Lower East Side, selling mountains of sweets, chocs, nuts and dried fruit at low prices. Mon 10am–6pm, Tues–Fri & Sun 9am–6pm, Sat 10am–5pm.

Li-Lac 40 Eighth Ave at Jane St ☎212 924 2280, ⓦli-lacchocolates.com; subway A, C, E, L, #1, #2, #3 to 14th St; map pp.96–97. Li-Lac's delicious chocolates have been handmade since 1923. One of the city's best treats for

30

30

those with a sweet tooth – try the fresh fudge or hand-moulded Lady Liberties and Empire States. Mon–Thurs 11am–8pm, Fri & Sat 11am–9pm, Sun 11am–7pm.

M&M's World 1600 Broadway, at W 48th St ⬤ mmsworld .com; map p.141. Yes, a multi-storey emporium dedicated solely to M&Ms – check out the candy wall on the second floor, packed with thousands of milk, peanut and speciality chocolate dots. Daily 10am–midnight.

★ **Mast Brothers Chocolate** 111 N 3rd St, Williamsburg ⬤ 718 388 2625, ⬤ mastbrotherschocolate.com; subway L to Bedford Ave; map p.236. Once you've tried the handmade artisan chocolate here, you'll be utterly hooked; the delicate dark chocolate with almonds and sea salt is a mind-bending treat. Quality comes at a price – it's around $9 a bar. Daily noon–7pm.

MUSIC

The age of **music stores** is fading fast. Of the large chains, only J&R Music remains, as Virgin closed its doors in 2009. Nevertheless, a few excellent independent record stores survive in the East and West villages and, increasingly, in Brooklyn.

Academy Records & CDs 12 W 18th St, between Fifth and Sixth aves ⬤ 212 242 3000, ⬤ academy-records .com; subway F, M to 14th St; map p.114. Used, rare and/or hard-to-find CDs and LPs (especially classical, rock and jazz) are the Academy's forte. Mon–Wed & Sun 11am–7pm, Thurs–Sat 11am–8pm.

Downtown Music Gallery 13 Monroe St, between Catherine and Market sts ⬤ 212 473 0043, ⬤ downtown musicgallery.com; subway F to East Broadway; map p.71. New York's most comprehensive selection of avant-garde jazz, contemporary classical, progressive rock and related styles, on used CD, LP and DVD. Mon–Wed noon–6pm, Thurs–Sun noon–8pm.

Generation Records 210 Thompson St, between Bleecker and W 3rd sts ⬤ 212 254 1100, ⬤ generation records.com; subway A, B, C, D, E, F, M to W 4th St; map pp.96–97. The focus here is on hardcore, metal and punk with some indie. New CDs and vinyl upstairs, used goodies downstairs. It also gets many of the imports the others don't have, plus fine bootlegs. Mon–Thurs & Sun 11am–10pm, Fri & Sat 11am–11pm.

★ **Halcyon** 57 Pearl St, at Water St, DUMBO, Brooklyn ⬤ 718 260 9299, ⬤ halcyontheshop.com; subway F to York St; map p.215. A trusted source for dance music, but covers jazz to techno. It now carries drum & bass and import titles from defunct-yet-revered Lower East Side store Breakbeat Science, now an online-only operation. Radio shows, listening parties and a general air of music-nerd

community make this a top pick. Mon, Wed & Sat noon–8pm, Tues, Thurs & Fri noon–9pm, Sun noon–6pm.

House of Oldies 35 Carmine St, between Bleecker St and Bedford St ⬤ 212 243 0500, ⬤ houseofoldies.com; subway A, B, C, D, E, F, M to W 4th St, #1 to Houston St; map pp.96–97. Just what the name says – oldies but goldies of all kinds from the 1950s to the 1970s. Vinyl only. Tues–Sat 10am–5pm.

Jazz Record Center 236 W 26th St, Room 804, between Seventh and Eighth aves ⬤ 212 675 4480, ⬤ jazzrecordcenter.com; subway #1 to 28th St; map p.107. The place to come for rare or out-of-print jazz LPs from the dawn of recording through the bebop revolution, avant-jazz and beyond. They also have rare books, videos and memorabilia. Mon–Sat 10am–6pm.

Other Music 15 E 4th St, between Broadway and Lafayette St ⬤ 212 477 8150, ⬤ othermusic.com; subway #6 to Astor Place; map p.88. This homespun place is an excellent spot for "alternative" CDs, both old and new, that can otherwise be hard to find. Stocking less indie on vinyl than it once did, and now leaning toward experimental and electronica, the store retains the same ever-friendly and knowledgeable staff. Mon–Fri 11am–9pm, Sat noon–8pm, Sun noon–7pm.

★ **Permanent Records** 181 Franklin St, at Huron St, Greenpoint ⬤ 718 383 4083, ⬤ permanentrecords .info; subway G to Greenpoint Ave map p.236. Friendly little shop stocking new and used LPs, CDs, DVDs, singles

---

GREENMARKETS

Several days each week, long before sunrise, hundreds of farmers from Long Island, the Hudson Valley and parts of Pennsylvania and New Jersey set out in trucks to transport their fresh-picked bounty to New York City, where they are joined by bakers, cheesemakers and other artisans at **greenmarkets**. These are run by the city authorities, roughly one to four days a week, and are busiest from June to September. Usually, you'll find apple cider, jams and preserves, flowers and plants, maple syrup, fresh meat and fish, pretzels, cakes and breads, herbs, honey – not to mention occasional live-worm composts and basil ice cream.

To find the greenmarket nearest to you, call ⬤ 212 788 7476 or visit ⬤ grownyc.org; the largest and most popular is held in Union Square, at E 17th Street and Broadway, year-round on Monday, Wednesday, Friday and Saturday from 8am to 6pm.

and 12 inches in all genres – you'll find some classics in the $1 section. Daily noon–8pm.

Record Grouch 986 Manhattan Ave, between Huron and India sts, Greenpoint ☎718 389 0122, ⊛record grouch.blogspot.com; subway G to Greenpoint Ave;

map p.236. Another Greenpoint gem and a must for all vinyl aficionados: they buy, sell or trade records in all genres, for reasonable prices. And yes, owner Doug Pressman can be a bit of a grouch, it's part of the appeal. Daily noon–8pm.

SPORTS

There are quite a number of sporting-goods outlets in the city – from cookie-cutter chain stores and mom-and-pop cycle shops to multistorey sneaker pleasure-domes. Check them out for merchandise as well as for their wealth of information about sports in and around the city.

30

Bicycle Renaissance 430 Columbus Ave, at W 81st St ☎212 724 2350, ⊛bicyclerenaissance.com; subway B, C to 81st St; map p.183. A classy place with competitive prices, custom-bike building and usually, same-day service. Specialized and Cannondale bikes, and Carrera and Pinarello frames in stock. Mon–Fri 10.30am–7pm, Sat & Sun 10am–5pm.

BLADES West 156 W 72nd St, between Broadway and Columbus Ave ☎212 787 3911, ⊛blades.com; subway #1, #2, #3 to 72nd St; map p.183. Also downtown; see website. Rent or buy rollerblades, skateboards and the like. Handy for Central Park. Mon–Sat 10am–8pm, Sun 10am–7pm.

Eastern Mountain Sports (EMS) 530 Broadway, at Spring St ☎212 966 8730, ⊛ems.com; subway N, R to Prince St, #6 to Spring St; map p.64. Top-quality merchandise covering almost all outdoor sports, including skiing and kayaking. Mon–Sat 10am–9.30pm, Sun 11am–8pm.

Mason's Tennis Mart 56 E 53rd St, at Park Ave ☎212 755 5805, ⊛masonstennis.com; subway E, M to Fifth Ave-53rd St; map p.123. New York's last remaining tennis speciality store – they let you try out all rackets. Mon–Fri 10am–7pm, Sat 10am–6pm, Sun noon–6pm.

NBA Store 590 Fifth Ave, between W 47th and W 48th sts ☎212 515 6221, ⊛nba.com/nycstore; subway B, D, F, M to 47–50th St; map p.123. This is the temporary

location of New York's shrine to basketball (check the website for details on the new flagship store), a vast space selling merchandise for all the NBA teams, not just the much-maligned NY Knicks. Mon–Sat 10am–9pm, Sun 11am–7pm.

Niketown 6 E 57th St, at Fifth Ave ☎212 891 6453, ⊛nike.com; subway N, R to Fifth Ave-59th St; map p.123. You can enter this five-floor sports-shoe temple through an atrium in Trump Tower, or through the front entry lined with basketball-court hardwood. Then, you can join the masses and purchase Nike clothing and accessories at full price. Mon–Sat 10am–8pm, Sun 11am–7pm.

Super Runners Shop 1337 Lexington Ave, at E 89th St ☎212 369 6010, ⊛superrunnersshop.com; subway #4, #5, #6 to 86th St; map p.169. Multiple other locations. Experienced runners work at all seven locations; co-owner Gary Muhrcke won the first NYC Marathon in 1970. Mon–Fri 10am–7.30pm, Sat 10am–6pm, Sun 10am–5pm.

Yankees Clubhouse Shop 245 W 42nd St, between Seventh and Eighth aves ☎212 768 9555, ⊛newyork .yankees.mlb.com; subway N, R, Q, S, #1, #2, #3, #7 to Times Square-42nd St; map p.141. In case you want that celebrated "NY" logo on your clothing, this emporium has all things related to the legendary baseball team (2009 World Series winners). Mon–Sat 9am–midnight, Sun 10am–9pm.

TOYS

Disney Store 1540 Broadway, at E 58th St ☎212 626 2910, ⊛ disneystore.com; subway N, R, Q, S, #1, #2, #3, #7 to Times Square-42nd St; map p.141. Disney's flagship Times Square store is a paradise for kids, with Disney toys, clothes and all their favourite characters from Mickey Mouse and Pooh to Nemo and Buzz Lightyear. Daily 10am–1am.

★ **FAO Schwarz** 767 Fifth Ave, at E 58th St ☎212 644 9400, ⊛fao.com; subway N, R to Fifth Ave-59th St; map p.123. The classic New York toy store since 1862, with everything from a massive Barbie collection to a vintage Chevrolet pedal car that costs over $1000. Even adults will be bowled over by the size, choice and quality of goods on offer. You can play with lots of them, too, before you buy. Mon–Thurs 10am–7pm, Fri & Sat 10am–8pm, Sun 11am–6pm.

Lego Store 620 Fifth Ave, at W 50th St ☎212 245 5973, ⊛lego.com; subway B, D, F, M to 47–50th St-Rockefeller Center; map p.123. Landmark Rockefeller Center store, famed for its giant displays, florid murals and Lego models of New York. Mon–Sat 10am–8pm, Sun 11am–7pm.

Toys R Us 1514 Broadway, at W 44th St ☎646 366 8800, ⊛ toysrus.com; subway S, #1, #2, #3, #7 to Times Square-42nd St; map p.141. Colossal branch of the toy store chain, with a 60ft Ferris wheel inside, a life-sized animatronic T-Rex dinosaur and a 4000-square-foot Barbie house; it's filled with everything from toys to trains to video games. Mon–Fri & Sun 10am–10pm, Sat 10am–11pm.

NEW YORK MARATHON

Sports and outdoor activities

If measured by sheer number of teams and the coverage devoted to them, New York ranks as the number-one sports city in America. TV stations broadcast most regular-season games and all post-season games in the big four American team sports – baseball, football, basketball and ice hockey. Baseball is a vital part of New York culture; even tepid sports fans have some allegiance to either the Yankees or the Mets. Tickets can on occasion be hard to find (for certain games, impossible) and most don't come cheap. Still, nothing compares to the chill (or heat) of the arena, the vibrant green of the outfield grass, the anticipation that comes from pre-game introductions and the camaraderie of a home-field crowd.

Many participatory activities in the city are either free or fairly affordable and take place in all kinds of weather. New Yorkers are passionate about jogging – there are plenty of places to take a scenic run – and you can swim at local pools or borough beaches. However, even with the help of the Parks Department (❏311, ⓦnycgovparks .org) it can be hard to find facilities for some sports (like tennis), especially if you are not a city resident. To this end, many locals spend $50–100 (or more) a month to be members of private health clubs; you can sometimes get a free trial week or a discounted month at one of the major ones (the YMCAs, New York Sports Clubs, Crunch, etc), particularly if you use the address where you are staying in New York.

TICKETS AND VENUES

Tickets For most sporting events, these can be booked ahead with a credit card through Ticketmaster (❏1 800 745 3000, or ❏1 866 448 7849, ⓦticketmaster.com) and collected at the gate, though it's cheaper – and of course riskier for popular events – to try to pick up tickets on the night of the event, at the venue. You can also call or go to the stadium's box office and buy advance tickets. Numerous internet brokers sell secondary tickets (tickets that are resold by agencies or individuals); prices are set according to supply and demand, so can be cheaper or substantially more, depending on the importance of the game and the seats. Try ⓦstubhub.com, ⓦrazorgator.com and ⓦticket liquidator.com. If you can't score a ticket, consider watching the game at a sports bar (see p.334).

Barclays Center 620 Atlantic Ave at Flatbush, Downtown Brooklyn ❏917 618 6700, ⓦbarclayscenter .com; subway B, D, N, Q, R, #2, #3, #4, #5 to Atlantic Ave–Barclays Center, C to Lafayette Ave, G to Fulton St. The Brooklyn behemoth debuted in Sept 2012 and plays host to basketball's Nets; it will also be home to hockey's Islanders beginning with the 2015–16 season. Box office Mon–Fri 10am–6pm, Sat noon–4pm.

Citi Field 126th St and Roosevelt Ave, Willets Point, Queens ❏718 507 8499, ⓦnewyork.mets.mlb.com; subway #7 to Mets-Willets Point. The newish home of the New York Mets takes its cues from old-fashioned stadiums like Ebbets Field, former stomping ground of the departed Brooklyn Dodgers. Box office Mon–Fri 9am–5.30pm, Sat 9am–3pm, later on game days; closed off-season.

Madison Square Garden Seventh Ave, between 31st and 33rd sts ❏212 465 6741, ⓦthegarden.com;

subway A, C, E, #1, #2, #3 to 34th St-Penn Station. Hockey's Rangers and basketball's Knicks are the primary tenants of this famous, just-renovated arena which even has extra seating on suspended bridges high above the action (see p.142). Box office Mon–Sat 9am–6pm.

MetLife Stadium Off routes 3, 17 and New Jersey Turnpike exit 16W, East Rutherford, New Jersey ❏201 935 8500, ⓦmetlife.com. Regular buses from Port Authority Bus Terminal on 42nd St and Eighth Ave. Box office Mon–Fri 9am–5pm.

Nassau Veterans Memorial Coliseum 1255 Hempstead Turnpike, Uniondale, Long Island ❏516 794 9300, ⓦnassaucoliseum.com. Not very accessible other than by car. If you don't have your own transportation, take the Long Island Railroad to Hempstead, then bus #N70, #N71 or #N72 from Hempstead bus terminal, one block away. Another option, which may be safer at night, is to catch the LIRR to Westbury or Hempstead and take a cab (5–10min) to the stadium. Box office Mon–Fri 9.30am–4.45pm.

Prudential Center 165 Mulberry St, between Edison Place and Lafayette St, Newark, New Jersey ❏973 757 6000 or ❏757 6600, ⓦprucenter.com. The home of the New Jersey Devils is just two blocks from Newark Penn Station, easily accessible by NJ Transit, Amtrak and PATH trains from Manhattan. Box office Mon–Fri 11am–6pm.

Yankee Stadium 161st St and River Ave, South Bronx ❏718 293 6000, ⓦnewyork.yankees.mlb.com; subway B, D, #4 to 161st St. Yankee Stadium is right next door to where the old one was; get to the game early and visit Monument Park, where all the Yankee greats are memorialized. Box office Mon–Fri 9am–5pm, Sat 10am–4pm.

31

BASEBALL

The two Major League Baseball (MLB) teams – **New York Mets** (which compete in the East Division of the National League) and **New York Yankees** (East Division of the American League) – play for what seems the better part of the year; try to make time to see a game if your visit coincides with a homestand by either. Spring Training exhibition games take place in Florida from late Feb to late March, with the regular season (in New York) beginning right after and running through Sept; Oct is playoff time. The organizations also have minor-league squads that play in the area.

NEW YORK YANKEES

Reciting the achievements of the Yankees (also known as "The Bronx Bombers") over the decades can get tedious. They are the team with the most World Series titles (27 up

to the end of 2012) and they have been in the playoffs more than half of the past ninety seasons: an almost-unheard-of success rate for major-league sports. Their major rivals are the Boston Red Sox; bitter feelings can be traced back to

LOCAL BASEBALL HISTORY

In the early 1840s, the **New York Knickerbocker Club** played "base ball" near Madison Square in Manhattan, before moving to Elysian Fields, across the Hudson River in Hoboken, New Jersey. There, on June 26, 1846, they laid down the basic rules (the "Knickerbocker Rules") of the game of baseball, as it is played to this day. For half the twentieth century, New York was home to three Major League Baseball (MLB) teams: the **New York Giants** and the **Brooklyn Dodgers**, who represented the National League, and the **New York Yankees**, who represented the American League. Additionally, in the years before MLB was integrated, the Negro League had several notable teams based in the city. The almost-decade between 1947 and 1956 was the golden age of baseball in New York, with a Yankees team first led by Joe DiMaggio, then by Mickey Mantle, steamrolling their opponents, and barrier-breaking heroes (not to mention great players) like Jackie Robinson and Roy Campanella playing for the Dodgers. This period ended abruptly in 1957, when the Giants and Dodgers bolted to California at the end of the season – though the city has mostly forgotten the Giants, old-time Brooklyn residents are still scarred by the loss of the Dodgers. New York was bereft of a National League franchise until the Mets arrived at the Polo Grounds in 1962, moving two years later to Shea Stadium and, most recently (on the same site as Shea), Citi Field, in Flushing, Queens.

31

1920, when former Red Sox star pitcher Babe Ruth was traded to the Yankees. If you can get a ticket to see a game between the two, or a "Subway Series" tilt, when the Bombers face their cross-town adversaries, the Mets, in June interleague play, you won't be disappointed. Tickets start close to $20 for the bleachers (stands) and range up to $300 for the best seats (see p.389).

NEW YORK METS

The Mets have often been regarded as the ugly bridesmaids – or, perhaps more optimistically, the loveable losers – of the city; their last championship, in 1986 (one of two in their fifty-year history), feels awfully long ago. Still, they have some exciting young pitchers and prospects, plenty of die-hard fans and an attractive stadium, Citi Field, to showcase the team. Most tickets cost between $15 and $125 (see p.389).

MINOR-LEAGUE BASEBALL

Attending a minor-league baseball game is great fun. Not only do you get the chance to see up-and-coming players compete with those hanging on for one last shot at The Show, but the crowds are smaller, the seats are better and tickets much cheaper. The season lasts for the better part of the year: the regular season runs from April to the end of Sept, and the post-season series takes place in Oct.

Staten Island Yankees ☎718 720 9265, ⊚staten island.yankees.milb.com. The first new baseball franchise in New York in several decades debuted in 1999: they play in the Class A New York–Penn League (June–early Sept). Catch them at the Richmond County Bank Ballpark at St George, within a two-minute walk of the Staten Island ferry terminal. Tickets $14–16.

Brooklyn Cyclones ☎718 449 8497, ⊚brooklyn cyclones.com. After a 43-year absence, baseball returned to Brooklyn in 2001 in the form of the Cyclones, an affiliate of the Mets which plays in the same New York–Penn League as the Staten Island Yankees. The beautiful, oceanside stadium (MCU Park) is at the former Steeplechase Park in Coney Island. Tickets $9–17.

AMERICAN FOOTBALL

The **National Football League (NFL)** regular season stretches from September till the end of December. New York's teams are the **Jets** and the **Giants**; both play at the New Meadowlands Stadium, which is, in fact, not in New York at all – it's part of the Meadowlands Sports Complex in New Jersey. **Tickets** for both teams are always officially sold out well in advance, but you can often pick up tickets (legally) from secondary-broker websites such as ⊚stubhub.com (see p.389).

NEW YORK GIANTS

The Giants have a long and proud history dating back to the 1920s, having won eight NFL titles (including four Super Bowl championships), most recently in 2012. Due to the long waiting list for season tickets, the Giants (☎201 935 8222, ⊚giants.com) actually encourage current ticket-holders to sell their unused seats to people further down on the list; you have to join the waiting list (by mail) to have a shot at these tickets. Tickets at MetLife Stadium start at $85 (see p.389).

NEW YORK JETS

Founded in 1960 as part of the upstart American Football League, the Jets (☎973 549 4600, ⊚newyorkjets.com), originally known as the Titans, share MetLife Stadium with the Giants. They've endured a lot of lean times (really, most of their existence) and are still trying to get back to their first Super Bowl since 1969, when they beat the heavily favoured Baltimore Colts 16–7. Secondary websites offer the best deals on tickets, but they'll still be quite pricey (see p.389).

PROFESSIONAL BASKETBALL

The **National Basketball Association (NBA)** regular season begins in Nov and runs till the end of April. The two professional teams in the New York area are the **New York Knicks** (Knickerbockers), who play at Madison Square Garden, and the **Brooklyn Nets**, whose venue is the Barclays Center. There is also a **women's professional team** in New York, the **WBNA Liberty**; tickets to see them play are easier to come by.

NEW YORK KNICKS

It hasn't been easy being a Knicks (⊕nba.com/knicks) fan in the new millennium, even though the venerable franchise is one of the most recognizable in any sport. Madison Square Garden – despite current renovations – is one of the less attractive stadiums in North America; their last championship win was way back in 1973; the team suffered through nine consecutive losing seasons from 2001 to 2010 (finally breaking that streak in the 2010–11 season); and after all that, tickets are virtually impossible to come by – and astronomically expensive when procured. At least these days, Carmelo Anthony and his cohort have brought the buzz back to the arena. Expect list prices to start at $70.

BROOKLYN NETS

The Nets (⊕nba.com/nets) began life in 1967 as the New Jersey Americans. Led by legendary Julius Erving ("Dr J"), they won two championships (1974 and 1976) playing on Long Island before joining the NBA. With a resurgence in the early 2000s, they made the finals twice in a row, and once again seem to be on the uptick – thanks in no small part to billionaire owner Mikhail Prokhorov's willingness to spend whatever it takes. Nets tickets are easier to come by than for the Knicks, but the team is not shrinking from taking on its Hudson River rivals in the battle for city supremacy – at least on a marketing and salary-expense level. Tickets at the Barclays Center (see p.389) start at $30.

NEW YORK LIBERTY

The **Women's National Basketball Association (WNBA)** season opens when the NBA season ends and runs through the summer to its playoffs in Sept. The league jumped off in 1997, with the New York team, the Liberty, finishing as runners-up for the title; despite making the playoffs almost every year and appearing in four finals, the Liberty have yet to win the championship. Games are at Madison Square Garden, and prices are low compared with those for the Knicks. You can usually get a ticket; call ☎ 1 212 465 6766, go to ⊕wnba.com/liberty, or pick some up at Madison Square Garden (see p.389). Ticket prices: $11–250.

31

COLLEGE BASKETBALL

The college basketball season begins in Nov and ends with "**March Madness**", in which conference tournaments are followed by a 68-team competition to select a national champion. **The NCAA (National Collegiate Athletic Association)** Tournament may be the most exciting, eagerly anticipated sporting event in the US. **Madison Square Garden** (see p.389) provides the setting for pre-season tournaments and the semifinals and finals of the **National Invitational Tournament**, which takes the best of the rest that don't make it to the NCAA Tournament. Metropolitan-area

FIVE NEW YORK SPORTS LEGENDS

It's impossible to set criteria by which to choose the five most legendary New York sports figures. With sincere apologies to Derek Jeter, Yogi, The Mick (they can't all be Yankees, can they?) and a whole host of others (John McEnroe, Tom Seaver, every member of the 1955 Brooklyn Dodgers), here's a starter list to get the ball rolling, so to speak.

Joe DiMaggio (1914–1999) Yankees Hall of Fame centerfielder whose career was highlighted by his untouchable 56-game hitting streak in 1941. Nicknames: The Yankee Clipper, Joltin' Joe.

Walt Frazier (1945–) Current Knicks television announcer was their star point-guard for their titles in 1970 and 1973; worth catching on the tube for his zany fashion sense and zanier use of language. Nickname: Clyde.

Mark Messier (1961–) The longtime (Canadian-born) Edmonton Oiler was the captain, best player and emotional leader of the Rangers' hockey team when they won their only Stanley Cup of the last seventy years, in 1994. Nicknames: The Moose, The Messiah.

Joe Namath (1943–) Not the best quarterback of all time, but the one with the most swagger and style; guaranteed the Jets victory in Super Bowl III (their only one), then backed it up on the field. Nicknames: Broadway Joe, Joe Willie.

George Herman "Babe" Ruth (1895–1948) Came to the Yankees from the Red Sox in one of the most lopsided deals in history; went on to hold the all-time home-run title for around forty years and the single-season record nearly as long. The greatest baseballer of all-time? Nicknames: The Babe, The Bambino, The Sultan of Swat.

STREET BASKETBALL

Free of the image-building and marketing that makes the NBA so superficial, and the by-the-books officiating of the NCAA, **street basketball** presents the game in its purest and, arguably, most attractive form. New York City is the capital of playground hoops, with a host of asphalt legends: Lew Alcindor (Kareem Abdul-Jabbar), Wilt Chamberlain, Julius Erving and Stephon Marbury are a few who have made it to the pros, though others who never made the transition, like Earl "The Goat" Manigault, were said to be just as skilled. If you want to play yourself, **Hoops Nation** by Chris Ballard is an invaluable (if, by now, somewhat dated) guide to basketball courts in the five boroughs (and across the nation) and a useful primer in the etiquette of pickup ball; the courts in **Rucker Park** (155th St and Eighth Ave in Harlem) are the most celebrated, though the ones right outside the **West 4th Street** courts (Sixth Ave between West 3rd and West 4th sts) are likely more convenient to stop by for a look. Scout out the next NBA superstar – or watch for current ones dropping by for an off-season tune-up.

31

colleges pursuing hoop dreams include NYU (Manhattan; ⓦgonyuathletics.com), Columbia (Manhattan; ⓦgocolumbialions.com), St John's (Queens; ⓦredstormsports.com), Fordham (Bronx; ⓦfordhamsports.com), Wagner (Staten Island; ⓦwagnerathletics.com), St Francis (Brooklyn; ⓦsfuathletics.com) and Long Island (Brooklyn; ⓦliuathletics.com) universities; it's easy enough to get tickets for games on any of the university athletics websites.

ICE HOCKEY

There are two professional **hockey** teams in New York: the **Rangers**, who play at Madison Square Garden, and the **Islanders**, whose venue is transitioning from Nassau Coliseum on Long Island to the Barclays Center in Brooklyn. In addition, the **New Jersey Devils** play out at the Prudential Center in Newark. All three compete in the Atlantic Division of the Eastern Conference of the National Hockey League (NHL). The season lasts throughout the winter and into early spring, when the playoffs take place.

NEW YORK RANGERS

One of the six original NHL teams, the Rangers (☎ 212 465 6000, ⓦ rangers.nhl.com) were founded in 1926 and won the Stanley Cup – awarded to the winner of the playoffs – three times in the following fifteen years. According to hockey lore, giddy from their 1940 playoff-finals victory over the Toronto Maple Leafs, the Madison Square Garden owners paid off their $3 million mortgage and celebrated by burning the deed in Lord Stanley's cup – an act of desecration that provoked a curse upon the franchise and its fans. The Rangers ended their 54-year championship drought in 1994, but this has been followed by another long period of mediocre performance. Tickets at Madison Square Garden (see p.389) cost $50–370.

NEW YORK ISLANDERS

Founded in 1972, the Islanders (☎ 1 800 882 4753, ⓦ islanders.nhl.com) were fortunate enough to string together their four Stanley Cups in consecutive years

(1980–83) and thus qualify as a bona fide hockey dynasty. Since then, however, it's been mostly downhill. Tickets at Nassau Coliseum (see p.389) cost $30–250, though starting in the 2015–16 season, the team will be playing at Brooklyn's Barclays Center.

NEW JERSEY DEVILS

The nomadic New Jersey Devils franchise (ⓦ devils.nhl.com) was founded in 1974 as the Kansas City Scouts and moved to New Jersey (after a brief stint as the Colorado Rockies in Denver) in 1982. A succession of mediocre seasons was interrupted when the Devils beat the heavily favoured Detroit Red Wings in four straight games to win the 1995 Stanley Cup. They regained the Cup in 2003; since then, the team has frequently put together strong seasons but been disappointing in the playoffs – and has gone through an almost revolving door of coaches. Tickets are $30–400 and available at the Prudential Center (see p.389).

SOCCER

The game of **soccer** (European football) continues to grow in popularity in America, thanks in part to World Cup results and the importing of some international (if usually aged) stars to the professional league, which has been expanding and increasing its exposure. Though soccer coverage is not as extensive in the US as it is abroad, it's not too hard to catch on TV and in sports bars (see box, p.334); in the city, interest is likely to grow with the introduction of a new team, the expansion New York City FC (ⓦ nycfc.com), which came together from a joint venture between baseball's Yankees and the Premier League's Manchester City. They are likely to begin playing in 2015, though at time of writing their home venue was yet to be determined.

NEW YORK RED BULLS
The New York Red Bulls (☎1 877 727 6223, ⓦnewyork
redbulls.com), who play at the purpose-built Red Bull Arena in
Harrison, New Jersey, are for now the metropolitan area's sole

Major League Soccer representatives. Their best-known
players are probably international veterans Thierry Henry
(France) and Tim Cahill (Australia). The MLS season runs from
April to Nov. Ticket prices: $23–73.

HORSE RACING

Aqueduct 110-00 Rockaway Blvd, South Ozone Park,
Queens ☎718 641 4700, ⓦnyra.com/aqueduct;
subway A to Aqueduct North Conduit Ave or Aqueduct
Racetrack. This spot in Queens has racing from late Oct to
April. It's also allied with a new casino, Resort Worlds
Casino New York City (ⓦrwnewyork.com), a slot-machine
heaven. Racetrack admission is free; valet parking at the

casino entrance costs $10 weekdays, $20 weekends.
Belmont 2150 Hempstead Turnpike, Elmont ☎516 488
6000, ⓦnyra.com. Elmont, Long Island, is home to the
Belmont Stakes (held in June), one of the three races in
which 3-year-olds compete for the Triple Crown. Belmont is
open late April to July and Sept to Oct; tickets range from $3
to $5 (more for the Belmont Stakes). Valet parking costs $5.

TENNIS

US Open Championships The top US tennis event of the
year; held late Aug/early Sept at the National Tennis Center
in Flushing Meadows–Corona Park, in Queens. Tickets go
on sale the first week or two of June at the Billie Jean King
National Tennis Center's box office (☎718 760 6200,
ⓦusopen.org; Mon–Fri 9am–5pm), though you can pre-
buy through Ticketmaster (☎1 800 745 3000 or ☎1 866
673 6849, ⓦticketmaster.com). Promenade-level seats at
the stadium cost $50–70 (better seats can cost several
hundred dollars) for evening games, while day-passes start
at $56 (those are grounds only and don't include Arthur
Ashe Stadium access; day-tickets for that start around $75);
though big-name matches are frequently saved for the
main stadium in the evening, it's plenty of fun to go during
the day and wander to the outer courts, where you can get

very close to the action. If events are sold out, keep trying
up to the day of the event because corporate tickets are
often returned.
Playing tennis There's not a great deal of court space in
New York, so finding an affordable one can be tough. For
information on all city courts, including those in Central Park
(☎212 360 8133 for permits, ☎212 280 0205 for
reservations; best to reserve ahead), go to ⓦnyc.gov/parks;
the ones at Prospect Park are also nice (open year-round, with
a bubble cover in winter). Most city parks require a permit to
play, which runs $200 for the year (seniors $20, under 18
$10), though you can buy one-off single sessions for $15; the
courts are open April–Nov. Hudson River Park has three
decent courts that are free to all and work on a first-come,
first-served basis (West St between Canal and Houston).

31

BEACHES

New York's **beaches** aren't worth a trip to the city in and of
themselves, but they can be a cool summer escape from
Manhattan. Most are only a MetroCard ride away.
Brighton Beach Brooklyn; subway B, Q to Brighton
Beach. Technically the same stretch as Coney Island Beach,
but less crowded and populated mainly by the local Russian
community. Stop on Brighton Beach Ave at one of the many
Russian supermarkets to get picnic supplies.
Coney Island Beach Brooklyn; subway B, D, F, Q to
Coney Island-Stillwell Ave. One of the city's most popular
bathing spots, jam-packed on summer weekends. The
Atlantic here is only moderately dirty, and there's a good,
reliable onshore breeze.

Jacob Riis Park Queens; subway #2, #5 to Flatbush
Ave, then #Q35 bus, or A to Rockaway Park, then #Q35
or #Q22. Good sandy stretches and very pristine, though
damage from Hurricane Sandy in Oct 2012 was extensive.
Orchard Beach The Bronx; subway #6 to Pelham Bay
Park, then bus #Bx5 or #Bx12 to Orchard Beach. This
manmade beach is a wide, crescent-shaped strand, fronted by
a decaying pavilion and lots of volleyball and basketball courts.
Rockaway Beach Queens; subway A, C to any stop
along the beach. This seven-mile strip has historically
been the best for surf – so good that the Ramones wrote a
song about it. The beach reopened in May 2013 after
Hurricane Sandy ripped up the boardwalk.

CYCLING

New York has more than 100 miles of **cycle paths**; those in Central Park, Riverside Park, Hudson River Park and the East
River Promenade are among the nicest. Three sources do an excellent job of providing specific cycling routes and maps,
laws and regulations, and other relevant info: the bike-advocacy organization Transportation Alternatives (☎212 629
8080, ⓦtransalt.org), which has some good maps; the New York City Department of City Planning (ⓦnyc.gov), which has
a wealth of information available as part of their BND (Bicycle Network Development) project; and ⓦnycbikemaps.com,
with extensive bike maps for all five boroughs, information on cycling events and links to other relevant sites. Perhaps most
exciting, a new **bike share program**, shepherded by Mayor Bloomberg, is making bike transport much more accessible

JAMMERS AND GOOGLIES

There are a lot of small-time organized sports that competitors take plenty seriously, even if they don't attract the attention that the major teams and sports do. Going to watch can be fun, not to mention inexpensive and accessible.

Gotham Girls Roller Derby ☎888 830 2253, ⓦgothamgirlsrollerderby.com. Four borough teams (Brooklyn Bombshells, Queens of Pain, Manhattan Mayhem and the Bronx Gridlock; the players' nicknames are just as – if not more – colourful) compete against one another in this fast-paced, bruising skate-fest; tickets are around $20 and take

place in venues around the city.
Commonwealth Cricket League ⓦcommon wealthcric.com. The biggest cricket league in the city plays in the newly renovated fields of Van Cortlandt Park's parade grounds (see p.257). Given a multimillion-dollar makeover in 2013, the new complex brings cricket to the Bronx.

31

for New Yorkers and visitors (see below). By law, you must wear a **helmet** when riding your bike on the street. Most bike stores rent bicycles by the day or hour. Refer to websites such as ⓦ bikenewyork.org for a list of rental shops.

USEFUL CONTACTS

Bicycle Habitat 244 Lafayette St ☎212 431 3315, ⓦbicyclehabitat.com; subway B, D, F, M to Broadway-Lafayette, N, R to Prince St, #6 to Spring St. Known for an excellent repair service, they also offer rentals, tune-ups and advice. Mon–Wed & Sat 10am–7pm, Thurs & Fri 8am–8pm, Sun 10am–6pm.

Citi Bike ☎855 245 3311, ⓦcitibikenyc.com. This new initiative involves hiring bikes from the thousands locked up at various locations around the city. You can either be a member ($95/year) and use a bike free of charge for short rides (45min; longer spells incur extra charges), unlocking it with your personalized key, or you can just get day ($9.95) or week passes ($25), which will give you a code to access the bike (30min maximum for each ride). Bikes can be returned to any station – check the website for a map of kiosks with available bikes and parking slots.

Five Borough Bike Club ☎347 688 2925, ⓦ5bbc.org. This club organizes rides throughout the year, including the Montauk Century, where riders can choose routes varying between 65 and 140 miles from New York to Montauk, Long Island.

New York Cycle Club ⓦnycc.org. A two-thousand-member club that offers many different rides every weekend and some weekdays.

SBR 203 W 58th St between Seventh Ave and Broadway ☎212 399 3999, ⓦsbrshop.com; subway A, B, C, D, #1 to 59th St-Columbus Circle, N, R to Seventh Ave-57th St. Besides cycling, running and swimming gear, they offer mechanical services and private cycling coaching. Central Park Bike Tours (☎212 541 8759, ⓦcentralparkbiketours.com), within the shop, rents out bikes by the hour or day ($15–50). Mon–Sat 9am–8pm, Sun 11am–6pm.

BOATING

Chelsea Piers ☎212 336 6777 or ☎212 627 1825, ⓦsail-nyc.com. Join the crew of the *Adirondack* and *America*, two beautiful wooden schooners, which sail from Pier 62. During the 2hr tour of lower New York Harbor, passengers can take the wheel, help hoist the sails or just enjoy the surroundings; there's also *The Manhattan*, a yacht that sails from here. Sightseeing, jazz and sunset cruises are available throughout the week; check the website for schedule and prices (a basic 1.5hr yacht sightseeing sail is $42; 2hr schooner trip is $64).

Downtown Boathouse Hudson River Pier 40, 72nd St and Pier 96 (Clinton Cove) at 56th St ⓦdowntown boathouse.org. Free kayaks and canoes can be hired May–Oct at weekends (9am–6pm, shorter hours at 72nd St);

also available on weekdays at Pier 96 June–Aug (5–7pm) and Thurs (same hours) at Pier 40.

Loeb Boathouse East Side of Central Park, between 74th and 75th sts ☎212 517 2233, ⓦthecentral parkboathouse.com. Rowboats and kayaks for rent April–Nov (daily 10am–dusk). Rates are $12 for the first hour, $2.50 per additional 15min, plus $20 deposit.

Seaport Museum South Street Seaport ☎212 748 8786, ⓦsouthstreetseaportmuseum.org. A number of historic ships are docked at the Seaport Museum harbour; though many are somewhat endangered and either being repaired or in need of repair, the 125-year-old *Pioneer* schooner does public sails.

BOWLING

Brooklyn Bowl 61 Wythe Ave, between 11th and 12th sts, Williamsburg, Brooklyn ☎718 963 3369, ⓦbrooklynbowl.com; subway L to Bedford Ave. As much a

nightspot (see p.345) as a bowling alley, in a renovated industrial warehouse; upscale bar food by the Blue Ribbon group and lots of borough-brewed beers too. Lanes

$20–25/30min, shoe rental $4.95. Mon–Fri 6pm–2am (sometimes later on Fri), Sat noon–4am, Sun noon–2am. **Frames** 550 Ninth Ave at 40th St, second floor in Port Authority ☎212 268 6909, ⓦframesnyc.com; subway A, C, E to 42nd St-Port Authority, or N, Q, R, #1, #2, #3, #7 to Times Square-42nd St. If you desire a different location in

which to bowl, look no further than this full-service, modern alley in Port Authority Bus Terminal (see p.143). Mon–Thurs $7 per game per person before 5pm, $10.50 evenings; Sat & Sun $10.50; shoe rental $6. Mon–Wed noon–midnight, Thurs noon–1am, Fri noon–3am, Sat 11am–3am, Sun 11am–11pm.

FISHING

Sometimes the amount of concrete in New York can make you forget that the city is actually surrounded by water, much of it teeming with **fish**. Call the New York State Department of Health's Environmental Health Information line (☎1 800 458 1158) for the latest tips on clean water and if you should toss your catch in the frying pan or back into the current.

Big City Fishing Pier 25 (N Moore St), Pier 46 (Charles St), Pier 63 (W 23rd St), Pier 84 (W 44th St) ☎212 627 2020, ⓦhudsonriverpark.org. Hudson River Park Trust runs this free summer programme at 1pm until early Sept on different days: Tues at pier 46, Thurs at Pier 25 and Sun at piers 63 and 84. The trust

provides free fishing rods, reels and bait (as well as instruction) on a first-come, first-served basis, with a 30min limit when others are waiting. Common species caught include American eel, striped bass, black sea bass, fluke and snapper – all fish are returned to the river at the end of the day.

31

GOLF

Manhattan has no public **golf courses**, though there is a two-level driving range at Chelsea Piers (☎212 336 6400). Recommended among those in the outer boroughs are the following, all of which are subject to low and generally standardized prices (if you don't have your own clubs, you can rent); full information is available at ⓦnycparks.org, ⓦamericangolf.com, ⓦgolfnyc.com and ⓦnycteetimes.com. The fee for eighteen holes on weekdays before noon is $39, $31 thereafter; weekend rates are $48 before noon, $39 thereafter. Non-residents must pay an additional fee of $8. The biggest issue you'll face is pace of play; it's frequently slow once you're out on the links, with rounds of up to six hours possible.

Dyker Beach Golf Course 86th St and Seventh Ave, Dyker Heights, Brooklyn ☎718 836 9722; subway R to 86th St. Noted for its striking views of the Verrazano Narrows, Dyker is also one of the more convenient local courses, just a few blocks from the subway.
La Tourette 1001 Richmond Hill Rd, Staten Island

☎718 351 1889. An excellent place to play a round; very well kept, and with a driving range.
Van Cortlandt Park Golf Course Van Cortlandt Park S and Bailey Ave, Bronx ☎718 543 4595; subway #1 to Van Cortlandt Park or #4 to Woodlawn. The oldest eighteen-hole public golf course in the country.

HEALTH AND FITNESS: POOLS, GYMS AND BATHS

You can join one of the city's **recreation centres** (ⓦnycparks.org) for $100–150 per year (ages 18–54), $25 (seniors) or free (under 18). All have gym facilities; some hold fitness and other classes, and most have an indoor and/or outdoor pool.

New York Spa Castle 131-10 Eleventh Ave, College Point, Queens ☎718 939 6300, ⓦnyspacastle.com; subway #7 to Main St-Flushing, then walk to shuttle bus at Union St and 39th Ave. If the Russian baths (see p.396) are too old-school for your tastes, hit this thoroughly modern spot out in Queens for saunas, massages and even an outdoor pool (open in winter, too). Towels, soap and uniforms are provided, but

you'll need to bring a swimsuit and beach towel for the outdoor pool. Weekdays $35, weekends $45. Daily 6am–midnight, though some areas have more limited hours.
Riverbank State Park ⓦ 145th St and Riverside Drive ☎212 694 3600. Beautiful facility built on top of a waste refinery in Harlem. Tennis courts, an outdoor track, an ice-skating rink (Nov–March; $5; skate rental $6) and several

---

TOP 5 SPACES FOR ACTIVE TYPES

Note that these are a selective and subjective list of (mainly) outdoor highlights at each park.
Central Park For running, biking, paddling and boating (see p.110).
Chelsea Piers For hockey, rock climbing and volleyball (see p.109).
Hudson River Park For boating, biking and skateboarding (see p.104).
Prospect Park For Frisbee, hiking and horseback riding (see p.225).
Van Cortlandt Park For cricket, cross-country running and fishing (see p.257).

FIVE MINI GOLF COURSES

If it seems too much trouble to play a round of eighteen on the links, consider the fun – and family-friendly – alternative of a game of mini-golf.

Flushing Meadows Golf Center Flushing Meadows–Corona Park (daily 8am–midnight; $8.75, under 13 $6.75; T 718 271 8182).

Governors Island Summers only (Sat & Sun 10am–6pm; free).

Pier 25 Hudson River Park, Tribeca (mid-April–May daily noon–6pm, June–mid-Nov 10am–8 or 10pm, depending on weather; $5, under 14 $4; T 212 766 1104, W pier25.com).

Randalls Island Golf Center 1 Randalls Island (Mon 10.30am–11pm, Tues–Sun 7am–11pm; $9, under 13 $7; T 212 427 5689, W randallsislandgolfcenter.com).

Rocket Park Mini Golf New York Hall of Science, Flushing Meadows Corona Park (April–Dec Mon–Fri 9.30am–4.30pm, Sat & Sun 10am–5.30pm; 6, ages 2–17 $5; T 718 699 0005).

indoor facilities including a roller-skating rink ($1.50; skate rental $6) and Olympic-sized swimming pool ($2, seniors and ages 5–15 $1). Park admission is free. Daily 6am–11pm.

Russian & Turkish Baths 268 E 10th St between First Ave and Ave A T 212 674 9250, W russianturkishbaths.com. A neighbourhood landmark, with saunas (the Russian one is intensely hot), steam rooms (the aromatherapy room is the pick of these) and an ice-cold pool for a bracing change-of-pace, as well as a seasonal sun deck, massage parlour and a juice bar/restaurant. Free towel, robe, slippers and shorts are provided; admission $35, plus an additional fee for massages and other extras. Highly recommended. Mon, Tues, Thurs & Fri noon–10pm, Wed 10am–10pm, Sat 9am–10pm, Sun 8am–10pm; men only Thurs till 5pm & Sun till 2pm; women only Wed till 2pm; co-ed otherwise (shorts are mandatory and dispensed on-site if you need a pair).

HORSERIDING

Jamaica Bay Riding Academy 7000 Shore Parkway, Brooklyn T 718 531 8949, W horsebackride.com; subway B, D, Q to Sheepshead Bay then 5min taxi ride. Trail riding, both Western and English, around the eerie landscape of Jamaica Bay. $37 for a guided 40min ride; lessons $85/hr. Roughly 9am–5pm.

Kensington Stables 51 Caton Place at E 8th St, Prospect Park, Brooklyn T 718 972 4588, W kensingtonstables.com; subway F to Fort Hamilton Pkwy. Horses and classes available for rides along Prospect Park's 3.5-mile bridle path for $37/hr. Private lessons are $34/30min, $57/hr. Daily 10am–sunset.

ICE-SKATING

New York's freezing winter weather makes for good **ice-skating**, and there are plenty of parks in which to do it. Just don't try it on any old pond or lake: the ice can be deceptively thin.

Citi Pond at Bryant Park T 212 661 6640, W thepondatbryantpark.com; subway B, D, F, M, #7 to 42nd St-Bryant Park. Skate in a busy, scenic and (just) slightly less touristy spot than Rockefeller Center (free, rental $14). Nov–Feb Sun–Thurs 8am–10pm, Fri & Sat 8am–midnight.

Lasker Rink 110th St, Central Park T 212 534 7639, W laskerrink.com. This lesser-known ice rink is at the northern end of Central Park and is used as a pool in summer. Much cheaper ($7, under 12 $4, skate rental $6) but less accessible than the Wollman Rink. Nov–March hours vary, but usually Mon–Thurs 10am–3.45pm, Fri 10am–11pm, Sat 1–11pm, Sun 12.30–4.30pm.

Rockefeller Center Ice Rink between 49th and 50th sts, off Fifth Ave T 212 332 7654, W rinkatrockcenter.com; subway B, D, F, M to 47–50th St-Rockefeller Center. It's a quintessential New York scene, lovely to look at but with long queues and high-ish prices ($25, under 11 $12, rentals $10). Oct–April Mon–Thurs 8.30am–10.30pm, Fri 8.30am–midnight, Sat 8am–midnight, Sun 8am–10.30pm.

Sky Rink Pier 61 T 212 336 6100, W chelseapiers.com; subway C, E to 23rd St. Ice-skate year-round at this indoor rink at Chelsea Piers ($10, rentals $5). Mon 1.30–5pm, Tues & Thurs 3–5pm, Fri 1.30–5.20pm, Sat & Sun 1–3.50pm.

Wollman Rink 62nd St, Central Park T 212 439 6900, W wollmanskatingrink.com. Lovely rink ($17, under 12 $6, rentals $7), where you can skate against the backdrop of the lower Central Park skyline – incredibly impressive at night. Nov–March Mon & Tues 10am–2.30pm, Wed & Thurs 10am–10pm, Fri & Sat 10am–11pm, Sun 10am–9pm.

JOGGING AND RUNNING

Jogging is still very much the number-one fitness pursuit in the city. The most popular venues are Central Park, Hudson

River Park and the Battery City Esplanade. A favourite circuit in Central Park is the 1.58 miles around the reservoir; just make sure you jog in the right direction along with everyone else: counterclockwise. For company on your runs, contact the New York Road Runners (☎212 860 4455, ⓦnyrr.org), who sponsor many races and fun runs every year.

POOL AND PING PONG

Along with bars and nightclubs, a good option for an evening in Manhattan is to play **pool** or **ping pong**. You can frequently find dive bars with pool tables; ping pong requires a bit more searching – although in addition to a few dedicated clubs, some outdoor places also have tables for public use (like Bryant Park, where it's free; see p.125).

Fat Cat 75 Christopher St, at Seventh Ave ☎212 675 6056, ⓦfatcatmusic.org; subway #1 to Christopher St-Sheridan Square. A somewhat dingy, fun subterranean space with ping pong, pool tables and other gaming options, not to mention free live music that runs till very late. Tables $5.50/hr per person weekdays, $6.50/hr per person weekends. Mon–Thurs 2pm–5am, Fri & Sat noon–5am.
SPIN New York 48 E 23rd St, between Madison and Park aves ☎212 982 8802, ⓦnewyork.spingalactic.com; subway R, #6 to 23rd St. A sprawling ping-pong centre with sixteen tables, a full restaurant and plenty of star power – actress Susan Sarandon is a co-owner; plenty of fun-oriented tournaments held, and it's as much a social and nightlife place as anything (see p.347). Tables $10/30min before 6pm, $20/30min after (50 percent less for members). Mon 11am–midnight, Tues & Wed 11am–1am, Thurs 11am–2am, Fri & Sat 11am–4am, Sun 11am–10pm.

YOGA

New York is a great place to try **yoga** for the first time, with classes offered throughout the day at scores of locations. You'll find all difficulty levels and numerous styles; like much of the Western world, the ancient practice has a large following in fitness clubs where it tends to be regarded as just another gym class (with aerobic hybrids like Yogalates), though there are plenty of traditional forms like *jivamukti*, and classes where breathing is more important than how many calories you burn. Yoga studios will also be able to tell you where to practise martial arts and Pilates. If you intend to take a number of sessions, you may want to purchase a **New York Yoga PassBook**, an excellent deal at $75 for hundreds of free visits and classes at workshops throughout the city and suburbs (☎212 808 0765, ⓦhealth-fitness.org/newyork_yoga). From spring till autumn, many outdoor classes are free; check *Time Out New York* magazine or websites such as ⓦnewyorkcityyoga.com for listings. A few reliable spots include:

Iyengar Yoga 150 W 22nd St, 11th floor, between Sixth and Seventh aves ☎212 691 9462, ⓦiyengarnyc .org; subway F, M, #1 to 23rd St. Dedicated to the practices of BKS Iyengar, this studio allows drop-ins for classes ($25 for nonmembers). Classes 8am–7.30pm, earlier some nights.

Yoga Vida 99 University Place, at E 12th St; also 666 Broadway ☎212 675 6056, ⓦyogavida.com; subway L, N, Q, R, #4, #5, #6 to 14th St-Union Sq. Modest prices (from $14 for a one-off class to $145 monthly unlimited pass) make this *vinyasa*-oriented place, which has a few beginner classes every day, a local favourite. Classes 7am–10pm.

NEW YORK CITY MARATHON

Every year on the first Sunday in November – save 2012, when Hurricane Sandy forced the event's cancellation – 37,000 runners come to New York to run the **New York City Marathon** (ⓦnycmarathon.org). Along with the competitors come the fans: on average, two million people turn out each year to watch the runners try to complete the 26.2-mile course, which starts in Staten Island, crosses the Verrazano-Narrows Bridge and passes through all the other boroughs before ending in Central Park.

If you are a **runner**, you can try to take part, but beware: the competition is fierce before the race even starts. Not everyone who submits the necessary entry forms is chosen to participate; race veterans (who have run fifteen or more New York marathons), qualified New York Road Runners (NYRR; ⓦnyrr.org) members who have completed at least nine official races during the calendar year, and those who have applied and been rejected for the last three NYC marathons receive guaranteed entry, which can also be (completely legitimately) procured for you by a travel agent in your home country. **Applications** must be sent by mid-April (check ⓦnycmarathon.org for exact date) for that year's race, and you must be at least 18 years old on race day.

HALLOWEEN PARADE, GREENWICH VILLAGE

Parades, festivals and events

New York City takes its numerous parades and festivals extremely seriously. They are often political or religious in origin, but as in most of the world, whatever their official reason for existing, they are generally just an excuse for music, food and dance. Almost every large ethnic group in the city – from the Irish to Puerto Ricans – holds an annual get-together, often using Fifth Avenue as the main drag; in general, it is a big mistake to drive, take a taxi or ride the buses anywhere near these. In addition, the city also hosts numerous annual special events, everything from America's oldest dog show to the New York City Marathon. Watch out also for street fairs, which tend to take place every weekend through the summer in different locations throughout the city.

FESTIVAL CALENDAR

JANUARY

New York Jewish Film Festival Mid- to late Jan; ☎ 212 496 3809, ⊕ thejewishmuseum.org/NYJFF and ⊕ filmlinc.com. Screenings of complex, provocative Jewish films with an international bent, as well as some rare oldies. Most films are shown at Lincoln Center's Walter Reade Theater.

Lunar (Chinese) New Year Usually Jan or Feb; ⊕ explorechinatown.com. A noisy, joyful occasion celebrated for two weeks along and around Mott St in Chinatown, as well as in Sunset Park in Brooklyn and Flushing in Queens.

Restaurant Week Late Jan to early Feb; also July ☎ 212 484 1200, ⊕ restaurantweek.com. For about ten weekdays, you can get prix-fixe three-course lunches at some of the city's finest establishments for around $24, or three-course dinners for $35. This can be quite a saving at restaurants like *Aquavit* and *Nobu*, though the limited menus don't always show off the cuisine at its best, and you must make reservations months in advance for the most desirable places.

Winter Antiques Show Late Jan; ☎ 718 292 7392, ⊕ winterantiquesshow.com. Foremost American antiques show takes over the Park Avenue Armory, 643 Park Ave at E 67th St, for one week. $20/day.

FEBRUARY

Empire State Building Run-Up Early Feb; ☎ 212 860 4445, ⊕ nyrr.org. Sponsored by the New York Road Runners, contenders race up the 1576 steps of this New York City landmark.

Outsider Art Fair Early Feb; ☎ 212 777 5218, ⊕ outsiderartfair.com. Leading dealers of outsider, primitive, visionary and intuitive art exhibit their collections at Center 548, 548 W 22nd St, Fri–Sun. $20/day.

Westminster Kennel Club Dog Show Mid-Feb; ☎ 212 213 3165, ⊕ westminsterkennelclub.org. Second only to the Kentucky Derby as the oldest continuous sporting event in the country (dating back to 1877), this show at Madison Square Garden welcomes 2500 canines competing for best in breed, along with legions of fanatic dog-lovers. Tickets $25/day.

MARCH

St Patrick's Day Parade March 17; ☎ 212 484 1222, ⊕ saintpatricksdayparade.com. Based on an impromptu march through the Manhattan streets by Irish militiamen on St Patrick's Day in 1762, this parade is a draw for every Irish band and organization in the US (and often Ireland itself), and it's impressive for the sheer mobs of people – no cars or floats are allowed. Starting around 11am at St Patrick's Cathedral on Fifth Ave and 44th St (following 8.30am Mass), it heads uptown to 86th St.

Greek Independence Day Parade Late March; ☎ 718 204 6500, ⊕ greekparade.org. Not as long or as boozy as St Pat's, more a patriotic nod to the old country from floats of pseudo-classically dressed Hellenes. When Independence Day (March 25) falls in the Orthodox Lent, the parade is shifted to April or May. It usually kicks off from 60th St and Fifth Ave and runs up to 79th St.

New Directors, New Films Late March to early April; ☎ 212 875 5638, ⊕ newdirectors.org. Lincoln Center and MoMA present this two-week series, one of the city's best, but rarely surrounded by hype. Films range from the next indie hits to obscure, never-to-be-seen-again works of genius, and the majority of the film-makers are from other countries. Tickets ($15) go on sale several weeks before the beginning of the festival, and films with a lot of buzz will sell out.

Pier Antiques Show March & Nov; ☎ 212 255 0020, ⊕ stellashows.com. Largest metropolitan antiques fair, including vintage clothing, on Pier 94, Twelfth Ave at 55th St; admission $15/day.

APRIL

Affordable Art Fair Early April; ☎ 212 255 2003, ⊕ affordableartfair.com/newyork/. Don't let the name fool you; four days of quality art sales for which everything is priced less than $10,000 (half costs under $5000, and lots

32

STREET FAIRS

In various sections of the city on weekend afternoons in the spring, summer and autumn, **street fairs** close a stretch of several blocks to traffic to offer pedestrians T-shirts, curios and gut-busting snacks like sausage sandwiches and fried dough. Unfortunately, once you've seen one, you've seen them all, as the vendors are rarely neighbourhood-specific. You'll find the most local flavour at the raucously tacky **Feast of San Gennaro** (see p.402), which could be called the prototypical street fair.

Street fairs are usually listed on ⊕ nycstreetfairs.com or in *Time Out New York* and neighbourhood newspapers. Smaller **block parties**, sponsored by community groups rather than business organizations, are more intimate affairs, generally with one side-street closed to cars, kids performing, politicos popping in to shake hands and everyone taking part in a huge pot-luck meal. They're typically not advertised, however, so consider yourself lucky to stumble upon one.

THE BROADWAY BOMB

One of Manhattan's greatest spectacles is also technically illegal. Since 2000, the **Broadway Bomb** has been an 8.5-mile longboard race down Broadway from 116th Street to the Charging Bull statue at Bowling Green. Some 800–1000 skaters dodge trucks and taxis in what is dubbed, accurately, as "the most dangerous longboard race in the world". Watching the skaters thrash towards the bull at the end of the race is a thrilling, if bizarre experience – check skate shops or ⓦbroadwaybomb.com to find out when the next event takes place. So far, attempts to stop the event have failed; in 2012 hundreds of boarders ignored an offical cancellation by court order and heavy police presence.

under $1500), held at the Metropolitan Pavilion, 125 W 18th St – but for $15 a day, it's the best contemporary art museum in the world.

Easter Parade Easter Sun; ☎212 360 8111, ⓦnycgo .com. Evoking the old fashion parade on the city's most stylish avenue, hundreds of people promenade up Fifth Ave, from 49th to 57th sts (10am–4pm) in elaborate, flower-bedecked Easter bonnets. These days, it's more like Halloween, with people using it as an excuse to dress up in wacky costumes.

New York Antiquarian Book Fair Early April; ☎212 944 8291, ⓦnyantiquarianbookfair.com. Sellers of rare books, letters, drawings, etc, exhibit at the Park Avenue Armory over four days. Get free appraisals of up to five items on "Discovery Day". Admission $20/day.

Tribeca Film Festival Late April to early May; ☎212 941 400, ⓦtribecafilmfestival.org. This glitzy two-week fest presents an admirable mix of soon-to-be-blockbusters and indie work, including shorts and international films. Purchase tickets ($8; $16 after 6pm) well in advance.

MAY

Sakura Matsuri (Cherry Blossom Festival) Early May; ☎718 623 7200, ⓦbbg.org. Music, art, dance, traditional fashion and sword-fighting demonstrations celebrate Japanese culture and the brief, sublime blossoming of the Brooklyn Botanic Garden's (see p.228) two hundred cherry trees. Free with garden admission ($10).

Five Boro Bike Tour First Sun in May; ☎212 932 2453, ⓦbikenewyork.org. Cars are banished from the route of this 42-mile ride through all five boroughs, and some 30,000 cyclists take to the streets. It's $86 to take part (and free to watch).

Ukrainian Festival Mid-May; ☎212 674 1615, ⓦbrama.com/stgeorge. This weekend festival (sponsored by St George Church) sees East 7th St – between Second and Third aves – filled with marvellous Ukrainian costumes, folk music and dance, plus foods and traditional crafts such as egg-painting.

Salute to Israel Parade Late May or early June; ☎212 245 8200, ⓦsalutetoisrael.com. Since 1964 this celebration of Israeli independence attempts to display unity within New York's ideologically and religiously diverse Jewish community. On Fifth Ave, between 57th and 79th streets, rain or shine.

JUNE

Museum Mile Festival First Tues evening; ☎212 606 2296, ⓦmuseummilefestival.org. On Fifth Ave from E 82nd to E 105th sts. Nine museums, including the Museum of the City of New York, the Cooper Hewitt, the Guggenheim, the Neue Galerie and the Met, are open free 6–9pm, and the street is closed down for a massive block party.

American Crafts Festival Early June; ☎973 746 0091, ⓦcraftsatlincoln.org. Over two weekends in June, entertainment and food accompany four hundred juried displays at Lincoln Center. Free admission.

National Puerto Rican Day Parade Second Sun; ☎718 401 0404, ⓦnationalpuertoricandayparade.org. The largest of several buoyant Puerto Rican celebrations in the city: seven hours of bands, flag-waving and baton-twirling from 44th to 86th sts on Fifth Ave, with an estimated two million people in attendance.

Mermaid Parade First Sat on or after June 21; ☎718 372 5159, ⓦconeyisland.com. At this outstanding event, participants dress like mermaids, fish and other sea creatures, and saunter through Coney Island, led by assorted offbeat celebs. A Mermaid Ball with burlesque entertainment follows.

Pride Week Third or fourth week of June; ☎212 807 7433, ⓦnycpride.org. The world's biggest lesbian, gay, bisexual and transgender Pride event kicks off with a rally in Bryant Park and ends with a march down Fifth Ave, a street fair in Greenwich Village and a huge last-night dance.

Dyke March Fourth Sat; ☎212 479 8520, ⓦnycdykemarch.tumblr.com. This technically illegal march rallies a diverse group of lesbian and bisexual women, from youngsters to topless grannies, at Bryant Park, to protest discrimination.

JULY

Independence Day July 4; ☎212 494 4495. The fireworks – above either the East River wor Hudson River – are visible from all over Manhattan, but the best places to view them are along the waterfront (and Brooklyn or Jersey depending on which river is being used), starting at about 9pm.

HOWL! Festival Usually early June; w howlfestival.com. Long weekend devoted to the Beats and especially Allen Ginsberg (a reading of *Howl!* opens the festival), with artists, poets and performers in and around Tompkins Square Park.

Restaurant Week Mid-July. See p.399.

Festa del Giglio Mid-July; t 718 384 0223, w olmcfeast .com. Since 1903, Havemeyer St between N 8th and N 11th sts in Williamsburg is taken over by this twelve-day Italian Catholic street festival ("Giglio" means lily), which culminates around July 16th, the feast day of Our Lady of Mount Carmel, with a procession of a giant wooden boat and a figure of St Paulinus on an 85ft tower.

Mostly Mozart Late July to late Aug; t 212 875 5766, w mostlymozart.org. More than forty concerts and Mozart-themed events at Lincoln Center, in the longest-running indoor summer festival in the US.

Washington Square Music Festival July; t 212 252 3621, w washingtonsquaremusicfestival.org. Since 1953, a series of classical, jazz and big-band concerts, every Tues at 8pm, at this outdoor venue (rain space is St Joseph's Church, 371 Sixth Ave). Free.

AUGUST

Charlie Parker Jazz Festival Third week w cityparksfoundation.org. Weekend festival of jazz celebrating the legacy of Charlie Parker, who spent the last years of his life in the East Village. Concerts at Tompkins Square Park and in Harlem.

Harlem Week All month; t 212 862 8473, w harlemweek.com. What began as a week-long festival around Harlem Day (a huge Sunday block party on W 135th St, between Fifth and St Nicholas aves) has stretched into a month of African, Caribbean and Latin performances, lectures and parties; some events in July, Sept and Oct, too.

Hong Kong Dragon Boat Festival First weekend in Aug; t 718 767 1776, w hkdbf-ny.org. Flushing Meadows–Corona Park is the site of this highly competitive race of 38ft-long sculls; live entertainment, an arts and crafts market and a dumpling-eating contest round out the weekend.

New York International Fringe Festival Mid- to late Aug; t 212 279 4488, w fringenyc.com. With more than two hundred companies performing at various downtown venues, this cutting-edge series is the biggest for performance art, theatre, dance, puppetry and more.

SEPTEMBER

West Indian-American Day Parade and Carnival Labor Day; t 718 467 1797, w wiadca.com. Brooklyn's largest parade, modelled after the carnivals of Trinidad and Tobago, features music, food, dance, floats with enormous sound systems and scores of steel-drum bands – not to mention more than a million attendees.

Broadway on Broadway Mid-Sept (usually Sun); t 212 869 1890, w broadwayonbroadway.com. One

32

SUMMER OUTDOOR FUN

Summer arts programmes are nice treats for those who stay in the city through the muggiest months. As most of these shows are free or at least very cheap, they're swarmed with fun-seeking New Yorkers – plan on arriving very early to stake out a picnic spot on the grass, and book tickets ahead when possible.

Blues BBQ Festival Aug; t 212 627 2020, w hudsonriverpark.org. Best blues bands from across the country combine with best city BBQ restaurants for a fabulous summer day on the river. Pier 54 at W14th St. Free.

Bryant Park Summer Film Festival Mid-June to mid-Aug; t 212 512 700, w bryantpark.org. Each Monday night (8–9pm) picnickers watch classic films like *Breakfast at Tiffany's* on the lush lawn of Bryant Park. Get there very early and bring a blanket. Free.

Celebrate Brooklyn May–Aug; t 718 855 7882, w bricartsmedia.org/celebrate. One of New York's longest-running free music series, at the bandstand in Prospect Park and Brooklyn Bridge Park; great Latin performances, among others.

Midsummer Night Swing July; t 212 875 5766, w midsummernightswing.org. In Lincoln Center's Damrosch Park, W 62nd St at Amsterdam Ave, Tuesday to Saturday evenings, learn a different dance en masse each night to the rhythm of live swing, mambo, merengue, samba or country. Lessons at 6.30pm; music and dancing at 7.30pm. Tickets $17.

River to River Festival June–July; w rivertorivernyc .com. Big-name performers in pop, World Music and dance take to the stage in Battery Park, the World Financial Center and elsewhere in Lower Manhattan. Free.

Rooftop Films May–Aug; t 718 417 7362, w rooftopfilms.com. Set on factory roofs and in public parks in Brooklyn and Manhattan, this movie series offers nifty backdrops for watching hip indie shorts. Tickets $10.

Shakespeare in the Park June–Aug; t 212 539 8500, w shakespeareinthepark.org. See p.156.

SummerStage June–Aug; t 212 360 2777, w cityparksfoundation.org/summerstage. See p.156.

day of free performances featuring songs by casts of the major Broadway musicals, culminating in a shower of confetti; held in Times Square.

Feast of San Gennaro Ten days in mid-Sept; ☎ 212 226 6427, ⓦ sangennaro.org. Since 1927, this festival has celebrated the patron saint of Naples along Mulberry St and its environs in Little Italy, with a cannoli-eating contest, midway games and tasty things to eat. In three parades (the largest is Sept 19, the saint's day), a San Gennaro statue is carried through the streets with donations pinned to his cloak.

German-American Steuben Parade Third Sat; ☎ 347 263 7376, ⓦ germanparadenyc.org. A celebration of German-American traditions that began in Queens, and now runs from 64th St to 86th St (once the heart of German Yorkville), starting at noon.

African-American Day Parade Late Sept; ☎ 212 384 3080, ⓦ africanamericandayparade.org. Drum lines, step-dancers, politicians, the Boys Choir of Harlem and other participants march through Harlem from W 111th St and Adam Clayton Powell Jr Blvd to W 136th St, in the largest black parade in America.

DUMBO Arts Festival Late Sept; ☎ 718 488 8588, ⓦ dumboartsfestival.com. More than two hundred resident artists show their work in open studios, bands perform and bizarre installations fill the streets in the stylish waterfront neighbourhood in Brooklyn.

New York Burlesque Festival Late Sept; ⓦ thenewyork burlesquefestival.com. Since 2003 this annual four-day event has spotlighted New York's booming modern burlesque scene, with performers from all over the world at various venues throughout Manhattan and Brooklyn.

Atlantic Antic Late Sept; ☎ 718 875 8993, ⓦ atlanticave.com. Massive, chaotic and incredibly entertaining street festival of food, art, music, shopping and festivities in the heart of Brooklyn (one mile of Atlantic Ave from Hicks St to Fourth Ave).

New York City Wine & Food Festival Late Sept to mid-Oct; ⓦ corporate.nycwineandfoodfestival.com. The Food Network and *Food & Wine* magazine team up to present the city's biggest food festival, with big-name television and cookbook personalities giving talks and demonstrations, and Meatpacking District restaurants hosting specially priced dinners. Tickets are expensive, but the proceeds go to charity.

New York Film Festival Late Sept to mid-Oct; ☎ 212 875 5600, ⓦ filmlinc.com. One of the world's leading film festivals unreels at Lincoln Center; tickets ($20) can be very hard to come by, as anticipated art hits get their debuts here.

OCTOBER

Pulaski Day Parade First Sun; ⓦ pulaskiparade.org. Held on Fifth Ave (29th St to 53rd St from 12.30pm) since 1937 for the celebration of Polish heritage, beginning with Mass at St Patrick's Cathedral – it's named after the famous Polish general who fought for America in the Revolutionary War (he was killed in Charleston in 1779).

New Yorker Festival Early Oct; ⓦ newyorker.com/festival. Literary, music and film celebrities hobnob on stage with *New Yorker* editors, writers and cartoonists at this three-day festival, held at venues throughout the city. Tickets sell out quickly; sign up online for the Festival Wire to get advance notification of events by email.

Columbus Day Parade Second Mon; ☎ 212 249 9923, ⓦ columbuscitizensfd.org. On Fifth Ave between 49th and 79th streets, 35,000 marchers commemorate Italian-American heritage and the day America was put on the map. Parallel events celebrate the heritage of Native Americans and other indigenous peoples.

Village Halloween Parade Oct 31; ⓦ halloween-nyc .com. In America's largest Halloween celebration, starting at 7pm on Sixth Ave at Spring St and making its way up to W 23rd, you'll see spectacular costumes, giant puppets, bands and any other bizarre stuff New Yorkers can muster. Get there

---

TOP 5 NEW YORK TRADE SHOWS

New York plays host to major expos, trade shows and conventions almost every week of the year – the following are some of the best.

Chocolate Show Nov ☎ 212 777 3455, ⓦ chocolate show.com. The largest show in the US completely dedicated to chocolate, with some 65 chocolate companies on display at the Metropolitan Pavilion, 125 W18th St.

International Artexpo NY End March, early April; ☎ 641 472 2257, ⓦ artexponewyork.com. The world's largest fine-art trade show, usually held on Pier 94, 711 Twelfth Ave. Tickets $20.

International Fashion Jewellery & Accessory-New York May; ☎ 212 563 1800, ⓦ jewelrytradeshows.com.

Major expo for all things glittery, usually held at the *Affinia Hotel*, 371 Seventh Ave.

New York Comic Con Oct; ⓦ newyorkcomiccon.com. The largest pop-culture event (and geek fest) on the East Coast. Bring your light saber. Jacob K. Javits Convention Center, 655 W 34th St. Single-day tickets $30–50.

New York International Gift Fair End Jan, and Aug; ☎ 212 204 1060, ⓦ nyigf.com. Showcasing everything from housewares to artisan jewellery, held at the Jacob K. Javits Convention Center, 655 W 34th St.

MACY'S PARADE INFLATION EVE

See Mickey Mouse and the other characters being inflated the night before **Macy's Thanksgiving Day Parade**. It's not as crowded as on parade day, and you can wander around the feet of these giants and experience something not broadcast to every home in America. The huge nylon balloons are set up on West 77th and West 81st streets between Central Park West and Columbus Avenue at the American Museum of Natural History.

early for a good viewing spot; marchers (anyone in costume is eligible) line up at 6.30pm. (A tamer children's parade usually takes place earlier that day in Washington Square Park.)

NOVEMBER

New York City Marathon First Sun; ☎212 423 2249, ⓦingnycmarathon.org. Some 37,000 runners from all over the world – from the champs to regular folks in goofy costumes – assemble for this high-spirited 26.2-mile run on city pavements through the five boroughs. One of the best places to watch is Central Park South, almost at the finish line.

Veterans Day Parade Nov 11; ☎212 693 1476. The United War Veterans sponsor this annual event on Fifth Ave from 23rd to 59th sts. Ceremony at 10.15am, salute and parade at 11am.

Macy's Thanksgiving Day Parade Thanksgiving Day; ☎212 494 4495, ⓦmacys.com. A made-for-TV extravaganza, with big corporate floats, dozens of marching bands from around the country and Santa Claus's first appearance of the season. Some two million spectators watch it along Central Park West from W 77th St to Columbus Circle, and along Broadway down to Herald Square, 9am–noon.

Rockefeller Center Christmas Tree Lighting Late Nov; ☎212 632 3975, ⓦrockefellercenter.com. Switching on the lights on the enormous tree in front of the ice rink begins the holiday season, in a glowing moment

sure to warm even the most Grinch-like heart. The crowds, however, can be oppressive.

African Diaspora Film Festival Late Nov to early Dec; ☎212 864 1760, ⓦnyadff.org. Films from throughout the world, by and about people of African descent, are shown at several Manhattan venues.

DECEMBER

Hanukkah Celebrations Usually mid-Dec. During the eight nights of this Jewish feast, a menorah-lighting ceremony takes place at Brooklyn's Grand Army Plaza (☎718 778 6000), and the world's largest menorah is illuminated on Fifth Ave near Central Park (☎212 736 8400).

SantaCon Mid-Dec; ⓦnycsantacon.com. Wildly popular, nonsensical Santa Claus convention where folks dressed in Santa costume go on a huge bar crawl around the city. It's a bit like a giant student booze-up – it's fun if you join in, but it can be extremely annoying if you don't.

Kwanzaa Dec 26–Jan 1; ☎212 568 1645, ⓦafrican folkheritagecircle.org. Celebrations city-wide honouring African-American heritage (the festival was established in the US in the 1960s), including a storytelling show by the African Folk Heritage Circle in Harlem.

New Year's Eve in Times Square Dec 31; ☎212 768 1560, ⓦtimessquarenyc.org. Several hundred thousand revellers party in the cold and well-guarded streets – a crowd-management nightmare, so take the subway and get where you're going early.

32

LITERARY FESTIVALS

American Crossword Puzzle Tournament Early March; ⓦcrosswordtournament.com. Usually held in the *Brooklyn Bridge Marriott*, Brooklyn, over three days; participants tackle eight original crosswords, with scoring based on accuracy and speed. Evening games and guest speakers. Spectators from $30, competitors $255.

Brooklyn Book Festival Mid-Sept; ⓦbrooklyn bookfestival.org. The largest free literary event in New York, presenting an array of national and international literary stars.

Little Red Lighthouse Festival Early Oct; ⓦnycgovparks.org. Special guest reading of Hildegarde Swift's children's classic, *The Little Red Lighthouse*, in Fort Washington Park.

Moby Dick Marathon Mid-Nov; ⓦmobydick marathonnyc.org. Marathon-style reading of Herman Melville's American classic, *Moby Dick*, over three days in book stores across the city (the book was published on Nov 14, 1851; Melville was born here in 1819).

New York Book Festival Late June; ⓦnewyork bookfestival.com. Open-air book competition and fair held in front of the Naumburg Bandshell in Central Park, with book sales, literary readings and live music.

Pynchon In Public Day ⓦpynchoninpublic.com. Various events to celebrate the novelist Thomas Pynchon's birthday, which falls on May 8.

BRONX ZOO

Kids' New York

New York can be quite a wonderful place to bring children. Obvious attractions like museums, theatres, skyscrapers, ferry rides and the city's numerous parks will certainly thrill them, but a visit with kids may also give you reason to appreciate simpler pleasures, from watching street entertainers to introducing youngsters to strange foods and fascinating neighbourhoods like Chinatown. The city is full of high-calibre free events aimed at children, especially in the summer: puppet shows, garden plantings, cultural celebrations, park festivals and storytelling hours at local bookstores are all excellent ways to entertain. Many museums and theatres also feature specific children's programmes. What follows are details on some attractions especially appealing to kids, but make sure to phone ahead for specific times, prices and the like to avoid any disappointment.

ESSENTIALS

Getting around Once in the city, your main problem won't be finding things to do with your kids but transporting them; subways are the fastest way to get around and are perfectly safe – as a bonus, children under 44 inches (112cm) ride free on the subway and buses when accompanied by an adult. Though some natives navigate the streets and subway stairs with pushchairs, most prefer to keep infants conveniently contained in a backpack or front carrier. Indeed, many attractions do not accommodate pushchairs, though some will keep yours temporarily while you visit – call ahead for details. If all else fails, or if you want some quiet time to enjoy the city's more mature

offerings, it's easy to hire a babysitter (see box, below).

Listings To find out what's available when you're in town, see the detailed NYCkidsARTS Cultural Calendar (ⓦ nyc-arts.org/kids). *Time Out New York* magazine (and the extra-specialized *TONY Kids*), the *Village Voice* and websites such as ⓦ gocitykids.parentsconnect.com, ⓦ mommypoppins .com and ⓦ achildgrows.com are also valuable resources. A solid directory of family-oriented events all around the city is available through NYC & Company, the marketing and tourism bureau, at 810 Seventh Ave, between 52nd and 53rd streets (Mon–Fri 9am–6pm, Sat & Sun 9am–5pm; ☎ 212 484 1200, ⓦ nycgo.com).

MUSEUMS

You could spend an entire holiday just checking out the city's many museums, almost all of which contain something fascinating for kids. The following is a brief overview of the ones that tend to evoke special enthusiasm. See the appropriate Guide chapters for more details on these and other museums.

American Museum of Natural History and the Rose Center for Earth and Space Central Park West, between 77th and 81st sts ☎ 212 769 5100, ⓦ amnh .org; subway B, C to 81st St-Museum of Natural History. Daily 10am–5.45pm, Rose Center until 8.45pm on first Fri of month; IMAX shows every hour on the half-hour daily 10.30am–4.30pm. Suggested donation $19, ages 2–12 $10.50 (includes the Rose Center). Special exhibits and IMAX additional charge; combination packages available. One of the best museums of its kind, this enormous complex is filled with bones, stuffed animals and other natural objects (more than 30 million in all). Your first stop should be the Fossil Halls on the Fourth Floor, where you'll find towering dinosaur skeletons. Elsewhere, a full-scale herd of elephants dominates the Akeley Hall of African Mammals; a 94ft-long blue whale hangs over the Milstein Hall of Ocean Life; the Hall of Biodiversity re-creates a Central African rainforest; and the seasonal Butterfly Conservatory is a sure bet for younger children. Just across from the Hall of Biodiversity, the Rose Center for Earth and Space features two high-tech theatres and the Cosmic Pathway, an evolutionary timeline.

Brooklyn Children's Museum 145 Brooklyn Ave, at St Mark's Ave ☎ 718 735 4400, ⓦ brooklynkids.org; subway #3 to Kingston Ave. Tues–Sun 10am–5pm, extended hours third Thurs of month (during which admission free); $9. Founded in 1899, this was the world's

first museum designed specifically for children. It's full of authentic ethnological, historical and technological artefacts with which kids can play (or pretend to shop or make pizza), plus live animals and a "Water Wonders" play area for smaller children.

Children's Museum of Manhattan 212 W 83rd St, between Broadway and Amsterdam Ave ☎ 212 721 1233, ⓦ cmom.org; subway #1 to 86th St. Tues–Fri & Sun 10am–5pm, Sat 10am–7pm, first Fri of month until 8pm; $11. This participatory museum, founded in 1937, has five floors full of imaginative, frequently rotating displays that involve a lot of clambering around.

Children's Museum of the Arts 103 Charlton St, between Hudson and Greenwich sts ☎ 212 274 0986, ⓦ cymany.org; subway C, E to Spring St, #1 to Houston St. Mon & Wed noon–5pm, Thurs & Fri noon–6pm, Sat & Sun 10am–5pm; $11, pay what you wish Thurs 4–6pm. At this gallery, children are encouraged to look at different types of art and then create their own with paints, paper, clay, fabric and other simple media. Holiday special events are particularly interesting – African mask-making for Kwanzaa, for example. Admission includes various dance, movie and music programmes on weekends.

Houdini Museum of New York 3rd Floor, 421 Seventh Ave, at 33rd St ☎ 212 244 3633, ⓦ houdinimuseumny .com; subway A, C, E, #1, #2, #3 to 34th St-Penn Station. Mon–Sat 11am–6pm, Sun 11am–5pm. It might be a bit

BABYSITTING

Most hotels can arrange babysitting services for you, or you can look up recommendations on the websites mentioned in this chapter's Essentials (see above). You could also get in touch with the Babysitters' Guild (☎ 212 682 0227, ⓦ babysittersguild.com) who do extensive screening on its caregivers and have been around for ninety-plus years.

33

of overstatement to rate this a museum, but most of the floor space at the Fantasma Magic shop is given over to Houdini memorabilia: straitjackets, cuffs, vintage advertisements and pictures, among various tricks of the trade.

Intrepid Sea, Air & Space Museum Pier 86, W 46th St, at Twelfth Ave ☎ 212 245 0072, ⓦ intrepidmuseum.org; subway A, C, E to 42nd St-Port Authority. April–Sept Mon–Fri 10am–5pm, Sat & Sun 10am–6pm; Oct–March Tues–Sun 10am–5pm; $24, ages 7–17 $19, ages 3–6 $12. Even non-military-minded kids will be impressed by the massive scale of this aircraft-carrier-cum-museum – not to mention the huge collection of aeroplanes and helicopters. The site includes a 15,000-square foot space for hands-on learning, in which children can climb a cargo net, experience (via computer) life on a ship and (for older kids or adults) simulate aircraft launches; kids can also marvel at the newly transplanted *Enterprise* space shuttle. One of the more unusual programmes involves the possibility of sleeping over on the ship: Operation Slumber takes place on Saturdays for groups of kids 6–17 years old (there is adult supervision; $120 per person).

New York City Fire Museum 278 Spring St, between Hudson and Varick sts ☎ 212 691 1303, ⓦ nycfiremuseum.org; subway C, E to Spring St, #1 to Houston St. Daily 10am–5pm; suggested donation $8, 12 and under $5. A sure hit with the preschool crowd, this space pays pleasing homage to New York City's firefighters. On display are fire engines from yesteryear (horse drawn and steam powered), helmets, dog-eared photos and a host of motley objects on three floors of a former fire station; a 9/11 memorial is on hand as well. A neat and appealing display, even though it's not fully interactive.

New York Hall of Science 47-01 111th St, at 46th Ave, Flushing Meadows–Corona Park, Queens ☎ 718 699 0005, ⓦ nysci.org; subway #7 to 111th St. April–Aug Mon–Fri 9.30am–5pm, Sat & Sun 10am–6pm; Sept–March same hours except closed Mon; $11, kids $8, free Sept–June Fri 2–5pm & Sun 10–11am. Housed in a cylindrical tower built for the 1964–65 World's Fair, this is one of the top science museums in the country. A highlight is the giant, outdoor Science Playground (open April–Dec; an additional $4), where kids can clamber around as they learn about scientific principles. Located in Queens, the Hall of Science makes for a good day-trip combined with a visit to any of the attractions in Flushing–Corona Park: Queens Zoo, the nearby Queens Museum of Art, or the park itself.

FIVE GREAT PLAYGROUNDS

Heckscher Playground Central Park. See p.152

Imagination Playground South Street Seaport. See p.54

Pier Six Brooklyn Bridge Park. See p.217

Pier 51 Hudson River Park. See p.104

Science Playground New York Hall of Science. See below

New York Transit Museum Old subway entrance at Schermerhorn St and Boerum Place, Brooklyn ☎ 718 694 1600, ⓦ mta.info/mta/museum; subway #2, #3, #4, #5 to Borough Hall, A, C, F, R to Jay St-MetroTech. Tues–Fri 10am–4pm, Sat & Sun 11am–5pm; $7, ages 3–17 $5. Also: Transit Museum Gallery and Store at Grand Central Terminal, open daily; free. Housed in an abandoned 1930s subway station, this museum offers more than a hundred years of transportation memorabilia, including old subway cars and buses dating back to the turn of the twentieth century. Frequent activities for kids include underground tours, workshops and an annual bus festival – all best for younger schoolkids (and there are usually plenty of them running around here). It's a quick hop on the subway, but if you don't want to go to Brooklyn, at least stop in to the museum's annexe at Grand Central in Manhattan, which has its own rotating exhibits.

South Street Seaport Museum 12 Fulton St ☎ 212 748 8600, ⓦ southstreetseaportmuseum.org; subway #2, #3, #4, #5 to Fulton St, A, C, J to Broadway-Nassau; Tues–Sun 10am–6pm; $15. South Street Seaport's dock is home to a small fleet of historic ships: you can look round the *Ambrose*, at Pier 17, and boat rides are available on the *Pioneer* (both seasonal), though other boats are in the midst of restoration. The museum's holdings, in galleries across a few warehouses, may seem staid in comparison to the boats – at least as far as kids' attention goes.

Staten Island Children's Museum Snug Harbor Cultural Center, 1000 Richmond Terrace, Staten Island ☎ 718 273 2060, ⓦ statenislandkids.org; bus #S40 from Ferry Terminal; June–Aug Tues–Sun 10am–5pm, Sept–May Tues–Sun noon–5pm; $6. Expect, among other things, giant chess sets, a small-scale playhouse, a great exhibit about bugs that includes a human-size anthill and an outdoor play area on the water where kids can sail boats and learn about oysters.

SIGHTS AND ENTERTAINMENT

Non-museum sights mostly comprise the various parks and gardens that help make New York a greener city than some might imagine. There's plenty of ongoing progress in that area, too: the Brooklyn waterfront between Dumbo and the Heights has undergone massive kid-friendly redevelopment, and similar things have taken place on Manhattan's west side.

Bronx Zoo Bronx River Parkway at Fordham Rd ☎718 367 1010, ⓦbronxzoo.org; subway #2, #5 to East Tremont Ave. April–Oct Mon–Fri 10am–5pm, Sat & Sun 10am–5.30pm; Nov–March daily 10am–4.30pm; $16.95, ages 3–12 $11.95; pay what you wish on Wed; parking $15. The largest urban zoo in America, with thrilling permanent exhibits – check out Wild Asia by monorail (May–Oct only; $4), the lush rainforest of JungleWorld and the Congo Gorilla Forest. Kids can watch penguins being fed, get up close with Siberian tigers or ride a giant bug on an insect-themed carousel. Highly recommended for an all-day excursion, particularly in spring, when many baby animals are born. Be prepared for small additional fees to certain exhibits.

Brooklyn Botanic Garden 900 Washington Ave ☎718 623 7200, ⓦbbg.org; subway #2, #3 to Eastern Parkway. March–Oct Tues–Fri 8am–6pm, Sat & Sun 10am–6pm; Nov–Feb Tues–Fri 8am–4.30pm, Sat & Sun 10am–4.30pm; $10, under 12 free; free Tues, Sat before noon, Nov–Feb weekdays; subway #2, #3 to Eastern Parkway, #4, #5 to Franklin Ave, B, Q to Prospect Park. This gorgeous landscape behind the Brooklyn Museum of Art is very child-friendly, with giant carp in the ponds and ducks to chase around. Kids will enjoy the City Farmers and Discovery Garden programmes, and parents can drop in for the flower-arranging classes (dried and silk), garden tutorials and *tai chi* sessions. Families crowd the place for seasonal events like the Cherry Blossom Festival in late April/early May.

Brooklyn Bridge Park ⓦbrooklynbridgepark.org. A number of piers along the once-downtrodden waterfront by Dumbo and Brooklyn Heights have been refashioned for family fun. The main prize for kids is Pier 6, at the end of Atlantic Avenue, where giant slides, an enormous sandbox, various climbing contraptions and, best of all, a waterpark for hot summer days, rule the roost; there's a pop-up pool at Pier 2 and other highlights along the way. Some choice food-vendors and great views make it good for adults too.

New York Aquarium Surf Ave, at W 8th St, Coney Island, Brooklyn ☎718 265 3474, ⓦnyaquarium .com; subway F, Q to W 8th St-New York Aquarium. June–Aug Mon–Fri 10am–6pm, Sat & Sun 10am–7pm; Sept, Oct, April & May Mon–Fri 10am–5pm, Sat & Sun 10am–5.30pm; Nov–March daily 10am–4.30pm. $14.95, ages 3–12 $10.95. Although it dates to 1896, the aquarium has very modern-looking exhibits dedicated to jellyfish and sea horses, along with ten thousand other underwater animals. Open-air sea-lion shows and various feedings are held several times daily. This is also the site of the famous Coney Island boardwalk and amusement parks: older children and teens will find it a good spot to people-watch or enjoy the thrill of riding the Cyclone and the WonderWheel (see p.233).

New York Botanical Garden 2900 Southern Blvd, at Fordham Road and Bronx River Parkway, Bronx (across from the Bronx Zoo) ☎718 817 8700, ⓦnybg.org; subway B, D, #4 to Bedford Park. Tues–Sun 10am–6pm, closes 5pm most of Jan & Feb; all-garden pass $25, ages 2–12 $10, grounds-only $10, ages 2–12 $2, parking $12. One of America's foremost public gardens, with an enormous conservatory showcasing a rainforest and other types of ecosystems, plus the 12-acre Everett Children's Adventure Garden, which includes a maze and various hands-on science lessons.

Sony Wonder Technology Lab 550 Madison Ave, at 56th St ☎212 833 8100, ⓦsonywondertechlab.com; subway #4, #5, #6 to 59th St-Lexington Ave, E, M to Fifth Ave. Tues–Sat 9.30am–5.30pm; free. Sony's gee-whiz exhibit space emphasizes the marvels of the digital age, and although it's a bit corporate-slick, tech-minded kids will enjoy creating their own video games and trying out TV editing, animation, even simulated open-heart surgery. This is a hugely popular attraction, so be sure to make reservations (you can do this up to three months in advance); same-day tickets are sometimes available as well.

CENTRAL PARK

Year-round, Central Park provides sure-fire entertainment for children; in the summer, it becomes one giant playground. The following are merely a few of the highlights; for detailed information on these and other sights, see Chapter 13.

The Carousel Mid-park at 64th St. For $2.50, children can take a (surprisingly fast) spin on the country's largest hand-carved horses.

Central Park Zoo Fifth Ave, at 64th. A small but enjoyable spot, with sea lions, penguins, monkeys and the Tisch Children's Zoo.

Hans Christian Andersen statue 72nd St, on the east side, just west of the boat pond. June–Sept

Sat 11am–noon. A fifty-year tradition of hosting storytelling sessions.

Loeb Boathouse East side at 72nd St. Rent a rowboat on the Central Park lake and enjoy the views, or take a gondola ride in the evening. Bike rentals available too.

Wollman Memorial Rink East side at 62nd St. Ice-skating during the winter; in the summer it's Victorian Gardens, an old-fashioned amusement park.

33

SHOPS

Apple Store 767 Fifth Ave, between 58th and 59th sts ☎ 212 336 1440, ⓦ apple.com; subway N, Q, R to Fifth Ave-59th St, F to 57th St ; map p.123 (plus four other locations). The Apple Store teems with gadget-loving kids, looking for the latest technology in cool shopping surroundings. The one on Fifth Ave, where you descend down a giant glass cube, might be your best bet. Daily 24hr.

Bank Street Bookstore 610 W 112th St, at Broadway ☎ 212 678 1654, ⓦ bankstreetbooks.com; subway #1 to 110th St; map p.183. The first floor of this store – affiliated with Bank Street College of Education – is filled with children's books and games, while the second floor is devoted to nonfiction books and educational materials. Frequent special events and afternoon story hours. Daily 8am–10pm.

Books of Wonder 18 W 18th St, between Fifth and Sixth aves ☎ 212 989 3270, ⓦ booksofwonder.com; subway F, M to 14th St, #1 to 18th St; map p.114. Showpiece kids' bookstore, with a great Oz section, plus story hour on Sunday at noon and author appearances Saturday in the spring and autumn. Mon–Sat 11am–7pm, Sun 11am–6pm.

Brooklyn Superhero Supply Store 372 Fifth Ave, between Fifth and Sixth sts, Park Slope, Brooklyn ☎ 718 499 9884, ⓦ superherosupplies.com; subway F, G, R to Fourth Ave ; map p.226. Want a unique souvenir for your young one? This Dave Eggers brainchild has everything an aspiring superhero will need, from jars of antimatter and omnipotence to capes. Money goes to a nonprofit dedicated to creative writing and education for kids – which takes place behind a hidden door in back. Daily 11am–5pm.

FAO Schwarz 767 Fifth Ave, at 58th St ☎ 212 644 9400, ⓦ fao.com; subway N, Q, R to Fifth Ave; map p.123. This multistorey toy emporium features an on-site ice-cream parlour, a whole wing dedicated to Lego and the legendary danceable floor piano featured in the 1988 film *Big*. Very popular (and very expensive). Mon–Thurs & Sun 10am–8pm, Fri & Sat 10am–9pm.

Midtown Comics 200 W 40th St, at Seventh Ave; three other locations in the city ☎ 212 302 8192, ⓦ midtowncomics.com; subway N, Q, R, #1, #2, #3 to Times Square-42nd St; map p.123. Vintage action figures and other collectibles abound, but the walls and shelves full of comics and character books make this a true teenager's dream. Mon–Sat 8am–midnight, Sun noon–8pm.

Red Caboose 23 W 45th St, between Fifth and Sixth aves, lower level ☎ 212 575 0155, ⓦ theredcaboose .com; subway B, D, F, M, #7 to 42nd St-Bryant Park; map p.123. A unique, cluttered subterranean shop specializing in models, particularly trains and train sets. Mon–Fri 11am–7pm, Sat 11am–5pm.

Sony Store 550 Madison Ave, at 56th St ☎ 212 833 8800; subway 4, #5, #6 to 59th St-Lexington Ave, E, M to Fifth Ave-53rd St; map p.123. The latest technology from a giant in the industry, though it's more a place to gawk at – and try out the latest games in the spacious downstairs – than buy items to take with you. Mon–Sat 10am–7pm, Sun 11am–6pm.

Space Kiddets 26 E 22nd St, between Park Ave and Broadway ☎ 212 420 9878, ⓦ spacekiddets.com; subway N, R, #6 to 23rd St; map p.114. Show your baby's musical taste with a CBGB onesie or a Van Halen T-shirt from this funky clothes shop that stocks infant to pre-teen sizes; vintage toys can be found at the shop around the block (46 E 21st St). Mon, Tues, Fri & Sat 10.30am–6pm, Wed & Thurs 10.30am–7pm, Sun 11am–5pm.

Tannen's Magic Studio 45 W 34th St, Suite 608, between Fifth and Sixth aves ☎ 212 929 4500, ⓦ tannens.com; subway B, D, F, M, N, Q, R to 34th St-Herald Square; map p.123. Your kids will never forget a visit to the largest magic shop in the world, with nearly 8000 props, tricks, and magic sets. The staff is made up of magicians who perform free shows throughout the day. Mon–Fri 11am–6pm, Sat & Sun 10am–4pm.

THEATRE, CIRCUSES AND OTHER ENTERTAINMENT

BAMfamily Brooklyn Academy of Music, 30 Lafayette Ave ☎ 718 636 4100, ⓦ bam.org. This series (2013 was the first year with a true "season", Jan–May) presents public performances for families on weekends, as well as the international BAMkids Film Festival (usually early Feb).

Big Apple Circus Cunningham Park, Fresh Meadows, Queens & Damrosch Park, Lincoln Center ☎ 212 721 6500 for ticketing, ☎ 212 268 2500 for administration, ⓦ bigapplecircus.org. Small circus that performs in late spring in the eastern portion of Queens, and then comes back again later in the year (around late Oct) to a tent next to the Met Opera House. Tickets $20–60.

New Victory Theater 209 W 42nd St, at Broadway ☎ 646 223 3010, ⓦ newvictory.org. The city's first theatre for families, located in a grand old renovated Times Square space, presents a rich mix of theatre, music, dance, storytelling, film and puppetry, in addition to pre- and

---

TOP 5 CHILD-FRIENDLY RESTAURANTS

Bubby's Tribeca p.296
Dinosaur Bar-B-Que Harlem p.319
Peking Duck House Chinatown p.299
Sarita's Mac & Cheese East Village p.302
Trattoria Zero Otto Novo Bronx p.327

NEW YORK WITH TEENS

For many teenagers, the sights and sounds of New York (paired with a little well-placed downtime) will be fascinating enough, particularly if they have certain obsessions.

Art MoMA (see p.128) has free teen nights – with pizza – and other dedicated events and workshops for kids.

Fashion Wander to the Fashion Institute of Technology, which has a free museum (see p.111) or go for a free makeup consultation at Sephora, 555 Broadway in Soho (plus fifteen other city locations).

Games Head to Washington Square Park (see p.95) or Bryant Park to see – or join – chess players in action.

Music Hush Birthplace of Hip Hop Tours (see p.251) introduce people to what made the Bronx the epicentre of hip-hop street culture – though youngsters may also want to check out sites in Brooklyn, like the newly dubbed Adam Yauch Park, in Brooklyn Heights, or in Queens' Hollis, made famous by Run DMC.

Sports Pier 62 on Chelsea's waterfront boasts a skate park, part of Hudson River Park (not Chelsea Piers), open from 8am until sunset.

post-performance workshops. Affordable shows (most tickets $14–38) run 1–2hr, and some are quite popular. In keeping with the cultural calendar that much of the city runs on, the theatre is dark (no performances) during the summer.

Puppetworks 338 Sixth Ave, at Fourth St, Park Slope, Brooklyn ☎718 965 3391, ⓦpuppetworks.org; subway F, G to Seventh Ave. Founded back in 1980, the not-for-profit Puppetworks puts on child-friendly shows – frequently adapted from familiar fairy tales – in an intimate setting; tickets usually around $10.

Ringling Brothers and Barnum & Bailey Circus ⓦringling.com. This large touring circus arrives in New York on a mile-long train in late March and stays for an extended run. Traditionally, the home has been Madison Square Garden, with the residence preceded by an elephant procession from the rail yards in Queens to the west side of Manhattan (though it did a recent stint at the Barclays Center). Check papers and websites for schedule, location and if the walk will take place. Tickets $25–150.

Streb Laboratory for Action Mechanics (S.L.A.M.) 51 N 1st St, Williamsburg, Brooklyn ☎718 384 6491, ⓦstreb.org. MacArthur-grant-winning choreographer Elizabeth Streb has developed a dynamic, physical dance style she calls Pop Action – go for one of the company's inspiring performances in its raw Brooklyn warehouse, or sign kids up for the week-long S.L.A.M. Summer Camps in July. The space also offers trampoline work, trapeze fun and basic tumbling; most classes are Tues–Thurs though it's open all week.

Trapeze School New York Pier 40, Hudson River Park, at Canal St; also South Street Seaport ☎212 242 8769, ⓦnewyork.trapezeschool.com. Two-hour classes on the flying trapeze, for ages 6 and up, start at $72 (including a one-time $22 registration fee) and include an amazing view over the Hudson River from high atop the rig. Parents must accompany children – but if this seems too daunting, you can just go sit in the park and watch the intrepid high-flyers practise their moves. Book well in advance.

KING KONG

Contexts

History

To Europe she was America, to America she was the gateway of the earth. But to tell the story of New York would be to write a social history of the world. H.G. Wells

Early days and colonial rule

Long before the arrival of European settlers, several Native American tribes inhabited New York; the **Lenni Lenape** tribe – part of the **Algonquin** nation – was the largest and most populous in the area that is now New York City. Although descendants of the Algonquins and other tribes still live on Long Island's Shinnecock reservation, the appearance of Europeans in the sixteenth century essentially destroyed their settled existence.

Giovanni da Verrazano was the first explorer to discover Manhattan. An Italian in the service of French king Francis I, he had set out to find the Pacific's legendary Northwest Passage, but like his countryman Christopher Columbus, had been blown off-course into what would become New York Harbor in 1524. Verrazano returned to France to woo the court with tales of fertile lands and friendly natives, but it was nearly a century before the powers of Europe were tempted to follow him.

In 1609 **Henry Hudson**, an Englishman employed by the **Dutch East India Company**, landed at Manhattan, sailing his ship, the *Half-Moone*, upriver as far as Albany. Hudson found that the route did not lead to the Northwest Passage, which he, too, had been commissioned to discover – but in charting its course for the first time he gave his name to the mighty river. Returning home, Hudson was persuaded to embark on another expedition, this time under the British flag. He arrived in Hudson Bay in the dead of winter, the temperature below freezing and his mutinous crew doubting his ability as a navigator; he, his son and several loyal sailors were set adrift in a small boat on the icy waters where, presumably, they froze to death.

British fears that they had lost the upper hand in the newly discovered land proved justified when the Dutch established a trading post at the most northerly point on the river that Hudson had reached, **Fort Nassau**, and quickly seized the commercial advantage. In 1624, four years after the Pilgrims had sailed to Massachusetts, thirty families left Holland to become New York's first European settlers, most sailing up to Fort Nassau. But a handful – eight families in all – stayed behind on a small island they called Nut Island because of the many walnut trees there: today's Governors Island. The community slowly grew as more settlers arrived, and the little island became crowded; the **settlement of Manhattan**, taken from the Lenape word *Manna-Hata* meaning "Island of the Hills", began when families from Governors Island moved across the water.

The Dutch gave this new outpost the name **New Amsterdam**, and in 1626 the Dutch West India Company sent over **Peter Minuit** to govern the small community. Among his first, and certainly more politically adroit, moves was to buy the whole of Manhattan Island from the Native Americans for trinkets worth sixty guilders (the equivalent of $24, at least according to a nineteenth-century historian); whether the Native Americans from whom Minuit "bought" the land had the same concept of permanent ownership as the Dutch is another matter altogether.

1609	**1624**	**1626**	**1664**
English explorer Henry Hudson, working for the Dutch, sails past Manhattan upriver as far as Albany	Dutch colony established on Governors Island	Peter Minuit arrives as governor, moves the Dutch settlement to Manhattan, which is named New Amsterdam	Revolt against Gov. Peter Stuyvesant's rule coincides with surrender to British naval troops, who rename the colony New York

As the colony slowly grew, a string of governors succeeded Minuit, the most famous of them **Peter Stuyvesant** or "Peg Leg Pete", a seasoned colonialist from the Dutch West Indies who'd lost his leg in a scrape with the Spanish. Under his leadership New Amsterdam doubled in size, population and fortifications, with an encircling wall (today's **Wall Street** follows its course) and a rough-hewn fort on what is now the site of the Customs House built to protect the settlement from the encroaching British. Stuyvesant also built himself a farm (*bouwerij* in Dutch) nearby, giving Manhattan's Bowery district its name.

Meanwhile, the **British** were steadily and stealthily building up their presence to the north. They asserted that all of America's east coast, from New England to Virginia, was theirs, and in 1664 Colonel Richard Nicholls was sent to claim the lands around the Hudson for King Charles II. To reinforce his sovereignty, Charles sent along four warships and enough troops to land on Nut and Long islands. Angered by Stuyvesant's increasingly dictatorial leadership and the high taxes levied by the Dutch West India Company, the Dutch settlers refused to defend the colony against the British. Captain Nicholls' men took New Amsterdam, renamed it **New York** in honour of Charles II's brother, the Duke of York, and started what was to be a hundred-odd years of British rule, a period interrupted only briefly in 1673 when the Dutch again gained, then lost, power in the region.

Revolution

By the 1750s the city had reached a population of sixteen thousand, spread roughly as far north as Chambers Street. As the community grew, it also operated increasingly independently of the British, but England reasserted control in 1763, when France conceded sovereignty over most of explored North America. Within a year the British had riled colonists by imposing punitive taxes and requisitioning private dwellings and inns. Skirmishes between British soldiers and the insurrectionist **Sons of Liberty** culminated in January 1770 with the fatal stabbing of a colonist in New York City.

New York did not play a large role in the **War of Independence**, due to several decisive defeats in the autumn of 1776, first in Brooklyn in the vicinity of Prospect Park, then in Westchester County (the Bronx), with the British pushing the Americans ever northward. Though the Patriots were under the command of George Washington himself, the campaign was a disaster, ending with the routing of three thousand American troops at Fort Washington and the occupation of the city by the British for the remainder of the war.

Lord Cornwallis's **surrender** to the Americans in October 1783 marked the end of the Revolutionary War, and a month later New York was finally liberated. Washington – an infinitely sharper commander than he was in the early days of the conflict – was there to celebrate, riding in triumphal procession down Canal Street and saying farewell to his officers at **Fraunces Tavern**, a facsimile of which stands at the end of Pearl Street. Soon after, New York became the fledgling nation's capital, and, on April 30, 1789, Washington its first president. The seat of the federal government was transferred to the District of Columbia a year later.

1776	1789	1792	1825
British naval vessels arrive to capture New York after the Declaration of Independence	George Washington takes oath as America's first President on Wall Street	Buttonwood Agreement, signed by 24 stockbrokers on Wall Street, signals beginning of New York Stock Exchange	Opening of the Erie Canal makes New York a major shipping port

Immigration and civil war

In 1790 the first official census of Manhattan numbered the population around 33,000. Business and trade were steadily increasing, with the forerunner of the New York Stock Exchange created under a buttonwood tree on Wall Street in the early 1800s and ferry services established between New York and Albany, and between Brooklyn and Manhattan.

In 1825, the completion of the **Erie Canal** (running from the Hudson River across the state to the Great Lakes) opened up internal trade and increased demand for cheap labour. The first waves of **immigrants**, mainly **Irish** and **German**, began to arrive in the mid-nineteenth century, the former forced out by famine, the latter by the failed revolutions of 1848–49. Though traders grew wealthy, the city could not handle the arrival of so many people all at once: epidemics of yellow fever and cholera were common, exacerbated by poor water supplies, unsanitary conditions and the poverty of most of the newcomers, not least in the Lower East Side where two of the largest communities – **Italians** and **Eastern Europeans** (many of them Jewish) – shared one of the most notorious slum areas of its day.

When the **Civil War** broke out in 1861, New York sided with the Union (North) against the Confederates (South). While the city saw little hand-to-hand fighting, it was fertile ground for much of the liberal thinking that had informed the war. In 1863, an unjust **conscription law** provoked the draft riots, with impoverished New Yorkers (especially Irish immigrants) burning buildings, looting shops and lynching African-Americans; more than a thousand people were killed.

The late nineteenth century

After the Civil War, New York began to assume the mantle as the wealthiest and most influential city in the nation by dint of its skilled immigrant workers, distribution networks and financial resources. Broadway developed into the main thoroughfare, with grand hotels, restaurants and shops catering to the rich; newspaper editors **William Cullen Bryant** and **Horace Greeley** founded the *Evening Post* and the *Tribune*, respectively; and the city became a magnet for intellectuals, with **Washington Irving** and **James Fenimore Cooper** among notable residents. **Cornelius Vanderbilt** controlled a vast shipping and railroad empire from here, and **J.P. Morgan**, the banking genius, was instrumental in organizing financial mergers, creating the nation's first major corporations.

The latter part of the nineteenth century was in many ways the city's golden age: elevated railways (**Els**) sprang up to transport people quickly and cheaply around the city; **Thomas Edison** lit the streets with his new electric light bulb, powered by the nation's first commercial power plant, on Pearl Street; and in 1883, the **Brooklyn Bridge** was unveiled. In 1898, New York City – formerly just Manhattan – assumed its current size by officially incorporating Brooklyn, Staten Island, Queens and the part of Westchester County known as the Bronx. All this expansion stimulated the city's cultural growth. **Walt Whitman** eulogized the city in his poems, and **Henry James** recorded its manners and mores in novels like *Washington Square*. Along Fifth Avenue, **Richard Morris Hunt** built palaces for the wealthy robber-barons who had plundered Europe's collections of fine art – collections that would eventually find their way into the newly opened **Metropolitan Museum**.

1830–50	1835	1856–71	1858
First wave of mass immigration, principally German and Irish. The Lower East Side developed	Great Fire of New York destroys most buildings on the southern tip of Manhattan around Wall Street	The city is ruled by a corrupt group of politicians known as Tammany Hall, headed by William "Boss" Tweed	First Chinese immigrants arrive in what would become Manhattan's Chinatown

Turn-of-the-century development

In 1898, boosted by the first wave of Asian immigrants, New York's population topped three million for the first time, making it the largest city in the world. Nearly half its residents were foreign-born, with **Ellis Island**, the depot that processed arrivals, handling two thousand people a day. Many immigrants worked in sweatshops for the city's growing, notoriously exploitative garment industry. Although workers began to strike for better pay and conditions, it took the **Triangle Shirtwaist Factory** fire (see p.95) to rouse public and civic conscience; within months the state passed 56 factory-reform measures, and unionization spread through the city.

On the upside of New York's capitalist expansion, the early 1900s saw some of the city's wealth delving into adventurous new architecture. In Soho classical facades were mass-produced from **cast iron**, and the **Flatiron Building** of 1902 announced the arrival of what was to become the city's trademark – the skyscraper. **Stephen Crane**, **Theodore Dreiser** and **Edith Wharton** all wrote stories about the city, and in 1913 the **Armory Exhibition** of paintings by Picasso, Duchamp and others caused a sensation. Skyscrapers pushed ever higher, and in 1913 a building that many consider the *ne plus ultra* of the genre, downtown's **Woolworth Building**, was completed. **Grand Central Terminal** also opened that year, celebrating New York as the gateway to the continent.

The war years and the Depression: 1914–45

As New York benefited from the trade and commerce generated by World War I, there was – perhaps surprisingly – little conflict between the various European communities crammed into the city, and few attacks on Germans.

Prohibition was passed in 1920 in an attempt to sober up the nation, but New York paid little heed. Under the helm of **Mayor Jimmy Walker**, who was quoted as saying, "No civilized man goes to bed the same day he wakes up", the city entered the Jazz Age. Writers as diverse as **Damon Runyon**, **F. Scott Fitzgerald** and **Ernest Hemingway** portrayed the excitement of the times, and musicians such as **George Gershwin** and **Benny Goodman** packed nightclubs with their new sound. Bootleg liquor ran freely in speakeasies all over town. The **Harlem Renaissance** soared to prominence, propelled by writers like **Langston Hughes** and **Zora Neale Hurston**, and music from **Duke Ellington**, **Cab Calloway** and **Billie Holiday**.

The **Wall Street Crash** of 1929 brought the party to an abrupt end. On October 24, known as "**Black Tuesday**", sixteen million shares were traded in a panicked sell-off; five days later, the New York Stock Exchange collapsed, losing $125 million ($1.5 billion in today's dollars). Millions lost their savings; banks, businesses and industries shut their doors. By 1932 approximately one in four New Yorkers was out of work, and shantytowns, known as "Hoovervilles" (after then-President Hoover, widely blamed for the Depression), had sprung up in Central Park to house the jobless and homeless.

Surprisingly, during this period three of New York's most beautiful skyscrapers were built – the **Chrysler Building** in 1930, the **Empire State** in 1931 (though it stood near-empty for years), and in 1932 the **Rockefeller Center** – but this impressive spate of construction was of little immediate help to those in Hooverville, Harlem or other depressed parts of the city. It fell to **Fiorello LaGuardia**, Jimmy Walker's successor, to run the crisis-strewn city. He did so with stringent taxation, anti-corruption and

1886	1898	Early 20th century	1920s
The Statue of Liberty, a gift from the French people to America, is unveiled	The outer boroughs of Brooklyn, Queens, the Bronx and Staten Island are incorporated into New York City	The first skyscrapers built, including the Flatiron Building (1902) and the Woolworth Building (1913)	Despite Prohibition, economic confidence brings Jazz Age and Harlem Renaissance

social-spending programmes that won him public approval. Simultaneously, President Roosevelt's **New Deal** supplied funds for roads, housing and parks, the latter undertaken by controversial Parks Commissioner **Robert Moses**. Under LaGuardia and Moses, the most extensive public-housing programme in the country was undertaken; the Triborough, Whitestone and Henry Hudson bridges were completed; fifty miles of new expressway and five thousand acres of new parks were designed and built; and, in 1939, the airport in Queens that still bears the legendary mayor's name was opened. That same year in Queens, New York hosted the **World's Fair**, in Flushing Meadows–Corona Park; the year-long event focused largely on technology and the future.

The country's entry into **World War II** in 1941 saw New York take on a top-secret role: the **Manhattan Project**, wherein scientists at Columbia University performed the experiments crucial to the creation of the first atomic weapon.

The postwar years to the 1960s

After World War II, New York regained its top-dog status in the fields of finance, art and communications, both in the US and the world, its intellectual and creative community swollen by European refugees. The city was the obvious choice as the permanent home of the **United Nations Organization**: lured by Rockefeller-donated land on the east side of Manhattan, the UN started construction in 1947; the Secretariat building in the complex introduced the glass curtain wall to Manhattan.

But even as the city, like the rest of the country, experienced a postwar boom, uniquely urban pressures were building. Immigrants from Puerto Rico and elsewhere in Latin America once more crammed East Harlem, the Lower East Side and other poor neighbourhoods, as did blacks from poor rural areas. Racial disturbances and riots started flaring up in what had for two hundred years been one of the more liberal of American cities. One response to the problem was a general exodus of the white middle classes – the **Great White Flight** as the media labelled it – out of New York. Between 1950 and 1970 more than a million families left the city. Things went from bad to worse during the 1960s with **race riots** in Harlem and Bedford-Stuyvesant in Brooklyn.

The **World's Fair** of 1964, again in Flushing Meadows, was a white elephant to boost the city's international profile, but on the streets the calls for civil liberties for blacks and withdrawal from Vietnam were, if anything, stronger than in most of the rest of the country. What few new buildings went up during this period seemed wilfully to destroy much of the best of earlier traditions. In particular, the eyesore that is **Madison Square Garden**, built over the old **Pennsylvania Station**, is still lamented as one of the city's worst architectural blunders; however, the **Verrazano-Narrows Bridge**, which linked Brooklyn to Staten Island, was an elegant, minimalist engineering addition.

The 1970s and 1980s

Manhattan reached **crisis point** in 1975 as companies, along with their employees, began leaving the city, lured by cheap land and low taxes in the suburbs. Even after municipal securities were sold, New York ran up a debt of millions of dollars. Essential

1939	Late 1940s to 1950s	1950	1965
Jazz legend Charlie Parker moves to New York, where he helps create Bebop	The East Village becomes home to the Beat poets – Jack Kerouac, Allen Ginsberg and William Burroughs	United Nations established in New York	Malcolm X is assassinated at Washington Heights' Audubon Ballroom

services, long shaky due to underfunding, were ready to collapse. Ironically, the mayor who oversaw this fiasco, **Abraham Beame**, was an accountant.

Three things saved the city: the **Municipal Assistance Corporation**, which was formed to borrow the money the city could no longer get its hands on; the 1977 election of **Edward I. Koch** as mayor, a man whose tough talking helped reassure jumpy corporations; and, in a roundabout way, the plummeting of the dollar on the world currency market following the rise of oil prices in the 1970s. This last factor, combined with cheap transatlantic airfares, brought European tourists into the city en masse for the first time.

The city's slow reversal of fortunes coincided with the completion of two face-saving building projects: the former **World Trade Center** was a gesture of confidence by the Port Authority of New York and New Jersey, which financed it; and the 1977 construction of the **Citicorp** (now Citigroup) **Center** added modernity and prestige to its environs on Lexington Avenue. Meanwhile, the raucous nightlife scene that started in the mid-1970s was best exemplified by hotspot **Studio 54**, where drugs and illicit sex were the main events off the dancefloor.

The real-estate and stock markets boomed during the 1980s, ushering in another era of Big Money. A spate of construction gave the city more eye-catching, though not necessarily well-loved, architecture, notably **Battery Park City**, and master builder **Donald Trump** provided glitzy housing for the super-wealthy. The stock market dip in 1987 started yet another downturn, and Koch's popularity waned. In 1989, he lost the Democratic mayoral nomination to **David Dinkins**, a 61-year-old black ex-marine who went on to beat Republican Rudolph Giuliani, a hard-nosed US attorney, in a tightly contested election. Even before the votes were counted, though, pundits forecasted that the city was beyond any mayoral healing. New York slipped, hard and fast, into a **massive recession**: in 1989 the city's budget deficit ran at $500 million. Of the 92 companies that had made the city their base in 1980, only 53 remained, the others having moved to cheaper pastures; and one in four New Yorkers was officially classed as poor – a figure unequalled since the Depression. By the end of 1990, the budget deficit was $1.5 billion.

The 1990s: the Giuliani years

Throughout 1991 the effects of these financial problems on the city's ordinary people became more and more apparent: homelessness increased; some public schools became no-go zones with armed police and metal detectors at the gates; and a garbage-workers' strike left piles of rubbish rotting on the streets. In 1993 New York, traditionally a Democratic city, elected **Rudolph Giuliani** – the city's first Republican mayor in 28 years.

The voters were rewarded: Giuliani's first term ushered in a dramatic upswing in New York's prosperity. Remarkable decreases in crime and a revitalized economy helped spur the tourism industry to some of its best years ever. Giuliani emerged as a very proactive mayor and one quite happy to take credit for making the streets safer and city bureaucracy leaner. While he made enemies among progressives for gutting rent stabilization laws and providing massive tax-breaks to corporations for moving to or remaining in the city (even as he reduced payments to the poor), Giuliani was handily

1969	1972	1977	1979
The Stonewall Riots in Greenwich Village inaugurate the gay-rights movement	World Trade Center Towers are built, dramatically altering the New York skyline	New York City Blackout (25hr): city suffers looting and civil unrest	The first hip-hop record, *Rapper's Delight*, released by The Sugarhill Gang (actually from New Jersey)

re-elected to a second term in 1997. The city's economy continued to grow, and a series of civic improvements, including the cleaning up of Times Square, the renovation of Grand Central Terminal and the influx of chain stores into Harlem ensued. Several high-profile incidents involving shocking allegations of **police brutality** marred Giuliani's second term, but these issues would all be superseded by events that would shake not just the city but the whole country – and cause the locals to lean on Giuliani once more.

9/11

As if the dot-com bust in the spring of 2001 wasn't hobbling enough, New York City was hit by the worst terrorist attack of the modern era on **September 11, 2001**. The story is now horribly familiar: two hijacked planes crashed into the Twin Towers of the World Trade Center, and, as the flaming fuel melted their steel frames, the towers collapsed. In all, 2750 people, including 343 firefighters, were killed in the catastrophe.

Over the next nine months, workers carted off 1.5 million tonnes of steel and debris, and by March 2002 the site was clear, well ahead of schedule (some would later ask if the job was perhaps done too quickly: several thousand Ground Zero workers continue to have chronic breathing problems as a result of not wearing ventilators and not following other environmental precautions at the site). So assured was his guidance throughout the ordeal that if Rudolph Giuliani had been able to run again, he most certainly would have won in a landslide. The law at the time, however, precluded him from running for a third term – he set his sights on the presidency instead – and so on January 1, 2002, businessman **Michael Bloomberg** replaced him as mayor.

The Bloomberg era

Though he had no prior political experience, Bloomberg, also a Republican (at least in name – as it's New York City, he not surprisingly has liberal views on same-sex marriage, gun control and a variety of other social issues), proved himself an able leader, using his corporate know-how to shore up the city's shaky finances and reorganize the school system. One of the mayor's most controversial acts was to follow California's lead and **ban smoking** in bars, clubs and all restaurants in 2003. Bar owners, naturally, fought the move, but it turned out to be good for business. In 2005 Bloomberg won re-election to a second term, during which he signed a law banning "trans-fats" in New York restaurants, unveiled a plan to replace the city's thirteen thousand taxicabs with hybrid vehicles (though it later got tripped up in the court system), and proposed a congestion pricing scheme to reduce traffic in Manhattan similar to the one in London.

In autumn 2007 the economy began to slump once more, as Wall Street registered heavy losses connected to the subprime mortgage crisis. The following year was a tough one for the city and some of its political figures. On Wall Street, investment banking giant **Bear Stearns** hit rock bottom and was bought out by JP Morgan, and later in the year **Lehman Brothers** declared bankruptcy. The real-estate market finally began to cave in and numerous construction projects were put on hold due to lack of funds. The 2008 presidential election season ended up as a disappointment for both Giuliani and

1987	1989	1993	2001
Black Monday: the stock exchange crashes and the Dow Jones index plunges 508 points in one day	David Dinkins becomes first black mayor of New York City, defeating Ed Koch and Rudolph Giuliani	Rudolph Giuliani is elected mayor – the city's first Republican mayor in 28 years	Twin Towers are destroyed in September 11 terrorist attacks; entrepreneur Michael Bloomberg succeeds Giuliani

the state's junior senator, **Hillary Rodham Clinton**, who lost their bids for the Republican and Democratic nominations, respectively (though Clinton became Secretary of State under President Barack Obama). Meanwhile, Bloomberg pushed a change through the city council to allow him to stand for a third stint in the fall of 2009; he won a closer-than-expected vote over Comptroller William Thompson.

The following year the economy finally began to rebound, a spate of new hotels opened and construction sped up both on the buildings around the World Trade Center site and on the long-awaited arena in Brooklyn's Atlantic Yards; meanwhile, the High Line and Hudson River Park developments helped spur revitalization on Manhattan's west side. Bloomberg presided over some difficult times, facing criticism for each event – one of the largest snowstorms in city history just after Christmas 2010; some unpopular (and, eventually, failed) appointments to high positions in the Department of Education; and, in October 2012, Hurricane Sandy (see box, p.249). The last of these shook the city like nothing since 9/11, disrupting subway lines, washing away shoreline houses and creating the need for heavy rebuilding in neighbourhoods from the Financial District (namely around South Street Seaport) to Far Rockaway. Meanwhile, a citywide bike-sharing plan – which almost immediately became the nation's largest such enterprise, with more than 40,000 members signed up within a month – was established; the long-debated Second Avenue subway line picked up speed in its construction; and the fight over Bloomberg's soda ban (an attempt to eradicate the sale of sugary drinks over sixteen ounces, overturned by the Manhattan Supreme Court) raged on.

The 2013 race to succeed Bloomberg as mayor saw a largely uninspiring field run, including disgraced Queens congressman Anthony Wiener; emerging late from the pack to win the Democratic primary was progressive Bill de Blasio, poised to be the first Democrat elected as mayor in 24 years.

2006	2008	2009	2012
7 World Trade Center finished, first in WTC rebuilding	US mortgage crisis hits Wall Street: Lehman Brothers goes bankrupt; several other merchant banks are sold	Michael Bloomberg is re-elected mayor for a third time	Hurricane Sandy makes landfall in New York City on October 29; roughly 800,000 in the area lose power

Books

Since the number of books about or set in New York is so vast, what follows is necessarily selective – use it as a place to begin further sleuthing. Most of the books listed are currently in print, but those that aren't should be available on websites such as ⓦabebooks.co.uk or ⓦamazon.co.uk.

ESSAYS, MEMOIRS AND NARRATIVE NONFICTION

Josh Alan Friedman *Tales of Times Square.* Expanded in 2007, the book chronicles activities on and around the square between 1978 and 1984, pornography's golden age, documenting a culture under siege by impresarios, pimps and 25-cent thrills.

William Grimes *Appetite City: A Culinary History of New York City.* The former *New York Times* restaurant critic engagingly traces the rise of the city's restaurants from way stations and early taverns to the glamour of today's celebrity-driven institutions.

Pete Hamill *Downtown: My Manhattan.* Former *Post* (and *Daily News*) editor Hamill is an authentic city voice. This isn't just his memoir of the island, though; it skilfully takes in centuries of New York characters and vanished settings along the way.

Phillip Lopate *Waterfront: A Walk Around Manhattan.* Somewhere between a guide, rumination and history, this book weaves personal observation of the city's waterfront today with its historical evolution – and works in a lot of salient quotes from literary types along the way.

Phillip Lopate (ed) *Writing New York.* A massive literary anthology of both fiction and nonfiction writings on the city, with selections by authors from Washington Irving to Tom Wolfe.

Federico García Lorca *Poet in New York.* The Andalusian poet and dramatist spent nine months in the city around the time of the 1929 Wall Street Crash. This collection of over thirty poems reveals his feelings on loneliness, greed, corruption, racism and mistreatment of the poor.

Frank McCourt *'Tis.* In the follow-up memoir to the phenomenon that was *Angela's Ashes*, McCourt relates life in NYC – concentrating on his time teaching in the public-school system – once he's left Ireland behind.

★ **Joseph Mitchell** *Up in the Old Hotel.* Mitchell's collected *New Yorker* essays are works of sober, if manipulative, genius, definitively chronicling NYC characters and situations with a reporter's precision and near-perfect style.

Jan Morris *Manhattan '45.* Morris's best piece of writing on Manhattan, reconstructing New York as it greeted returning GIs in 1945. Effortlessly written, fascinatingly anecdotal and marvellously warm about the city.

Georges Perec and Robert Bober *Ellis Island.* A brilliant, moving, original account of the "island of tears": part history, part meditation and part interviews. Some of the stories are heartbreaking (between 1892 and 1924 there were 3000 suicides on the island); the pictures even more so.

Suze Rotolo *A Freewheelin' Time: A Memoir of Greenwich Village in the Sixties.* Bob Dylan's formative years in the Village are recounted by his smart and sensitive girlfriend of four years, Suze Rotolo, who also talks about her own artistic pursuits and her family's devotion to communism.

Patti Smith *Just Kids.* The story of Smith's relationship with photographer Robert Mapplethorpe, as they and a cast of artists and musicians hang out in the *Chelsea Hotel* and generally define the art-punk ethos of 1970s New York City.

HISTORY, POLITICS AND SOCIETY

★ **Herbert Asbury** *The Gangs of New York.* First published in 1928, this fascinating telling of the seamier side of New York is essential reading. Full of historical detail, anecdotes and character sketches of crooks, the book describes New York mischief in all its incarnations and locales.

Edwin G. Burrows and Mike Wallace *Gotham: A History of New York City to 1898.* Enormous and encyclopedic in its detail, this is a serious history of the development of New York, with chapters on everything from its role in the Revolution to reform movements to its racial make-up in the 1820s.

★ **Robert A. Caro** *The Power Broker: Robert Moses and the Fall of New York.* Despite its imposing length, this brilliant and searing critique of New York City's most powerful twentieth-century figure is one of the most important books ever written about the city and its environs. Caro's book brings to light the megalomania and manipulation responsible for the creation of the nation's largest urban infrastructure.

George Chauncey *Gay New York: The Making of the Gay Male World 1890–1940.* Definitive, revealing account of the city's gay subculture.

Irving Howe *World of Our Fathers: The Journey of the East*

European Jews to America and the Life They Found and Made. The title more or less says it all. If you're looking for a narrative about how Jewish immigrant experience played out in New York City's Lower East Side, you'll find a stirring and sweeping account of it right here.

Kenneth T. Jackson (ed) The Encyclopedia of New York. Massive, engrossing and utterly comprehensive guide to just about everything in the city. Did you know that Truman Capote's real name was Streckford Persons?

Roger Kahn The Boys of Summer. This account of the 1950s Brooklyn Dodgers by a beat writer who covered them is considered one of the classic baseball reads.

David Levering Lewis When Harlem Was in Vogue. Much-needed account of the Harlem Renaissance, a brief flowering of the arts in the 1920s and 1930s that was suffocated by the dual forces of the Depression and racism.

★ **Jonathan Mahler** Ladies and Gentlemen, the Bronx Is Burning: 1977, Baseball, Politics, and the Battle for the Soul of a City. Incredible portrait of the city as it was in the late 1970s, weaving together Yankee Reggie Jackson's conflicts with manager Billy Martin, the duel between Mario Cuomo and Ed Koch, the birth of punk rock, the hunt for serial killer Son of Sam, the blackout and looting, and more.

Legs McNeil and Gillian McCain Please Kill Me. An oral history of punk music in New York, artfully constructed by juxtaposing snippets of interviews as if the various protagonists (artists, financiers, impresarios) were in a conversation. Sometimes hilarious, often quite bleak.

Dan Okrent Great Fortune: The Epic of Rockefeller Center. Everything you ever wanted to know about the construction of one of New York's cultural and architectural high-water marks: fascinating stories of the Rockefeller family, the designers, the art commissioned (and, in one case, removed) and much more.

★ **Luc Sante** Low Life: Lures and Snares of Old New York. This chronicle of the city's seamy side between 1840 and 1919 is a pioneering work. Full of outrageous details usually left out of conventional history, it reconstructs the day-to-day life of the urban poor, criminals and prostitutes with shocking clarity.

Russell Shorto The Island at the Centre of the World. Before New York was New York it was New Amsterdam; Shorto delivers a much-needed and highly readable account of this largely forgotten chapter in the city's history, using newly researched Dutch sources. Shorto's central thesis – that it was the freedom-loving and multicultural Dutch city that laid the roots of modern New York – is highly compelling.

Gay Talese Fame and Obscurity. Talese deftly presents interviews with New York City's famous (Sinatra, DiMaggio, etc) and its obscure (bums, chauffeurs, etc), offering not only a window into the heart of NYC, but that of human existence.

Jennifer Toth Mole People. A creepy sociological study of the people who live below NYC streets, in the dark reaches of the subway tunnel system. You may never again ride the subway without your face plastered to the window looking for signs of human life.

ART, ARCHITECTURE AND PHOTOGRAPHY

Lorraine Diehl The Late Great Pennsylvania Station. The anatomy of a travesty. How could a railroad palace, modelled after the Baths of Caracalla in Rome, stand for only fifty years before being destroyed? The pictures alone warrant the price.

Horst Hamann New York Vertical. This beautiful book pays homage to the New York skyscraper, and is filled with dazzling black-and-white vertical shots of Manhattan, accompanied by witty quotes from famous and obscure folk.

★ **Jane Jacobs** The Death and Life of Great American Cities. Landmark 1961 screed authored by Robert Moses' nemesis, and railing against urban over-planning.

David McCullough Great Bridge: The Epic Story of the Building of the Brooklyn Bridge. The story of the father-and-son Roebling team who fought the laws of gravity, sharp-toothed competitors and corrupt politicians to build a bridge that has withstood the test of time and become one of NYC's most noted landmarks.

Jed Perl New Art City. A thoughtful look at the artists (some household names, like de Kooning; some less so, like Hans Hoffman) who defined the 1940s, 50s and 60s of the New York scene – and how New York helped define them.

Jacob Riis How the Other Half Lives. Photojournalism reporting on life in the Lower East Side at the end of the nineteenth century. Its original publication in 1890 awakened many to the plight of New York's poor.

Stern, Melins and Fishman/Stern, Gilmartin and Massengale/Stern, Gilmartin and Mellins/Stern, Mellins and Fishman/Stern, Fishman and Tilove New York 1880/1900/1930/1960/2000. These five exhaustive tomes contain all you'll ever want or need to know about architecture and the organization of the city.

★ **N. White, E. Willensky and F. Leadon** (eds) AIA Guide to New York. The definitive contemporary guide to the city's architecture – witty, immensely informative and opinionated – and useful as an on-site reference; look for the 2010 edition, which is the latest.

OTHER GUIDES

Richard Alleman The Movie Lover's Guide to New York. More than two hundred listings of corners of the city with cinematic associations: TV and film locations, stars' childhood homes and final resting places, and more. Interestingly written, painstakingly researched.

★ **Federal Writers' Project** The WPA Guide to New

York City. Originally written in 1939 and subsequently reissued, this detailed guide offers a fascinating look at life in New York City when the Dodgers played at Ebbetts Field, a trolley ride cost five cents and a room at the *Plaza* was $7.50. A surprising amount of description remains apt.

Rob Grader *The Cheap Bastard's Guide to New York City*. If the title doesn't immediately turn you off, this frequently updated guide is the book for you.

Eric Sanderson *Mannahatta*. Get this for the illustrations, charts and maps if nothing else: it's a geographic, ecological history of the city that is bound to give you new perspectives on what Manhattan was before becoming such a densely populated island.

FICTION

Julia Alvarez *How the Garcia Girls Lost Their Accents*. Four Latina sisters are uprooted from their privileged life in the Dominican Republic to the Bronx in this compelling look at the modern immigrant experience.

Paul Auster *The New York Trilogy: City of Glass, Ghosts and The Locked Room*. Three Borgesian investigations into the mystery, madness and murders of contemporary NYC.

★ **James Baldwin** *Another Country*. Baldwin's best-known novel, tracking the feverish search for meaningful relationships among a group of 1960s New York bohemians.

Lawrence Block *When the Sacred Ginmill Closes*. Tough to choose between Block's perfectly pitched Matthew Scudder suspense novels, all set in the city; this might be the most compelling, with Hell's Kitchen, downtown Manhattan and far-flung parts of Brooklyn expertly woven into a dark mystery.

Truman Capote *Breakfast at Tiffany's*. Far sadder and racier than the movie, this novel is a rhapsody to New York in the early 1940s, tracking the dissolute youthful residents of an uptown apartment building and their movements about town.

Caleb Carr *The Alienist*. This 1896-set thriller evokes old New York to perfection. The heavy-handed psychobabble grates at times, but the story line (the pursuit of one of the first serial killers) is still involving. Best for its descriptions of New York as well as saliva-inducing details of meals at long-gone restaurants.

Michael Chabon *The Amazing Adventures of Kavalier and Clay*. A wartime fantasy of Jewish youths in Brooklyn and their fascination with all forms of escapism – magic, radio and, most important, comic strips.

Reed Farrel Coleman *Walking the Perfect Square*. Coleman's mysteries contain one of the genre's great (relatively) unknown creations: Brooklyn detective-cum-wine store operator Moe Prager, a very flawed protagonist. This, the first, flashes back between the late Seventies and late Nineties; the plot is involving enough but most importantly sets the scene for Prager's emotional development.

Stephen Crane *Maggie: A Girl of the Streets*. An 1893 melodrama about a girl growing up in a Lower East Side slum. Although luridly overdescribed, its groundbreaking naturalism brought deserved acclaim to *Red Badge of Courage* author Crane; the fictional counterpart to Riis's work.

Don DeLillo *Underworld*. Following the fate of the baseball hit out of the park to win the 1951 pennant for the New York Giants, DeLillo's sprawling novel offers a counterhistory of twentieth-century America. His luminous prose is spellbinding even when the story feels faintly ridiculous.

Jennifer Egan *A Visit from the Goon Squad*. Egan's Pulitzer Prize-winning "novel" – really, a series of loosely connected short stories that jump around in time and space – bristles with energy, imagination and musical reference; many take place in or around New York, including one in a disquieting version of the city's future.

★ **Ralph Ellison** *Invisible Man*. The definitive, if sometimes long-winded, novel of what it's like to be black and American, using Harlem and the 1950s race riots as a backdrop.

★ **Paula Fox** *Desperate Characters*. A depressing, engrossing drama about a faded marriage in 1960s Brooklyn, this slim book is exquisitely crafted and brilliantly observed.

Oscar Hijuelos *Our House in the Last World*. A warmly evocative novel of a Cuban immigrant's life in New York from before the war to the present day.

Chester Himes *The Crazy Kill*. Himes wrote violent, fast-moving and funny thrillers set in Harlem; this and *Cotton Goes to Harlem* are among the best.

Henry James *Washington Square*. Skilful and engrossing examination of the mores and strict social expectations of genteel New York society in the late nineteenth century.

Sue Kaufman *Diary of a Mad Housewife*. This is a classic dissection of 1960s New York, satirically chronicling the antics of a group of social climbers along with the disintegration of a marriage.

★ **Jonathan Lethem** *Motherless Brooklyn*. Brooklyn author sets this quirky suspense novel in Cobble Hill and its environs, where a Tourette's sufferer tries to track down his boss's killer. See also his subsequent *The Fortress of Solitude*, which treats childhood and gentrification with great wit and sensitivity, or *Chronic City*, a kind of send-up of Manhattan.

Colum McCann *Let the Great World Spin*. Though set in the 1970s, its touchstone of Philip Petit's tightrope walk across the new towers of the World Trade Center – then zooming to the ordinary lives of the people below – make it clear that the effects of 9/11 are the true social subject of this involving novel.

Alice McDermott *Charming Billy*. Billy is a poetry-loving drunkard from Queens, looking to bring his Irish love over to New York City. National Book Award winner.

Jay McInerney *Bright Lights, Big City*. A trendy, "voice of a generation" book when it came out in the 1980s, it made first-time novelist McInerney a household name. The story follows a struggling New York writer in his job as a fact-checker at an important literary magazine (a thinly disguised *New Yorker*), and from one cocaine-sozzled nightclub to another. Still amusing.

Emma McLaughlin and Nicola Kraus *The Nanny Diaries: A Novel*. A delicious and nimble comic novel, culled from the authors' own experiences nannying to the wealthy families of the Upper East Side; later made into an entertaining film with Scarlett Johansson.

Joseph O'Neill *Netherland*. Bringing together threads about friendship, marriage, cricket, the immigrant experience and 9/11, this literary novel, if at times overwritten, ranks as one of the more important and memorable New York stories of the past decade.

Dorothy Parker *Complete Stories*. Parker's tales are, at times, surprisingly moving, depicting New York in all its glories, excesses and pretensions with perfect, searing wit.

★ **Richard Price** *Lush Life*. With perfect pitch for the language of the streets, Richard Price tells the sprawling story of the murder of a bartender on today's Lower East Side, a place where struggling writers, old Jewish immigrants, drug dealers, cops and club kids uneasily coexist.

Judith Rossner *Looking for Mr Goodbar*. A disquieting book, tracing the life – and eventual demise – of a female teacher in search of love in volatile and permissive 1970s New York.

Henry Roth *Call It Sleep*. Roth's novel traces the awakening of a small immigrant child to the realities of life among the slums of the Jewish Lower East Side. Read more for the evocations of childhood than the social comment.

Paul Rudnick *Social Disease*. Hilarious, often incredible send-up of Manhattan night-owls. Very New York, very funny.

J.D. Salinger *The Catcher in the Rye*. Salinger's gripping novel of adolescence, following Holden Caulfield's sardonic journey of discovery through the streets of New York. A classic.

Hubert Selby, Jr *Last Exit to Brooklyn*. When first published in Britain in 1966, this novel was tried on charges of obscenity. Even now it's a disturbing read, evoking the sex, immorality, drugs and violence of Brooklyn in the 1960s with fearsome clarity.

Betty Smith *A Tree Grows in Brooklyn*. A classic, and rightly so – a courageous Irish girl learns about family, life and sex against a vivid prewar Brooklyn backdrop. Totally absorbing.

Rex Stout *The Doorbell Rang*. Stout's Nero Wolfe is perhaps the most intrinsically "New York" of all the literary detectives based in the city, a larger-than-life character who, with the help of his dashing assistant, Archie Goodwin, solves crimes from the comfort of his sumptuous midtown brownstone. Wonderfully evocative of the city in the 1940s and 1950s.

Colm Tóibín *Brooklyn*. Another immigrant story, this time via Ireland to 1950s Brooklyn; a methodical, literary work that rewards your patience and persistence.

Jess Walter *The Zero*. This dark, hallucinatory and probing satire, set just after 9/11, may set your head spinning like that of its protagonist – who endures memory loss, a self-inflicted gunshot wound and an unusual mission that he has no idea why he's on.

Lauren Weisberger *The Devil Wears Prada*. A satirical snapshot of New York's cut-throat magazine world, this *roman à clef* from *Vogue* editor Anna Wintour's former assistant is pleasant enough, but the film version with Meryl Streep is even better.

★ **Edith Wharton** *Age of Innocence*. A withering, deftly drawn picture of New York high society at the beginning turn of the twentieth century and how rigid social convention keeps two sensitive, ill-fated lovers apart. See also Wharton's astounding *House of Mirth* and her classic stories *Old New York*.

Tom Wolfe *Bonfire of the Vanities*. Set all around New York City, this sprawling novel skewers 1980s status-mongers to great effect.

New York on film

With its skyline and rugged facades, its mean streets and swanky avenues, its electric energy and edgy attitude, New York City is a natural-born movie star. From the silent era's cautionary tales of young lovers ground down by the metropolis, through the smoky location-shot *noirs* of the 1940s, right through to the Lower East Side and Brooklyn indies of the past few decades, New York has probably been the most filmed city on earth. What follows is a selection not just of the best New York movies but the most New York of New York movies – movies that capture the city's atmosphere, pulse and style; movies that celebrate its diversity or revel in its misfortunes; and movies that, if nothing else, give you a pretty good idea of what you're going to get before you get there.

TEN NEW YORK CLASSICS

Breakfast at Tiffany's (Blake Edwards, 1961). The most charming and cherished of New York movie romances, starring Audrey Hepburn as party girl Holly Golightly. Hepburn and George Peppard run up and down each other's fire escapes and skip along Fifth Avenue, taking in the New York Public Library and that jewellery store.

Do the Right Thing (Spike Lee, 1989). Set over 24 hours on the hottest day of the year in Brooklyn's Bed-Stuy – a day on which the melting pot reaches boiling point – Spike Lee's colourful, stylish masterpiece moves from comedy to tragedy to compose an epic song of New York.

The Godfather Part II (Francis Ford Coppola, 1974). Flashing back to the early life of Vito Corleone, Coppola's great sequel re-created the Italian immigrant experience at the turn of the century, portraying Corleone quarantined at Ellis Island and growing up tough on the meticulously re-created streets of Little Italy.

King Kong (Merian C. Cooper and Ernest B. Schoedsack, 1933). *King Kong* paints a vivid picture of Depression-era Manhattan, and gives us the city's most indelible movie image: King Kong straddling the Empire State Building and swatting at passing planes.

Manhattan (Woody Allen, 1979). This black-and-white masterpiece, one of the truly great eulogies to the city, details the self-absorptions, lifestyles and romances of middle-class intellectuals, to the tune of a Gershwin soundtrack.

On the Town (Gene Kelly and Stanley Donen, 1949). Three sailors get 24 hours' shore leave in NYC and fight over whether to see the sights or chase the girls. Starring Gene Kelly, Frank Sinatra and Ann Miller flashing her legs in the Museum of Natural History, this was the first musical taken out of the studios and onto the streets. Smart, cynical and satirical with a bunch of terrific numbers.

On the Waterfront (Elia Kazan, 1954). Few images of New York are as unforgettable as Marlon Brando's rooftop pigeon coop at dawn and those misty views of the New York Harbor (actually shot just over the river in Hoboken), in this unforgettable story of long-suffering longshoremen and union racketeering.

Shadows (John Cassavetes, 1960). Cassavetes' debut film is a New York movie *par excellence*: a New Wave melody about jazz musicians, young love and racial prejudice, shot with bebop verve and jazzy passion in Central Park, Greenwich Village and even the MoMA sculpture garden.

Sweet Smell of Success (Alexander Mackendrick, 1957). Broadway as a nest of vipers. Gossip columnist Burt Lancaster and sleazy press-agent Tony Curtis eat each other's tails in this snappy, cynical study of showbiz corruption. Shot on location and mostly at night, in steely black and white. Times Square and the Great White Way never looked so alluring.

Taxi Driver (Martin Scorsese, 1976). A long night's journey into day by the great chronicler of the city's dark side. Scorsese's New York is hallucinatorily seductive and thoroughly repellent in this superbly unsettling study of obsessive outsider Travis Bickle (Robert De Niro).

FIVE NEW YORK STORIES

Basquiat (Julian Schnabel, 1996). Haunting portrait of the artist as a young (doomed) man, rising from spray-painting graffiti and living in a box in a Lower East Side park to taking the New York art world by storm in the early 1980s. David Bowie plays a sensitive Andy Warhol.

The Cruise (Bennett Miller, 1998). A documentary portrait of a true New York eccentric, Timothy "Speed" Levitch, a Dostoyevskian character with a baroque flair for language and an encyclopedic knowledge of local history, who takes puzzled tourists on guided "cruises" around the city, on which he rails against the tyranny of the grid plan and rhapsodizes about "the lascivious voyeurism of the tour bus".

Man on Wire (James Marsh, 2008). This documentary on Philippe Petit's astounding tightrope walk between the Twin Towers in 1974 is illuminating both about the feat and the character of the man behind it.

Pollock (Ed Harris, 2000). From a cramped Manhattan apartment to the barren nature of the Hamptons, abstract artist Jackson Pollock drips on canvases and battles his wife (Oscar-winner Marcia Gay Harden), fame and drink. Harris is powerful in the title role.

Unmade Beds (Nicholas Barker, 1998). This poignant, occasionally hilarious and beautifully stylized documentary about four single New Yorkers looking for love in the personal columns, visualizes the city as one endless Edward Hopper painting, full of lonely souls biding time in rented rooms.

FIVE FILMS ABOUT MODERN NEW YORK

The 25th Hour (Spike Lee, 2002). Lee stacks his film flick (based on an excellent first novel by David Benioff) with an impressive cast, headed by Ed Norton as a drug dealer on the last day before he goes to prison, ricocheting round between friends and lovers. Bleak but gripping.

The Devil Wears Prada (David Frankel, 2006). A delicious turn by Meryl Streep as an Anna Wintour-clone propels this story of a young woman who arrives in the city with high journalistic ambitions but can only find work at a glamorous fashion magazine (a thinly disguised *Vogue*); based on a popular novel (see p.422).

Frances Ha (Noah Baumbach, 2012). Greta Gerwig is the centre of attention in this breezy black-and-white

flick that aims for a retro feel, but its twentysomething-trying-to-make-it-in-the-big-city theme is totally up to date.

It's Kind of a Funny Story (Anna Boden and Ryan Fleck, 2010). Frequently cited as a modern-day *One Flew Over the Cuckoo's Nest*, this has a much lighter touch, following the travails of a depressed Brooklyn high-school student who checks himself into a psychiatric ward.

Roger Dodger (Dylan Kidd, 2002). A self-important advertising exec (Campbell Scott) takes his nephew (Jesse Eisenberg) on an alcohol-fuelled tour of the city in search of sex, plumbing the depths of his own depravity. Extremely witty, if hard to watch.

FIVE FILMS ABOUT NEW YORK'S PAST

The Age of Innocence (Martin Scorsese, 1993). The upper echelons of New York society in the 1870s brought gloriously to life. Though Scorsese restricts most of the action to drawing rooms and ballrooms, look out for the breathtaking matte shot of a then-undeveloped Upper East Side.

The Crowd (King Vidor, 1928). "You've got to be good in that town if you want to beat the crowd." A young couple try to make it in the big city but are swallowed up and spat out by the capitalist machine. A bleak vision of New York in the 1920s, and one of the great silent films.

The Last Days of Disco (Whit Stillman, 1998). About the most unlikely setting for Stillman's brand of square WASPy talkfests would be the bombastic glittery

bacchanals that were Studio 54 in its late-1970s heyday, which is what makes this far more enjoyable than the same season's overly literal and melodramatic *54* (Mark Christopher, 1998).

Radio Days (Woody Allen, 1987). Woody contrasts reminiscences of his loud, vulgar family in 1940s Rockaway with reveries of the golden days of radio and the glamour of Times Square.

Summer of Sam (Spike Lee, 1999). The dark summer of 1977 – the summer of the "Son of Sam" killings, a blistering heatwave, power blackouts, looting, arson and the birth of punk – provides the perfect backdrop for Lee's sprawling tale of paranoia and betrayal in an Italian-American enclave of the Bronx.

FIVE NEW YORK COMEDIES

Annie Hall (Woody Allen, 1977). Oscar-winning autobiographical comic romance, which flits from reminiscences of Alvy Singer's childhood living beneath the Coney Island Cyclone to life and love in uptown Manhattan, is a valentine both to ex-lover co-star Diane Keaton and to the city. Simultaneously clever, bourgeois and very winning.

Elf (Jon Favreau, 2003). A Will Ferrell vehicle with an actual heart, in which a young orphan mistakenly gets carried off to the North Pole, is brought up as an elf, then goes as an

adult to Manhattan to find his real father. Dad (James Caan) works in the Empire State Building; the romantic interest (Zooey Deschanel) works at Gimbel's; and the climactic scenes take place in and around Central Park.

The Out-of-Towners (Arthur Hiller, 1969). If you have any problems getting into town from the airport take solace from the fact that they can be nothing compared to those endured by Jack Lemmon and Sandy Dennis – for whom everything that can go wrong does go wrong – in Neil Simon's frantic comedy.

So This Is New York (Richard Fleischer, 1948). A bomb on its initial release, this rarely shown but edgy and innovative comedy plants three Midwesterners among the sharpies and operators of 1930s New York. The voiceover by star Henry Morgan (an Indiana salesman thoroughly unimpressed by the big city) is sublimely sarcastic.

The Squid and the Whale (Noah Baumbach, 2005). A sometimes-uncomfortable but quite funny and resonant coming-of-age story in Park Slope, Brooklyn; the title refers to an exhibit in the Ocean Life section of the American Museum of Natural History.

FIVE NEW YORK NIGHTMARES

After Hours (Martin Scorsese, 1985). Yuppie computer programmer Griffin Dunne inadvertently ends up on a nightlong odyssey into the Hades of downtown New York, a journey that goes from bad to worse to awful as he encounters every kook south of 14th Street. Amazing footage of pre-gentrified Soho.

American Psycho (Mary Harron, 2000). This stylized adaptation of the Bret Easton Ellis novel succeeds largely due to Christian Bale, pulling off some blacker-than-black comedy in his role as a securities trader consumed by designer labels, the ladder of success and Huey Lewis lyrics.

The Lost Weekend (Billy Wilder, 1945). Alcoholic Ray Milland is left alone in the city with no money and a desperate thirst. The film's most famous scene is his long trek up Third Avenue (shot on location) trying to hawk his typewriter to buy booze, only to find all the pawn shops closed for Yom Kippur.

Rosemary's Baby (Roman Polanski, 1968). Mia Farrow and John Cassavetes move into their dream New York apartment and think they have problems with nosy neighbours – but that's just until Farrow gets pregnant and hell, literally, breaks loose. Arguably the most terrifying film ever set in the city.

The Taking of Pelham One Two Three (Joseph Sargent, 1974). Just when you thought it was safe to get back on the subway. A gang of mercenary hoods hijacks a train on its way through midtown and threatens to start killing one passenger per minute if their million-dollar ransom is not paid within the hour.

FIVE WALKS DOWN THE MEAN STREETS

The French Connection (William Friedkin, 1971). Plenty of heady Brooklyn atmosphere in this sensational Oscar-winning cop thriller starring Gene Hackman, whose classic car-and-subway chase takes place under the Bensonhurst Elevated Railroad.

Mean Streets (Martin Scorsese, 1973). Scorsese's brilliant breakthrough film breathlessly follows small-time hood Harvey Keitel and his volatile, harum-scarum buddy Robert De Niro around a vividly portrayed Little Italy before reaching its violent climax.

Midnight Cowboy (John Schlesinger, 1969). The odd love story between Jon Voight's bumpkin hustler and Dustin Hoffman's touching urban creep Ratso Rizzo plays out against both the seediest and swankiest of New York locations. The only X-rated film to receive an Oscar for Best Picture.

Prince of the City (Sidney Lumet, 1981). Lumet is a die-hard New York director, and this is his New York epic. A corrupt narcotics detective turns federal informer to assuage his guilt, and Lumet takes us from drug busts in Harlem to the cops' suburban homes on Long Island, to federal agents' swanky pads overlooking Central Park.

Superfly (Gordon Parks Jr, 1972). Propelled by its ecstatic Curtis Mayfield score, this blaxploitation classic about one smooth-looking drug dealer's ultimate score is best seen today for its mind-boggling fashion excess and almost documentary-like look at the Harlem bars, streets, clubs and diners of thirty-odd years ago. Also see Parks' *Shaft*, released a year earlier.

FIVE NEW YORK GROOVES

42nd Street (Lloyd Bacon, 1933). One of the best films ever made about Broadway – though the film rarely ventures outside the theatre. Starring Ruby Keeler as the young chorus girl who has to replace the ailing leading lady: she goes on stage an unknown and, well, you know the rest.

A Great Day in Harlem (Jean Bach, 1994). A unique jazz documentary that spins many tales around the famous Art Kane photograph for which the cream of New York's jazz world assemble on the steps of a Harlem brownstone one August morning in 1958. Using home-movie footage of the event and present-day interviews, Bach creates a wonderful portrait of a golden age.

Guys and Dolls (Joseph L. Mankiewicz, 1955). The great Broadway musical shot entirely on soundstages and giving as unlikely a picture of Times Square hoodlums (all colourfully suited sweetie-pies) as was ever seen. And a singing and dancing Marlon Brando to boot.

Saturday Night Fever (John Badham, 1977). What everybody remembers is the tacky glamour of flared white pantsuits and mirror-balled discos, but *Saturday Night Fever* is actually a touching and believable portrayal of working-class youth in the 1970s, Italian-American Brooklyn and the road to Manhattan.

West Side Story (Robert Wise and Jerome Robbins, 1961). Sex, singing and Shakespeare in a hyper-cinematic Oscar-winning musical (via Broadway) about rival street gangs.

Small print and index

A ROUGH GUIDE TO ROUGH GUIDES

Published in 1982, the first Rough Guide – to Greece – was a student scheme that became a publishing phenomenon. Mark Ellingham, a recent graduate in English from Bristol University, had been travelling in Greece the previous summer and couldn't find the right guidebook. With a small group of friends he wrote his own guide, combining a highly contemporary, journalistic style with a thoroughly practical approach to travellers' needs.

The immediate success of the book spawned a series that rapidly covered dozens of destinations. And, in addition to impecunious backpackers, Rough Guides soon acquired a much broader readership that relished the guides' wit and inquisitiveness as much as their enthusiastic, critical approach and value-for-money ethos.

These days, Rough Guides include recommendations from budget to luxury and cover more than 200 destinations around the globe, as well as producing an ever-growing range of eBooks and apps.

Visit **roughguides.com** to see our latest publications.

Rough Guide credits

Editors: Rachel Mills, Ann-Marie Shaw, Helen Abramson
Layout: Ankur Guha
Cartography: Katie Bennett
Picture editor: Tim Draper
Proofreader: Diane Margolis
Managing editor: Mani Ramaswamy
Assistant editor: Prema Dutta
Production: Charlotte Cade
Cover design: Tim Draper, Ankur Guha, Wilf Matos and Dan May

Editorial assistant: Olivia Rawes
Senior pre-press designer: Dan May
Creative operations manager: Jason Mitchell
Operations coordinator: Helen Blount
Publisher: Joanna Kirby
Publishing director (Travel): Clare Currie
Commercial manager: Gino Magnotta
Managing director: John Duhigg

Publishing information

This fourteenth edition published February 2014 by
Rough Guides Ltd,
80 Strand, London WC2R 0RL
11, Community Centre, Panchsheel Park,
New Delhi 110017, India
Distributed by Penguin Random House
Penguin Books Ltd,
80 Strand, London WC2R 0RL
Penguin Group (USA)
345 Hudson Street, NY 10014, USA
Penguin Group (Australia)
250 Camberwell Road, Camberwell,
Victoria 3124, Australia
Penguin Group (NZ)
67 Apollo Drive, Mairangi Bay, Auckland 1310,
New Zealand
Penguin Group (South Africa)
Block D, Rosebank Office Park, 181 Jan Smuts Avenue,
Parktown North, Gauteng, South Africa 2193
Rough Guides is represented in Canada by Tourmaline
Editions Inc. 662 King Street West, Suite 304, Toronto,
Ontario M5V 1M7
Printed in Singapore by Toppan Security Printing Pte. Ltd.

MIX
Paper from responsible sources
FSC FSC™ C018179

Help us update

We've gone to a lot of effort to ensure that the fourteenth edition of **The Rough Guide to New York City** is accurate and up-to-date. However, things change – places get "discovered", opening hours are notoriously fickle, restaurants and rooms raise prices or lower standards. If you feel we've got it wrong or left something out, we'd like to know, and if you can remember the address, the price, the hours, the phone number, so much the better.

Please send your comments with the subject line "**Rough Guide New York City Update**" to ✉ mail @uk.roughguides.com. We'll credit all contributions and send a copy of the next edition (or any other Rough Guide if you prefer) for the very best emails.

Find more travel information, connect with fellow travellers and plan your trip on ⊕ roughguides.com

Acknowledgements

Andrew Rosenberg would like to thank Rachel Mills for her keen editorial eye and her patience; fellow author and collaborator Stephen Keeling; Mani Ramaswamy at RG HQ; Barbara Russo, Cindy VandenBosch, Brittnie Mabry, Sara Lieber, Laura Washington, Alanna Schindelwolf, Tim Wroten, Glen Whitney and Cindy Lawrence for their assistance during research; and, for the love, company, support and ideas, Melanie and Jules.

Stephen Keeling would like to thank Victor Ozols, Seth Fineberg, Gordon Polatnick, Marion Emmanuelle and the team at AvroKO, Darren Wan at Red Egg, fellow author Andrew Rosenberg, Rachel Mills and Annie Shaw for their fine editing and Tiffany Wu, whose love and support made this book possible.

ABOUT THE AUTHORS

Andrew Rosenberg is a freelance copy editor and sometimes writer. He lives in Brooklyn with his wife, Melanie; son, Jules; and cats, Caesar and Louise. You can contact him about anything in the book at ❷nycroughguide @gmail.com.

Stephen Keeling has lived in New York City since 2006. He worked as a financial journalist for seven years before writing his first travel guide and has written several titles for Rough Guides, including books on Puerto Rico, New England, Florida and Canada.

Martin Dunford is the author of Rough Guides to Rome, Italy, Amsterdam and Norfolk & Suffolk, among others, and is a freelance writer and editor and founder of the UK travel website ❿coolplaces.co.uk. He lives in London and Norfolk, with his wife Caroline and two daughters.

Readers' updates

Thanks to all the readers who have taken the time to write in with comments and suggestions (and apologies if we've inadvertently omitted or misspelt anyone's name):

Lindsey Anderson, Philip Basford, Rosie Blass, Laura Buhl, Andria Chin, Radmila Daniell, John Figaro, Cathy Guppey, Joanne Gibbons, Dan Harvey, Marianne Hoogeveen, Linda Maxson, Ranjit Madgavkar, Sheryn Omeri, Sue Wall, Eric Westberg and Hywel Williams.

Photo credits

All photos © Rough Guides except the following:
(Key: t-top; c-centre; b-bottom; l-left; r-right)

p.1 Corbis:Allan Baxter
p.2 Getty Images: Superstudio
p.4 Getty Images: Siegfried Layda
p.6 4Corners: Degree
p.7 Alamy: dbimages (b); Stacy Walsh (c) Getty Images: Wayne Eastep (t)
p.8 Getty Images: Siegfried Layda (b); Michael Yamashita (t)
p.10 Alamy: Danita Delimont
p.11 Getty Images: Luis Vega
p.12 Axiom Photographic Agency: Katja Neinemann
p.13 Getty Images: Pete Seaward (t)
p.14 Getty Images: Mitchell Funk
p.15 Corbis: Erik Lesser (b); MATTES René (c); Getty Images: Jim McIsaac (t)
p.16 Getty Images: Brad Barket (b); Jorg Greuel (t)
p.17 Alamy: Randy Duchaine (bl); Arcaid Images (br); Getty Images: Marvin E Newman (t)
p.18 Alamy: Richard Levine (c); Corbis: Jon Hicks (t); Getty Images: Gavin Hellier (b)
p.19 Alamy: Ann E Parry (c); Corbis: Rudy Sulgan (b); Getty Images: Travelstock44 - Juergen Held (t)
p.36 Getty Images: Harald Sund
p.51 Getty Images: Ben Cooper (bl); Herald Sund (tl); Camille Tokerud (tr); STAN HONDA (br)
p.56 Getty Images: Allan Baxter
p.62 Alamy: Patrick Batchelder
p.69 Alamy: Richard Green
p.77 Alamy: Richard Levine
p.86 Alamy: World Travel Library
p.94 SuperStock: Hemis
p.101 Alamy: Wendy Connett (br); SuperStock: Ambient Images (bl); Jean-Pierre Lescourre (tr)
p.105 Corbis: GH

p.112 Getty Images: Ellen Stagg
p.117 Getty Images: Picture Garden
p.121 Getty Images: Berthold Trenkel
p.135 Getty Images: Siegfried Layda (t)
p.139 Getty Images: Image Source
p.149 Getty Images: Piotr Powietrzynski
p.157 Corbis: Massimo Borchi
p.167 Getty Images: Christian Kober
p.177 Getty Images: Mitchell Funk (b)
p.196 Alamy: Ambient Images
p.212 Alamy: Randy Duchaine
p. 237 Alamy: Pegaz
p.249 Getty Images: Luca Trovato
p.257 Getty Images: Nick Laham (br); Rob Tringali (tr, bl); Jim McIsaac (tl)
p.259 Alamy: Ambient Images
p.276 Axiom Photographic Agency: Jenny Acheson
p.291 Getty Images: Frank Whitney (br)
p.321 Alamy: Ted Pink
p.333 Getty Images: Cory Schwartz
p.350 Alamy: Sandra Baker
p.361 Getty Images: Stan Honda
p.368 Alamy: Alex Segre
p.388 Getty Images: Don Emmert
p.398 Getty Images: Mario Tama
p.410 Getty Images: John Kobal Foundation

Front Cover: I Love NY Big Apple artwork © Travel Pictures Ltd
Back Cover: Financial District at dusk © Sylvain Sonnet/ Getty Images (t); Statue of Liberty souvenirs © Brian Jannsen (br); Wall Street sign © Ocean/Corbis (bl)

Index

Maps are marked in grey

N

U

V

W

Y

Z

Maps

Index

New York

Listings key

■ Accommodation

● Restaurant/café

■ Bar/nightlife

● Shop

City plan

The **city plan** on the pages that follow is divided as shown on the right:

Map symbols

🛥	Boat
✡	Synagogue
✿	Buddhist temple
☪	Mosque
▲	Peak
⊠	Gate
⊥	Gardens
⛳	Golf course
)(	Bridge
✚	Hospital
⊠	Post office
ⓘ	Tourist office
@	Internet access
🏛	Monument
🕯	Lighthouse
◆	Point of interest
✝	Church
◯	Stadium
▦	Building
✝ ⊡	Cemetery
⬚	Park/forest
☐	Beach

N

0	200

yards

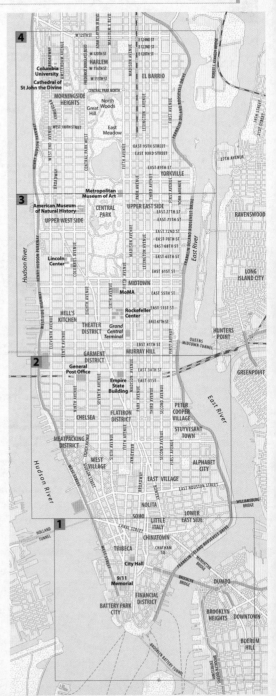

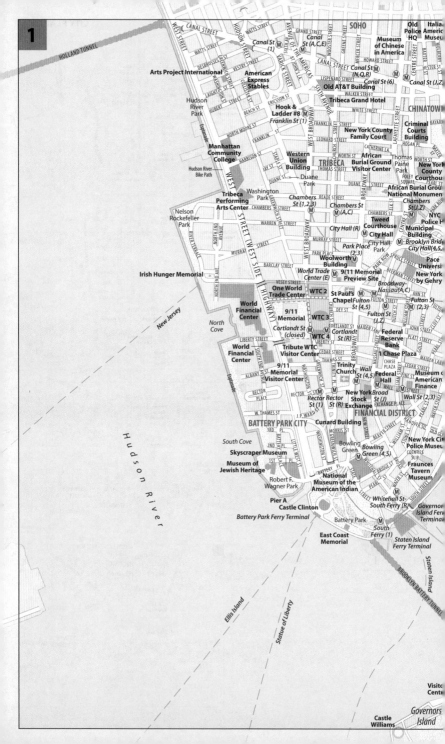

HOLLAND TUNNEL

SOHO

Old Italia
Police America
HQ Muse

CANAL STREET
WATTS STREET
HUDSON STREET
WEST STREET
AVENUE OF THE AMERICAS
GRAND STREET
WOOSTER STREET
GREENE STREET
MERCER STREET
CENTRE STREET
MULBERRY STREET

Canal St
(1)

Museum
of Chinese
in America

Canal
St (A,C,E)

HOWARD STREET
Canal St
(N,Q,R)

HESTER ST

Arts Project International
DESBROSSES STREET
VESTRY STREET

American
Express
Stables

VARICK STREET

SIXTH AVENUE
Old AT&T Building

LISPENARD STREET
Canal St (6)

Canal St (J,Z)

WALKER STREET
LAIGHT STREET

Hudson
River
Park

HUBERT STREET
BEACH STREET

Hook &
Ladder #8
Franklin St (1)

WEST BROADWAY

Tribeca Grand Hotel

WHITE STREET

LAFAYETTE STREET

CHINATOW

BAYAR

NORTH MOORE STREET
FRANKLIN STREET

FRANKLIN STREET
CHURCH STREET

New York County
Family Court

LEONARD STREET

HOGAN PL

Criminal
Courts
Building

Manhattan
Community
College

HARRISON STREET

Western
Union
Building

TRIBECA

WORTH ST
THOMAS STREET

CATHERINE LA

African
Burial Ground
Visitor Center

Thomas
Paine
Park

WORTH ST

New York
County
Courthou

Hudson River
Bike Path

JAY ST

—Duane
Park

DUANE

CHURCH STREET

BROADWAY

DUANE STREET

FOLEY
SQUARE

CLARK S

African Burial Grou
National Monumen

Tribeca
Performing
Arts Center

Washington
Park

Chambers
St (1,2,3)

READE STREET
CHAMBERS STREET

Chambers St
(M)(A,C)

CENTRE STREET

Chambers
St(J,Z)

Nelson
Rockefeller
Park

CHAMBERS STREET

WARREN STREET

WEST STREET (WEST SIDE)
NORTH END AVENUE

City Hall (R)

WEST BROADWAY

Tweed
Courthouse

City Hall

NYC
Police H

RIVER TERRACE

MURRAY STREET

City Hall
Park

Municipal
Building

Brooklyn Brid
City Hall (4,5,

BARCLAY STREET
PARK PLACE

Park Place
(2,3)

PARK ROW

BEEKMAN STREET

Woolworth
Building

VESEY STREET

World Trade
Center (E)

9/11 Memorial
Preview Site

SPRUCE STREET

Pace
Universi

New York
by Gehry

Irish Hunger Memorial

One World
Trade Center

WEST STREET (WEST) HIGHWAY

WTC 2

St Paul's
Chapel

DEY ST
Fulton
St (4,5)

Broadway-
Nassau(A,C)

Fulton
St (2,3)

FULTON

New Jersey

North
Cove

World
Financial
Center

9/11
Memorial

WTC 3

Cortlandt St
(closed)

WTC 4

Cortlandt
St (R)

Fulton
St (J,Z)

MAIDEN LANE

JOHN STREET
PLATT STREET

World
Financial
Center

LIBERTY STREET

Tribute WTC
Visitor Center

GREENWICH STREET

CEDAR STREET
THAMES ST

LIBERTY ST

Federal
Reserve
Bank

WILLIAM STREET

Esplanade

9/11
Memorial
Visitor Center

ALBANY STREET

Trinity
Church

Wall
St (4,5)

1 Chase Plaza

CHASE
PLAZA

CEDAR STREET

PINE STREET

Maiden Lan

Museum o
American
Finance

RECTOR
PLACE

Rector
St (1)

Rector
St (R)

Federal
Hall

New York
Stock
Exchange

Wall
St (J)

WALL
STREET

EXCHANGE PLACE

Wall St (2,3)

WATER STREET

W. THAMES ST

J. P. WARD ST

BATTERY PARK CITY

3RD PL

Cunard Building

BROAD STREET

FINANCIAL DISTRICT

BEAVER STREET

HANOVER ST

OLD SL

South Cove

2ND PL

Skyscraper Museum

LITTLE WEST ST
GREENWICH STREET

Bowling
Green

Bowling
Green (4,5)

WILLIAM STREET

New York Cit
Police Museu

QUENTIES
SLIP

Museum of
Jewish Heritage

1ST PL

Robert F.
Wagner Park

National
Museum of the
American Indian

BATTERY PL

PEARL STREET

STATE STREET

Fraunces
Tavern
Museum

Hudson River

Pier A
Castle Clinton

Battery Park Ferry Terminal

Whitehall St-
South Ferry (R)

SOUTH STREET

Governor
Island Fer
Termina

Battery Park

South
Ferry (1)

East Coast
Memorial

Staten Island
Ferry Terminal

BROOKLYN BATTERY TUNNEL

Staten Island

Ellis Island

Statue of Liberty

Visito
Cente

Castle
Williams

Governors
Island

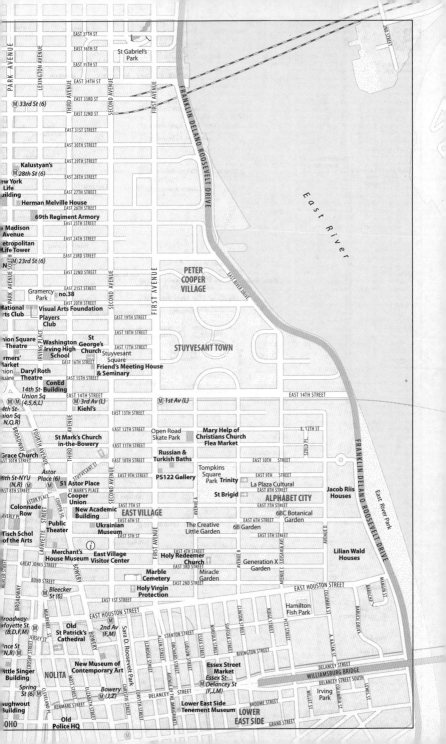

3

WEST 81ST STREET

81st St–
Museum of Natural
History (B,C)

Delacorte
Theater

Metropol
Museum o

WEST 80TH STREET

Rose Center for
Earth & Space
(Hayden Planetarium)

Shakespeare
Garden

79th St (1) Ⓜ

79TH STREET

WEST 79TH STREET

Swedish
Cottage

79TH STREET TRANSVERSE

Turtle Pond

79TH ST

**79th Street
Boat Basin**

WEST 78TH STREET

American Museum
of Natural History

Belvedere
Castle &
Vista Rock

CENTRAL PARK EAST DRIVE

WEST 77TH STREET

Swedish
Marionette
Theatre

The Ramble

WEST 76TH STREET

The New-York
Historical Society

UPPER WEST SIDE

Kenilworth Apartments

Alice
Wonder
Statu

WEST 75TH STREET

San Remo Apartments

Loeb
Boathouse

WEST 74TH STREET

**Eleanor Roosevelt
Monument**

Lake

Bow
Bridge

Hans Christian
Andersen Statue

WEST 73RD STREET

Bethesda
Terrace &
Fountain

Conserva
P

RIVERSIDE DRIVE

**72nd Street Kayaking
(Downtown
Boathouse)**

WEST 72ND STREET

72nd St
(1,2,3) Ⓜ

Dakota Building

72nd St (B,C)

Strawberry
Fields

Cherry Hill
Fountain

OLMSTEAD DRIVE

WEST 71ST STREET

Majestic Apartments

TERRACE DRIVE

Naumberg
Bandshell

WEST 70TH STREET

Rumsey Play
(Summerst

W. 69TH ST

BROADWAY

WEST 69TH STREET

FREEDOM PLACE

COLUMBUS

AVENUE

CENTRAL PARK WEST

WEST 68TH STREET

WEST 67TH STREET

Sheep Meadow

THE MALL

H u d s o n   R i v e r

HENRY HUDSON PARKWAY

66th St–
Lincoln Center (1) Ⓜ

WEST 66TH STREET

Tavern on
the Green

CENTRAL PARK WEST DRIVE

Walter Reade
Theater

Alice Tully
Hall

American Folk
Art Museum

65TH STREET TRANSVERSE

Dairy

WEST 65TH STREET

Lincoln
Center

Avery Fisher Hall

Carousel

Chess & Checkers
Pavilion

Ce
P
Z

WEST 64TH STREET

Fountain

New York Society
for Ethical Culture

Wollman Memorial
Ice Skating Rink

CENTRAL PARK SOUTH DRIV

David H. Koch
Theater

WEST 63RD STREET

David Rubenstein
Atrium

Heckscher
Playground

WEST 62ND STREET

WEST END AVENUE

Museum of
Biblical Art

Victorian
Gardens

The
Pond

WEST 61ST STREET

59th St–
Columbus Circle
(1,A,B,C,D)

WEST 60TH STREET

Church of St Paul
the Apostle

COLUMBUS
CIRCLE

CENTRAL PARK SOUTH

The P
Hot

WEST 59TH STREET

Time Warner
Center

Gainsborough
Studios

WEST 58TH STREET

AMSTERDAM AVENUE

Museum of
Arts & Design

57th St–7th Av
(N,Q,R) Ⓜ

57th St (F) Ⓜ

WEST 57TH STREET

Hearst Tower

Carnegie Hall

WEST 56TH STREET

SIXTH AVENUE

WEST 55TH STREET

BROADWAY

WEST 54TH STREET

Ed Sullivan Theater

7th Av (B,D,E) Ⓜ

Museun
Modern

WEST 53RD STREET

NY Convention &
Visitors Bureau ⓘ

Paley Cente
for Media

**Dewitt
Clinton
Park**

WEST 52ND STREET

AXA Equitable
Center

Top
the R

WEST 51ST STREET

Time-Life
Building

Radio City
Music Hall

50th St (C,E) Ⓜ

50th St (1) Ⓜ

WEST 50TH STREET

WEST SIDE HIGHWAY

ELEVENTH AVENUE

TENTH AVENUE

NINTH AVENUE

**HELL'S
KITCHEN**

WEST 49TH STREET

Brill Building

49th St
(N,Q,R) Ⓜ

GE Building
("30 Rock")

Rockefell
Center

WEST 48TH STREET

47th–50th Sts–Ⓜ
Rockefeller
Center (B,D,F,M)

WEST 48TH

Pier 86

WEST 47TH STREET

TKTS

ⓘ

EIGHTH AVENUE

DIAMOND

Hudson River Bike Path

WEST 46TH STREET

Music Box
Theatre

DUFFY
SQ

Times Square
Museum &
Visitor Center

WEST 46TH STRE

**The Intrepid
Sea-Air-Space Museum**

Shubert
Theatre

**THEATER
DISTRICT**

Lyceum
Theatre

WEST 45TH STREET

General So
of Mecha
& Tradesr

Pier 83

WEST 44TH STREET

Helen Hayes
Theatre

TIMES
SQUARE

Discovery
Times Square

International
Center of
Photography

(Circle Line)

WEST 43RD STREET

42nd St–
Port Authority
Bus Terminal (A,C,E)

WEST 43RD STREET

New Victory
Theatre

5th Av

WEST 42ND STREET

Times Square–
42nd St
(1,2,3,7,N,Q,R,S) Ⓜ

42nd St–Ⓜ
Bryant Park
(B,D,F,M)

Bryan
Park

**Lucky Strike
Lanes**

WEST 41ST STREET

Port Authority
Bus Terminal

WEST 41ST STREET

WEST 40TH STREET

WEST 40TH STREET

LINCOLN TUNNEL

WEST 39TH STREET

New York
Times Building

WEST 39TH STREET

**Jacob Javits
Convention
Center**

WEST 38TH STREET

**GARMENT
DISTRICT**

WEST 38TH STREET

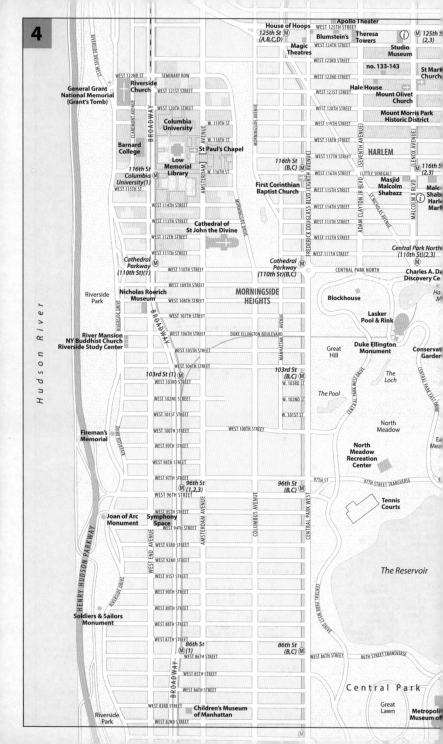

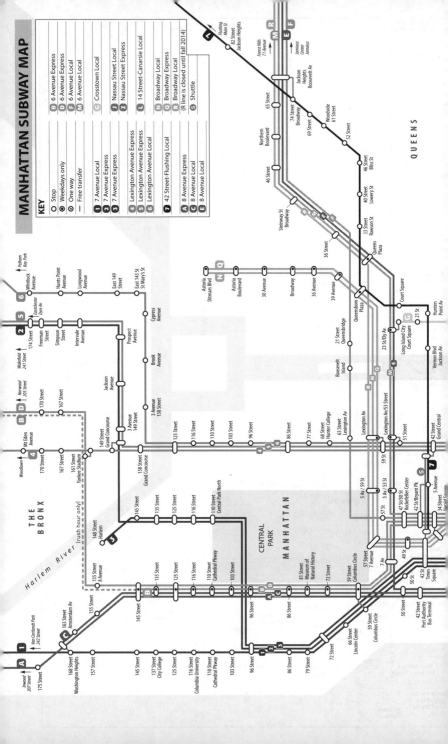

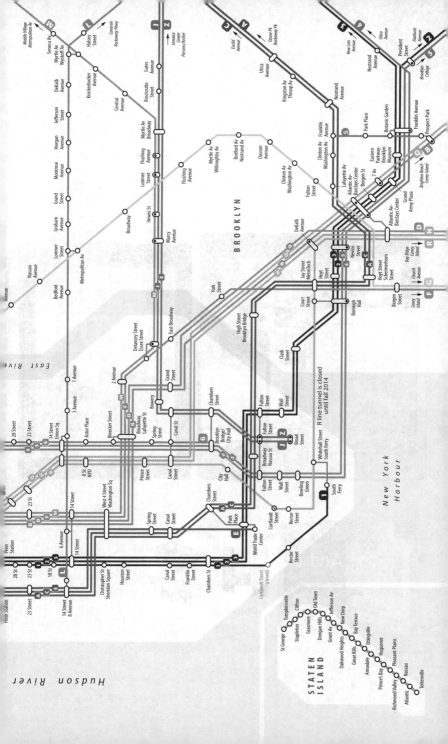